Lec[illegible] in Control and Information Sciences

Edited by A.V. Balakrishnan and M. Thoma

16

Stochastic Control Theory and Stochastic Differential Systems

Proceedings of a Workshop of the „Sonderforschungsbereich 72 der Deutschen Forschungsgemeinschaft an der Universität Bonn“ which took place in January 1979 at Bad Honnef

Edited by
M. Kohlmann and W. Vogel

Springer-Verlag
Berlin Heidelberg New York 1979

Editors
Dr. M. Kohlmann, Bonn
Prof. Dr. W. Vogel, Bonn

With 15 Figures

ISBN 3-540-09480-6 Springer-Verlag Berlin Heidelberg NewYork
ISBN 0-387-09480-6 Springer-Verlag NewYork Heidelberg Berlin

Printed in Germany

Printing and binding: Beltz Offsetdruck, Hemsbach/Bergstr.
2060/3020-543210

PREFACE

This book contains the contributions to a workshop on stochastic control theory and stochastic differential systems at the University of Bonn in January 1979.The main aim of this conference was to give a compact and possibly rather complete presentation of the present state of the art and - in particular - of the scope of methods used in stochastic system theory,in order to stimulate the interest of scientists and students working in other areas of stochastics,in engineering sciences,in econometrics,etc..Thus the success of the conference depended on the willingness of the lecturers to meet our request to give an as understandable as possible introduction into stochastic system theory from their different points of viewing the various problems.As we know that most of the lecturers spent considerable time to make the surveys on their research understandable for non-experts,and as they had a remarkable patience in answering questions and in explaining their works during the conference several times,we want to take this opportunity to express them our deep thanks.We also have to thank them for their careful preparation of their manuscripts.

The first part of this volume presents survey lectures on different topics and methods of stochastic system theory.Thus this part may be seen as an introductory compendium for non-experts.These surveys written by fourteen excellent scientists whose names stand for a special way of seeing the problems of stochastic system theory cover the broad spectrum of problems and methods of the art.

The second part of this book contains all research reports presented during the conference.These papers give a glimpse into the present state of research in the field of stochastic system theory.We hope that the ideas and methods presented there will contribute toward the second aim of the workshop,namely to enforce the cooperation of scientists working on stochastic differential systems and the interchange of ideas.

We gratefully acknowledge the financial support of the Sonderforschungsbereich 72 of the Deutsche Forschungsgemeinschaft and the hospitality of the Elly-Hölterhoff-Stiftung in Bad Honnef,where the conference took place.Finally,we would like to thank Mrs. I.Kreuder, Dr. N.Christopeit,Dr. K.Helmes and many students of the University of Bonn,who helped us organize the workshop.

Bonn,January 1979

Michael Kohlmann
Walter Vogel

CONTENTS :

CONTENTS :

LIST OF PARTICIPANTS

D'Alessandro,P.
University of Rome
Italy

Andreadakis,E.
Imperial College, London
Great Britain

Arnold,L.
Universität Bremen
BRD

Balakrishnan,A.V.
University of California
Los Angeles
USA

Barth,T.
Universität Tübingen

Basar,T.
Marmara Scientific and Industrial
Research Institute
Turkey

Beekes,B.
Universität Bonn
BRD

Bensoussan,A.
Institut de Recherche
d'Informatique et d'Automatique
Domaine de Voluceau-Rocquencourt
France

Bertsch,E.
TU Berlin
BRD

Bismut,J.M.
Universite de Paris-Sud
France

Bock,H.G.
Universität Bonn
BRD

Brémaud,P.
Laboratoire de Recherche
d'Informatique et d'Automatique
Le Chesnay
France

Cansever,D.
Yenileven 20.B.4
Istanbul
Turkey

Christopeit,N.
Universität Bonn
BRD

Cleef,H.J.
Universität Bonn
BRD

Curtain ,R.
Rijksuniversiteit Groningen
The Netherlands

Davis,M.H.A.
Imperial College of Science
and Technology
London
Great Britain

Deistler,M.
Technische Universität Wien
Österreich

Dempster,M.A.H.
University of Oxford
Great Britain

Deppe,H.
Universität Bonn
BRD

Doshi,B.
State University New Jersey
USA

Duncan,T.E.
Universty of Kansas
USA

Ehrhardt,M.
Universität Bremen
BRD

Eisele,T.
Universität Heidelberg
BRD

Elliott,R.J.
University of Hull
Great Britain

Ferroni,A.
Universita Firenze
Italy

Frehse,J.
Universität Bonn
BRD

Friedman,A.
Northwestern University
Evanston
Illinois
USA

Fujisaki,M.
University of Tokio
Japan

Gallisch,E.
Universität Bonn
BRD

Gans,A.
Universität Bonn
BRD

Gasser,T.
Zentralinstitut Seel. Gesundheit
Mannheim
BRD

Gattinger,M.
Universität Erlangen-Nürnberg
BRD

Gaul,W.
Universität Bonn
BRD

Gollan,B.
Universität Würzburg
BRD

Graef,F.
Universität Erlangen-Nürnberg

Grigelionis,B.
Mosklu Akademija
UDSSR

Härdle,W.
Institut für Mineralogie
Heidelberg
BRD

Hazewinkel,M.
Erasmus University
Rotterdam
The Netherlands

Helmes,K.
Universität Bonn
BRD

Herkenrath,U.
Universität Bonn
BRD

Jacod,J.
Université de Rennes
France

Jammernegg,W.
Universität Graz
Österreich

Janssen,K.
Universität Düsseldorf
BRD

Johannson,V.
Universität Bonn
BRD

Kalin,D.
Universität Bonn
BRD

Kendall,W.S.
The University Hull
Great Britain

Kistner,A.
Universität Stuttgart
BRD

Klasing,J.
Universität Bonn
BRD

Kliemann,W.
Universität Bremen
BRD

Koch,G.
University of Rome
Italy

Kohlmann,M.
Universität Bonn
BRD

Kolonko,M.
Universität Bonn
BRD

Krener,A.J.
University of California
Davis
USA

Kunita,H.
Kyushu University
Hakozaki Fukuoka
Japan

Kushner,H.J.
Brown University
USA

Langen,H.J.
Universität Bonn
BRD

Linhart,H.
Statistik und Ökonometrie
Göttingen
BRD

Lüchters,G.
Universität Bonn
BRD

Maurer,H.
Universität Münster
BRD

Mann,E.
Universität Bonn
BRD

Mazziotto,G.
Centre National d'Etude de
Telecommunication
Bagneux
France

De Mey,G.
Ghent State University
Belgien

Meyer zu Hörste,U.
Universität Bonn
BRD

Miesen,K.
Universität Bonn
BRD

Moro,A.
Universita Firenze
Italy

Mosco,U.
Universita di Roma
Italy

Oettli,W.
Universität Mannheim
BRD

Paaß,G.
GMD St.Augustin
BRD

Pardoux,E.
IRIA Le Chesnay
France

Plachky,D.
Westfälische Wilhelms-Universität
Münster
BRD

Plein,K.
Universität Bonn
BRD

Rao,M.M.
Université de Strasbourg
France

Reimnitz,P.
Universität Bonn
BRD

Ressel,P.
Universität Münster
BRD

Rinaldi,A.
University of Rome
Italy

Rishel,R.
University of Kentucky
Lexington
USA

Rümelin,W.
Universität Bremen
BRD

Russek,A.
Polish Academy of Science
Polen

Rustem,B.
London School of Economics
Great Britain

Sänger,G.
Universität Bonn
BRD

Sassano,A.
University of Rome
Italy

Sawitzki,G.
Ruhr-Universität Bochum
BRD

Schäl,M.
Universität Bonn
BRD

Schmitz,K.J.
Universität Bonn
BRD

Schroeter,K.H.
Institut für Mineralogie
Heidelberg
BRD

van Schuppen,J.H.
Washington University
Saint Louis,Missouri
USA

Segall,A.
Israel Institut of Technology
Haifa
Israel

Sentis,R.
IRIA, Le Chesnay
France

Shiryayev,A.
Mathemathisches Institut
Moskau
UDSSR

Shreve,S.E.
University of Delaware
Nework,Delaware
USA

Sommer,U.
Universität Bremen
BRD

Stang,U.
Universität Bonn
BRD

Stoer,J.
Universität Würzburg
BRD

Süß,P.
Berlin
BRD

Szpirglas,J.
Centre National d'Etude
de Telecommunication
Bagneux
France

Tarres,R.
Centre Universitaire
Tlemcen
Algerien

Theodorescu,R.
Universite Laval
Quebec
Kanada

Varaiya,P.
University of California
Berkeley
USA

Väth,R.
Universität Bayreuth
BRD

Vogel,W.
Universität Bonn
BRD

von Weizäcker,H.
Universität Kaiserslautern
BRD

Walk,H.
Universität Essen
BRD

Warns,R.
Universität Bonn
BRD

Werner,H.J.
Universität Bonn
BRD

Witting,H.
Universität Freiburg
BRD

Yor,M.
Universite de Paris VI
France

Zabczyk,J.
Polish Academy of Sciences
Warschau
Polen

Zerrweck,K.E.
Universität Bonn
BRD

Zink,H.
Heidelberg
BRD

PART I :

SURVEY LECTURES

Lecturers: A.V.Balakrishnan , A.Bensoussan , J.M.Bismut , R.F.Curtain , M.H.A.Davis , T.E.Duncan , R.J.Elliott , A.Friedman , H.Kushner , R.Rishel , J.van Schuppen , J.Zabczyk

WHITE NOISE MODELS IN NON-LINEAR FILTERING AND CONTROL*

A.V. Balakrishnan

Department of System Science
University of California
Los Angeles, California 90024

1. INTRODUCTION

In loose terms, any non-linear operation on observed data is referred to as "non-linear filtering". The basic model for observed data is that of a well-defined stochastic process ("signal" or "system response") with an additive "noise" process to account for the limiting unavoidable error brought in by the sensor (measuring instrument).

Thus, letting $y(t)$ represent the observed process, we have:

$$y(t) = s(t) + N(t), \quad 0 < t \tag{1.1}$$

where $s(t)$ is the *signal* and $N(t)$ is the *noise*. Here, "t" represents time and $y(s)$, $0 \le s \le t$ is usually referred to as *the observed time history up to time* t, starting at some arbitrary point in time which is normalized to zero. A basic question that arises is whether the time variable t should be treated as *continuous* or *discrete*. In this paper, we shall consider the continuous-time (*continuous parameter*) model for the reason that in current engineering applications of interest (viz., aircraft flight-test data reduction), although all processing is done by a digital computer, the sampling rate in the A-D converter is sufficiently high so that using a time-continuous model to derive the optimal processing is more efficient that discretizing the model. Of course, the use of a continuous-time model increases the level of sophistication of the mathematical theory required. In particular, the noise model used becomes more complex.

The noise process $N(t)$ is, to begin with, not as well-defined as the signal. About all that one can say for the process is that, since it accounts for the (*non-systematic*) instrumentation error and can often be ascribed to thermodynamic origin, it can be modeled as a stationary Gaussian process with a spectral density which is constant over a range of frequencies wider than the frequency range of the signal (since the instrument, if well designed, is not suppost to "distort" the signal). In the absence of precise information about the noise bandwidth, which is characteristically the case in practice, it has been customary in the early engineering literature to translate the concept of "large" bandwidth to infinite bandwidth and refer to it as

*Research supported in part under AFOSR grant no. 732942, Applied Math.Divn. USAF.

white noise. Of course, such a process must have infinite variance and leads to conceptual mathematical difficulties. Fortunately, so long as operations on the data are confined to *linear* operations, this does not create any real stumbling block and *asymptotic* considerations can take care of matters, as in the Kalman Filter, for example.

Serious difficulties at the instrumentation level arise, however, as soon as we wish to consider non-linear operations. Indeed, the simplest non-linear operation of squaring the instantaneous values (considering, say, $\|y(t)\|^2$), leads to ambiguous interpretations in the asymptotic sense of *infinite* bandwidth.

This was the situation in about 1960, when a different noise model, purported to be more *rigorous*, was introduced (see [1] and the many references therein). This proceeds as follows. First, we rewrite (1.1) in the *integrated* version:

$$\begin{aligned} Y(t) &= \int_0^t y(s)ds \\ &= \int_0^t s(\sigma)d\sigma + \int_0^t n(\sigma)d\sigma \quad . \end{aligned} \tag{1.2}$$

If, formally, $N(t)$ is *white noise* with spectral density matrix D, we see that

$$E\left(\int_0^t N(s)ds\right)\left(\int_0^t N(s)ds\right)^* = tD \quad . \tag{1.3}$$

But next these authors make the all-important step; make, in other words, the transition to:

$$Y(t) = \int_0^t s(\sigma)d\sigma + W(t) \quad , \tag{1.4}$$

where $W(t)$ is now a Wiener process. Of course,

$$E[W(t)W(t)^*] = tD \quad ,$$

and in this sense the theory is *more rigorous*, for now there is nothing ambiguous about the Wiener process. Moreover, there is a crucial advantage that, for (1.4), one can lift bodily the well-developed apparatus of the Ito stochastic integral and concomitant mathematical theory. One result in particular (in many ways, the triumph of the Ito theory) is: the (time-continuous) likelihood ratio (of signal-plus-noise to noise alone, $0 \le t \le T \le \infty$) for the Wiener process model (1.4) can be expressed in closed form:

$$\text{Exp} -\tfrac{1}{2}\left\{\int_0^T [\hat{s}(t),\hat{s}(t)]dt - 2\int_0^T [\hat{s}(t),dY(t)]\right\} , \tag{1.5}$$

where

$$s(t) = E[s(t)\ B_Y(t)] ,$$

where $B_Y(t)$ is the sigma-algebra generated by $Y(s)$, $0 \le s \le t$. The salient feature of this formula is the second term, which is an Ito integral.

This is indeed a remarkable formula, mathematically impeccable. But unfortunately, it simply does *not* apply to our model either in *theory* or in *practice*. It does not apply in *theory* because, in the first place, the Ito integral is defined only with probability one and all sample paths $Y(t)$ under our model (1.1) have probability zero. Contrariwise, the sample paths $Y(t)$ under model (1.2) are *not* absolutely continuous in t with respect to Lebesgue measure, with probability one. (This becomes of significance when we consider problems of stochastic control -- see [4].) But even more important, the formula (1.5) has no operational meaning for our model (1.2) for, according to (1.2), we can only substitute for dY in (1.5) by $y(t)dt$, and this would be completely wrong (unless the operations involved on $Y(\cdot)$ are totally linear as in the trivial case where the signal is deterministic). It does *not* have an operational meaning because it was derived in the first place on the basis of an artificial model created only for mathematical convenience! Indeed, this situation is not atypical. One of the major advantages of the Ito integral is that *any* non-linear operation on $Y(\cdot)$ represented by the Wiener process model (1.4) can be represented as an Ito integral in $Y(\cdot)$. Thus, we can indeed express any non-linear operation, the only problem being that such a formula does not have an operational meaning for our model (1.2) ! It is interesting that the promulgators of both the Ito likelihood-ratio formula and non-linear filtering based on (1.4) (of which there is now an enormous "engineering" literature) apparently never bothered to use their formulas on any real data!

Fortunately, it turns out that the situation can be rectified by going back to the earlier asymptotic notion of white noise but now exploiting the notion of Gauss measure -- of weak distributions on Hilbert Spaces. Of course, we cannot present an adequate exposition of the theory here. The basic concepts and results are treated briefly in Section 2. These are based on the pioneering work of Siegel and Gross [2], and Sazonov [3]. Section 3 is devoted to the white-noise version of the likelihood ratio which plays a fundamental role in Communication and Control Theory. Section 4 deals with Non-Linear Filtering.

Space does not permit inclusion of stochastic control problems with the white-noise observational model. Suffice it to say here that the main difference is the lack of existence of optimal controls on the white-noise model. It turns out that such existence for the Wiener process model is bought at the expense of ruling out all smooth trajectories as having zero probability. (A strong solution may exist for the differential equation characterizing the optimal control in the Wiener process model but only for sample paths which are not absolutely continuous.) An excellent example is provided by the quadratic control problem for a linear system, but with a hard constraint on the control and noisy observed data, so that the problem again involves non-linear operations on the data. (See [4] for details.)

2. BASIC NOTIONS

2.1 Weak Distributions

Let H denote a real separable Hilbert space. Let C denote the algebra of cylinder sets with finite-dimensional Borel bases. Let μ denote a finitely additive measure on C such that it is a probability measure on any class of cylinder sets with bases in a fixed finite-dimensional subspace, with the usual consistency property as the dimension is changed. Such a finitely additive or *cylinder* measure is also referred to as a *Weak Distribution*. The characteristic function of a weak distribution is defined by:

$$C(h) = \int_H e^{i[x,h]} \, d\mu(x) \quad , \qquad h \in H \quad ,$$

the integral being definable as a Lebesgue integral. We need consider only weak distributions whose characteristic function is continuous. We note that the distribution is completely specified by the characteristic function.

Our basic *probability triple* will be (H,C,μ) . A typical example of a weak distribution for us is the *Gauss measure* with characteristic function:

$$C(h) = \text{Exp} - \tfrac{1}{2} \, [h,h] \quad .$$

An immediate question that arises is of course: when is a finitely additive measure actually countably additive? The answer to this is provided by the following:

THEOREM 2.1 (Sazonov [3]) The finitely additive probability measure is countably additive if and only if the characteristic function is continuous in the trace-norm topology of H .

We recall that the trace-norm topology is a locally convex topology defined by the seminorms:

$$C(x) = \sqrt{[Sx,x]} \quad ,$$

where S is a non-negative self-adjoint linear bounded operator on H into H, which is nuclear (or *trace-class*). Such an operator is also referred to as a *nuclear covariance operator*.

An important consequence of the Sazonov theorem is the following. Let L denote any Hilbert-Schmidt operator mapping H into possibly different real separable Hilbert space H_r. If $C(\cdot)$ is the characteristic function (assumed continuous) of μ, then $C(L^*h)$ defines a characteristic function of a countably additive measure on H_r. In particular then, we see that μ can be extended to be countably additive on the inverse images of any Hilbert-Schmidt operator.

Let $\mathcal{B}$ denote the Borel sigma algebra of H. Then any weak distribution can be extended to be countably additive on $\mathcal{B}$ by imbedding H in H', the algebraic dual of H, via essentially the Kolmogorov extension theorem. But such an extension is at the expense of introducing sets (events) which are artificial, and furthermore (and this is crucial) the outer measure of H may be rendered zero.

For example, let us consider the Gauss measure on ℓ_2. Then we know it can be extended via the Kolmogorov theorem to countably additive on R^∞, the class of all real sequences, yielding in fact the Wiener measure on R^∞. Of course, the Wiener measure of ℓ_2 is zero.

The main difficulty in working with (H,C,μ) concerns the notion of a random variable. Let $f(\cdot)$ denote any Borel measurable function mapping H into H_r. Since μ may not even be defined on the inverse images of Borel sets in H_r, much less countably additive on them, we do not have the luxury of having every Borel measurable function as a random variable. Indeed, this is too large a class for us from the physical point of view; and thus we introduce the notion of a *physical* random variable.

First of all, we shall consider only functions $f(\cdot)$ which are continuous. Now, if $f(\cdot)$ is a continuous function and P_n is any monotone sequence of projections on H converging (strongly) to the identity, then $f(P_n x)$ converges to $f(x)$ for each x in H. Moreover, $f(P_n x)$ is C-measurable and μ is countably additive on the inverse images, for each n. We shall call $f(\cdot)$ a *physical random variable*, p.v.r. for short, if the sequence of random variables $\{f(P_n x)\}$ is Cauchy in probability and, for each h in H_r :

$$C(h) = \lim_n C_n(h) \quad ,$$

where

$$C_n(h) = \int_H e^{i[f(P_n x),h]}\, d\mu(x)$$

and the limit $C(h)$ is independent of the particular approximating projection sequence chosen. In most cases of interest to us, the sequences will be actually equivalent. Let μ_n denote the measure on H_r induced by $f(P_n\cdot)$:

$$\mu_n(\mathbb{B}) = \mu(f(P_n\cdot)^{-1}\,\mathbb{B}) \quad ,$$

where $\mathbb{B}$ is a Borel set in H_r. Then μ_n is weakly Cauchy and, defining the limiting measure by μ_f, we see that μ_n converges weakly to μ_f, and we now simply define:

$$\Pr.(f(x) \in \mathbb{B}) = \mu_f(\mathbb{B}) \; .$$

Note that any continuous function of a p.r.v. is a p.r.v.

From now on, we shall consider only weak distributions with finite second moment:

$$\int_H [x,h]^2\, d\mu(x) \qquad \text{is continuous in } h \; .$$

Hence,

$$\int_H [x,h][x,g]\, d\mu(x) = [Rh,g] \quad ,$$

where R is self-adjoint, non-negative definite linear bounded operator on H into H. And of course conversely.

A simple sufficient condition for a p.r.v. is:

THEOREM 2.2 Let $f(\cdot)$ be a function mapping H into H_r such that it is uniformly continuous in the S-topology. Let $g(\cdot)$ be any continuous function mapping H_r into another separable Hilbert space. Then

$$q(x) = g(f(x))$$

defines a p.r.v.

Proof Let P_n denote any sequence of finite-dimensional projections converging strongly to the identity. Let $\varepsilon > 0$ be given. Then we can find a nuclear covariance S such that

$$\|f(x) - f(y)\| < \varepsilon \quad , \quad \text{for all } x,y \text{ such that } [(S(x-y),x-y] < 1 \quad .$$

Hence, it follows that

$$\Pr.(\|f(P_n x) - f(P_m x)\| \geq \varepsilon) \leq \Pr.\ [S(P_n - P_m)x,(P_n - P_m)x] \geq 1$$

and, by the Chebychev inequality, the right side is

$$\leq \text{Tr.}(P_n - P_m)\,S\,(P_n - P_m)R$$

$$= \text{Tr.}(P_n - P_m)\,R\,(P_n - P_m)S \quad ,$$

which is less than ε, for all n,m sufficiently large. Hence, $f(P_n x)$ is Cauchy in probability. We can readily see by a similar argument that all such Cauchy sequences are actually equivalent. Hence, f(x) defines a p.r.v. and, $g(\cdot)$ being continuous, so is $g(f(\cdot))$, as required.

Remark: Note that $q(\cdot)$ is continuous at the origin in the S-topology.

As a simple illustrative example of the theorem, we see that

$$[Lx,x] = f(x)$$

is a p.r.v. if $(L+L^*)$ is nuclear, since we can write:

$$[Lx,x] = [R_2x,x] - [R_1x,x] \quad ,$$

where R_1 and R_2 are nuclear covariances, and

$$[R_2x,x] = g(\sqrt{R_2}\,x) \quad ,$$

where

$$g(y) = [y,y]$$

is continuous in y and, of course, $\sqrt{R_2}$ is Hilbert-Schmidt and hence, $[R_2x,x]$ defines a p.r.v., and so does $[R_1x,x]$. In this particular example, the condition that $[L+L^*]$ be nuclear is also necessary. (See [5].)

Not all functions of interest in non-linear filtering are of the type described in the Theorem. In fact, the characterization provided by the Theorem is inadequate in the two primary cases of interest, as we shall see.

2.2 *Radon-Nikodym Derivatives of Weak Distributions*

Let μ_1 and μ_2 denote two weak distributions on H. We need to define what we shall mean by the Radon-Nikodym derivative of μ_2 with respect to μ_1. Let $f(\cdot)$ denote a mapping of H into the positive reals. Suppose $f(\cdot)$ is a p.r.v. with respect to μ_1 and such that, for any cylinder set C in H, we have:

$$\lim_n \int_C f(P_n x)\,d\mu_1(x) = \mu_2(C) \quad ,$$

where P_n is any sequence of finite-dimensional projections converging strongly to the identity. Then we shall call $f(\cdot)$ the Radon-Nikodym derivative of μ_2 with respect to μ_1.

Here is a canonical (for us) example. Suppose μ_1 is Gauss measure and μ_2 is defined by the characteristic function:

$$C_2(h) = C(h) \ \text{Exp} - \tfrac{1}{2}\ [h,h] \quad ,$$

where $C(h)$ is the characteristic function of a countably additive probability measure μ_S on the Borel sigma-algebra of H. Then the Radon-Nikodym derivative of μ_2 with respect to Gauss measure is given by:

$$f(h) = \int_H \text{Exp} - \tfrac{1}{2}\ \{[x,x] - 2[x,h]\}\ d\mu_S \quad . \tag{2.1}$$

For a proof, see [6]. If P_n is the usual approximating sequence of finite-dimensional projections, $\{f(P_n x)\}$ is actually Cauchy in the mean of order one. This verification is immediate from the fact that $f(P_n h)$ is equivalent to:

$$f_n(h) = \int_H \text{Exp} - \tfrac{1}{2}\ \{\ \|P_n x\|^2 - 2[P_n x,h]\}\ d\mu_S \quad ,$$

and the latter is well known to be an L_1-Martingale.

2.3 *White Noise*

We are now in a position to make a precise definition of what we shall mean by *white noise* (or, more properly, *non-linear white noise* in order to distinguish it from the notion of the generalized or distributional white noise of Gelfand [7]; our emphasis is on non-linear operations).

Let, for each T, $0 < T \leq \infty$,

$$W(T) = L_2((0,T);H)$$

denote the L_2-space over the Hilbert space H , real seperable. By white noise in $(0,T)$, we shall mean the triple: $(W(T), C(T), \mu_G)$ where μ_G is the Gauss measure on $C(T)$, the cylinder sets with finite-dimensional Borel Bases in $W(T)$. Note that we have then white noise in $W(t)$, for every $t \leq T$.

Let

$$W_r(T) = L_2((0,T);H_r) \quad ,$$

where H_r is a real separable Hilbert space, possibly different from H . Let $f(\cdot)$ be any continuous function mapping $W(T)$ into $W_r(T)$. Then, in a slight modification of our previous definition, we shall call $f(\cdot)$ a p.r.v. with respect to the Gauss measure or a *white noise integral* if $\{f(T_n x)\}$ is Cauchy in probability for any sequence T_n of Hilbert-Schmidt (linear) Volterra operators mapping $W(T)$ into $W(T)$, and converging strongly to the identity. It is apparent from a perusal of the proof of Theorem 2.2 that any functions satisfying the condition of the theorem is a white noise signal. So is the R-N derivative defined by (2.1).

3. *LIKELIHOOD RATIO*

We can now make our data model more precise. Thus, we have:

$$y(t) = S(t) + N(t) \quad , \quad 0 < t < T \quad ,$$

where we specify the noise $N(t)$ to be white noise in $[0,T]$ with

$$W(T) = L_2((0,T);H) \quad ,$$

where H is a real separable Hilbert space. We assume that the signal $S(t)$ is a lot smoother. More specifically, we take it to be a well-measurable stochastic process $S(t,\omega)$ with range in H, where ω denotes sample points in Ω; $(\Omega, \mathbb{B}, p)$ being the usual probability triple. We assume further that:

$$\int_0^T E(\|S(t,\omega)\|^2)dt < \infty \quad ,$$

and further that:

$$E(\|S(t,\omega)\|^2) < \infty$$

actually for each t in $[0,T]$. Since $S(\cdot,\omega)$ yields a measurable mapping on into $W(T)$, denoting the sample paths of white noise by N, we have the abstract version of our data model:

$$y(\cdot) = S(\cdot,\omega) + N \quad .$$

Assuming now that the signal and noise are independent, we can calculate the characteristic function of the weak distribution μ_y induced by $y(\cdot)$ as:

$$C_y(h) = (\text{Exp} - \tfrac{1}{2}\,[h,h]) \cdot \int_\Omega \text{Exp} - i[S(\cdot,\omega),h]\; dp \quad .$$

As we have seen, the cylinder measure μ_y is absolutely continuous with respect to the Gauss measure, with derivative given by the p.r.v.:

$$q(h) = \int_\Omega \text{Exp} - \tfrac{1}{2}\left\{\int_0^T \|S(t,\omega)\|^2\,dt - 2\int_0^T [S(t,\omega),h(t)]dt\right\}dp \quad .$$

To cast this into the more useful likelihood-ratio form, we need to introduce the notion of *conditional expectation* with respect to the observation process $y(\cdot)$ as a p.r.v. Let $P(t)$, for each t, $0 < t < T$, denote the projection of $W(T)$ into $W(t)$ as a subspace:

$$P(t)f = g \quad ; \quad g(s) = \begin{cases} f(s) \quad , & 0 \le s \le t \\ 0 \quad , & \text{otherwise.} \end{cases}$$

Let $f(t,\omega)$ be any real-valued random variable measurable $\mathbb{B}$, for fixed t. Let P_n denote any usual approximating sequence of finite-dimensional projections. We assume that $f(t,\omega)$ has finite first moment. Then, for each n, the conditional expectation:

$$E(f(t,\omega) \mid P_n\, P(t)y)$$

is of course well defined, and is an L_1 martingale, and Cauchy in L_1. Suppose now that there exists a function $g(P(t)y)$ such that the Cauchy sequences

$$\{g(P_n\, P(t)y)\} \quad \text{and} \quad \{E(f(t,\omega) \mid P_n\, P(t)y)\}$$

are equivalent. We define the conditional expectation to be the p.r.v. $g(P(t)y)$, and denote it $\hat{f}(t;y)$.

We also need to extend our definition to functions $f(t,\omega)$ measurable $\mathbb{B}$, (with fixed t) with range in H. In this case, we only need to consider L_2 variables:

$$E(\|f(t,\omega)\|^2) < \infty \ .$$

Now, of course, the conditional expectation

$$E(f(t,\omega) \mid P_n\, P(t)y)$$

yields an H-valued sequence, Cauchy in L_2 over H. Hence, if the Cauchy sequences

$$\{g(P_n\, P(t)y)\} \quad \text{and} \quad \{E(f(t,\omega) \mid P_n\, P(t)y)\}$$

are equivalent in probability, we call $g(P(t)u)$ the *conditional expectation of* $f(t,\omega)$ *given* $P(t)y$, and denote it $\hat{f}(t,y)$.

We can then show (see [8] for the proofs) that

$$q(h) = \text{Exp} - \tfrac{1}{2}\left\{\int_0^T [\hat{S}(t,h),\ \hat{S}(t,h) - 2h(t)]dt + \int_0^T r(t,h)dt\right\}$$

where $\hat{S}(t;y)$ is the conditional expectation of $S(t,\omega)$ given $P(t)y$, for which we hive the Bayes formula:

$$\hat{S}(t,y) = \int_\Omega S(t,\omega)\, B(t,\omega,y)dp \ ,$$

where

$$B(t,\omega,y) = \frac{\text{Exp} - \tfrac{1}{2}\displaystyle\int_0^t [S(\sigma,\omega),\ S(\sigma,\omega) - 2h(\sigma)]\, d\sigma}{\displaystyle\int_\Omega \text{Exp} - {}^1{}_2\left\{\int_0^t [S(\sigma,\omega),\ S(\sigma,\omega) - 2h(\sigma)]d\right\} dp} \ .$$

The function $r(t,y)$ is non-negative and is defined by the *conditional* mean square error:

$$r(t,y) = \int_\Omega \|S(t,\omega)\|^2\, B(t,\omega,y)dp - \|\hat{S}(t,y)\|^2 \ .$$

In what is easily the most useful case of the likelihood ratio, in which the signal process is also Gaussian, the function $r(t,y)$ is independent of y. For more on this special case, see [6]. In particular, the formula has been tested on actual (as opposed to simulated) data arising in an aircraft flight control application [9].

4. *NON-LINEAR FILTERING*

The *non-linear filtering* problem is that of evaluating $\hat{S}(t,y)$ in the case where $S(t,\omega)$ cannot be assumed to be Gaussian. As noted in the Introduction, this problem has been considered so far in the Wiener process version of the model. The main results of the latter are to be found in [1] and [11] .

Here, we shall examine the problem in our white noise setting. Our first result is that the *innovation process*:

$$\nu(t) = y(t) - \hat{S}(t,y) \quad , \quad 0 < t < T \quad ,$$

is a white noise process in $W(T)$. In other words, if we define the mapping $\phi(\cdot)$ on $W(T)$ into itself by:

$$\phi(y) = g \quad ; \qquad g(t) = \hat{S}(t,y) \quad , \ \text{a.e.} \quad 0 < t < T \ ,$$

then

$$\int_{W(T)} \text{Exp} - i\ [P_n y - \phi(P_n y), h] \cdot d\mu_y = C_n(h)$$

converges to

$$\text{Exp} - \tfrac{1}{2}\ [h,h]$$

for any sequence of finite-dimensional projections P_n converging strongly to the identity. For a proof, see [10].

Let us now specialize H to R_m in order to consider next the *conditional density* problem of non-linear filtering. Here, the signal process is specified by means of a stochastic differential equation, and the problem is to characterize the *conditional density of* $S(t,\omega)$ *given the data* $P(t)y$.

As potentially the most useful case, we shall consider a time-invariant system where the signal is given by:

$$S(t) = C(x(t)) \tag{4.1}$$

$$d\,x(t) = F(x(t))dt + \sigma(x(t))dW(t) \quad , \tag{4.2}$$

where the differential is taken in the Ito sense, $x(\cdot) \in R_m$, and $x(0)$ is independent of the Wiener process $W(t)$, and posseses a probability density denoted $p(t,x)$. We remark that we could also have expressed the stochastic equation in the white noise sense (as in [5]), but this is immaterial since all that is needed is a mechanism for specifying uniquely the probability distributions of the signal process. Here, we actually prefer the Ito version, since the infinitesimal generator (denote it by L) of the process $x(t)$ is more directly deduced from the equation. Of course, we assume the usual sufficient conditions on $F(\cdot)$ and $\sigma(\cdot)$ to guarantee a unique strong solution to (4.2), as can be found for example in [11]. We assume furthermore that the process has a transition density.

As is customary in non-linear filtering theory, we shall actually seek to characterize the conditional density of $x(t)$ given the data $y(s)$, $s < t$. In principle, this is more general since $\hat{S}(t;y)$ is only the first moment of $C(x)$, and can be computed from the conditional density, as indeed can any desired moment, the second moment being particularly desirable.

Things are not quite so straightforward since, as is well known, the evolution equation satisfied by the conditional density contains implicitly in it the first moment. Nevertheless, the evolution equation for the conditional density is usually what is derived in non-linear filtering theory based on the Wiener process noise model. Our objective here is to derive the similar equation based on our non-linear white noise model, with special attention to the noticeable differences. In this vein, we shall make the same assumptions as in the Wiener process theory, as may be found for example in [1]. These conditions do not depend on the noise model used. Of course, we do assume that the signal has finite energy:

$$\int_0^T E(\|Cx(t,\cdot)\|^2)dt < \infty \quad . \tag{4.3}$$

Leaving the details of the derivation to [10], let $f(\cdot)$ denote any infinitely differentiable function, mapping R_m into R_i and vanishing outside a compact subset. Define (the conditional expectation):

$$f(x(t,\cdot);P(t)y = \frac{\int_\Omega f(x(t,\omega))(\mathrm{Exp} - \tfrac{1}{2}\int_0^t \{\|S(\sigma,\omega)\|^2 - 2[S(\sigma,\omega),y(\sigma)]\}d\sigma)dp}{\int_\Omega (\mathrm{Exp} - \tfrac{1}{2}\int_0^t \{\|S(\sigma,\omega)\|^2 - 2[S(\sigma,\omega),y(\sigma)]\}d\sigma)dp} \tag{4.4}$$

Fix $y(\cdot)$ in $W(T)$. Let $r(t;x;P(t)y)$ denote for each t the Baire function over R_m defined by

$$r(t;x(t;\omega);P(t)y) = \frac{E(\mathrm{Exp} - \tfrac{1}{2}\int_0^t \{\|S(\sigma,\omega)\|^2 - 2[S(\sigma,\omega),y(\sigma)]\}d\sigma \mid x(t,\omega))}{E(\mathrm{Exp} - \tfrac{1}{2}\int_0^t \{\|S(\sigma,\omega)\|^2 - 2[S(\sigma,\omega),y(\sigma)]\}d\sigma)} \quad . \qquad (4.5)$$

Next, define:

$$p(t;x;P(t)y) = r(t;x;P(t)y)p(t,x) \quad .$$

Then, since:

$$f(x(t,\cdot);P(t)y) = \int_{R_m} f(x)p(t;x;P(t)y)d|x| \quad ,$$

it is natural to call $p(t;x;P(t)y)$ the conditional density of $x(t,\omega)$, given $y(s)$, $s<t$. By direct differentiation of (4.4), we obtain that (see [10]) the conditional density will satisfy the evolution equation:

$$\begin{aligned} p(t;x;P(t)y) &= L^*(p(t; \ ;P(t)y))(x) \\ &+ [C(x) - \hat{S}(t;y),y(t) - \hat{S}(t;y)]\ p(t;x;P(t\ y) \\ &+ \tfrac{1}{2}(P(t;y) - \|C(x) - \hat{S}(t;y)\|^2)\ p(t;x;P(t)y) \quad , \end{aligned} \qquad (4.6)$$

where we have assumed that $p(t;\cdot;P(t)y)$ belongs to the domain of L^* , the distribution adjoint of L . The main thing to note is the appearance of the third term in parentheses which do not appear in the Wiener process version of this equation; (see [1] for the Wiener process version). If the conditional density is to be calculated from observed $y(\cdot)$ according to model (1.1), then the Wiener process version has no operational meaning, while (4.5) does. The equation now explicitly contains the second conditional moment. It is a stochastic partial differential in that it contains the forcing term involving $y(\cdot)$; it is actually *bilinear* in the $y(t) - \hat{S}(t,y)$ innovation and, the latter being white noise, it is of the kind treated in [5].

REFERENCES

[1] R.S. Lipster and A.N. Shiryayev: "Statistics of Random Processes," Springer-Verlag, New York, 1978.

[2] L. Gross: Harmonic Analysis on Hilbert Space, Memoirs of the American Mathmatical Society, 1963.

[3] V. Sazonov: A Remark on Characteristic Functions, Theory of Probability and Applications, 1958.

[4] A.V. Balakrishnan: On Stochastic Bang-Bang Control, Int.Symp. on Stochastic Differential Systems, Vilnius, August, 1978, Proceedings (to be published by Springer-Verlag, 1979).

[5] A.V. Balakrishnan: Stochastic Bilinear Partial Differential Equations, in "Variable Structure Systems," edited by R. Mohler and A. Ruberti, Springer-Verlag, 1975.

[6] A.V. Balakrishnan: Radon-Nikodym Derivatives of a Class of Weak Distributions of Hilbert Spaces, Journal of Applied Mathematics and Optimization, vol.3, 1977, 209-225.

[7] I.M. Gelfand and N. Ya. Vilenkin: "Generalized Functions, Vol.IV", Academic Press, 1964.

[8] A.V. Balakrishnan: Likelihood Ratios for Signals in Additive White Gaussian Noise, Journal of Applied Mathematics and Optimization, vol.3, 1977, 341-356.

[9] K.W. Iliff: "Identification and Stochastic Control with Application to Flight Control in Turbulence," Dissertation UCLA, 1973 (UCLA-ENG-7340, 1973).

[10] A.V. Balakrishnan: Non-Linear White Noise Theory, in "Multivariate Analysis V," edited by P.R. Krishnaiah, Academic Press, 1979.

[11] I. Gikhman and A.V. Skhorokhod: "Stochastic Differential Equations," Springer-Verlag, 1970.

OPTIMAL IMPULSIVE CONTROL THEORY

Alain BENSOUSSAN (*)

We present in this survey some of the main ideas concerning impulse control theory. We have chosen the following framework. The process is a non degenerate diffusion stopped at the exit of a bounded regular domain of R^n. The control is excited by impulses, which modify the state of the system instantaneously. The cost involves an integral cost and a variable cost (depending on the size of the jump).

We mainly develop in this presentation the semi-group approach which is sufficient to prove the existence of an optimal impulse control. However, other analytic approaches of the characterization of the optimal cost are possible and in general are more convenient for the applications. We briefly mention them. Since the optimal stopping time problem is a necessary step to solve the impulse control problem, we present the main results of that theory also. The article ends with comments and remarks concerning other problems and extensions.

CONTENTS

(*) Université Paris IX-Dauphine and IRIA/LABORIA

1. THE MODEL PROBLEM

1.1. Notations.

Let $(\Omega,\mathcal{A},P)$ be a probability space, $\mathfrak{F}^t$ be a family of sub σ-algebras of $\mathcal{A}$, $\mathfrak{F}^s \leq \mathfrak{F}^t$ for $s \leq t$, and $\mathcal{A} = \mathfrak{F}^\infty$. Let also $w(t)$ be an n dimensional Wiener process, which is an $\mathfrak{F}^t$ martingale. We consider functions $g(x) : R^n \to R^n$, $\sigma(x) : R^n \to \mathcal{L}(R^n;R^n)$ such that :

(1.1) $\quad g\ ,\ \sigma$ are bounded

(1.2) $\quad |g(x)-g(x')| + |\sigma(x)-\sigma(x')| \leq C|x-x'|\ .$ (1)

By virtue of (1.2), one can solve the stochastic differential equation :

(1.3) $\quad dy = g(y)dt + \sigma(y)dw(t) \quad , y(o)= x$

where x is given.

An impulsive control W is defined as follows :

(1.4) $\quad W = \{\theta^1,\xi^1;\ldots;\theta^i,\xi^i;\ldots\}$

where the θ^i are $\mathfrak{F}^t$ stopping times, $\theta^i \leq \theta^{i+1}$ and $\theta^i \to +\infty$ a.s. as $i \to +\infty$, $\theta^i = +\infty$ is possible, ξ^i is $\mathfrak{F}^{\theta^i}$ measurable, $\xi^i \geq 0$, $\xi^i \in R^n$.

To an impulsive control W, one associates the controlled trajectory :

(1.5)
$$\left|\begin{array}{l} dy = g(y)dt + \sigma(y)dw(t) + \sum_i \xi_i\ \delta(t-\theta_i) \\ y(o) = x \end{array}\right.$$

The cad lag process $y(t)$ is well defined on $[o,\infty[$, since $\theta^i \to +\infty$ a.s.

Let now $\mathcal{O}$ be a bounded regular domain of R^n, and :

(1.6) $\quad \tau_x = \inf\{t \geq 0 \mid y(t) \notin \bar{\mathcal{O}}\}$,

(1.7) $\quad f \geq 0\ ,\ f \in L^p(\mathcal{O}),\ p > \frac{n}{2}$

(1.8) $\quad \alpha \geq 0\ ,\ k > 0$

(1.9)
$$\left|\begin{array}{l} c(\xi)\ :\ (R^n)^+ \to R^+, \text{ non decreasing, continuous and sub additive} \\ c(\xi) \to +\infty \text{ as } |\xi| \to +\infty,\ c(o) = 0. \end{array}\right.$$

---

(1) the norm of the matrix σ is given by :

$$|\sigma|^2 = \operatorname{tr} \sigma\sigma^*$$

One defines the cost functional :

(1.10) $$J_x(W) = E\Big[\int_0^{\tau_x} f(y(t))\, e^{-\alpha t} dt + \sum_i (k+c(\xi_i))\, e^{-\alpha\theta_i} \chi_{\theta_i < +\infty}\Big]$$

This functional is well defined, with the possible value $+\infty$. The problem consists in characterizing the function

(1.11) $$u(x) = \operatorname*{Inf}_W J_x(W)$$

and obtaining an optimal control.

1.2. Remarks.

We can replace $J_x(W)$ by

$$J'_x(W) = E\Big[\int_0^{\tau_x} f(y(t))\, e^{-\alpha t} dt + \sum_i (k+c(\xi_i))\, e^{-\alpha\theta_i} \chi_{\theta_i < \tau_x}\Big]$$

Clearly :

$$\operatorname{Inf} J'_x(W) = \operatorname{Inf} J_x(W).$$

This means that one should not exert any jump, after the exit of $y(t)$ from $\bar{\mathcal{O}}$.

Let $\mathcal{B}_0$ be the class of Borel sets of R^n, such that their closure does not contain 0. Let $A \in \mathcal{B}_0$, we define

$\nu(t,A)$ = number of jumps on $]0,t]$ of the process $y(t)$, whose value belongs to A.

Since $y(t)$ is cad lag, $\nu(t,A)$ is well defined for $A \in \mathcal{B}_0$.

One defines on $R^+ \times R^n$ a measure by setting, if $\Delta =]t,t+\Delta t[$

$$\nu(\Delta,A) = \nu(t+\Delta t,A) - \nu(t,A).$$

Clearly, we have :

(1.12) $$J_x(W) = E\Big[\int_0^{\tau_x} f(y(t))\, e^{-\alpha t} dt + \int_0^\infty\int_{R^n} (k+c(z))\, e^{-\alpha t}\, \nu(dt,dz)\Big]$$

which has a meaning since the integrand is positive.

Denoting by $\emptyset$ the impulse control for which all the $\theta_i = +\infty$. Then $y(t)$ is continuous, and :

$$u(x) \le J(x)(\emptyset) = E\Big[\int_0^{\tau_x} f(y(t))\, e^{-\alpha t} dt\Big] \le C_0.$$

It is thus clear, that we may restrict the class of impulse controls which are admissible, such that they satisfy :

$$(1.13)\qquad k\,E\int_0^\infty e^{-\alpha t}\,\nu(dt;R^n) + E\int_0^\infty\int_{R^n} c(z)\,e^{-\alpha t}\,\nu(dt,dz) \le C_o$$

In particular, it follows that :

$$(1.14)\qquad E\,\nu(t;R^n) \le \frac{C_o\,e^{\alpha t}}{k}\ ,\quad \forall t$$

It is convenient to give a weak formulation of (1.5). Let us consider the canonical space

$$\Omega = D[0,\infty;R^n]\ ,\quad x(t) = \omega(t)\ ,\quad \mu^t = \sigma(x(s),s\le t\,),$$

$$\mu = \mu^\infty = \text{Borel } \sigma\text{-algebra on } \Omega.$$

We also use the notation $\nu(t,A)$ for the number of jumps of the process $x(t)$. A control will be a probability measure P^x, on Ω, μ such that

$$(1.15)\qquad \left|\begin{array}{l} P^x[x(o) = x] = 1 \\ E^{P^x}\nu(t;R^n) \le \dfrac{C_o\,e^{\alpha t}}{k}\ ,\quad E^{P^x}\displaystyle\int_0^\infty\int_{R^n} c(z)\,e^{-\alpha t}\,\nu(dt,dz) \le C_o \end{array}\right.$$

and for $\varphi \in \Phi(R^n)$

$$(1.16)\qquad \left|\begin{array}{l} \varphi(x(t)) + \displaystyle\int_0^t A\varphi(x(s))ds - \int_0^t\int_{R^n}(\varphi(x(s)+z) - \varphi(x(s)))\nu(ds,dz) \\ \text{is a } P^x,\ \mu^t \text{ martingale.} \end{array}\right.$$

The last integral in (1.16) makes sense, by virtue of (1.15). We have set

$$(1.17)\qquad A\varphi(x) = -g(x)\cdot\nabla\varphi(x) - \sum_{ij} a_{ij}(x)\,\frac{\partial^2\varphi}{\partial x_i\partial x_j}$$

where

$$a = \tfrac{1}{2}\,\sigma\sigma^*\ ,\quad a = a_{ij}.$$

We have now the payoff :

$$(1.18)\qquad J(P^x) = E^{P^x}\Big[\int_0^\tau f(x(t))\,e^{-\alpha t}dt + \int_0^\infty\int_{R^n}(k+c(z))\,e^{-\alpha t}\,\nu(dt,dz)\Big]$$

and

$$(1.19)\qquad u(x) = \inf_{P^x} J(P^x)$$

Such a formulation is useful to remove the Lipschitz properties of g, σ.

2. REVIEW ON OPTIMAL STOPPING

2.1. Notations.

We assume (1.1), (1.2) and $\mathcal{O}$ bounded regular. We also assume (1.7), $\alpha \geq 0$. We consider a function ψ such that

(2.1) $$\psi \in C^0(\bar{\mathcal{O}}) \ , \ \psi|_\Gamma \geq 0 \ , \ \Gamma = \partial\mathcal{O}$$

Let θ be an $\mathcal{F}^t$ stopping time. One sets :

(2.2) $$J_x(\theta) = E\Big[\int_0^{\tau_x \wedge \theta} e^{-\alpha t} f(y(t))dt + \psi(y(\theta)) \chi_{\theta<\tau_x} e^{-\alpha\theta}\Big] ,$$

and

(2.3) $$u(x) = \operatorname*{Inf}_\theta J_x(\theta).$$

We denote by $\Phi(t)$ the semi-group corresponding to the diffusion stopped at the exit of $\mathcal{O}$, i.e.

(2.4) $$\Phi(t)h(x) = E\, h(y(t\wedge\tau_x)), \text{ if } h \text{ is Borel bounded.}$$

2.2. Semi-group approach.

One considers the following problem. To find $u(x)$ such that :

(2.5) $$u \in C^0(\bar{\mathcal{O}}) \ , \ u|_\Gamma = 0$$

(2.6) $$u(x) \leq \int_0^t \Phi(s)(f\,\chi_{\mathcal{O}})(x)\, e^{-\alpha s} ds + \Phi(t)u(x)\, e^{-\alpha t}$$

(2.7) $$u(x) \leq \psi(x) \qquad \forall x \in \bar{\mathcal{O}} .$$

In this paragraph, we will assume that :

(2.8) $$f \text{ Borel bounded, } \alpha > 0$$

(2.9) $$\Phi(t) : B_0(\bar{\mathcal{O}}) \to C_0(\bar{\mathcal{O}}) \ , \ \forall t > 0$$ [(1)]

This assumption amounts to a non degeneracy assumption on the diffusion matrix a. Then we can state the :

---

(1) where $B_0(\bar{\mathcal{O}})$ is the set of bounded Borel functions which vanish on Γ, and $C_0(\bar{\mathcal{O}})$ the set of continuous functions which are 0 on the boundary of $\mathcal{O}$.

Theorem 2.1.

Under the assumptions (1.1), (1.2), $\mathcal{O}$ bounded regular, (2.1), (2.8), (2.9) then the set of functions satisfying (2.5), (2.6), (2.7) is non empty and has a maximum element, denoted by $u(x)$. This function $u(x)$ satisfies (2.3), and there exists an optimal stopping time $\hat{\theta}_x$, i.e., such that :

$$u(x) = J_x(\hat{\theta}_x).$$

This optimal stopping time $\hat{\theta}_x$ is defined by :

$$\hat{\theta}_x = \inf \{t \geq 0 \mid u(y(t)) = \psi(y(t))\}.$$

Proof : From (2.9), (2.4) it follows that the function :

$$z = \int_0^\infty e^{-\alpha t} \Phi(t)(f\chi_{\mathcal{O}})dt \in C_0(\bar{\mathcal{O}})$$

and by the semi group property satisfies and is the unique solution of the functional equation :

$$z = \int_0^t e^{-\alpha s} \Phi(s)(f\chi_{\mathcal{O}})ds + e^{-\alpha t} \Phi(t)z \ , \quad \forall t \geq 0.$$

Clearly,

$$z(x) = E\int_0^{\tau_x} e^{-\alpha t} f(y(t))dt.$$

One next considers the penalized problem, defined as follows. To find $u_\varepsilon \in C_0(\bar{\mathcal{O}})$, such that :

$$u_\varepsilon = \int_0^\infty e^{-\alpha t} \Phi(t)(f\chi_{\mathcal{O}} - \tfrac{1}{\varepsilon}(u_\varepsilon-\psi)^+)dt \tag{2.10}$$

We show that there exists one and only one solution of (2.9) $u_\varepsilon \in C_0(\bar{\mathcal{O}})$. Indeed, let $w \in C_0(\bar{\mathcal{O}})$, and define $T_\varepsilon w = z$, by

$$z = \int_0^\infty e^{-(\alpha+\frac{1}{\varepsilon})t} \Phi(t)(f\chi_{\mathcal{O}} + \frac{\psi \wedge w}{\varepsilon})dt. \tag{2.11}$$

Since $\psi|_\Gamma \geq 0$,$\psi \wedge w \in C_0(\bar{\mathcal{O}})$, and thus $z \in C_0(\bar{\mathcal{O}})$. Hence T_ε maps $C_0(\bar{\mathcal{O}})$ into itself. The map T_ε is a contraction, since :

$$\|z_1 - z_2\| \leq \int_0^\infty e^{-(\alpha+\frac{1}{\varepsilon})t} \frac{\|w_1 - w_2\|}{\varepsilon} dt = \frac{\|w_1 - w_2\|}{1 + \varepsilon\alpha}$$

A fixed point of T_ε satisfies the equation :

$$z = \int_0^\infty e^{-(\alpha+\frac{1}{\varepsilon})t} \Phi(t)[f\chi_{\mathcal{O}} - \frac{(z - \psi)^+}{\varepsilon} + \frac{z}{\varepsilon}] dt \tag{2.12}$$

which is equivalent to (2.10). Therefore there exists one and only one solution of (2.10) belonging to $C_0(\bar{\mathcal{O}})$. The fact that (2.10) and (2.12) are equivalent can be seen as follows.

Let us set

$$z = \int_0^\infty e^{-\alpha t}\,\Phi(t)g\,dt \quad , \quad \text{with } g \in B_0(\bar{\mathcal{O}})$$

then :

$$z = \int_0^\infty e^{-(\alpha+\frac{1}{\varepsilon})t}\,\Phi(t)(g + \frac{z}{\varepsilon})dt.$$

Indeed, using the relation

$$z = \int_0^t e^{-\alpha s}\,\Phi(s)g\,ds + e^{-\alpha t}\,\Phi(t)z$$

we have :

$$\int_0^\infty e^{-(\alpha+\frac{1}{\varepsilon})t}\,\Phi(t)\,\frac{z}{\varepsilon}\,dt = \int_0^\infty \frac{e}{\varepsilon}^{-\frac{t}{\varepsilon}}\,[z - \int_0^t e^{-\alpha s}\,\Phi(s)g\,ds]dt =$$

$$= z + \int_0^\infty \frac{d}{dt}\,e^{-\frac{t}{\varepsilon}}\,(\int_0^t e^{-\alpha s}\,\Phi(s)g\,ds)dt$$

and performing an integration by parts, we recover the desired relation.

We can give the interpretation of u_ε as follows. Let $v(t)$ be a process adapted to $\mathcal{F}^t$, such that $0 \leq v(t) \leq 1$.

Such a process will be called an admissible control for the penalized problem by setting :

$$(2.13) \qquad J_x^\varepsilon(v) = E[\int_0^{\tau_x} e^{-(\alpha t+\frac{1}{\varepsilon}\int_0^t v(s)ds)}\,(f(y(t)) + \frac{1}{\varepsilon}\,v(t)\,\psi(y(t)))dt]$$

We note that, since the stopped process is a Markov process then u_ε satisfies the property :

$$\int_0^{t\wedge\tau_x} e^{-\alpha t}(f(y(t)) - \frac{1}{\varepsilon}(u_\varepsilon(y(t)) - \psi(y(t)))^+)dt +$$

$$e^{-\alpha t\wedge\tau_x}\,u_\varepsilon(y(t\wedge\tau_x)) \text{ is an } \mathcal{F}^t \text{ martingale.}$$

Using a standard lemma on martingales, it is easy to check the relation :

$$(2.14) \qquad u_\varepsilon(x) = E[\int_0^{\tau_x} e^{-(\alpha t+\frac{1}{\varepsilon}\int_0^t v(s)ds)}\,(f(y(t)) - \frac{1}{\varepsilon}(u_\varepsilon(y(t)) - \psi(y(t)))^+ + \frac{u_\varepsilon(y(t))v(t)}{\varepsilon})dt].$$

From this, it readily follows that :

$$(2.15) \qquad u_\varepsilon(x) = \operatorname*{Inf}_v J_x^\varepsilon(v) = J_x^\varepsilon(\hat{v}_\varepsilon)$$

where

$$\hat{v}_\varepsilon(t) = \begin{cases} 1 & \text{if} \quad u_\varepsilon(y(t)) > \psi(y(t)) \\ 0 & \text{if} \quad u_\varepsilon(y(t)) \leq \psi(y(t)) \end{cases}$$

We now show that (cf. J.L.MENALDI)

(2.16) $$u_\varepsilon(x) \leq u_{\varepsilon'}(x) \quad \text{if} \quad \varepsilon \leq \varepsilon'.$$

Indeed, we have, as easily seen

$$T_\varepsilon u_{\varepsilon'} - u_{\varepsilon'} = \int_0^\infty e^{-(\alpha+\frac{1}{\varepsilon})t} \Phi(t)(u_{\varepsilon'} - \psi)^+(\tfrac{1}{\varepsilon'} - \tfrac{1}{\varepsilon})dt \leq 0$$

The operator T_ε being obviously monotone, it follows that

$$T_\varepsilon^k u_{\varepsilon'} \leq u_{\varepsilon'}$$

and letting $k \to +\infty$, we obtain (2.16).

Let us denote for a while by :

$$w(x) = \operatorname*{Inf}_\theta J_x(\theta)$$

We are going to show that

(2.17) $$u_\varepsilon \to w \quad \text{in } C^0(\bar{\mathcal{O}})$$

Indeed, by the martingale property seen above, we have if θ is a stopping time

(2.18) $$E\, e^{-(\alpha\, \theta\wedge\tau_x + \frac{1}{\varepsilon}\int_0^{\theta\wedge\tau_x} v(s)ds)} u_\varepsilon(y(\theta\wedge\tau_x)) +$$

$$+ E\int_0^{\theta\wedge\tau_x} e^{-(\alpha t+\frac{1}{\varepsilon}\int_0^t v(s)ds)} (f(y(t)) - \tfrac{1}{\varepsilon}(u_\varepsilon(y(t)) - \psi(y(t)))^+ +$$

$$+ \frac{u_\varepsilon(y(t))v(t)}{\varepsilon})dt = u_\varepsilon(x).$$

Let :

$$\hat{\theta}_\varepsilon = \inf\{t \geq 0 \mid u_\varepsilon(y(t)) \geq \psi(y(t))\}$$

which is an $\mathcal{F}^t$ stopping time, since u_ε, ψ are continuous.

Clearly,

$$\hat{v}_\varepsilon(t) = 0 \quad \text{if} \quad t < \hat{\theta}_\varepsilon.$$

Taking in (2.18), $v(t) = \hat{v}_\varepsilon(t)$, $\theta = \hat{\theta}_\varepsilon$, and noting that by virtue of the continuity of the process $y(t)$,

$$u_\varepsilon(y(\hat{\theta}_\varepsilon \Lambda \tau_x)) = \psi(y(\hat{\theta}_\varepsilon))\chi_{\hat{\theta}_\varepsilon < \tau_x} ,$$

then; one has

$$u_\varepsilon(x) = J_x(\hat{\theta}_\varepsilon).$$

Hence

$$u_\varepsilon(x) \geq w(x)$$

We next obtain an estimate from above for $u_\varepsilon(x)$.

Let θ be an arbitrary $\mathfrak{F}^t$ stopping time, we define

$$v_\theta(t) = \begin{vmatrix} 0 & \text{if } t < \theta \\ 1 & \text{if } t \geq \theta \end{vmatrix}$$

We have :

$$J_x^\varepsilon(v_\theta) - J_x(\theta) = E[\int_{\theta \Lambda \tau}^{\tau} f(y(t))\, e^{-\alpha t} \exp - \frac{t - \theta \Lambda \tau}{\varepsilon} dt +$$

$$+ \int_{\theta \Lambda \tau}^{\tau} \frac{\psi(y(t))}{\varepsilon} \; e^{-\alpha t} \exp - \frac{t - \theta \Lambda \tau}{\varepsilon} dt - \psi(y(\theta))\psi_{\theta < \tau}\, e^{-\alpha\theta}]$$

$$= I + II.$$

Since f is bounded, we have :

$$I \leq ||f||\, \varepsilon \; .$$

For II, we may write, if $\delta > 0$

$$II = E[\int_{\theta \Lambda \tau}^{\tau \Lambda (\theta \Lambda \tau + \delta)} \frac{1}{\varepsilon}[\psi(y(t)) - \psi(y(\tau \Lambda \theta)] \exp - \alpha(\tau \Lambda \theta) \exp - \frac{t - \theta \Lambda \tau}{\varepsilon} dt$$

$$+ \int_{\theta \Lambda \tau}^{\tau \Lambda (\theta \Lambda \tau + \delta)} \frac{1}{\varepsilon} \psi(y(t))(e^{-\alpha t} - e^{-\alpha(\tau \Lambda \theta)}) \exp - \frac{t - \theta \Lambda \tau}{\varepsilon} dt +$$

$$- \psi(y(\theta))\chi_{\theta < \tau}\, e^{-\alpha\theta} \exp - \frac{1}{\varepsilon}(\tau \Lambda (\theta + \delta) - \theta)$$

$$+ \int_{\tau \Lambda (\theta \Lambda \tau + \delta)}^{\tau} \frac{1}{\varepsilon} \psi(y(t))\, e^{-\alpha t} \exp - \frac{t - \theta \Lambda \tau}{\varepsilon} dt] = II_1 + II_2 + II_3$$

$$= II_1 + II_2 + II_3 + II_4.$$

We have

$$II_1 \leq C\, E \sup_{\theta \Lambda \tau \leq t \leq \tau \Lambda (\theta \Lambda \tau + \delta)} |\psi(y(\tau \Lambda \theta))| \exp - \alpha\, \theta \Lambda \tau$$

$$II_2 \leq C\, \delta$$

$$II_4 \leq C \exp - \frac{\delta}{\varepsilon}$$

$$II_3 = -E\, \psi(y(\theta))\chi_{\tau-\delta\leq\theta<\tau}\, e^{-\alpha\theta} \exp - \frac{\tau-\theta}{\varepsilon} -$$

$$- E\, \psi(y(\theta))\psi_{\theta<\tau-\delta}\, e^{-\alpha\theta} \exp - \frac{\delta}{\varepsilon}$$

$$\leq - E(\psi(y(\theta)) - \psi(y(\tau)))\chi_{\tau-\delta\leq\theta<\tau}\, e^{-\alpha\theta} \exp - \frac{\tau-\theta}{\varepsilon} + C \exp - \frac{\delta}{\varepsilon}$$

$$\leq C[\exp - \frac{\delta}{\varepsilon} + E \sup_{\tau-\delta\leq t\leq\tau} |\psi(y(t)) - \psi(y(\tau))| \exp -\alpha\tau].$$

Let us set :

$$\rho(\lambda) = \sup_{\substack{\xi_1,\xi_2 \in \bar{\mathcal{O}} \\ |\xi_1-\xi_2| \leq \lambda}} |\psi(y(t)) - \psi(y(\tau))|\, e^{-\alpha\tau} \leq$$

$$\leq E \sup_{\tau-\delta\leq t\leq\tau} |\psi(y(t)) - \psi(y(\tau))|\chi_{\tau\leq T} + C\, e^{-\alpha T}$$

and

$$E \sup_{\tau-\delta\leq t\leq\tau} |\psi(y(t)) - \psi(y(\tau))|\chi_{\tau\leq T} \leq \rho(h) +$$

$$+ C\, E\, \chi_{\sup_{\tau-\delta\leq t\leq\tau} |y(t)- y(\tau)| \geq h}\, \chi_{\tau\leq T}$$

$$\leq \rho(h) + \frac{C}{h^{2m}} E \sup_{\tau-\delta\leq t\leq\tau} |y(t)- y(\tau)|^{2m} \chi_{\tau\leq T}.$$

Let N be equal to $[\frac{T}{k}]$. We have :

$$E \sup_{\tau-\delta\leq t\leq\tau} |y(t)- y(\tau)|^{2m} \chi_{\tau\leq T} = E\, \chi_{\tau\leq T} \sum_{p=o}^{n} \chi_{pk<\tau\leq(p+1)k} \times$$

$$\times \sup_{\tau-\delta\leq t\leq\tau} |y(t)- y(\tau)|^{2m}$$

$$\leq E \sum_{p=o}^{N} C_m\, E \sup_{(pk-\delta)^+\leq t\leq(p+1)k} |y(t) - y(pk-\delta)^+)|^{2m}$$

$$\leq C'_m\, (k+\delta)^m\, \frac{T}{k}.$$

Chosing $h = \delta^{1/10}$, $m = \frac{5}{2}$, $k = \delta$, $T = \frac{1}{\delta^{\frac{1}{2}}}$,

we finally obtain :

$$II_3 \leq C[\exp - \frac{\delta}{\varepsilon} + \exp - \frac{\alpha}{\delta^{\frac{1}{2}}} + \rho(\delta^{1/10}) + \delta^{\frac{1}{2}}].$$

Similarly :

$$II_1 \leq C[\exp - \frac{\alpha}{\delta^{\frac{1}{2}}} + \rho(\delta^{1/10}) + \delta^{\frac{1}{2}}].$$

Gathering results, it follows that :

$$J_x^{\varepsilon}(v_\theta) - J_x(\theta) \leq C[\varepsilon + \delta + \delta^{\frac{1}{2}} + \rho(\delta^{1/10}) + \exp - \frac{\alpha}{\delta^{\frac{1}{2}}} + \exp - \frac{\delta}{\varepsilon}]$$

hence

$$u^{\varepsilon}(x) - w(x) \leq C[\varepsilon + \delta + \delta^{\frac{1}{2}} + \rho(\delta^{1/10}) + \exp - \frac{\alpha}{\delta^{\frac{1}{2}}} + \exp - \frac{\delta}{\varepsilon}]$$

Letting first ε go to 0, then δ go to 0, we obtain (2.17).

We note that :

$$w(x) \leq J_x(o) \leq \psi(x) \quad \text{if } x \in \mathcal{O}.$$

Moreover, since $w|_\Gamma = 0 \leq \psi|_\Gamma$, we have :

$$w(x) \leq \psi(x) \quad \forall x \in \bar{\mathcal{O}}.$$

Now from (2.10), it follows that :

$$u_\varepsilon = \int_0^t e^{-\alpha s} \Phi(s) f\chi_{\mathcal{O}} ds + e^{-\alpha t} \Phi(t) u_\varepsilon$$

and from the convergence of u_ε towards w in $C_o(\bar{\mathcal{O}})$, it follows that w is solution of (2.4), (2.5), (2.6).

Now if u is a solution of (2.4), (2.5), (2.6), then using again the Markov property of the stopped process $y(t \wedge \tau_x)$, we see that :

$$e^{-\alpha t} u(y(t \wedge \tau)) + \int_0^t e^{-\alpha s} \chi_{\mathcal{O}} f(y(s \wedge \tau))ds \text{ is a lower martingale.}$$

From this and (2.6), it is easy to check that :

$$u(x) \leq J_x(\theta)$$

hence :

$$u \leq w .$$

Therefore, w is the maximum element of the set of functions satisfying (2.5), (2.6), (2.7).

It remains to show that $\hat{\theta}_x$ is optimal. If $u(x) = \psi(x)$, then $\hat{\theta}_x = 0$ a.s., which is clearly optimal. Therefore, we may assume $u(x) < \psi(x)$. Then $\hat{\theta}_x > 0$ a.s. Let $\delta > 0$, such that

$$u(x) < \psi(x) - \delta$$

and

$$\theta_x^\delta = \inf \{t \geq 0 \mid u(y(t)) \geq \psi(y(t)) - \frac{\delta}{2}\}.$$

Hence for $t \in [0,\theta_x^\delta \Lambda \tau_x]$, we have $y(t) \in \bar{\mathcal{O}}$, and $\psi(y(t)) - u(y(t)) \geq \frac{\delta}{2}$.

Let ε_δ such that :

$$\varepsilon \leq \varepsilon_\delta \text{ implies } \|u_\varepsilon - u\|_{C^o(\bar{\mathcal{O}})} \leq \frac{\delta}{4}.$$

Therefore, we have :

$$\varepsilon \leq \varepsilon_\delta \text{ and } t \in [0,\theta_x^\delta \Lambda \tau_x] \text{ implies } u_\varepsilon(y(t)) \leq u(y(t)) + \frac{\delta}{4}$$

$$\leq \psi(y(t)) - \frac{\delta}{2} + \frac{\delta}{4} = \psi(y(t)) - \frac{\delta}{4}.$$

Therefore :

$$\hat{\theta}_\varepsilon \geq \theta_x^\delta \Lambda \tau_x.$$

Hence :

$$u_\varepsilon(x) = E[u_\varepsilon(y(\theta_x^\delta \Lambda \tau_x)) \exp - \alpha\, \theta_x^\delta \Lambda \tau_x + \int_0^{\theta_x^\delta \Lambda \tau_x} f(y(t))e^{-\alpha t}dt].$$

Letting ε go to 0, we obtain :

$$w(x) = E[w(y(\theta_x^\delta \Lambda \tau_x))\exp - \alpha\, \theta_x^\delta \Lambda \tau_x + \int_0^{\theta_x^\delta \Lambda \tau_x} f(y(t))e^{-\alpha t}dt].$$

Letting $\delta \downarrow 0$, it is easy to check, using the continuity of the process $y(t)$ and of the function u, that $\theta_x^\delta \uparrow \hat{\theta}_x$. Therefore, in the above equality, we can replace θ_x^δ by $\hat{\theta}_x$. From the definition of $\hat{\theta}_x$, this implies $w(x) = J_x(\hat{\theta}_x)$, which proves that $\hat{\theta}_x$ is optimal, and completes the proof of the theorem.

■

By some slight modifications of the proof of theorem 2.1, one can prove the following property. Let θ, θ' be two $\mathcal{F}^t$ stopping times with $\theta \leq \theta'$, and let $\tilde{y}(t)$ be the diffusion starting in η at time θ, where η is $\mathcal{F}^\theta$ measurable, i.e.

$$(2.19) \qquad \begin{cases} d\tilde{y} = g(\tilde{y})dt + \sigma(\tilde{y})dw(t), \ t > \theta \\ \tilde{y}(\theta) = \eta \end{cases}$$

Let $\tilde{\tau}$ be the first exit time of $\tilde{y}(t)$ from the domain $\mathcal{O}$, after θ. Then, the maximum element of the set of functions satisfying (2.5), (2.6), (2.7) satisfies the relations

$$(2.20) \qquad u(y(\theta)) \leq E[\int_\theta^{\theta' \Lambda \tau} f(\tilde{y}(t))\, e^{-\alpha(t-\theta)}dt + u(\tilde{y}(\theta'))\, e^{-\alpha(\theta'-\theta)} \chi_{\theta' < \tau} | \mathcal{F}^\theta] \text{ a.s.,}$$

and if

$$\hat{\theta} = \inf\{t \geq \theta \mid u(y(t)) = \psi(y(t))\}$$

Then :

$$(2.21)\qquad u(y(\theta)) = E[\int_{\theta}^{\hat{\theta}\wedge\tau} f(\tilde{y}(t))\, e^{-\alpha(t-\theta)}dt + u(\tilde{y}(\hat{\theta}))\, e^{-\alpha(\hat{\theta}-\theta)}\, \chi_{\hat{\theta}<\tau} \mid \mathcal{F}^{\theta}] \text{ a.s.}$$

2.3. Analytic approach.

The problem of interest here is two fold. Firstly, to obtain some regularity properties of the function $u(x)$, and secondly to characterize it in a more convenient way than saying it is the maximum element of the set of functions satisfying (2.5), (2.6), (2.7). We introduce the differential operator :

$$(2.22)\qquad A = -g_i \frac{\partial}{\partial x_i} - a_{ij} \frac{\partial^2}{\partial x_i \partial x_j}$$

where

$$a = \tfrac{1}{2}\sigma\sigma^*$$

We assume here the uniform ellipticity condition :

$$(2.23)\qquad \sum_{i,j} a_{ij}\xi_i\xi_j \geq \beta|\xi|^2 \quad , \quad \forall\xi \in R^n \quad , \beta > 0.$$

Since a_{ij} is Lipschitz, we may rewrite A in the variational form :

$$A = -\frac{\partial}{\partial x_i} a_{ij} \frac{\partial}{\partial x_j} + a_i \frac{\partial}{\partial x_i}$$

with $\quad a_i = -g_i + \frac{\partial}{\partial x_j} a_{ij}$.

Let $H^1(\mathcal{O}) = \{z \in L^2(\mathcal{O}), \frac{\partial z}{\partial x_i} \in L^2(\mathcal{O})\}$ and $H^1_o(\mathcal{O})$ = closure of $\mathcal{D}(\mathcal{O})$ in $H^1(\mathcal{O})$.

We define the bilinear form on $H^1_o(\mathcal{O})$

$$a(u,v) = \Sigma\int_{\mathcal{O}} a_{ij} \frac{\partial u}{\partial x_j} \frac{\partial v}{\partial x_i}\, dx + \Sigma\int_{\mathcal{O}} a_i \frac{\partial u}{\partial x_i}\, v dx .$$

Then, from standard results on variational inequalities (G. STAMPACCHIA [1], J.L. LIONS - G. STAMPACCHIA [1]), there exists one and only one solution u of :

$$(2.24)\qquad \left| \begin{array}{l} a(u,v-u) + \alpha(u,v-u) \geq (f,v-u) \\ \forall v \in H^1_o(\mathcal{O}) \ , \ v \leq \psi \ \text{ and } u \in H^1_o(\mathcal{O}) \ , \ u \leq \psi. \end{array} \right.$$

The important result is that this function u coincides with maximum element of (2.5), (2.6), (2.7). This is shown by considering the penalized problem

$$(2.25)\qquad \left| \begin{array}{l} Au_\varepsilon + \alpha u_\varepsilon + \frac{1}{\varepsilon}(u_\varepsilon-\psi)^+ = f \quad , u_\varepsilon|_\Gamma = 0 \quad u_\varepsilon \in W^{2,p}(\mathcal{O}), \\ \qquad \forall p \geq 2. \end{array} \right.$$

which has one and only one solution by standard results on P.D.E. Moreover u_ε coïncides with the solution of (2.10). Now one checks that $u_\varepsilon \to u$ solution of (2.24), say in $H_0^1(\mathcal{O})$ weakly, which completes the proof of the desired result. The characterization (2.24) besides giving some information on the derivatives of u, is very convenient from the numerical point of view.

Let us also mention to end this section, that if ψ is regular, i.e., if $\psi \in W^{2,p}(\mathcal{O})$, then u can also be characterized uniquely as the solution of :

$$(2.26)\qquad \begin{cases} Au + \alpha u \leq f \quad \text{a.e.} \\ u \leq \psi \ , \ u|_\Gamma = 0 \ , \quad u \in W^{2,p}(\mathcal{O}), \quad \forall p \geq 2 \\ (u-\psi)(Au + \alpha u - f) = 0. \end{cases}$$

For details, see A. BENSOUSSAN - J.L. LIONS [1].

An additional advantage of the formulations (2.24), (2.26) is that one can weaken the assumption on f and α ($\alpha = 0$ and $f \in L^p(\mathcal{O})$, $p > \frac{n}{2}$ are possible) relying on results from P.D.E.

3. SOLUTION OF THE IMPULSIVE CONTROL PROBLEM

We now return to the problem posed in the first paragraph.

3.1. Semi-group approach.

We formulate the following problem. To find u(x) such that :

$$(3.1)\qquad u(x) \leq \int_0^t \Phi(s)\, \chi_{\mathcal{O}} f(x)\, e^{-\alpha s} ds + \Phi(t) u(x) e^{-\alpha t} \ , \quad \forall t$$

$$(3.2)\qquad u \in C_0(\bar{\mathcal{O}}) \ , \quad u(x) \leq Mu(x) \quad \forall x,$$

where we have set in (3.2) :

$$(3.3)\qquad Mu(x) = k + \operatorname*{Inf}_{\xi \geq 0} (u(x+\xi) + c(\xi)).$$

It is understood implicitly that if $u \in C_0(\bar{\mathcal{O}})$, it is extended outside $\bar{\mathcal{O}}$ by setting $u=0$ in $R^n - \bar{\mathcal{O}}$. With that convention, it is easy to check that :

$$(3.4)\qquad Mu(x) = k + \operatorname*{Inf}_{\substack{\xi \geq 0 \\ \xi + x \in \bar{\mathcal{O}}}} (u(x+\xi) + c(\xi)).$$

Moreover, since: $c(\xi)$ is continuous, $c(\xi) \to +\infty$ as $|\xi| \to \infty$, there exists, by standard measurable selection theorems a mapping $\hat{\xi}(x)$, which is measurable, such that $x + \hat{\xi}(x) \in \bar{\mathcal{O}}$, and :

$$u(x+\hat{\xi}(x)) + c(\hat{\xi}(x)) = \operatorname*{Inf}_{\substack{\xi\geq 0 \\ \xi+x\in\bar{\mathcal{O}}}} (u(x+\xi) + c(\xi)).$$

We are going to prove the following :

Theorem 3.1.

We assume (1.1), (1.2), (1.7), (1.8), (1.9), (2.8), (2.23).

Then, the set of functions satisfying (3.1), (3.2) is not empty and admits a maximum element, also denoted by $u(x)$. Moreover :

(3.5) $$u(x) = \operatorname*{Inf}_{W} J_x(W)$$

and there exists an optimal impulse control $\hat{W}$.

Proof : We define an iterative process. Let us set :

$$u^o(x) = \int_0^\infty \Phi(t)\, \chi_{\mathcal{O}} f(x)\, e^{-\alpha t} dt$$

which belongs to $C_o(\bar{\mathcal{O}})$. Having defined $u^{n-1} \in C_o(\bar{\mathcal{O}})$, one defines $u^n \in C_o(\bar{\mathcal{O}})$, as the maximum element of the set of functions satisfying :

(3.6) $$\begin{cases} u^n(x) \leq \int_0^t \Phi(s)\, \chi_{\mathcal{O}}\, f(x)\, e^{-\alpha s} ds + \Phi(t) u^n(x)\, e^{-\alpha t} \\ u^n \in C_o(\bar{\mathcal{O}}) \;,\quad u^n(x) \leq M u^{n-1}(x). \end{cases}$$

By theorem 2.1, u^n is well defined and is the infimum of an optimal stopping time problem.

We have :

(3.7) $$0 \leq u^{n+1} \leq u^n \leq u^o.$$

Indeed, from (3.6), we see that $u^1 \leq u^o$. Since M is order preserving, one checks by induction that $u^{n+1} \leq u^n$, hence (3.7). In particular, we obtain :

(3.8) $$u^n \downarrow u \text{ point wise} \quad , \quad 0 \leq u \leq u^o.$$

We are now going to use an argument inspired form HANOUZET - JOLY [ ]. Let for $\psi \in C(\bar{\mathcal{O}})$, $\psi|_\Gamma \geq 0$, $\sigma(\psi)$ denote the maximum element of the set :

$$z \in C_o(\bar{\mathcal{O}}) \;,\quad z \leq \psi$$

$$z \leq \int_0^t \Phi(s)\, \chi_{\mathcal{O}} f\, e^{-\alpha s} dt + \Phi(t) z\, e^{-\alpha t}.$$

We notice that σ is concave, since :

$$\sigma(\lambda\psi_1 + (1-\lambda)\psi_2) \geq \lambda\, \sigma(\psi_1) + (1-\lambda)\sigma(\psi_2)$$

for $\lambda \in [0,1]$. The operator M being order preserving and also concave, it follows that :

$$S = \sigma M : C_o(\bar{\mathcal{O}}) \to C_o(\bar{\mathcal{O}}) \text{ is concave, and order preserving.}$$

Now since $u^o \in C_o(\bar{\mathcal{O}})$, there exists $\lambda > 0$ such that

$$\lambda\, u^o(x) \leq k = M(o) \quad , \forall x \tag{3.9}$$

Since $u^o \geq 0$, we may without loss of generality assume that $\lambda \in]0,1[$.

Let now $v,w \in C_o(\bar{\mathcal{O}})$, $v,w \geq 0$, and $\beta \in [0,1]$ such that

$$v(x) - w(x) \leq \beta\, v(x) \quad , \quad \forall x$$

Then, we have :

$$Sv(x) - Sw(x) \leq (1-\lambda)\, \beta\, Sv(x) \quad \forall x. \tag{3.10}$$

Indeed, by assumption :

$$w \geq (1-\beta)v$$

Since S is order preserving and concave :

$$Sw \geq S((1-\beta)v)$$
$$\geq (1-\beta)Sv + \beta S(o).$$

Using the fact that :

$$S(o) \geq \lambda\, u^o$$

which follows from (3.9) and

$$\lambda u^o = \lambda \int_o^t \Phi(s)\, \chi_{\mathcal{O}} f\, e^{-\alpha s}\, ds + \lambda\, \Phi(t) u^o\, e^{-\alpha t}$$
$$\leq \int_o^t \Phi(s)\, \chi_{\mathcal{O}} f\, e^{-\alpha s}\, ds + \Phi(t)(\lambda u^o) e^{-\alpha t} \ ,$$

We obtain :

$$Sw \geq (1-\beta)Sv + \beta\lambda u^o.$$

However, for any v, $Sv \leq u^o$, hence

$$Sw \geq (1-\beta)Sv + \beta\lambda\, Sv = Sv(1-\beta(1-\lambda))$$

hence the property (3.10).

We now apply (3.10). We first note that since $u^1 \geq 0$, we have

$$u^o - u^1 \leq u^o$$

hence

$$Su^o - Su^1 \leq (1-\lambda)\, Su^o \qquad \text{i.e;}$$

$$u^1 - u^2 \leq (1-\lambda)u^1$$

where we have used the fact that :

$$u^{n+1} = Su^n.$$

Applying (3.10) again, we get :

$$u^2 - u^3 \leq (1-\lambda)^2 u^2.$$

Therefore, in general we obtain :

$$u^m - u^{m+1} \leq (1-\lambda)^m u^m \leq (1-\lambda)^m u^o \tag{3.11}$$

Applying (3.11) inductively, it follows that :

$$u^{m+1} - u^{m+2} \leq (1-\lambda)^{m+1} u^o$$

......

$$u^{n-1} - u^n \leq (1-\lambda)^{n-1} u^o \quad , \text{ for } n > m.$$

Adding up :

$$u^m - u^n \leq (1-\lambda)^m[1+(1-\lambda)+\ldots+(1-\lambda)^{n-m-1}]u^o$$

$$\leq \frac{(1-\lambda)^m}{\lambda} u^o$$

From (3.8) follows the estimate :

$$u^m - u \leq \frac{(1-\lambda)^m}{\lambda} u^o \leq \frac{C}{\lambda}(1-\lambda)^m. \tag{3.12}$$

Hence $u \in C_o(\bar{\mathcal{O}})$. Let us note that if

$$u^o \leq M(o) \ , \quad \text{i.e.} \quad \lambda = 1,$$

then $Sv = u^o \quad \forall v$

hence $u^n = u^o = u$, which is consistent with (3.12). Letting $n \to +\infty$, we see that u satisfies the relations (3.1), (3.2).

Let us check that u is the maximum element of the set of function satisfying (3.1), (3.2). Let z be a function satisfying (3.1), (3.2). Clearly $z \leq u^o$. Assuming that $z \leq u^{n-1}$, and noting that (from theorem 2.1),

$$u^n = \inf_\theta E[\int_0^{\theta\Lambda\tau_x} f(y(t))\, e^{-\alpha t}dt + Mu^{n-1}(y(\theta))\chi_{\theta<\tau_x} e^{-\alpha\theta}]$$

we see that :

$$u^n \geq \inf_\theta E[\int_0^{\theta\Lambda\tau_x} f(y(t))\, e^{-\alpha t}dt + Mz(y(\theta)\chi_{\theta<\tau_x} e^{-\alpha\theta}] \tag{3.13}$$

But the function on the right hand side of (3.13) is (from theorem 2.1), the maximum element of the set of functions ϕ such that :

$\psi \in C_o(\bar{\mathcal{O}})$, $\psi \leq Mz$

$$\psi \leq \int_0^t \Phi(s)\, \chi_{\mathcal{O}} f\, e^{-\alpha s} ds + \Phi(t)\, \psi\, e^{-\alpha t}.$$

Since z is such a function, then $u^n \geq z$.

Going to the limit, we see that $u \geq z$. Hence u is the maximum element. Let us now prove (3.5) and define an optimal impulse control. Let W be an arbitrary impulse control. Let us define :

$y^o(t)$ = diffusion process (g,σ) starting in x, at time 0.

$y^1(t)$ = diffusion process (g,σ) starting in $y^o(\theta^1)+\xi^1$ at time θ^1,

....

$y^{i+1}(t)$ = diffusion process (g,σ) starting in $y^i(\theta^{i+1})+\xi^{i+1}$ at time θ^{i+1}

....

Let also τ^i be the first exit time of $y^i(t)$ from $\mathcal{O}$, after θ^i. It is clear that :

$$y(t) = y^i(t) \text{ for } t \in [\theta^i,\theta^{i+1}[,$$

and also :

$$\theta^{i+1}\Lambda\tau^i = \theta^{i+1}\Lambda\tau \quad i=0,1....$$

Let us consider the maximum element u of (3.1), (3.2).

From the convergence of the u^n, we have

$$u(x) = \operatorname*{Inf}_{\theta} E\left[\int_0^{\theta\Lambda\tau_x} f(\tilde{y}(t))e^{-\alpha t}dt + Mu(\tilde{y}(\theta))\chi_{\theta<\tau_x}\, e^{-\alpha\theta}\right] \tag{3.14}$$

Therefore u is also the maximum element of (2.5), (2.6), (2.7) with ψ = Mu. Using the property (2.19), we can write

$$u(y^i(\theta^i)) \leq E\Big[\int_{\theta^i}^{\theta^{i+1}\Lambda\tau^i} f(y^i(t))\, e^{-\alpha(t-\theta^i)}dt + Mu(y^i(\theta^{i+1})) \times \tag{3.15}$$

$$\times\, e^{-\alpha(\theta^{i+1}-\theta^i)}\, \chi_{\theta^{i+1}<\tau^i} \Big| \mathcal{F}^{\theta^i}\Big]$$

hence :

$$Eu(y(\theta^i))\, e^{-\alpha\theta^i}\chi_{\theta^i<\tau} \leq E\Big[\int_{\theta^i}^{\theta^{i+1}\Lambda\tau} f(y(t))\, e^{-\alpha t}dt +$$

$$+ (k+c(\xi^{i+1}))\, e^{-\alpha\theta^{i+1}} + u(y(\theta^{i+1})) . e^{-\alpha\theta^{i+1}}\, \chi_{\theta^{i+1}<\tau}\Big]$$

Adding up and using the fact that $\theta^i \to +\infty$ a.s., it follows :

(3.16) $$u(x) \leq J_x(W).$$

Let us now define :

$$\tilde{\theta}^o = 0 \quad , \hat{\theta}^o = 0$$

$$d\hat{y}^o = g(\hat{y}^o)dt + \sigma(\hat{y}^o)dw(t) \quad , \hat{y}^o(0) = x$$

$$\hat{\tau}^i = \inf\{t \geq 0 \mid \hat{y}^i(t) \notin \mathcal{O}\}$$

$$\tilde{\theta}^{i+1} = \inf\{t \geq \tilde{\theta}^i \mid u(\hat{y}^i(t)) = Mu(\hat{y}^i(t))\}$$

$$\hat{\theta}^i = \begin{cases} \tilde{\theta}^i & \text{if } \tilde{\theta}^i < \hat{\tau}^{i-1} \\ +\infty & \text{if not.} \end{cases}$$

$$\hat{\xi}^{i+1} = \hat{\xi}(\hat{y}^i(\hat{\theta}^{i+1})) \text{ if } \hat{\theta}^{i+1} < +\infty \quad , \hat{\xi}^{i+1} = 0 \text{ if } \hat{\theta}^{i+1} = +\infty ,$$

$$d\hat{y}^{i+1} = g(\hat{y}^{i+1})dt + \sigma(\hat{y}^{i+1})dw(t) \quad , t > \hat{\theta}^{i+1}$$

$$\tilde{y}^{i+1}(\hat{\theta}^{i+1}) = \hat{y}^i(\hat{\theta}^{i+1}) + \hat{\xi}^{i+1} .$$

We set :

$$\hat{W} = \{\hat{\theta}^i, \hat{\xi}^i\}$$

and :

$$\hat{y}(t) = \hat{y}^i(t) , \quad \text{for} \quad t \in [\hat{\theta}^i, \hat{\theta}^{i+1}[$$

$$\hat{\tau} = \inf\{t \geq 0 \mid \hat{y}(t) \notin \bar{\mathcal{O}}\}$$

We first note that :

(3.17) $$\hat{\theta}^{i+1} \wedge \hat{\tau}^i = \hat{\theta}^{i+1} \wedge \hat{\tau} = \tilde{\theta}^{i+1} \wedge \hat{\tau}^i$$

and :

(3.18) $$\hat{\theta}^i \geq \hat{\tau} \quad \text{implies} \quad \hat{\theta}^i = +\infty.$$

Therefore, we can write :

$$Eu(\hat{y}^i(\hat{\theta}^i))\, e^{-\alpha\hat{\theta}^i} = E\Big[\int_{\hat{\theta}^i}^{\tilde{\theta}^{i+1} \wedge \hat{\tau}^i} f(\hat{y}^i(t))\, e^{-\alpha t} dt + $$
$$+ Mu(\hat{y}^i(\tilde{\theta}^{i+1}))\, e^{-\alpha\tilde{\theta}^{i+1}} \chi_{\tilde{\theta}^{i+1} < \hat{\tau}^i}\Big]$$

Using (3.17), (3.18) and the fact that :

$$Mu(\hat{y}^i(\hat{\theta}^{i+1})) = k + c(\hat{\xi}^{i+1}) + u(\hat{y}^{i+1}(\hat{\theta}^{i+1})) \quad , \text{if } \hat{\theta}^{i+1} < \infty,$$

we obtain :

$$Eu(\hat{y}(\hat{\theta}^i))\, e^{-\alpha\hat{\theta}^i} = E\Big[\int_{\hat{\theta}^i \wedge \hat{\tau}}^{\hat{\theta}^{i+1} \wedge \hat{\tau}} f(\hat{y}(t))\, e^{-\alpha t} dt + (k + c(\hat{\xi}^{i+1}))e^{-\alpha\hat{\theta}^{i+1}} +$$

$$+ u(\hat{y}(\hat{\theta}^{i+1}))\, e^{-\alpha\hat{\theta}^{i+1}} \chi_{\hat{\theta}^{i+1} < \hat{\tau}}\Big].$$

Adding up, for i running from 0 to I, we obtain :

$$(3.19) \qquad u(x) = E\Big[\int_0^{\hat{\theta}^{I+1} \wedge \hat{\tau}} f(\hat{y}(t))e^{-\alpha t} dt + \sum_{i=1}^{I+1} (k + c(\hat{\xi}^i))\, e^{-\alpha\hat{\theta}^i} +$$

$$+ u(\hat{y}(\hat{\theta}^{I+1}))\, e^{-\alpha\hat{\theta}^{I+1}} \chi_{\hat{\theta}^{i+1} < \hat{\tau}}\Big].$$

From (3.19) it follows that :

$$E \sum_{i=1}^{\infty} e^{-\alpha\hat{\theta}^i} < +\infty$$

which implies that $\hat{\theta}^1 \to +\infty$ a.e. Hence $\hat{W}$ is an admissible impulse control. Letting $I \to +\infty$ in (3.19) it follows that :

$$u(x) = J_x(\hat{W})$$

This completes the proof of the theorem.

3.2. Analytic approach.

In the same way as in paragraph 2.3, it is important to obtain regularity results on u and to give a better characterization of the maximum element of (3.1), (3.2). We first indicate what is the analogue of (2.23). Namely :

$$(3.20) \qquad \left| \begin{array}{l} a(u,v-u) + \alpha(u,v-u) \geq (f,v-u) \\ \forall v \in H_0^1(\mathcal{O}),\ v \leq Mu\ ,\quad u \in H_0^1(\mathcal{O}),\ u \leq Mu. \end{array} \right.$$

This formulation is called a quasi-variational inequality. It has one and only one solution which coïncides with the maximum element of (3.1), (3.2).

The analogue of (2.25) is the following :

$$(3.21) \qquad \left| \begin{array}{l} Au + \alpha u \leq f \\ u \leq Mu\ ,\quad u|_\Gamma = 0\ ,\quad u \in W^{2,p}(\mathcal{O})\ ,\quad p \geq 2,\ p < \infty \\ (u - Mu)(Au + \alpha u - f) = 0 \end{array} \right.$$

The regularity $W^{2,p}(\mathcal{O})$ of u has been one of the most challenging difficulties. It has first been proved by JOLY-MOSCO-TROIANELLO [1] in the case of constant a_{ij}, then more recently by CAFFARELLI-FRIEDMAN [1] and MOSCO [1] in the general case. We can also weaken the assumptions on f, α.

3.3. Interpretation of the penalized problem.

The penalized problem associated with (3.1), (3.2) is defined as follows :

$$(3.22)\qquad u_\varepsilon = \int_0^\infty \Phi(t)(\chi_{\mathcal{O}} f - \tfrac{1}{\varepsilon}(u_\varepsilon - Mu_\varepsilon)^+)e^{-\alpha t}dt \quad , \quad u_\varepsilon \in C_0(\bar{\mathcal{O}})$$

This is not the penalized problem corresponding to an optimal stopping time problem with $\psi = Mu$. Nevertheless we have :

Theorem 3.2.

The assumptions are those of Theorem 3.1. Then :

$$(3.23)\qquad u_\varepsilon \downarrow u \text{ pointwise as } \varepsilon \downarrow 0$$

Proof : The existence and uniqueness of the solution of (3.22) is proved by a fixed point argument. Indeed (3.22) is equivalent to :

$$u_\varepsilon = \int_0^\infty e^{-(\alpha+\frac{1}{\varepsilon})t}\,\Phi(t)(\chi_{\mathcal{O}} f + \frac{u_\varepsilon \wedge Mu_\varepsilon}{\varepsilon})dt \,.$$

Defining the mapping $\mathcal{T}_\varepsilon : C_0(\bar{\mathcal{O}}) \to C_0(\bar{\mathcal{O}})$, by

$$\mathcal{T}_\varepsilon z = \int_0^\infty e^{-(\alpha+\frac{1}{\varepsilon})t}\,\Phi(t)(\chi_{\mathcal{O}} f + \frac{z\wedge Mz}{\varepsilon})dt$$

and using the fact that :

$$\|Mz_1 - Mz_2\|_{C_0(R^n)} \leq \|z_1 - z_2\|_{C_0(R^n)}$$

$$\|z_1 \wedge Mz_1 - z_2 \wedge Mz_2\| \leq \|z_1 - z_2\|$$

it is clear that $\mathcal{T}_\varepsilon$ is a contraction. We also have

$$\mathcal{T}_\varepsilon u_{\varepsilon'} - u_{\varepsilon'} = \int_0^\infty e^{-(\alpha+\frac{1}{\varepsilon})t}\,\Phi(t)(u_{\varepsilon'} - Mu_{\varepsilon'})^+(\tfrac{1}{\varepsilon'} - \tfrac{1}{\varepsilon})dt \leq 0$$

if $\varepsilon \leq \varepsilon'$. Hence $u_\varepsilon \leq u_{\varepsilon'}$. Since $\mathcal{T}_\varepsilon^k\, 0 \geq 0$, $u_\varepsilon \geq 0$.

Hence u_ε converges towards w pointwise. To identify w, we rely on Q.V.I. theory (Quasi variational inequality).

The function u_ε is solution of :

(3.23) $$a(u_\varepsilon,v) + \alpha(u_\varepsilon,v) + \frac{1}{\varepsilon}((u_\varepsilon - Mu_\varepsilon)^+,v) = (f,v)$$

$$\forall v \in H_o^1 , \quad u_\varepsilon \in H_o^1$$

Moreover, we have

(3.24) $$u_\varepsilon \geq u$$

Indeed, defining the sequence u_ε^n by $u_\varepsilon^o = u^o$, and

$$u_\varepsilon^{n+1} = \int_o^\infty \Phi(t)(\chi_{\mathcal{O}} f - \frac{1}{\varepsilon}(u_\varepsilon^{n+1} - Mu_\varepsilon^n)^+)\, e^{-\alpha t} dt$$

we have from the property of the penalized problem of the optimal stopping time problem, $u_\varepsilon^1 \geq u^1$, then inductively $u_\varepsilon^n \geq u^n$. Going to the limit we obtain (3.23).

Let $v \in H_o^1$, such that $v \leq Mu$. Hence $v \leq Mu^\varepsilon$.

Therefore :

$$((u_\varepsilon - Mu_\varepsilon)^+, v-u^\varepsilon) \leq ((u_\varepsilon - Mu_\varepsilon)^+, Mu_\varepsilon - u_\varepsilon) \leq 0$$

hence :

$$a(u_\varepsilon, v-u_\varepsilon) + \alpha(u_\varepsilon, v-u_\varepsilon) \geq (f, v-u_\varepsilon)$$

from which it easily follows that $u_\varepsilon \to u$ in $H_o^1(\mathcal{O})$ weakly. Hence u=w. The desired result (3.23) follows.

We note that from Dini's theorem $u_\varepsilon \to u$ in $C_o(\bar{\mathcal{O}})$ ∎

Let us now give the interpretation of u_ε. We first note that

(3.25) $$-\frac{1}{\varepsilon}(u_\varepsilon - Mu_\varepsilon)^+ = \operatorname*{Inf}_{m(x;R^n) \leq \frac{1}{\varepsilon}} \int [k + c(z) + u_\varepsilon(x+z) - u_\varepsilon(x)]\, m(x,dz)$$

where m $(x;A)$ is a positive measure on R^n, and $m(x;A)$ depends measurably on x, for A fixed Borel subset of R^n.

Let us go back to the notation at the end of §1. To a finite measure $m_\varepsilon(x;A)$, such that $m_\varepsilon(x;R^n) \leq \frac{1}{\varepsilon}$ and $m_\varepsilon(x;\{0\}) = 0$, one can associate a probability measure P_ε^x on Ω, μ, such that

(3.26) $$P_\varepsilon^x[x(o)=x] = 1$$

for $\varphi \in \mathcal{D}(R^n)$

$$(3.27)\qquad \varphi(x(t)) + \int_0^t A\varphi(x(s))ds - \int_0^t\int_{R^n} (\varphi(s)+z) - \varphi(x(s))\nu(ds,dz)$$

is a P_ε^x, μ^t martingale.

and :

$$(3.28)\qquad \nu(t,A) - \int_0^t m_\varepsilon(x(s);A)ds \quad \text{is a measure martingale.}$$

We define the payoff :

$$(3.29)\qquad J(P_\varepsilon^x) = E^{P_\varepsilon^x}\left[\int_0^\tau f(x(t))e^{-\alpha t}dt + \int_0^\infty\int_{R^n} (k+c(z))e^{-\alpha t}\,\nu(dt,dz)\right]$$

then :

$$(3.30)\qquad u_\varepsilon(x) = \operatorname*{Inf}_{P_\varepsilon^x} J(P_\varepsilon^x).$$

Clearly, we can restrict the choice of $m_\varepsilon(x;A)$ such that :

$$E^{P_\varepsilon^x}\int_0^t m_\varepsilon(x(s);R^n)ds \le \frac{C_0\, e^{\alpha t}}{k}$$

$$E^{P_\varepsilon^x}\int_0^\infty\int_{R^n} c(z)\, e^{-\alpha t}\, m_\varepsilon(x(t),dz)dt \le C_0$$

i.e;, P_ε^x satisfies all the conditions requested on P^x.

4. OTHER PROBLEMS AND REMARKS

Remark 4.1. : One can consider evolution problems. The semi-group approach extends with easy changes. Difficulties are found in studying the regularity of the function $u(x,t)$, since it depends now on time. The Q.V.I. approaches in the stationary and non stationary cases are significantly different. See MIGNOT-PUEL [1], BENSOUSSAN-LIONS [2].

Remark 4.2. : One can study impulsive control problems for other type of processes (diffusion with reflexions, semi-Markov processes, Levy processes, random evolutions, etc..). See A. BENSOUSSAN-J.L. LIONS [3], J.L. MENALDI [1], M. ROBIN [1], R.F. ANDERSON- A. FRIEDMAN [1], A.Friedman - M.Robin [1], etc...

Remark 4.3. : A purely probabilistic approach along the lines of C. STRIEBEL [1], has been considered by J.P. LEPELTIER - B.MARCHAL [1].

Remark 4.4. : One can consider differential games with impulse controls (A. BENSOUSSAN - J.L. LIONS [4]).

Remark 4.5. : It is possible to consider problems of stochastic control coupled with impulse control. This leads to non linear semi-groups $\Phi(t)$ in the formulation (3.1), (3.2), (see A. BENSOUSSAN - J.L. LIONS [3]).

Remark 4.6. : The shape of the continuation region, i.e . $C = \{x \mid u(x) < Mu(x)\}$ is an important open problem. For results in particular cases see BENSOUSSAN - BREZIS - FRIEDMAN [1], BENSOUSSAN FRIEDMAN [1], FRIEDMAN - ROBIN [1], ANDERSON - FRIEDMAN [1].

Remark 4.7. : Numerical techniques have been given by M. GOURSAT [1], J.P. QUADRAT [1], H.J. KUSHNER [1].

Remark 4.8. : In many applications, the impulses influence the state of the system only after some delay, once the decision has been taken. For details see M. ROBIN [1].

REFERENCES :

R.F. ANDERSON - A. FRIEDMAN [1], A quality control problem and quasi-variational inequalities, Arch. Rational Mech. Anal., 63 (1977), pp. 205-252.

A. BENSOUSSAN - H. BREZIS - A. FRIEDMAN [1], Estimates on the free boundary for quasi-variational inequalities, Comm. in Partial Differential Equations 2(3), 297-321 (1977).

A. BENSOUSSAN - A. FRIEDMAN [1], On the support of the solution of a system of quasi-variational inequalities of evolution. Journal of Math. Anal. and Applic.

A. BENSOUSSAN - J.L. LIONS [1], Applications des inéquations variationnelles en contrôle stochastique, Dunod, Paris, 1978.

A. BENSOUSSAN - J.L. LIONS [2], Contrôle impulsionnel et temps d'arrêt : inéquations variationnelles et quasi-variationnelles d'évolution, Cahiers de Mathématiques de la Décision, Université Paris IX-Dauphine, n° 7523.

A. BENSOUSSAN - J.L. LIONS [3], Contrôle Impulsionnel et Inéquations Quasi-Variationnelles, Dunod, Paris, to be published.

A. BENSOUSSAN - J.L. LIONS [4], Differential games with impulse times, Proceedings IEEE Conference on Decision and Control, Phoenix, November 1974.

A. BENSOUSSAN - J.L. LIONS [5], Optimal impulse and continuous control : method of non linear quasi-variational inequalities, Uspehi Math. Nauk, Dedicated to Academician Professor N.S. Nicholski, Moscou 1975, Tome 134, pp. 5-22.

L. CAFFARELLI - A. FRIEDMAN [1], Regularity of the solution of the quasi-variational inequality for the impulse control problem, I, II, to be published.

A. FRIEDMAN - M. ROBIN [1], the free boundary for variational inequalities with non local operators, SIAM Journal Control and Optimization, Vol. 16, n°2, March 1978.

M. GOURSAT - J.P. QUADRAT [1], Analyse numérique d'inéquations quasi-variationnelles elliptiques associées à des problèmes de contrôle impulsionnel, IRIA-Laboria Report, Aug. 1976, n°186.

B. HANOUZET - J.L. JOLY [1], Convergence uniforme des itérés définissant la solution d'une inéquation quasi-variationnelle abstraite, Note C.R.A.S. Paris, 1978.

J.L. JOLY - U. MOSCO - G.M. TROIANLELLO [1], On the regular solution of a quasi-variational inequality connected to a problem of stochastic impulse control, Journal Math. Analysis and Applications, to be publihed, also C.R.A.S. t. 279, Série A, 1974, p. 937.

H.J. KUSHNER [1], Probability Methods for Approximations in Stochastic Control and for Elliptic Equations, Academic Press (1977), New York.

J.P. LEPELTIER - B. MARCHAL [1], Techniques probabilistes dans le contrôle impulsionnel, to be published.

J.L. LIONS - G. STAMPACCHIA[1], Variational inequalities, Comm. Pure Applied Math. XX (1967), pp. 493-519.

J.L. MENALDI [1], Thesis, Paris, 1979.

F. MIGNOT - J.P. PUEL [1], Solution Maximum de certaines inéquations d'évolution paraboliques et inéquations quasi-variationnelles paraboliques, C.R.A.S., 280, Série A (1975), p. 259.

U. MOSCO [1], Personal communication.

J.P. QUADRAT [1], Thesis, Paris 1979.

M. ROBIN [1], Contrôle impulsionnel des processus de Markov, Thesis, Paris 1977.

G. STAMPACCHIA [1], Formes bilinéaires coercitives sur les ensembles convexes, C.R. Acad. Sc. Paris, t. 258 (1964), 4413-4416.

C. STRIEBEL [1], Martingale conditions for the optimal control of a continuous time stochastic system, International Workshop on Stochastic Filtering and control, Los Angeles, (May 1974).

AN INTRODUCTION TO DUALITY IN

RANDOM MECHANICS

by

Jean-Michel Bismut

Université Paris-Sud

Département de Mathématiques

91405 Orsay

1. INTRODUCTION.

Problems of deterministic control appear classically in mechanics in the following form [1] :

. x is a state variable varying in a n-dimensional manifold $\mathbf{M}$.

L is a function defined on the tangent bundle $T(\mathbf{M})$ of $\mathbf{M}$ with values in R. An extremum of

$$(1.1) \qquad \int_0^T L(x,\dot{x})dt$$

must be found among all differentiable paths $t \longrightarrow x_t$, with speed $\dot{x}$, with fixed x_0 and x_T.

This is the so-called Lagrangian formulation of the problem.

Under well known assumptions [1], the problem may be put in a Hamiltonian form.

Let us assume that for each $x \in \mathbf{M}$, $\dot{x} \longrightarrow L(x,\dot{x})$ is strictly convex and differentiable on $T_x(M)$.

The Hamiltonian function is then defined on the cotangent bundle $T^*(\mathbf{M})$ by Legendre transformation, i.e :

$$(1.2) \qquad H(x,p) = \sup_{\dot{x} \in T_x(\mathbf{M})} \langle p,\dot{x}\rangle - L(x,\dot{x}).$$

It is then known [1]-[16], under growth conditions on L, that for each $x \in M$, $p \longrightarrow H(x,p)$ is a strictly convex differentiable function on $T_x^*(M)$. Under classical assumptions, H may be supposed to be differentiable on $T^*(M)$.

dH defines then an element of $T^*(T^*(M))$. $T^*(M)$ is endowed with a canonical symplectic 2-form ω given by

$$\omega = \sum_1^n dp_i \wedge dx_i$$

ω defines then a canonical one to one mapping from $T^*_{(x,p)}(T^*(M))$ in $T_{(x,p)}(T^*(M))$: if $\phi \in T^*_{(x,p)}(T^*(M))$, $I\phi \in T_{(x,p)}(T^*(M))$ is given by : $\omega(I\phi, Y) = \langle \phi, Y \rangle$ when $Y \in T_{(x,p)}(T^*(M))$.

Hamilton -Jacobi equations may then be written in intrinsic form on $T^*(M)$

$$\frac{d(x,p)}{dt} = IdH(x,p) \tag{1.3}$$

In Coordinate form (1.3) may be written as :

$$\frac{dx}{dt} = \frac{\partial \mathcal{H}}{\partial p} \qquad \frac{dp}{dt} = \frac{-\partial \mathcal{H}}{\partial x} \tag{1.4}$$

There is a one-to-one correspondence between the extremums of (1.1) and the solutions of (1.4) by :

$$(x,\dot{x}) \in T(M) \longrightarrow (x,\ p = \frac{\partial L}{\partial \dot{x}}) \in T^*(M)$$

The problem of finding an intrinsic Lagrangian or Hamiltonian formulation for a stochastic control is much more difficult. It is in fact well known by Ito's stochastic calculus [14] that if w is a m-dimensional brownian motion, and if

$$x = x_0 + \int_0^t \dot{x}dt + \int_0^t H.dw \tag{1.5}$$

is a semi-martingale with values in R^n, then if Φ is a C^∞ mapping $R^n \longrightarrow R^n$,

$$\Phi(x_t) = \Phi(x_0) + \int_0^t (\Phi'(x)\dot{x} + \frac{1}{2}\tilde{H}\Phi''H)dt + \int_0^t \Phi'(x).Hdw.$$

This implies that if x a semi-martingale with values in a manifold written in a coordinate system as (1.5), then $H \in T_x(M)$ but $(x,\dot{x},H)$ is not intrinsically defined.

The Hamiltonian intrinsic formulation of an optimization problem of stochastic control is then much more difficult that in deterministic control and requires technical developements out of the reach of this survey [10].

We will not try to present here the intrinsic analog of (1.3) in stochastic control, but only the coordinate analog of (1.4), which requires that the manifold M is in fact R^n. We will point out some "intrinsic" quantities appearing in the computations, i.e. quantities invariant by any diffeomorphism of R^n. In particular a stochastic process $p_t \in T^*_{x_t}(M)$ is defined, which is the analogous of p in (1.4).

This paper is not a review paper, but only an introductory paper to random mechanics, based mostly on our own work . We will not always be entirely rigorous. In particular integrability conditions will not be given, but the gaps may be easily filled. Moreover we will deal essentially with the topics covered in our review paper [11], i.e. with variational methods on semi-martingales, and not with any other problem, like optimal stopping, impulse control, where Lagrange multiplier techniques may also be efficiently used (e.g. [9]). For a complete coverage of the relation between the approach used here and previous work, we refer also to [11] and references therein.

Section 2 is devoted to stochastic Lagrangian variational techniques, and section 3 to a stochastic Hamiltonian formalism. In section 4, the stochastic analog of Pontryagin maximum principle is given.

In section 5, backward stochastic differential equations are reviewed. In section 6, in presence of convexity, the Hamiltonian equations are shown to derive from two dual problems of optimization on semi-martingales in the sense of Rockafellar [16]. In section 7, some examples of dual problems are explicited. Extensions are indicated in section 8.

Some knowledge of stochastic integration and martingale theory [14] is necessary to read the whole paper.

2. THE VARIATIONAL PROBLEM

$(\Omega, \mathfrak{F}, P)$ is a complete probability space endowed with an increasing right continuous sequence of complete σ-fields $\{\mathfrak{F}_t\}_{t\geq 0}$. w is a m-dimensional brownian motion adapted to $\{\mathfrak{F}_t\}_{t\geq 0}$.

ℓ_0 and ℓ_T are two differentiable functions defined on R^n with values in R. L is a function defined on $(\Omega \times R) \times R^n \times R^n \times (R^n)^m$ which is such that

. for $(x,\dot{x},H)$ $R^n \times R^n \times (R^n)^m$

$$(\omega,t) \longrightarrow L(\omega,t,x,\dot{x},H)$$

is an adapted process (i.e. measurable and for each t,

$$\omega \longrightarrow L(\omega,t,x,\dot{x},H) \text{ is } \mathcal{F}_t\text{-measurable})$$

. for $(\omega,t) \in \Omega \times R^+$, $(x,\dot{x},H) \longrightarrow L(\omega,t,x,\dot{x},H)$ is a C^∞ function.

L_{22} is the space of adapted measurable processes y with values in R^n such that

$$\|y\|_{22} = (E\int_0^T |y|^2 dt)^{1/2} < +\infty$$

Two $dP \otimes dt$ equivalent processes y and y' are identified.

L_2^t is the set of R^n-valued square-integrable $\mathcal{F}_t$-measurable functions.

S is the set of semi-martingales which may be written as

$$(2.1) \qquad x = x_0 + \int_0^t \dot{x} ds + \int_0^t H.dw$$

where $(x_0,\dot{x},H) \in L_2^0 \times L_{22} \times (L_{22})^m$.

We consider the criterion I defined on S by :

$$(2.2) \qquad x \longrightarrow I(x) = E\Big[\int_0^T L(\omega,t,x,\dot{x},H)dt + \ell_0(x_0) + \ell_T(x_T)\Big].$$

All the necessary assumptions are done on L,ℓ_0,ℓ_T for (2.2) to make sense.

The problem is then to find as extremum for I on S. We have then the fundamental result [3]-[11].

<u>THEOREM</u> 2.1. A sufficient condition for I to be extremum at $x \in S$ is that there exists $(p_0,\dot{p},H')$ $L_2^0 \times L_{22} \times (L_{22})^m$ and a R^n-valued square-integrable martingale M null at time 0, such that $Mw_1,\dots,Mw_n$ are martingales, satisfying the following conditions :

if p is the semi-martingale

$$(2.3) \qquad p_t = p_0 + \int_0^t \dot{p} ds + \int_0^t H'.dw + M_t$$

then :

$$P = \frac{\partial L}{\partial \dot{x}}$$

$$\dot{P} = \frac{\partial L}{\partial x}$$

$$H' = \frac{\partial L}{\partial H}$$

$$P_o = \frac{\partial \ell_o}{\partial x_o} \quad , \quad P_T = \frac{-\partial \ell_T}{\partial x_T}.$$

Proof : We use a classical variational technique.

Let x defined by (2.1) be an element of S.

Let $\partial x \in S$ be an increment of x in S, i.e.

(2.4) $$\partial x_t = \partial x_o + \int_o^t \partial \dot{x} ds + \int_o^t \partial H . dw$$

Then

(2.5) $$\partial I(x) = E\{\int_o^T (\frac{\partial L}{\partial x} \partial x + \frac{\partial L}{\partial x} \partial \dot{x} + \frac{\partial L}{\partial H} \delta H) dt + \frac{\partial \ell_o}{\partial x} \delta x_o + \frac{\partial \ell_T}{\partial x} \partial x_T)\}.$$

Let us then assume that p is given by (2.2). Then by proposition I.1 of [3] which follows from an application of Ito's calculus and a uniform integrability argument, we have :

(2.6) $$E < p_T, \partial x_T > = E\{ < p_o, x_o > + \int_o^T (< p, \partial \dot{x} > + < \dot{p}, \partial x > + < H', \partial H >) dt\}$$

Then from (2.5), (2.6), it follows that if $p_o = \frac{\partial \ell_o}{\partial x_o}$, $p_T = \frac{-\partial \ell_T}{\partial x_T}$, $p_t = \frac{\partial L}{\partial \dot{x}}$, then

(2.7) $$\partial I(x) = E\int_o^T [< (\frac{\partial L}{\partial x} - \dot{p}), \partial x > + < (\frac{\partial L}{\partial H} - H'), \partial H >] dt.$$

It is then clear that if the conditions (2.3) are verified, $\partial I(x) = 0$ □.

Remark 2.1. When L, ℓ_o, ℓ_T are convex functions, the given condition are sufficient for I to be minimum at x. **They are necessary for extremality under standard assumptions.**

Remark 2.2. If x is constrained by $x(0) = x_o$, there is no condition on p_o (except that it must be in L_2^o).

Remark 2.3. If $(\Omega, \mathcal{F}_t, H)$ is the sequence of σ-fields $\sigma(w_s \mid s \leq t)$, it is classical that $M = 0$ ([13], p. 135).

3. HAMILTONIAN FORMALISM

Because of the non intrinsic character of the $(\dot{x},\dot{p})$, the hamiltonian formalism which we will develop now is - at least apparently - non intrinsic. It is not coordinate invariant.

We assume L to be strictly convex in the variables with respect to which the Legendre transform will be taken. In the next paragraph, we do not write explicitly any dependence on (ω,t).

Let $\mathcal{H}, \mathcal{H}', M$ be functions defined by :

$$
(3.1)\quad \begin{cases}
\mathcal{H}(x,p,H) = \sup\limits_{\dot{x}} <p,\dot{x}> - L(x,\dot{x},H) \\
\mathcal{H}'(x,p,H') = -\sup\limits_{\dot{x},H}\{ <p,\dot{x}> + <H',H> - L(x,\dot{x},H) \\
\qquad = -\sup\limits_{H}\{<H',H> + \mathcal{H}(x,p,H)\} \\
M(p,\dot{p},H') = \sup\limits_{x,\dot{x},H} <\dot{p},x> + <p,\dot{x}> + <H',H> - L(x,\dot{x},H)
\end{cases}
$$

where $<H',H>$ is $\sum_1^m <H_i',H_i>$.

ℓ_o^* and ℓ_T^* are the Legendre transforms of ℓ_o and ℓ_T, which we assume to be strictly convex.

Then under classical conditions, $\mathcal{H}, \mathcal{H}', M, \ell_o^*, \ell_T^*$ are differentiable functions.

We have then:

THEOREM 3.1. Under convexity assomptions, the necessary conditions of theorem 2.1 are equivalent to each of the following systems :

$$
(3.2)\quad \begin{cases}
dx = \frac{\partial\mathcal{H}}{\partial p} dt + H dw \\
x(0) = x_o \\
dp = \frac{-\partial\mathcal{H}}{\partial x} dt - \frac{\partial\mathcal{H}}{\partial H} dw + dM \\
p_o = \frac{\partial \ell_o}{\partial x_o} \qquad p_T = \frac{-\partial \ell_T}{\partial x_T}
\end{cases}
$$

$$(3.3)\quad \begin{cases} dx = \dfrac{-\partial \mathcal{H}'}{\partial p}\, dt - \dfrac{\partial \mathcal{H}'}{\partial H'}\, dw \\ x(0) = x_0 \\ dp = \dfrac{\partial \mathcal{H}'}{\partial x}\, dt + H'.dw + dM \\ p_0 = \dfrac{\partial \ell_0}{\partial x_0}, \quad p_T = \dfrac{-\partial \ell_T}{\partial x_T}. \end{cases}$$

$$(3.4)\quad \begin{cases} (2.1) \text{ and } (2.3) \text{ are verified} \\ x = \dfrac{\partial M}{\partial \dot{p}} \\ \dot{x} = \dfrac{\partial M}{\partial p} \\ H = \dfrac{\partial M}{\partial H'} \\ x_0 = \dfrac{\partial \ell_0^*}{\partial p_0}, \quad x_T^* = \dfrac{+\partial \ell_T^*(-p_T)}{\partial p_T}. \end{cases}$$

In particular the criterion

$$(3.5)\qquad p \longrightarrow J(p) = E\left\{\int_0^T M(p,\dot{p},H')dt + \ell_0^*(p_0) + \ell_T^*(-p_T)\right\}$$

is extremal among all the semi-martingales p which are written as in (2.3).

Proof : This is clear from the equivalence [16]

$$p_0 = \frac{\partial \ell}{\partial x}(x_0) \iff x_0 = \frac{\partial \ell_0^*}{\partial p}(p_0)$$

and the subsequent relations for the other functions. □.

Remark 3.1. Let us note that function $\mathcal{H}$ is not intrinsically defined (i.e. coordinate invariant), but that (x,p) is an intrinsic process with values in $T^*(M)$ (here $M = R$). This follows in particular from the non intrinsic character of $\dot{x}$ and $\dot{p}$.

(3.3) and (3.4) are given to prove the total symetry of x and p.

This symetry is in fact revealed by the fact that p is also the solution of the extremal problem (3.5).

4. THE MAXIMUM PRINCIPLE

We study now the control of the differential equations on R^n.

$$
(4.1) \qquad \begin{aligned} dx &= f(\omega,t,x,u)dt + \sigma(\omega,t,x,u)dw \\ x(0) &= x \end{aligned}
$$

where u varies in a compact manifold U and is still adapted to $\{\mathcal{F}_t\}$.

M is taken to be R^n.

f,σ are adapted in (ω,t), uniformly Lipchitz in x, continuous in u, and verify classical growth conditions to ensure existence and uniqueness of the solution of (4.1).

We want to find an extremum for the criterion

$$
(4.2) \qquad u \underset{I}{\longrightarrow} E\left(\int_0^T L(\omega,t,x,u)dt + \ell_T(x_T)\right)
$$

where L is a function defined on $\Omega \times R \times R^n \times U$ verifying assumptions similar to f and σ, with values in R, and ℓ_T is as in section 3.

We assume then f,σ,L to be C^∞ in the variables x,u and ℓ_T to be C^∞ in x_T.

We have then :

THEOREM 4.1. A sufficient condition for I to be extremal at u is that there exists $(p_0,H) \in L_2^0 \times (L_{22})^m$, and a square integrable martingale null at time 0 M such that $Mw_1, Mw_2, \ldots, Mw_m$ are martingales and verifying the following system :

$$
(4.3) \qquad \left\{ \begin{aligned} & dx = f(t,x,u)dt + \sigma(t,x,u)dw \\ & x(0) = x_0 \\ & dp = -\left(\left\langle p,\frac{\partial f}{\partial x}\right\rangle + \left\langle H,\frac{\partial \sigma}{\partial x}\right\rangle - \frac{\partial L}{\partial x}\right) + H.dw + dM \\ & p_T = -\frac{\partial \ell_T}{\partial x_T} \\ & \left\langle p,\frac{\partial f}{\partial u}\right\rangle + \left\langle H,\frac{\partial \sigma}{\partial u}\right\rangle - \frac{\partial L}{\partial u} = 0. \end{aligned} \right.
$$

Proof. Let $\delta u \in T_u(U)$ be an increament of u. It may be easily proved, by using the techniques of Gikhman-Skorokhod in [17] that x depends differentiably on u at least in the L_2 sense, and that moreover

$$(4.4) \qquad \begin{cases} \partial x = (\frac{\partial f}{\partial x}\partial x + \frac{\partial f}{\partial u}\partial u)dt + (\frac{\partial \sigma}{\partial x}\partial x + \frac{\partial \sigma}{\partial u}\partial u)dw \\ \partial x(0) = 0 \end{cases}$$

Then

$$(4.5) \qquad \partial I = E\{\int_0^T (< \frac{\partial L}{\partial x}, \partial x > + < \frac{\partial L}{\partial u}, \partial u >)dt + < \frac{\partial \ell_T}{\partial x}, \partial x_T > \}$$

Let us assume that p is a solution of equation (4.3). Then, by Ito's formula :

$$(4.6) \qquad E < p_T, \partial x_T > = E\int_0^T \{ < p, \frac{\partial f}{\partial x}\partial x + \frac{\partial f}{\partial u}\partial u > - << p, \frac{\partial f}{\partial x} >$$

$$+ < H, \frac{\partial \sigma}{\partial x} > - \frac{\partial L}{\partial x}, \partial x > + < H, \frac{\partial \sigma}{\partial x}\partial x + \frac{\partial \sigma}{\partial u}\partial u > \}dt$$

$$= E\int_0^T \{ < p, \frac{\partial f}{\partial u} > + < H, \frac{\partial \sigma}{\partial u} > + < \frac{\partial L}{\partial x}, \partial x > \}dt$$

which implies :

$$(4.7) \qquad \partial I = E\int_0^T \{ < \frac{\partial L}{\partial u} - < p, \frac{\partial f}{\partial u} > - < H, \frac{\partial \sigma}{\partial u} > , \partial u > \}dt.$$

The theorem follows. □

<u>Remark</u> 4.1. Let us note that $(\frac{\partial L}{\partial x}, \frac{\partial L}{\partial u}) \in T^*_{(x,u)}(M \times U)$, and is then an intrinsic quantity.

Moreover, $< p, \partial x >$ being intrinsic, the Meyer decomposition of the semi-martingale $< p_t, \partial x_t >$ is intrinsic, i.e. is ∂x_t is written as in (2.4), we have

$$(4.8) \qquad < p_t, \partial x_t > = < p_o, \partial x_o > + \int_0^t (< p, \partial\dot{x} > + < \dot{p}, \partial x > + < H', \partial H >)dt + \int_0^t \{ < p, \partial H > + < H', \partial x > \}dw + \int_0^t < dM, \partial x > .$$

$< p, \partial\dot{x} > + < \dot{p}, \partial x > + < H', \partial H >$ is then intrinsically defined, (i.e. invariant by a diffeomorphism of R^n).

Because $\dot{x} = f(x,u)$, $H = \sigma(x,u)$, we have :

$$(4.9)\qquad \begin{aligned} \partial\dot{x} &= \frac{\partial f}{\partial x}\,\partial x + \frac{\partial f}{\partial u}\,\partial u \\ \partial H &= \frac{\partial \sigma}{\partial x}\,\partial x + \frac{\partial \sigma}{\partial u}\,\partial u \end{aligned}$$

$(\dot{p} + \langle p,\frac{\partial f}{\partial x}\rangle + \langle H',\frac{\partial \sigma}{\partial x}\rangle\ ,\ \langle p,\frac{\partial f}{\partial u}\rangle + \langle H',\frac{\partial \sigma}{\partial u}\rangle)$ is then an element of $T^{*}_{x,u}(M \times U)$. The equality given in (4.3) is then an equality between intrinsic quantities. $\tilde{\mathcal{H}}$ is not intrinsically defined, but $(\dot{p} + \frac{\partial \mathcal{H}}{\partial x}, \frac{\partial \mathcal{H}}{\partial u}) \in T^{*}_{(x,u)}(M \times U)$.

We give now an "Hamiltonian" formulation of the result as in [11]. This is not a formulation in the rigorous Legendre transformation sense, but it helps to underline the similarity with the deterministic Pontryagin principle.

$\tilde{\mathcal{H}}$ is a function defined by

$$\tilde{\mathcal{H}}(\omega,t,x,p,\sigma,H,u) = \langle p,f(\omega,t,x,u)\rangle + \langle H,\sigma(\omega,t,x,u)\rangle - L(\omega,t,x,u).$$

Then (4.3) may be written

$$(4.10)\qquad \left\{ \begin{aligned} dx &= \frac{\partial \tilde{\mathcal{H}}}{\partial p}\,dt + \frac{\partial \tilde{\mathcal{H}}}{\partial H}\,dw \\ x(0) &= x \\ dp &= \frac{-\partial \tilde{\mathcal{H}}}{\partial x}\,dt + \frac{\partial \tilde{\mathcal{H}}}{\partial \sigma}\,dw + dM \\ p_T &= \frac{-\partial \ell_T}{\partial x_T} \\ \frac{\partial \tilde{\mathcal{H}}}{\partial u} &= 0. \end{aligned} \right.$$

($\frac{\partial \tilde{\mathcal{H}}}{\partial \sigma}$ represents H. This notation is not entirely correct).

<u>Remark</u> 4.1. Under convexity assumptions, it is proved in [3]-theorem V.1 that one needs only compactness and metrisability for U and that condition $\frac{\partial \tilde{\mathcal{H}}}{\partial u} = 0$ may be replaced by

$$(4.11)\qquad \max_{v \in U} \tilde{\mathcal{H}}(v) = \tilde{\mathcal{H}}(u) \quad dP \otimes dt \text{ a.e.}$$

5. BACKWARD STOCHASTIC DIFFERENTIAL EQUATIONS

We will not give here sufficient conditions for an optimal couple (x,p) to exist. These conditions rely on functional analysis arguments developped in [2]-[3]-[4]-[5].

We want here to underline that equations (3.3) or (4.3) show that p is solution of stochastic differential equations with a terminal condition. This fact, which dit not arise any special difficulty in deterministic control, generates supplementary difficulties in optimal stochastic control.

Let us consider for example the equation in (4.3) :

$$(5.1)\qquad \begin{cases} dp = -\left(< p, \frac{\partial f}{\partial x} > + < H, \frac{\partial \sigma}{\partial x} > - \frac{\partial L}{\partial x}\right) + H.dw + dM \\ p_T = \frac{-\partial \ell_T}{\partial x_T}. \end{cases}$$

Let A and $B_1,\dots,B_m$ be the matrices defined by

$$(5.2)\qquad \begin{aligned} A &= \frac{\partial f}{\partial x} \\ B_i &= \frac{\partial \sigma_i}{\partial x} \quad (i=1,\dots,m). \end{aligned}$$

Then we may write

$$p_t = q_t + \int_0^t \frac{\partial L}{\partial x}\, ds$$

where q is a solution of

$$(5.3)\qquad \begin{cases} dq = (-A^* p - B^* H)dt + H.dw + dM \\ q_T = \frac{-\partial \ell_T}{\partial x_T} - \int_0^T \frac{\partial L}{\partial x}\, ds. \end{cases}$$

Then if A,B are bounded and if $-R_T = \frac{\partial \ell_T}{\partial x_T} + \int_0^T \frac{\partial L}{\partial x}\, ds \in L_2^T$, the following is proved in [5-Theorem I.2, Theorem I.4.] :

THEOREM 5.1. If Z is the unique solution of

$$\left\{\begin{array}{l} dZ = ZA^{*}dt + ZB^{*}dw \\ Z(0) = I \end{array}\right. \tag{5.4}$$

Z has invertible values, and moreover q_t may be obtained by :

$$q_t = Z_t^{-1} E^{\mathcal{F}_t} Z_T R_T \tag{5.5}$$

(the right continuous version of the martingale $E^{\mathcal{F}_t} Z_T R_T$ is of course considered).

The backward stochastic differential equation may then be explicitly solved.

6. DUALITY IN STOCHASTIC CONTROL

We saw in section 3 that if L, ℓ_0, ℓ_T are strictly convex functions, then extremality is equivalent to minimalityand that in (3.4), both x and p are solutions of optimization problems.

In the deterministic case we know by the work of Rockafellar [15] that the problems of minimizing I and J are dual to each other in the sense of convex analysis [16]-[18].

It is then natural to prove that there is an implicit duality between the two problems in the stochastic case. This was in fact the starting point of [3].

Let $L_{2\infty}$ be the set of $dP \otimes dt$ classes of adapted processes y such that :

$$\|y\|_{2\infty} = [E(\operatorname*{supess}_{0 \leq t \leq T} |y_t|^2)]^{1/2} < +\infty.$$

S' is the set of semi-martingales which may be written as in (2.3). S is already defined in (2.1).

For $(y,b) \in L_2^{\infty} \times L_2^T$, $\Phi_{\ell,L}^{y,b}$ is the function defined on S' by :

$$x = (x_0, \dot{x}, H, M) \xrightarrow[\Phi_{\ell,L}^{y,b}]{} \left\{\begin{array}{ll} E\{\int_0^T L(\omega,t,x+y,\dot{x},H)dt + \ell_0(x_0) + \ell_T(x_T - b)\} & \text{if } x \in S \text{ (i.e. } M = 0) \\ +\infty \text{ elsewhere.} & \end{array}\right. \tag{6.1}$$

$\phi_{\ell,L}$ is defined on $L_2^\infty \times L_2^T$ by :

(6.2) $$\phi_{\ell,L}\ (y,b) = \inf_{x \in S'} \phi_{\ell,L}^{y,b}(x)$$

$\phi_{m,M}^{y,b}$ is defined on S' by :

(6.3) $$p = (p_o,\dot{p},H',M) \longrightarrow E\{\int_0^T M(\omega,t,p+y,\dot{p},H')dt + \ell_o^*(p_o) + \ell_T^*(-p_T+b))$$

$\phi_{m,M}$ is defined on $L_2^\infty \times L_2^T$ by :

(6.4) $$\phi_{M,M}(y,b) = \inf_{p \in S'} \phi_{m,M}^{y,b}(p).$$

I is extended to all S' by taking the value $+\infty$ on S'/S . J is defined on S' as in (3.5).

A duality between S' and $L_2^\infty \times L_2^T$ is defined by

(6.5) $$< p,(y,b) > = E(\int_0^T < \dot{p},y > dt + < p_T,b >)$$

Let us recall that if F is a convex function defined on $L_2^\infty \times L_2^T$, the dual function F^* of F is defined on S' by

$$F^*(p) = \sup_{(y,b)} < p,(y,b) > - F((y,b)).$$

The following result is proved in [3]-Theorem III.1, under simple conditions on L,ℓ_o,ℓ_T :

<u>THEOREM</u> 6.1. $\phi_{\ell,L}$ and $\phi_{M,M}$ are convex functions on $L_2^\infty \times L_2^T$ and their duals are given by :

(6.5) $$\phi_{\ell,L}^* = J$$
$$\phi_{m,M}^* = I$$

This result allows as to interpret the problem of minimizing I and J on S' as dual problems in the sense of [16]. In particular p is in fact a Lagrange multiplier associated to the problem of minimizing

(6.6) $$E\{\int_0^T L(\omega,t,X,\dot{x},H)dt + \ell_0(x_0) + \ell_T(x_T)\}$$

when the evolution constraint

(6.7) $$x_t = x_0 + \int_0^t \dot{x}ds + \int_0^t Hdw$$

is verified.

Similarly, x is a Lagrange multiplier relative to p.

The conditions given in Theorem 6.1 are then analyzed in [3] as classical coextremality conditions which characterize the optimums of two dual minimization problems.

7. EXAMPLES

We will give here a few examples illustrating the techniques previously developped. The reader is referred to [2], [3], [4], [5],[8], [11], for more complete explanations.

a) Control of densities ([8],[11]).

Let $A \in L_2^T$, and b a bounded function from $\Omega \times R^+ \times U$ with values in R^m, adapted in (ω, t) and continuous in u.

Let Z be the unique solution of

(7.1) $$\begin{cases} dZ = Z < b(\omega,t,u),dw > \\ Z(0) = 1 \end{cases}$$

Z is then given by :

(7.2) $$Z_t = \exp\{\int_0^t < b,dw > - \frac{1}{2}\int_0^t |b|^2 ds\}$$

Let $A_T \in L_2^T$. We want to minimize the criterion

(7.3) $$u \longrightarrow E(Z_T A_T)$$

It is well known [12], [8], [11], that this problem arises in the control of the drift of a stochastic differentail equation with a fixed non degenerate diffusion term, by means of the Girsanov transformation.

It is proved in [8] that the techniques of section 4 apply. $\tilde{\mathcal{H}}$ is given by :

$$\tilde{\mathcal{H}} = Z < H,b > \quad . \tag{7.4}$$

Then equations(4.10)-(4.11) may be written :

$$\begin{aligned} &dp = - < H,b > dt + Hdw + dM \\ &p_T = - A_T \\ &\max < H,b > \quad . \end{aligned} \tag{7.5}$$

Moreover by (5.5), p may be written as :

$$p_t = \frac{-E^{\mathcal{F}_t} Z_T A_T}{Z_t} \tag{7.6}$$

p_t is then a conditional expectation relative to $\mathcal{F}_t$ of A_T for the measure Q defined on $\mathcal{F}_T$ by :

$$dQ = Z_T dP. \tag{7.7}$$

$- p_t$ is then equal to the martingale of costs for the new measure dQ.

This is a form of the maximum principle of Davis- Varaiya [12]. We refer to [8]- [11] for more details.

Let us note here that Z is in fact a density of probability, and then a "pure real", and that there is here no need of finding an "intrinsic" definition of the various quantities appearing in the maximum principle.

In [8] - Proposition 3.2, the following is proved:

<u>Theorem</u> 7.1. The dual problem of the minimizing of (7.3) consists of the minimization of $E(p_0)$ over all real process $p \in S'$ verifying :

$$\begin{aligned} &p_T = -A_T \\ &\dot{p} + \phi(\omega,t,H') \leq 0 \end{aligned} \tag{7.7}$$

where

$$\phi(\omega,t,H') = \sup_{u \in U} < H',b(\omega,t,u) > \tag{7.8}$$

b) <u>The linear-quadratic case</u>, [4], [5], [11].

We consider the equation

(7.8)
$$dx = (Ax + Cu)dt + (Bx + Du)dw$$
$$x(0) = x_o$$

and the criterion

(7.9)
$$\frac{1}{2}(E\int_o^T (|Mx|^2 + \langle Nu,u \rangle)dt + E|M_1 \; x_T|^2)$$

where $A,B,C,D,M,N,$ are adapted bounded processes, N has self-adjoint values, and is such that there exists $\lambda > 0$ for which

$$\langle Nu,u \rangle \geq \lambda |u|^2$$

and M_1 is $\mathcal{F}_T$-measurable and bounded.

A complete analysis of this example is carried over in [4], [5], [11].

Equations (4.10) may be written :

(7.10)
$$\tilde{\mathcal{H}} = -\frac{1}{2}(|Mx|^2 + \langle Nu,u \rangle \;) + \langle p,Ax + Cu \rangle + \langle H,Bx + Du \rangle$$
$$dp = (M^*Mx - A^*p - B^*H)dt + Hdw + dM$$
$$p_T = -M_1^* M_1 x_T$$
$$Nu = C^*p + B \; H.$$

As indicated in [11], if M and M_1 have an inverse, the dual problem may be written as the minimizing on S' of the criterion

(7.11)
$$E \langle p_o,x_o \rangle + \frac{1}{2}E(\int_o^T (|M^{*-1}(\dot{p} + A^*p + B^*H)|^2 dt + \langle N^{-1}(C^*p + D^*H),C^*p + D^*H \;\rangle)dt + |M_1^{*-1} p_T|^2).$$

c) <u>Relation with the dynamic programining equation</u> [3], [11].

We go back to assumptions of section 4. If f, σ , L do not depend on ω ,we are then in the case of the control of Markov systems.

Let us assume formally that u is a function of (t,x) and that p is a C^2 function of (t,x). Then by using Ito's stochastic calculus, (4.3) may be written

(7.12)
$$\frac{\partial p}{\partial t} + \langle \frac{\partial p}{\partial x},f \rangle + \frac{1}{2}\,\sigma_k^i \sigma_k^j p_{x_i x_j} = -\langle p,\frac{\partial f}{\partial x} \rangle - \langle \frac{\partial p}{\partial x}\,\sigma,\frac{\partial \sigma}{\partial x} \rangle + \frac{\partial L}{\partial x}\,.$$

Moreover :

$$\text{(7.13)} \qquad < p, \frac{\partial f}{\partial u} > + < \frac{\partial p}{\partial x}\sigma, \frac{\partial \sigma}{\partial u} > - \frac{\partial L}{\partial u} = 0.$$

But (7.13) is equivalent to saying that

$$\text{(7.14)} \qquad \frac{\partial}{\partial u}(< p, f > + \frac{1}{2}\sigma_k^i \sigma_k^j \frac{\partial p^i}{\partial x_j} - L) = 0.$$

But by the dynamic programming equation [19], p. 105, we have :

$$\text{(7.15)} \qquad \frac{\partial V}{\partial t} = -\sup_u (< \frac{\partial V}{\partial x}, f > + \frac{1}{2}\sigma_k^i \sigma_k^j V_{x_i x_j} - L)$$

where V is the function

$$\text{(7.16)} \qquad V(t,x) = -\inf_u E_x(\int_t^T L(s,x,u)ds + \ell_T(x_T))$$

where u is in the form $u(t,x)$, and lipchitz in x, and x_t is the solution of (4.1).

By identifying formally (7.13), (7.14) and (7.15), we see that

$$\text{(7.17)} \qquad p = \frac{\partial V}{\partial x}.$$

p is then the gradient of the gain function V, as in deterministic control.

Let us underline that this reasoning is formal ; to be rigorously justified it requires the optimal u to be a lipchitz feedback function of x.

8. EXTENSIONS

The duality formulation of an optimal control problem has been extended in [7] to the control of a general semi-martingale with jumps.

Moreover supply constraints of type

$$\int_0^{+\infty} |u|^2 dt \leq 1$$

are handled in [6] with Lagrange multipliers techniques.

- REFERENCES -

[1] ARNOLD V. Les méthodes mathématiques de la mécanique classique. Editions Mir : Moscou 1974.

[2] BISMUT J.M. Analyse convexe et probabilités. Thèse, Université Paris VI: 1973.

[3] BISMUT J.M. Conjugate convex functions in optimal stochastic control, J. of Math. Anal. Appl., 44 , 384-404 (1973).

[4] BISMUT J.M. Linear quadratic optimal stochastic control with random coefficients. SIAM J. of control, 14, 419-444 (1976).

[5] BISMUT J.M. Contrôle des systèmes linéaires quadratiques. Applications de l'intégrale stochastique. Séminaire de Probabilités, XII, pp. 180-264. Lecture Notes in Mathematics n° 649. Berlin-Heidelberg-New-York : Springer 1978.

[6] BISMUT J.M. An example of stochastic control with constraints. SIAM. J. of Control, 12, 401-418 (1974).

[7] BISMUT J.M. Duality methods in the control of semi-martingales. Proceedings of the Conference on the Analysis and Optimization of stochastic systems. To appear in 1979.

[8] BISMUT J.M. Duality methods in the control of densities. SIAM J. of control and Opt., 16, 771-777 (1978).

[9] BISMUT J.M. Dualité convexe, temps d'arrêt optimal et contrôle stochastique. Z. Wahrscheinlichkeitstheorie, verw. Gebiete, 38, 169-198 (1977).

[10] BISMUT J.M. Principes de mécanique aléatoire : to appear (1979).

[11] BISMUT J.M. An introductory approach to duality in optimal stochastic control. SIAM Review, 20, 62-78 (1978).

[12] DAVIS M.H.A. and VARAIYA P.P. Dynamic Programming conditions for partially observable stochastic systems. SIAM.J. Control 11, 226-261 (1973).

[13] MEYER P.A. Intégrales stochastiques I,II,III. Séminaire de probabilités n° 1. Lecture Notes in Mathematics n° 39, 71-141. Berlin-Heidelberg-New-York: Springer 1967.

[14] MEYER P.A. Cours sur les intégrales stochastiques. Séminaire de Probabilités n° X, pp 245-400. Lecture Notes in Mathematics n° 511- Berlin-Heidelberg-New-York: Springer 1976.

[15] ROCKAFELLAR R.T. Conjugate convex functions and the calculus of variations. J. Math. Anal. and Appl. 32. 174 -222 (1970).

[16] ROCKAFELLAR R.T. Convex Analysis. Princeton Univ. Press. Princeton 1970.

[17] GIKHMAN I.I. and SKOROKHOD A.V.
Introduction to the Theory of Random Processes, Philadelphia : W.B. Saunders Company 1969.

[18] MOREAU J.J. Fonctionnelles Convexes, Séminaire d'équations aux dérivées partielles. Collège de France 1966-1967.

LINEAR STOCHASTIC ITÔ EQUATIONS IN HILBERT SPACE

Ruth F. Curtain
Mathematics Institute
University of Groningen

CONTENTS

1. INTRODUCTION

It is well-known that large classes of linear systems described by parabolic and hyperbolic partial differential equations and delay equations can be formulated as differential equations on a suitable abstract Banach using semigroup theory. This semigroup description is appealing because the notation is reminiscent of that for finite dimensional systems and it provides a unified mathematical framework for studying the classical systems concepts such as controllability, observability and stabilizibility for a wide class of linear infinite dimensional systems [11]. Similarly, infinite dimensional stochastic systems can be modelled as stochastic Itô equations on an appropriate Hilbert space and problems such as filtering and the linear quadratic gaussian control problem yield solutions analogous to the finite dimensional case. For a detailed account of this approach to infinite dimensional systems theory see [11], and for surveys of various aspects of this see [9], [10] and [12].

This survey concerns itself with a larger class of linear stochastic systems, namely those with a state-dependent noise term, which have been studied in [5], [13], [14], [18], [20] and [21] using the same semigroup approach as in [11]. Existence and uniqueness of strong and mild solutions of stochastic abstract evolution equations are discussed in detail together with examples of stochastic delay, parabolic and second order partial differential equations. Recent results on the second order and sample path stability of mild solutions of these equations are surveyed and again illustrated by examples. The second order stability results are crucial for the solution of the stochastic regulation problem with state and control dependent noise and quadratic cost proved in [21] and briefly surveyed here. Finally extensions to time-dependent system operators, nongaussian noise processes, boundary noise, limited sensing and control stochastic operators, delayed observation and control action and nonlinear systems are briefly discussed.

It should be noted that the approach given here is but one approach to the study of infinite dimensional linear stochastic systems. There are many others, and the major ones which model the same physical systems (that is delay or distributed systems with additive noise disturbances) can be found in [1], [2], [3], [24].

2. ABSTRACT EVOLUTION EQUATIONS

We shall use the following standard theory of semigroups[19].

Definition 2.1 Strongly continuous semigroup.

A strongly continuous semigroup T_t on a Banach space Z is a map $T_t : R^+ \to L(Z)$, which satisfies

(2.1) $T_{t+s} = T_t T_s$

(2.2) $T_o = I$

(2.3) $||T_t z_o - z_o|| \to 0$ as $t \to 0+$ $\forall z_o \in Z$.

Useful consequences of the definition are the following

(2.4) $||T_t|| \leq Me^{\omega t}$

for some constants M, ω with $M \geq 0$. Furthermore, T_t uniquely defines a closed, linear densely-defined operator A by

(2.5) $Az_o = \lim_{h \to o+} [(T_t z_o - z_o)/h]$,

for all z_o, such that $T_t z_o$ is differentiable. A is called the infinitesimal generator of T_t and (2.5) implies that

(2.6) $\frac{d}{dt}(T_t z_o) = AT_t z_o = T_t Az_o$ $\forall z_o \in D(A)$.

Conversely, certain classes of closed linear operators A generate semigroups and sufficient conditions for this are well-known (Hille-Yoshida theorem [19]). In fact in our applications, A is usually specified and describes the evolution of a dynamical sytsem on Z

(2.7) $\dot{z} = Az$, $z(0) = z_o \in D(A)$.

Then from (2.6), (2.7) has the unique solution $z(t) = T_t z_o$. The classes of linear systems, which can be formulated by an abstract evolution equation such as (2.7) on some suitable Banach space include ordinary differential equations, delay equations, parabolic and hyperbolic partial differential equations, integral equations and combinations of these. To be more specific we give some examples.

Example 2.1 Ordinary differential equations on $Z = R^n$

(2.8) $\dot{z} = Az$; $z(0) = z_o$,

where $A \in L(R^n)$ is a matrix and $T_t = e^{At}$.

Example 2.2 Delay equations

(2.9) $\dot{x}(t) = \int_{-b}^{o} dN(\theta)\, x\,(t + \theta)$

where $N(\cdot)$ is a function of bounded variation from $[-b, 0]$ into the space of $n \times n$ matrices. It is possible to formulate (2.9) as an abstract equation on $C(-b, 0; R^n)$, but for our purposes the Hilbert space $M^2(-b, 0; R^n)$ is more convenient ([4], [17]). M^2 is the quotient space of $L_2(-b, 0; R^n)$ under the norm

$$(2.10) \qquad ||h||^2_{M^2} = ||h(0)||^2_{R^n} + \int_{-b}^{0} ||h(\theta)||^2_{R^n} \, d\theta .$$

and $\qquad M^2 \cong R^n \times L_2(-b, 0; R^n)$.

The new state $z(t) \in M^2$ is defined to be

$$(2.11) \qquad z(t) = (x(t), \quad x(t + \theta)) \qquad -b \leq \theta \leq 0.$$

and it satisfies the following equation on M^2

$$(2.12) \qquad \dot{z} = \tilde{A}z; \quad z(0) = h, \quad h \in D(\tilde{A})$$

where $\tilde{A}$ is given by

$$(2.13) \qquad (\tilde{A}h)(\theta) = \begin{cases} \int_{-b}^{0} dN(\theta)h(\theta); & \theta = 0 \\ \dfrac{dh}{d\theta} ; & \theta \neq 0 \end{cases}$$

and

$$(2.14) \qquad D(\tilde{A}) = \{(a, h); \quad h \in W_2^1(-b,0; R^n); \quad a = h(0)\}$$

and $\qquad W_2^1(-b,0; R^n) = \{h \in L_2(-b, 0; R^n); \quad Dh \in L_2(-b, 0; R^n)\}$,

where Dh is the distributional derivative of h.

Furthermore $\tilde{A}$ generates a strongly continuous semigroup $\tilde{T}_t$ on M^2 and the solution of (2.12) can be used to recover the solution of (2.9), via

$$(2.15) \qquad x(t) = z(t) \; (\theta = 0).$$

Example 2.3 Parabolic equations [11]

$$(2.16) \qquad \frac{\partial z}{\partial t} = \sum\sum_{i,j=1}^{n} \frac{\partial}{\partial x_i} \left(a_{ij}(x) \frac{\partial z}{\partial x_j}\right)$$

$$z(x, 0) = z_o(x); \quad z|_{\partial\Omega} = 0,$$

where $\Omega \subset R^n$ is sufficiently smooth, $a_{ij} \in L_\infty(\Omega)$ and

$$(2.17) \qquad \sum_{i,j=1}^{n} a_{ij}(x)\xi_i\xi_j \geq \alpha(\xi_1^2 + \cdot \quad \cdot + \xi_n^2) \qquad \text{for some } \alpha > 0, \; \xi_i \in R.$$

Then (2.16) becomes an evolution equation on $Z = L_2(\Omega)$.

(2.18) $\dot{z} = Az; \quad z(0) = z_o \in D(A)$

where

(2.19) $$Az = \sum_{i,j=1}^{n} \frac{\partial}{\partial x_i}(a_{ij}(x) \frac{\partial z}{\partial x_j})$$

and

(2.20) $$D(A) = \{h \in Z: \; h_x, h_{xx} \in Z \text{ and } h\big|_{\partial\Omega} = 0\}$$

Example 2.4 Second order equations [11]

(2.21) $$v_{tt} + \alpha v_t + Av = 0; \quad v(0) = v_o, \quad v_t(0) = v_1$$

where A is a positive self adjoint operator or a Hilbert space H with domain D(A), for example A given by (2.19), and $\alpha > 0$. Then $Z = D(A^{\frac{1}{2}}) \times H$ is a Hilbert space under the inner product

(2.22) $$\langle z, \bar{z} \rangle_Z = \langle A^{\frac{1}{2}} z_1, A^{\frac{1}{2}} \bar{z}_1 \rangle_H + \langle z_2, \bar{z}_2 \rangle_H$$

where $z = \begin{pmatrix} z_1 \\ z_2 \end{pmatrix}, \quad \bar{z} = \begin{pmatrix} \bar{z}_1 \\ \bar{z}_2 \end{pmatrix}.$

Furthermore (2.21), can be formulated as a first order evolution equation on Z.

(2.23) $\dot{z} = \tilde{A}z; \; z(0) = z_o \in D(\tilde{A})$

where $z(t) = \begin{pmatrix} v(t) \\ \bar{v}_t(t) \end{pmatrix}, \quad z_o = \begin{pmatrix} v_o \\ \bar{v}_1 \end{pmatrix}$ and

(2.24) $\tilde{A} = \begin{pmatrix} 0 & I \\ -A & -\alpha I \end{pmatrix}$ and $D(\tilde{A}) = D(A) \times D(A^{\frac{1}{2}})$.

Often one has inhomogeneous systems such as

(2.25) $\dot{z} = Az + f(t); \quad z(0) = z_o.$

If Z is finite demensional, (2.24) has the unique solution

(2.26) $$z(t) = T_t z_o + \int_o^t T_{t-s} f(s)ds$$

for all $z_o \in Z$ and $f \in L_1(0, t_1; Z)$.

However for infinite dimensional Z, one must improve smoothness conditions on f(t) to ensure that (2.26) is differentiable or even in D(A). To avoid these complications it is convenient to define (2.26) to be the mild solution of (2.25) for all $z_o \in Z$ and $f \in L_1(0, t_1; Z)$ ([11]). Roughly speaking, mild solutions correspond to weak solutions for partial differential equations, whereas for inhomogeneous delay equations the mild solution is in fact strong. This is due to the fact that an inhomogeneous term in (2.9), f(t), gives rise to an inhomogeneous term (f(t), 0) in (2.12).

The stability properties of (2.26) depend on the semigroup T_t and from the bound (2.4), we have the following definition.

Definition 2.2 Stability.

We say that T_t or its generator A is stable if in (2.4), $\omega < 0$.

In general the stability of T_t is not determined by the spectrum of A, although for certain classes of sytsems this does hold, in particular for our examples 2.1 - 2.4. See [25] and [26].

In § 5 we shall need the concept of stabilizibility.

Definition 2.3 Stabilizibility.

Given A, the infinitesimal generator of a strongly continuous semigroup T_t, on a Banach space Z and $B \in L(U, Z)$ where U is another Banach space, we say that (A, B) is stabilizible if there exists a $K \in L(Z, U)$ such that $A - BK$ generates a stable semigroup.

3. STOCHASTIC LINEAR EVOLUTION EQUATIONS IN HILBERT SPACE

The linear [1)] stochastic differential equation in finite dimensions is

$$dx(t) = Ax(t)dt + Bx(t)dw_1(t) + D(t)dw_2(t); \; x(0) = x_0 \tag{3.1}$$

where $x \in R^n$, $w_1(t) \in R^{k1}$, $w_2(t) \in R^{k2}$ are mutually independent Wiener processes and $B \in L(R^n, L(R^{k1}, R^n))$, $D(t) \in L(R^{k2}, R^n)$. In order to generalize (3.1) to infinite dimensions we need to define a Hilbert space valued Wiener Process (see [11]).

Definition 3.1 A Wiener process w(t) on a Hilbert space K is an K-valued stochastic process on $(0, t_1)$, such that $w(t) \in L_2(\Omega, p; K)$ and

$$E\{w(t)\} = 0 \tag{3.2}$$

$$Cov\{w(t) - w(s)\} = E\{(w(t) - w(s)) \circ (w(t) - w(s))\} = (t - s)W, \tag{3.3}$$

where $W \in L(K)$ is positive and nuclear.

(3.4) $w(s_4) - w(s_3)$ and $w(s_2) - w(s_1)$ are independent whenever

$$0 \leq s_1 \leq s_2 \leq s_3 \leq s_4 \leq t_1.$$

(3.5) w(t) has continuous sample paths on $[0, t_1]$.

(For a review of basic facts on probability theory and stochastic processes in Banach spaces see [10] or [11]).

There are alternative definitions of an abstract Wiener process (cf. [2]) but they are equivalent. In fact definition 3.1 implies that w(t) has the representatio

1) Often linear is reserved for the case B = 0 and bilinear for the case D = 0.

(3.6) $$w(t) = \sum_{i=o}^{\infty} \beta_i(t) e_i,$$

where $\{e_i\}_{i=o}^{\infty}$ is a complete orthonormal basis for K formed by augmenting the eigenvectors of W_1 and $\beta_i(t)$ are mutually orthogonal real Wiener processes with incremental covariance parameters λ_i or 0, where λ_i are the eigenvalues of W. Furthermore $\Sigma\, \lambda_i < \infty$, since W is nulcear. Other properties of w(t) are

(3.7) $$E\{||w(t) - w(s)||^2\} = \text{trace } W(t-s),$$

(3.8) $$E\{||w(t) - w(s)||^4\} \le 3(\text{trace } W)^2\ (t-s)^2.$$

The decomposition (3.6) gives us a simple way to define a stochastic integral with respect to random integrands $\Phi \in B_2$

(3.9) $$B_2(K,H) = \left\{ \begin{array}{l} \Phi \text{ is an } L(K,H) \text{ valued stochastic process, adapted to the sigma} \\ \text{fields generated by } w(t) \text{ and such that } E\{\int_o^{t_1} ||\Phi(t)||^2_{L(K,H)} dt\} < \infty. \end{array} \right.$$

Then for $\Phi \in B_2$, the following is well-defined, see [6]

(3.10) $$\int_{t_o}^{t_1} \Phi(s) dw(s) = \sum_{i=o}^{\infty} \int_{t_o}^{t} \Phi(s) e_i d\beta_i(s)$$

Moreover,

(3.11)a $$E\{\int_o^{t_1} \Phi(s) dw(s)\} = 0$$

(3.11)b $$E\{||\int_{t_o}^{t} \Phi(s) dw(s)||^2\} \le \text{trace } W\ \ E\{\int_{t_o}^{t_1} ||\Phi(s)||^2 ds\}.$$

See also [2] and [22] for different approaches to the definition of (3.10).

We wish to consider the infinite dimensional analogue of (3.1), namely

(3.12) $$dz(t) = Az(t)dt + Bz(t)dw_1(t) + D(t)dw_2(t) + g(t)dt;\ z(0) = z_o,$$

where $z_o \in L_2(\Omega, p; H)$, A is the infinitesimal generator of the strongly continuous semigroup T_t on H, $g \in L_2(0, t_1, H)$, w_1 and w_2 are mutually independent Wiener processes on Hilbert spaces K_1 and K_2 with incremental covariance operators W_1 and W_2, respectively, and $D \in B_2(K_2,H)$, $B \in L(H, L(K_1, H))$. z_o is independent of w_1 and w_2. Versions of such equations have been studied in [5], [7], [8], [20], [23] and [24], and here we follow the development in [5] with slight modifications.

Definitions 3.2 z(t) is a strong solution of (3.12) if $z(t) \in D(A)$ w.p. 1 for almost all t, $\int_o^{t_1} ||Az(s)|| ds < \infty$ w.p. 1, and z(t) has continuous sample paths almost all of which satisfy

(3.13) $$z(t) = z_o + \int_o^t Az(s)ds + \int_o^t Bz(s)dw_1(s) + \int_o^t D(s)dw_2(s) + \int_o^t g(s)ds.$$

This turns out to be a very strong requirement for infinite dimensional systems and so it is useful to consider a weaker concept as in [5] or [8].

Definition 3.3 z(t) is a mild solution of (3.12) if z(t) is a well-defined H valued stochastic process and satisfies w.p. 1.

(3.14) $$z(t) = T_t z_o + \int_o^t T_{t-s} Bz(s)dw_1(s) + \int_o^t T_{t-s} D(s)dw_2(s) + \int_o^t T_{t-s} g(s)ds.$$

In [5] it is proved that this concept of mild solution is equivalent to z(t) satisfying either of

(3.15) $$z(t) = z_o + A\int_o^t z(s)ds + \int_o^t Bz(s)dw_1(s) + \int_o^t D(s)dw_2(s) + \int_o^t g(s)ds,$$

(3.16) $$<z(t),h> = <z_o, h> + \int_o^t <z(s), A^*h> ds + \int_o^t <Bz(s)dw_1 + D(s)dw_2(s), h> + \int_o^t <g(s), h> ds,$$

for arbitrary $h \in D(A^*)$.

By theorem 3.17 in [5], (3.12) has a unique mild solution under our assumptions and $z(t) \in C(0,t_1; L_2(\Omega, p; H)$. Combining results from [8] and [5], we can show that sufficient conditions for (3.12) to have a strong solution are the following

(3.17) $$T_t z_o, T_{t-s}D(s)e_i^2 \; T_{t-s}g(s), T_{t-s}Bz(s)h \in D(A) \text{ w.p. } 1$$

for $h \in K_1$ and e_i^2, the eigenvalues of W_2

(3.18) $$\int_o^t ||A\, T_{t-s}g(s)||ds < \infty \text{ w.p. } 1,$$

(3.19) $$\sum_{i=o}^{\infty} \lambda_i^2 \int_o^t ||A\, T_{t-s}\, D(s)e_i^2\, ||^2\, ds < \infty$$

(3.20) $$\sum_{i=o}^{\infty} \lambda_i^1 \int_o^t E\{||A\, T_{t-s}Bz(s)e_i^1\, ||\}^2\, ds < \infty$$

where (e_i^1, λ_i^1) and (e_i^2, λ_i^2) are the eigenvector, eigenvalue pairs for the nuclear operators W^1 and W^2. For finite dimensional equations these assumptions are automatically satisfied and for T_t analytic (3.17) is too and (3.18) - (3.20) are essentially restrictions on the size of the noise terms. In particular for parabolic partial differential equations we do get strong solutions for sufficiently small noise terms, whereas for delay and hyperbolic equations we never do. However, it is possible to show that the mild solution of most hyperbolic and delay equations considered in applications does have continuous sample paths. This is important if we wish to consider stochastic stability.

Example 3.1 (3.1) has unique strong solutions.

Example 3.2 Stochastic Delay Equations

$$(3.21)\quad \begin{cases} dx(t) = \int_{-b}^{o} dN(\theta)\, x(t+\theta)dt + Bx(t)dw_1(t) + Ddw_2(t) \\ x(0) = h(0) \end{cases}$$

where $N(\cdot)$ is as in example (2.9), w_1 and w_2 are mutuallly independent Brownian motions in R^{k_1} and R^{k_2}; respectively and $D \in \mathcal{L}(R^{k_2}; R^n)$, $B \in \mathcal{L}(R^n, \mathcal{L}(R^{k_1}, R^n))$.Then analogously to Example 2.2 the M^2 version is

$$(3.22)\quad dz = \tilde{A}z(t)dt + \tilde{B}z(t)dw_1(t) + \tilde{D}dw_2(t),$$

where $\tilde{B} \in \mathcal{L}(M^2, \mathcal{L}(R^{k_1}, M^2)$ and $\tilde{D} \in \mathcal{L}(R^{k_2}, L^2)$ are

given by

$$(3.23)\quad \tilde{D}k = \begin{cases} Dk & ; \quad \theta = 0 \\ 0 & \quad\;\; \theta \neq 0 \end{cases} \qquad \text{for } k \in R^{k_2}$$

$$(3.24)\quad (\tilde{B}h)k = \begin{cases} Bh(0)k & ; \quad \theta = 0 \\ 0 & ; \quad \theta \neq 0 \end{cases} \qquad \begin{matrix} \text{for } k \in R^{k_1} \\ h \in M^2 \end{matrix},$$

In [11], it is explained that (3.22) can never have strong solutions since $z(t) \notin \mathcal{D}(\tilde{A})$. However, because of the degenerate nature of $\tilde{D}$ and $\tilde{B}$, $z(t)$ does have continuous sample paths in M^2.(This was first proved in [27]).

Example 3.3 Stochastic Parabolic Equations

Let $H = L_2(\Omega)$ as in example 2.3, then a distributed Wiener process is

$$(3.25)\quad w(t) = \sum_{i=o}^{\infty} \beta_i(t)e_i$$

where e_i are the eigenvectors of A in H and $\beta_i(t)$ are mutually independent Wiener process with incremental covariance λ_i, $\sum_{i=o}^{\infty} \lambda_i < \infty$. The stochastic version of (2.18) is

$$(3.26)\begin{cases} dz(t) = Az(t)dt + Bz(t)dw_1(t) + Ddw(t) \\ z(o) = z_o . \end{cases}$$

where we suppose that $w(t)$ is given by (3.25), but $w_1(t)$ is a standard scalar Brownian motion, independent of $w(t)$, and $B, D \in \mathcal{L}(H)$.

Now A generates an analytic semigroup and so $T_t : H \to D(A)$ and so conditions for strong solutions reduce to

(3.27) $\sum_{i=o}^{\infty} \lambda_i \int_0^t ||AT_{t-s} De_i||^2 ds < \infty$

(3.28) $\int_0^t E\{||AT_{t-s} Bz(s)||\}^2 ds < \infty$

and these must be checked for the particular semigroup. If the semigroup T_t is not known explicitly, then one can impose the stronger conditions

(3.27)' $\sum_{i=o}^{\infty} \lambda_i ||ADe_i||^2 < \infty$

(3.28)' $\int_0^t E\{||ABz(s)||^2\} dt < \infty$

In [11] the heat equation in one dimension was considered with B = 0 and it was found that strong solutions were obtained if $\sum_{i=1}^{\infty} i^2 \lambda_i < \infty$, a restriction on the size of the noise disturbance.

Example 3.4 Stochastic Second Order Equations

A typical type of second order stochastic equations found in applications is formally described by

(3.29) $$\begin{cases} v_{tt} + \alpha v_t + Av + \xi_1 v_t + \xi_2 v + \xi_3 = 0 \\ v(0) = v_o, \quad v_t(0) = v_1 \end{cases}$$

where ξ_1 and ξ_2 are scalar white-noise processes and ξ_3 is distributed. As in [13] or [14] the corresponding stochastic evolution equation on $Z = D(A^{\frac{1}{2}}) \times H$ is

(3.30) $$\begin{cases} dz_t = \tilde{A} z dt + \begin{pmatrix} 0 & 0 \\ B_1 & 0 \end{pmatrix} z dw_1(s) + \begin{pmatrix} 0 & 0 \\ 0 & B_2 \end{pmatrix} z dw_2(s) + \begin{pmatrix} 0 \\ D \end{pmatrix} dw_3(s) \\ z(0) = z_o. \end{cases}$$

where w_1 and w_2 are standard scalar Wiener process and w_3 is a K-valued Wiener process with covariance W_3. w_1, w_2, w_3 and z_o are mutually independent and $D \in \mathcal{L}(K, H)$, $B_1 \in \mathcal{L}(D(A^{\frac{1}{2}}), H)$ and $B_2 \in \mathcal{L}(H)$. In [14] it us shown that although (3.30) does not have a strong solution, its mild solution has continuous simple paths.

4. STOCHASTIC CALCULUS IN HILBERT SPACE

In finite dimensions it is well known that functions of stochastic processes obey a different type of calculus and in [6] the following generalization to Hilbert spaces was proved.

Theorem 4.1 Itô's lemma

Suppose that $g(\cdot,\cdot) : [0, t_1] \times H \rightarrow R^1$ is continuous H is a Hilbert space and z(t) is an H-valued stochastic process defined by

$$(4.1) \qquad z(t)=z(0) + \int_0^t \Phi(s)ds + \int_0^t \psi(s)dw(s).$$

We say that z(t) has the stochastic differential

$$(4.2) \qquad dz(t) = \Phi(t)dt + \psi(t)dw(t)$$

Suppose the following assumptions hold

(a) $g(\cdot,\cdot)$ is twice Fréchet differentiable on H for each $t \in [0,t_1]$ and once differentiable in t on $[0, t_1]$.

(b) $g_t(\cdot,\cdot)$, $g_z(\cdot,\cdot)$, $g_{zz}(\cdot,\cdot)$ are continuous on $[0, t_1] \times H$,

(c) w(t) is an K-valued Wiener process with covariance matrix W, where K is a Hilbert space,

(d) $\Phi(t)$ as an H-valued process adapted to w_t and $\in L_1(0, t_1; H)$ w.p. 1,

(e) $\Psi(t)$ is an $\mathcal{L}(H, K)$-valued measurable stochastic process adapted to w_t and $E\{\int_0^{t_1} ||\Psi(t)||^4 dt\} < \infty$

Then $x(t) = g(t,z(t))$ has the stochastic differential

$$dx(t) = [g_t(t,z(t)) + \langle g_z(t,z(t)), \Phi(t)\rangle + \tfrac{1}{2}\,\mathrm{trace}\{\Psi(t)W\Psi^*(t)\; g_{zz}(t,z(t))\}]dt$$
$$+ \langle g_z(t), z(t)), \Psi(t)dw(t)\rangle.$$

In fact, one can prove a similar result for Hilbert space valued maps, but for applications we are usually interested in functionals of stochastic processes, for example $\langle z(t), z(t)\rangle$ or some Lyapunov function, (see [21]). Unfortunately, Theorem 4.1 can only be applied to strong solutions of stochastic differential equations like (3.12), see [21] on [14]. This means that for strong solutions z(t) of (3.12), we can deduce the following

$$(4.3) \qquad \langle z(t),z(t)\rangle - \langle z(0), z(0)\rangle = \int_0^t [2\langle z(s), Az(s) + g(s)\rangle + \mathrm{trace}\{D(s)W_2D^*(s)\} +$$
$$+ \mathrm{trace}\{Bz(s)W_1(Bz(s))^*\}]ds,$$
$$+ 2\int_0^t \langle Az(s), Bz(s)dw_1(s)\rangle + 2\int_0^t \langle Az(s), D(s)dw_2(s)\rangle,$$

and taking expectations of (4.3) using (3.11) (a), we obtain an equation for the second moments

$$(4.4)\qquad E\{||z(t)||^2\} = E\{||z(0)||^2\} + 2\int_0^t E\{<z(s),\ Az(s) + g(s)>\}\,ds$$

$$+ \int_0^t E\{||D(s)W_2^{\frac{1}{2}}||^2\}ds + \int_0^t E\{||Bz(s)W_1^{\frac{1}{2}}||^2\}ds$$

In [14] an approximation argument was used to obtain equations for the energy and its expectation for the mild solution of Example 3.4 for $\xi_3 = 0$. They are

$$(4.5)\qquad ||v_t||^2_H + ||A^{\frac{1}{2}}v||^2_H - ||v_1||^2_H - ||A^{\frac{1}{2}}v_o||^2_H = -2\alpha\int_o^t||v_s||^2ds$$

$$+ \int_o^t(||B_1v||^2_H + ||B_2v_s||^2_H)ds + 2\int_o^t<v_s, B_1v>\,dw_1(s) + 2\int_o^t <v_s,\ B_2v_s>dw_2(s).$$

$$(4.6)\qquad E\{||v_t||^2 + ||A^2v||^2_H\} - E\{||v_1||^2 + ||A^{\frac{1}{2}}v_o||^2\}$$

$$= -2\alpha\int_o^t E\{||v_s||^2\}ds + \int_o^t (E\{||B_1v||^2_H\} + E\{||B_2v_s||^2_H\})ds$$

where $||v_t||^2_H + ||A^{\frac{1}{2}}v||^2_H$ represents the energy of the system. Moment equations for parabolic and second order systems were also obtained in [24]. using a nonsemigroup approach. Their usefulness in infinite dimensions is for proving properties of solutions as in [24] and in particular sample path stability properties as in [18]and [14], which we shall discuss in the next section.

5. STABILITY OF LINEAR STOCHASTIC EVOLUTION EQUATIONS

This aspect of stochastic evolution equations has only recently been investigated in [14], [18], [21] and [30]. First we define the concept of mean square stability for the system as in [18], [21],[30]

$$(5.1)\qquad z(t) = T_tz_o + \int_o^t T_{t-s}Bz(s)dw_1(s)$$

where H and K_1 are Hilbert spaces, $w_1(t)$ is a K-valued Wiener process, $z_o \in H$, $B_1 \in L(H,\ \mathcal{L}(K,H)$ and T_t is a semigroup on H.

Definition 5.1 (5.1) is a mean square stable if for each $z_o \in H$, the mild solution of (5.1) satisfies

$$(5.2)\qquad \int_o^\infty E\{||z(s)||^2_H\}ds < \infty.$$

Ichikawa in [21] establishes the following stochastic Lyapunov theorem.

Theorem 5.1

(5.1) is mean square stable if and only if there exists a self adjoint nonnegative operator $P \in L(H)$, which is a solution of

(5.3) $$2 < Ah, Ph >_H + <h, h>_H + \text{trace } [(Bh)^* P(Bh)W_1] = 0 \qquad \text{for } h \in D(A).$$

(W_1 is the covariance matrix of $w_1(t)$).

Furthermore, (5,1) is mean square stable if and only if for all $z_o \in H$

(5.4) $$E\{||z(s)||^2_H\} \leq C e^{-\omega t} ||z_o||^2_H$$

for some constants c, $\omega > 0$.

Easily verifiable sufficient conditions for the existence of a solution to P were given by Haussmann in [18].

Theorem 5. [18]

(5.1) is mean square stable if T_t is stable and

(5.5) $$||\int_o^\infty T_t^* \, \Delta T_t \, dt||_H < 1$$

where $<\Delta h, k>_H = \text{trace } \{(Bh)^*(Bk)W_1\}$ for $h, k \in H$.

Zabczyk [30] obtains necessary and sufficient conditions for systems of Lurie type

(5.6) $$z(t) = T_t z_o + \sum_{i=1}^{p} \int_o^t T_{t-s} B_i z(s) dw^i(s); \qquad t \geq 0$$

where $w^i(t)$ are scalar mutually independent Wiener processes and B_i; $i = 1, \ldots, p$ satisfy for $z \in H$

(5.7) $$B_i(z) = b_i <c_i, z>_H$$

where $b_i, c_i \in H$.

Theorem 5.3 [30].

The system (5.6) is mean square stable if and only if T_t is stable and the spectral radius of the matrix $D = (d_{kj})_{k,j = 1,\ldots p}$ is less then 1, where

(5.8) $$d_{kj} = \int_o^\infty |<T_t b_k, c_j>|^2 dt.$$

Ichikawa in [21] has also defined mean square stability for the system

$$(5.9) \qquad z(t) = T_t z_o + \int_0^t T_{t-s} Bz(s)dw_1(s) + \int_0^t T_{t-s} Ddw_2(s)$$

where w_2 is a Wiener process on another Hilbert space K_2 and $D \in L(K_2H)$. w_2 is assumed to be independent of w_1.

<u>Definition 5.2</u> (5.3) is mean square stable if for each $z_o \in H$

$$(5.10) \qquad \lim_{t_1 \to \infty} \frac{1}{t_1} \int_o^{t_1} E\{||z(s)||_H^2\}ds < \infty.$$

The proved in [13], that (5.9) is mean square stable if and only if (5.1) is, and moreover

$$(5.11) \qquad \lim_{t_1 \to \infty} \frac{1}{t_1} \int_o^{t_1} E\{||z(s)||^2{}_H\}ds = \text{trace } \{D^*PDW_2\}$$

where P is the solution of (5.3).

The Markov process defined by (5.9) has an invariant measure μ associated with it defined by

$$(5.12) \qquad P_t(z, B) = \text{prob}\{z(t) \in B | z(0) = z_o\}$$

for an arbitrary Borel set B of H and

$$(5.13) \qquad \int_H |z|^2 \mu(dz) = \text{trace } \{D^*PDW_2\}.$$

Sample path stability properties were first treated in [18] primarily for systyms where T_t is analytic. It seems that the strongest stability properties of (5.1) for an infinite dimensional state space are the following.

<u>Definition 5.3</u> <u>Asymptotic stability properties</u>

(a) (5.1) is <u>pathwise exponentially bounded</u> if there exist constants C, $\beta > 0$ and $T(\omega) < \infty$, such that for $t > T(\omega)$

$$(5.14) \qquad ||z(t)||^2 \leq C\, E\{||z(0)||^2\}e^{-\alpha t} \quad \text{w.p. } 1.$$

(b) (5.1) <u>is asymptotically stable relative to finite dimensional initial</u>

$$\text{prob } \{\lim_{\eta \downarrow o} \sup \{\sup_{t>o} ||z_t|| : ||z_o|| < \eta;\ z_o \in H_f\} = 0\} = 1$$

where H_f is a <u>finite</u> dimensional subspace of H.

Haussmann gives different sets of sufficient conditions for systems to have the asymptotic stability properties of Definition 5.3, depending on whether he uses a semigroup or Pardoux [24] description. This best results use the nonsemigroup description of Pardoux [24], which basically say that for the class of linear parabolic systems studied in [24], if they satisfy (5.2), they also have the asymptotic stability properties of Definition 5.3. To prove these results using a semigroup description, Haussmann assumes that T_t is analytic and in addition

(5.15) $\qquad ||AT_tB(x)e_i|| \leq f(t)||x|| \quad$ for $\quad$ all $x \in H$,

where $\{e_i\}$ is the completed set of eigenvalues of W_1 and $f \in L_2(0,t_1)$, (5.15) is very restrictive, but can in fact be avoided, by using the results (4.3) and (4.4) of § 4, unavailable to Haussmann at that time. He used instead the moment equations in [24] and hence a different mathematical framework. However his methods apply equally well to [4.3] and [4.4] and it is then possible to prove the following (cf [14]).

Theorem 5.4 (unpublished)

Consider (5.1), where T_t has an infinitesimal generator $A = A_o + B$, with A_o self adjoint nonnegative and B a linear operator $B : D(A_o^{\frac{1}{2}}) \to D(A_o^{\frac{1}{2}})$. Then if $D : D(A_o^{\frac{1}{2}}) \to A(A_o^{\frac{1}{2}})$ and the mild solution of (5.4) is mean square stable, then it is also pathwise exponentially bounded and asymptotically stable relative to finite dimensional initial conditions.

Theorem 5.4 can be applied to parabolic equations and here we present the example considered in [18].

Example 5.1 Heated rod of length π.

(5.16)
$$\begin{cases} dz = (\dfrac{\partial^2}{\partial x^2} + a)z\,dt + b\,z\,dw \\ z(t,0) = 0 + z(t,\pi); \quad z(0,x) = z_o(x) \end{cases}$$

where w(t) is a scalar standard Wiener process and a, b are constants. Then on $H = L_2(0,1)$, $A = \dfrac{\partial^2}{\partial x^2} + a$ generates the semigroup T_t given by

(5.17)
$$(T_th)(x) = \sum_{n=1}^{\infty} e^{-(n^2-a)t} \sin nx \int_0^{\pi} \sin n\pi h(y)dy$$

and T_t is stable if $a < 1$. The conditions of theorem 5.4 are satisfied and (5.5) yields $b^2 < 2(1 - a)$. Hence if $a < 1$ and $b^2 < 2(1 - a)$ we have mean square stability and the asymptotic stability properties of defintion 5.3

Theorem 5.4 cannot be applied to second order systems or delay equations, but similar asymptotic stability results can be obtained using the special structure of these systems.

Theorem 5.5 Second order systems [13].

Consider the mild solution of (3.30) with D = 0. If the state vector $z(t) = \binom{v}{v_t}$ is mean square stable with respect to the norm $||z(t)||_Z = (||v_t||_H^2 + ||A^{\frac{1}{2}}v||_H^2)^{\frac{1}{2}}$, then it also has the asymptotic stability properties of definition 5.3.

In [25] conditions for the stability of $\tilde{A}$ are given in terms of the spectrum of A for $\alpha > 0$ and these results are exploited in [14] to obtained stability results for a large class of second order systems including that of example 3.4.

Example 5.2 [14] The vibration of a panel in supersonic flow subjected to random end loads.

$$(5.18) \quad \begin{cases} v_{tt} + \alpha v_t + (f + c\xi)v_{xx} + v_{xxxx} = 0 \\ v(0,t) = 0 = v(1,t) = v_{xx}(0,t) = v_{xx}(1,t) \end{cases}$$

where α, f and c are nonrandom constants, $\alpha > 0$ and ξ is a standard scalar white noise process. Let $H = L_2(0,1)$ and define

$$(5.19) \quad A = \frac{\partial^4}{\partial x^4} + f\frac{\partial^2}{\partial x^2}$$

with $D(A) = \{h \in H: h(0) = 0 = h(1) = h_{xx}(0) = h_{xx}(1)\}$

A is self adjoint and positive if $f < \pi^2$ and its eigenvalues are bounded below by $\pi^2(\pi^2 - f^2)$. Constructing $\tilde{A}$ as in example 2.4, from the results of [25] we obtain that $\tilde{A}$ is stable if $f < \pi^2$ and $\alpha > 0$. Furthermore, $||T_t|| \leq e^{-\omega t}$, where

$$(5.20) \quad \omega \geq \frac{2\alpha\pi^2(\pi^2 - f^2)}{4\pi^2(\pi^2 - f^2) + 2\ (\alpha^2 + 4\pi^2(\pi^2 - f^2))^{\frac{1}{2}}}$$

Condition (5.5) yields $c^2 < 2\omega$ and so, we obtain the asymptotic stability properties for this example if $\alpha > 0$, $f < \pi^2$ and

$$c^2 < \frac{4\alpha\pi^2(\pi^2 - f^2)}{4\pi^2(\pi^2 - f^2) + \alpha(\alpha^2 + 4\pi^2(\pi^2 - f^2))^{\frac{1}{2}}}.$$

For delay equations, as remarked by Haussmann in [18] one can use the finite dimensionality to deduce asymptotic stability from the mean square stability in the abstract M^2 space. We conclude this section with a delay example considered in both [18] and [30].

Example 5.3 Delay equations of Lurie type

Consider (3.21), where D = 0 and B is given by

$$(5.21) \quad B(x)w = \sum_{i=1}^{K_1} B_i x w_i = \sum_{i=1}^{K_1} b_i < c_i, x > w_i$$

where $B_i = b_i < c_i, \cdot >$ is an $n \times n$ matrix. Then from Theorem 5.3, we have mean square stability if and only if

$$(5.22) \qquad \sup \{ \operatorname{Re} \lambda : \det [\int_{-b}^{o} e^{\lambda\theta} dN(\theta) - \lambda I] = 0\} < 0$$

and the absolute values of the eigenvalues of $D = (d_{kj})_{k,j=1\ldots n}$ are strictly less than one, where

$$(5.23) \qquad d_{kj} = \int_{o}^{\infty} | < y_t^{b_k}, c_j > |^2 dt$$

and $y_t^{b_k}$ is the solution of the deterministic delay equation

$$(5.24) \qquad y^{b_k} = \int_{-h}^{o} dN(\theta) y(t+\theta); \qquad y^{b_k}(\theta) = 0 \text{ , } \theta \in [-b, 0]. \quad y^{b_k}(0) = b^k$$

Now since (3.21) is finite dimensional, one can argue as in [18] to prove that under (5.22) and (5.23) we have asymptotic stability of the sample paths to zero w.p. 1.

6. STOCHASTIC OPTIMAL CONTROL

In [10],[11] and [12] can be found accounts of the standard linear stochastic control or regular problem in infinite dimensions. By the standard stochastic regular problem is meant the minimization of a cost functional quadratic in the control $u(t)$ and the state $z(t)$, where the state is given by a general system of the from (3.12), with $g(t) = B_c(t)u(t)$, but $B \equiv 0$; that is no state-dependent noise.
Recently in [21], Ichikawa has considered a more general stochastic regulator problem allowing for both control and state-dependent noise. Specifically, he considered the mild solution of the following system

$$(6.1) \qquad \begin{cases} dz(t) = (Az(t) + B_c u(t)dt + D(x(t)dw_1(t) + Fdw_2(t) + C(u(t)dw_3(t) \\ z(0) = z_o \end{cases}$$

where A is the generator of the strongly continuous semigroup T_t on the Hilbert space H, $w_i(t)$; $i = 1, 2, 3$ are mutually indepdent Wiener processes on Hilbert spaces K_i, and have incremental variance operator W^i, $z_o \in H$, $u(t)$ takes values in the Hilbert space U, $B_c \in L(U, H)$, $C \in L(U, L(K_3, H))$, $D \in L(H, L(K_1, H))$, $F \in L(K_2, H)$. The cost functional to be minimized is

$$(6.2) \qquad J(u) = E\{ < Gz(t_1), z(t_1) > \} + \int_{o}^{t_1} E\{ < Mz(t), z(t) > + < Nu(t), u(t) > \} dt$$

where $G, M \in L(H)$, $N, N^{-1} \in L(U)$ and $G, M \geq 0$, $N > 0$.

Admissible controls are those adapted to the sigma field generated by $\{w_i(s);\ 0 \leq s \leq t;\ i = 1, 2, 3\}$ and statisfying $\int_0^{t_1} E\{||u(t)||^2\}dt < \infty$. From Theorem 3.17 in [5] it follows that feedback controls of "Lipschitz-type" are admissible; that is for

(6.3) $\quad u(t) = k(t, x)$

where $k : [0, t_1] \times H \to U$ is measurable and

(6.4) $\quad ||k(t, x)||_U \leq c(1 + ||x||_H)$

(6.5) $\quad ||k(t, x) - k(t, y)||_U \leq c||x - y||_H, \quad c > 0,\ x, y \in H.$

Using a dynamic programming argument, Ichikawa in [12] proves the following.

Theorem 6.1

Under the above assumptions there exists a unique admissible optimal control of a linear feedback type given by

(6.6) $\quad u^*(t) = -[N + \Gamma(Q(t)]^{-1} B^* Q(t)z(t)$

where $\Gamma \in L(L(H), L(U))$ is defined by

(6.7) $\quad <\Gamma(S)u,v> = \text{trace } C^*(v)SC(u)W^3 \quad \forall S \in L(H), \quad u, v \in U,$

and $Q(t)$ is the unique solution in the class of self adjoint, nonnegative strongly continuous $L(H)$-valued functions of

$$(6.8)\quad \begin{cases} \frac{d}{dt} <Q(t)x,x> + 2<Ax, Q(t)x> + <Mx,x> + <\Delta(Q(t)x,x> = \\ \qquad\qquad <Q(t)B(N + \Gamma(Q(t))^{-1} B^*Q(t)x, x> \\ Q(t_1) = G \qquad\qquad \text{for } x \in D(A) \end{cases}$$

where (6.9) $<\Delta(s)x,y> = \text{trace } \{D^*(y)SD(x)W^1\} \qquad \forall x,y \in H,\ S \in L(H).$

The minimum cost is

(6.10) $\quad J(u^*) = <Q(0)z_o, z_o> + \int_0^{t_1} \text{trace}(F^*Q(t)FW^2)dt.$

It is worthwhile to compare these results with those of the standard stochastic regulator problem, namely with $D = 0 = C$ in (6.1). For the finite time case, $t_1 < \infty$, Theorem 6.1 yields precisely the usual results. For the infinite time case we quote the following result from [10].

Theorem 6.2

Consider (6.8) with $D = C = 0$. If (A,B) and $(A^*, M^{\frac{1}{2}})$ [1)] are stabilizible, then the

---

1) Equivalently $(M^{\frac{1}{2}}, A)$ is detectable.

solution of (2.8) converges strongly as $t_1 \to \infty$ to the unique solution $Q \geq 0$ of the algebraic Riccati equation

$$(6.11) \qquad 2 < Ax, Qx > + < Mx, x > + < QBN^{-1}B^*Qx, x > = 0, \qquad x \in D(A).$$

The stochastic regulator problem on the infinite interval does not appear to have been studied explicitly in the literature, although it follows easily from Theorem 6.2 and the results in [21] for the more general case. However, it is not a special case of the D = 0 = C case and so we outline the arguments here.

We now define admissible controls to be time invariant feedback controls satisfying (6.5), which produce a Markov process with an invariant measure μ_k, such that $\int_H ||z||^2\mu_k\ (dz) < \infty$, we can pose the problem of finding an admissible control $u = k(z)$ which minimizes the cost

$$(6.12) \qquad J(u) = \int_H \{<Mz, z> + <Nk(z), k(z)> \}\ \mu_k(dz).$$

From Definition 5.2, we see that for linear feedback controls $u = -kz$, admissible controls produce mean square stable mild solutions. Furthermore, from Theorem 5.1, we see that $u = -kz$ is admissible if A - BK is stable. So stabilizibility of (A, B) is sufficient for the stochastic control problem on $[0, \infty)$ with cost (6.12) to be well-posed. In particular, assuming that (A, B) and $(A^*, M^{\frac{1}{2}})$ are stabilizible, the following feedback control

$$(6.13) \qquad u^* = -N^{-1}B^*Q\ z,$$

where Q is the unique solution of (6.11) is admissible, since $(A-BN^{-1}B^*Q)$ is stable (Cor. 4.17 [11]). Adapting the arguments in § 4.3 [11], it can be shown that (6.13) is optimal and the optimal cost is

$$(6.14) \qquad J(u^*) = \text{trace}\ \{F^*QFW^2\}.$$

<u>Theorem 6.3</u>

Consider the control problem for (6.1) with D = C = 0 and cost (6.12). If (A, B) and $(A^*, M^{\frac{1}{2}})$ are stabilizible, there exists a unique optimal control given by (6.13) with minimal cost(6.14).

Let us return now to the development of the state and control dependent noise case in [21]; that is $D \neq 0$, $C \neq 0$, but F = 0 in (6.1) and G = 0, $t_1 = \infty$ in (6.2). Admissible controls are now time invariant controls satisfying (6.4), (6.5) and in addition produce mild solutions of (6.1) which satisfy

$$(6.15) \qquad E\ \{||z(t)||^2\} \to 0 \text{ as } \quad t \to \infty.$$

The control problem is meaningful of (A, B, C, D) is stabilizible in the following sense.

<u>Definition 6.1</u> (A, B, C, D) defining (6.1) with F = 0 is <u>stabilizible</u> if the e exists a $K_1 \in L(H, U)$ such that the feedback control law $u = - K_1 z$ produces a mean square stable solution z(t), i.e z(t) statisfies Definition 5.1 .

In this case, we say that $(A - BK_1, C, D)$ is <u>stable</u>. Necessary and sufficient conditions for stabilizibility are given in terms of Lyapunov-type equations.

<u>Lemma 6.1</u>

(A, B, C, D) is stabilizible if and only if these exists $K_1 \in L(H, U)$ and $0 \leq P_1 \in L(H)$ such that

$$(6.16) \qquad 2 <(A - BK_1)x , P_1 x> + < [K_1^* \Gamma(P_1) K_1 + \Delta(P_1)]x,x> = - <x, x> \text{ for } x \in D(A)$$

Unfortunately the conditions for the existence of an optimal control in the state and control dependent noise case are not the same as for Theorem 6.3. One key condition is a weaker condition than (6.16), namely the esistence of $K_1 \in L(K, U)$ and $0 \leq Q_1 \in L($ satisfying

$$(6.17) \qquad 2 <(A - BK_1)x, Q_1 x > + <(M + K_1^* NK)x, x > + <[\Delta(Q_1) + K_1^* \Gamma(Q_1) K_1]x, x> = 0,$$

$$\text{for} \qquad x \in D(A).$$

This is only necessary for the stability of $(A - BK_1, C, D)$ but it is sufficient for the existence of a solution $0 \leq Q \in L(H)$ of the algebraic Riccati equation determining the optimal cost

$$(6.18) \qquad 2 <Ax, Qx> + <[M + \Delta(Q) - QB[N + \Gamma(Q)]^{-1} B^* Q]x,x> = 0 \qquad x \in D(A).$$

In order to assume that the optimal control law is admissible it is necessary to assume a second key condition, namely the existence of $J \in L(H)$, such that $A - JM^{\frac{1}{2}}$ produces a stable semigroup S_t with the estimate

$$(6.19) \qquad ||S_t|| \leq C e^{-\alpha t} \quad \text{and moreover}$$

$$(6.20) \qquad C^2 ||D||^2 \text{ trace } W^1 < \infty$$

The existence of $J \in L(H)$ statisfying (6.19) and (6.20) is stronger that the detectability of $(M^{\frac{1}{2}}, A)$ needed in theorem 6.3. The existence of (K_1, Q_1) satisfying (6.17) and J satisfying (6.19), (6.20) are together sufficient for the stability of $(A - BK_1, C, D)$, and hence for an optimal solution to the control problem.

<u>Theorem 6.4</u>

For the problem with F = G = 0 and $t_1 = \infty$, if there exists a $K_1 \in L(H, U)$, such that $(A - BK_1, C, D)$ is stable, then there exists a unique optimal admissible control given by

$$(6.21) \qquad u^* = - [N + \Gamma(Q)]^{-1} B^* Qz$$

where Q is the unique solution of (6.14). Furthermore the minimum cost is

(6.22) $J(u^*) = \langle Qz_o, z_o\rangle$.

Finally the $F \neq 0$ case can be treated as before for the degenerate $D = 0 = C$ case; that is the admissible controls are feedback controls which produce Markov processes with invariant measures. The cost is again (6.12) and G is not necessarily zero.

Theorem 6.5

For the problem (6.1), (6.12) on $t_1 = \infty$, if there exists a $K_1 \in \mathcal{L}(H,U)$ such that $(A - BK_1, C, D)$ is stable, then there exists a unique optimal control given by (6.21) and the miminum cost is given by

$$J(u^*) = \text{trace } \{F^*QFW^2\}.$$

The next obvious step is to consider incomplete on noisy observations, but this has only been solved for the case $C = 0 = D$ and is fully described in [10], [11] and [12].

7. EXTENSIONS OF MORE GENERAL SYSTEMS

There are many possible extensions of this theory. All that is attempted here is the physical motivation of these extensions, the types of mathematical complications involved and relevant references.

a) Time-dependent Systems

This means basically that all operators can be time dependent and the physical motivation is obvious. For A(t) time dependent, one can define solutions in terms of a mild evolution operator $U(t,s) \in L(H)$, see for example chapter 9 of [11] for a discussion of systems describable by mild evolution operators. Mild and strong solutions can be defined as before and similar existence and uniqueness results can be proved, see for example [8] and [20]. The stochastic control problem on the finite time interval discussed in [6] also has an analogue for the time-dependent case. For a diffrent approach to time-dependent distributed systems, see [2], [3] and [24].

b) Martingale Noise Processes

In [22], $\int_o^t \Phi(t)dM_t$ is defined for $\Phi \in B_2$ as before and M_t a very general class of right continuous martingale. Using this general theory, several authors have considered stochastic differential equations with a general noise process of the type '$\Phi(t)dM_t$', see for example [23], [5] and [24]. Basically, the same sort of results hold except that even the strong solutions will not in general have continuous sample paths. The nongaussianness will of couse make a difference to the filtering theory as discussed in [10] § VII C. The physical motivation for this generalization is that some stochastic disturbances are not of gaussian white noise type and could for example be poission-type. A simpler approach to modelling nongaussian noise disturbances as they arise in applications is given in [8].

c) Limited Sensing and Control in Distributed Systems

An example of limited control is the following

$$Bu = u(x_o)$$

where $u \in L_2(0,1)$ and $x_o \in (0,1)$. B is then an unbounded, uncloseable operator from $L_2(0,1)$ to R. Although it is bounded from C(0,1), for control problems we need to work with Hilbert spaces. Similarly for observation operators $y(t) = Cz(t)$, we often wish to measure "at points". For second order distributed systems, such operators represent no mathematical problem because of the choice of spaces (see [13]). but for parabolic systems it is an awkward mathematical problem. One solution to this problem is given in [15],[16] and [11] chapter 8. For stochastic evolution equations it means working with mild solutions, never strong ones. Some existence theorems are given in [20] and filtering and control problems are discussed in [11], chapter 8.

d) Boundary Noise and Stochastic Operators

Although the physical motivation here is slightly different, namely noise occuring through the boundary conditions or via the partial differential operators, it is mathematically the same problem as in (c) and the same remarks apply. See also [1] and [24].

e) Delayed Observation and Control Action

In example 3.2, the delays occurred only in the A operator and the theory described in § 3 does not cover the case for delays in the other operators. Again this results in unbounded operators, but of a different sort to those in [c]and [d]. Some results in this direction can be found in [5] and [20].

f) Nonlinear Evolution Operators

In fact this lies outside the scope of this survey, but as it is a natural extension I recommend the references [3], [5], [11] and [24].

REFERENCES

1. A.V. Balakrishnan, Applied Functional Analysis. Springer Verlag, 1976.
2. A. Bensoussan, Filtrage Optimal des Systemes Lineaires, Dunod, 1971.
3. A. Bensoussan, Control of Stochastic Partial Differential Equations, p. 209-245, "Distributed Parameter Systems: Identification, Estimation and Control", Ed. W.H. Ray and F.G, Lainiotis, 1978. Marcel Dekker.
4. J.G. Borisovic, and A.S. Turbabin, On the Cauchy Problem for Linear Non-homogeneous differential equations with retarded arguments. Soviet Math. Dokl., 10(1969), p. 401 - 405.
5. A. Chojnowska-Michalik, Stochastic Differential Equations in Hilbert Spaces and their Applocations. Ph. D. Thesis, Institute of Mathematics Polish Academy of Sciences, 1976.

6. R.F. Curtain, and P.L. Falb, Itô's Lemma in Infinite Dimensions. J. Math. Anal. and Appl., 1970, Vol. 31, p. 434 - 448.

7. R.F. Curtain and P.L. Falb, Stochastic Differential Equations in Hilbert Space, J. Diff. Eqns. 10(1971) p. 412 - 430.

8. R.F. Curtain, Stochastic Evolution Equations with General White Noise Disturbance. J. Math. Anal. and Appl. 1977, 60 p. 570 - 595.

9. R.F. Curtain, and A.J. Pritchard, A Semigroup Approach to Infinite Dimensional Systems Theory. Proc. IMA Conf. 'Recent Developments in Control', Leicester, U.K. 1976.

10. R.F. Curtain, Estimation and Stochastic Control for Linear Infinite Dimensional Systems, " p. 45 - 56 "Probabilistic Analysis and Related Topics", Volume 1, 1978, Academic Press.

11. R.F. Curtain and A.J. Pritchard, Infinite Dimensional Linear Systems Theory. Lecture Notes in Control and Information Sciences. Vol. 8, 1978, Springer Verlag.

12. R.F. Curtain, A semigroup Approach to the LQG Problem for Infinite Dimensional Systems, Proc. IEEE, 1978.

13. R.F. Curtain, Mathematical Models for Random Vibration Problems. International Symposium of the Analysis and Optimization of Stochastic Systems, Oxford, U.K., 1978.

14. R.F. Curtain, Asymptotic Stability of Second Order Linear Stochastic Partial Differential Equations, 1978 (Submitted to SIAM J. Applied Mathematics).

15. R.F. Curtain, and A.J. Pritchard, An Abstract Theory for Unbounded Control Action for Distributed Parameter Systems. SIAM J. Control 15, pp. 566 - 611.

16. R.F. Curtain, Linear Stochastic Control for Distributed Systems with Boundary Control, Boundary Noise and Point Observations. Control Theory Centre Report No. 46, 1976, University of Warwick, Coventry, England.

17. M.C. Delfour, and S.K. Mitter, Hereditary Differential Systems with Constant. Delays I: General case, J. Diff. Eqns. 12 (1972) p. 213 - 235.

18. U.G. Haussmann, Asymptotic Stability of the Linear Itô Equation in Infinite Dimensions. J. Math. Anal. and Appl. 65 (1978) p. 219 - 235.

19. E. Hille, and R.S. Phillips, Functional Analysis and Semigroups. Colloq. Amer. Math. Soc. 31, 1957.

20. A. Ichikawa, Linear Stochastic Evolution Equations in Hilbert Space. Control Theory Centre Report No. 51. University of Warwick, 1976 (To appear in J. Diff. Eqns).

21. A. Ichikawa, Dynamic Programming Approach to Stochastic Evolution Equations. Control Theory Centre Report No. 60. University of Warwick, 1977. (To appear in SIAM J. Control + Opt., 1979).

22. M. Metivier, Integrale Stochastique par rapport a des processus a valeurs dans un espace de Banach relexif. The Prob. and Appl. Tom. 19, 1974.

23. M. Metivier, and G. Pistone, Une formule d'isometrie pour l'integrale stochastique hilbertienne et equations d'evolution lineaires stochastiques. Z. Wahrschein. 33 (1975) p. 1 - 18.

24. E. Pardoux, Doctoral Thesis, L"Université de Paris Sud, Centre d'Orsay, 1978.

25. A.J. Pritchard, and J. Zabczyk, Stabilizibility of Infinite Dimensional Systems. Control Theory Centre Report, University of Warwick, U.K., No. 70, 1977.

26. M. Slemrod, Asymptotic Behaviour of C_0 Semigroup as Determined by the Spectrum of the generator, Indiana, J. 25 (1976) pp. 783 - 792.

27. R. Vinter, A Representation of Solutions to Stochastic Delay Equations. Imperial College of Science and Technology. Dept. of Computing and Control Report, 1975.

28. R. Vinter, Semigroup on Product Spaces and Applications to Initial Value Problems with Nonlocal Boundary Conditions. Proc. 2nd IFAC Symposium on the Control of Distributed Paramter Systems. University of Warwick, 1975.

29. J. Zabczyk, A semigroup Approach to Boundary Value Control. Ibid.

30. J. Zabczyk, On Stability of Infinite Dimensional Linear Stochastic Systems. Proc. Banach Centre. Prob. Semester, Warsaw, 1976.

MARTINGALE METHODS IN STOCHASTIC CONTROL *

M.H.A. Davis
Laboratory for Information and Decision Systems
Massachusetts Institute of Technology
Cambridge, Massachusetts 02139

CONTENTS

1. INTRODUCTION

The status of continuous-time stochastic control theory ten years ago is admirably summarized in Fleming's 1969 survey paper [40]. The main results, of which a very brief outline will be found in §2 below and a complete account in the book [41], concern control of completely-observable diffusion processes, i.e. solutions of stochastic differential equations. Formal application of Bellman's "dynamic programming" idea quickly leads to the "Bellman equation" (2.3), a quasi-linear parabolic equation whose solution, if it exists, is easily shown to be the value function for the control problem. At this point the probabilistic aspects of the problem are finished and all the remaining work goes into finding conditions under which the Bellman equation has a solution. The reason why dynamic programming is a fruitful approach in stochastic control is precisely that these conditions are so much weaker than those required in the deterministic case. As regards problems with *partial observation* the best result was Wonham's formulation of the "separation theorem" [78] which he proved by reformulating the problem as one of complete observations, with the "state" being the conditional mean estimate produced by the Kalman filter; see §6 below.

* Work supported by the U.S. Air Force Office of Sponsored Research under Grant AFOSR 77-3281 and by the Department of Energy under Contract EX-76-A-01-2295.

The dynamic programming approach, while successful in many applications, suffers from many limitations. An immediate one is that the controls have to be smooth functions of the state in order that the resulting stochastic differential equation (2.1) have a solution in the Ito sense. This rules out, for example, "bang-bang" controls which arise naturally in some applications (e.g. [3]). Thus a weaker formulation of the solution concept seems essential for stochastic control; this was provided by Stroock and Varadhan [71] for Markov processes and by various forms of measure transformations, beginning with the Girsanov Theorem [43], for more general stochastic systems; these are outlined in §3. But even with the availability of weak solution concepts it seems that the Bellman equation approach is essentially limited to Markovian systems and that no general formulation of problems with partial observations is possible (A Bellman equation for partially observed diffusions was formally derived by Mortensen [65], but just looking at it convinces one that some other approach must be tried).

Since 1969 a variety of different approaches to stochastic control have been investigated, among them the following (a very partial list). Krylov [51] has studied generalized solutions of the Bellman equation; methods based on potential theory [5] and on convex analysis [7] have been introduced by Bismut; necessary conditions for optimality using general extremal theory have been obtained [44] by Haussmann; a reformulation of dynamic programming in terms of nonlinear semigroups has been given by Nisio [66]; variational inequality techniques have been introduced by Bensoussan and Lions [4], and computational methods systematically developed by Kushner [54].

This survey outlines the so-called "martingale approach" to stochastic control. It is based on the idea of formulating Bellman's "principle of optimality" as a *submartingale inequality* and then using Meyer's submartingale decomposition [63] to obtain local conditions for optimality. This is probably the most general form of dynamic programming and applies to a very general class of controlled processes, as outlined in §5 below. However, more specific results can be obtained when more structure is introduced, and for this reason we treat in some detail in §§4,6 the case of stochastic differential equations, for which the best results so far are available. Other specific cases are outlined in §7.

I have attempted to compile, in §9, a fairly complete list of references on this topic and related subjects. Undoubtedly this list will suffer from important omissions, but readers have my assurance that none of these is intentional. It should also be mentioned that no systematic coverage of martingale representation theorems has been attempted, although they are obviously germane to the subject.

2. CONTROL OF DIFFUSION PROCESSES

To introduce the connection between dynamic programming and submartingales, let us consider a control problem where the n-dimensional *state process* x_t satisfies the Ito stochastic differential equation

$$dx_t = f(t, x_t, u_t)dt + \sigma(t, x_t)dw_t \tag{2.1}$$

$$x_0 = \xi \in R^n$$

Here w_t is an n-dimensional Brownian motion and the components of f and σ are C^1 functions of x, u, with bounded derivatives. The *control* u_t is a feedback of the current state, i.e. $u_t = u(t, x_t)$ for some given function $u(t, x)$ taking values in the *control set* U. If u is Lipschitz in x, then (2.1) is a stochastic differential equation satisfying the standard Ito conditions and hence has a unique strong solution x_t. The cost associated with u is then

$$J(u) = E[\int_0^T c(t, x_t, u_t)dt + \Phi(x_T)]$$

where T is a fixed terminal time and c, Φ are, say, bounded measurable functions. The objective is to choose the function $u(\cdot,\cdot)$ so as to minimize J(u). An extensive treatment of this kind of problem will be found in Fleming and Rishel's book [41].

Introduce the *value function*

$$V(t, x) = \inf_u E_{(t, x)}[\int_t^1 c(s, x_s, u_s)ds + \Phi(x_T)] \tag{2.2}$$

Here the subscript (t, x) indicates that the process x_s starts at $x_t = x$, and the infimum is over all control functions restricted to the interval [t, T]. Formal application of Bellman's "principle of optimality" together with the differential formula suggests that V should satisfy the *Bellman equation*:†

$$V_t + 1/2 \sum_{i,j} (\sigma\sigma')_{ij} V_{x_i x_j} + \min_{u \in U} [V'_x f(t, x, u) + c(t,x,u)] = 0 \tag{2.3}$$

$$(t, x) \in [0, T[\times R^n$$

$$V(T, x) = \Phi(x), \quad x \in R^n \tag{2.4}$$

($V_t = \partial V/\partial t$ etc., and V_t, V_x etc. are evaluated at (t, x) in (2.3)). There is a "verification theorem" [41 ,§ VI 4] which states that if V is a solution of (2.3), (2.4) and u^o is an admissible control with the property that

$$V'_x(t,x)\ f(t,x,u^\circ(t,x)) + c(t,x,u^\circ(t,x)) = \min_{u \in U} [V'_x(t,x)\ f(t,x,u) + c(t,x,u)]$$

then u° is optimal. Conditions under which a solution of (2.3), (2.4) is guaranteed will be found in [41 ,§ VI 6]. Notable among them is the *uniform ellipticity* condition: there exists $\kappa > 0$ such that

$$\sum_{ij} (\sigma\sigma')_{ij} \xi_i \xi_j \geq \kappa |\xi|^2 \tag{2.5}$$

for all $\xi \in R^n$. This essentially says that noise enters every component of equation (2.1), whatever the coordinate system.

---

† A prime denotes vector or matrix transposition.

Let us reformulate these results in martingale terms, supposing the conditions are such that (2.3), (2.4) has a solution with suitable growth properties (see below). For any admissible control function u and corresponding trajectory x_t define a process M_t^u as follows:

$$(2.6) \qquad M_t^u = \int_0^t c(s, x_s, u_s)ds + V(t, x_t)$$

Note that M_t^u is the minimum expected *total* cost given the evolution of the process up to time t. Expanding the function $V(t, x_t)$ by the Ito rule gives

$$(2.7) \qquad M_t^u = V(0,\xi) + \int_0^t [V_t + 1/2 \sum_{ij}(\sigma\sigma')_{ij} V x_i x_j + V_x' f^u + c]ds + \int_0^t V_x \sigma dw$$

where $f^u(t,x) = f(t, x, u(t, x))$. But note from (2.3) that the integrand in the second term of (2.7) is always non-negative. Thus this term is an *increasing process*. If u is optimal then the integrand is identically zero. Assuming that the function V is such that the last term is a martingale, we thus have the following result:

(2.8) *For any admissible* u, M_t^u *is a submartingale and* u *is optimal if and only if* M_t^u *is a martingale.*

The intuitive meaning of the submartingale inequality is clear: the difference

$$E[M_t^u \mid x_r, r \leq s] - M_s^u$$

is simply the expected cost occasioned by persisting in using the non-optimal control over the time interval [s, t] rather than switching to an optimal control at time s. The other noteworthy feature of this formulation is that an optimal control is constructed by minimizing the *Hamiltonian*

$$H(t,x,V_x,u) = V_x' f(t,x,u) + c(t,x,u)$$

and, conveniently, the "adjoint variable" V_x is precisely the function that appears in the integrand of the stochastic integral term in (2.7).

Abstracted from the above problem, the "martingale approach" to stochastic control of systems with complete observations (i.e. where the controller has exact knowledge of the past evolution of the controlled process) consists of the following steps:

1. Define the value function V_t and conditional minimal cost processes M_t^u as in (2.2), (2.6)
2. Show that the "principle of optimality" holds in the form (2.8)
3. Construct an optimal policy by minimizing a Hamiltonian, where the adjoint variable is obtained from the integrand in a stochastic integral representation of the martingale component in the decomposition of the submartingale M_t^u.

In evaluating the cost corresponding to a control policy u in the above problem, all that is required is the sample space measure induced by the x_t process with control u. It is also convenient to note that the cost can always be regarded as a terminal cost by introducing an extra state variable x_t° defined by

$$(2.9) \qquad dx_t^\circ = c(t, x_t, u_t)dt + dw_t^\circ$$

where w_t° is an additional Brownian motion, independent of w_t. Then since $E\, w_T^\circ = 0$ we have

$$(2.10) \qquad J(u) = E\,[x_T^\circ + \Phi(x_T)] \quad = \quad E\,[\tilde{\Phi}(x_T^\circ, x_T)]$$

Let C denote the space of R^{n+1}- valued continuous functions on [0, T] and (F_t) the increasing family of σ-fields generated by the coordinate functions $\{\chi_t\}$ in C. Since (2.1), (2.9) define a process (x_t°, x_t) with a.s. continuous sample functions, this induces a measure, say μ_u, on (C, F_T) and the cost can be expressed as

$$J(u) = \int_C \Phi(\chi_T^\circ, \chi_T)\, \mu_u(d\chi)$$

It turns out that each μ_u is absolutely continuous with respect to the measure μ induced by (x_t°, x_t) with $f \equiv c \equiv 0$. Thus in its abstract form the control problem has the following ingredients:

(i) A probability space (Ω, F_T, μ)

(ii) A family of measures $(\mu_u, u \in U)$ absolutely continuous with respect to μ (or, equivalently, a family of positive random variables (ℓ_u) such that $E\,\ell_u = 1$ for each $u \in U$)

(iii) An F_Y-measurable random variable $\tilde{\Phi}$

The problem is then to choose $u \in U$ so as to minimize $E_u \Phi = E[\ell_u \tilde{\Phi}]$. In many cases it is possible to specify the Radon-Nikodym derivative ℓ_u directly in order to achieve the appropriate sample-space measure. We outline this idea in the next section before returning to control problems in section 4.

3. ABSOLUTELY CONTINUOUS CHANGES OF MEASURE

Let (Ω, F, P) be a probability space and $(F_t)_{0\leq t\leq 1}$ be an increasing family of sub-σ-fields of F such that

(3.1)
(i) Each F_t is completed with all null sets of F

(ii) (F_t) is right-continuous: $F_t = \bigcap_{s>t} F_s$

(iii) F_o is the completion of the trivial σ-field $\{\emptyset, \Omega\}$.

(iv) $F_1 = F$

Suppose P_u is a probability measure such that $P_u \ll P$. Define

$$(3.2) \qquad L_1 = dP_u/dP$$

and

$$(3.3) \qquad L_t = E\,[L_1 | F_t]$$

Then L_t is a positive martingale, $EL_t = 1$, and $L_o = 1$ a.s. in view of (3.1) (iii). According to [63 , VI T4] there is a modification of (L_t) whose paths are right-continuous with left hand limits (we denote $L_{t-} = \lim_{s\uparrow t} L_s$). Define

$$T = 1 \wedge \inf \{t: L_t \wedge L_{t-} = 0\}$$

$$T_n = 1 \wedge \inf\{t: L_t < 1/n \}$$

Then $T_n\uparrow$, $T_n \le T$ and Meyer shows in [64 , VI] that $L_t(\omega) = 0$ for all $t > T(\omega)$, a.s.

Suppose (X_t) is a given non-negative *local* martingale of (F_t) with $X_o=1$ a.s. Then X_t is always a *supermartingale*, since, if s_n is an increasing sequence of localizing times and $s<t$, using Fatou's lemma we have:

$$x_s = \lim_n X_{s\wedge s_n} = \lim_n E[X_{t\wedge s_n}|F_s] \geq E[\lim_n\inf X_{t\wedge s_n}|F_s] = E[X_{t\wedge s_n}|F_s]$$

It follows that $EX_t \leq 1$ for all t and X_t is a martingale if and only if $EX_1 = 1$. This is relevant below because we will want to use (3.2), (3.3) to *define* a measure P_u from a given process L_t which, however, is *a priori* only known to be a local martingale.

Let (M_t) be a local martingale of (F_t) and consider the equation

$$L_t = 1 + \int_0^t L_{s-}dM_s \tag{3.4}$$

It was shown by Doléans-Dade [28] (see also [64 , IV 25], that there is a unique local martingale (L_t) satisfying this, and that L_t is given explicitly by

$$L_t = \exp\,(M_t - 1/2 <M^c, M^c>_t) \prod_{s\leq t} (1 + \Delta M_s)\, e^{-\Delta M_s}$$

Here M_t^c is the "continuous part" of the local martingale M_t (see [64, IV 9] and the countable product is a.s. absolutely convergent. We denote $L_t = \mathcal{E}(M)_t$ (the "Doléans-Dade exponential").

Suppose $\Delta M_s \geq -1$ for all (s,ω). Then L_t is a non-negative local martingale, and hence according to the remarks above is a martingale if and only if $EL_1 = 1$. Its utility in connection with measure transformation lies in the following result, due to van Schuppen and Wong [69].

(3.5) *Suppose* $EL_1 = 1$ *and define a measure* P_u *on* (Ω, F_1) *by* (3.2). *Let* X *be a local martingale such that the cross-variation process* <X, M> *exists. Then* $\tilde{X}_t := X_t - <X, M>_t$ *is a* P_u *local martingale.*

Note that from the general formula connecting Radon-Nikodym derivatives and conditional expectations we have

$$E_u(\hat{X}_t|F_s) = \frac{E[L_t\hat{X}_t|F_s]}{L_s} \tag{3.6}$$

and consequently $\hat{X}_t$ is a P_u-local martingale if and only if $\hat{X}_tL_t$ is a P-local martingale One readily verifies that this is so with X_t defined as above, using the general change of variables formula for semimartingales [64 , IV 21].

Conditions for the existence of <X, M> are given by Yoeurp [79]. Recall that the "square brackets" process $[X, M]$ is defined for any pair of local martingales X, M by

$$[X, M] = \langle X^c, M^c\rangle_t + \sum_{s\leq t} \Delta X_s \Delta M_s$$

Yoeurp defines $\langle X, M\rangle$ as the dual predictable projection (in the sense of Dellacherie [27]) of $[X, M]$, when this exists and gives conditions for this [79, Thm. 1.12]. (This definition coincides with the usual one [52] when X and M are locally square integrable.) In fact a predictable process A such that $X-A$ is a P_u-local martingale exists *only* when these conditions are satisfied (see also [64, VI 22]).

An exhaustive study of conditions under which $E\mathcal{E}(M)_1 = 1$ is given by Lepingle and Memin in [57]. A typical condition is that $\Delta M > -1$ and

$$(3.7) \qquad E\left[\exp\left(1/2 \ \langle M^c, M^c\rangle_1\right)\prod_{t\leq 1} (1+\Delta M_t) \exp\left(\frac{-\Delta M_t}{1+\Delta M_t}\right)\right] < \infty$$

This generalizes an earlier condition for the continuous case given by Novikov [67]. We will mention more specific results for special cases below; see also references [2],[3], [12], [13], [30], [36], [43], [56], [60], [77].

Let us now specialize the case where X_t is a Brownian motion with respect to the σ-fields F_t, and M_t is a stochastic integral

$$M_t = \int_0^t \phi_s dX_s$$

where ϕ_s is an adapted process satisfying

$$(3.8) \qquad \int_0^t \phi_s^2 ds < \infty \qquad \text{a.s. for each } t$$

Then $\langle M^c, M^c\rangle_t = \langle M, M\rangle_t = \int_0^t \phi_s^2\, ds$ and $\langle M, X\rangle_t = \int_0^t \phi_s ds$ so that

$$(3.9) \qquad L_t = \exp\left(\int_0^t \phi_s dX_s - 1/2\int_0^t \phi_s^2\, ds\right)$$

and

$$(3.10) \qquad B_t := X_t - \int_0^t \phi_s ds$$

in a P_u-local martingale (assuming $EL_1 = 1$). Since X_t has continuous paths, $\langle X, X\rangle_t$ is the sample path quadratic variation of X_t [52] and this is invariant under absolutely continuous change of measure. It follows from (3.10), since the last term is a continuous process of bounded variation, that

$$\langle B, B\rangle_t^{(P_u)} = \langle X, X\rangle_t^{(P)} = t$$

and hence that B_t *is a* P_u *-Brownian motion,* in view of the Kunita-Watanabe characterization [64, III 102]. This is the original "Girsanov theorem" [43]. A full account of it will be found in Chapter 6 of Liptser and Shiryaev's book [60]. In particular, theorem 6.1 of [60] gives Novikov's condition: $EL_1 = 1$ if ϕ satisfies (3.7) and

$$(3.11) \qquad E\exp\left(1/2\int_0^1 \phi_s^2 ds\right) < \infty$$

The Girsanov theorem is used to define "weak solutions" in stochastic differential equations. Suppose $f : [0, 1] \times C \to R$ is a bounded non-anticipative functional on the space of continuous functions and define

$$\phi(t, \omega) = f(t, x(\cdot,\omega))$$

where x_t is a P-Brownian motion as above. Then (3.11) certainly holds and from (3.10) we see that under measure P_u the process x_t satisfies

$$dx_t = f(t, x)dt + dB_t \tag{3.12}$$

where B_t is a P_u-Brownian motion, i.e. (x_t, F_t, P_u) is a "weak solution" of the stochastic differential equation (3.12). (It is not a "strong" or "Ito" solution since B does not necessarily generate x; a well-known example of Tsyrelson [72], [60, §4.4.8] shows that this is possible). The reader is referred to [60] for a comprehensive discussion of weak and strong solutions, etc. Suffice it to say that the main advantage of the weak solution concept for control theory is that there is no requirement that the dependence of f on x in (3.12) be smooth (e.g., Lipschitz as the standard Ito conditions require), so that such things as "bang-bang" controls [3], [21] fit naturally into this framework.

4. CONTROLLED STOCHASTIC DIFFERENTIAL EQUATIONS-COMPLETE

This problem, a generalization of that considered in §2, is the one for which the martingale approach has reached its most definitive form, and it seems worth giving a self-contained outline immediately rather than attempting to deduce the results as special cases of the general framework considered in §5. The results below were obtained in a series of papers: Rishel [68], Beneš [2], Duncan and Varaiya [30], Davis and Varaiya [25], Davis [16], and Elliott [34].

Let Ω be the space of continuous functions on [0, 1] to R^n, (w_t) the family of coordinate functions and $F_t^\circ = \sigma\{w_s, s \leq t\}$. Let P be Wiener measure on (Ω, F_1°) and F_t be the completion of F°_t with null sets of F_1°. Suppose $\sigma : [0, 1] \times \Omega \to R^{n\times n}$ is a matrix-valued function such that

$$\begin{aligned} &\text{(i) } \sigma_{ij}(\cdot,\cdot) \text{ is } F_t\text{- predictable} \\ &\text{(ii) } |\sigma_{ij}(t, x) - \sigma_{ij}(t, y)| \leq K \sup_{0\leq s\leq t} |x_s - y_s| \\ &\text{(iii) } \sigma(t, x) \text{ is non-singular for each } (t, x) \text{ and } |(\sigma^{-1}(t, x))_{ij}| \leq K \end{aligned} \tag{4.1}$$

(Here K is a fixed constant, independent of t, i, j). Then there exists a unique strong solution to the stochastic differential equation

$$dx_t = \sigma(t, x)dw_t, \quad x_o \in R^n \text{ given.}$$

Now let U be a compact metric space, and $f: [0, 1] \times C \times U \to R^n$ a given function which is continuous in $u \in U$ for fixed $(t, x) \in [0, 1] \times C$, an F_t-predictable process as a function of (t, x) for fixed $u \in U$, and satisfies

(4.2) $$|f(t, x, u)| \le K(1 + \sup_{s \le t} |x_s|)$$

Now let U be the family of F^t-predictable U-valued processes and for $u \in U$ define

$$L_t(u) = \exp\left(\int_0^t (\sigma^{-1}(s,x)\ f(s,x,u_s))' dw_s - 1/2 \int_0^t |\sigma^{-1} f|^2 ds\right)$$

The Girsanov theorem as given in §3 above generalizes easily to the vector case, and condition (4.2) implies the vector version of Novikov's condition (3.10) (see [60, p. 221]). Thus $EL_1(u) = 1$ and defining a measure P_u by

$$\frac{dP_u}{dP} = L_1(u)$$

we see that under P_u the process x_t satisfies

(4.3) $$dx_t = f(t,x,u_t)dt + \sigma(t,x)dw_t^u$$

where w_t^u is a P_u-vector Brownian motion. The cost associated with $u \in U$ is now

(4.4) $$J(u) = E_u\left[\int_0^1 c(t,x,u_t)dt + \Phi(x_1)\right]$$

where c, Φ are bounded measurable functions and c satisfies also the same condition as f.

It is clear that σ must be non-singular if weak solutions are to be defined as above (cf. the uniform ellipticity conditions (2.5)), but an important class of "degenerate" systems is catered for, namely those of the form

(4.5) $$dx_t^1 = f^1(t,x_t^1, x_t^2)dt$$

(4.6) $$dx_t^2 = f^2(t,x_t^1,x_t^2,u_t)dt + \bar{\sigma}(t,x_t^1,x_t^2)dw_t$$

where $\bar{\sigma}$ is nonsingular and f^1 is Lipschitz in x_t^1 uniformly in (t,x_t^2). Then (4.5) has a unique solution $x_t^1 = \chi_t(x^2)$ for each given trajectory x^2, and (4.6) can be rewritten as

$$dx_t^2 = f^2(t,\chi_t(x^2),x_t^2,u_t)dt + \bar{\sigma}(t,\chi_t(x^2),x_t^2)dw_t$$

which is in the form (4.3). This situation arises when a scalar n'th-order differential equation is put into 1st-order vector form.

Fix $t \in [0,1]$ and define the conditional remaining cost at time t as

$$\psi_t^u = E_u\left[\int_t^1 c^u(x,s)ds + \Phi(x_1)\,|\,F_t\right]$$

(Here and below we will write $c(x,s,u_s)$ as $c^u(x,s)$ or c_s^u, and similarly for f). It is seen from the formula (3.6) that ψ_t^u only depends on u restricted to the interval [t,1] and since all measures P_u are equivalent the null sets up to which ψ_t^u is defined are also control-independent; in fact ψ_t^u is a well-defined element of $L_1(\Omega,F_t,P)$ for each $u \in U$. Since L_1 is a complete lattice we can define the lattice infimum

$$W_t = \bigwedge_{u\in U} \psi_t^u$$

as an F_t-measurable random variable. This is the *value function* (or *value process*). It satisfies the following *principle of optimality*, originally due to Rishel [68]: for each fixed $u\in U$ and $0\le t\le \tau\le 1$,

$$W_t \le E_u\left[\int_t^\tau c_s^u ds \middle| F_t\right] + E_u[W_\tau | F_t] \tag{4.7}$$

The proof of this depends on the fact that the family $[\psi_t^u : u\in U]$ has the "ε-lattice property": see §5 below. Now define

$$M_t^u = \int_0^t c_s^u\, ds + W_t$$

This has the same interpretation as in (2.6) above. Note that since x_0 is assumed to be a fixed constant,

$$\begin{aligned} M_0^u &= W_0 = \inf_{v\in U} J(v) \\ M_1^u &= \int_0^1 c_s^u ds + \Phi(x_1) = \text{"sample cost"} \end{aligned} \tag{4.8}$$

The statement of the principle of optimatlity is now exactly as in (2.8). Firstly (4.7) implies that M_t^u is a P_u-submartingale for each u. Now if M_t^u is a P_u-martingale then $E_u M_0^u = E_u M_1^u$ which implies u is optimal in view of (4.8), while if u is optimal then for any t,

$$W_0 = E_u\left[\int_0^t c_s^u ds + \psi_t^u\right].$$

Now for any control we have from (4.7)

$$W_0 \le E_u\left[\int_0^t c_s^u ds + W_t\right]$$

and hence

$$E_u[W_t - \psi_t^u] \ge 0 .$$

But by definition $W_t \le \psi_t^u$ a.s.; thus $W_t = \psi_t^u$ a.s. and therefore $M_t^u = E_u(M_1^u | F_t]$. So M_t^u is a martingale if and only if u is optimal.

Fix $u\in U$. A direct argument shows that the function $t\to EM_t^u$ is right continuous, and it follows from [63, VI T4] that M_t^u has a right-continuous modification. The conditions for the Meyer decomposition [63, VII T31] are thus met, so there exists a unique predictable increasing process A_t^u with $A_0^u = 0$ and a martingale N_t^u such that

$$M_t^u = W_0 + A_t^u + N_t^u$$

We now want to represent the martingale N_t^u as a stochastic integral. If the σ-fields F_t were generated by a Brownian motion then this representation would be a standard result [15], [52], [60], but here (4.3) is only a weak solution, so (w_t^u) does not necessarily generate (F_t). Nevertheless it was proved by Fujisaki, Kallianpur and Kunita [42] (see also [25], [60]) that all F_t-martingales are in fact stochastic integrals of w_t^u, i.e. there exists an adapted process g_t such that

$$\int_0^t |g_s|^2 ds < \infty \quad \text{a.s.}$$

and

$$(4.9) \qquad N_t^u = \int_0^t g_s \sigma_s dw_s^u .$$

From the definition of M_t^u we now have

$$(4.10) \qquad W_t = W_0 + \int_0^t g_s \sigma_s dw_s^u + A_t^u - \int_0^t c_s^u ds$$

Now take another control $v \in U$. By definition

$$M_t^v = \int_0^t c_s^v ds + W_t$$

and hence, using (4.3) and (4.10) we get

$$(4.11) \qquad M_t^v = W_0 + \int_0^t g_s \sigma_s dw_s^v + \Big[A_t^u + \int_0^t (H_s(v_s) - H_s(u_s))ds\Big]$$

where

$$(4.12) \qquad H_s(u_s) = g_s f(s,x,u_s) + c(s,x,u_s)$$

Now (4.11) gives a representation of M_t^v as a "special semimartingale" (= local martingale + predictable bounded variation process) under measure P_u and it is known that such a decomposition is unique [64,IV32]. But we know that M^v is a submartingale with decomposition

$$(4.13) \qquad M^v = W_0 + N_t^v + A_t^v$$

so the terms in (4.11), (4.13) must correspond. In particular this shows that *the integral* g *in* (4.9) *does not depend on the control* u. We can now state some conditions for optimality.

(4.14) A necessary condition. *If* $u^* \in U$ *is optimal then it minimizes* (a.s. dP x dt) *the Hamiltonian* H_s *of* (4.12)

Indeed, if u* is optimal then $A_t^{u^*} = 0$. Referring to (4.11) with u = u* we see that (4.14) is just the statement that the last term in (4.11) is an increasing process.

(4.15) A sufficient condition for optimality. *For a given control* u*, defined the P^{u^*} *-martingale*

$$p_t^* = E_{u^*}[M_1^{u^*} | F_t]$$

Then u* *is optimal if for any other* $u \in U$ *the process*

$$I_t^u = p_t^* + \int_0^t (c_s^u - c_s^{u^*})ds$$

is a P_u *-submartingale.*

This is evident since then

$$J(u^*) = I_0^u = E_u I_0^u \leq E_u I_1^u = J(u).$$

We can recast (4.15) as a local condition: since it is a martingale, p_t^* has a representation

$$p_t^* = J(u^*) + \int_0^t \tilde{g}_s \sigma_s dw_s^{u^*}$$

Now suppose that

(4.16) $\quad \tilde{H}_t(u_t) \leq \tilde{H}_t(v) \quad$ a.e. for all $v \in U$

where $\tilde{H}$ is as in (4.12) but with $\tilde{g}$ replacing g. Then a calculation similar to (4.11) shows that I_t^u is a local P_u-submartingale for any $u \in \mathcal{U}$; since $I_0^u = J(u^*)$, this implies that if T_n is a sequence of localizing times then

$$E_u[I_{1\wedge T_n}^u] \geq J(u^*)$$

But the process I_t^u is uniformly bounded and $I_{1\wedge T_n}^u \to I_1^u$ as $n\to\infty$, so that

$$E_u[I_{1\wedge T_n}^u] \to J(u).$$

Thus (4.16) is a sufficient condition for optimality and it is easily seen that if it is satisfied then $p_t^* = M_t^{u^*}$ and $\tilde{g}_t = g_t$, a.e. See [21] for an application.

Since the process g_t is defined independently of the existence of any optimal control it seems clear from the above that an optimal control should be constructed by minimizing the Hamiltonian (4.12). Under the conditions we have stated, an implicit function lemma of Beneš [1] implies the existence of a predictable process u_t^0 such that

$$H_t(u_t^0) = \min_{v \in U} H_t(v) \text{ a.e.}$$

Using (4.11) with $u = u^0$ gives

$$M_t^v \geq W_0 + \int_0^t g_s \sigma_s dw_s^v + A_t^{u^0}$$

and hence, taking expectations at t=1,

(4.17) $\quad E_v[A_1^{u^0}] \leq J(v) - W_0$

To show u^0 is optimal it suffices, according to the criterion (2.8), to show that $A_1^{u^0} = 0$ a.s. Here we need some results on compactness of the sets of Girsanov exponentials, due to Beneš [2] and Duncan and Varaiya [30]. Let A be the set of R^n-valued F_t-predictable processes ϕ satisfying

$$|\phi(t,x)| \leq \kappa(1 + \sup_{s\leq t} |x_s|), \quad (t,x) \in [0,1] \times \Omega$$

(thus $f^u \in A$ for $u \in \mathcal{U}$, see (4.2)) and let

$$D = \{\delta(\phi) : \phi \in A\}$$

where

$$\delta(\phi) = \exp\left(\int_0^1 (\sigma^{-1}\phi)' dw - 1/2 \int_0^1 |\sigma^{-1}\phi|^2 dt \right)$$

then Beneš' result is

(4.18) *D is a weakly compact subset of* $L_1(\Omega,F,P)$ *and $\ell>0$ a.s. for all $\ell \in D$.*

Returning to (4.17) we can, in view of (4.8), choose a sequence $u_n \in U$ such that $J(u_n) \downarrow W_0$ and hence such that for any positive integer N,

(4.19) $$E_{u_n}[A_1^{u^0} \wedge N] = E[\delta(f^{u^n})(A_1^{u^0} \wedge N)] \to 0, \quad n \to \infty.$$

In view of (4.18) there is a subsequence of $\delta(f^{u^n})$ converging weakly to some $\rho \in D$; hence from (4.19)

$$E[\rho(A_1^{u^0} \wedge N)] = 0$$

and it follows that $A_1^{u^0} = 0$ a.s. We thus have:

(4.20) *Under the stated conditions, an optimal policy* u^0 *exists, constructed by minimizing the Hamiltonian* (4.12).

Two comments on this result: firstly, it is possible to recast the problem so as to have a purely terminal cost by introducing an extra state x^0 as in (2.9), (2.10). However it is important *not to do this* here, since an extra Brownian motion w_t^0 is introduced as well, and there is then no way of showing that the optimal policy u^0 does not depend on w^0 - i.e. one gets a possibly "randomized" optimal policy this way. Secondly, the existence result (4.20) was originally proved in [2] and [30] just by using the compactness properties of the density sets. However one is then obliged to assume convexity of the "velocity set" $f(t,x,U)$ in order that the set $D(U) = \{\delta(f^u) : u \in U\}$ be convex (and can then be shown to be weakly closed). Finally it should be remarked that (4.20) is a much stronger result than anything available in *deterministic* control theory, the reason being of course that the noise "smooths out" the process.

A comparison of (2.3) and (4.12) shows that the process g_t plays the role of the gradient $V_x(t,x_t)$ in the Markov case, so that in a sense the submartingale decomposition theorems are providing us with a weak form of differentiation. The drawback with the martingale approach is of course that while the function V_x can (in principle) be calculated by solving the Bellman equation, the process g_t is only defined implicitly by (4.9), so that the optimality conditions (4.14) (4.15) do not provide a *constructive* procedure for calculating the optimal u^0, or for verifying whether a candidate control satisfies the necessary condition (4.14). Some progress on this has been made by Haussmann [44], but it depends on $u^0(t,x)$ being a smooth function of $x \in \Omega$, which is very restrictive.

Suppose u^0 is optimal and that the random variable

$$M_1^{u^0} = \int_0^1 c(s,x,u^0(s,x))ds + \Phi(x_1)$$

is Frechet differentiable as a function of $x\in\Omega$; then by the Riesz representation theorem there is, for each $x\in\Omega$ an R^n-valued Radon measure μ_x such that for $y\in\Omega$

$$M_1^{u^0}(x+y) = M_1^{u^0}(x) + \int_{[0,1]} y(s)\,\mu_x(ds) + o(||y||)$$

Since u^0 is optimal $M_t^{u^0}$ satisfies

$$M_t^{u^0} = J(u^0) + \int_0^t g_s \sigma_s dw_s^{u^0}$$

and Haussmann [45] [46] (see also [19]) shows that, under some additional smoothness assumptions, g_t is given by

$$g_t = E_{u^0}[\int_{]t,1]} \mu_x'(ds)\Psi(s,t)\,|\,F_t]$$

where $\Psi(s,t)$ is the (random) fundamental matrix solution of the linearized equation corresponding to (4.3) with $u = u^0$. Ths representation gives, in some cases, an "adjoint equation" satisfied by g_t, along the lines originally shown by Kushner [53].

Finally let us remark that in all of the above the state space of x_t is R^n. Some problems - for example, control of the orientation of a rigid body - are more naturally formulated with a differentiable manifold as state space. Such problems have been treated by Duncan [29] using versions of the Girsanov theorem etc. due to Duncan and Varaiya [31].

5. GENERAL FORMULATION OF STOCHASTIC CONTROL

The first abstract formulation of dynamic programming for continuous-time stochastic control problems was given by Rishel [68] who isolated the "principle of optimality" in a form similar to (4.7). The submartingale formulation was given by Striebel [70] who also introduced the important "ε-lattice property." Other papers formulating stochastic control problems in some generality are those of Boel and Varaiya [11], Memin [61], Elliott[37] [38], Boel and Kohlmann [9] [10], Davis and Kohlmann [23] and Brémaud and Pietri [14].

We shall sketch briefly a formulation, somewhat similar to that of [23], which is less general than that of Striebel [70] but sufficiently general to cover all of the applications considered in this paper.

The basic ingredients of the control problem are

(i) A probability space (Ω,F,P)

(ii) Two families (F_t), (Y_t) $(0\leq t\leq 1)$ of increasing, right-continuous, completed sub-σ-fields of F, such that $Y_t \subset F_t$ for each t.

(iii) A non-negative F_1-measurable random variable Φ.

(iv) A measurable space (U,Ξ)

(v) A family of control processes $\{\mathcal{U}_s^t,\ 0\leq s\leq t\leq 1\}$

Each control process $u\in\mathcal{U}_s^t$ is a Y_t-predictable U-valued function on $]s,t]\times\Omega$. The family $\{U_s^t\}$ is assumed to be closed under

restriction: $u \in U_s^t \to u|_{[s,\tau]} \in U_s^\tau$ for $s \leq \tau \leq t$

concatenation: $u \in U_s^\tau$, $v \in U_\tau^t \Rightarrow w \in U_s^t$ where

$$w(\sigma,\omega) = \begin{cases} u(\sigma,\omega) & \sigma \in]s,\tau] \\ v(\sigma,\delta) & \sigma \in]\tau,t] \end{cases}$$

(5.1)

finite mixing: $u,v \in U_s^t$, $A \in Y_s \to w \in U_s^t$ where

$$w(\sigma,\omega) = \begin{cases} u(\sigma,\omega), & \omega \in A \\ v(\sigma,\omega), & \omega \in A^c \end{cases}$$

We denote $U = U_0^1$ (In most cases U will consist of *all* predictable U-valued processes, but (5.1) is the set of conditions actually required for the principle of optimality below). A control $u \in U_0^t$ is assumed to determine a measure P_u on (Ω, F_t) which is absolutely continuous with respect to $P|_{F_t}$ such that $P_u|_{F_o} = P|_{F_0}$ and such that the assignment is compatible in the sense that if $u \in U_0^t$, $s < t$ and $v = u|_{[0,s]}$ (so that $v \in U_0^s$) then $P_v = P_u|_{F_s}$. If $u \in U_s^t$ and X is an F_t-measurable random variable, then $E_u X$ denotes expectation with respect to measure P_u. We finally assume that $E_u \Phi < \infty$ for all $u \in U$ and the problem is then to choose $u \in U$ so as to minimize $J(u) = E_u \Phi$.

The value process corresponding to $u \in U_0^t$ is

(5.2) $$W_t^u = \bigwedge_{v,t} E_v[\Phi|Y_t]$$

where "$\bigwedge_{v,t}$" denotes the lattice infimum in $L_1(\Omega, Y_t, P)$, taken over all $v \in U$ such that $v|_{[0,t]} = u$. Note that, in contrast to the situation in §4, W_t^u is in general *not* control-independent. We nevertheless have a result analogous to (2.8), namely

(5.3) W_t^u *is a submartingale for each* $u \in U$ *and is a martingale if and only if* u *is optimal.*

Note that by inclusion and using the compatability condition, for any $\tau > t$

$$W_t^u \leq \bigwedge_{v,\tau} E_v[\Phi|Y_t] = \bigwedge_{v,\tau} E_u[E_v[\Phi|Y_\tau]|Y_t]$$

so that the first statement of (5.3) is equivalent to the assertion that $\bigwedge_{v,\tau}$ and $E_u[\cdot|Y_t]$ may be interchanged, and according to Striebel [70] (see also [26] for a summary) this is possible if the random variables $E_v[\Phi|Y_t)$ have the ε-*lattice property*: if $v_1, v_2 \in U_t^1$ then there exists $v_3 \in U_t^1$ such that, with $\bar{v}_i$ denoting the concatenation of u and v_i,

(5.4) $$E_{\bar{v}_3}[\Phi|Y_t] \leq E_{\bar{v}_1}[\Phi|Y_t] \wedge E_{\bar{v}_2}[\Phi|Y_t] + \varepsilon \quad \text{a.s.}$$

Now it is evident that under assumptions (5.1) the set $\{E_v[\Phi|Y_t]\}$has the 0-lattice property, because given v_1, v_2 as above one only has to define

$$A = \{\omega : E_{\bar{v}_1}[\Phi|Y_t] \leq E_{\bar{v}_2}[\Phi|Y_t]\}$$

and, for $\tau \in]t,1]$,

$$v_3(\tau,\omega) = \begin{cases} v_1(\tau,\omega), & \omega \in A \\ v_2(\tau,\omega), & \omega \in A^c \end{cases}$$

Then (5.4) holds with $\varepsilon = 0$.

It is clear from the definition (5.2) that u is optimal if W_t^u is a P_u-martingale while conversely if u is optimal then for any $t \in [0,1]$

(5.5) $$E_u[W_0^u] = \inf_{v \in U} J(v) = J(u) = E_u[E_u[\Phi|Y_t]]$$

But by the submartingale property $E_u[W_0^u] \leq E_u[W_t^u]$ and this together with (5.2) and (5.5) implies that $W_t^u = E_u[\Phi|Y_t]$, i.e. W_t^u is a P_u-martingale.

Statement (5.3) is a general form of optimality principle but its connection with conventional dynamic programming is tenuous as there is a different value function for each control, reflecting the fact that past controls can affect the expectation of future performance. This is suggestive of Feldbaum's "dual control" idea, namely that an optimal controller will act so as to "acquire information" as well as to achieve direct control action.

The postulates of the general model above are not, as they stand, sufficient to ensure that there is a single value function if $Y_t = F_t$ (complete information). Let

(5.6) $$L_t(u) = E[\frac{dP_u}{dP}|F_t]$$

Now fix $s \in [0,1]$ and for $s \leq t \leq 1$ define

$$L_t(u,v) = \begin{cases} L_t(u)/L_s(v) & \text{if } L_s(v) > 0 \\ 1 & \text{if } L_s(v) = 0 \end{cases}$$

then $L_t(u,v)$ is a positive martingale and $L_s(u,v) = 1$. Then the following hypothesis ensures that there is a process W_t such that $W_t^u = W_t$ in case $Y_t = F_t$:

(5.7) *For any* $v \in U$, *and* $u_1, u_2 \in U$ *such that* $u_1|_{]s,1]} = u_2|_{]s,1]}$ *we have*

$$L_t(u_1,v) = L_t(u_2,v) \quad \text{for all } t \in]s,1]$$

See [61, Lemma 3.2]. Clearly the densities $L_t(u)$ of §4 above satisfy (5.7)

<u>A minimum principle - complete observations case</u>

If we are to use the principle of optimality (5.3) to obtain *local* conditions for optimality in the form of a minimum principle it is necessary to be more specific about how the densities $L_t(u)$ are related to the controls $u \in U$. This is generally through a transformation of measures as described in §3 above. A general formulation will be found in Elliott's paper [38] in this volume, but to introduce the idea let us consider the following rather special set-up.

Suppose $Y_t = F_t$ for each t, and let M_t be a given F_t-martingale with almost all paths continuous. Now take a function $\phi : [0,1]\times\Omega\times U\to R$ such that ϕ is a predictable process for each $u\in U$ and continuous in u for each fixed (t,ω), and for $u\in \mathcal{U}$ let ϕ^u denote the predictable process $\phi^u(t,\omega) = \phi(t,\omega,u(t,u))$. We suppose that for each $u\in\mathcal{U}$

$$(5.8)\qquad E\exp(1/2\int_0^1 (\phi_s^u)^2 d\langle M\rangle_s) < \infty$$

and that the measure P_u is defined by

$$\frac{dP_u}{dP} = \mathcal{E}(\int\phi^u dM)_1$$

(see §3). From (3.7), condition (5.8) ensures that P_u is a probability measure and that $P_u \approx P$. Now $L_t(u)$ (defined by (5.6)) satisfies the equation

$$L_t(u) = \int_0^t L_s(u)\phi_s^u\, dM_s$$

The uniqueness of the solution to this equation shows that condition (5.7) is satisfied, and hence that there is a single value process W_t, which can be shown to have a right-continuous modification [61], assuming *the cost function is bounded.* Then for any $u\in\mathcal{U}$, W_t has the submartingale decomposition

$$(5.9)\qquad W_t = W_0 + N_t^u + A_t^u$$

where N_t^u is a P_u-martingale and A_t^u a predictable increasing process. According to the translation theorem, the process

$$(5.10)\qquad dM_t^u = dM_t - \phi^u d\langle M\rangle_t$$

is a continuous P_u-martingale. Decompose N_t^u into the sum

$$N_t^u = \bar{N}_t^u + \tilde{N}_t$$

where $\bar{N}_t^u$ is in the stable subspace generated by M_t^u (see [64]) and $\tilde{N}_t$ is orthogonal to this stable subspace. There is a predictable process g_t such that

$$\bar{N}_t^u = \int_0^t g_s dM_s^u$$

Now consider another admissible control v. Using (5.9), (5.10), we see, as in (4.11), (4.12) above that W_t can be written

$$W_t = W_0 + \int_0^t g_s dM_s^u + \tilde{N}_t + \int_0^t g_s(\phi_s^v - \phi_s^u)d\langle M\rangle_s + A_t^u$$

Now $\tilde{N}_t$ *is a* P_v*-martingale,* since the Radon-Nikodym derivative $E_u[dP_v/dP_v|F_t]$ is in the stable subspace generated by M^u (see [37], [38]) and hence, by the uniqueness of the semi-martingale decomposition (5.9) we have

$$A_t^u = \int_0^t g_s(\phi_s^u - \phi_s^u)d\langle M\rangle_s + A_t^u$$

Since A_t^u is an increasing process and $A_t^u = 0$ if u is optimal, we have the following minimum principle:

(5.11) *If* $u \in U$ *is optimal and* v *is any admissible control then for almost all* ω

$$g_s \phi(s,\omega,u_s) \le g_s \phi(s,\omega,v_s) \quad \text{a.e. } (d\langle M \rangle_s)$$

In particular if U *consists of all predictable* U-*valued processes then*

$$g_s \phi(s,\omega,u_s) = \min_{v \in U} g_s \phi(s,\omega,v)$$

The importance of this type of result is that no martingale representation result is required, since the "orthogonal martingale" $\tilde{N}_t$ plays no role in the optimality conditions (things are somewhat more complicated if the basic martingale M_t is not continuous).

Partial observations case

Further progress in the case when $Y_t \neq F_t$ appears to depend on representation theorems for Y_t-martingales, although possibly a development similar to the above could be carried out. For each $u \in U$ the P_u-submartingale W_t^u is decomposed into the sum of a martingale and an increasing process. In Memin's paper it is assumed that all (Y_t,P)-martingales have a representation as a sum of stochastic integrals with respect to a continuous martingale and a random measure. It is shown in [48] that a similar representation then holds for (Y_t,P_u)-martingales since $P_u \ll P$. Using this some somewhat more specific optimality conditions can be stated, but these do not lead to useful results as no genuine minimum principle can be obtained. Rather than describe them we revert to the stochastic differential equation model of §4 for which better results have been obtained.

6. PARTIAL INFORMATION

Returning to the problem of §4, let us suppose that the state vector x_t is divided into two sets of components $x_t' = (y_t', z_t')$ of which only the first is observed by the controller. Define $Y_t = \sigma\{y_s, s \le t\}$. Then the class of admissible controls is the set N of Y_t-adapted processes with values in U. The objective is to choose $u \in N$ so as to minimize J(u) given by (4.4). Following Elliott [34] we will outline a *necessary condition* for optimality. Thus we suppose that $u^* \in N$ is optimal (and write c^*, E_* instead of c^{u^*}, E_{u^*}, etc.). Let

$$\psi_t^* = E_*\Big[\int_t^1 c_s^* ds + \Phi(x_1) \,\Big|\, F_t\Big]$$

and for any $u \in N$ define

$$N_t^u = \int_0^t c_s^u ds + \psi_t^*$$

Then N_t^* is an (F_t,P_*)-martingale and it is easily shown that

(6.1) (i) $E_*[N_t^* | Y_t]$ is a (Y_t,P_*)-martingale

(ii) $E^*[N_t^u | Y_t] \le E_*\, [E_u[N_{t+h}^u | F_t] | Y_t]$ for any $u \in U$ and $h > 0$

As in §4, we can represent N^*_t as a stochastic integral with respect to the Brownian motion $w^*_t = w^{u^*}_t$, i.e. there exists an F_t-adapted process g^*_t such that

$$(6.2)\qquad N^*_t = \psi^*_0 + \int_0^t g^*_s \sigma_s dw^*_s$$

Using an argument similar to that of (4.11)-(4.12) we see that N^u_t can be written

$$(6.3)\qquad N^u_t = \psi^*_0 + \int_0^t g^*_s \sigma_s dw^u_s + \int_0^t \Delta H^*_s(u) ds$$

where

$$\Delta H^*_s(u) = [g^*_s f(s,x,u_s) + c(s,x,u_s)] - [g^*_s f(s,x,u^*_s) - c(s,x,u^*_s)]$$

It now follows from (6.1) (ii) and (6.3) that

$$(1/h)E_*[E_u(\int_t^{t+h} \Delta H^*_s(u) ds | F_t) | Y_t] \geq 0$$

A rather delicate argument given in [34] shows that taking the limit as $h \downarrow 0$ gives $E_*[\Delta H^*_t(u) | Y_t] \geq 0$. We thus obtain the following minimum principle:

(6.4) *Suppose* $u^* \in N$ *is optimal and* $u \in N$. *Then there is a set* $T \subset [0,1]$ *of zero Lebesgue measure such that for* $t \notin T$

$$E_*[g^*_t f(t,x,u^*_t) + c(t,x,u^*_t) | Y_t] \leq E_*[g^*_t f(t,x,u_t) + c(t,x,u_t) | Y_t] \quad \text{a.s.}$$

where g^*_t *is the process of* (6.2).

This is a much better result than the original minimum principle (theorem 4.2 of [25]) since the optimal control minimizes the conditional expectation of a Hamiltonian involving a single "adjoint process" g^*. A similar result (including some average value state space constraints) was obtained by Haussmann [44] using the Girsanov formulation together with L.W. Neustadt's "general theory of extremals."

It is shown in [39] that a *sufficient condition* for optimality is that an inequality similar to (6.4) but with E_u replacing E_* should hold for all admissible u.

The disadvantage of the types of result outlined above is that they ignore the general cybernetic principle that in partially observable problems the conditional distribution of the state given the observations constitutes an "information state," on which control action should be based. In other words, the filtering operation is not explicitly brought in. Although there is a well-developed theory of filtering for stochastic differential equations [42], [60], it turns out to be remarkably difficult to incorporate this into the control problem. A look at the "separation theorem" of linear control [18], [78], [41 , chapter 7] will show why. The separation theorem concerns a linear stochastic system of the form

$$(6.5)\qquad \begin{aligned} dx_t &= Ax_t dt + \beta(u_t)dt + G dw^{1u}_t \\ dy_t &= Fx_t dt + R^{1/2} dw^{2u}_t \end{aligned}$$

where w^{1u}, w^{2u} are independent vector Brownian motions, the distribution of the initial state x_0 is normal, and the coefficient matrices can be time-varying. It is assumed that GG' and R are symmetric and strictly positive definite, that the controls u_t

take values in a compact set U and that the function β is continuous. The solution of (6.5) for a given Y_t-adapted control policy u_t is then defined by standard application of the Girsanov technique and the (non-quadratic) cost is given by

$$J(u) = E_u[\int_0^1 c(t,x_t,u_t)dt + \Phi(x_1)]$$

It is shown in [24] that *the conditional distribution of* x_t *given* Y_t *is normal,* with mean $\hat{x}_t$ and covariance Σ_t given by the Kalman filter equations:

$$(6.6)\qquad d\hat{x}_t = A\hat{x}_t dt + \beta(u_t)dt + \Sigma_t F'R^{-1/2}d\nu_t$$

$$\hat{x}_0 = Ex_0$$

$$(6.7)\qquad \dot{\Sigma} = A\Sigma + \Sigma A' + GG' - \Sigma F'R^{-1}F\Sigma$$

$$\Sigma(0) = \mathrm{cov}(x_0)$$

Here ν_t is the normalized innovations process

$$\nu_t = \int_0^t R^{-1/2}(dy - F\hat{x}_s ds)$$

which is a standard vector Brownian motion. Let us denote $K(t) = \Sigma_t F'R^{-1/2}$, and let $n(\cdot,x,t)$ be the normal density function with mean x and covariance Σ_t. Now define

$$\hat{c}(t,x,u) = \int_{R^n} c(t,\xi,u)n(\xi,x,t)d\xi,\quad \hat{\Phi}(x) = \int_{R^n}\Phi(\xi)n(\xi,x,t)d\xi$$

Then the cost J(u) can be expressed as

$$(6.8)\qquad J(u) = E_u[\int_0^1 \hat{c}(t,\hat{x}_t,u_t)dt + \hat{\Phi}(x_1)]$$

The original problem is thus seen to be equivalent to a "completely observable" problem (6.6), (6.8) with "state" $\hat{x}_t$ (this characterizes the entire conditional distribution since the covariance $\Sigma(t)$ is non-random). This suggests studying "separated controls" of the form $u_t = \psi(t,\hat{x}_t)$ for some given measurable function ψ: $[0,1]\times R^n \to U$. However, such controls are, in general, *not admissible:* admissible controls are *specified functionals* of y, whereas the random variable $\hat{x}_t$ depends on past controls $\{u_s, s\leq t\}$. One way round this difficulty is to consider (6.6)-(6.8) as an independent problem of the type considered in §4, i.e., to define the solution of (6.6) by Girsanov transformation on a new probability space, for separated controls $u(t,\hat{x})$. However we then run into the fresh difficulty that weak solutions of (6.6) are only defined if the matrix $K(t)K'(t)$ is strictly positive definite, which cannot happen unless the dimension of y_t is at least as great as that of x_t - a highly artificial condition. If this condition is met then we can apply (4.20) to conclude that there exists an optimal separated control, and an extra argument as in [18] shows that its cost coincides with $\inf_{u\in\mathcal{N}} J(u)$. If $\dim(y_t) < \dim(x_t)$ then some form of approximation must be resorted to.

With these elementary obstacles standing in the way of a satisfactory martingale treatment of the separation theorem, it is not surprising that a proper formulation of information states for nonlinear problems has not yet been given. It is possible that the Girsanov solution concept is still too strong to give existence of optimal controls for partially-observable systems in any generality.

7. OTHER APPLICATIONS

This section outlines briefly some other types of optimization problems to which martingale methods have been applied. The intention is merely to indicate the martingale formulation and not to give a survey of these problems as a whole: most of them have been extensively studied from other points of view and the associated literature is enormous. Nor is it claimed that the martingale approach is, in all cases, the most fruitful.

7.1 Jump processes

A jump process is a piecewise-constant right-continuous process x_t on a probability space (Ω,F,P) with values in, say, a complete separable metric space X with Borel σ-field S. It can be identified with an increasing sequence of times $\{T_n\}$ and a sequence of X-valued random variables $\{Z_n\}$ such that

$$x_t = \begin{cases} Z_n, & t\in[T_n,T_{n+1}[\\ z_\infty, & t\geq T_\infty \end{cases}$$

where $T_\infty = \lim_n T_n$ and z_∞ is a fixed element of X. (Generally $T_\infty = \infty$ a.s. in application.) Jump processes are useful models in operations research (queueing and inventory systems) and optical communication theory, among other areas. Their structure is analysed in Jacod [47], Boel, Varaiya and Wong [12] and Davis [17]. A jump process can be thought of as an integer valued random measure μ on $E = R^+ \times X$ defined by

$$\mu(\omega,dt,dz) = \sum_n \delta_{(T_n(\omega),\, X_n(\omega))}(dt,dz)$$

where δ_e is the Dirac measure at $e\in E$. Now let

$$F_t = \sigma\{\mu(]0,s] \times A),\ s\leq t,\ A\in S\} = \sigma\{x_s,\ s\leq t\}$$

and let P be the F_t-predictable σ-field on $R^+ \times\Omega$. A random measure μ is *predictable* if the process

$$(7.1) \qquad \int_{]0,t] \times X} g(\omega,s,z)\mu(\omega,ds,dz)$$

is predictable for all bounded measurable functions g on $(\Omega\times R^+\times X, P_* S)$. The fundamental result of Jacod [47] is that there is a unique predictable random measure ν such that

$$(7.2) \qquad E[\int_E g(s,z)\mu(ds,dz)] = E[\int_E g(s,z)\nu(ds,dz)]$$

for all g as above. ν is also characterized by the fact that for each $A\in S$, $\nu(]0,t] \times A)$ is the dual predictable projection (in the sense of Dellacherie [27]) of $\mu(]0,t],A)$, i.e. the process

$$q(t,A) = \mu(]0,t] \times A) - \nu(]0,t] \times A)$$

is an F_t -martingale. An explicit construction for ν in terms of the distributions of the (T_n, Z_n) sequence is given in [17]. We will denote by $\int g\,dq$ integrals of the form $(\int g\,d\mu - \int g\,d\nu)$ where $\int g\,d\mu$ and $\int g\,d\nu$ are defined as in (7.1); then the process

$$g\cdot q_t = \int_{]0,t]\times X} g\,dq$$

is an F_t-martingale for a suitable class of predictable integrands g, and the *martingale representation theorem* [12], [17], [47] states that all F_t-martingales are of this form for some g.

Denote

$$\Lambda_t = \nu(]0,t] \times X)$$

For each ω this is an increasing function of t and evidently the measure it defines on R^+ dominates that defined by $\nu(]0,t] \times A)$ for any $A\in S$. Thus there is a positive function $n(\omega,s,A)$ such that

$$\nu(]0,t] \times A) = \int_{]0,t]} n(\omega,s,A)\,d\Lambda_s \tag{7.3}$$

Owing to the existence of regular conditional probabilities it is possible to choose n so that it is measurable and is a probability measure in A for each fixed (s,ω). The pair (n,Λ) is called the *local description* of the process and has the interpretation that Λ_t is the *integrated jump rate*: roughly, $d\Lambda_s \approx P[x_{s+ds} \neq x_s | F_s]$ and $n(\omega,s,\cdot)$ is the *conditional distribution* of x_s given that $x_s \neq x_{s-}$.

Optimization problems arise when the local description of the process can be controlled to meet some objective. This is normally formulated [11], [22] by absolutely continuous change of measure, as in §3: we start with a "base measure" P on (Ω,F_1) with respect to which the jump process has a local description (n,Λ) and define a new measure P_u by

$$\frac{dP_u}{dP} = E(m^u)_1$$

where m^u is a (P,F_t) martingale. Under P_u the process x_t has a different local description which can be identified by the translation theorem (3.5). More specifically, it is supposed that the admissible controls U consist of F_t-predictable, (U,Ξ)-valued processes and that a real-valued measurable function ϕ on $(R^+\times\Omega \times X \times U,\ P*S*\Xi)$ is given. Denoting $\phi^u(t,\omega,z) = \phi(t,\omega,z,u(t,\omega))$ for $u\in U$, m^u is defined by

$$m^u_t(\omega) = \int_{]0,t]\times X} \phi^u(s,\omega,z)\,q(\omega,ds,dz)$$

The Doleans-Dade exponential (3.4) then takes the specific form

$$E(m^u)_t = \exp\Big(-\int_0^t \int_X \phi^u dn\, d\Lambda^c\Big) \prod_{T_i\le t} \Big(1+\phi^u(T_i,Z_i) - \Delta\Lambda_{T_i} \int_X \phi^u(T_i,z)\,n(T_i,dz)\Big)$$

$$\times \prod_{s\le t} \Big(1-\Delta\Lambda_s \int_X \phi^u(s,z)\,n(s,dz)\Big)$$

where Λ^c is the continuous part of Λ and the second product is taken over the countable set of s such that $\Delta\Lambda_s > 0$ and $s \notin \{T_1, T_2, \ldots\}$. Assuming that $E\mathcal{E}(M^u)_1 = 1$, x_t is, under measure P_u, a jump process with local description

$$(7.4)\qquad \begin{aligned} \Lambda_t^u &= \int_{]0,t]\times X} \Big((1 + \phi_s^u - \Delta\Lambda_s \int_X \phi^u dn\Big)\nu(ds,dz) \\ n^u(s,A) &= \frac{\int_A \big(1+\phi_s^u - \Delta\Lambda_s \int_X \phi^u dn\big)\, n(s,dz)}{\int_X \big(1 + \phi_s^u - \Delta\Lambda_s \int_X \phi^u dn\big)\, n(s,dz)} \end{aligned}$$

See [22], [36] for details of these calculations and conditions under which $E\mathcal{E}(m^u)_1 = 1$. Generally, only weak conditions on ϕ are needed to ensure that P_u is a probability measure on F_{T_n} for each n and hence on F_{T_∞}. If $T_\infty = \infty$ a.s. (P) then extra conditions on ϕ can be imposed to ensure that $T_\infty = \infty$ a.s.(P_u) and then P_u is a probability on F_t for each fixed t; see [77]. Let us suppose that the control problem is to choose $u \in \mathcal{U}$ so as to minimize

$$J(u) = E_u \Phi$$

where Φ is a bounded F_1-measurable random variable. Then the problem is in the general framework of §5 and furthermore we have a martingale representation theorem analogous to that of the Brownian case. Thus local conditions for optimality can be obtained by following the steps of §4.

Suppose $u^* \in \mathcal{U}$ is optimal. Then by the martingale representation theorem there is an integrand g such that

$$(7.5)\qquad E_*[\Phi|F_t] = J(u^*) + \int_{]0,t]\times X} g(s,z)q^*(ds,dz)$$

where $q^* = \mu - \nu^*$, and ν^* is the dual projection of μ under measure P_* (cf. (7.2)). Now let $u \in \mathcal{U}$ be any other control; then we can rewrite (7.5) in the form

$$(7.6)\qquad E_*[\Phi|F_t] = J(u^*) + \int_{]0,t]\times X} g\, dq^u + \int_{]0,t]\times X} g(d\nu^u - d\nu^*)$$

According to the criterion (5.3), $E_*[\Phi|F_t]$ is a P_u-submartingale, and hence the last term in (7.5) must be an increasing process. Using (7.3) and the specific forms of local description provided by (7.4), this statement translates into the following result:

(7.7) *Suppose* u^* *is optimal, let* g *be as in* (7.5) *and define*

$$h(t,z,\omega) = g(t,z,\omega) - \Delta\Lambda(t,\omega)\int_X g(t,\xi,\omega)n(t,d\xi,\omega)$$

Then for almost all ω

$$\int_X h(t,z)\phi(t,z,u_t^*)n(t,dz) = \min_{u\in U}\int_X h(t,z)\phi(t,z,u)n(t,dz) \quad \text{a.e. } (d\Lambda_t)$$

Thus, as in (4.14), the optimal control minimizes a "Hamiltonian." A sufficient condition for optimality similar to (4.15) can also be obtained. In the literature [12], [22], [77] various forms of Hamiltonian appear, depending on the nature of the cost function and the function ϕ. In [77] an existence theorem along the lines of (4.20) is obtained; however this only holds under very restrictive assumptions, related to the absolute continuity of the measures. In the Brownian case all the measures P_u are *mutually* absolutely continuous under very natural conditions, and this is crucial in the proof of the existence result, as is seen in (4.18), (4.19). In the jump process context mutual absolute continuity is very unnatural, but one is apparently obliged to insist on it if an existence result is to be obtained.

Finally, let us mention some other work related to the above. Optimality conditions for jump processes are obtained by Kohlmann [50] using Neustadt's extremal theory in a fashion analogous to Haussmann's treatment of the Brownian case [44]. Systems with both Brownian and jump process disturbances are dealt with in Boel and Kohlmann [9], [10] (based on a martingale representation theorem of Elliott [33]) and Lepeltier and Marchal [58]. The survey [13] by Brémaud and Jacod contains an extensive list of references on martingales and point processes.

7.2 Differential games [32], [35], [73], [74], [75], [76]

The set-up here is the same as that of §4 except that we suppose $U = U_1 x U_2 x \ldots x U_N$ where each U_i is a compact metric space. Then $\mathcal{U} = \mathcal{U}_1 x \ldots x \mathcal{U}_N$ where $\mathcal{U}_i$ is the set of F_t-predictable U_i-valued processes, and we assume that each $u^i \in \mathcal{U}_i$ is to be chosen by a *player* i with the objective of minimizing a *personal cost*

$$J_i(u) = J_i(u^1 \ldots u^N) = E_u[\int_0^1 c_i(s,x,u_s)ds + \Phi_i(x_1)]$$

(c_i and Φ_i satisfy the same conditions as c, Φ of §4). Thus each player is assumed to have perfect observations of the state process x_t.

Various solution concepts are available for this game [76]: $u^* = (u^{1*}, \ldots u^{N*})$ is

- *a Nash equilibrium* if there is no i and $u^i \in \mathcal{U}_i$ such that

  $J_i(u^{*1}, \ldots, u^{*(i-1)}, u^i, u^{*(i+1)}, u^{*N}) < J_i(u^*)$

- *efficient* if there is no $u \in \mathcal{U}$ such that

  $J_i(u) < J_i(u^*)$ for all i

- *in the core* if there is no subset $S \subset \{1,2\ldots,N\}$ and $u \in \mathcal{U}$ such that

  $J_i(v) < J_i(u^*)$ $\quad i \in S$

  where $v^i = u^i$ for $i \in S$ and $v^i = u^{i*}$ for $i \notin S$.

Thus an equilibrium point is one from which it does not pay any player to deviate unilaterally, a strategy is efficient if no strategy is better for everybody and a strategy is in the core if no coalition can act jointly to improve its lot. Evidently a core strategy is both efficient and an equilibrium, but equilibrium solutions are not necessarily efficient or conversely.

For $u \in \mathcal{U}$ denote $J'(u) = (J_1(u),\ldots,J_N(u))$ and let

$$\mathcal{J} = \{J(u) \mid u \in \mathcal{U}\}$$

This is a bounded subset of R^N, and a *sufficient* condition for efficiency of a strategy u^* is the existence of a non-negative vector $\lambda \in R^N$ such that

(7.8) $$\lambda' J(u^*) \leq \lambda' \xi \quad \text{for all } \xi \in \mathcal{J}$$

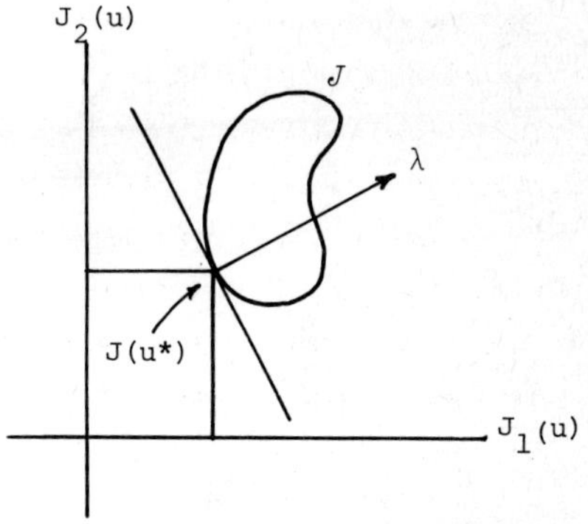

(see diagram for N=2). If $\mathcal{J}$ is convex, this condition is also necessary. It follows from results of Beneš [2] (see the remarks following (4.20)) that convexity of the set $(f(t,x,U),\ c'(t,x,U_1)\ldots,c^N(t,x,U_N)) \subset R^{n+N}$ implies convexity of $\mathcal{J}$. Now (7.8) says that u^* is optimal for the control problem of minimizing the weighted average cost $J_\lambda(u) = \sum_i \lambda^i J_i(u)$.

Fix $u^* \in \mathcal{U}$, and as in §4,, let $g^i, i=1,\ldots,N$, be adapted processes such that

$$E_{u^*}\left[\int_0^1 c_{is}^{u^*} ds + \Phi_i(x_1) \mid F_t\right] = J_i(u^*) + \int_0^t g_s^i \sigma_s dw_s^{u^*}$$

For any other strategy $u \in \mathcal{U}$ the right-hand side can be expressed, as in (4.11), as

$$J^i(u^*) + \int_0^t g_s^i \sigma_s dw^u + \int_0^t (H_s^i(u_s) - H_s^i(u_s^*))ds$$

where

$$H_s^i(u) = g^i f(t,x,u) + c_i(t,x,u)$$

Combining the remarks above with (4.16) shows that u^* is efficient if there exists $\lambda \in R^N$ such that

(7.9) $$\sum_i \lambda^i H^i(u_t^*) \leq \sum_i \lambda^i H^i(v), \qquad \text{a.e. for all } v \in U.$$

Under the convexity hypothesis, this condition is also necessary.

A strategy u^* is a Nash equilibrium if, for each i, u^{*i} minimizes $J_i(u^{*1},\ldots,u^{*(i-1)},u,u^{*(i+1)},\ldots,U^{*N})$ over $u \in \mathcal{U}_i$. Applying condition (4.16) we see that this will be the case if

(7.10) $$H^i(u_t^*) \leq H^i(v), \qquad \text{a.e. for all } v \in U_i, \quad i=1,2,\ldots,N$$

Thus u^* is an *efficient equilibrium* if u_t minimizes each "private" Hamiltonian as in (7.10) and also minimizes a "social" Hamiltonian (7.9) formed as a certain weighted average of these. Analogous conditions can be formulated under which u^* lies in the core.

For $(t,x,p_i,u) \in R^+ \times \Omega \times R^n \times U$ define the Hamiltonians

$$\overline{H}^i(t,x,p_i,u) = p_i' f(t,x,u) + c_i(t,x,u)$$

We say that the *Nash condition* holds if there exists for $i=1,\ldots,N$ measurable functions $u_i^0(t,x,p_1,\ldots,p_n)$ such that u_i^0 is a predictable process for each fixed $(p,u)=(p_1\ldots p_N,u)$

and

$$\bar{H}^i(t,x,p_i,u_1^0(t,x,p),\ldots,u_N^0(t,x,p)) \leq \bar{H}^i(t,x,p_i,u_1^0,\ldots,u_{i-1}^0,v,u_{i+1}^0,\ldots,u_N^0)$$

for all $v \in U_i$, for each $(t,x,p) \in R^+ \times \Omega \times R^{Nn}$. Uchida shows in [73] that *the game has a Nash equilibrium point if the Nash condition holds.* The proof is by a contradiction argument using the original formulation of the results of §4 as given in Davis and Varaiya [25]. Conditions under which the Nash condition holds are stated in [74].

Now consider the case N=2, $J_2(u) = -J_1(u)$, so that the game is 2-person, 0-sum. Then the core concept is nugatory, all strategies are efficient and an equilibrium is a *saddle point*, i.e. a strategy u* such that (denoting $J_1 = J$) for all $u \in \mathcal{U}$

$$J(u^{*1}, u^2) \leq J(u^{*1},u^{*2}) \leq J(u^1,u^{*2})$$

In this case the relevant condition is the *Isaacs' condition:* for each $(t,x,p) \in R^+ \times \Omega \times$

$$\max_{u_2 \in U_2} \min_{u_1 \in U_1} \bar{H}^1(t,x,p,u_1,u_2) = \min_{u_1 \in U_1} \max_{u_2 \in U_2} \bar{H}^1(t,x,p,u_1,u_2)$$

The main result is analogous to the above, namely that *a saddle strategy* u* *exists if the Isaacs' condition holds.* The argument, given by Elliott in [32], [35], is constructive, along the lines leading to the existence result (4.20) for the control problem. One considers first the situation where the minimizing player I announces his strategy $u_1 \in \mathcal{U}_1$ in advance. It is immediate from (4.20) that the maximizing player II has an optimal reply $u_2^0(u_1)$ to this. Now introduce the *upper value function*

$$W_t^+ = \bigwedge_{u_1 \in \mathcal{U}_1} E_{u_1,u_2^0(u_1)}\left[\int_t^1 c_1(s,x,u_1,u_2^0(u_1))ds + \Phi_1(x_1) \mid F_t\right]$$

An analysis of this somewhat similar to that of §4 shows that player I has a best strategy, i.e. a strategy $u_1^0 \in \mathcal{U}_1$, such that

$$J(u_1^0,u_2^0(u_1^0)) = \min_{u_1 \in \mathcal{U}_1} J(u_1,u_2^0(u_1))$$

If it is player II who announces his strategy first, then we can define in an analogous manner the *lower value* function W_t^-. In general $W_t^+ \geq W_t^-$, but if the Isaacs' condition holds then $W_t^+ = W_t^-$ and it follows that u* given by $u^{*1} = u_1^0$, $u^{*2} = u_2^0(u_1^0)$ is a saddle strategy.

A somewhat more restricted version of this result was given by Varaiya in [75], using a compactness-of-densities argument similar to that of Beneš [1] and Duncan and Varaiya for the control problem. No results are available if the players do not have complete observations. Some analogous results for a differential game including a jump process component are given in [49].

7.3 Optimal stopping and impulse control

In the conventional formulation of optimal stopping one is given a Markov process x_t on a state space S and a bounded continuous function ϕ on S, and asked to find a Markov time τ such that $E_x\phi(x_\tau) \geq E_x\phi(x_\sigma)$ for all $x \in S$ and Markov times σ. Let

$$\psi(x) = \sup_\sigma E_x \phi(x_\sigma)$$

Then under some regularity conditions ψ is the "least excessive majorant" of ϕ (i.e., $\psi(x) \geq \phi(x)$ and $\psi(x_t)$ is a supermartingale) and the first entrance time of x_t into the set $\{x: \phi(x) = \psi(x)\}$ is an optimal time. See [4], and the references there. If we define $X_t = \phi(x_t)$ and $W_t = \psi(x_t)$ then τ maximizes $E_x X$ and $\tau = \inf\{t: X_t = Z_t\}$. Thus the optimal stopping problem generalizes naturally as follows.

Let (Ω, F, P) be a probability space and $(F_t)_{t\geq 0}$ be an increasing, right-continuous, completed family of sub-σ-fields of F. Let T denote the set of F_t-stopping times and X_t be a given positive, bounded optional process defined on $[0,\infty]$. The optimal stopping problem is then to find $T \in T$ such that

$$EX_T = \max_{S \in T} EX_S$$

This problem is studied by Bismut and Skalli in [8]. The simplest case occurs when X_t satisfies the following hypothesis:

(7.11) *Let* $\{T_n, T\}$ *be stopping times such that* $T_n \uparrow T$ *or* $T_n \downarrow T$. *Then* $EX_{T_n} \to EX_T$.

Criteria under which (7.11) holds are given in [8].

An essential role in this problem is played by the *Snell envelope* of X_t, introduced by Mertens [62, Theorem 4]. He shows that the set of all supermartingales which majorize X_t has a smallest member, denoted W_t, which is characterized by the property that for any stopping time T and σ-field $G \subset F_T$,

$$E[W_T | G] = \operatorname{ess\,sup}_{S \geq T} E[X_S | G]$$

Thus in particular for each fixed time t

$$W_t = \operatorname{ess\,sup}_{S \geq t} E[X_S | F_t]$$

so that W_t is the *value function* for the optimal stopping problem. Under condition (7.11) W_t is *regular* [63, VII D33] and hence has the Meyer decomposition

$$W_t = M_t - B_t$$

where M_t is a martingale and B_t a *continuous* increasing process with $B_0=0$. Now define

$$D_0' = \inf\{t>0: B_t>0\}$$

and

$$A = \{(t,\omega): X_t(\omega) = W_t(\omega)\}$$

The *début* of A is the stopping time $D_0^A = \inf\{t: (t,\omega) \in A\}$. It is shown in [8] that $D_0^A \leq D_0'$ and that:

(7.12) *A stopping time* T *is optimal if and only if the graph of* T *is contained in* A *and* $T \leq D_0'$

In particular, both D_0^A and D_0' are optimal.

This result implies an optimality criterion similar to (5.3): if T is optimal then $B_{t\wedge T} = 0$ so that $W_{t\wedge T} = M_{t\wedge T}$ is a martingale, and conversely if $W_{t\wedge T}$ is a martingale then it is easily seen that T must satisfy the conditions of (7.12).

Analogous results can be obtained for processes more general than those satisfying (7.11); the details are more involved and only ε-optimal stopping times may exist.

Impulse control: Space precludes any detailed discussion of this topic, but it should be mentioned that a martingale treatment has been given by Lepeltier and Marchal [59]. In the simplest type of problem one has a stochastic differential equation

$$dx_t = f(x_t)dt + \sigma(x_t)dw_t$$

A *strategy* $\delta = \{T_n, Y_n\}$ consists of an increasing sequence of stopping times T_n and a sequence of random variables Y_n such that Y_n is F_{T_n}-measurable. The corresponding trajectory is x_t^δ defined by

$$x_0^\delta = x \text{ (given)}$$

$$\left.\begin{aligned} dx_t^\delta &= f(x_t^\delta) + \sigma(x_t^\delta)dw_t \\ x_{T_n}^\delta &= x_{T_n-}^\delta + Y_n \end{aligned}\right\} \quad t \in [T_n, T_{n+1}[$$

The strategy δ is to be chosen to minimize

$$J(\delta) = E[\sum_n I_{(T_n \le 1)} + \int_0^1 c(x_s^\delta)ds]$$

A value function and conditions for optimality can be obtained along the lines of §5. It is worth pointing out that the above system obviously has a Markovian flavor about it, and indeed it is shown in [59] that the value function is Markovian (i.e., at time t it depends on x^δ only through x_t^δ) even though the controls δ are merely assumed to be non-anticipative. Some further remarks on this are given in the next section.

7.4 Markovian systems

Let us return to the problem of §4 and suppose that the system equation and cost are

$$dx_t = f(t, x_t, u_t)dt + \sigma(t, x_t)dw_t^u$$

$$J(u) = E_u[\int_0^1 c(t, x_t, u_t)dt + \Phi(x_1)],$$

i.e., we have a diffusion model as considered in §2. In §4 the admissible controls U were general non-anticipative functionals but here it seems clear that feedback controls of the form $u(t, x_t)$ should be adequate. Denote by M the set of measurable functions $u: [0,1] \times R^n \to U$; then $M \subset U$ if we identify $u \in M$ with the process $u_t = u(t, x_t)$ and x_t is a Markov process under measure P_u. Thus we can define the *Markovian value function* $W^M(t,x)$ as (with obvious notation)

$$W^M(t,x) = \bigwedge_{u \in M} E_{t,x}^u[\int_t^1 c(s, x_s, u_s)ds + \Phi(x_1)]$$

The conjecture then is that $W^M(t, x_t) = W_t$ a.e. (W_t being defined as in §4) so that in particular

$$\inf_{u \in M} J(u) = \inf_{u \in U} J(u)$$

This is easily established (see [25, §6]) if it can be shown that W^M satisfies a principle of optimality similar to (4.7). However this is not clear, as there is still, to my knowldge, no direct proof that the class M satisfies the ε-lattic property. An argument along the lines given in §5 fails because it involves "mixing" two controls $u_1, u_2 \in M$ to form a control v by taking

$$v_s = \begin{cases} u_1(s,x_s) I_A \\ u_2(s,x_s) I_{A^c} \end{cases}$$

where $s \geq t$ and $A \in F_t$. But then v_s is of course no longer Markov. Thus the results presented in §6 of [23] must be regarded as incomplete.

This problem has been dealt with in the case of controlled Markov jump processes by Davis and Wan [26]. There it is possible to "mix" two controls in a more ingenious way which, however, uses the special structure of the sample paths very explicitly and hence does not generalize to other problems. An alternative approach would be to start with the value process W_t as previously defined and to show directly that $W_t = \tilde{W}(t,x_t)$ for some function $\tilde{W}$. This has been done by Lepeltier and Marchal [59] for impulse control problems but again the argument is very problem-specific.

My general conclusion from the above is that the direct martingale approach is not particularly well adapted to Markovian problems, and that more information can be obtained from methods such as those of Bismut [5] which are specially tailored for Markov processes.

8. CONCLUDING REMARKS

The successes of martingale methods in control are twofold: firstly the essence of the optimality principle is revealed in the general formulation (5.3), and in particular the fundamental difference between the situations of complete and of incomplete observations is clearly brought out; and secondly, the power of the submartingale decomposition provides, in effect, a weak form of differentiation which enables minimum principles and existence of optimal controls to be established with few technical restrictions. The drawbacks of the method are that it does not lead naturally to computational techniques, and there are difficulties in handling Markovian systems and problem formulations of the "separation principle" type.

Here are a few suggestions for further research.

(8.1) Obtain a more explicit characterization of the "adjoint process" g_t of §4. Comparisons with deterministic optimal control theory and other forms of stochastic minimum principle [6], [53] suggest that it should satisfy some form of "adjoint equation," yet little is known about this unless the optimal control is smooth [44].

(8.2) To my knowledge martingale methods have not been applied seriously to infinite-time problems (see Kushner [55] for some results using methods similar to those of Bismut [5]).

(8.3) The partially-observable problem continues to elude a satisfactory treatment. In particular there are no good existence theorems, and experience with the separation theorem (§6) suggests that these may be hard to get. My feeling is that the proper formulation of partially-observable problems must explicitly include filtering, since it is the conditional distribution of the state given the observations that is the true "state" of the system. A lot of information about nonlinear filtering is available [60] but, again using the separation principle as a cautionary tale, it is far from clear how to incorporate this into the martingale framework. Possibly some entirely different approach, such as Nisio's nonlinear semigroup formulation, will turn out to be more appropriate. See [20] for a step in this direction.

(8.4) Show that the ε-lattice property holds in some generality for Markovian systems with Markov controls (cf. §7.4).

(8.5) Give a constructive treatment of Uchida's result [73] on the existence of Nash equilibirum points in stochastic differential games.

(8.6) Is *mutual* absolute continuity of the measures P_u really necessary for the existence result (4.20)? If not then better existence results could possibly be obtained for problems such as controlled jump processes (§7.1) where mutual absolute continuity does not arise so naturally.

9. REFERENCES

SPm/LNMn Université de Strasbourg Séminaire de Probabilités m, Lecture Notes in Mathematics vol. n, Springer-Verlag, Berlin-Heidelberg-New York

SICON SIAM Journal on Control (and Optimization)

ZW Zeitschrift für Wahrscheinlichkeitstheorie und verwandte Gebiete

[1] V.E. Beneš, Existence of optimal strategies based on specified information, for a class of stochastic decision problems, SICON 8 (1970) 179-188

[2] V.E. Beneš, Existence of optimal stochastic control laws, SICON 9 (1971) 446-475

[3] V.E. Beneš, Full "bang" to reduce predicted miss is optimal, SICON 15 (1976) 52-8

[4] A. Bensoussan and J.L. Lions, Applications des inéquations varationelles en contrôle stochastique, Dunod, Paris, 1978

[5] J.M. Bismut, Théorie probabiliste du contrôle des diffusions, Mem. Americ. Math. Soc. 4 (1976), no. 167

[6] J.M. Bismut, Duality methods in the control of densities, SICON 16 (1978) 771-777

[7] J.M. Bismut, An introductory approach to duality in optimal stochastic control, SIAM Review 20 (1978) 62-78

[8] J.M. Bismut and B. Skalli, Temps d'arrêt optimal, théorie général des processus et processus de Markov, ZW 39 (1977) 301-313

[9] R. Boel and M. Kohlmann, Stochastic control over double martingales, in "Analysis and Optimization of Stochastic Systems" ed. O.L.R. Jacobs, Academic Press, New York/London 1979

[10] R. Boel and M. Kohlmann, Semimartingale models of stochastic optimal control with applications to double martingales, preprint, Institut für Angewandte Mathematik der Universität Bonn, 1977

[11] R. Boel and P. Varaiya, Optimal control of jump processes, SICON 15 (1977) 92-119

[12] R. Boel, P. Varaiya and E. Wong, Martingales on jump processes I and II, SICON 13 (1975) 999-1061

[13] P. Brémaud and J. Jacod, Processus ponctuels et martingales: resultats recents sur la modelisation et le filtrage, Adv. Appl. Prob. 9 (1977) 362-416

[14] P. Brémaud and J.M. Pietri, The role of martingale theory in continuous-time dynamic programming, Tech. report, IRIA, Le Chesnay, France, 1978

[15] J.M.C. Clark, The representation of functionals of Brownian motion by stochastic integrals, Ann. Math. Stat. 41 (1970) 1285-1295

[16] M.H.A. Davis, On the existence of optimal policies in stochastic control, SICON 11 (1973) 507-594

[17] M.H.A. Davis, The representation of martingales of jump processes, SICON 14 (1976) 623-638

[18] M.H.A. Davis, The separation principle in stochastic control via Girsanov solutions, SICON 14 (1976) 176-188

[19] M.H.A. Davis, Functionals of diffusion processes as stochastic integrals, submitted to Math. Proc. Camb. Phil. Soc.

[20] M.H.A. Davis, Nonlinear semigroups in the control of partially-observable stochastic systems, in Measure Theory and Applications to Stochastic Analysis, ed. G. Kallianpur and D. Kölzow, Lecture Notes in Mathematics, Springer-Verlag, to appear

[21] M.H.A. Davis and J.M.C. Clark, "Predicted Miss" problems in stochatic control, Stochastics 2 (1979)

[22] M.H.A. Davis and R.J. Elliott, Optimal control of a jump process, ZW 40 (1977) 183-202

[23] M.H.A. Davis and M. Kohlmann, Stochastic control by measure transformation: a general existence result, preprint, Institut für Angewandte Mathematik der Universität Bonn (1978)

[24] M.H.A. Davis and P.P. Varaiya, Information states for linear stochastic systems, J. Math. Anal. Appl. 37 (1972) 387-402

[25] M.H.A. Davis and P.P. Varaiya, Dynamic programming conditions for partially-observable stochastic systems, SICON 11 (1973) 226-261

[26] M.H.A. Davis and C.B. Wan, The principle of optimality for Markov jump processes, in "Analysis and Optimization of Stochastic Systems" ed. O.L.R. Jacobs, Academic Press, New York/London, 1979

[27] C. Dellacherie, Capacités et processus stochastiques, Springer-Verlag, Berlin, 1972

[28] C. Doléans-Dade, Quelques applications de la formule de changement de variables pour les semimartingales, ZW 16 (1970) 181-194

[29] T.E. Duncan, Dynamic programming criteria for stochastic systems in Riemannian manifolds, Applied Math. & Opt. 3 (1977) 191-208

[30] T.E. Duncan and P.P. Varaiya, On the solutions of a stochastic control system, SICON 9 (1971) 354-371

[31] T.E. Duncan and P.P. Varaiya, On the solutions of a stochastic control system II, SICON 13 (1975) 1077-1092

[32] R.J. Elliott, The existence of value in stochastic differential games, SICON 14 (1976) 85-94

[33] R.J. Elliott, Double martingales, ZW 34 (1976) 17-28

[34] R.J. Elliott, The optimal control of a stochastic system, SICON 15 (1977) 756-778

[35] R.J. Elliott, The existence of optimal strategies and saddle points in stochastic differential games, in Differential Games and Applications, ed. P. Hagedorn, Lecture Notes in Control and Information Sciences 3, Springer-Verlag, Berlin, 1977

[36] R.J. Elliott, Lévy systems and absolutely continuous changes of measure, J. Math. Anal. Appl. 61 (1977) 785-796

[37] R.J. Elliott, The optimal control of a semimartingale, 3rd Kingston Conference on Control Theory, Kingston, RI (1978)

[38] R.J. Elliott, The martingale calculus and its applications, this volume

[39] R.J. Elliott and P.P. Varaiya, A sufficient condition for the optimal control of a partially observed stochastic system, in "Analysis and Optimization of Stochastic Systems," ed. O.L.R. Jacobs, Academic Press, New York/London, 1979

[40] W.H. Fleming, Optimal continuous-parameter stochastic control, SIAM Rev. 11 (1969) 470-509

[41] W.H. Fleming and R.W. Rishel, Deterministic and stochastic optimal control, Springer-Verlag, New York, 1975

[42] M. Fujisaki, G. Kallianpur and H. Kunita, Stochastic differential equations for the nonlinear filtering problem, Osaka J. Math. 9 (1972) 19-40

[43] I.V. Girsanov, On transforming a certain class of stochastic processes by absolutely continuous substitution of measures, Theory of Prob. and Appls. 5, (1960) 285-301

[44] U.G. Haussmann, On the stochastic maximum principle, SICON 16 (1978) 236-251

[45] U.G. Haussmann, Functionals of Itô processes as stochastic integrals, SICON 16 (1978) 252-269

[46] U.G. Haussmann, On the integral representation of functionals of Ito processes, Stochastic 2 (1979)

[47] J. Jacod, Multivariate point processes: predictable projection, Radon-Nikodym derivatives, representation of martingales, ZW 31 (1975) 235-253

[48] J. Jacod and J. Memin, Caracteristiques locales et conditions de continuité absolue pour les semimartingales, ZW 35 (1976) 1-37

[49] M. Kohlmann, A game with Wiener noise and jump process disturbances, submitted to Stochastics

[50] M. Kohlmann, On control of jump process, preprint, Institut für Angewandte Mathematik der Universität Bonn, 1978

[51] N.V. Krylov, Control of a solution of a stochastic integral equation Theory of Prob. and Appls. 17 (1972) 114-131

[52] H. Kunita and S. Watanabe, On square-integrable martingales, Nagoya Math. Journal 30 (1967) 209-245

[53] H.J. Kushner, Necessary conditions for continuous-parameter stochastic optimization problems, SICON 10 (1972) 550-565

[54] H.J. Kushner, Probability Methods for Approximations in Stochastic Control and for Elliptic Equations, Academic Press, New York, 1977

[55] H.J. Kushner, Optimality conditions for the average cost per unit time problem with a diffusion model, SICON 16 (1978) 330-346

[56] E. Lenglart, Transformation des martingales locales par changement absolument continu de probabilités, ZW 39 (1977) 65-70

[57] D. Lepingle and J. Memin, Sur l'integrabilité uniforme des martingales exponentielles, ZW 42 (1978) 175-203

[58] J.P. Lepeltier and B. Marchal, Sur l'existence de politiques optimales dans le contrôle integro-differentiel, Ann. Inst. H. Poincaré 13 (1977) 45-97

[59] J.P. Lepeltier and B. Marchal, Techniques probabilistes dans le contrôle impulsionelle, Stochastics 2 (1979)

[60] R.S. Liptser and A.N. Shiryayev, Statistics of Random Processes, vols I and II, Springer-Verlag, New York, 1977

[61] J. Memin, Conditions d'optimalité pour un problème de contrôle portant sur une famille de probabilités dominées par une probabilité P, preprint, University of Rennes, 1977

[62] J.F. Mertens, Processus stochastiques généraux, applications aux surmartingales, ZW 22 (1972) 45-68

[63] P.A. Meyer, Probability and Potentials, Blaisdell, Waltham, MA, 1966

[64] P.A. Meyer, Un cours sur les intégrales stochastiques, SP10/LNM 511 (1976)

[65] R.E. Mortensen, Stochastic optimal control with noisy observations, Int. J. Control 4 (1966) 455-464

[66] M. Nisio, On a nonlinear semigroup attached to stochastic control, Pub. Res. Inst. Math. Sci., Kyoto, 12 (1976) 513-537

[67] A.A. Novikov, On an identity for stochastic integrals, Theor. Probability Appl. 17 (1972) 717-720

[68] R. Rishel, Necessary and sufficient conditions for continuous-time stochastic optimal control, SICON 8 (1970) 559-571

[69] J.H. van Schuppen and E. Wong, Transformations of local martingales under a change of law, Ann. Prob. 2 (1974) 879-888

[70] C. Striebel, Martingale conditions for the optimal control of continuous-time stochastic systems, 5th Symposium on nonlinear estimation and applications, San Diego, CA, 1974

[71] D.W. Stroock and S.R.S. Varadhan, Diffusion processes with continuous coefficients, Comm. Pure and Appl. Math. 22 (1969) 345-400, 479-530

[72] B.S. Tsyrelson, An example of a stochastic equation having no strong solution, Theory of Prob. and Appls. 20 (1975) 427-430

[73] K. Uchida, On the existence of a Nash equilibrium point in N-person nonzero sum stochastic differential games, SICON 16 (1978) 142-149

[74] K. Uchida, A note on the existence of a Nash equlibrium point in stochastic differential games, to appear in SICON

[75] P. Varaiya, Differential games, Proc. VI Berkeley Symposium on Math. Stat. and Prob., vol. 3, 687-697, Univ. of California Press, Berkeley, 1972

[76] P.P. Varaiya, N-person stochastic differential games, SICON 14 (1976) 538-545

[77] C.B. Wan and M.H.A. Davis, existence of optimal controls for stochastic jump processes, to appear in SICON

[78] W.M. Wonham, On the separation theorem of stochastic control, SICON 6 (1968) 312-326

[79] C. Yoeurp, Decompositions des martingales locales et formules exponentielles, SP10/LNM 511 (1976) 432-480

SR gewidmet
Dezember 1978

A GEOMETRIC APPROACH TO LINEAR CONTROL AND ESTIMATION*

T. E. Duncan**

1. Introduction.

Probably the first nontrivial example of the use of algebra and geometry in linear system theory was the solution of a mathematical problem posed in 1868 by J. C. Maxwell [26]. He proposed the problem of finding computable algebraic criteria to determine if a system of linear, constant coefficient ordinary differential equations is asymptotically stable. This problem had largely been solved in 1856 by Hermite [17] who related the computation of the Cauchy index [9] to the signature of a quadratic form. Subsequently, the complete solution was given by Routh [30] and Hurwitz [18].

While this early work in linear system theory used important algebro-geometric techniques much of the subsequent development did not. The work that was done during World War II and subsequently through the development of the space program relied heavily on the use of analysis for the solution of various problems in linear system theory. It has been only recently that algebra and geometry have again begun to play an important role in system theory. The purpose of this paper is to provide a brief review of some of the highlights of these results, to apply geometric techniques in the derivation and the analysis of the solutions of the linear quadratic optimization and Gaussian estimation problems, and to sketch how algebro-geometric techniques can be used to obtain solutions to problems that are related to the usual quadratic optimization and Gaussian estimation problems but are nontrivial generalizations of these problems. The natural geometric setting for the algebro-geometric techniques that are used for the solutions of the estimation and the optimization problems will be emphasized.

A number of reasons exist for the use of algebro-geometric techniques in system theory. A large number of objects in system theory are naturally algebraic or geometric. Transfer functions for linear, constant coefficient systems are matrices of rational functions which have been studied for more than a cen-

---

* Research supported by AFOSR Grant 77-3177 and as a guest of the SFB 72 of the Deutsche Forschungsgemeinschaft, Bonn.

** Institute of Applied Mathematics, University of Bonn, FRG and Department of Mathematics, University of Kansas, Lawrence, Kansas, 66045 USA.

tury in algebraic geometry. The relation between the input-output description and and the state space description of a linear system provides an important principal bundle and an algebraic variety. The Hankel matrix and its relation to realization theory have a natural geometric interpretation. Linear quadratic optimal control and linear Gaussian estimation and smoothing problems are naturally described geometrically in the Lagrangian Grassmannian. Algebro-geometric methods often give algebraic criteria, such as for the pole placement (or coefficient assignability) problem, which are relatively easy to compute. Solutions to some linear quadratic optimization and linear Gaussian estimation problems for linear pure delay time differential equations can be readily obtained from the solutions of these problems for linear constant coefficient ordinary differential equations by viewing the pure delay time systems geometrically as systems over rings. Posing system theory problems geometrically provides the setting for generalizations to nonlinear problems that have some hope of useful solutions and it provides the setting for the interaction with a large segment of contemporary mathematics.

2. Preliminaries.

To study a number of system theory notions geometrically it is necessary to introduce the concept of a Grassmannian. The Grassmannian, Grass(k, n), is the family of all k-planes (through the origin) in n - space. While this description is the most elementary geometrical picture of it, we have to be somewhat more precise to give a topology to this family. This will be accomplished by a number of methods. For some of our purposes the Grassmannian will be the family of complex planes, while in other applications the Grassmannian will be real planes. Some of the constructions of the Grassmannian over $\mathbb{R}$ or $\mathbb{C}$ will be naturally related while some will be more naturally considered only over $\mathbb{C}$. Let Grass $(k, n; \mathbb{R})$ (resp. Grass $(k, n; \mathbb{C})$) be the family of k-planes in $\mathbb{R}^n$ (resp. $\mathbb{C}^n$). Let $GL(k, n-k; \mathbb{R})$ (resp. $GL(k, n-k; \mathbb{C})$) be the subgroup of the general linear group which leaves fixed the k-space $z_{k+1} = \dots = z_n = 0$. The Grassmann manifold is the real (resp. complex) manifold $GL(n; \mathbb{R})/_{GL(k,n;\mathbb{R})}$ (resp. $GL(n; \mathbb{C})/_{GL(k,n-k;\mathbb{C})}$). Fixing the usual Riemannian (resp. Hermitian) metric in $\mathbb{R}^n$ (resp. $\mathbb{C}^n$) the Grassmannian can be identified with $O(n)/_{O(k,n-k)}$ (resp. $U(n)/_{U(n,n-k)}$) so that it is compact. In fact, it is the natural compactification in many physical problems. Another approach is to consider $\mathbb{C}^{kn}$ as the family of all $k \times n$ matrices where $k \leq n$. The subset S of all matrices of rank less than k is an algebraic subset so $\mathbb{C}^{kn} \setminus S$ is a Zariski open set where $GL(k; \mathbb{C})$ acts by left multiplication on

$\mathbb{C}^{kn} \setminus S$ and the quotient topological space by this action is Grass(k, n) which is clearly k-planes in n-space. Let U be the Zariski open set in $\mathbb{C}^{kn} \setminus S$ where the first k columns of the matrix are linearly independent. Since U is naturally isomorphic to $GL(k; \mathbb{C}) \times \mathbb{C}^{k(n-k)}$ the quotient of U is naturally identified with $\mathbb{C}^{k(n-k)}$. Since a similar description holds for any k linearly independent columns, Grass(k, n; $\mathbb{C}$) is covered by open sets that are isomorphic, as complex manifolds and as algebraic varieties, to $\mathbb{C}^{k(n-k)}$. $\mathbb{C}^{kn} \setminus S$ may also be considered as the family of all surjective maps from $\mathbb{C}^n$ to $\mathbb{C}^k$. Thus Grass (k, n; $\mathbb{C}$) may be considered as the family of all surjective maps from $\mathbb{C}^n$ to $\mathbb{C}^k$ modulo isomorphisms of $\mathbb{C}^k$. The Grassmannian, Grass(1, n; $\mathbb{C}$) (Grass(1, n; $\mathbb{R}$)) of all lines in n-space is denoted $\mathbb{P}^n(\mathbb{C})$ $(\mathbb{P}^n(\mathbb{R}))$ and is called complex (real) projective n-space. The projective space, $\mathbb{P}^1(\mathbb{C})$, is also called the Riemann sphere because it describes the two coordinate patches that are necessary to cover S^2 which by stereographic projection is $\mathbb{C} \cup \{\infty\}$.

Some of the recent algebro-geometric results in linear system theory will be briefly reviewed now. Let σ be a minimal scalar input-output system and let τ be its transfer function. Minimality of the system means that it is reachable and observable. Since the system is minimal, the rational function $\tau = {}^f/g$ has no cancellation of poles and zeros. Thus the pair (f, g) never takes the value (0, 0) for any $s \in \overline{\mathbb{C}}$ and this linear relation between input and output describes an element in $\mathbb{P}^1(\mathbb{C})$ for each s. Since the degree of g is strictly greater than the degree of f, the map $\tau: \mathbb{C} \longrightarrow \mathbb{P}^1(\mathbb{C})$ can be extended to infinity so that there is a map $\tau: \mathbb{P}^1(\mathbb{C}) \longrightarrow \mathbb{P}^1(\mathbb{C})$. A transfer function τ for an arbitrary minimal linear system can be written as fg^{-1} ([29]) so that $\tau: \mathbb{P}^1(\mathbb{C}) \longrightarrow$ Grass(m, m+p; $\mathbb{C}$) where m is the number of inputs and p is the number of outputs. This map τ can be also described directly from algebraic geometry without the use of the factorization fg^{-1}.

The state space description of a linear system is

$$\frac{dX}{dt} = FX + GU$$

$$Y = HX$$

Since an observer sees only the inputs and the outputs, it is natural to allow nonsingular coordinate transformations on the state space so there is an action on triples (F, G, H) given by $(F, G, H) \longmapsto (gFg^{-1}, gG, Hg^{-1})$ where $g \in GL(n; \mathbb{R})$. Thus it is natural to take a quotient by this group action. Given that the system is reachable (or minimal) it has been shown (Byrnes - Hurt [7]) that the quotient is geometric and quasi-projective. The algebraic variety obtained by this quotient is a nonsingular, irreducible variety of dimension $n(m+p)$ where m is the number of inputs, n is the state space dimension and p is the number of outputs. The principal bundle for this $GL(n;\mathbb{R})$ action is globally trivial only if $m = 1$.

The Hankel matrix, h, for a system σ can be obtained from the expansion of the transfer function τ at infinity. It provides some natural data from which a system σ can be realized in state space form. In addition, the rank of the infinite matrix h is the Mc Millan degree and the finiteness of the rank of a Hankel matrix is the necessary and sufficient condition for the corresponding meromorphic function to be rational.

If τ is a symmetric matrix, then the degree of the map $\tau: \mathbb{P}^1(\mathbb{R}) \longrightarrow \Lambda(n)$, where $\Lambda(n)$ is the Lagrangian Grassmannian, is the generalized Cauchy index that counts the components in the space of minimal transfer functions and is computed from the signature of the corresponding Hankel matrix (Brockett [3], Byrnes - Duncan [6]).

It is natural to view a transfer function τ as an element in $[\mathbb{P}^1(\mathbb{C}), Y]$, the homotopy class of maps from $\mathbb{P}^1(\mathbb{C})$ to the output space $Y = \mathrm{Grass}(m, m+p; \mathbb{C})$. Since $[\mathbb{P}^1, Y] = \pi_2(Y) \simeq H_2(Y; \mathbb{Z})$ by the Hurewicz isomorphism, the hyperplane $H \subset Y$ corresponding to the Plücker imbedding can be used to form the intersection pairing $(\cdot,\cdot)$ such that

$$(\cdot,\cdot) : H_2(Y;\mathbb{Z}) \times H_{2pm-2}(Y;\mathbb{Z}) \longrightarrow H_{2pm}(Y;\mathbb{Z}) = \mathbb{Z}.$$

The integer that is obtained by this computation for a minimal transfer function is the Mc Millan degree which is the minimal state space dimension (Hermann-Martin [16], Byrnes [5]).

It is well known in system theory (e.g. Brunovsky [4], Kalman [20]) that the Kronecker indices are the complete family of obstructions to feedback deformations of a minimal system. Grothendieck [14] gave a decomposition of vector bundles over the Riemann sphere, $\mathbb{P}^1(\mathbb{C})$, into a sum of line bundles. The degrees of these line bundles are the Kronecker indices (Hermann-Martin [16], Byrnes [5]).

3. Lagrangian Grassmannian

A special Grassmannian, the Lagrangian Grassmannian, appears in optimization and estimation problems, as well as in electrical networks, so that it will play a central role in the subsequent developments in this paper. It is a particular Grassmannian that also preserves a skew symmetric form. The Euclidean space, $\mathbb{R}^{2n}$, has three natural structures that can be preserved. The Euclidean structure or scalar product, which is $< x, x >$, is preserved by $O(2n)$. The complex sructure $J: \mathbb{R}^{2n} \longrightarrow \mathbb{R}^{2n}$ is given by $J(p, q) = (-q, p)$, where $z = p + iq$, and is preserved by $GL(n; \mathbb{C})$. Finally, the symplectic structure is given by the skew scalar product $[x, y] = < Jx, y > = - [y, x]$ and is preserved by the symplectic group $Sp(n)$. An automorphism that preserves two of these structures preserves the third so that
$O(2n) \cap GL(n; \mathbb{C}) = GL(n; \mathbb{C}) \cap Sp(n) = Sp(n) \cap O(2n) = U(n)$.
An n-plane in 2n-space is called Lagrangian if the skew scalar product of any two vectors in this plane are zero, equivalently π is a Lagrangian plane if $J\pi$ is orthogonal to π. The manifold of all (unoriented) Lagrangian planes of $\mathbb{R}^{2n}$ is called the Lagrangian Grassmannian, $\Lambda(n)$. As an extension of our previous discussion of Grassmannians we have $\Lambda(n) = U(n)/O(n)$.

Since we shall be primarily interested in the Lagrangian Grassmannian, some aspects of its topology will be described. Let the coordinates in $\mathbb{R}^{2n}$ be described as $x = (q, p)$ where $q = (q_1, \ldots, q_n)$ and $p = (p_1, \ldots, p_n)$ which is the phase space description from physics. Note that the planes $p = 0$ and $q = 0$ are Lagrangian. Let $\lambda \in \Lambda(n)$. Then there is a unitary automorphism that maps the plane $p = 0$ into λ. The square of the determinant of this mapping depends only on λ, so $\det^2 : \Lambda(n) \longrightarrow S^1$.

We have the following useful results ([1]).

<u>Lemma 1. The fundamental group of $\Lambda(n)$, $\pi_1(\Lambda(n))$, is $\mathbb{Z}$ (free cyclic) and its generator goes into the generator of S^1 by the map $\det^2$.</u>

<u>Corollary. $H_1(\Lambda(n), \mathbb{Z}) \simeq H^1(\Lambda(n), \mathbb{Z}) \simeq \pi_1(\Lambda(n)) = \mathbb{Z}$.</u>

The generator, α, of the cohomology group $H^1(\Lambda(n), \mathbb{Z})$ is the number of rotations of $\det^2$, that is, if $\gamma : S^1 \longrightarrow \Lambda(n)$ is a closed curve then $[\alpha, \gamma]$ is the degree of the composition $S^1 \xrightarrow{\gamma} \Lambda(n) \xrightarrow{\det^2} S^1$.

Another useful description of a Lagrangian plane is in terms of a generating function (Carathéodory [8], Arnol'd[1]).

Lemma 2. The plane π is Lagrangian if and only if there is a generating function $s(q) = 1/2 < Sq, q >$ such that

$$p = \frac{\partial S}{\partial q} .$$

Proof. Consider a simply connected neighborhood of the point (q_o, p_o) where $p = \tilde{p}(q)$. Let

$$\tilde{s}(q) = \int_{q_o}^{q} \tilde{p}(\tilde{q})\, d\tilde{q} .$$

By Stokes theorem, independence of the path of integration is equivalent to $d(pdq) = dp \wedge dq = 0$ on π. However, this is exactly the definition of a Lagrangian plane in terms of the skew scalar product being zero. By choosing the constant of integration appropriately $\tilde{s}$ can be taken as a quadratic form. ∎

Corollary. The manifold $\Lambda(n)$ has dimension $\frac{n(n+1)}{2}$.

In $\Lambda(n)$ there is an important singular cycle that is called the Maslov cycle (Maslov [25], Arnol′d [1]). Two descriptions will be given of it. Let $\Lambda^k(n)$ be the set of all $\lambda \in \Lambda(n)$ whose intersection with the Lagrangian plane $q = 0$ is k dimensional.

Lemma 3. $\bar{\Lambda}^1(n)$ determines an (unoriented) cycle of codimension 1 in $\Lambda(n)$.

Proof. The manifold $\Lambda(n)$ can be considered as algebraic. Since $\Lambda^k(n)$ is an open manifold of codimension $\frac{k(k+1)}{2}$ in $\Lambda(n)$, the closure $\bar{\Lambda}^1(n) = \bigcup_{k \geq 1} \Lambda^k(n)$ is an algebraic submanifold of codimension 1. Thus $\bar{\Lambda}^1(n)$ determines an (un - oriented) chain. Since the singularity of $\bar{\Lambda}^1(n)$ is $\bar{\Lambda}^2(n) = \bigcup_{k \geq 2} \Lambda^k(n)$ which has codimension 3 in $\Lambda(n)$, the homological boundary of the chain $\bar{\Lambda}^1(n)$ is 0. ∎

Another characterization for the singular cycle is obtained from the projection $\pi : \Lambda(n) \longrightarrow \mathbb{R}^n$ onto the plane $p=0$ given by $\pi(p, q) = q$. The set Σ of points of $\Lambda(n)$ where the rank of the differential of π is less than n is called the singularity of the mapping π. Σ is clearly the same as $\bar{\Lambda}^1(n)$.

The symplectic group that has been introduced with the notion of a Lagrangian Grassmannian and the skew scalar product will be briefly described because of its importance in optimization and estimation problems. The (real) symplectic group, $Sp(n)$, is the subgroup of $GL(2n;\mathbb{R})$ that satisfy

$$ {}^{t}gJg = J $$

where

$$ J = \begin{bmatrix} 0 & I_n \\ -I_n & 0 \end{bmatrix} $$

The Lie algebra sp(n) is the vector space of all matrices of the form

$$ X = \begin{bmatrix} X_1 & X_2 \\ X_3 & X_4 \end{bmatrix} $$

where X_j is an $n \times n$ matrix $j=1,\dots,4$ and the condition $JX + {}^{t}XJ = 0$ from ${}^{t}gJg = J$ implies that

$$ X_4 = -{}^{t}X_1 \qquad X_3 = {}^{t}X_3 \qquad X_2 = {}^{t}X_2 $$

The dimension of the manifold of this Lie group is $n^2 + 2n(n+1)/2 = 2n^2 + n$. The Hamiltonian equations are given in this Lie algebra.

4. Linear Deterministic Optimization and Stochastic Estimation.

The deterministic linear quadratic optimization problem will be studied initially to see some of the geometry in the optimization techniques. This optimization problem is described by the linear differential system

$$ \dot{X} = FX + Gu \tag{1} $$

$$ Y = HX \tag{2} $$

where $X \in \mathbb{R}^n$, $u \in \mathbb{R}^m$ and $Y \in \mathbb{R}^p$. A control is sought (say in D^o, the family of functions that have right and left limits and only a finite number of discontinuities) to minimize

$$ J(u) = \int_{t_o}^{t} \frac{1}{2}\left[< HX(t), HX(t) > + < u(t), u(t) > \right] dt + \frac{1}{2} < \mathbf{A}X(t_1), X(t_1) > $$

$$ = \int_{t_o}^{t} L(x,u,t)\, dt + \frac{1}{2} < \mathbf{A}X(t_1), X(t_1) > \tag{3} $$

where $\mathbf{A}$ is a nonnegative definite, symmetric matrix.

A simple lemma will be given for optimality (Carathéodory [8], Kalman [19]).

Lemma 4. Let $f: \mathbb{R}^n \times [t_o, t_1] \longrightarrow \mathbb{R}^m$ be a continuously differentiable function. Let $u^o = f$ and $\mathbf{A} = 0$. For $(x,t) \in \mathbb{R}^n \times [t_o, t_1]$ assume that

i) $L(x, u^o, t) = 0$

ii) $L(x, u, t) > 0$

for all $u \neq u^o$.

Then the optimal cost is zero and the optimal control is u^o.

Clearly the hypotheses of the lemma easily force the optimality of u^o.

It will be shown how this elementary result will give us the Hamilton- Jacobi equation and the Hamiltonian equations with their geometric interpretations.

Let $V : \mathbb{R}^n \times [t_o, t_1] \longrightarrow \mathbb{R}$ be a twice continuously differentiable function such that $V(x, t_1) = 1/2 < \mathbf{A}x, x >$. Consider the function

$$\tilde{L}(x, u, t) = L(x, u, t) + V_t(x, t) + < V_x(x, t), Fx + Gu >$$

Since the last two terms are an exact differential, the minimization problem formed by using $\tilde{L}$ instead of L in (3) gives the same optimal control. The necessary condition that $\tilde{L}$ has a minimum at u^o is that the first partial derivatives with respect to u are zero at u^o. This condition and $\tilde{L} = 0$ give the equations

$$G'V_x = -L_u(x, u^o, t) \qquad (4)$$

$$-V_t = L(x, u^o, t) + < V_x, Fx + Gu > \qquad (5)$$

From L it follows immediately that

$$u^o = -G'V_x \qquad (6)$$

Thus, if there is a V which satisfies the above equations (4 - 5) then the optimization problem is solved. With a view toward the subsequent developments in this paper define the dual or conjugate variable ξ as

$$\xi = V_x$$

and the Hamiltonian as

$$H(x, \xi, t) = L(x, -G'\xi, t) + < \xi, Fx + G(-G'\xi) > \qquad (7)$$

A smooth function satisfies (4 - 5) if and only if V is a solution of the Hamilton-Jacobi equation

$$V_t + H(x, V_x, t) = 0 \tag{8}$$

The corresponding Hamiltonian equations for the optimization problem are

$$\frac{dx}{dt} = \frac{\partial H}{\partial \xi} = Fx - GG'\xi \tag{9}$$

$$\frac{d\xi}{dt} = -\frac{\partial H}{\partial x} = -H'Hx - F'\xi \tag{10}$$

Equations of this form were apparently first used by Lagrange [23] but they were subsequently discovered by Hamilton [15] who used them systematically.

To view these equations geometrically some definitions are introduced. This geometrical picture developed in optics and mechanics.

Definition 1. A manifold M is said to be a Hamiltonian manifold (or possess a Hamiltonian structure) if there is a closed, nondegenerate two form Ω defined on M.

Remark. These manifolds are also called symplectic manifolds.

For our purposes M will be $\mathbb{R}^{2n}$ while usually in physics it is TN where N is an n-dimensional submanifold of $\mathbb{R}^{2n}$ and TN is the tangent bundle. If M is a finite dimensional Hamiltonian manifold, then it is even dimensional and there are local coordinates $(q_1, \ldots, q_n, p_1, \ldots, p_n)$ such that

$$\Omega = \Sigma\, dp_i \wedge dq_i \tag{11}$$

This latter property is Darboux's theorem.

An important family of vector fields on $M \times \mathbb{R}$ is given in the following definition.

Definition 2. The vector field $\tilde{X}$ is a Hamiltonian vector field if there is a function H on $M \times \mathbb{R}$ such that

$$\tilde{X}t = \langle \tilde{X}, dt \rangle \equiv 1$$

where t is the canonical coordinate on $\mathbb{R}$, regarded as a function on $M \times \mathbb{R}$, and

$$\tilde{X} \lrcorner (\pi^* \Omega - dH \wedge dt) = 0 \tag{12}$$

where $\pi : M \times \mathbb{R} \longrightarrow M$ is the projection and $\lrcorner$ is the interior product ([24]).

<u>Remark.</u> H is determined up to a function of t alone. This observation will be important for the subsequent study of stochastic optimization.

Let $\pi^*\Omega = \tilde{\Omega}$. Since $T(M \times \mathbb{R}) = T(M) \times \mathbb{R}^2$ the vector field $\tilde{X}$ at any point is given by $\tilde{X} = (X, \frac{\partial}{\partial t})$ where X is a time varying vector field on M. For each t

$$\tilde{X} \lrcorner \tilde{\Omega} = X(\cdot, t) \lrcorner \Omega \tag{13}$$

because Ω does not depend on dt and for each t

$$< \tilde{X}, dH > = < X(\cdot, t), dH(\cdot, t) > + \frac{\partial H}{\partial t} \tag{14}$$

Thus the equation (12) can be described by two equations, the terms involving dt and those that do not. Since for each fixed t

$$X(\cdot, t) \lrcorner \Omega = - dH(\cdot, t) \tag{15}$$

we have

$$\tilde{X} \lrcorner \tilde{\Omega} = - dH + \frac{\partial H}{\partial t} dt \tag{16}$$

In this form the equation simplifies naturally to the case where the Hamiltonian is not time varying to

$$X \lrcorner \Omega = - dH \tag{17}$$

To see how the local description of the Hamiltonian equations arise in this formulation let

$$\Omega = \Sigma\, dp_i \wedge dq_i \tag{18}$$

and

$$X = \Sigma \left(\mathbf{A}^i \frac{\partial}{\partial q^i} + B^i \frac{\partial}{\partial p^i} \right) \tag{19}$$

so

$$X \lrcorner \Omega = \Sigma \left(B^i dq_i - \mathbf{A}^i dp_i \right) \tag{20}$$

If

$$dF = \Sigma \left(\frac{\partial F}{\partial q^i} dq_i + \frac{\partial F}{\partial p^i} dp_i \right) \tag{21}$$

then the vector field X_{dF} that corresponds to the one form dF by the bijection (20) is

$$X_{dF} = \Sigma \left(\frac{\partial F}{\partial q^i} \frac{\partial}{\partial p^i} - \frac{\partial F}{\partial p^i} \frac{\partial}{\partial q^i} \right) \tag{22}$$

If $\tilde{X} = (X, \frac{\partial}{\partial t})$ is a Hamiltonian vector field, then $X(\cdot, t) \lrcorner \Omega = - dH(\cdot, t)$ and

$$X_{-dH(\cdot, t)} = \Sigma \left(\frac{\partial H}{\partial p^i} \frac{\partial}{\partial q^i} - \frac{\partial H}{\partial q^i} \frac{\partial}{\partial p^i} \right) \tag{23}$$

and if $(q^1(\cdot), \ldots, q^n(\cdot), p^1(\cdot), \ldots, p^n(\cdot))$ is an integral curve of this flow then it must satisfy the Hamiltonian differential equations

$$\frac{dq^i}{dt} = \frac{\partial H}{\partial p^i} \tag{24}$$

$$\frac{dp^i}{dt} = - \frac{\partial H}{\partial q^i} \tag{25}$$

Since we shall be interested in integrating Hamiltonian vector fields, we need one additional concept that is given in the following definition.

<u>Definition 3.</u> A diffeomorphism, $\tilde{\varphi} : M \times \mathbb{R} \longrightarrow M \times \mathbb{R}$, is called a <u>canonical transformation</u> if

i) $\tilde{\varphi}^* (\tilde{\Omega}) = \tilde{\Omega} - dW \wedge dt$ where W is some function depending on $\tilde{\varphi}$.

ii) $\tilde{\varphi}$ is time preserving, that is, $\tilde{\varphi}(x, t) = (\varphi(x, t), t)$ where $\varphi(\cdot, t) : M \longrightarrow M$ is a diffeomorphism for each t.

<u>Remark.</u> Since we are considering here only the linear theory, φ will be an evolution in the symplectic group. However, the above definition is useful for generalizations.

Let $\tilde{X}$ be a Hamiltonian vector field and let $\tilde{\varphi} : M \times \mathbb{R} \longrightarrow M \times \mathbb{R}$ be the flow generated by $\tilde{X}$ which passes through (x, 0) at time 0. The form of $\tilde{\varphi}$ $(\tilde{\varphi}(x, t) = (\varphi(x, t), t))$ implies that

$$\tilde{\varphi}^* \left(\frac{\partial}{\partial t} \right) = \tilde{X}_{\varphi(x, t)} \quad .$$

It will be shown that $\tilde{\varphi}$ is a canonical transformation. Since $X(\cdot, t) \lrcorner \Omega = - dH(\cdot, t)$ for each t, we have

$$\frac{d}{ds}\left(\varphi(\cdot, s)^{*} \Omega \right) = \varphi(\cdot, s)^{*} D_{X(\cdot, t)} \Omega = 0$$

where D_X is the Lie derivative. This equation implies that $\tilde{\varphi}^{*}\tilde{\Omega} = \tilde{\Omega} + \theta \wedge dt$. To determine θ it suffices to take the interior product with $\frac{\partial}{\partial t}$ because $\tilde{\Omega}$ does not depend on dt.

$$\frac{\partial}{\partial t} \lrcorner \tilde{\varphi}^{*} \pi^{*} \Omega = \tilde{\varphi}^{*} \left[\tilde{\varphi}^{*} \left(\frac{\partial}{\partial t}\right) \lrcorner \pi^{*} \Omega \right] = \tilde{\varphi}^{*} (\tilde{X} \lrcorner \pi^{*} \Omega) = \tilde{\varphi}^{*} \left(- dH + \frac{\partial H}{\partial t} dt \right) \tag{26}$$

Thus $\tilde{\varphi}$ is a canonical transformation and

$$W_{\tilde{\varphi}} = - \tilde{\varphi}^{*} H_X \tag{27}$$

We shall relate the determination of $W_{\tilde{\varphi}}$ to the Hamilton-Jacobi equation. Let $(q_1, \ldots, q_n, p_1, \ldots, p_n)$ be local coordinates such that $\Omega = \Sigma \, dp_i \wedge dq_i$. Let $V(q_1, \ldots, q_n, p_1, \ldots, p_n, t)$ be a function such that

$$\varphi_1 (q_1, \ldots, q_n, p_1, \ldots, p_n, t) = \left(q_1, \ldots, q_n, \frac{\partial V}{\partial q_1}, \ldots, \frac{\partial V}{\partial q_n}, t\right)$$

and

$$\varphi_2 (q_1, \ldots, q_n, p_1, \ldots, p_n, t) = \left(\frac{\partial V}{\partial p_1}, \ldots, \frac{\partial V}{\partial p_n}, p_1, \ldots, p_n, t\right)$$

are diffeomorphisms. Clearly $\tilde{\varphi} = \varphi_1 \circ \varphi_2^{-1}$ is a canonical transformation because each diffeomorphism φ_i $i = 1, 2$ acts only on the p´s or the q´s separately. Locally, any canonical transformation can be expressed by the composition of two such diffeomorphisms because Ω is preserved. It is claimed that

$$W_{\tilde{\varphi}} = \varphi_2^{-1 *} \frac{\partial V}{\partial t} \tag{28}$$

Recall that the condition for a canonical transformation, which is clear in this case, is that

$$\tilde{\varphi}^{*} \tilde{\Omega} = \tilde{\Omega} - dW \wedge dt$$

Since $\tilde{\Omega} = d(\Sigma p_i dq_i) = - d(\Sigma q_i dp_i)$, we have

$$\tilde{\varphi}^{*} \tilde{\Omega} - \tilde{\Omega} = d(\tilde{\varphi}^{*} \Sigma p_i dq_i + \Sigma q_i dp_i)$$

$$= d\,\varphi_2^{-1*}\left(\varphi_1^{*}\,\Sigma p_i dq_i + \varphi_2^{*}\,\Sigma q_i dp_i\right)$$

$$= d\,\varphi_2^{-1*}\left(\Sigma \frac{\partial V}{\partial q_i}\, dq_i + \Sigma \frac{\partial V}{\partial p_i}\, dp_i\right)$$

$$= d\,\varphi_2^{-1*}\left(dV - \frac{\partial V}{\partial t}\, dt\right)$$

$$= \varphi_2^{-1*}\, d\, dV - d\,\varphi_2^{-1*}\frac{\partial V}{\partial t} \wedge dt$$

$$= - d\left(\varphi_2^{-1*}\frac{\partial V}{\partial t}\right) \wedge dt$$

This verifies (28) and substituting into (27) we see that $\tilde{\varphi}$ is the solution if and only if

$$\varphi_2^{-1*}\frac{\partial V}{\partial t} + \tilde{\varphi}^* H = 0 \tag{29}$$

or equivalently ($\tilde{\varphi}^* H = \varphi_2^{-1*}\varphi_1^{*} H$)

$$\frac{\partial V}{\partial t} + H\left(q_1, \ldots, q_n, \frac{\partial V}{\partial q_1}, \ldots, \frac{\partial V}{\partial q_n}, t\right) = 0 \tag{30}$$

which is the Hamilton-Jacobi equation. Thus locally, the solution of the Hamilton-Jacobi equation is equivalent to the solution of the Hamiltonian equations.

Recalling the Hamiltonian for the linear quadratic optimization problem

$$H(x, \xi, t) = \frac{1}{2}\left[< Hx, Hx > + 2 < Fx, \xi > - < G'\xi, G'\xi > \right]$$

we have the Hamiltonian equations

$$\frac{dx}{dt} = Fx - GG'\xi$$

$$\frac{d\xi}{dt} = - H'Hx - F'\xi$$

From our calculations in the Lagrangian Grassmannian and with symplectic forms we know that x and ξ are related by a symmetric matrix so that the solution to the Hamilton-Jacobi equation is given by a quadratic form. The necessary and sufficient condition that a symmetric matrix , P, is this solution is that it satisfies the Riccati equation

$$- \frac{dP}{dt} = F'P + PF - PGG'P + H'H \tag{31}$$

$$P(t_1) = A$$

This equation is obtained by inserting the quadratic form in the Hamilton-Jacobi equation.

We can summarize our results for the linear deterministic optimization problem by the following theorem.

Theorem 1. Consider the linear deterministic optimization problem described by the linear differential system (1 - 2) and the cost functional (3). The optimal control is given by

$$u^{\circ}(t) = G' P(t) X(t)$$

where P is a solution of the Riccati equation (31).

While the Riccati equation for this optimization problem has been obtained from a computation with the Hamilton-Jacobi equation, a more geometric derivation of the Riccati equation will be obtained from the properties of the Lagrangian Grassmannian. Let V be the vector space $\mathbb{R}^{2n}$ and fix canonical coordinates on V. From these canonical coordinates on V there is a decomposition $V = U \oplus W$ where the canonical coordinates on U are $(q_1, \ldots, q_n, 0, \ldots, 0)$ and those on W are $(0, \ldots 0, p_1, \ldots, p_n)$. Let

$$U_{\mathbf{A}} = \{ w + \mathbf{A}w : A \in L_s(W, U), \ w \in W \}$$

where $L_s(W, U)$ is the family of symmetric linear transformations from W to U. Clearly $U_A = U_B$ if and only if $A = B$. Let

$$\Gamma(U) = \{ U_{\mathbf{A}} : \mathbf{A} \in L_s(W, U) \}$$

and

$$\varphi_U : \Gamma(U) \longrightarrow L_s(W, U) = \mathbb{R}^{\frac{n(n+1)}{2}}$$

where $\varphi_U(U_{\mathbf{A}}) = A$. It can be verified that $(\Gamma(U), \varphi_U)$ determines the differential structure for $\Lambda(n)$.

Let $\beta(t)$ be a curve in the symplectic group, Sp(n), such that

$$\beta^{-1} \frac{d\beta}{dt} = B \qquad \beta(0) = I \tag{32}$$

where B is in the Lie algebra of the symplectic group. Partition β and B into four $n \times n$ matrices such that

$$B = \begin{bmatrix} B_{11} & B_{12} \\ B_{21} & B_{22} \end{bmatrix}$$

$$\beta = \begin{bmatrix} \beta_{11} & \beta_{12} \\ \beta_{21} & \beta_{22} \end{bmatrix}$$

Then

$$\beta U_A = \{ \beta_{11} w + \beta_{12} A w + \beta_{21} w + \beta_{22} A w : A \in L_s(W, U) \}$$

$$= \{ [\beta_{11} + \beta_{12} A] w + [\beta_{21} + \beta_{22} A] w : A \in L_s(W, U) \}$$

If $\beta U_A \in \Gamma(U)$, then $(\beta_{11} + \beta_{12} A)$ is invertible so that

$$\beta(t) U_A = U_{X(t)}$$

where $X(t) = (\beta_{21}(t) + \beta_{22}(t) A) (\beta_{11}(t) + \beta_{12}(t) A)^{-1}$

The family of symmetric transformations , X(t), satisfies the Riccati equation

$$\frac{dX}{dt} = B_{21} + B_{22} X - X B_{11} - X B_{12} X \tag{33}$$

Now we consider the linear quadratic Gaussian estimation problem. This problem is described by the linear stochastic differential equations

$$dX_t = F X_t dt + G dB_t \tag{34}$$

$$dY_t = H X_t dt + d\tilde{B}_t \tag{35}$$

where (B_t) and $(\tilde{B}_t)$ are independent standard $\mathbb{R}^m$ and $\mathbb{R}^p$ dimensional Brownian motions respectively, $X(0) = X_o$ is a Gaussian random variable with zero mean and covariance P_o that is independent of $(B_t, \tilde{B}_t)$ and $Y(0) \equiv 0$. An estimate $\hat{X}_t$ is sought for X_t from the observations $(Y_s, \ 0 \le s \le t)$ that minimizes $E [< X_t - \bar{X}_t , X_t - \bar{X}_t >]$ over all such estimators $\bar{X}_t$. It is well known and easy to verify that $\hat{X}_t$ is the conditional mean $E [X_t / Y_s, \ 0 \le s \le t]$. An equation will be derived for $\hat{X}_t$.

Let

$$Z_t = \hat{X}_t - \hat{X}_o - \int_0^t F\hat{X}_s\,ds$$

It is elementary to verify that the process (Z_t) has orthogonal increments and from the Gaussian property of (X_t, Y_t), (Z_t) is a process of independent increments with respect to $\sigma(Y_s, 0 \leq s \leq t)$. From the equation (35) for (Y_t) it follows that this Brownian motion is a scaled version of the so-called innovations process $dY_t - H\hat{X}_t = d\overline{B}_t$. Rewriting the equation for (Z_t) we have

$$d\hat{X}_t = F\hat{X}_t dt + dZ_t$$

$$X_o \equiv 0$$

Equivalently, this equation can be written as

$$d\hat{X}_t = F\hat{X}_t dt + R(t)\,d\overline{B}_t \tag{36}$$

and it remains only to compute R(t). We have

$$\hat{X}_t = \int_0^t K(t,s)\,d\overline{B}_s$$

$$= \int_0^t \Phi(t,s)R(s)\,d\overline{B}(s)$$

where Φ is the fundamental solution of $\dot{X} = FX$. It follows from elementary projection properties that

$$K(t,s) = \frac{d}{ds} E[\,X_t\ \overline{B}'_s\,]$$

Computing $E[\,X_t\ \overline{B}'_s\,]$ we have

$$E[\,X_t\ \overline{B}'_s\,] = \int_0^s \Phi(t,u)\ P(u)\ H'(u)\,du$$

Thus $R(t) = P(t)H'(t)$ where $P(t) = E[\,(X_t-\hat{X}_t)(X_t-\hat{X}_t)'\,]$. Let $\tilde{X}_t = X_t - \hat{X}_t$. The equation for $\tilde{X}_t$ is

$$d\tilde{X}_t = (F - PH'H)\tilde{X}_t\,dt - PH'\,d\tilde{B}_t + G\,dB_t \tag{37}$$

Let Ψ be the fundamental solution of $\dot{X} = (F - PH'H)X$. Then

$$P(t) = E[\,\tilde{X}_t\ \tilde{X}'_t\,] = \Psi(t,0)\,P_o\,\Psi'(t,0) + \int_0^t \Psi(t,s)\,GG'\,\Psi'(t,s)\,ds +$$

$$+ \int_0^t \Psi(t,s)\, PH'HP\, \Psi'(t,s)\, ds$$

Differentiating this equation we obtain

$$\frac{dP}{dt} = FP + PF' + GG' - PH'HP \tag{38}$$

$$P(0) = P_o$$

The solution of the linear estimation problem is summarized in the following theorem.

Theorem 2. Consider the linear stochastic system described by (34 - 35). The conditional mean, $\hat{X}_t = E[X_t | Y_s, 0 \leq s \leq t]$, satisfies the stochastic equation

$$d\hat{X}_t = F\hat{X}_t dt + P(t) H'(dY_t - H\hat{X}_t dt)$$

$$\hat{X}_o \equiv 0$$

where P satisfies the Riccati equation (38).

Given the Riccati equation (38) we can characterize the solution to the linear estimation problem via the Hamiltonian equations. Making the obvious identifications there is a natural duality between the linear optimization problem and the linear estimation problem.

While the optimization and the estimation problems are naturally dual to one another, there is an asymmetry in the duality that occurs from the observations (dY_t) in the estimation problem. One could generalize the optimization problem so that there is a complete symmetry in the duality, but it is more natural for our purpose to consider the observations in the estimation problem directly. There is a natural pairing $< dY, HX > = < H'dY, X >$ so that the family $(H'dY_t)$ are linear functionals on the x-space and are therefore natural elements in the ξ-space. Since these objects are in the fibres of the (co-) tangent bundle, the elements in the fibres are naturally added and the symmetric linear transformation that acts on the ξ-variable also acts on the elements $(H'dY)$. Thus the optimal linear filter has the observations or the elements $(H'dY_t)$ as inputs.

5. Linear Stochastic Optimization

The final well known results from linear control theory that will be solved emphasizing a geometrical approach are two problems of quadratic optimization for linear Gaussian systems. The first problem will assume that complete observations of the state are available, while the second problem will assume that there are only partial, noisy observations of the state.

Initially, consider the linear stochastic system

$$dX_t = FX_t dt + CU_t dt + G\, dB_t \qquad (39)$$

$$X(0) = X_o$$

where the assumptions on (X_t), (B_t), F and G are the same as for the stochastic equation (34) and $C \in \mathrm{Hom}(\mathbb{R}^q, \mathbb{R}^n)$ and (U_t) is a stochastic process that is called the control. The family of admissible controls are maps $U: [0,T] \times \Omega \longrightarrow \mathbb{R}^q$ that are piecewise continuous functions of t for each $\omega \in \Omega$ and U_t is measurable with respect to (the completion of) the sub-σ-algebra $\sigma(X_s, 0 \leq s \leq t)$. An admissible control is sought that minimizes the functional

$$J(u) = \frac{1}{2} E[\int_0^T < QX_t, X_t > + < U_t, U_t > dt + < AX_T, X_T >] \qquad (40)$$

where A and Q are nonnegative, symmetric elements of $\mathrm{Hom}(\mathbb{R}^n, \mathbb{R}^n)$. At this point it is not clear that a minimizing control exists in the admissible family of controls and, in fact, for a general stochastic optimization problem, a more general class of admissible controls has to be allowed.

To solve this stochastic optimization problem it is most expedient to use a necessary and sufficient condition for optimality that will not be proved here. This result appears in various versions in the literature (e.g. Rishel [28], Davis-Varaiya [11], Duncan [12]). The result states that an optimal control is determined by the solution of the (generalized) Hamilton-Jacobi equation

$$V_t + \frac{1}{2} \mathrm{tr}(G' V_{xx} G) + \min_u (< V_x, Fx+Cu > + \frac{1}{2} < Qx, x > + \frac{1}{2} < u, u >) = 0$$

$$V(T,x) = < Ax, x > \qquad (41)$$

If the usual necessary condition for the minimization over the controls is applied, then this Hamilton-Jacobi equation can be expressed as

$$V_t + \frac{1}{2} \mathrm{tr}(G' V_{xx} G) + H(x, V_x, t) = 0 \qquad (42)$$

where

$$H(x, \xi, t) = \frac{1}{2} < Qx, x > + \frac{1}{2} < -C'\xi, -C'\xi > + < \xi, Fx + C(-C'\xi) > \qquad (43)$$

This equation has the same form as the Hamilton-Jacobi equation that was used to solve the deterministic optimization problem except for the additional term $\frac{1}{2}\operatorname{tr}(G'V_{xx}G)$ where tr is the trace and V_{xx} is the matrix of second partial derivatives. This term arises from the infinitesimal generator of the semigroup corresponding to the martingale term $(G\,dB_t)$.

To solve this equation it will be assumed that V_{xx} does not depend on x. If this assumption is correct then basically the solution is the same as for the deterministic optimization problem. This approach has been used by Wonham [34] (cf. also [10]). Recall that from the definition of Hamiltonian vector fields, the Hamiltonian is only determined up to a function of t alone.
From the solution of the deterministic optimization problem (Theorem 1) the assumption that V_{xx} does not depend on x is correct and the solution of (42) is given by

$$V(t,x) = \frac{1}{2}\left[\langle P(t)x, x\rangle + p(t) \right] \tag{44}$$

where

$$\frac{dp}{dt} = -\operatorname{tr}(G'PG) \tag{45}$$

$$-\frac{dP}{dt} = PF + F'P + Q - PCC'P \tag{46}$$

$$P(T) = A$$

$$p(T) = 0$$

Now the problem of stochastic optimization will be considered where only noisy, partial observations of the state are available. The linear stochastic system is

$$dX_t = FX_t dt + CU_t dt + G\,dB_t \tag{47}$$

$$dY_t = HX_t dt + d\tilde{B}_t \tag{48}$$

$$X(0) = X_o$$

$$Y(0) \equiv 0$$

where the terms in these equations satisfy the assumptions given for the equations (34-35) and (39) except that the family of admissible controls is different. In this problem the family of admissible controls will be all maps $U:[0,T]\times\Omega \to \mathbb{R}^q$ that are piecewise continuous in t for fixed $\omega \in \Omega$ and (U_t) is predictable with respect to (the completion of) the family of sub-σ-algebras $(\sigma(Y_s, 0 \leq s \leq t))$. The cost functional J is (40).

The optimal estimator for (47) is easily obtained from the optimal estimator for (34) by subtracting off the $(\sigma(Y_s, 0 \leq s \leq t))$ measurable vectors (CU_t). Specifically, the equation for the conditional mean is

$$d\hat{X}_t = F\hat{X}_t dt + CU_t dt + PH'(dY_t - H\hat{X}_t dt) \tag{49}$$

To show that the optimal control is the same as for the previous stochastic optimization problem it is only necessary to rewrite the cost functional in terms of $(\hat{X}_t)$. Using the orthogonality of the error $\tilde{X}$ and the optimal estimate $\hat{X}$, the cost functional J can be expressed as

$$J(u) = \frac{1}{2}\{E[\int_0^T < Q\hat{X}_t, \hat{X}_t > + < U_t, U_t > dt + < A\hat{X}_T, \hat{X}_T >] + + \int_0^T tr\ (PQ) + tr\ (P(T)A)\} \tag{50}$$

where P is the solution of (38). Since the last two terms in the equation for J do not depend on the control, it is clear that the optimal control is the same as it was for the stochastic optimization problem with complete observations which is the same as the optimal control for the deterministic problem.

The fact that the optimization and the estimation problems can be performed separately is called the separation principle.

5. Infinite Time Problems

The last topic to be considered in the linear control theory is the infinite time problems for deterministic control and stochastic estimation. By the duality of optimization and estimation it suffices to consider only one of these problems. The optimization problem will be considered here. For the infinite time problems the fundamental difficulty is that for some initial conditions the cost may be infinite for all controls so that the minimization problem is not well defined. Since the control problem can be formulated in the Lagrangian Grassmannian $\Lambda(n)$ by the Hamiltonian equations, it is natural to identify the subset (or sub-manifold) that is to be avoided.
Of course, this is the Maslov cycle that had been described in our discussion of the Lagrangian Grassmannian.

The condition that ensures a reasonable optimization problem is reachability. It is known (Wonham [35]) that the necessary and sufficient condition for pole placement or coefficient assignability of the characteristic polynomial for the equation

$$\dot{X} = FX + Gu$$

using state feedback is that the system is reachable.

With the stability for some feedback laws it trivially follows that the optimal system is asymptotically stable. The optimal feedback control is obtained from the steady state solution of the Riccati equation which is called the algebraic Riccati equation

$$0 = F'P + PF - PGG'P + H'H \tag{51}$$

6. Some Generalizations

To show the power of the geometric techniques that have been used in this paper a generalization of the optimization and estimation problems to some linear systems with pure delays will be sketched. A complete discussion of this problem is given in another paper in this volume (Duncan [13]). For simplicity of the discussion only the deterministic optimization problem will be described. Consider a linear pure delay time system where the delays occur only in the state matrix F and consider an optimization problem that is similar to the one described by the equations (1-2). For such a system the state equation can be viewed as a system over a ring of polynomials that are formed from the delays ([5, 21, 22, 33]). The linear system over this ring can be considered as a finitely generated, projective module and this module can be viewed as a vector bundle over the algebraic variety formed from the ring of polynomials (Serre [31]). Intuitively, the delays are treated as parameters of the system and the evaluation of these parameters has a precise geometrical picture. The conjecture of the global triviality of this bundle, known as the Serre conjecture, has been verified (Quillen [27], Suslin [32]). Thus the evaluation of the parameters is particularly simple. If the Hamiltonian equations are formed, then these equations describe a symplectic vector bundle and this bundle is also globally trivial (Bass [2]). Thus the form of the optimal system can be immediately demonstrated from the optimal system for linear systems without delays and an equation for the symmetric matrix that relates x and ξ can be obtained that is formally similar to the Riccati equation (31).

References

1. V.I. Arnol'd, Characteristic classes entering in quantization conditions, Funct. Anal. Appl. 1 (1967), 1 - 13.
2. H. Bass, Quadratic modules over polynomial rings, Contributions to Algebra, (H. Bass, P. Cassidy, J. Kovacic, eds.), 1 - 23, Academic Press, New York, 1977.
3. R.W. Brockett, Some geometric questions in the theory of linear systems, IEEE Trans. Auto. Control AC - 21 (1976), 444 - 455.
4. P. Brunovsky, A classification of linear controllable systems, Kybernetica 3 (1970)
5. C. Byrnes, On the control of certain deterministic infinite dimensional systems by algebro-geometric techniques, to appear in Amer. J. Math.
6. C.I. Byrnes and T.E. Duncan, Topological and geometric invariants arising in control theory, to appear.
7. C. Byrnes and N. Hurt, On the moduli of linear dynamical systems, Adv. in Math. Studies in Analysis 4 (1979), 83 - 122.
8. C. Carathéodory, Variationsrechnung und Partielle Differentialgleichungen Erster Ordnung, Teubner, Leipzig, 1935.
9. A. Cauchy, Calcul des indices des fonctions, J. L'École Polytechnique, 1835, 176 - 229.
10. M.H.A. Davis, Linear Estimation and Stochastic Control, Chapman and Hall, London, 1977.
11. M.H.A. Davis and P. Varaiya, Dynamic programming conditions for partially observable stochastic systems, SIAM J. Control 11 (1973), 226 - 261.
12. T.E. Duncan, Dynamic programming optimality criteria for stochastic systems in Riemannian manifolds, Appl. Math. Optim. 3 (1977), 191 - 208.
13. T.E. Duncan, An algebro-geometric approach to estimation and stochastic control for linear pure delay time systems, this volume.
14. A. Grothendieck, Sur la classification des fibrés holomorphes sur la sphère de Riemann, Amer. J. Math. 79 (1957), 121 - 138.
15. W.R. Hamilton, Trans. Roy. Irish Acad. 15 (1828), 69; 16 (1830), 1; 16 (1831), 93; 17 (1837), 1.
16. R. Hermann and C. Martin, Applications of algebraic geometry to systems

theory: the McMillan degree and Kronecker indices of transfer functions as topological and holomorphic system invariants, SIAM J. Control Optim. 16 (1978), 743 - 755.

17. C. Hermite, Sur les nombres des racines d'une équation algébrique comprises entre des limites données, J. Reine Angew. Math. 52 (1856), 39 - 51.

18. A. Hurwitz, Über die bedingungen unter welchen eine gleichung nur wurzeln mit negativen reelen theilen besitzt, Math. Ann. 46 (1895), 273 - 284

19. R. E. Kalman, Contributions to the theory of optimal control, Bol. Soc. Mat. Mex. 1960, 102 - 119.

20. R. E. Kalman, Kronecker invariants and feedback, Ordinary Differential Equations, (L. Weiss, ed.), Academic Press, New York, 1972.

21. E. W. Kamen, On an algebraic theory of systems defined by convolution operators, Math. Systems Theory 9 (1975), 57 - 74.

22. E. W. Kamen, An operator theory of linear functional differential equations, J. Differential Equations 27 (1978), 274 - 297.

23. J. L. Lagrange, Mémoire sur la théorie des variations des éléments des planètes, Mém. Cl. Sci. Math. Phys. Inst. France (1808), 1 - 72.

24. L. H. Loomis and S. Sternberg, Advanced Calculus, Addison-Wesley, Reading, Mass., 1968.

25. V. P. Maslov, Theory of Perturbations and Asymptotic Methods (in Russian) MGU, 1965.

26. J. C. Maxwell, On governors, Proc. Roy. Soc. London 16 (1868), 270 - 283.

27. D. Quillen, Projective modules over polynomial rings, Invent. Math. 36 (1976), 167 - 171.

28. R. Rishel, Necessary and sufficient dynamic programming conditions for continuous-time stochastic optimal control, SIAM J. Control 8 (1970), 559 - 571.

29. H. H. Rosenbrock, State-space and Multivariable Theory, Nelson, London, 1970.

30. E. J. Routh, A treatise on the stability of a given state of motion, Macmillan, London, 1877.

31. J. P. Serre, Modules projectifs et espaces fibrés à fibre vectorielle, Sém. Dubreil-Pisot, no. 23, 1957/58.

32. A. A. Suslin, Projective modules over a polynomial ring are free, Dokl. Akad. Nauk. S.S.S.R 229 (1976) (Soviet Math. Dokl. 17 (1976), 1160 - 1164).

33. N. S. Williams and V. Zakian, A ring of delay operators with applications to delay-differential systems, SIAM J. Control and Optim. 15 (1977), 247 - 255.

34. W. M. Wonham, Lecture Notes in Stochastic Control, Center for Dynamical

Systems, Brown University 1967.

35. W. M. Wonham, On pole assignment in multi-input controllable linear systems, IEEE Trans Auto. Contr. AC - 12 (1967), 660 - 665.

THE MARTINGALE CALCULUS AND APPLICATIONS

Robert J. Elliott

University of Hull, England

1. INTRODUCTION

We obtain below a necessary minimum principle for the optimum control of a general vector valued semimartingale. The system is controlled by changing the measure on the space trajectories; this in turn varies the local characteristics of the process, as is shown in the work of Jacod and Memin [11] . In a previous paper [6] , the minimum remaining cost process is represented as a predictable stochastic integral plus a (weakly) orthogonal martingale. In this paper we use integrals with respect to random measures associated with the process, and apply results of Jacod [9] , to show the remaining summand is strongly orthogonal to the space of stochastic integrals. This gives a more explicit Hamiltonian for the system and a much neater minimum principle than that obtained in [6] .

In section 2 the state process of the system is described, together with its associated continuous martingales and random measure. The state process in our previous paper [6] was one dimensional, but vector processes are now discussed. Stochastic integrals with respect to the random measure are defined in section 3 together with a representation result. It is well known, (see [12] for example), that integrals with respect to random measures are a generalization of the optional stochastic integrals of Meyer [14] . Admissible controls are described in section 4 and the cost process in section 5. In section 6 results are given which state how our semimartingales and their local characteristics behave under any other measure which is obtained by use of an admissible control. The minimum principle is obtained in section 7.

Diffusions and Ito processes

$x_t = x_o + \int_{[o,t]} f(s,x,u)\, ds + \int_{[o,t]} \sigma(s,x) dw_s, x_t \in R^m$, as discussed by Davis and Varaiya [2] and Elliott [5] , are examples of semimartingales. A Poisson process $N_t = (N_t - \lambda t) + \lambda t$ is another example, and semimartingales can be associated with a multivariate point process in a natural way, (see Davis and Elliott [1]). The formulation below, and consequently the class of processes covered by our theory, is, therefore, very general. The author is grateful to the Division of Applied Mathematics of Brown University for its hospitality through the summer of 1978, during which some of the ideas in this paper were developed.

2. THE STATE PROCESS

Suppose (Ω, F, P) is a probability space, and that, for $t \in [o,1]$, X_t is a stochastic process defined on Ω with values in R^m. All processes will be right continuous with left-hand limits. Write $F_t = \sigma\{X_s : s \le t\} \subset F$ for the σ -field generated by X up to time t. We shall suppose that on (Ω, F_t, P) X_t is a semimartingale, that is X_t has a decomposition:

$$X_t = X_o + M_t + A_t.$$

Here M_t is a local martingale and A_t is a process of finite variation, (that is, A_t is F_t adapted and its sample paths are locally of bounded variation.) This decomposition is not in general unique. However, the jumps of the process, $\Delta X_s = X_s - X_{s-}$, are unamibiguously defined, and if $X_t = X_o + \bar{M}_t + \bar{A}_t$ is a second decomposition then

$$M^c = \bar{M}^c$$

where M^c, (resp. $\bar{M}^c$) , is the continuous part of the martingale M , (resp. $\bar{M}$).

The martingale $M^c = (M^{c1}, \dots, M^{cm})$ is m-dimensional and we shall suppose that $B_{ij} = < M^{ci}, M^{cj} > = 0$ a.s. (P) if $i \neq j$. This condition could be relaxed; see [10] p. 43.

If B denotes the Borel σ-field on R^m, write P for the predictable σ-field on $\Omega \times [o,1]$ and $\tilde{P}$ for the product σ-field $P \times B$ on $\tilde{\Omega} = \Omega \times [o,1] \times R^m$.

We wish to consider the random measure μ determined by the jumps of X, that is

$$\mu(\omega; dt, dx) = \sum_s I_{\{\Delta X_s \neq o\}} \varepsilon(s, \Delta X_s)(dt, dx), \quad \text{(see [8] and [11])}.$$

A related measure M^P_μ can be defined on $(\tilde{\Omega}, \tilde{P})$ by putting

$$M^P_\mu (X) = E((X * \mu)_1)$$

for any non-negative $\tilde{P}$ measurable function X defined on $\tilde{\Omega}$. Here

$$(X*\mu)_t(\omega) = \int_{[o,t] \times R^m} X(s,y)\mu(\omega; ds, dy).$$

The fundamental result of [7] then states there is a unique predictable random measure ν , defined on $(\tilde{\Omega}, \tilde{P})$, such that, if $X*\mu$ is a locally integrable process, then $(X*\mu)_t - (X*\nu)_t$ is a local martingale. ν is called the dual predictable projection of μ.

As in [8], Proposition 2.3, a version of ν exists which satisfies

$\nu(\omega:\{t\} \times E) \le 1$. Following Jacod , write

$$a_t = \nu(\{t\} \times R^m) \text{ and } \hat{U}_t = \int_{R^m} U(t,x)\nu(\{t\},dx)$$

for every function on $\tilde{\Omega}$ for which the integral exists. Note that

$$a_t = \hat{1}_t, \text{ and } \hat{U}_t = 0 \text{ if } a_t = 0.$$

Write $\quad J = \{a > 0\}$, $\nu^c = I_{J' \times R^m}.\nu$, and $\nu^d = I_{J \times R^m}.\nu = \nu - \nu^c$,

where J' is the complement of J.

$$D \text{ will denote } \{\Delta X \neq 0\} = \{(\omega,s): \mu(\omega;\{s\} \times R^m) = 1\}.$$

For any ω the section of D is countable,that is, adapting the terminology of Dellacherie, D is minced. (Dellacherie [3] suggests 'scanty' as a translation of 'mince', but 'minced' does suggest the property of being chopped - up).D can then be written as $D^a \cup D^i$, where D^a, (resp. D^i), is the accessible, (resp. totally inaccessible), part of D, and is a countable union of graphs of accessible, (resp. totally inaccessible), stopping times. D^p is then the smallest predictable set containing D^a, and D^p is a countable union of graphs of predictable stopping times. It is not difficult to see that

$$D^p = \{a > o\} = J, \text{ and } D^p \setminus D = \{o < a < 1\}.$$

3. STOCHASTIC INTEGRALS

Following [8] we wish to define two types of integral with respect to μ.

DEFINITION 3.1. For a $\tilde{P}$ measurable function W write

$$W' = (W - \hat{W}) I_{\{|W - \hat{W}| > 1\}} + \hat{W} I_{\{|\hat{W}| > 1\}} ,$$

$$W'' = W - W' ,$$

$$C(W)_t = (I_{\{a = o\}} (|W'| + W''^2)) * \nu_t$$

$$+ \sum_{s \le t} (\widehat{(W''^2)}_s - (\hat{W}''_s)^2 + \widehat{|W' - \hat{W}'|}_s$$

$$+ (1 - a_s)|\hat{W}'_s|).$$

Here we take $C(W)_t = + \infty$ if one of the terms is not defined.

$G_{loc}(\mu)$ is then defined to be the set of processes W which are $\tilde{P}$ measurable and for which $C(W)_t$ is a process of locally integrable variation.

If $W \in G_{loc}$,a discontinuous local martingale $W * (\mu - \nu)$ can be defined,and

$$\Delta(W*(\mu - \nu))_t = I_D(t)W(t,\Delta X_t) - \hat{W}_t.$$

DEFINITION 3.2 Write $\mathcal{O}$ for the optional σ-field on $\Omega \times [o,1]$, and $\tilde{\mathcal{O}}$ for the product σ-field $\mathcal{O} \times \mathcal{B}$ on $\tilde{\Omega}$. If $W : \tilde{\Omega} \to R$ is $\mathcal{O}$ measurable we can consider the measure $W.\mu$.

$K(\mu)$ is the set of $\tilde{\mathcal{O}}$ measurable functions W such that $W.\mu$ is σ-finite. If $W \in K(\mu)$ the conditional expectation $M_\mu(W|\tilde{P})$ can be defined.

DEFINITION 3.3. Suppose $V \in K(\mu)$ is such that $M_\mu(V|\tilde{P}) = 0$.

Write $\quad V' = VI_{\{|V|>1\}} - M_\mu(VI_{\{|V|>1\}} \mid P),$

and $\quad V'' = V - V'$

$H_{loc}(\mu)$ is then the set of $V \in K(\mu)$ such that $M_\mu(V|\tilde{P}) = 0$

and $\quad (V''^2 + |V'|) * \mu$ is a process of locally integrable variation.

If $V \in H_{loc}(\mu)$ a discontinuous local martingale $V*\mu$ can be defined, and $\Delta(V*\mu)_t = I_D(t)\ V(t, \Delta X_t)$.

The following theorem is then proved in [8]:

THEOREM 3.4. Suppose M is a (real valued) local martingale on (Ω, F_t, P) and that $M_o = 0$. Then the process $\Delta M \in K(\mu)$.

Write $\quad U = M_\mu(\Delta M|\tilde{P}), \quad V = \Delta M - U,$

and $\quad W = U + (1 - a)^{-1}\ \hat{U}I_{\{a < 1\}}.$

Then $\quad V \in H_{loc}(\mu),\ W \in G_{loc}(\mu)$

and $\quad M = W*(\mu - \nu) + V*\mu + Y,$ where Y is a local martingale satisfying $\Delta Y = 0$ on D.

REMARKS 3.5 Let us proceed further with this representation. The local martingale Y has a unique decomposition into the sum of a continuous local martingale Y^c and a discontinuous martingale Y^d. Because $< M^{ci}, M^{cj} > = 0$ if $i \neq j$, the stable subspace, generated by $M^{ci}, \ldots, M^{cm}$ in the space of locally square integrable martingales, consists of all sums of stochastic integrals with respect to the M^{ci}. Therefore, there exists an m-dimensional predictable process $H = (H^1, \ldots, H^m)$, and a continuous local martingale N^c, such that

$$Y^c = \sum_{i=j}^{m} H^i.M^{ci} + N^c = H.M^c + N^c$$

and $\quad < M^{ci}, N^c > = 0$ for $i=1,\ldots,m$.

Now $\Delta Y = \Delta Y^d$. Let us consider those jumps of Y which occur on $D^p \setminus D$. In fact, because $\Delta Y^d = 0$ on D this is the same as considering the jumps of Y which occur on D^p. We know that $D^p = \cup [\![T_n]\!]$, for some countable family of predictable stopping times T_n. The jump of Y at T_n is $\Delta Y_{T_n} = Y_{T_n} - Y_{T_n -}$, and $Y_{T_n -} = E[Y_{T_n} | F_{T_n -}]$.

The process $M_n^d(t) = \Delta Y_{T_n} I_{t \geq T_n}$ is a martingale on (Ω, F_t, P), and $M_t^d = \sum_n M_n^d(t)$ is a discontinuous local martingale whose jumps are ΔY_{T_n} at the times T_n. In fact M^d is the term X^3 in the decomposition given in Theorem 4 of [9].

Writing $N^d = Y^d - M^d$ we see that N^d is a discontinuous local martingale such that $\Delta N^d = 0$ on $D^p \cup D$. Summarizing the above, therefore, we have the following result:

THEOREM 3.5. Suppose M is a local martingale on (Ω, F_t, P). Then, with the above notation,

$$M_t = W*(\mu - \nu)_t + V*\mu_t + \sum_n \Delta Y_{T_n} I_{t \geq T_n} + H.M_t^c + N_t^c + N_t^d .$$

Here $\langle M^{ci}, N^c \rangle = 0$, $i = 1, \ldots, m$

and $\Delta N^d = 0$ on $D^p \cup D$.

4. ADMISSIBLE CONTROLS

Suppose the space of control values is a compact metric space U, with the Borel σ-field $\mathcal{U}$. Let ϕ denote a $P \times \mathcal{U}$ measurable function from $\Omega \times [o,1] \times U$ to $(R^m, \mathcal{B})$, and ψ denote a $\tilde{P} \times \mathcal{U}$ measurable function from $\tilde{\Omega} \times U$ to $(R, \mathcal{B})$. A control function u is defined to be a predictable function from $(\Omega \times [o,1], P)$ to $(U, \mathcal{U})$. Write ϕ_s^u for $\phi(\omega, s, u(\omega, s))$ and ψ_s^u for $\psi(\omega, s, x, u(\omega, s))$.

DEFINITION 4.1. A control function $u(\omega, s)$ is called an admissible control over the time interval $[r,t] \subset [o,1]$ if

i) for $\sigma \leq t$ the stochastic integrals

$$N_\sigma^c(u) = \int_{[r,\sigma]} \phi_s^u \, dM_s^c = \sum_1^m \int_{[r,\sigma]} \phi_s^{iu} \, dM_s^{ci}$$

and

$$N_\sigma^d(u) = \int_{[r,\sigma] \times R^m} \psi_s^u \, d(\mu - \nu) = \psi^u*(\mu - \nu)_\sigma - \psi^u*(\mu - \nu)_r,$$

are square integrable martingales,

ii) $\Delta N_s^d(u) = (\psi_s^u I_D(s) - \hat{\psi}_s^u) > -1$ a.s.

for $s \in [r,t]$,

iii) if $\varepsilon(N_s(u))$ denotes the martingale exponential of $N_s(u) = N_s^c(u) + N_s^d(u)$

then $E[\varepsilon(N_t(u)) | F_r] = 1$ a.s.

Write N_r^t for the set of admissible controls over $[r,t]$, and N for N_o^1

REMARKS 4.2. By construction, $N^c(u)$ is the continuous part of the martingale $N(u)$, and $N^d(u)$ is the discontinuous part. From the exponential formula of Doléans-Dade [4]:

$$\varepsilon(N_\sigma(u)) = exp(N_\sigma(u) - \tfrac{1}{2}\sum_1^m \int_{[r,\sigma]} (\phi_s^{iu})^2 d < M^{ci},M^{ci} >_s) \prod_{s \le \sigma} (1+\Delta N_s^d(u))e^{-N_s^d(u)}.$$

Note that $\Delta N_s^d(u)$ is given in (ii) above.

DEFINITION 4.3. If $u \in N$ is an admissible control, a new probability measure P^u can be defined on (Ω,F) by putting

$$\frac{dP^u}{dP} = \varepsilon(N_1(u)).$$

Write E_u for the expectation with respect to P^u . From condition 4.1.(ii), $\varepsilon(N_1(u)) \neq 0$ *a.s.*, so P is also absolutely continuous with respect to P^u.

Finally, we shall suppose that the set of admissible controls is closed under concatenation , that is if $u \in N_r^s$, and $v \in N_s^t$, then the control $w \in N_r^t$,

where $$w(\omega,\sigma) = \begin{cases} u(\omega,\sigma) & r \le \sigma \le s \\ v(\omega,\sigma) & s < \sigma \le t \end{cases}$$

5. THE COST PROCESS

Suppose g is a bounded measurable function defined on R^m and let the total cost associated with the process be $g(X_1)$.

If a control u is used up to time t , and a control v is used from time t to time 1 , so that a control $w \in N$, constructed as above, is used over the whole time interval, then the expected final cost, given F_t , is

$$E_w[g(X_1)|F_t].$$

From §24.4 of Loève [13], this is

$$E[\varepsilon_o^t(N_t(u))\varepsilon_t^1(N_1(v))g(X_1)|F_t].\ E[\varepsilon_o^t(N_t(u))\varepsilon_t^1(N_1(v))|F_t]^{-1}$$

$$= E[\varepsilon_t^1(N_1(v))g(X_1)|F_t],$$

because $\varepsilon_o^t(N_t(u))$ is F_t measurable and $E[\varepsilon_t^1(N_1(v))|F_t] = 1$ *a.s.*

Therefore ,the expected final cost, given F_t, is independent of the control used up to time t.

DEFINITION 5.1. Define

$$Y_t = \inf_{v \in N_t^1} E[\varepsilon_t^1(N_1(v))g(X_1)|F_t].$$

Because $L^1(\Omega, F_t, P)$ is a complete lattice, this minimum exists and is an F_t adapted process.

The admissible controls are F_t adapted, in fact predictable, so the optimality principle of Striebel [15], (see also [2]), applies to this control problem and states:

THEOREM 5.2.

i) $u^* \in N$ is optimal if and only if Y_t is a martingale on (Ω, F_t, P^{u^*}).

ii) in general, for $u \in N$ Y_t is a submartingale on (Ω, F_t, P^u).

The local characteristics of the semimartingale X under a measure P^u will now be described. Recall that, for a locally square integrable martingale M on (Ω, F, P), $< M,M >^P$ is the unique predictable increasing process such that $M^2 - < M,M >^P$ is a locally square integrable martingale. We write P to indicate the quadratic variation process is associated with measure P. The continuous martingales M^{ci}, $i = 1, \dots m$, that occur in the decomposition of X are certainly locally square integrable and from [14] , page 379, we have the following result:

PROPOSITION 6.1. Under the measure P^u, M^{uci}, $i = 1,\dots,m$, is a continuous local martingale where

$$M_t^{uci} = M_t^{ci} - \int_{[o,t]} \phi_s^{iu} \, d < M^{ci}, M^{ci} >_s^P.$$

Furthermore,

$$< M^{uci}, M^{ucj} >^{P^u} = < M^{ci}, M^{cj} >^P = 0 \quad \text{if } i \neq j.$$

From theorem 3.8. of [11] we have the following description:

PROPOSITION 6.2 Suppose, as above, that ν is the dual predictable projection of μ under the measure P. Then, under measure P^u, ν^u is the dual predictable projection, where $\nu^u = \nu + \psi^u \nu - \hat{\psi}^u \nu = \nu + \psi^u \nu^c + \Sigma(\psi^u - \hat{\psi}^u)\nu^d$.

NOTATION 6.3. For $u \in N$ and ψ^u as in Definition 4.1. write

$$\tilde{\psi}_s^u = \psi_s^u I_D(s) - \hat{\psi}_s^u = \Delta N_s^d .$$

Then $\tilde{\psi}^u_s = 0$ for $(\omega,s) \notin D^p \cup D$.

From now on we shall make the following hypothesis:

HYPOTHESIS 6.4. There is an optimal control $u^* \in N$.

From Theorems 3.5 and 5.2., therefore, we have the following representation for the minimum remaining cost process Y_t.

THEOREM 6.5. On (Ω, F_t, P^{u^*}) the process Y_t is a martingale, and so

$$Y_t = Y_0 + W*(\mu - \nu^{u^*})_t + V*\mu_t + \Lambda_t$$
$$+ H.M_t^{u^*c} + N_t^c + N_t^d$$

Here $M^{u^*c} = (M^{u^*c1},\dots,M^{u^*cm})$, $H = (H^1,\dots,H^m)$ and from 6.1.

$$M_t^{u^*ci} = M_t^{ci} - \int_{[o,t]} \phi_s^{iu} d < M^{ci}, M^{ci} >_s^P .$$

Also $\nu^{u^*} = \nu + \psi^{u^*}\nu - \tilde{\psi}^{u^*}\nu$ and $W \in G_{loc}^{P^{u^*}}(\mu)$.

$$V \in H_{loc}^{P^{u^*}}(\mu), \text{ and } \Lambda_t = \sum_n \Delta Q_{T_n} I_{t \geq T_n}$$

where $\Delta Q_{T_n} = Q_{T_n} - Q_{T_n-} = Q_{T_n} - E_{u^*}[Q_{T_n} | F_{T_n-}]$,

and T_n is a countable family of predictable stopping times, the union of whose graphs is $D^p \setminus D$. (Because the measures are equivalent, this is true for all P^u.)

$< M^{u^*ci}, N^c >^{P^{u^*}} = 0$ for $i=1,\dots,m$ and $\Delta N^d = 0$ on $D^p \cup D$. (The set D is the same under all measures P^u, as is the set $D^p \setminus D$.)
We now investigate the process Y_t under the other measures P^u.

PROPOSITION 6.6. N^c is a continuous local martingale under any other measure P^u.

PROOF. As in Proposition 6.1., the predictable quadratic variation of a continuous local martingale is independent of the measure, so writing $\tilde{N}^c$ for the unique continuous local martingale part of N^c, when N^c is considered as a semimartingale under P, we have

$$< M^{u^*ci}, N^c >^{P^{u^*}} = < M^{ci}, \tilde{N}^c >^P = 0 . \qquad i=1,..,m.$$

Therefore, by 6.1.

$$\tilde{N}_t^c - \sum_1^m \int_{[o,t]} \phi_s^{iu^*} d < M^{ci}, \tilde{N}^c >_s^P = \tilde{N}_t^c$$

is the continuous local martingale part of $\tilde{N}^c$, when $\tilde{N}^c$ is considered a semimartingale under P^{u^*}.

By uniqueness, this must be N^c. So $N^c = \tilde{N}^c$, and N^c is a continuous local martingale under P. For any other $u \in N$

$$N_t^c - \sum_1^m \int_{[o,t]} \phi_s^{iu}\, d < M^{ci}, N^c >_s^P = N_t^c$$

is a continuous local martingale on (Ω, F_t, P^u).

PROPOSITION 6.7. Recalling that

$$\frac{dP^{u*}}{dP} = \varepsilon(N_1(u^*)) \neq 0 \ a.s.$$

we have $\Delta R_s^{-1} = -\Psi_s^{u*} R_s^{-1}$ where $R_s = \varepsilon(N_s(u^*))$, as given in 4.2.

PROOF. From the differentiation formula

$$\frac{1}{R_t} = 1 - \int_{[o,t]} \frac{dR_s}{R_{s-}^2} + \int_{[o,t]} \frac{d < R^c, R^c >_s^P}{R_{s-}^3}$$

$$+ \sum_{o<s\leq t} \left(\frac{1}{R_s} - \frac{1}{R_{s-}} + \frac{\Delta R_s}{R_{s-}^2}\right).$$

Now

$$R_t = 1 + \sum_1^m \int_{[o,t]} R_{s-} \phi_s^{iu*} dM_s^{ci} + (R_{s-}\Psi_{s-}^{u*}) * (\mu - \nu)_t$$

so

$$\Delta R_s = R_{s-}\Psi^{u*}, \text{ and } \Delta R_s = 0 \text{ for } (\omega, s) \notin D^P \cup D.$$

$$\left(\frac{1}{R_s} - \frac{1}{R_{s-}} + \frac{\Delta R_s}{R_{s-}^2}\right) = \frac{\Delta R_s^2}{R_{s-}^2 R_s} = \frac{(\Psi_s^{u*})^2}{R_s}$$

so finally

$$\Delta R_s^{-1} = -\frac{\Delta R_s}{R_{s-}} + \frac{\Delta R_s^2}{R_s^2 R_s} = -\Psi_s^{u*} R_s^{-1}.$$

Again we see that $\Delta R_s^{-1} = 0$ if $(\omega, s) \notin D^P \cup D$.

COROLLARY 6.8. N^d is a local martingale under any other measure P^u.

PROOF. From Proposition 6.7.

$$\Delta R_s^{-1} = 0 \quad (\omega, s) \notin D^P \cup D.$$

Therefore, $[N^d, R^{-1}]_t = \sum_{s\leq t} \Delta N_s^d \Delta R_s^{-1} = 0$, because $\Delta N^d = 0$ on $D^P \cup D$.

The process $B_t = \int_{[o,t]} R_s \, d[N^d, R^{-1}]_s$ of [14] page 377 is, therefore, zero,

so by Theorem 24 of [14] N^d is a local martingale under P.

Because $\Delta(\varepsilon(N(u)))_s = \Psi_s^u$ we have $[N^d, \varepsilon(N(u))] = 0$,

and the same theorem implies that N^d is a martingale under P^u for any $u \in N$.

7. A MINIMUM PRINCIPLE

In this section it is shown that an optimal control must minimize a certain Hamiltonian associated with the system.

THEOREM 7.1. Suppose u^* is an optimal control. Then there are:

a) predictable processes α, H^i, β_i, $i=1,\dots,m$,

b) a $\tilde{P}$ measurable process W,

c) a family of transition probability measures $B^c(\omega,t,dx)$ from $(\Omega \times [0,\infty],P)$

d) a positive measure ρ on $(\Omega \times [0,\infty],P)$, and

e) an optional process Q,

such that 1) almost surely $(d\rho)$ u^* minimizes the Hamiltonian

$$\sum_1^m \beta_i H^i (\phi^{iu} - \phi^{iu^*}) + \int_{R^m} \alpha W(\psi^u - \psi^{u^*}) B^c(\omega,t,dx)$$

and 2) on the set $J = D^p$, u^* minimizes the Hamiltonian

$$\widehat{(W_s + Q_s)}\, \widehat{(\psi_s^u - \psi_s^{u^*})} - (\hat{W}_s + \hat{Q}_s)(\hat{\psi}_s^u - \hat{\psi}_s^{u^*}).$$

PROOF. Under an optimal control u^* the minimum remaining cost Y_t is a martingale on (Ω, F_t, P^{u^*}) and we know, from Theorem 6.5., that Y_t has a representation:

$$Y_t = Y_o + Y_t^c + Y_t^d$$

where $\quad Y_t^c = H.M_t^{u^*c} + N_t^c \qquad (7.1)$

and $\quad Y_t^d = W*(\mu - \nu^{u^*})_t + V*\mu_t + \Lambda_t + N_t^d. \qquad (7.2)$

For any other control $u \in N$, Y_t is a submartingale on (Ω, F_t, P^u), and so Y_t has a unique Doob-Meyer decomposition

$$Y_t = Y_o + M_t^u + A_t^u,$$

into the sum of a martingale M_t^u and a predictable increasing process A_t^u. However, we can re-write the right hand side of (7.1) as:

$$Y_t^c = H.M_t^{uc} + \sum_{i=1}^m \int_{[0,t]} H^i . (\phi^{iu} - \phi^{iu^*}) d < M^{ci}, M^{ci} >_s^P + N_t^c.$$

Here $\quad M_t^{uci} = M_t^{ci} - \int_{[0,t]} \phi_s^{iu}\, d < M^{ci}, M^{ci} >_s^P$

and N_t^c are martingales under the measure P^u.

Turning to the discontinuous martingale Y_t^d we know from Corollary 6.8 that N_t^d is a martingale under any other measure P^u. Furthermore, N_t^d only has jumps on the complement of $D^p \cup D$.

Write $\quad K_t = W*(\mu - \nu^{u^*})_t + V*\mu_t + \Lambda_t$

and $\quad Z_t = E_{u^*}[\frac{dP^u}{dP^{u^*}} | F_t]$

$$= \varepsilon\,(N_t\,(u)).\ \varepsilon(N_t(u^*))^{-1}.$$

Then K_t only has jumps on $D^p \cup D$, equal to jumps of the minimum cost process Y_t. These jumps are, therefore, bounded. We also wish to introduce the P^{u^*} martingale

$$L_t = \int_0^t \frac{dZ_s}{Z_{s-}}\ .$$

Then the process

$$[K,L\,]_t = \sum_{s\le t} \Delta K_s \Delta\, L_s$$

is of locally integrable variation so, by Theorem 1-13 of [16] , its dual predictable projection $< K,L >_t^{P^{u^*}}$ exists.

Now $$\Delta\, L_s = Z_{s-}^{-1}\ \Delta\, Z_s$$

$$= Z_{s-}^{-1} . Z_{s-} . (\psi_s^u - \hat{\psi}_s^u - \psi_s^{u^*} + \hat{\psi}_s^{u^*})\ (1 + \psi_s^{u^*} - \hat{\psi}_s^{u^*})^{-1}$$

$$= (\psi_s^u - \hat{\psi}_s^u - \psi_s^{u^*} + \hat{\psi}_s^{u^*})\ (1 + \psi_s^{u^*} - \hat{\psi}_s^{u^*})^{-1}.$$

Write

$$[K\,,\,L\,]_t = A_t + B_t$$

where

$$A_t = \sum_{s\le t} I_{J'} . \Delta\, K_s \Delta\, L_s$$

$$B_t = \sum_{s\le t} I_{J'} \Delta K_s \Delta\, L_s\ .$$

On $J' = (D^p)'$ $\Delta\,\Lambda$ and $\hat{W}$ are zero, so the P^{u^*} dual predictable projection

$$A_t^3 = (I_{J'}\ \Delta\, L\,(W + V)*\ \mu)_t^3 = [M_\mu^{P^{u^*}}\ (I_{J'} . \Delta\, L\,(W + V)\ |\ \tilde{P}\ ]*\nu^{u^*} \qquad \text{by [8].}$$

Now $I_{J'}$ and $\Delta\, L$ are $\tilde{P}$ measurable Also, $M_\mu^{P^{u^*}}\ (W\ |\ \tilde{P}) = W$ and, by construction, $M_\mu^{P^{u^*}}\ (V\ |\ \tilde{P}) = 0$.

Therefore,

$$A_t^3 = (I_{J'} . W . \Delta\, L\,)\ *\ \nu^{u^*}\ .$$

But $$\nu^{u^*} = (1 + \psi^{u^*} - \psi^{u^*}) .\ \nu \qquad \text{and } I_{J'} . \nu = \nu^c$$

so

$$A_t^3 = W(\psi^u - \psi^{u^*})\ *\ \nu_t^c \quad (\text{ because } \hat{\psi}^u = \hat{\psi}^{u^*} = 0 \text{ on } J').$$

The set $J = D^p$ is the union of the graphs of a countable family of predictable stopping times $\{T_n\}$, and these can be chosen so that B_t is of locally integrable variation. Write B_t in the form

$$B_t = \sum_n C_n \, I_{[\![T_n, \infty [\![}, \text{ where } C_n = \Delta K_{T_n} . \Delta L_{T_n}$$

$$= (I_D . \hat{W}_{T_n} - W_{T_n} + I_D . V_{T_n} + \Delta \Lambda_{T_n}). \Delta L_{T_n} .$$

Then , from Dellacherie [3], the P^{u*} dual predictable projection

$$B_t^3 = \sum_n E_{u*} [C_n \mid F_{T_n -}]. I_{[\![T_n, \infty [\![} .$$

Now

$$E_{u*} [I_D V_{T_n} \mid F_{T_n -}] = E_{u*} [E_{u*} [I_D V_{T_n} \mid F_{T_n -} \vee \sigma(\Delta X_{T_n}) \mid F_{T_n -}] = 0,$$

so

$$E_{u*} [C_n \mid F_{T_n -}] = \int_{R^m} (I_D W_{T_n} - \hat{W}_{T_n} + \Delta \Lambda_{T_n}) (\psi^u_{T_n} - \hat{\psi}^u_{T_n} - \psi^{u*}_{T_n} + \hat{\psi}^{u*}_{T_n}). \nu(\{T_n\}, dx)$$

from Lemma (2.2) of [8]. Recalling that $\Delta \Lambda_{T_n} = Q_{T_n} - Q_{T_n -}$ this is equal to

$$\Gamma = \widehat{W\psi^u} - \widehat{W\psi^{u*}} - \hat{W} \hat{\psi}^u + \hat{W} \hat{\psi}^{u*} + \widehat{Q\psi^u} - \widehat{Q\psi^{u*}} - \hat{Q} \hat{\psi}^u + \hat{Q} \hat{\psi}^{u*} \text{ evaluated at } T_n .$$

Therefore,

$$B_t^3 = \sum_n \Gamma_{T_n} I_{t \geq T_n} = \sum_{s \leq t} \Gamma_s .$$

The P^{u*} dual predictable projection of $[K, L]_t$ is $A_t^3 + B_t^3$

$$= W(\psi^u - \psi^{u*}) * \nu_t^c + \sum_{s \leq t} \Gamma_s ,$$

so from Theorem 24 of [14] $K_t^u = K_t - A_t^3 - B_t^3$ is a P^u local martingale.

Write

$$Y_t = Y_o + H.M_t^{uc} + N_t^c + K_t^u + N_t^d + \sum_{i=1}^m \int_{[o,t]} H^i . (\phi^{iu} - \phi^{iu*}) d\langle M^{ci}, M^{ci} \rangle_s^P + A_t^3 + B_t^3 .$$

The first four processes in this decomposition are local P^u martingales; the final three processes are predictable. Consequently, under the measure P^u, the process Y_t is a special semimartingale in the sense of Meyer [14]. This decomposition into the sum of a local martingale and a predictable process is then unique, and so must be the same as the Doob-Meyer decomposition. The sum of the final three terms above is, therefore, the increasing process

$$A_t^u = \sum_{i=1}^m \int_{[o,t]} H^i . (\phi^{iu} - \phi^{iu*}) d\langle M^{ci}, M^{ci} \rangle_s^P + W(\psi^u - \psi^{u*}) * \nu_t^c + \sum_{s \leq t} \Gamma_s .$$

As in Jacod [7], we can find a $\tilde{P}$ measureable partition $\tilde{\Omega}_n$ of $\tilde{\Omega}$, such that $M_\mu^P (\tilde{\Omega}_n) < \infty$ for each n.

Write $\nu_n^c = I_{\Omega_n} . \nu^c$.

Then for each n, there is a family of transition probabilities B_n^c $(\omega, t; dx)$, from

$(\Omega \times [0,\infty], P)$ to R^m, such that

$$d\nu_n^c = B_n^c \cdot dA_n^c \quad , \text{ where } A_n^c(\omega, ds) = \nu_n^c(\omega, ds, R^m).$$

For any (ω, t) only one transition probability B_n^c will be non-zero, so we can write $B^c = \sum_n B_n^c$.

Consider the measure

$$\rho(\omega, ds) = \sum_{i=1}^{m} d<M^{ci}, M^{ci}> + dA^c \text{ where } dA^c = \sum_n dA_n^c .$$

Because dA^c is absolutely continuous with respect to ρ there is a Radon-Nikodym derivative α such that $dA^c = \alpha d\rho$. Similarly, for $i=1,\dots,m$ $d<M^{ci}, M^{ci}>$ is absolutely continuous with respect to $d\rho$, so there are Radon-Nikodym dervivatives β_i such that $d<M^{ci}, M^{ci}> = \beta_i d\rho$. We can, therefore, write the increasing process as

$$A_t^u = \sum_{i=1} \int_{[0,t]} H^i . (\phi^{iu} - \phi^{iu*}) \beta_i d\rho + \int_{[0,t]} \int_{R^m} W(\psi^u - \psi^{u*}) B^c(\omega, s; dx) d\rho$$

$$+ \sum_{s \le t} [\widehat{(W_s + Q_q)(\psi_s^u - \psi_s^{u*})} - (\hat{W}_s + \hat{Q}_s)(\hat{\psi}_s^u - \hat{\psi}_s^{u*})]$$

The integrand (and summands) in the increasing process A^u must be non - negative, so the minimum principle takes the final form:

i) almost surely $d\rho$ the optimal control minimizes the Hamiltonian

$$\sum_{i=1}^{m} \beta_i . H_s^i (\phi_s^{iu} - \phi_s^{iu*}) + \int_{R^m} \alpha_s W_s(\psi_s^u - \psi_s^{u*}) B^c(\omega, s; dx).$$

ii) on the set $J = D^p$ the optimal control minimizes the Hamiltonian

$$\widehat{(W_s + Q_s)(\psi_s^u - \psi_s^{u*})} - (\hat{W}_s + \hat{Q}_s)(\hat{\psi}_s^u - \hat{\psi}_s^{u*}).$$

ACKNOWLEDGEMENT: The author is indebted to Jean Jacod for carefully reading this work, and for many valuable comments.

REFERENCES

1. DAVIS, M.H.A. and ELLIOTT, R.J. Optimal Control of a jump process. Zeits für Wahrs. 40, 183-202 (1977).

2. DAVIS, M.H.A. and VARAIYA, P. Dynamic programming conditions for partially observable systems. S.I.A.M. Jour. Control 11, 226-261 (1973).

3. DELLACHERIE, C. Capacités et processus stochastiques. Berlin-Heidelberg-New York. Springer 1972.

4. DOLEANS-DADE, C. Quelques applications de la formule de changement de variables pour les semimartingales, Zeits. für Wahrs. 16, 181-190 (1970).

5. ELLIOTT, R.J. A stochastic mimimum principle, Bull. Amer. Math Soc. 82, 944-946 (1976).

6. ELLIOTT, R.J. The optimal control of a semimartingale. Proceedings of the Third Kingston Conference on Differential Games and Control Theory. To be published by M. Dekker, New York.

7. JACOD, J. Multivariate point processes, predictable projections, Radon-Nikodym derivatives, representation of martingales. Zeits für Wahrs 31. 235-253 (1975).

8. JACOD, J. Un théorème de représentation pour les martingales discontinus. Zeits für Wahrs 34, 225-245 (1976).

9. JACOD, J. Sur la construction des intégrales stochastiques et les sous-espaces stables de martingales. Sem. Prob. Stasbourg Xl. Lecture Notes in Math. 581. Springer-Verlag, Berlin-Heidelberg-New York. 1977.

10. JACOD, J. A general theorem of representation for martingales. Proceedings of Symposia on Pure Mathematics, Vol. 31, American Math. Society, Providence R.I. 1977.

11. JACOD, J. and MEMIN, J. Caractéristiques locales et conditions de continuité absolue pour les semi-martingales. Zeits für Wahrs. 35, 1-37 (1976).

12. JACOD, J. and YOR, M. Etude des solutions extrémales et représentation intégrale de solutions pour certains problèmes de martingales. Zeits für Wahrs. 38, 83-125 (1977).

13. LOEVE. M. Probability theory, 3rd. Ed. Van Nostrand. Princeton 1963.

14. MEYER, P. A. Un cours sur le intégrales stochastiques. Sem. Prob. Strasbourg X. Lecture Notes in Math. 511 Springer-Verlag. Berlin-Heidelberg-New York.1976.

15. STRIEBEL, C. Martingale conditions for the optimal control of continuous time stochastic systems. International Workshop on Stochastic Filtering and Control, Los Angeles, May 1974.

16. YOEURP, C. Decompositions des martingales locales et formules exponentielles. Sem. Prob. Strasbourg X. Lecture Notes in Math. 511. Springer-Verlag Berlin-Heidelberg-New York. 1976.

INTERACTION BETWEEN STOCHASTIC DIFFERENTIAL EQUATIONS AND PARTIAL DIFFERENTIAL EQUATIONS

Avner Friedman
Northwestern University
Evanston, Ill. 60201/USA

1. DEGENERATE ELLIPTIC EQUATIONS

Consider the differential operator

$$Lu \equiv \frac{1}{2} \sum_{i,j=1}^{n} a_{ij}(x) \frac{\partial^2 u}{\partial x_i \partial x_j} + \sum_{i=1}^{n} b_i(x) \frac{\partial u}{\partial x_i} + c(x)u \tag{1.1}$$

with coefficients which are Lipschitz continuous in the closure $\bar{D}$ of a bounded domain D in R^n, and assume that

$$\sum_{i,j=1}^{n} a_{ij}(x)\xi_i\xi_j \geq \mu|\xi|^2 \qquad (x \in \bar{D},\ \xi \in R^n,\ \mu > 0)$$

$$c(x) \leq 0.$$

Let f, ϕ be functions defined on $\bar{D}$ and ∂D, respectively, f Hölder continuous and ϕ continuous; here ∂D, the boundary of D, is assumed to belong to C^3. Consider the Dirichlet problem

$$Lu = f \quad \text{in } D, \tag{1.2}$$

$$u = \phi \quad \text{on } \partial D. \tag{1.3}$$

It is well known that this problem has a unique classical solution.

Since the matrix $a(x) = (a_{ij}(x))$ is positive definite and uniformly Lipschitz continuous in $\bar{D}$, there exists a square matrix $\sigma(x) = (\sigma_{ij}(x))$ which is symmetric, positive definite and uniformly Lipschitz continuous in $\bar{D}$ such that $a(x) = \sigma^2(x)$. We extend $\sigma(x)$ into R^n so that it remains uniformly Lipschitz continuous; $b(x) = (b_1(x),\dots,b_n(x))$ is extended similarly into R^n.

Consider the system of stochastic differential equations

$$d\xi(t) = \sigma(\xi(t))dw(t) + b(\xi(t))dt. \tag{1.4}$$

Denote by τ the exit time of $\xi(t)$ from D. It is easy to show that $E_x\tau < \infty$ for any $x \in D$. Using Ito's formula one can easily prove:

Theorem 1.1. The solution u of (1.3) can be represented in the form

$$u(x) = E_x\phi(\xi(\tau))e^{\int_0^\tau c(\xi(s))ds} - E_x \int_0^\tau f(\xi(t))e^{\int_0^t c(\xi(s))ds} . \tag{1.5}$$

Consider now the case where the operator L is degenerate, i.e., $(a_{ij}(x))$ is positive semi-definite. If $a_{ij} \in C^2(U)$, U a neighborhood of $\bar{D}$, then there still exists a uniformly Lipschitz symmetric matrix $\sigma(x)$ for $x \in R^n$ such that $a(x) = \sigma^2(x)$ [17]. The formula (1.5) then defines a function $u(x)$, and the question arises: in what sense is $u(x)$ a solution (or the solution) of the Dirichlet problem (1.2),(1.3)?

Consider for example the degenerate elliptic equations in R^2:

(1.6) $$u_{xx} - u_t = 0,$$

(1.7) $$u_{xx} + u_t = 0,$$

and take D to be the rectangle $-1 < x < 1$, $0 < t < T$. It is well known that the correct boundary conditions for (1.6) are

$$u = \phi \quad \text{on } x = \pm 1, \text{ and on } t = 0,$$

whereas for (1.7)

$$u = \phi \quad \text{on } x = \pm 1, \text{ and on } t = T.$$

To study the general case we divide the boundary ∂D into four sets:

$$\Sigma_3 = \{x \in \partial D;\ \Sigma a_{ij}\nu_i\nu_j > 0\},$$

$$\Sigma_2 = \{x \in \partial D;\ \Sigma a_{ij}\nu_i\nu_j = 0,\ \Sigma b_i\rho_{x_i} + \tfrac{1}{2}\Sigma a_{ij}\rho_{x_ix_j} < 0\},$$

$$\Sigma_1 = \{x \in \partial D;\ \Sigma a_{ij}\nu_i\nu_j = 0,\ \Sigma b_i\rho_{x_i} + \tfrac{1}{2}\Sigma a_{ij}\rho_{x_ix_j} > 0\},$$

$$\Sigma_0 = \{x \in \partial D;\ \Sigma a_{ij}\nu_i\nu_j = 0,\ \Sigma b_i\rho_{x_i} + \tfrac{1}{2}\Sigma a_{ij}\rho_{x_ix_j} = 0\},$$

where $\rho(x) = \mathrm{dist}(x,\partial D)$, $\nu = (\nu_1,\ldots,\nu_n)$ the inward normal ($\nu = \mathrm{grad}\,\rho$ on ∂D). These sets can be given probabilistic interpretation.

A point $x^0 \in \partial D$ is called a <u>regular point</u> if for any $\delta > 0$

$$\lim_{\substack{x \to x^0 \\ x \in D}} P_x\{\tau < \infty;\ |\xi(\tau) - x^0| < \delta\} = 1.$$

It can be shown [30] that every point $x^0 \in \Sigma_2 \cup \Sigma_3$ is regular. On the other hand, the set $\mathrm{int}(\Sigma_0 \cup \Sigma_1)$ is unattainable from D, i.e.,

$$P_x\{\tau < \infty,\ \xi(\tau) \in \mathrm{int}(\Sigma_0 \cup \Sigma_1)\} = 0 \quad \text{if } x \in D.$$

The set Σ_1 is not even stable [a set $\Gamma \subset \partial D$ is <u>stable</u> if for any D-neighborhood U of Γ and for any $\varepsilon > 0$ there is a D-neighborhood U_ε of Γ such that

$$P_x\{\xi(t) \in U \quad \text{for all } 0 \le t < \tau\} > 1 - \varepsilon$$

for all $x \in U_\varepsilon$]; see [21], [22].

In the example of (1.6), the boundary $x = \pm 1$ belongs to Σ_3, the boundary $t = 0$ lies in Σ_2, and the boundary $t = T$ is contained in Σ_1.

The above considerations indicate that if $\tau < \infty$ then $\xi(\tau)$ should lie in $\overline{\Sigma_2 \cup \Sigma_3}$ whereas if $\tau = \infty$ then $\xi(t)$ either approaches Σ_0 or stays in D away from the boundary.

It is often more convenient to work with τ' = hitting time of $R^n \setminus \bar{D}$ instead of τ. It is known [32] that $P_x(\tau' = \tau) = 1$ a.e. in $x \in D$.

Theorem 1.2 [32]. _Assume that either_ $\sup_{x \in D} E_x \tau' < \infty$ _or_ $c(x) \leq -\alpha < 0$. _Then the function_ $u(x)$ _defined by_ (1.5) _with_ τ _replaced by_ τ' _is the unique solution of_

$$u \in L^\infty(D),$$

$$Lu = f \quad \text{weakly},$$

$$u(x) \to \phi(x^0) \quad \text{if } x \to x^0,\ x^0 \in \Sigma_2 \cup \Sigma_3.$$

Further, $u(x)$ _is continuous a.e. in_ D; _if_ $\Sigma_2 \cup \Sigma_3$ _is a closed set then_ $P_x(\tau' = \tau) = 1$ _and_ $u(x)$ _is continuous for all_ $x \in D$.

It may be recalled that the traditional methods of elliptic estimates and regularization used to study degenerate equations make very restrictive assumptions on the type of degeneracy, on the smoothness of the coefficients, or on $c(x)$ (assuming $c(x) \leq -\alpha$, α "sufficiently large"); see [26] and the references given there. These methods however establish higher regularity of the solution.

A more delicate situation arises when $P_x(\tau = \infty) > 0$ whereas $c(x) \leq 0$ or $c(x) \equiv 0$; in this case the integrand in (1.5), on the set $\tau = \infty$, is not "killed" by $\exp\left[\int_0^\infty c(\xi(s))ds\right]$, and thus one is faced with the problem of studying the asymptotic behavior of paths $\xi(t)$ that remain in D for all times. If such paths converge to a boundary point ζ, then ζ must necessarily belong to Σ_0, whereas if some paths remain in a compact subset of D (and, say, $c \equiv 0$) then the Dirichlet problem does not make sense.

Work in this direction was done in [22],[31]; see also [21]. We shall describe a special case for $n = 2$.

Assume that $\Sigma_2 \cup \Sigma_3$, Σ_1, Σ_0 each consists of a finite number of C^3 curves; further, there exists a function $R(x)$ in $C^2(\bar{D})$ coinciding with $\text{dist}(x,\Sigma_2 \cup \Sigma_3)$ and with $1-\text{dist}(x,\Sigma_1)$ in ε_0-neighborhoods of $\Sigma_2 \cup \Sigma_3$ and Σ_1 respectively, $\varepsilon_0 < R < 1-\varepsilon_0$ elsewhere in D, and grad $R(x) \neq 0$ except for a finite number of points in D where $\Sigma a_{ij} R_{x_i x_j} > 0$.

We also assume that

$$(a_{ij}(x)) \text{ is positive definite in } D, \quad c(x) \equiv 0.$$

Set

$$\mathcal{A}_\rho(x) = \frac{1}{2} \Sigma a_{ij} \rho_{x_i} \rho_{x_j},$$

$$\mathcal{B}_\rho(x) = \Sigma b_i \rho_{x_i} + \frac{1}{2} \Sigma a_{ij} \rho_{x_i x_j}$$

$$Q_\rho = \frac{1}{\rho}\left(\mathcal{B}_\rho - \frac{1}{\rho}\mathcal{A}_\rho\right)$$

where $\rho(x) = \text{dist}(x,\Sigma_0)$ and assume

$$Q_\rho(x) \leq -\theta < 0 \quad \text{if } \rho(x) \leq \varepsilon_1 \quad (\varepsilon_1 > 0).$$

We can represent Σ_0 in the form

$$x_1 = f(s), \quad x_2 = g(s) \quad (s = \text{length parameter}).$$

Introducing coordinates $y_1 = s$, $y_2 = \rho$, the stochastic system transforms into

$$dy_j = \sum_{k=1}^{2} \tilde{\sigma}_{jk}(y)dw_k + \tilde{b}_j(y)dt \qquad (j = 1,2).$$

Let

$$\tilde{\sigma}(s) = \left(\sum_k (\tilde{\sigma}_{1k}(s,0))^2\right)^{1/2}, \qquad \tilde{b}(s) = \tilde{b}_1(s,0)$$

and introduce the 1-dimensional elliptic operator

$$\tilde{L}_0 v = \frac{1}{2}\tilde{\sigma} v'' + \tilde{b}v'.$$

Suppose s_0 is a point of degeneracy, i.e., $\tilde{\sigma}(s_0) = 0$. If $b(s_0) > 0$ (< 0) we call s_0 a <u>positive shunt</u> (<u>negative shunt</u>); if $b(s_0) = 0$ and

$$Q_0(s_0) \equiv \lim_{t\to s_0}\left[\frac{\tilde{b}(t)}{t-s_0} - \frac{\tilde{\sigma}^2(t)}{(t-s_0)^2}\right] < 0$$

then we call s_0 a <u>stable trap</u>.

We now assume that on Σ_0 there exist a finite number of stable traps $\zeta_1,\ldots,\zeta_m$ and between each two ζ_i, ζ_{i+1} $\tilde{L}_0$ has a finite number of points of degeneracy, all being either positive shunts or negative shunts.

<u>Theorem 1.3</u>. <u>Under the foregoing assumptions, for any continuous function</u> ϕ <u>on</u> $\Sigma_2 \cup \Sigma_3$ <u>and for any given numbers</u> $g_1,\ldots,g_m$ <u>there exists a unique classical solution</u> u <u>of</u>

(1.8) $$Lu = 0 \quad \underline{\text{in}}\ D,$$

(1.9) $$u(x) \to \phi(x^0) \quad \underline{\text{if}}\ x \to x^0, \quad x^0 \in \Sigma_2 \cup \Sigma_3,$$

(1.10) $$u(x) \to g_i \quad \underline{\text{if}}\ x \to \zeta_i \quad (1 \leq i \leq m).$$

<u>The solution is given by</u>

(1.11) $$u(x) = E_x\{\phi(\xi(\tau)I_{\tau<\infty}\} + \sum_{i=1}^{m} g_i P_x\{\tau = \infty,\ \xi(t) \to \zeta_i \ \underline{\text{if}}\ t \to \infty\}.$$

Under different conditions on the coefficients of L in a neighborhood of ζ_i one replaces (1.10) by

$$u(x) \to g_{i,1} \ \text{if } x \in V_{i,1},\ x \to \zeta_i, \quad u(x) \to g_{i,2} \ \text{if } x \in V_{i,2},\ x \to \zeta_i$$

where $V_{i,1}$, $V_{i,2}$ are two "half D-neighborhoods" of ζ_i.

It would be interesting to find sufficient conditions on a_{ij}, b_i which will imply that $\xi(t)$ visits any neighborhood of a portion Γ of Σ_0, spending roughly "equal time" near each point of Γ (for instance, spiralling around a closed curve Γ in a "regular" manner). In this case one would expect the condition

$$\int_\Gamma u = \gamma \qquad (\gamma \text{ a prescribed number})$$

to be added to the Dirichlet boundary conditions.

2. SINGULAR PERTURBATIONS

Consider the uniformly elliptic operator

$$L_\varepsilon u = \frac{\varepsilon}{2} \sum_{i,j=1}^{n} a_{ij}(x) \frac{\partial^2 u}{\partial x_i \partial x_j} + \sum_{i=1}^{n} b_i(x) \frac{\partial u}{\partial x_i} \qquad (\varepsilon > 0)$$

with uniformly Lipschitz continuous coefficients in a bounded domain D with C^2 boundary, and set $Lu = L_1 u$. We shall be interested in the following problems.

Problem 1. Denote by u_ε the solution of the Dirichlet problem

$$(2.1) \qquad \begin{aligned} L_\varepsilon u &= 0 \quad \text{in } D, \\ u_\varepsilon &= \phi \quad \text{on } \partial D. \end{aligned}$$

Find the behavior of $u_\varepsilon(x)$ as $\varepsilon \to 0$.

Problem 2. Denote by λ_ε, ϕ_ε the principal eigenvalue and eigenfunction of

$$(2.2) \qquad \begin{aligned} L_\varepsilon w &= -\lambda w \quad \text{in } D, \\ w &= 0 \quad \text{on } \partial D. \end{aligned}$$

Find the behavior of λ_ε, ϕ_ε as $\varepsilon \to 0$; here ϕ_ε is normalized by

$$\int_D \phi_\varepsilon^2 dx = 1, \qquad \phi_\varepsilon > 0 \quad \text{in } D.$$

The solution of (2.1) can be written in the form

$$(2.3) \qquad u_\varepsilon(x) = E_x \phi(\xi^\varepsilon(\tau^\varepsilon))$$

where

$$d\xi^\varepsilon(t) = \varepsilon^{1/2} \sigma(\xi^\varepsilon(t)) dw(t) + b(\xi^\varepsilon(t)) dt;$$

σ is the positive square root of (a_{ij}), and τ^ε is the exit time of $\xi^\varepsilon(t)$ from D. The behavior of τ^ε as $\varepsilon \to 0$ depends in a crucial way on the behavior of the solutions of the ordinary differential equations

$$(2.4) \qquad \frac{dx}{dt} = b(x), \quad x(0) \in D.$$

Suppose all solutions of (2.4) leave $\bar{D}$ in finite time τ_x^0 (depending on the initial point $x(0) = x$). Since

$$(2.5) \qquad \sup_{0 \le t \le T} |\xi_x^\varepsilon(t) - \xi_x^0(t)| \xrightarrow{P} 0 \quad \text{as } \varepsilon \to 0 \quad (\text{for any } T < \infty)$$

where $\xi_x^\varepsilon(t)$ $(\varepsilon \ge 0)$ is the solution $\xi^\varepsilon(t)$ with $\xi_x^\varepsilon(0) = x$, it follows that

$$u_\varepsilon(x) \to u_0(x) \equiv \phi(\xi_x^0(\tau_x^0)) \quad \text{as } \varepsilon \to 0.$$

Consider now the other extreme case where

$$(2.6) \qquad b(x)\cdot\nu(x) < 0 \quad (x \in \partial D)$$

where ν is the outward normal. This condition implies that the solutions of (2.4) cannot reach ∂D in any time $t > 0$. Thus $\tau_x^0 = \infty$.

We shall assume:

(A) There is a point $x^0 \in D$ such that every solution of (2.4) enters a given neighborhood of x^0 in finite time. Further, x^0 is a stable equilibrium point for (2.4) in the sense that $b(x^0) = 0$ and all the eigenvalues of the Jacobian matrix of $a^{-1}b$ at x^0 have negative real parts.

Denote by C_T the space of n-dimensional continuous functions $\zeta(t)$, $0 \le t \le T$, with the uniform topology.

Introduce the functional

$$I_T(\zeta) = \int_0^T \left(\left\|\frac{d\zeta(t)}{dt} - b(\zeta(t))\right\|_{a^{-1}(\zeta(t))}\right)^2 dt$$

if $\zeta(t)$ is absolutely continuous ($I_T(\zeta) = \infty$ if ζ is not absolutely continuous) and

$$\|X\|_{a^{-1}(x)} = (\Sigma\, a_{ij}^{-1}(x) X_i X_j)^{1/2}, \qquad (a_{ij}^{-1}(x)) = \text{inverse of } (a_{ij}(x)).$$

Let

$$V(y) = \inf I_T(\zeta), \quad y \in \partial D,$$

where ζ varies in C_T, $\zeta(0) = x^0$, $\zeta(T) = y$, $\zeta(t) \in D$ if $0 < t < T$, $0 < T < \infty$.

$V(y)$ is called a _quasi potential_. It measures in some sense the amount of work required to move a particle from x^0 to y against the dynamical system (2.4). It is easy to verify that $V(y)$ is Lipschitz continuous. Denote by Σ the set of points on ∂D where $V(y)$ (restricted to ∂D) achieves its minimum.

Theorem 2.1. _If_ $\phi \equiv$ const. $= C$ _on_ Σ, _then (under the conditions_ (2.6),(A)) $u_\varepsilon(x) \to C$ _uniformly on compact subsets of_ D.

This result is due to Ventcel and Freidlin [36]. Their proof is based on the following asymptotic estimates for any open set G and any closed set H in the space C_T:

(2.7) $$\varliminf_{\varepsilon\to 0} [2\varepsilon \log P_x^\varepsilon(G)] \geq -\inf_{\omega \in G_x} I_T(\omega),$$

(2.8) $$\varlimsup_{\varepsilon\to 0} [2\varepsilon \log P_x^\varepsilon(H)] \leq -\inf_{\omega \in H_x} I_T(\omega),$$

where P_x^ε is P_x induced by $\xi^\varepsilon(t)$ and

$$G_x = \{\omega \in G;\ \omega(0) = x\}, \quad H_x = \{\omega \in H;\ \omega(0) = x\}.$$

For proofs see also [21].

In case Σ does not reduce to one point, if $\phi \not\equiv$ const. on Σ, then the problem of computing the limit of u_ε (if existing) is still open, except in the case where L is selfadjoint, i.e.,

(2.9) $$b = \frac{1}{2} a\nabla\psi \quad \text{in } D, \quad \text{for some function } \psi.$$

In this case one can show that $V(y) = 4\psi(y)$ for $y \in \Sigma$. Consider the Dirichlet problem

(2.10) $$L_\varepsilon u + \varepsilon \sum_{i=1}^{n} b_i^1 \frac{\partial u}{\partial x_i} = 0 \quad \text{in } D,$$
$$u = \phi \quad \text{on } \partial D$$

where

$$b_j^1 = \frac{1}{2}\sum_{k=1}^{n} \frac{\partial a_{jk}}{\partial x_k} + \frac{1}{2}\sum_{k=1}^{n} a_{jk}\frac{\partial \psi^1}{\partial x_k} \quad \text{for some } \psi^1.$$

Notice that if a_{jk} = const. then we can take $\psi^1 = 0$, $b_j^1 = 0$ so that (2.10) reduces to (2.1).

Set

(2.11) $$C = \lim_{\varepsilon\to 0} \frac{\int_{\partial D} e^{\psi/\varepsilon} e^{\psi^1} (b\cdot\nu)\phi dS}{\int_{\partial D} e^{\psi/\varepsilon} e^{\psi^1} (b\cdot\nu) dS}$$

if this limit exists.

Theorem 2.2. *Let* (2.6),(A),(2.9) *hold. If* C *exists then the solution* u_ε *of* (2.10) *satisfies*: $u_\varepsilon(x) \to C$ *uniformly in compact subsets of* D.

For the Dirichlet problem

(2.12) $$\frac{\varepsilon}{2}\sum_{j,k=1}^{n} \frac{\partial}{\partial x_j}\left(a_{jk}\frac{\partial u}{\partial x_k}\right) + \sum_{j=1}^{n} b_j \frac{\partial u}{\partial x_j} = 0 \quad \text{in } D,$$
$$u = \phi \quad \text{on } \partial D$$

one can establish a similar result (if (2.6),(A),(2.9) hold) with

$$C = \lim_{\varepsilon \to 0} \frac{\int_{\partial D} e^{\psi/\varepsilon}(b\cdot\nu)\phi\, dS}{\int_{\partial D} e^{\psi/\varepsilon}(b\cdot\nu)\, dS} . \tag{2.13}$$

The formulas (2.11),(2.13) for lim u_ε were discovered heuristically by Matkovsky and Schuss [29] and proved by Kamin [24] and Devinatz and Friedman [14]. The latter proof exploits probabilistic considerations.

We now turn to Problem 2.

Lemma 2.3. *Define*

$$\Lambda = \sup\{\lambda \geq 0, \quad \sup_{x \in D} E_x e^{\lambda\tau} < \infty\}.$$

Then $\Lambda = \lambda_0$ *where* λ_0 *is the principal eigenvalue of* L.

For proof, see [21].

Theorem 2.4. *Let* (2.6) *and* (A) *hold. Then the principal eigenvalue* λ_ε *satisfies:*

$$-2\varepsilon \log \lambda_\varepsilon \to V^* \quad \text{if } \varepsilon \to 0 \qquad (V^* = \min_{y \in \partial D} V(y)). \tag{2.14}$$

Theorem 2.5. *If in addition to* (2.6),(A), $a_{ij} \equiv \delta_{ij}$ *and* $b = \nabla\psi$, *then the principal eigenfunction* ϕ_ε *satisfies*

$$\phi_\varepsilon(x) \to \text{const.} = C \quad \Big(\int_D C^2 dx = 1\Big) \tag{2.15}$$

uniformly in compact subsets of D *and boundedly in* D.

The proof of Theorem 2.4 (which was originally asserted by Ventcel [34]) is proved in Friedman [19]. The proof of Theorem 2.5 is due to Devinatz and Friedman [13]. The proofs use the Ventcel-Freidlin estimates (2.7),(2.8) and (in the case of Theorem 2.5) some elliptic estimates.

Theorem 2.5 holds for general a_{ij} provided $a^{-1}b = \nabla\psi$ in a neighborhood of x^0. It remains an open question to prove the theorem without this restriction.

In the case where all solutions of (2.4) leave $\bar{D}$ in a finite time, Ventcel [35] proved that

$$\lambda_\varepsilon \sim c/\varepsilon$$

where

$$c = \lim_{T \to \infty} \frac{1}{T} \inf_\zeta \{I_T(\zeta);\ \zeta(t) \in D \quad \text{for } 0 \leq t \leq T\}.$$

He uses the estimates (2.7),(2.8).

Other results are known on the behavior of λ_ε, ϕ_ε for different types of conditions on b(x) (but the methods are not probabilistic). In the selfadjoint case, a more precise formula for λ_ε (than in Theorem 2.4) was derived heuristically in

Matkovsky and Schuss [29] and recently proved by Kamin [25].

The Ventcel-Freidlin estimates have been used to obtain the asymptotic behavior of other quantities; for instance, the Green function $q_\varepsilon(t,x,y)$ of the parabolic operator $L_\varepsilon - \partial/\partial t$ (see [20],[21],[33]). Probabilistically,

$$q_\varepsilon(t,x,A) = P_x\{\xi^\varepsilon(s) \in D \quad \text{for } 0 \leq s \leq t, \quad \xi^\varepsilon(t) \in A\}$$

$$= \int_A q_\varepsilon(t,x,y)dy.$$

Similarly, the fundamental solution $p_\varepsilon(t,x,y)$ can be represented in the form

$$\int_A p_\varepsilon(t,x,y)dy = P_{x,0}(\xi(t) \in A).$$

Define

$$I_t^D(x,y) = \inf_\zeta I_t(\zeta)$$

where ζ varies over the function in C_T, $\zeta(0) = x$, $\zeta(t) = y$, $\zeta(s) \in D$ for $0 \leq s \leq t$;

$$I_t(x,y) = \inf_\zeta I_t(\zeta),$$

where ζ varies in C_T, $\zeta(0) = x$, $\zeta(t) = y$.

<u>Theorem 2.6</u>. <u>For any</u> x, y <u>in</u> D, t > 0,

$$\lim_{\varepsilon\to 0}[2\varepsilon \log p_\varepsilon(t,x,y)] = -I_t(x,y), \tag{2.16}$$

$$\lim_{\varepsilon\to 0}[2\varepsilon \log q_\varepsilon(t,x,y)] = -I_t^D(x,y). \tag{2.17}$$

For proofs, see [20],[21].

Let

$$I_t(x,\partial D) = \inf I_t(\zeta)$$

where ζ varies in C_T, $\zeta(0) = x$, $\zeta(s) \in \partial D$ for some $s \in [0,t]$.

<u>Theorem 2.7</u>. <u>For any</u> $x \in D$, $t > 0$,

$$\lim_{\varepsilon\to 0}[2\varepsilon \log P_x(\tau^\varepsilon \leq t)] = -I_t(x,\partial D). \tag{2.18}$$

Theorem 2.7 was first proved in [36] by means of the estimates (2.7),(2.8). More recently Fleming [16] gave another proof based on ideas from the theory of stochastic control.

The Ventcel-Freidlin estimates have been extended by Anderson and Orey [4] to solutions of stochastic differential equations which exist in a given domain D, and are reflected into D as soon as they hit the boundary. They also derive the analog of (2.17) for the Neumann function.

3. STOCHASTIC CONTROL

Consider the stochastic system (1.4) and introduce the cost functional

$$
J_x(\tau) = E_x\Big[\int_0^\tau e^{-\alpha t} f(\xi(t))dt + e^{-\alpha\tau}\phi(\xi(\tau))I_{\tau<\tau_0} + e^{-\alpha\tau} h(\xi(\tau))I_{\tau=\tau_0}\Big] \qquad (\alpha > 0) \tag{3.1}
$$

where τ_0 = exit time from D, and τ is any stopping time $\leq \tau_0$. Consider the problem of studying the function

$$
V(x) = \inf_\tau J_x(\tau)
$$

and finding $\bar{\tau}$ such that $V(x) = J_x(\bar{\tau})$. This is a stopping time problem. It is well known [10] (see also [21]) that there exists a unique solution u of the (so called) variational inequality

$$
\begin{aligned}
Lu + f &\geq 0 \quad \text{a.e. in } D,\\
u &\leq \phi \quad \text{in } D,\\
(Lu + f)(u - \phi) &= 0 \quad \text{a.e. in } D,\\
u &= h \quad \text{on } \partial D
\end{aligned} \tag{3.2}
$$

and $u \in W^{2,p}(D)$ for any $1 < p < \infty$; here we make some smoothness assumptions on f,ϕ,h and ∂D, and $h \leq \phi$ on ∂D. Further [7],

$$
\begin{aligned}
V(x) &= u(x)\\
\bar{\tau} &= \text{hitting time of the set } \{u = \phi\} \cup \partial D.
\end{aligned} \tag{3.3}
$$

The sets $C = \{u < \phi\}$, $S = \{u = \phi\}$ are called the continuation set and the stopping set respectively. The set $\Gamma = \partial C \cap D$ is called the free boundary.

In view of (3.3), the study of $\bar{\tau}$ reduces to the study of the free boundary. One is interested in the following questions:

(i) estimate the support of C;

(ii) find the smoothness properties of Γ;

(iii) study the shape of Γ.

There has been a lot of work on these questions; especially since it was discovered in recent years that many physical problems can be transformed into (3.2) or into other types of variational inequalities. The methods used in studying (i)-(iii) are usually those of partial differential equations, but results regarding (i),(iii) may be anticipated by the probabilistic interpretation.

Let us mention another model which corresponds to a zero sum game. The payoff functional is

$$J_x(\sigma,\tau) = E_x\Big[\int_0^{\sigma\wedge\tau} e^{-\alpha t} f(\xi(t))dt + e^{-\alpha\sigma}\,\phi_1(\xi(\sigma))I_{\substack{\sigma<\tau\\ \sigma<\tau_0}}$$

$$+ e^{-\alpha\tau}\,\phi_2(\xi(\tau))I_{\substack{\tau\le\sigma\\ \tau\le\tau_0}} + e^{-\alpha\tau_0}\,h(\xi(\tau_0))I_{\tau_0\le\sigma\wedge\tau}\Big];$$

the player that controls σ tries to minimize the payoff, whereas the player that controls τ tries to maximize the payoff. A pair (σ^*,τ^*) is called a saddle point if

$$J_x(\sigma^*,\tau) \le J_x(\sigma^*,\tau^*) \le J_x(\sigma,\tau^*)$$

for all σ, τ. The number

$$V(x) = J_x(\sigma^*,\tau^*)$$

is called the value of the game.

Assume that $\phi_2 \le \phi_1$ in D. Consider the variational inequality

$$(3.4)\qquad \begin{aligned} &Lu + f \ge 0 \quad \text{a.e. where } u > \phi_2,\ x \in D,\\ &Lu + f \le 0 \quad \text{a.e. where } u < \phi_1,\ x \in D,\\ &\phi_2 \le u \le \phi_1 \quad \text{in } D,\\ &u = h \quad \text{on } \partial D. \end{aligned}$$

It is known to have a unique $W^{2,p}$ solution (for any $1 < p < \infty$) and again we have (see [18],[27])

$$(3.5)\qquad V(x) = u(x);$$

further,

$$\sigma^* = \text{hitting time of the set } \{u = \phi_1\},$$

$$\tau^* = \text{hitting time of the set } \{u = \phi_2\}.$$

The function ϕ in the variational inequality (3.2) is called the constraint function; similarly ϕ_1, ϕ_2 are the constraint functions in the variational inequality (3.4). There are stochastic optimization problems which lead to problems of the type (3.2), or (3.4), in which the constraint is not a priori known; in fact, it depends on the unknown solution u.

These types of problems are called quasi variational inequalities (q.v.i.) and so far only partial results are known regarding existence, uniqueness and regularity of the solution; much less is known regarding the free boundary.

For instance, consider a non-zero sum stochastic game (which generalizes the previous model in the sense that each player has his own cost functional, and one seeks a Nash equilibrium point). The study of the equilibrium point reduces to a system of two q.v.i. for which only the existence of a weak solution is known (see [6]).

The best known q.v.i. is the one which arises in the impulse control problem [8]. Here one is to choose a sequence of stopping times

$$\theta^1 < \theta^2 < \cdots$$

and a sequence of random variables

$$\zeta^1, \zeta^2, \ldots$$

and solve (1.4) in each interval $\theta^i < t < \theta^{i+1}$ subject to the initial condition

$$\xi|_{t=\theta^i} = \xi(\theta^i - 0) + \zeta^i.$$

We can represent this process in the form:

$$d\xi(t) = \sigma(\xi(t))dw(t) + b(\xi(t))dt + \sum_i \zeta^i \delta(s - \theta^i).$$

We now consider the cost functional

$$(3.6) \qquad J_x(\theta,\zeta) = E_x\Big[\int_0^\tau e^{-\alpha t} f(\xi(t))dt + \sum_i e^{-\alpha\theta_i} I_{\theta_i < \tau} + e^{-\alpha\tau} h(\xi(\tau)) I_{\tau < \infty}\Big]$$

where τ = exit time from D. (One can also take $D = R^n$, $h \equiv 0$.)

Set

$$V(x) = \inf_{(\theta,\zeta)} J_x(\theta,\zeta).$$

Consider the q.v.i.

$$(3.7) \qquad \begin{aligned} Lu + f &\geq 0 \quad \text{a.e. in } D, \\ u &\leq Mu \quad \text{in } D, \\ (Lu + f)(u - Mu) &= 0 \quad \text{a.e. in } D, \\ u &= h \quad \text{on } \partial D \end{aligned}$$

where

$$(Mu)(x) = 1 + \inf_{\substack{y \geq 0 \\ x+y \in D}} u(x + y)$$

($y = (y_1,\ldots,y_n)$ is ≥ 0 if $y_i \geq 0$ for all i). Bensoussan and Lions [9] proved that, under suitable assumptions on h, f (ensuring that there exist functions v satisfying $v = h$ on ∂D, $v \leq Mv$) there exists a continuous solution u satisfying (3.7) in some weak sense, and

$$(3.8) \qquad V(x) = u(x);$$

further, the optimal times θ^i are the hitting times of the set $\{u = Mu\}$, and the optimal ζ^i satisfy

$$Mu(x) = 1 + u(x + \zeta^i) \quad \text{if } x = \xi(\theta^i - 0).$$

Recently Caffarelli and Friedman [11],[12] have proved that the solution is $W^{2,\infty}_{\ell oc}$; for L with constant coefficients this was proved earlier by Joly, Mosco and Troianiello [23]. The next question is the study of the free boundary. Here there are only some results on the support of the sets where $\{u < Mu\}$ or which $\{u = Mu\}$; see [5].

In all the above problems the stopping times were Markov times. In some problems of partial observation, we are given a Markov process $\xi(t)$ and the random times to be chosen are stopping times with respect to a family $\mathcal{F}_t$ of σ-fields such that

$$\mathcal{F}_t \subsetneqq \sigma\{\xi(s),\ 0 \leq s \leq t\} \equiv \mathcal{G}_t.$$

We are then required to optimize a functional which depends on the chosen stopping times. There are no standard procedures as to how to proceed in transforming the optimization problem into a variational inequality or some other system of differential inequalities. The trouble is that the infimum of the cost functional, $V(x)$, does not have the Markovian property which is essential, for instance, in establishing (3.3), (3.5), or (3.8). However, in some models one is able to "Markovianize" the problem:

Suppose $\mathcal{G}_t$ can be "factored" into $\mathcal{F}_t$ plus a finite dimensional space, say of dimension m. Then by conditioning the information of this space on $\mathcal{F}_t$, we are able to construct an m-dimensional Markov process $p(t)$ which is "sufficient statistics." The cost functional can then be expressed in terms of the p-process, and variational inequalities (or q.v.i.) then emerge.

The oldest example of this type occurs in linear filtering theory. For more recent results (for nonlinear equations) with models arising in quality control and in reliability theory, see [1],[2],[3].

Up to now we considered control problems in which the control variables were stopping times. But control variables may occur in other forms; for instance, as non-anticipative functions, or as switching variables. We shall consider here the latter case.

Thus we consider a sequence of stochastic differential equations

$$d\xi^k(t) = \sigma^k(\xi^k(t))dw(t) + b^k(\xi^k(t))dt \tag{3.9}$$

where σ^k is the positive square root of the matrix (a^k_{ij}).

Let $v(t)$ be any Borel measurable function with values in $\{1,2,3,\ldots\}$. We call v a <u>control function</u> and denote by V the set of all controls. To each $v \in V$ we define the trajectory $\xi^v(t)$ by

$$d\xi^v(t) = \sigma^{v(t)}(\xi^v(t))dw(t) + b^{v(t)}(\xi^v(t))dt \tag{3.10}$$

with initial condition $\xi^v(0) = x$. Thus $\xi^v(t)$ coincides with $\xi^k(t)$ "as long as" $v(t) = k$. The construction of a continuous process $\xi^v(t)$ and its uniqueness can be proved by successive approximations.

We now introduce a cost functional which depends on a sequence of given functions $f^k(x)$, for which

$$|D^\beta f^k(x)| \leq C \quad (|\beta| \leq 2,\ x \in R^n,\ C > 0),$$

namely

$$J_x(v) = E_x \int_0^\infty e^{-\alpha t} f^{v(t)}(\xi^v(t))dt \qquad (\alpha \geq 0).$$

Consider the problem of finding

$$(3.11) \qquad V(x) = \inf_{v \in V} J_x(v).$$

This is a problem of optimizing the running cost $f = \{f^k\}$ when one is allowed to switch freely from one stochastic system to another.

Krylov [28] proved the following result.

Theorem 3.1. *If α is sufficiently large then*

$$(3.12) \qquad V \in W^{2,p}_{\ell oc}(R^n) \quad \textit{for all } 1 < p < \infty,$$

$$(3.13) \qquad \inf_k \{L^k V(x) + f^k(x)\} = 0 \quad \textit{a.e. in } R^n,$$

and V *is uniquely determined by* (3.12), (3.13) *and its growth condition at* ∞.

Equation (3.13) is called the *Bellman equation*. Krylov's proof is probabilistic and does not extend to the corresponding problem in a domain D, $D \neq R^n$ (which will be defined in detail below).

Now let D be a bounded domain with C^2 boundary ∂D, and define a cost functional

$$(3.14) \qquad J_x(v) = E_x \int_0^T e^{-\alpha t} f^v(\xi^v(t))dt$$

where T is the exit time from D; let V(x) be again defined by (3.11).

Consider the problem of characterizing V(x) as the solution of the Dirichlet problem for the Bellman equation:

$$(3.15) \qquad \begin{aligned} &\inf_k \{L^k u(x) + f^k(x)\} = 0 \quad \text{a.e. in } D, \\ &u = 0 \quad \text{on } \partial D. \end{aligned}$$

The following result is due to Evans and Friedman [15]. (J. P. Lions and J. L. Manaldi informed us that they have another proof of this result.)

Theorem 3.2. *Assume that the coefficients a^k_{ij} are constants. Then, for any* $\alpha \geq 0$, *there exists a unique solution* u *of* (3.15) *such that*

$$u \in W^{1,\infty}_0(G) \cap W^{2,\infty}_{\ell oc}(G),$$

and $u \equiv V$.

Even though the proof is by p.d.e. methods, the main idea of its outline is probabilistically motivated, namely, we begin by solving the system

$$-L^i u^i + \beta_\varepsilon(u^i - u^{i+1}) - f^i = 0 \quad \text{in } D,$$

$$u^i = 0 \quad \text{on } \partial D \quad (1 \le i \le m)$$

where $u^{m+1} = u^1$ and $\beta_\varepsilon(t) \to \infty$ if $t > 0$, $\varepsilon \to 0$, $\beta_\varepsilon(t) = 0$ if $t < 0$. Each $u^i(x)$ roughly represents the optimal cost of a cost functional which is a modification of (3.14) in the sense that switching from i to i+1 entails a cost β_ε. Thus it is expected that when $\varepsilon \to 0$ and then $m \to \infty$, the u^i will each converge to the solution of (3.15); the proof shows that is the case.

REFERENCES

[1] R. F. Anderson, Optimal stopping in a reliability problem, Stochastic Analysis, pp. 1-23, Academic Press, New York, 1978.

[2] R. F. Anderson and A. Friedman, A quality control problem and quasi variational inequalities, J. Rat. Mech. Analys., 63 (1977), 205-252.

[3] R. F. Anderson and A. Friedman, Multi-dimensional quality control problems and quasi variational inequalities, Trans. Amer. Math. Soc., to appear.

[4] R. F. Anderson and S. Orey, Small random perturbation of dynamical systems with reflecting boundary, Nagoya Math. J., 60 (1976), 189-216.

[5] A. Bensoussan, H. Brezis and A. Friedman, Estimates on the free boundary for quasi variational inequalities, Comm. in P.D.E., 2 (1977), 297-321.

[6] A. Bensoussan and A. Friedman, Nonzero sum stochastic differential games with stopping times and new free boundary problems, Trans. Amer. Math. Soc., 231 (1977), 275-327.

[7] A. Bensoussan and J. L. Lions, Problèmes de temps d'arrêt optimal et inéquations variationnelles paraboliques, Applicable Analysis, 3 (1973), 267-294.

[8] A. Bensoussan and J. L. Lions, Nouvelle methodes en contrôle impulsionnel, Appl. Math. Optimization, 1 (1975), 289-312.

[9] A. Bensoussan and J. L. Lions, Sur le contrôle impulsionnel et les inéquations quasi variationnelles d'evolution, C.R. Acad. Sci. Paris, 280 (1975), 1049-1053.

[10] H. Brezis, Problèmes unilatéraux, J. Math. pures et appl., 51 (1972), 1-168.

[11] L. A. Caffarelli and A. Friedman, Regularity of the solution of the quasi variational inequality for the impulse control problem, Comm. in P.D.E., 3 (1978), 745-753.

[12] L. A. Caffarelli and A. Friedman, Regularity of the solution of the quasi variational inequality for the impulse control problem II, Comm. in P.D.E., 3 (1978), to appear.

[13] A. Devinatz and A. Friedman, Asymptotic behavior of the principal eigenfunction for singularly perturbed Dirichlet problem, Indiana Univ. Math. J., 27 (1978), 143-157.

[14] A. Devinatz and A. Friedman, The asymptotic behavior of a singularly perturbed Dirichlet problem, Indiana Univ. Math. J., 27 (1978), 527-537.

[15] C. L. Evans and A. Friedman, Optimal stochastic switching and the Dirichlet problem for the Bellman equation, to appear.

[16] W. H. Fleming, Exist probabilities and optimal stochastic control, to appear.

[17] M. I. Freidlin, On the factorization of nonnegative definite matrices, Theor. Probability Appl., 13 (1968), 354-358.

[18] A. Friedman, Stochastic games and variational inequalities, Archive Rat. Mech. Analys., 51 (1973), 321-346.

[19] A. Friedman, The asymptotic behavior of the first real eigenvalue of a second order elliptic operator with small parameter in the highest derivatives, Indiana Univ. Math. J., 22 (1973), 1005-1015.

[20] A. Friedman, Small random perturbations of dynamical systems and applications to parabolic equations, Indiana Univ. Math. J., 24 (1974), 533-553; Erratum, ibid, 25 (1975), p. 903.

[21] A. Friedman, Stochastic Differential Equations and Applications, vol. 2, Academic Press, New York, 1976.

[22] A. Friedman and M. A. Pinsky, Dirichlet problem for degenerate elliptic equations, Trans. Amer. Math. Soc., 186 (1973), 359-383.

[23] J. L. Joly, U. Mosco and G. M. Troianiello, On the regular solution of a quasi-variational inequality connected to a problem of stochastic impulse control, J. Math. Anal. Appl., 61 (1977), 357-369.

[24] S. Kamin, Elliptic perturbation of a first order operator with a singular point, Indiana Univ. Math. J., to appear.

[25] S. Kamin, to appear.

[26] J. J. Kohn and L. Nirenberg, Degenerate elliptic-parabolic equations of second order, Comm. Pure Appl. Math., 20 (1967), 797-872.

[27] N. V. Krylov, Control of Markov processes and W-spaces, Math. SSSR-Izv., 5 (1971), 233-266.

[28] N. V. Krylov, Control of a solution of stochastic integral equation, Theor. Probability Appl., 17 (1972), 114-130.

[29] B. J. Matkowsky and Z. Schuss, On the exit problem for randomly perturbed dynamical systems, SIAM J. Appl. Math., 33 (1977), 365-382.

[30] M. A. Pinsky, A note on degenerate diffusion processes, Theor. Probability Appl., 14 (1969), 502-506.

[31] M. A. Pinsky, Stochastic stability and the Dirichlet problem, Comm. Pure Appl. Math., 27 (1974), 311-350.

[32] D. Stroock and S. R. S. Varadhan, On degenerate elliptic-parabolic operators of second order and their associated diffusions, Comm. Pure Appl. Math., 25 (1972), 651-713.

[33] S. R. S. Varadhan, Diffusion processes in a small time interval, Comm. Pure Appl. Math., 20 (1967), 659-685.

[34] A. D. Ventcel, On the asymptotic behavior of the greatest eigenvalue of a second order elliptic differential operator with a small parameter in the highest derivatives, Soviet Math. Dokl., 13 (1972), 13-17.

[35] A. D. Ventcel, On the asymptotic behavior of the first eigenvalue of a differential operator of the second order with small parameter in the highest derivatives, Theor. Probability Appl., 20 (1975), 599-602.

[36] A. D. Ventcel and M. I. Freidlin, On small random perturbations of dynamical systems, Russian Math. Surveys, 25 (1970), 1-56.

APPROXIMATION OF SOLUTIONS TO DIFFERENTIAL EQUATIONS WITH RANDOM INPUTS BY DIFFUSION PROCESSES

Harold J. Kushner
Division of Applied Mathematics
Brown University
Providence, Rhode Island 02912

November, 1978

ABSTRACT

Let $y^{\varepsilon}(\cdot)$ denote a random process whose bandwidth, loosely speaking, goes to ∞ as $\varepsilon \to 0$. Consider the family of differential equations $\dot{x}^{\varepsilon} = g(x^{\varepsilon},y^{\varepsilon}) + f(x^{\varepsilon},y^{\varepsilon})/\alpha(\varepsilon)$, where $\alpha(\varepsilon) \to 0$ as $\varepsilon \to 0$. The question of interest is: does the sequence $\{x^{\varepsilon}(\cdot)\}$ converge in some sense and if so which, if any, ordinary or Itô differential equation does it satisfy? Normally, the limit is taken in the sense of weak convergence. The problem is of great practical importance, for such questions arise in many practical situations arising in many fields. Often the limiting equation is nice and can be treated much more easily than can the $x^{\varepsilon}(\cdot)$. In any case, in practice approximations to properties of the $x^{\varepsilon}(\cdot)$ are usually sought in terms of ε and some limit. To illustrate these points, as well as a related stability problem, we give a practical example which arises in the theory of adaptive arrays of antennas.

The topic of convergence has seen much work, starting with the fundamental papers of Wong and Zakai, and followed by others, including Khazminskii, Papanicolaou and Kohler, etc. From a non-probabilistic point of view, it has been dealt with by McShane and Sussmann. In this paper, we discuss a rather general and efficient method of getting the correct limits. The idea exploits some general semigroup approximation results of Kurtz, and often not only gets better results than those obtained by preceding methods, but is also easier to use.

---

*This research was supported in part by the Air Force Office of Scientific Research under AF-AFOSR 76-3063, in part by the National Science Foundation under NSF-Eng 77-12946, and in part by the Office of Naval Research under N0014-76-C-0279-P0002.

1. INTRODUCTION

Let $y^{\varepsilon}(\cdot)$ denote a stationary random process whose "bandwidth" goes to ∞ as $\varepsilon \to 0$, and define the R^r-valued process $x^{\varepsilon}(\cdot)$ by the O.D.E.

$$\dot{x}^{\varepsilon} = g(x^{\varepsilon},y^{\varepsilon}) + f(x^{\varepsilon},y^{\varepsilon})/\alpha(\varepsilon), \quad x_0 = x(0) \text{ given,} \tag{1.1}$$

where $\alpha(\varepsilon) \to 0$ as $\varepsilon \to 0$, and $Ef(x,y^{\varepsilon}) = 0$ for each x. In this paper, we address the question: as $\varepsilon \to 0$, what is the limit of $\{x^{\varepsilon}(\cdot)\}$; in particular, does it satisfy an ordinary or Itô stochastic differential equation, and if so, what is that equation. The question arises frequently in applications in many areas. Often $y^{\varepsilon}(\cdot)$ is a rather arbitrary process and yet the limit is a nice Markov process satisfying, say, an Itô equation. Then many functionals of $x^{\varepsilon}(\cdot)$ can be approximated by functionals of the limit and the parameter ε, for small ε. In applications, this is often done, either explicitly or implicitly. In Sections 2 and 6, one particular important application will be discussed.

The problem has been around for some time and is a crucial aspect of the problem of modelling the processes which arise in practice by mathematically tractable processes. Perhaps, the first mathematical treatment was given by Wong and Zakai [1], [2] who dealt with equations of the form

$$\dot{x}^{\varepsilon} = g(x^{\varepsilon}) + f(x^{\varepsilon})y^{\varepsilon}, \tag{1.2}$$

where $y^{\varepsilon}(\cdot)$ was (more or less) the derivative of a polygonal approximation $Y^{\varepsilon}(\cdot)$ to a Wiener process, and $Y^{\varepsilon}(\cdot)$ converged to that process as ε went to zero. Much subsequent was done on the following form. Let $\alpha(\varepsilon) = \varepsilon$, suppose that $y(\cdot)$ is a stationary bounded process and $\rho(\cdot)$ a measurable function which satisfy the strong mixing condition (1.3).

$$\int_0^{\infty} \rho^{1/2}(s)ds < \infty \tag{1.3a}$$

$$|P\{B|A\} - P\{B\}| \leq \rho(\tau) \tag{1.3b}$$

for each t,τ and each $B \in \mathscr{B}(y_s, s \geq \tau + t)$ and $A \in \mathscr{B}(y_s, s \leq t)$. Let $y^{\varepsilon}(t) = y(t/\varepsilon^2)$. Motivation for this scaling is given in the next subsection. (We write the values of a process $y(\cdot)$ as either $y(t)$ or y_t, depending on notational convenience.)

Under (1.3) and other conditions on g and f, (1.1) was dealt with by Khazminskii [3], Papanicolaou [5], Papanicolaou and Kohler [4], Papanicolaou and Blankenship [6] and Kushner [7]. The last reference obtained perhaps the most general results (for the time invariant case) and allowed cases where $y^{\varepsilon}(\cdot)$ could contain (approximations to) impulsive jumps, and also where $y(\cdot)$ is unbounded but the form $f(x,y) = f(x)y$ was used.

Let C_0^i denote the space of real-valued functions on R^r which go to zero as $|x| \to \infty$, together with their first i^{th} mixed partial derivatives, and let $\hat{C}^i$ denote the subset with compact support. Let subscript x denote gradient, and define the operator A on $\hat{C}^2$ by

$$(1.4)\quad Ak(x) = Eg'(x,y_s)k_x(x) + \int_0^{\infty} Ef'(x,y_s)(f'(x,y_{s+\tau})k_x(x))_x d\tau$$

$$\equiv \sum_i b_i(x)\frac{\partial k(x)}{\partial x_i} + \frac{1}{2}\sum_{i,j} a_{ij}(x)\frac{\partial^2 k(x)}{\partial x_i \partial x_j}\ .$$

In references [3]-[7], it was proved (under various conditions on $f,g,y(\cdot)$) that $x^{\varepsilon}(\cdot)$ converged weakly to a diffusion process $x(\cdot)$ whose generator on $\hat{C}^2$ functions is the operator A of (1.4).

References [4] and [6] contain a wealth of ideas on the approximation and related problems. The methods used in [7] are based on general semigroup approximation methods of Kurtz [8]. They have a number of advantages over previous methods, being somewhat easier to use and giving better results in many cases. The method will be described and used in Section 3.

Most past work has dealt with showing that $x(\cdot)$ is a good approximation to $x^{\varepsilon}(\cdot)$ in some sense. Only recently (see, e.g. [13]) has the question of dealing with the control and stability properties of $x^{\varepsilon}(\cdot)$ in terms of those of $x(\cdot)$ been considered. Reference [14] deals with the reversed problem: finding $x^{\varepsilon}(\cdot)$ which are easier to work with than $x(\cdot)$.

Discussion of properties of $y^{\varepsilon}(\cdot)$ as $\varepsilon \to 0$. As $\varepsilon \to 0$ in (1.1) the process $f(x^{\varepsilon},y^{\varepsilon})/\alpha(\varepsilon)$ is "increasingly compressed", hence (loosely speaking) the bandwidth goes to ∞. If $f(x,y)$ were not divided by $\alpha(\varepsilon)$, then the average energy in the process $f(x_t^{\varepsilon},y_t^{\varepsilon})/\alpha(\varepsilon)$ (over any finite interval) would tend to zero as $\varepsilon \to 0$ and the f term would play no role in the limit. To see the rough idea most simply, let $y^{\varepsilon}(\cdot)$ be scalar valued, let $f(x,y) = f(x)y$, let $R(\cdot)$ and $S(\cdot)$ denote the correlation function and spectral density of a stationary process $y(\cdot)$, consider the special case where $y_t^\varepsilon = y(t/\varepsilon^2)$ and let $R^\varepsilon(\cdot)$ and $S^\varepsilon(\cdot)$ denote the correlation function and spectral density of $y^\varepsilon(\cdot)$. Then $R^\varepsilon(t) = R(t/\varepsilon^2)/\alpha^2(\varepsilon)$ and

$$S^\varepsilon(w) = \int_{-\infty}^{\infty} e^{iwt}R^\varepsilon(t)dt = \int_{-\infty}^{\infty} e^{iwt}R(t/\varepsilon^2)dt/\alpha^2(\varepsilon) = \varepsilon^2 S(\varepsilon^2 w)/\alpha^2(\varepsilon).$$

Unless $\alpha(\varepsilon) = \varepsilon$, the energy per unit bandwith either blows up $(\varepsilon/\alpha(\varepsilon) \to \infty)$ or goes to zero $(\varepsilon/\alpha(\varepsilon) \to 0)$. When $\alpha(\varepsilon) = \varepsilon$, $R^\varepsilon(0) = R(0)/\varepsilon^2 \to \infty$. If the "magnitude" of $y^\varepsilon(t)/\varepsilon$ did not go to ∞ as $\varepsilon \to \infty$, then the energy per unit bandwidth would go to zero. So, in order to get a constant energy per unit bandwidth as $\varepsilon \to 0$, we need both a time compression (t/ε^2 scale) and an amplitude magnitication $(\alpha(\varepsilon) = \varepsilon)$. Use of this remark will be made in the next section.

In Section 5, we illustrate the technique of [7] on an important class of problems not explicitly treated previously. For each ε, let $\{s_i^\varepsilon, i \geq 0\}$, denote a stationary process. Define $s^\varepsilon(\cdot)$ as the function which is equal to s_i^ε on the interval $[i,i+1)$, set $\xi_t^\varepsilon = s^\varepsilon(t/\varepsilon)$, and let s_i^ε be "small"; i.e., $Ef(x,s_i^\varepsilon) = 0$, $\operatorname{var} f(x,s_i^\varepsilon) \approx \varepsilon$ and define $x^\varepsilon(\cdot)$ by

$$\dot{x}^\varepsilon = g(x^\varepsilon,\xi^\varepsilon) + f(x^\varepsilon,\xi^\varepsilon)/\varepsilon,\ x(0) = x_0. \tag{1.5}$$

The exact forms of the conditions to be used are stated in Section 5. The form (1.5) is chosen partly to illustrate the method. That $\xi^\varepsilon(\cdot)$ is piecewise constant makes the calculations a little easier, but is not a particularly crucial assumption. We will treat the case where $f(\cdot,\cdot)$ is linear in its second argument: $f(x,s) = f(x)s$.

Equation (1.5) is also important from the point of view of applications. Consider the scalar valued discrete parameter sequence $X_{n+1}^\varepsilon = X_n^\varepsilon + h(X_n^\varepsilon,s_n^\varepsilon)$ where $Eh(x,s_i^\varepsilon) \equiv \varepsilon p(x)$ and $\operatorname{var} h(x,s_i^\varepsilon) = \sigma^2(x)\varepsilon$. Then, setting $q(x,s_i^\varepsilon) = h(x,s_i^\varepsilon) - Eh(x,s_i^\varepsilon)$ yields the discrete parameter version of (1.5):

$$X_{n+1}^\varepsilon = X_n^\varepsilon + \varepsilon p(X_n^\varepsilon) + q(X_n^\varepsilon,s_n^\varepsilon). \tag{1.6}$$

Let $\bar{x}^\varepsilon(\cdot)$ denote a piecewise linear interpolation of $\{X_n^\varepsilon\}$ which is linear in each $[\varepsilon n,\varepsilon n+\varepsilon)$ and equals X_n^ε at εn. Then the slope of $\bar{x}^\varepsilon(\cdot)$ is $\rho(X_n^\varepsilon) + q(X_n^\varepsilon,s^\varepsilon(\varepsilon n/\varepsilon))/\varepsilon$ in $[\varepsilon n,\varepsilon n+\varepsilon)$. Thus, (1.5) is a continuous parameter version of $\{X_n^\varepsilon\}$. The limits of $\bar{x}^\varepsilon(\cdot)$ and of $\{x^\varepsilon(\cdot)\}$ are not necessarily the same, although in many cases we can find g and g such that $x^{\varepsilon}(n\varepsilon) = X_n^{\varepsilon}$ for all ε, n.

Let us suppose that in (1.1), $\alpha(\varepsilon) = \varepsilon$ and $y^{\varepsilon}(t) = y(t/\varepsilon^2)$. Equation (1.5) differs from equation (1.1) in that the $\xi^{\varepsilon}(t)$ essentially become small in some sense as $\varepsilon \to 0$. But the scaling is also different (less compression), t/ε being used in lieu of t/ε^2. Equation (1.5) (and (1.6)) correspond to a problem where, as $\varepsilon \to 0$, more and more random effects affect the system, but where the individual effects became smaller and smaller. Let $f(x,s) = f(x)s$ and write $\xi^{\varepsilon}(t)/\varepsilon = [s^{\varepsilon}(t/\varepsilon)/\sqrt{\varepsilon}]/\sqrt{\varepsilon}$, bringing the form (1.5) into that of (1.1) but with $\sqrt{\varepsilon}$ replacing ε and $s^{\varepsilon}(t/\varepsilon)/\sqrt{\varepsilon}$ replacing $y^{\varepsilon}(t)$. But now, as $\varepsilon \to 0$, $s^{\varepsilon}(t/\varepsilon)/\sqrt{\varepsilon}$ might become unbounded. Owing to this, the methods used for (1.1) (at least when $y(\cdot)$ was assumed bounded) need to be modified a little for use here.

In Section 2, we discuss a currently important problem concerning "adaptive" antenna arrays, which illustrates one particular value derived from the type of limit results with which we are concerned. Sections 3 and 4 describe Kurtz's [8] interesting method for proving tightness and weak convergence of a sequence of not necessarily Markov processes. Henceforth, x^{ε} is used only for the solution to (1.5). Convergence of the finite dimensional distributions of $x^{\varepsilon}(\cdot)$ to those of a particular diffusion $x(\cdot)$ is proved in Section 5. Also, Section 5 proves tightness of $\{X^{\varepsilon}(\cdot)\}$. Together these results yield that $x^{\varepsilon}(\cdot)$ converges weakly to $x(\cdot)$. In Section 6, we return to the antenna problem, and treat the problem of weak convergence and get a moment estimate for the adapting parameters, and discuss a related stability problem.

The use of weak convergence methods seems quite natural for our problem. Often w.p.1 results are meaningless, since usually only one system (a fixed ε) is to be studied, and we seek approximations to its properties in terms of ε and properties of the limit.

2. A PROBLEM IN ADAPTIVE ANTENNA ARRAYS

Let $n(\cdot) = (n_1(\cdot),\ldots,n_r(\cdot))$ denote a "wide band" complex valued stochastic process. We are given an array of r antennas with received signal plus noise $v(t) = s(t) + n(t) = \{s_i(t) + n_i(t)\}$, $s_i(t)$ and $n_i(t)$ being complex valued. The $v(t)$ is multiplied by a complex valued weight w, and the object is to find the weights which maximize the ratio of signal to noise power in the output $w'v(t)$. The problem is important and of great current interest (see the papers in [9] or [10] and references contained therein). The signal frequency is known, the signals received by the antennas differ only in the phase. Let * denote complex conjugate. Let $S_0^* = (1, \exp i\phi_2, \ldots, \exp i\phi_r)$, where ϕ_j is the phase of $s_j(t)$ relative to that of $s_1(t)$, and let S be proportional to S_0. With $\bar{M} = En^*(t)n'(t)$, the optimum weight is $w = k\bar{M}^{-1}S^*$, for any constant $k > 0$.

In many applications, $\bar{M}$ is time varying, due to deliberate jamming attempts, or due to more natural phenomena. In fact, in many applications $n(\cdot)$ is a strong competing signal which we wish to "tune out" and its covariance may vary, depending on the particular use to which the system is put. We suppose (as is often the case - e.g., in pulsed radar) that the signal power is much less than the noise power, so that $\bar{M} \approx Ev^*(t)v'(t)$.

A very useful and relatively simple mechanism for adapting the weights (see, e.g. [10]) can be constructed. The relevant equation is $(M_t = v^*(t)v'(t))$

$$\tau\dot{w} + (GM+I)w = G_0S^*, \tag{2.1}$$

where τ is a scalar system time constant and G and G_0 are system gains. Since M is the "square" of a wide band process, if the bandwidth (BW) goes to infinity and the energy per unit BW does not go to zero, (2.1) becomes meaningless. In practice, we are interested in both Ew_t and in an equation for an approximation to $w_t - Ew_t$ for wide BW noise.

A commonly used "engineering" heuristic argument says that since $M(\cdot)$ is wide band and $w(\cdot)$ is much smoother than $M(\cdot)$, the two are essentially independent and $EM(t)w(t) \approx EM(t)Ew(t)$ and that Ew_t approximately equals $\bar{w}_t$, the solution to

$$\dot{\bar{w}} + (G\bar{M}+I)\bar{w} = G_0S^*. \tag{2.2}$$

Of course (2.2) does not give the correct value of Ew_t, even as an approximation, unless the energy per unit BW of the noise is very small. To see this, simply consider the scalar case where $\tau\dot{w} + (Gn^2+1)w = G_0$; solve it and take expectations. Since (2.2) is widely used, we must find an interpretation with respect to which it makes sense. If (2.2) is an asymptotic result, then it must be satisfied by a limit of solutions to (2.1) (or their expectations), as some parameter tends to say, ∞. The comments below are illustrative of the usefulness of the limit results to which this paper (and references [3]-[7]) are devoted.

Let σ^2 denote the sum of the eigenvalues of $\overline{M}$. In practice, often a rough estimate of a quantity proportional to σ^2 (the noise power) is made, and an automatic gain control mechanism is used to adjust G, usually decreasing G as the estimate of σ^2 increases. Such a mechanism is crucial to the proper scaling of (2.1), and we assume its use. In fact, suppose that for some number K, $G = K/\sigma^2$. Then (approximately, actually, since we ignore the "signal" component of M) with $\delta M = M - \overline{M}$,

$$\tau\dot{w} + [K\overline{M}/\sigma^2 + K(\delta M)/\sigma^2 + I]w = G_0S^*. \tag{2.3}$$

As the BW of $n(\cdot)$ tends to ∞, the effects of $K(\delta M)w/\sigma^2$ become negligable (a consequence of the type of argument in [7], Sections 6 and 7, under reasonable assumptions on $n(\cdot)$) and the limit is precisely the solution of (2.2). For concreteness, we consider the case arising from (1.1) where $n_t = y(t/\varepsilon^2)/\varepsilon$ and $y(\cdot)$ is a stationary bounded process and $\varepsilon = 1/\sigma$. Set $\overline{M}_0 = Ey_t^*y_t', \delta\tilde{M}_t^\varepsilon = [y^*(t/\varepsilon^2)y'(t/\varepsilon^2) - \overline{M}_0]$. Write δM_t as $\delta M_t^\varepsilon \equiv \delta\tilde{M}_t^\varepsilon/\varepsilon^2$ and use $\delta\tilde{M}_t$ for $\delta\tilde{M}_t^1$.

Now, define $\delta w_t = w_t - \overline{w}_t$ and $u^\varepsilon = \sigma\delta w$. Then

$$\begin{aligned} &\tau\dot{u}^\varepsilon + [K\overline{M}/\sigma^2 + I]u^\varepsilon + K(\delta M^\varepsilon/\sigma^2)u^\varepsilon + K(\delta M^\varepsilon/\sigma)\overline{w} = 0, \\ &\dot{u}^\varepsilon = -\frac{1}{\tau}[K\overline{M}_0 + I]u^\varepsilon - \frac{K}{\tau}(\delta\tilde{M}^\varepsilon)u^\varepsilon - \frac{K}{\tau}\left(\frac{\delta\tilde{M}^\varepsilon}{\varepsilon}\right)\overline{w}. \end{aligned} \tag{2.4}$$

As $BW \to \infty$, the effects of $K(\delta M^\varepsilon/\sigma^2)u$ disappear and $K(\delta M^\varepsilon/\sigma)\overline{w}$ becomes "white noise", in the sense that there is a standard Wiener process $B(\cdot)$ such that the limit process has the law of $u(\cdot)$ in

$$\tau du + [K\overline{M}_0 + I]udt + QdB = 0, \quad u(0) = 0. \tag{2.5}$$

Q is obtainable by the method of Theorem 5. We return to this problem in Section 6, and deal with the convergence problem and a related stability problem when all quantities are <u>not</u> complex valued, to simplify the notation.

3. CONVERGENCE OF FINITE DIMENSIONAL DISTRIBUTIONS

In reference [8], Kurtz gave some fairly general methods for showing convergence to a Markov process of a sequence of non-Markov processes, either in the sense of weak convergence or in the sense of convergence of finite dimensional distributions. In this section and in the next, we briefly describe his method. Later we apply it, together with an idea in [5], [6], to get limit results in a fairly efficient manner.

Sections 3 and 4 are identical to Sections 2 and 3 of [7].

Let $(\Omega,P,\mathscr{F})$ denote a probability space, $\{\mathscr{F}_t\}$ a nondecreasing sequence of sub σ-algebras of $\mathscr{F}$, let $\mathscr{L}$ denote the space of progessively measurable real valued processes $k(\cdot)$ on $[0,\infty)$, adapted to $\{\mathscr{F}_t\}$ and such that $\sup_t E|k(t)| < \infty$. Let k^ε and k be in $\mathscr{L}$. Define the limit "p-lim" by p-lim $k^\varepsilon = k$ iff $\sup_{\varepsilon>0}\sup_t E|k^\varepsilon(t)| < \infty$ and $E|k^\varepsilon(t) - k(t)| \to 0$ for each t as $\varepsilon \to 0$. For each $s > 0$, define the operator $\mathscr{T}(s): \mathscr{L} \to \mathscr{L}$ by $\mathscr{T}(s)k$ = function in $\mathscr{L}$ whose value at t is the random variable $E_{\mathscr{F}_t} k(t+s)$. There is a version which is progressively measurable ([8], Appendix) and we always assume that this is the one which is used. The $\mathscr{T}(s)$, $s \geq 0$, are a semigroup of linear operators on $\mathscr{L}$. Let $\hat{\mathscr{L}}_0$ denote the subspace of p-right continuous functions. If the limit $\text{p-lim}_{s\to 0} [\frac{1}{s}(\mathscr{T}(s)k-k)]$ and exists and is in $\hat{\mathscr{L}}_0$, we call it $\hat{A}k$ and say that $k \in \mathscr{D}(\hat{A})$. The operators $\mathscr{F}(s)$ and $\hat{A}$ are analogous to the semigroup and weak infinitesimal operator of a Markov process. Among the properties to be used later is ([8], equation (1.9))

$$\mathscr{T}(s)k - k = \int_0^s \mathscr{T}(\tau)\hat{A}k\,d\tau, \quad k \in \mathscr{D}(\hat{A}), \tag{3.1a}$$

or, equivalently,

$$E_{\mathscr{F}_t} k(t+s) - k(t) = \int_0^s E_{\mathscr{F}_t} \hat{A}k(t+\tau)\,d\tau, \quad \text{for each } t \geq 0. \tag{3.1b}$$

If, for some process $Z^\varepsilon(\cdot)$, $\mathscr{F}_t = \mathscr{B}(Z^\varepsilon_s, s \leq t)$, we may write $\mathscr{F}^\varepsilon_t, T^\varepsilon_t$ and $\hat{A}^\varepsilon$ for $\mathscr{F}_t$, $\mathscr{T}(t)$ and $\hat{A}$, resp.

The following Theorem (a specialization of [8], Theorem 3.11) is our main tool for dealing with (1.1) or (1.5).

<u>Theorem 1</u>. <u>Let</u> $Z^\varepsilon(\cdot) = x^\varepsilon(\cdot), \xi^\varepsilon(\cdot)$, $\varepsilon > 0$, <u>denote a sequence of</u> $R^{r+r'}$ <u>valued right continuous processes</u>, $x(\cdot)$ <u>a</u> (R^r<u>-valued</u>) <u>Markov process with semigroup</u> T_t <u>mapping</u> C_0 <u>into</u> C_0 <u>and which is strongly continuous</u> (<u>sup norm</u>) <u>on</u> C_0. <u>For some</u> $\lambda > 0$ <u>and dense set</u> D <u>in</u> C_0, <u>let</u> Range $(\lambda - A|_D)$ <u>be dense in</u> C_0 (<u>sup norm</u>, A = <u>infinitesimal operator of</u> $x(\cdot)$). <u>Suppose that, for each</u> $k \in D$, <u>there is a sequence</u> $\{k^\varepsilon\}$ <u>of progressively measurable functions adapted to</u> $\{\mathscr{F}^\varepsilon_t\}$ <u>and such that</u>

$$\text{p-lim}[k^\varepsilon - k(x^\varepsilon(\cdot))] = 0 \tag{3.2}$$

$$\text{(3.3)} \qquad \text{p-lim}[\hat{A}k^{\varepsilon} - Ak(x^{\varepsilon}(\cdot))] = 0.$$

Then, if $x^{\varepsilon}(0) \to x(0)$ weakly, the finite dimensional distributions of $x^{\varepsilon}(\cdot)$ converge to those of $x(\cdot)$.

Equations (3.2) and (3.3) are equivalent to (the limits are taken for each t as $\varepsilon \to 0$)

$$\text{(3.2')} \qquad \sup_{\varepsilon,t} E|k^{\varepsilon}(t) - k(x^{\varepsilon}(t))| < \infty, \; E|k^{\varepsilon}(t) - k(x^{\varepsilon}(t))| \to 0$$

$$\text{(3.3')} \qquad \sup_{\varepsilon,t} E|\hat{A}^{\varepsilon}k^{\varepsilon}(t) - Ak(x^{\varepsilon}(t))| < \infty, \; E|\hat{A}^{\varepsilon}k^{\varepsilon}(t) - Ak(x^{\varepsilon}(t))| \to 0.$$

4. TIGHTNESS

Let $\xi^{\varepsilon}(\cdot), x^{\varepsilon}(\cdot)$ denote the functions in the model (1.5). Let $\mathscr{F}_t^{\varepsilon}$ denote $\mathscr{B}(\xi_u^{\varepsilon}, u \leq t)$ and write E_t^{ε} for $E_{\mathscr{F}_t^{\varepsilon}}$.

Again, we describe results from [8]. Let $D^r[0,\infty)$ denote the space of R^r valued functions on $[0,\infty)$ which are right continuous on $[0,\infty)$ and have left hand limits on $(0,\infty)$. Note that $x^{\varepsilon}(\cdot) \in D^r[0,\infty)$ w.p.1. Suppose that the finite dimensional distributions of $x^{\varepsilon}(\cdot)$ converge to those of a process $x(\cdot)$, where $x(\cdot)$ has paths in $D^r[0,\infty)$ w.p.1. Then, as noted in [8], bottom of page 628, $\{x^{\varepsilon}(\cdot)\}$ is tight in $D^r[0,\infty)$ if $\{k(x^{\varepsilon}(\cdot))\}$ is tight in $D[0,\infty)$ for each $k \in \hat{C}$. ($\hat{C}$ is used there, but it can be replaced by $\hat{C}^3$ or by any set of functions dense in $\hat{C}$ in the sup norm.) It follows from [8], Theorem 4.20, that $\{k(x^{\varepsilon}(\cdot))\}$ is tight in $D[0,\infty)$ if $x_0^{\varepsilon} \to x_0$ weakly and if, for each real $T > 0$, there is a random variable $\gamma_{\varepsilon}(\delta)$ such that

$$\text{(4.1)} \qquad E_t^{\varepsilon}\gamma_{\varepsilon}(\delta) \geq E_t^{\varepsilon} \min\{1, [k(x_{t+u}^{\varepsilon}) - k(x_t^{\varepsilon})]^2\},$$

for all $0 \leq t \leq T$, $0 \leq u \leq \delta \leq 1$, and

$$\text{(4.2)} \qquad \lim_{\delta\to 0} \overline{\lim_{\varepsilon\to 0}} E\, \gamma_{\varepsilon}(\delta) = 0.$$

In [8], p. 629, Kurtz suggests a method of getting the $\gamma_{\varepsilon}(\delta)$. This method is developed in Theorem 2 and is used in the sequel. The k^{ε} below will be obtained in the same manner as we will obtain the k^{ε} needed in Theorem 1. We have $(||k|| = \sup_x |k(x)|)$

$$(4.3)\qquad E_t^\varepsilon[k(x_{t+u}^\varepsilon) - k(x_t^\varepsilon)]^2 \le 2||k||\ |E_t^\varepsilon k(x_{t+u}^\varepsilon) - k(x_t^\varepsilon)| + |E_t^\varepsilon k^2(x_{t+u}^\varepsilon) - k^2(x_t^\varepsilon)|.$$

Theorem 2. Let $k \in \hat{C}^3$, and let there be a sequence $\{k^\varepsilon\}$ in $\mathscr{L}$, where $(k^\varepsilon)^i \in \mathscr{D}(\hat{A}^\varepsilon)$, $i = 1,2$, and such that, for each real $T > 0$ there is a random variable M^ε such that

$$(4.4)\qquad \sup_{t\le T}|k^\varepsilon(t) - k(x_t^\varepsilon)| \to 0 \quad \text{in probability as } \varepsilon \to 0,$$

$$(4.5)\qquad \sup_{t\le T}|A^\varepsilon(k^\varepsilon(t))^i| \le M_\varepsilon,\quad i = 1,2,\quad \lim_N \sup_\varepsilon P\{M_\varepsilon > N\} = 0.$$

Then $\{k(x^\varepsilon(\cdot))\}$ is tight in $D[0,\infty)$.

Proof: We need only show tightness of $\{k^\varepsilon(\cdot)\}$ on $[0,T]$. By (3.1)

$$E_t^\varepsilon(k^\varepsilon(t+u))^i - (k^\varepsilon(t))^i = \int_0^u E_t^\varepsilon \hat{A}^\varepsilon(k^\varepsilon(t+\tau))^i d\tau,$$

from which (4.3) and (4.5) yield that there is a $\gamma_\varepsilon(\delta)$ satisfying (4.1) and (4.2) for $\{k^\varepsilon(\cdot)\}$. Then (4.4) and tightness of $\{k^\varepsilon(\cdot)\}$ imply tightness of $\{k(x^\varepsilon(\cdot))\}$. Q.E.D.

5. CONVERGENCE OF THE SEQUENCE $\{x^\varepsilon(\cdot)\}$ OF (1.5)

We follow the general line of development in [7], using the ideas in Sections 3 and 4.

Assumptions:

(A1) Let $f(x,s) = f(x)s$. The functions $g(\cdot,\cdot)$ and $f(\cdot)$ are continuous, the first (second, resp.) function having continuous first (second, resp.) mixed partial x-derivatives.

(A2) There is a constant K such that

$$|f(x)| + |g(x,s)| \le K(1+|x|).$$

(A3) $\{s_i^\varepsilon\}$ is bounded (uniformly in ε) and stationary and $Es_i^\varepsilon \equiv 0$.

Define $\mathscr{F}_i^\varepsilon = \mathscr{B}(s_j^\varepsilon, j \le i)$, $\mathscr{F}_t^\varepsilon = \mathscr{B}(\xi_s^\varepsilon, s \le t)$ and let E_i^ε and E_t^ε denote the corresponding conditional expectation operators.

Throughout the sequel, K denotes a constant, whose value may change from usage to usage. Also in (A4b,c), we let s_i^ε denote an arbitrary scalar component of itself. It seems to be most convenient to use (A4) in its given form. Other forms, more closely resembling strong mixing can be given. Strong mixing would imply the second part of (A4a) and (A4b,d). But something like (A4c) would still be required, because we need the ε dependence there.

(A4) a. There are μ_j and $\delta > 0$ such that $\sum_j \mu_j^{1/2} < \infty$ and

$$E|s_i^\varepsilon|^2 \le K\varepsilon, \quad |E_i^\varepsilon s_{i+j}^\varepsilon| \le K\mu_j.$$

b. $|E_i^\varepsilon s_{i+j}^\varepsilon s_{i+j+k}^\varepsilon - Es_{i+j}^\varepsilon s_{i+j+k}^\varepsilon| \le K\mu_j$

c. $E^{1/2}|E_i^\varepsilon s_{i+j}^\varepsilon s_{i+j+k}^\varepsilon - Es_{i+j}^\varepsilon s_{i+j+k}^\varepsilon|^2 \le K\mu_j\varepsilon^{1/2+\delta}$

d. $\sum_j |E_i^\varepsilon g(x,s_{i+j}^\varepsilon) - Eg(x,s_{i+j}^\varepsilon)| < \infty,$

$$\sum_j |E_i^\varepsilon g_x(x,s_{i+j}^\varepsilon) - Eg_x(x,s_{i+j}^\varepsilon)| < \infty.$$

Let the expectation of the sums in (d) go to zero as $\varepsilon \to 0$, uniformly on bounded x-sets.

Define the operators A_t^ε and $\bar{A}^\varepsilon$ by $(k(\cdot) \in \hat{C}^2)$

(5.1) $$A_t^\varepsilon k(x) = E\int_0^\infty f'(x,\xi_t^\varepsilon)[k_x'(x)f(x,\xi_{t+u}^\varepsilon)]_x du/\varepsilon^2$$

$$= E\int_0^\infty f'(x,s^\varepsilon(t/\varepsilon))[k_x'(x)f(x,s^\varepsilon(u+t/\varepsilon))]_x du/\varepsilon$$

and

$$\bar{A}^\varepsilon k(x) = \lim_{N\to\infty}\frac{1}{N}\int_0^N A_{t+s}^\varepsilon k(x)ds.$$

Let $i = [t/\varepsilon]$, which equals the nearest integer to t/ε which is not larger than t/ε. Then

(5.2) $$A_t^\varepsilon k(x) = \frac{1}{\varepsilon}\sum_{j=1}^\infty Ef'(x,s_0^\varepsilon)[k_x'(x)f(x,s_j^\varepsilon)]_x$$

$$+ \frac{1}{\varepsilon}Ef'(x,s_0^\varepsilon)[k_x'(x)f(x,s_0^\varepsilon)]_x(\varepsilon[t/\varepsilon] + \varepsilon - t)/\varepsilon.$$

Note that $\bar{A}^{\varepsilon}$ is A_t^{ε} but with $(\varepsilon[t/\varepsilon] + \varepsilon - t)/\varepsilon$ replaced by 1/2.

(A5) The sum in (5.2) converges uniformly in ε for each x and $k(\cdot)$. Hence also uniformly in x, since $f(x,s) = f(x)s$. There are matrix and vector valued functions $a(\cdot)$ and $b(\cdot)$, resp., such that $(\bar{g}^{\varepsilon}(x) = Eg(x,s_i^{\varepsilon}))$

(5.3)
$$\bar{A}^{\varepsilon}k(x) + k_x'(x)\bar{g}^{\varepsilon}(x) \to b'(x)k_x(x) + \frac{1}{2}\sum_{i,j} a_{ij}(x)\partial^2 k(x)/\partial x_i \partial x_j \equiv Ak(x)$$

uniformly in x for each k.

(A6) A is the restriction to $\hat{C}^2$ of the strong infinitesimal operator of a strong Markov diffusion process (with no finite escape time) with semigroup T_t, which maps C_0 into C_0 and is strongly continuous on C_0.

(A7) For some real $\lambda > 0$, the set $(\lambda - A)\hat{C}^2$ is dense in C_0.

We note that it is enough to use $\hat{C}^3$ in (A5) and (A6).

Remark on bounding the coefficients. In our case (since $f(x,s) = f(x)s$) there is a matrix $\sigma(\cdot)$ such that $a(\cdot) = \sigma(\cdot)\sigma'(\cdot)$. Suppose that b, σ, are locally Lipschitz and that $x(\cdot)$, the diffusion with coefficients $\sigma(\cdot), b(\cdot)$, has no finite escape time w.p.1. Then $x(\cdot)$ has a representation as a solution to an Itô equation, and can be defined on Wiener process space. We say that $x^N(\cdot)$ is an N-truncation of $x(\cdot)$ if its drift and diffusion coefficients $b^N(\cdot), \sigma^N(\cdot)$ are bounded and equal $b(\cdot), \sigma(\cdot)$ in $S_N = \{x: |x| \le N\}$, and are obtained by a bounding of g and f. The process $x^N(\cdot)$ can be defined on the same Wiener process space on which $x(\cdot)$ is defined, and then equals $x(\cdot)$ up until the first exit time from S_N (which $\to \infty$ w.p.1 as $N \to \infty$). If for each N, Theorem 2 (and, of course, (A6)-(A7)) is true for some N-truncation, then it is true as stated.

Remark on the conditions. (A6) and (A7) are required for the use of (the semigroup approximation) Theorem 1. (A7) is equivalent to the strong infinitesimal operator of the T_t of (A6) being the closure of the operator A of (5.3) acting on $\hat{C}^2$ (or on any set dense in $\hat{C}^2$ in the norm $||k||_2 = \sup_x(|k(x)| + |k_x(x)| + |k_{xx}(x)|)$).

This condition does not seem to be very restrictive. As noted above it is often only necessary to verify it for some $x^N(\cdot)$ truncation for each N. If the coefficients are bounded and uniformly twice continuously differentiable, then ([11], Chapter 8.4) T_t maps C_0^2 into C_0^2 and is strongly continuous on C_0^2 with respect to norm $||k||_2$. We can then replace C_0 by C_0^2 in (A5), (A6) and in Theorem 1 and consider T_t as acting on C_0^2 rather than on C_0.

In Theorem 3, we apply Theorem 1 to get convergence of finite dimensional distributions of $\{x^\varepsilon(\cdot)\}$ to those of $x(\cdot)$ on an arbitrary time interval $0,T$. Tightness (Theorem 4) is a little harder to get, owing to the fact that $f(x,\xi_t^\varepsilon)/\sqrt{\varepsilon}$ is not necessarily uniformly bounded as $\varepsilon \to 0$ (see remarks in Section 1), and some additional conditions must be used.

Theorem 3. *Under (A1) to (A7), the finite dimensional distributions of $x^\varepsilon(\cdot)$ converge to those of $x(\cdot)$ as $\varepsilon \to 0$, where $x(\cdot)$ is the diffusion with infinitesimal operator A (on $\hat{C}^2$ functions) and initial condition x_0.*

Remark. Give $k \in \hat{C}^3$, the main work in using Theorem 1 is in finding a suitable k^ε and proving (3.2)-(3.3). Following a basic idea in [5], [6], we will define functions k_1^ε and k_2^ε such that $k^\varepsilon = k + k_1^\varepsilon + k_2^\varepsilon$ does the job. The k_i^ε are constructed to guarantee that p-lim $k_i^\varepsilon = 0$ and $\hat{A}^\varepsilon k^\varepsilon = Ak$ plus terms going to zero in the sense of p-lim.

Proof: Part 1. Let $k \in \hat{C}^3$. Then it is easy to check that $k_0^\varepsilon(\cdot) \equiv k(x^\varepsilon(\cdot)) \in \mathcal{D}(\hat{A}^\varepsilon)$ and that (write $x = x_t^\varepsilon$, $\xi = \xi_t^\varepsilon$)

$$\hat{A}^\varepsilon k_0^\varepsilon(t) = k_x'(x)[g(x,\xi) + f(x,\xi)/\varepsilon].$$

Part 2. We now define $k_1^\varepsilon(t) = k_1^\varepsilon(x_t,t)$ in such a way that $\hat{A}^\varepsilon k_1^\varepsilon(t)$ cancels the $k_x'(x)f(x,\xi)/\varepsilon$ term of $\hat{A}^\varepsilon k_0^\varepsilon(t)$. Define

$$k_1^\varepsilon(x,t) = \int_0^\infty E_t^\varepsilon k_x'(x)(f(x,\xi_{t+s}^\varepsilon)/\varepsilon)ds. \tag{5.4}$$

By (A3), (A4), $(i = [t/\varepsilon])$

$$|k_1^\varepsilon(x,t)| \le \sum_{j=0}^\infty |E_i^\varepsilon k_x'(x)f(x,s_{i+j}^\varepsilon)| \le K \sum_j \mu_j. \tag{5.5}$$

Thus, k_1^ε is bounded. By (A4a), $E|E_i^\varepsilon k_x'(x)f(x,s_{i+j}^\varepsilon)| \le K\sqrt{\varepsilon}$. Thus (5.5) is bounded above by $K\varepsilon^{1/4}\sum_j \mu_j^{1/2}$ and, hence, p-lim $k_1^\varepsilon = 0$.

Note that $k_1^\varepsilon(x,t)$ is differentiable with respect to x. In fact,

$$(5.6)\qquad k_{1,x}^\varepsilon(x,t) = \int_0^\infty E_t^\varepsilon[k_x'(x)f(x,\xi_{t+s}^\varepsilon)/\varepsilon]_x ds$$

which is well defined for each ε. We can readily show that $\sup_t E|E_t^\varepsilon k_1(x_{t+\delta}^\varepsilon,\xi_{t+\delta}^\varepsilon) - k_1^\varepsilon(x_t^\varepsilon,\xi_t^\varepsilon)|/\delta$ is bounded as $\delta \to 0$ and that

$$(5.7)\qquad \text{p-lim}[E_t^\varepsilon k_1^\varepsilon(x_{t+\delta}^\varepsilon,t+\delta) - k_1^\varepsilon(x_t^\varepsilon,t)]/\delta$$

$$= \text{p-lim}[E_t^\varepsilon k_1^\varepsilon(x_{t+\delta}^\varepsilon,t+\delta) - k_1^\varepsilon(x_t^\varepsilon,t+\delta)]/\delta$$

$$+ \text{p-lim}[E_t^\varepsilon k_1^\varepsilon(x_t^\varepsilon,t+\delta) - k_1^\varepsilon(x_t^\varepsilon,t)]/\delta$$

$$= (k_{1,x}^\varepsilon(x_t^\varepsilon,t))'\dot{x}_t^\varepsilon - k_x'(x_t^\varepsilon)f(x_t^\varepsilon,\xi_t^\varepsilon)/\varepsilon$$

$$\equiv \hat{k}_{1,x}(x_t^\varepsilon,t) + \tilde{k}(x_t^\varepsilon,t)/\varepsilon$$

where $\dot{x}_t^\varepsilon = g(x_t^\varepsilon,\xi_t^\varepsilon) + f(x_t^\varepsilon,\xi_t^\varepsilon)/\varepsilon$. Thus $k_1^\varepsilon \in \mathcal{D}(\hat{A}^\varepsilon)$ and $\hat{A}^\varepsilon k_1^\varepsilon$ is given by (5.7). The second term on the r.h.s. of (5.7) cancels a term of $\hat{A}^\varepsilon k_0^\varepsilon$. Also the term in $\hat{k}_{1,x}^\varepsilon(x_t^\varepsilon,t)'\dot{x}_t^\varepsilon$ which arises from the g term goes to zero in the p-lim sense as $\varepsilon \to 0$.

Part 3. Now k_2^ε is to be defined such that $\hat{A}^\varepsilon k_2^\varepsilon(t)$ equals $\hat{A}k(x_t^\varepsilon)$ minus the dominant term in $k_{1,x}^\varepsilon(x_t^\varepsilon,t)'\dot{x}_t^\varepsilon$ plus terms which go to zero in the p-lim sense as $\varepsilon \to 0$. Set $k_2^\varepsilon(t) = k_2^\varepsilon(x_t^\varepsilon,t)$ where

$$(5.8)\qquad k_2^\varepsilon(x,t) = \int_0^\infty ds\left\{\int_0^\infty E_t^\varepsilon \frac{f'(x,\xi_{t+s}^\varepsilon)}{\varepsilon}\left[k_x'(x)\,\frac{f(x,\xi_{t+s+u}^\varepsilon)}{\varepsilon}\right]_x du - A_{t+s}^\varepsilon k(x)\right\}$$

$$+ \int_0^\infty E_t^\varepsilon k_x'(x)[g(x,\xi_{t+s}^\varepsilon) - \bar{g}^\varepsilon(x)]ds = \tilde{k}_2^\varepsilon(x,t) + \hat{k}_2^\varepsilon(x,t).$$

The last term of k_2^ε goes to zero uniformly in x, as $\varepsilon \to 0$; also (with $x = x_t^\varepsilon$) it is in $\mathcal{D}(\hat{A}^\varepsilon)$ and $\hat{A}^\varepsilon\hat{k}_2^\varepsilon(x,t) = k'(x)\bar{g}^\varepsilon(x)$ plus terms going to zero in the p-lim sense minus $k_x'(x)g(x,\xi_t^\varepsilon)$. This last term cancels a term of $\hat{A}^\varepsilon k_0^\varepsilon(t)$. We need to deal only with the first term of (5.8). Recall that $A_{t+s}^\varepsilon k(x)$ is just the expected value of the integral with respect to u of the coefficient of E_t^ε.

Owing to the integration with respect to s in (5.8) A^{ε}_{t+s} can (and will) be replaced by $\bar{A}^{\varepsilon}$ with little required change in the subsequent arguments. Next, we show that $\tilde{k}^{\varepsilon}_2$ is well-defined and p-lim $\tilde{k}^{\varepsilon}_2 = 0$. To simplify the notation, assume the scalar case and let f^{ε}_j represent either $f(x,s^{\varepsilon}_j)$ or $f_x(x,s^{\varepsilon}_j)$. All bounds and convergences are uniform on bounded x-sets.

We have $(i = [t/\varepsilon])$

$$|\tilde{k}^{\varepsilon}_2(t)| \leq K \sum_{i,j} |E^{\varepsilon}_i f^{\varepsilon}_{i+j} f^{\varepsilon}_{i+j+k} - Ef^{\varepsilon}_{i+j} f^{\varepsilon}_{i+j+k}|.$$

By (A4a,b) the i,j^{th} term is bounded above by $K\mu_j$ and also by $K\mu_k$, hence by $K(\mu_j\mu_k)^{1/2}$ which implies that the sum is bounded. Also, by (A4a,c), p-lim $\tilde{k}^{\varepsilon}_2 = 0$. It can also be readily shown that $\tilde{k}^{\varepsilon}_2 \in \mathscr{D}(\hat{A}^{\varepsilon})$. We need only show that $\hat{A}^{\varepsilon}\tilde{k}^{\varepsilon}_2$ = minus argument of the outer integral of $\tilde{k}^{\varepsilon}_2$ (at $s = 0$) plus $\tilde{k}^{\varepsilon}_{2,x}(x^{\varepsilon}_t,t)'\dot{x}^{\varepsilon}_t$ and that p-lim $\tilde{k}^{\varepsilon}_{2,x}(x^{\varepsilon}_t,t)'\dot{x}^{\varepsilon}_t = 0$. If this is true, then we have $\hat{A}^{\varepsilon}(k(x^{\varepsilon}_t) + k^{\varepsilon}_1(t) + k^{\varepsilon}_2(t)) = Ak(x^{\varepsilon}_t)$ plus terms whose p-lim is zero, and the proof will be completed. That $\hat{A}^{\varepsilon}\tilde{k}^{\varepsilon}_2$ has the asserted form is not hard to show, and we only show that p-lim $(\dot{x}^{\varepsilon})'\tilde{k}^{\varepsilon}_{2,x} = 0$.

To get $\tilde{k}^{\varepsilon}_{2,x}$, we can differentiate under the integral in (5.8). With the use of the above f^{ε}_i notation, $\tilde{k}^{\varepsilon}_{2,x}(t)'x^{\varepsilon}_t$ is bounded by a finite (the number not depending on ε) sum of terms of the type $(i = [t/\varepsilon])$

$$(5.9) \qquad Q^{\varepsilon} = |f^{\varepsilon}_i/\varepsilon| \sum_{i,j} |E^{\varepsilon}_i f^{\varepsilon}_{i+j} f^{\varepsilon}_{i+j+k} - Ef^{\varepsilon}_{i+j} f^{\varepsilon}_{i+j+k}|.$$

By (A4), $E^{1/2}|f^{\varepsilon}_i|^2 \leq K\varepsilon^{1/2}$ and $E^{1/2}|E^{\varepsilon}_i f^{\varepsilon}_{i+j} f^{\varepsilon}_{i+j+k}|^2 \leq KEE^{\varepsilon}_i|f^{\varepsilon}_{i+j}|\mu_k \leq K\varepsilon^{1/2}\mu_k$. This and (A4c) implies that

$$E^{1/2}|E^{\varepsilon}_i f^{\varepsilon}_{i+j} f^{\varepsilon}_{i+j+k} - Ef^{\varepsilon}_{i+j} f^{\varepsilon}_{i+j+k}|^2 \leq K\varepsilon^{(1+\delta)/2}(\mu_j\mu_k)^{1/2}.$$

Thus, by (A4) again, $E|Q^{\varepsilon}| \leq K\varepsilon^{\delta/2}$; hence, p-lim $(\dot{x}^{\varepsilon})'\tilde{k}^{\varepsilon}_{2,x} = 0$. Q.E.D.

<u>Tightness</u>. To prove tightness (which together with the convergence of finite dimensional distributions yields weak convergence of $\{x^{\varepsilon}(\cdot)\}$ to $x(\cdot)$, we make use of Theorem 2. Both (4.4) and (4.5) must be shown for each $k \in \hat{C}^3$. They do not follow from (A1)-(A7). In order to simplify matters we use (A8) also.

(A8) <u>Let</u> $s_i^\varepsilon = L_\varepsilon w_i^\varepsilon$, <u>where</u> L_ε <u>is a matrix (bounded uniformly in</u> ε) <u>and</u> $\{w_i^\varepsilon, i \geq 0\}$ <u>is a Markov chain for each</u> ε. <u>There are matrices</u> ρ_j^ε <u>such that</u> $\sum_j |\rho_j^\varepsilon| < \infty$ <u>and where the convergence is uniform in</u> ε, <u>and</u> $E_i^\varepsilon w_{i+j}^\varepsilon = \rho_j^\varepsilon w_i^\varepsilon$. <u>We use</u> E_i^ε <u>to denote conditioning on</u> $(w_j^\varepsilon, j \leq i)$. <u>Let</u> $E|w_i^\varepsilon|^7 \leq K\varepsilon^{7/2}$ <u>and</u> $|E_i^\varepsilon w_{i+j}^\varepsilon (w_{i+j}^\varepsilon)' - Ew_{i+j}^\varepsilon (w_{i+j}^\varepsilon)'| \leq \rho_j^\varepsilon (|w_i^\varepsilon|^2 + K\varepsilon)$.

<u>Remark</u>. Condition (A8) is quite realistic. For example, let $w_{n+1}^\varepsilon = Bw_n^\varepsilon + \beta_n^\varepsilon$, where the eigenvalues of B are inside the unit circle and for each ε, $\{\beta_n^\varepsilon\}$ is a sequence of truncated independent identically distributed Gaussian random variables with covariance bounded above by $K\varepsilon$. Then (we use scalar case for illustration) $E_i^\varepsilon (w_{i+j}^\varepsilon)^2 = B^{2j}(w_i^\varepsilon)^2 + \sum_{k=0}^{j-1} (\text{var } \beta_n^\varepsilon) B^{2k}$ and $|E_i^\varepsilon (w_{i+j}^\varepsilon)^2 - E(w_{i+j}^\varepsilon)^2| \leq |B|^{2j}(w_i^\varepsilon)^2 + \sum_{k=j}^{\infty} (\text{var } \beta_n^\varepsilon)|B|^{2k}$ where var $\beta_n^\varepsilon \leq K\varepsilon$.

<u>Theorem 4</u>. <u>Under</u> (A1) <u>to</u> (A8), $\{x^\varepsilon(\cdot)\}$ <u>is tight on</u> $D^r[0,\infty)$ <u>and converges weakly to the diffusion</u> $x(\cdot)$ <u>of Theorem 3 as</u> $\varepsilon \to 0$.

<u>Proof</u>. Tightness of $\{k(x^\varepsilon(\cdot))\}$ on $D[0,T]$ needs to be shown, for arbitrary T and $k \in \hat{C}^3$. Define k_i^ε as in Theorem 3. Since k_i^ε, $i = 0,1,2$, are bounded, and $k^\varepsilon \in \mathcal{D}(\hat{A}^\varepsilon)$, then $(k^\varepsilon)^2 \in \mathcal{D}(\hat{A}^\varepsilon)$ and $\hat{A}^\varepsilon (k^\varepsilon)^2 = 2k^\varepsilon \hat{A}^\varepsilon k^\varepsilon$. By Theorem 2 and the estimates of Theorem 3 we only need to show that for each $\delta > 0$ $(i = 1,2)$ $P\{\sup_{t<T} |k_i^\varepsilon(t)| \geq \delta\}^2 \to 0$ as $\varepsilon \to 0$ and that $(\tilde{k}_{2,x}^\varepsilon)'\dot{x}^\varepsilon$ is bounded on $[0,T]$ by some random variable $M_\varepsilon(T)$ such that $\sup_\varepsilon P\{M_\varepsilon(T) \geq A\} \to 0$ as $A \to \infty$. (All the other components of $\hat{A}^\varepsilon k^\varepsilon$ have this property by the estimates in Theorem 3.)

By (A8) (using <u>scalar case</u> notation where convenient)

$$\sup_{t\leq T} |k_1^\varepsilon(t)| \leq K \sup_{i\leq [T/\varepsilon]} \sum_{j=0}^{\infty} |E_i^\varepsilon s_{i+j}^\varepsilon| \leq K \sup_{i\leq [T/\varepsilon]} |w_i^\varepsilon| \tag{5.10}$$

$$\begin{aligned}\sup_{t\leq T} |\tilde{k}_2^\varepsilon(t)| &\leq K \sup_{i\leq [T/\varepsilon]} \sum_{j,k=0}^{\infty} |E_i^\varepsilon s_{i+j}^\varepsilon s_{i+j+k}^\varepsilon - Es_{i+j}^\varepsilon s_{i+j+k}^\varepsilon| \\ &\leq K \sup_{i\leq [T/\varepsilon]} |w_i^\varepsilon|^2 + K\varepsilon.\end{aligned} \tag{5.11}$$

Similarly

$$(5.12)\qquad \sup_{t\le T}|\tilde{k}^{\varepsilon}_{2,x}(t)'x^{\varepsilon}_t| \le K\frac{|s^{\varepsilon}_i|}{\varepsilon}\sum_{j,k=0}^{\infty}|E^{\varepsilon}_i s^{\varepsilon}_{i+j}s^{\varepsilon}_{i+j+k} - Es^{\varepsilon}_{i+j}s^{\varepsilon}_{i+j+k}|$$

$$\le K \sup_{i\le[T/\varepsilon]}\frac{|w^{\varepsilon}_i|^3}{\varepsilon} + K_0|w^{\varepsilon}_i|.$$

By the comments in the first paragraph and the bounds (5.10)-(5.12) we need only show that

$$(5.13)\qquad P^{\varepsilon} \equiv P\{\sup_{i\le[T/\varepsilon]}|w^{\varepsilon}_i| \ge A\varepsilon^{1/3}\} \to 0$$

as $\varepsilon \to 0$ for each positive A. Bounding (5.13) and using Chebychev's inequality yields

$$P^{\varepsilon} \le \sum_{i=0}^{[T/\varepsilon]} P\{|w^{\varepsilon}_i| \ge A\varepsilon^{1/3}\} \le (\frac{T}{\varepsilon}+2)\frac{E|w^{\varepsilon}_i|^7}{A^7\varepsilon^{7/3}} \le \frac{K\varepsilon^{1/6}}{A^7},$$

from which we get that (5.10), (5.11) go to zero as desired and that (5.12) is bounded as desired. In fact (5.12) goes to zero in probability as $\varepsilon \to 0$. Q.E.D.

6. CONVERGENCE AND STABILITY FOR THE ADAPTIVE ANTENNA PROBLEM

We use the same notation as in Section 2. The symbols E^{ε}_t and E_t refer to expectation conditioned on $y(s)$, $s \le t/\varepsilon^2$ and $y(s)$, $s \le t$, resp. Write $K_0 = (K\bar{M}_0+I)/\tau$. As in Section 2, $y(\cdot)$ is a (not necessarily piecewise constant) stationary right continuous and bounded process. The quantities are not complex valued here, to simplify the notation. In general, deal with the real and imaginary parts separately. Assume

(B1) $\int_0^{\infty}|E_t\delta\tilde{M}_{t+s}|ds$ <u>is bounded uniformly in</u> t,ω.

Define the operator A^0_t (on $\hat{C}^2$ functions) by ($\bar{w}_t$ is not random)

$$A^0_t k(u) = \frac{K^2}{\tau^2}\int_0^{\infty}\bar{w}'_t E\delta\tilde{M}'_0 k_{uu}(u)\delta\tilde{M}_s\bar{w}_t ds.$$

(B2) $\int_0^{\infty}ds\int_0^{\infty}|E_t\delta\tilde{M}_{t+s}\delta\tilde{M}'_{t+s+v} - E\delta\tilde{M}_{t+s}\delta\tilde{M}'_{t+s+v}|dv$

<u>is bounded uniformly in</u> t,ω.

(B3) Either let E_t be the expectation conditioned on $\bigcap_{\rho>0} \mathscr{B}(y(s), s \le t + \rho)$ (and similarly for E_t^ε) or else $E_{t+\rho} y_{t+s} \to E_t y_{t+s}$ and $E_{t+\rho} y_{t+s} y'_{t+\tau} \to E_t y_{t+s} y'_{t+\tau}$ (and also for 3rd order terms) in probability as $\rho \downarrow 0$, for each positive t, s, τ.

Both (B1) and (B2) follow from the strong mixing condition (1.3).

Define the operator A_t by $A_t k(u) = -k'_u(u) K_0 u + A_t^0 k(u) \equiv -k'_u(u) K_0 u + \frac{1}{2} \sum_{i,j} p_{ij}(t) \partial^2 k(u)/\partial u_i \partial u_j$. Set $\{p_{ij}\} = P = QQ'$.

Theorem 5. Under (B1)-(B3), $\{u^\varepsilon(\cdot)\}$ converges weakly in $D^r[0,\infty)$ to the diffusion (2.5) with generator A_t and initial condition $u(0) = 0$.

The proof follows the lines of that of Theorem 3 quite closely, except, of course, that the integrals cannot necessarily be written as sums. Also, due to the scaling and to the fact that $y(\cdot)$ is bounded, tightness is more easily proved than in Section 5. In particular, $k_i^\varepsilon \to 0$ as $\varepsilon \to 0$ $(i = 1,2)$ and so does $(k_{2,u}^\varepsilon)' \dot{u}^\varepsilon$, all uniformly on $[0,\infty)$. Theorem 5 is also a consequence of the results in [4] (under their mixing condition (3.1) on $y(\cdot)$, which implies (B1)-(B2)), [6] (for Markovian $y(\cdot)$) or [7]. We will give only the relevant k_i^ε.

Let $k \in \hat{C}^3$. Then $k_i^\varepsilon(t) = k_i^\varepsilon(u_t^\varepsilon, t)$, where we use

$$k_1^\varepsilon(u,t) = \frac{-K}{\tau} \int_0^\infty E_t^\varepsilon k'_u(u) \left[\delta \tilde{M}_{t+s}^\varepsilon u + \frac{\delta \tilde{M}_{t+s}}{\varepsilon} \overline{w}_t \right] ds$$

$$k_2(u,t) = \frac{K^2}{\tau^2} \int_0^\infty ds \left\{ \int_0^\infty \overline{w}'_t E_t^\varepsilon \frac{(\delta \tilde{M}_{t+s+v})'}{\varepsilon} k_{uu}(u) \frac{\delta \tilde{M}_{t+s}}{\varepsilon} \overline{w}'_t dv - A_t^0 k(u) \right\}.$$

We have $\hat{A}^\varepsilon k^\varepsilon = A_t k$ plus terms which to to zero (uniformly in ω, t) as $\varepsilon \to 0$.

An extension of Theorem 5. Theorem 5 is not very satisfactory, since we are usually interested in $u^\varepsilon(\cdot)$ for large times, and would like some estimates of how close the tails ($[T,\infty)$ sections, for large T) are to the tail of (2.5). The weak convergence result of Theorem 5 does not give this to us. In Theorem 6, we show that

$$(6.1) \qquad \sup_{t>0,\varepsilon \text{ small}} E|u^\varepsilon(t)|^2 \text{ is bounded}$$

$$(6.2) \qquad \{u^\varepsilon(T+\cdot),\ T > 0,\ \varepsilon \text{ small}\} \text{ is tight in } D^r[0,\infty).$$

From these, we get the more satisfactory conclusion of Theorem 6. As noted after the proof, the method is not sharp enough to get good estimates for how small ε must be in order for (6.1)-(6.2) to hold.

Theorem 6. Assume (B1)-(B3). Then (6.1) and (6.2) hold and as $\varepsilon \to 0$, $T \to \infty$ in any way at all, $\bar{u}^\varepsilon(T+\cdot)$ converges weakly to the stationary solution to (2.5). Also, if $u^\varepsilon(T+\cdot)$ converges weakly to a process $u^\varepsilon(\cdot)$ as $T \to \infty$, then $u^\varepsilon(\cdot)$ converges weakly to the stationary solution of (2.5). (Indeed, it can be easily shown from (6.1) and the stationarity of $y(\cdot)$ that $\{u^\varepsilon(T+\cdot),\ T > 0\}$ is tight for each small ε.)

Proof: Only a sketch will be given. The stability idea is essentially that in [6], except that it is used in a slightly different way and that Kurtz's results must be used since $y(\cdot)$ is not assumed to be Markovian. Let P be a positive definite symmetric matrix such that $u'Pu \equiv k(u)$ is a Liapunov function for $\dot{u} = -K_0 u$, and $C = -(K_0'P+PK_0)$ is negative definite. In the proofs of Theorems 3, 4, 5, it was required that $k(\cdot) \in \hat{C}^3$. Our $k(\cdot)$ here is not in $\hat{C}^3$, but it makes little difference in the proofs. This is because $y(\cdot)$ is bounded and because we could use the form $\int_t^T E_t^\varepsilon(\cdot)$ for the k_i^ε and get estimates (6.1) for $t \le T$, and which do not depend on T. In order to simplify the argument, we ignore the fact that $k(\cdot) \notin \hat{C}^3$.

We have (use $u = u_t^\varepsilon$, $\bar{w} = \bar{w}_t$, $\delta M^\varepsilon = \delta M_t^\varepsilon$)

$$\hat{A}^\varepsilon k(u) = -u'Cu - \frac{K}{\tau} u'[(\delta\tilde{M}^\varepsilon)'P + P(\delta\tilde{M}^\varepsilon)]u - \frac{K}{\tau}[u'P\frac{\delta\tilde{M}^\varepsilon\bar{w}}{\varepsilon} + \bar{w}'(\frac{\delta\tilde{M}^\varepsilon}{\varepsilon})'Pu].$$

Following the method of Theorem 4, define k_1^ε such that $\hat{A}^\varepsilon k_1^\varepsilon$ cancels all the terms of $\hat{A}^\varepsilon k(u)$, except for the first. Set $k_1^\varepsilon(t) = k_1^\varepsilon(u_t^\varepsilon, t)$ where

$$(6.3) \qquad k_1^\varepsilon(u,t) = \frac{-K}{\tau}\int_0^\infty E_t^\varepsilon u'[(\delta\tilde{M}_{t+s}^\varepsilon)'P + P\delta\tilde{M}_{t+s}^\varepsilon u]ds$$

$$- \frac{K}{\tau\varepsilon}\int_0^\infty E_t^\varepsilon[u'P\delta\tilde{M}_{t+s}^\varepsilon\bar{w} + \bar{w}'(\delta\tilde{M}_{t+s}^\varepsilon)'Pu]ds.$$

Note that, by the change of variable $s/\varepsilon^2 \to s$,

$$(6.4)\quad k_1(u,t) = \frac{-K\varepsilon^2}{\tau}\int_0^\infty E_t^\varepsilon u'[\delta\tilde{M}(s+t/\varepsilon^2)'P + P\delta\tilde{M}(s+t/\varepsilon^2)]u\,ds$$
$$- \frac{K\varepsilon}{\tau}\int_0^\infty E_t^\varepsilon[u'P\delta\tilde{M}(s+t/\varepsilon^2)\overline{w} + \overline{w}'\delta\tilde{M}(s+t/\varepsilon^2)'Pu]ds.$$

Now,

$$(6.5)\qquad \hat{A}^\varepsilon k_1^\varepsilon(u,t) = -(\text{last two terms of } \hat{A}^\varepsilon k(u)) + (k_{1,u}^\varepsilon(u,t))'\dot{u}^\varepsilon.$$

The function $k_2^\varepsilon(t)$ is chosen in a way such that $\hat{A}^\varepsilon k_2^\varepsilon(t)$ cancels the part of the last term of (6.5) which is not $O(\varepsilon)$ (to see which terms are $O(\varepsilon)$ or $O(1)$, change variables $s/\varepsilon^2 \to s$). Thus set

$$(6.6)\qquad k_2^\varepsilon(t) = \frac{2K^2}{\tau^2\varepsilon^2}\int_0^\infty ds\int_0^\infty [E_t^\varepsilon \overline{w}_t'(\delta\tilde{M}_{t+s}^\varepsilon)'P\delta\tilde{M}_{t+s+v}^\varepsilon \overline{w}_t - C_t]dv$$

where

$$C_t = (2K^2/\tau^2)\int_0^\infty E\overline{w}_t'(\delta\tilde{M}_0)'P\delta\tilde{M}_s,\overline{w}_t ds.$$

Now,

$$\hat{A}^\varepsilon k_2^\varepsilon(t) = -(\text{dominant part of last term in (6.5)} + C_t.$$

By a change of variables $s/\varepsilon^2 \to s$, $v/\varepsilon^2 \to v$ and (B2), it can be verified that $k_2^\varepsilon = O(\varepsilon^2)$.

Combining the foregoing together with (B1)-(B2) yields, for $k^\varepsilon = k + k_1^\varepsilon + k_2^\varepsilon$, $u = u_t^\varepsilon$,

$$\hat{A}^\varepsilon k^\varepsilon(t) = -u'Cu + C_t + B_\varepsilon(u,\overline{w}_t)\varepsilon,$$
$$k(u) \le k^\varepsilon(u,t) + \varepsilon|\overline{B}_\varepsilon(u,\overline{w}_t)|,$$

where $B_\varepsilon(\cdot)$ and $\overline{B}_\varepsilon(\cdot)$ are both the sum of quadratic forms in u and bilinear forms in $(u,\overline{w}_t)$ and with coefficients that are bounded uniformly in ε,ω,t.

By (3.1) and the above estimates, there are positive real C,α and ε_0 such that for $\varepsilon \le \varepsilon_0$,

$$(6.7) \qquad Ek(u_s^\varepsilon) \le Ek^\varepsilon(u_0^\varepsilon) - \alpha \int_0^s Ek(u_v^\varepsilon)dv + \int_0^s C\,dv + \varepsilon|\overline{B}_\varepsilon(u_s^\varepsilon,\overline{w}_s)|.$$

Since $u_0^\varepsilon = 0$, (6.7) implies (6.1).

Given (6.1), it is not hard to show, via the method of Section 4 (see also Section 5 of [7]) that (6.2) holds. Also, the limit of any weakly convergent sequence (as $\varepsilon \to 0$) must converge to some solution of (2.5).

We only need to show that as $\varepsilon \to 0$, $T \to \infty$, any subsequence converges to the stationary solution of (2.5). Fix $T_1 > 0$ and take a convergent subsequence of $\{u^\varepsilon(T+\cdot)\}$ ($\varepsilon \to 0$, $T \to \infty$). Take a further subsequence of the subsequence, such that the $[T-T_1,\infty)$ sections are weakly convergent also. Let $\overline{u}(\cdot)$ and $\overline{\overline{u}}(\cdot)$ denote the weak limits on $D^r[0,\infty)$ of the $[T,\infty)$ and $[T-T_1,\infty)$ sections, resp. Then $\overline{u}(\cdot)$ is just the $[T_1,\infty)$ section of $\overline{\overline{u}}(\cdot)$. In particular, $\overline{u}(0) = \overline{\overline{u}}(T_1)$. Since $\{u^\varepsilon(t)\}$ is tight and T_1 arbitrary and $\dot{u} = -K_0 u$ asymptotically stable, we get that any limit as $T \to \infty$, $\varepsilon \to 0$ must be the stationary solution of (2.5). Q.E.D.

<u>Remark</u>. Theorem 6 is preferable to Theorem 5, but since ε_0 depends on the maximum magnitude of $y(\cdot)$, we do not get a good estimate of the stability region. Some other approach seems to be needed for this. We have tried to combine the above ideas with the ideas in stochastic stability for linear systems with coefficient variations (such as those based on Gronwall's Lemma [15]-[17]) but without much success so far.

REFERENCES

[1] E. Wong and M. Zakai, "On the relationship between ordinary and stochastic differential equations", Int. J. Engin. Science, (1965), <u>3</u>, 213-229.

[2] E. Wong and M. Zakai, "On the convergence of ordinary integrals to stochastic integrals", Ann. Math. Statist. <u>36</u>, 1560-1564.

[3] R. Z. Khasminskii, "A limit theorem for solutions of differential equations with random right hand sides", Theory of Prob. and Applic., (1966), <u>11</u>, 390-406.

[4] G. C. Papanicolaou and W. Kohler, "Asymptotic theory of mixing stochastic ordinary differential equations", Comm. Pure and Appl. Math., (1974), <u>27</u>, 641-668.

[5] G. C. Papanicolaou, "Some probabilistic problems and methods in singular perturbations", Rocky Mountain Journal of Math., (1976), <u>6</u>, 653-674.

[6] G. Blankenship and G. C. Papanicolaou, "Stability and control of stochastic systems with wide-band noise disturbances", SIAM J. on Appl. Math., (1978), 34, 437-476.

[7] H. J. Kushner, "Jump diffusion approximations for ordinary differential equations with random right hand sides", submitted to SIAM J. on Control; see also LCDS Report 78-1, September 1978, Brown University.

[8] T. G. Kurtz, "Semigroups of conditional shifts and approximation of Markov processes", Ann. Prob., (1975), 4, 618-642.

[9] IEEE Trans. on Antennas and Propagation, (1976), AP-24. Special Issue on Adaptive Antenna Arrays.

[10] L. E. Brennan, E. L. Pugh and I. S. Reed, "Control-loop noise in adaptive antenna arrays", IEEE Trans. on Aerospace and Electronic Systems, (1971), AES-7, 254-262.

[11] I. I. Gikhman and A. V. Skorokhod, Introduction to the Theory of Random Processes, (1965), Saunders, Philadelphia.

[12] P. Billingsley, Convergence of Porbability Measures, (1968), John Wiley and Sons, New York.

[13] G. L. Blankenship and G. C. Papanicolaou, "Stability and control of stochastic systems with wide-band noise disturbances", (1978), preprint.

[14] H. J. Kushner, Probability Methods for Approximations for Elliptic Equations and Optimal Stochastic Control Problems, Academic Press, New York, 1977.

[15] E. F. Infante, "On the stability of some linear autonomous random systems", (1968), ASME J. Appl. Mech., 35, 7-12.

[16] F. Kozin and C. M. Wu, "On the stability of linear stochastic differential equations", (1973), ASME J. Appl. Mech., 40, 87-92.

[17] G. Blankenship, "Stability of linear differential equations with random coefficients", (1977), IEEE Trans. on Automatic Control, AC-22, 834-838.

OPTIMAL CONDITIONS AND SUFFICIENT STATISTICS FOR CONTROLLED JUMP PROCESSES

Raymond Rishel

University of Kentucky
Lexington, Kentucky 40506

I. INTRODUCTION

A number of different optimality conditions [1] [3] [4] [9] have been given for partially observed jump processes. In this paper we show how the concept of sufficient statistics can be used to give the relationship between these optimality conditions for the case of a partially observed jump Markov process. An understanding of the relationship between these conditions gives insight into the question of which conditions should be used in computing optimal controls and can also be a guide in setting up numerical algorithms.

These results have been discussed from a slightly different point of view in [6]. The purpose of this paper is to show the role of sufficient statistics in obtaining the correspondence between the optimality conditions.

II. FORMULATION OF THE OPTIMAL CONTROL PROBLEM

In this paper a partially observed jump process will be a process

$$x = (y,z) \tag{1}$$

which has two integer valued components y and z. The component y is considered as observed and z as unobserved. When x takes on only a finite number of different values in each finite interval there will be a one-to-one correspondence

$$x(\cdot) \leftrightarrow (y_0, z_0, \tau_1, y_1, z_1, \tau_2, \ldots) \tag{2}$$

between paths of x and the succession of states x takes on and times of jumps between states.

Let

$$\begin{aligned} n(t) &= \{\text{no. of jumps of } x \text{ in } [0,t]\} \\ k(t) &= \{\text{no. of jumps of } y \text{ in } [0,t]\} \end{aligned} \tag{3}$$

Then when $n(t) = n$, x on $[0,t]$ corresponds to

$$(y_0 z_0, \tau_1 y_1, z_1, \ldots, \tau_n, y_n, z_n) \tag{4}$$

and if when $n(t) = n$ we also have $k(t) = k$, we must have $k \leq n$ and y on $[0,t]$ corresponds to

(5) $$(\bar{y}_0, \bar{\tau}_1, \ldots, \bar{\tau}_k, \bar{y}_k)$$

where $(\bar{y}_0, \ldots, \bar{y}_k)$ are $(y_0, \ldots, y_n)$ with repetitions suppressed and $\bar{\tau}_1, \ldots, \bar{\tau}_k$ is that subset of $\tau_1, \ldots, \tau_n$ for which there is a jump of y at each $\bar{\tau}_i$.

For brevity denote

(6) $$X_n = (y_0, z_0, \tau_1, y_1 z_1, \ldots, \tau_n, y_n z_n)$$

and

$$Y_k = (\bar{y}_0, \bar{\tau}_1, \bar{y}_1, \ldots, \bar{\tau}_k, \bar{y}_k) .$$

Call X_n the history up to the time of the n-th jump and Y_k the corresponding observed history. In the remainder of the paper we shall always use (i,j) to denote the current state of X_n ; that is we shall always use (i,j) to denote the value of (y_n, z_n) .

A partially observed controlled jump Markov process will be determined by a controlled conditional jump rate

(7) $$q(t,i,j,u) ,$$

a controlled conditional state jump distribution

(8) $$\pi[(\ell,m) \mid (i,j),t,u] ,$$

and the specification of a control. A control will be a family of functions $u(t,Y_k)$ of time and the various measurement histories Y_k . The values of the control are to lie on a closed set U . For a control given by a family of functions $\{u(t,Y_k)\}$, to define a corresponding controlled process specify that the conditional distribution of the time of the next jump and the conditional distribution of the location of the location of the next jump of the controlled process are given by

(9) $$P\{\tau_{n+1} > t \mid X_n\} = e^{-\int_{\tau_n}^{t} q(s,i,j,u(s,Y_k))ds}$$

and

(10) $$P\{(y_{n+1}, z_{n+1}) = (\ell,m) \mid X_n, \tau_{n+1}\} = \pi[(\ell,m) \mid (i,j), \tau_{n+1}, u(\tau_{n+1}, Y_k)]$$

In these expressions, Y_k is the measurement history corresponding to X_n , and as mentioned previously $(y_n, z_n) = (i,j)$. Let (x_0, y_0) have a fixed initial distribution P_{ij} that is

(11) $$P_{ij} = P(x_0 = i, y_0 = j) .$$

In terms of these conditional distributions and the initial distribution of x_0, y_0 construct finite dimensional distributions of the variables of the sequence

$$(y_0, z_0, \tau_1, y_1, z_1, \tau_2, y_2, z_2, \ldots) \tag{12}$$

and then extend this to a probability measure in the usual way. Define a controlled process x by defining

$$x(t) = \begin{cases} (y_0, z_0) & \text{if } 0 \le t < \tau_1 \\ \\ (y_n, z_n) & \text{if } \tau_n \le t < \tau_{n+1} \end{cases} . \tag{13}$$

Assume $q(t,i,j,u)$ is bounded in this case this procedure defines a process which has a finite number of jumps in each finite interval [3] pp. 494.

For the process constructed the measurement of $y(s)$, $0 \le s \le t$, corresponds to the measurement history $Y_{k(t)}$. The control applied at time t is $u(t, Y_{k(t)})$. Often we shall abbreviate by writing $u(t)$ for $u(t, Y_{k(t)})$. It can be seen from (9) that

$$\lim_{\Delta t \downarrow 0} \frac{1}{\Delta t} P\{t \le \tau_{n+1} < t+\Delta t \mid \tau_n \le t < \tau_{n+1}, X_n\} = q(t,i,j,u(t,Y_k)) \tag{14}$$

almost surely with respect to Lebesgue measure as a function of t. Thus $q(t,i,j,u)$ is the conditional jump rate. From (10) $\pi[(\ell,m) \mid (i,j),t,u]$ is the conditional distribution of the location of the next jump.

Since these depend only on the current values (t,i,j,u) of the time, state, and control; we shall call the process constructed a partially observed controlled jump Markov process. This is somewhat a misnomer because the conditional distributions (9) and (10) can depend on the past measurements and thus the future evolution of the process constructed can depend on the past measurements and the process need not be Markov. However we shall use the terminology partially observed controlled jump Markov process even though the process need not be Markov.

To formulate the optimization problem let $c(t,i,j,u)$ denote a cost rate. Let T denote a fixed time. The control problem is to find the control in the class of controls so that the corresponding expected cost

$$E\{\int_0^T c(s,y(s),z(s),u(s))ds\} \tag{15}$$

is a minimum.

III. MINIMUM PRINCIPLE OPTIMALITY CONDITIONS

In [3] optimality conditions in the form of a minimum principle were given for this problem. The following slight reformulation of these conditions can be shown to hold. The minimum principle of [3] is expressed in terms of equations for the conditional remaining cost conditioned with respect to the number of jumps up to time t

and the corresponding jump history of the past of the entire process.

Let $u(t,Y_k)$ denote an optimal control and

$$J_u(t,X_n) = E\{\int_t^T c(s,y(s),z(s),u(s))ds \,|\, n(t)=n,X_n\} \tag{16}$$

Define $H(t,X_n,u)$ by

$$H(t,X_n,u)=c(t,i,j,u)+q(t,i,j,u)[\sum_{\substack{\ell m\\(\ell,m)\neq(i,j)}} J_u(t,X_n,t,\ell,m,u)\pi[(\ell,m)\,|\,(i,j),t,u] - J_u(t,X_n)] \tag{17}$$

In (17), $(t,X_n,t,\ell,m,u) = (t,X_{n+1},u)$,that is (17) involves J_u evaluated at a history X_{n+1} with $n+1$ jumps, where the history X_{n+1} agrees with X_n for the first n jumps, the $n+1$-st jump takes place exactly at the current time t and is to the state (ℓ,m) .

The minimum principle asserts that on $(\tau_n,T]$, $J_u(t,X_n)$ is the solution of

$$\frac{d}{dt} J_u(t,X_n) = -H(t,X_n,u(t,Y_k)) \tag{18}$$

with boundary condition

$$J_u(T,X_n) = 0 \tag{19}$$

and for Lebesgue measure almost every t the minimum condition

$$\min_{u\in U} E\{H(t,X_{n(t)},u)\,|\,k(t) = k,Y_k\} = E\{H(t,X_{n(t)},u(t,Y_k))\,|\,k(t) = k,Y_k\} \tag{20}$$

is satisfied.

IV. OPTIMAL ESTIMATION RESULTS

To describe other optimality conditions it will be necessary to have some results on optimal estimation of jump processes.

Define the conditional probability that the unobserved state $z(t)$ is j given that k jumps of the observed process $y(t)$ have occurred up to time t and the measurement jump history is Y_k by:

$$P_j(t,Y_k) = P[z(t)=j\,|\,k(t)=k,Y_k] \tag{21}$$

Let $P(t,Y_k)$ denote the vector whose components are given by (21). We shall use the notation P for a possible value of $P(t,Y_k)$.

Define the quantities

$$r[(\ell,m)\,|\,t,i,P,u] = \sum_j \pi[(\ell,m)\,|\,(i,j),t,u]q(t,i,j,u)P_j \tag{22}$$

$$r[\ell\,|\,t,i,P,u] = \sum_m r[(\ell,m)\,|\,t,i,P,u] \tag{23}$$

(24) $$r(t,i,P,u) = \sum_{\ell} r[\ell|t,i,P,u]$$

The proof of the following theorem which interprets [22]-[24] as conditional jump rates can be given in a manner similar to that of Theorem 1 of [5].

Theorem IV-1: *For Lebesgue measure almost every* t

(25) $$\lim_{\Delta t \downarrow 0} \frac{1}{\Delta t}[P[t<\tau_{n+1}<t+\Delta t\ (y(\tau_{n+1}),z(\tau_{n+1}))=(\ell,m)|k(t)=k,Y_k]=r[(\ell,m)|t,i,P(t,Y_k),u(t,Y_k)]$$

(26) $$\lim_{\Delta t \downarrow 0} \frac{1}{\Delta t} P[t<\tau_{n+1}<t+\Delta t,y(\tau_{n+1})=\ell|k(t)=k,Y_k] = r[\ell|t,i,P(t,Y_k),u(t,Y_k)]$$

(27) $$\lim_{\Delta t \downarrow 0} \frac{1}{\Delta t} P[t,<\tau_{n+1}<t+\Delta t|k(t)=k,Y_k] = r[t,i,P(t,Y_k),u(t,Y_k)]$$

The following theorem, which is well known [2] [5] [7] [8] [10] but is usually stated in a different form, gives filtering formulas for the conditional probabilities $P(t,Y_k)$.

Theorem IV-2:

On $(\bar{\tau}_k,T]$, $P(t,Y_k)$ *satisfies the system of differential equations*

(28) $$\frac{d}{dt} P_j(t,Y_k) = [r(t,i,P(t,Y_k),u(t,Y_k)) - q(t,i,j,u(t,Y_k))]P_j(t,Y_k)$$
$$+ \sum_{\substack{\ell m \\ \ell \neq i}} \pi[(i,j)|(\ell,m),t,u(t,Y_k)]\ q(t,\ell,m,u(t,Y_k))\ P_m(t,Y_k)$$

At $\bar{\tau}_k$ *if the current state of* Y_{k-1} *is* i *and* $Y_k = (Y_{k-1},\bar{\tau}_k,\ell)$ *then* $P(\bar{\tau}_k,Y_k)$ *and* $P(\bar{\tau}_k,Y_{k-1})$ *are related by*

(29) $$P_m(\bar{\tau}_k,Y_k) = P_m^+(\bar{\tau}_k,\ell,i,P(\bar{\tau}_k,Y_{k-1}),u(\bar{\tau}_k,Y_{k-1}))$$

where

(30) $$P_m^+(t,\ell,i,P,u) = \frac{r[(\ell,m)|t,i,P,u]}{r[\ell|t,i,P,u]} .$$

The final Theorem on estimation gives the structure of the conditional distributions of the observed process. For jump Markov processes it is given in [7]. The present case may be obtained by extending results of [5].

Theorem VI-3: *The observed process* $y(t)$ *is a jump process with conditional distribution of the time of the next jump given by*

(31) $$P[\bar{\tau}_{k+1} \leq t|Y_k] = \int_{\bar{\tau}_k}^{t} r(s,i,P(s,Y_k),u(s,Y_k))e^{-\int_{\tau_k}^{s} r(\tau,i,P(\tau,Y_k),u(\tau,Y_k))d\tau} ds$$

and conditional distribution of the state at the next jump given by

(32) $$P[Y_{k+1}=\ell|Y_k,\tau_{k+1}] = \mu[\ell|\tau_{k+1},i,P(\tau_{k+1},Y_k),u(\tau_{k+1},Y_k)]$$

where

(33) $$\mu[\ell|t,i,P,u] = \frac{r[\ell|t,i,P,u]}{r[t,i,P,u]}$$

V. DYNAMIC PROGRAMMING OPTIMALITY CONDITIONS

Let u be any given control. For each t , let $\mathcal{U}_t$ denote the class of controls v which agree with u up to time t . Let $M_t = \sigma\{y(s);\ 0 \le s \le t\}$ denote the σ-field generated by the observed process corresponding to a control v of $\mathcal{U}_t$. Since each of these controls agree up to time t , the σ-fields M_t will be the same for each of the controls $v \in \mathcal{U}_t$.

Let

(34) $$J_v(t,\omega) = E[\int_t^T c(s,x(s),v(s))ds|M_t] .$$

Call a control $u_t \in \mathcal{U}_t$ *optimal from time* t *onward* if

(35) $$J_{u_t}(t,\omega) \le J_v(t,\omega)$$

almost surely for each $v \in \mathcal{U}_t$.

In [5] necessary and sufficient conditions for there to be controls u_t which are optimal from time t onward were given. Rather restrictive hypotheses were assumed in [5] to obtain the necessity of these conditions. An examination of the proof of the sufficiency of these conditions shows these restrictive assumptions are not needed to demonstrate the sufficiency of the conditions. Thus the following theorem gives a sufficient condtion for there to be controls u_t which are optimal from time t onward for each t .

Theorem V-1: *For each control* u *let there be functions* $W_u(t,Y_k)$ *such that* $W_u(t,Y_k)$ *are bounded and are Lipschitzian as functions of* t *, which satisfy*

(36) $$W_u(t,Y_k) = W_v(t,Y_k)$$

if $u = v$ *on* $[0,t]$, *and*

(37) $$\frac{d}{dt} W_u(t,Y_k) + \sum_j c(t,i,j,u(t,Y_k))P_j(t,Y_k)$$

$$+ r(t,i,P(t,Y_k),u(t,Y_k))[\sum_\ell W_u(t,Y_k,t,\ell)\mu(\ell|t,i,P(t,Y_k),u(t,Y_k))-W_u(t,Y_k)] \ge 0$$

for Lebesgue measure almost every t *on* $(\tau_k,T]$. *For each control* u *and each time* t *, let there be controls* $u_t \in \mathcal{U}_t$ *such that*

(38) $$\frac{d}{ds} W_{u_t}(s,Y_k) + \sum_j c(s,i,j,u_t(s,Y_k))\ P_j(s,Y_k)$$

$$+ r(s,i,P(s,Y_k),u_t(s,Y_k))\{\sum_\ell W_{u_t}(s,Y_k,s,\ell)\mu[\ell|s,i,P(s,Y_k),u_t(s,Y_k)]-W(s,Y_k)\} = 0$$

for Lebesgue measure almost every s *on* [t,T] . *Then* u_t *are optimal from time* t *onward.*

VI. SUFFICIENT STATISTICS - DYNAMIC PROGRAMMING CONDITIONS

Some thought about the optimization problem leads one to suspect that knowledge of the current state of the observed process and the conditional probabilities of the unobserved process should suffice for making decisions. Based on this intuitive idea, let us define (i,P) to be *sufficient statistics for the dynamic programming conditions* if there is a solution of these conditions and an "optimal control" of the form

$$W(t,i,P) \qquad u(t,i,P) \quad . \tag{39}$$

That is if it is possible to express $W_u(t,Y_k)$ and $u_t(s,Y_k)$ by (40) and (41) below so that (36) - (38) are satisfied

$$W_u(t,Y_k) = W(t,i,P_u(t,Y_k)) \tag{40}$$

$$u_t(s,Y_k) = \begin{cases} u(s,Y_k) & \text{if } 0 \leq s \leq t \\ u(s,i,P_{u_t}(s,Y_k)) & \text{if } t < s \leq T \end{cases} \tag{41}$$

Where $P_u(t,Y_k)$ and $P_{u_t}(s,Y_k)$ are the solutions of (28) and (29) corresponding to the controls u and u_t.

If there were solutions of the optimality conditions of the form (39), formally differentiating the relationship (40) and using (37) leads to the formula

$$W_t(t,i,P)+W_p(t,i,P)\dot{P}(t,i,P,u) + \sum_j c(t,i,j,u)P_j + r(t,i,P,u)[\sum_\ell W(t,\ell,P^+(t,\ell,i,P,u))\mu[\ell|t,i,P,u] - W(t,i,P)] \geq 0 \tag{42}$$

Where the j-th component of $\dot{P}(t,i,P,u)$ is defined from (28) by

$$\dot{P}_j(t,i,P,u) = [r(t,i,P,u) - q(t,i,j,u)]P_j + \sum_{\substack{\ell m \\ \ell \neq i}} \pi[(i,j)|(\ell,m),t,u]q(t,\ell,m,u)]P_m \tag{43}$$

In (37) $W_u(t,Y_k,t,\ell) = W_u(t,Y_{k+1})$ where $Y_{k+1} = (Y_k,t,\ell)$. Since if $Y_{k+1} = (Y_k,t,\ell)$, (29) implies $P(t,Y_{k+1}) = P^+(t,\ell,i,P(t,Y_k),u(t,Y_k))$ and (40) makes the correspondence

$$W_u(t,Y_{k+1}) = W(t,\ell,P_u(t,Y_{k+1})) \ ;$$

in obtaining (42) from (37) $W_u(t,Y_{k+1})$ is replaced by $W(t,\ell,P^+(t,\ell,i,P,u))$. Similarly to (42) formal differentiation of (40), (38) and (41) lead to

(44) $W_t(t,i,P) + W_p(t,i,P)\dot{P}(t,i,P,u(t,i,P)) + \sum_j c(t,i,j,u(t,i,p)P_j$

$+ r(t,i,P,u(t,i,P))[\sum_\ell W(t,\ell,P^+(t,\ell,i,P,u(t,i,P))\mu[\ell|t,i,P,u(t,i,P)] - W(t,i,P)] = 0$

Formulas (42) and (44) are equivalent to the partial differential equation

(45) $\underset{u\in U}{\mathrm{Min}}\Big\{W_t(t,i,P) + W_p(t,i,P)\dot{P}(t,i,P,u) + \sum_j c(t,i,j,u)P_j$

$+ r(t,i,P,u)[\sum_\ell W(t,\ell,P^+(t,\ell,i,P,u))\mu[\ell|t,i,P,u]-W(t,i,P)]\Big\}$

$= W_t(t,i,P) + W_P(t,i,P)\dot{P}(t,i,P,u(t,i,P)) + \sum_j c(t,i,j,u(t,i,P))P_j$

$+ r(t,i,P,u(t,i,P))[\sum_\ell W(t,\ell,P^+(t,\ell,i,P,u(t,i,P)))\mu[\ell|t,i,P,u(t,i,P)] - W(t,i,P)] = 0$

A special case of this partial differential equation was considered by Segall in [9]. He used filtering formulas and the Doleans-Dade-Meyer stochastic differential rule to show that a smooth solution of this partial differential equation gave a sufficient condition for optimality. Since his arguement was very similar to Wonham's [12] proof of the separation principle, he called these optimality conditions a generalized separation principle. For this reason we shall call (45) the *separated dynamic programming partial differential equation*. The preceeding discussion and Theorem VI-1 below give us our first comparison of optimality conditions. We have seen that if (i,P) were sufficient statistics for the dynamic programming conditions that a formal argument led to the conditions given by Segall [8]. Conversely Theorem VI-1 implies that a continuously differentiable solution of the separated dynamic programming partial differential equation will give a solution of the dynamic programming sufficiency conditions.

Theorem VI-3. *If* W(t,i,P) *is a continuously differentiable solution of the separated dynamic programming equation and if* u(t,i,P) *is a control which achieves the minimum in this equation which is continuously differentialbe in* (t,P) , *then for any given control* u *and time* t *the control defined by*

(46) $$u_t(s,Y_k) = \begin{cases} u(s,Y_k) & \text{if } 0 \le s \le t \\ u(s,i,P(s,Y_k)) & \text{if } t < s \le T \end{cases}$$

is optimal from time t *onward.*

Proof:

Corresponding to any control $u(t,Y_k)$ define $W_u(t,Y_k)$ by

(47) $$W_u(t,Y_k) = W(t,i,P(t,Y_k))$$

Where $P(t,Y_k)$ is the solution of (28) (29) corresponding to the control u . Similarly if $Y_{k+1} = (Y_k,t,\ell)$ define

$$(48)\qquad W_u(t,Y_{k+1}) = W_u(t,\ell,P^+(t,\ell,i,P(t,Y_k),u(t,Y_k)))$$

Since (47) implies that on $[\bar{\tau}_k,T]$

$$(49)\quad \frac{d}{dt} W_u(t,Y_k) = W_{u_t}(t,i,P(t,Y_k)) + \sum_r W_{uP_r}(t,i,P(t,Y_k))\dot{P}_r(t,i,P(t,Y_k),u(t,Y_k))$$

the separated dynamic programming equation (45) implies

$$(50)\quad \frac{d}{dt} W_u(t,Y_k) + \sum_j c(t,i,j,u(t,Y_k))P_j(t,Y_k)$$
$$+ r(t,i,P(t,Y_k),u(t,Y_k))[\sum_{\ell\neq i} W_u(t,Y_k,t,\ell)\mu(\ell|t,i,P(t,Y_k),u(t,Y_k))-W_u(t,Y_k)] \geq 0$$

on $(\bar{\tau}_k,T]$.

Since $u(t,i,P)$ achieves the minimum in the separated dynamic programming equation, the definition of $u_t(s,Y_k)$, (49) and the separated dynamic programming equation (45) imply

$$(51)\quad \frac{d}{ds} W_{u_t}(s,Y_k) + \sum_j c(s,i,j,u_t(s,Y_k))P_j(s,Y_k)$$
$$+ r(s,i,P(s,Y_k),u_t(s,Y_k))[\sum_{\ell\neq i} W_{u_t}(s,Y_k,s,\ell)\mu[\ell|s,i,P(s,Y_k),u_t(s,Y_k)]-W_{u_t}(s,Y_k)] = 0$$

on $[t,T]$.

Thus we see that the conditions of Theorem V-1 are satisfied.

VII. SUFFICIENT STATISTICS - MINIMUM PRINCIPLE

We can also look for sufficient statistics for the minimum principle. Since $J_{u^*}(t,X_n)$ involves conditioning with respect to the past of both the unobserved and observed processes, we might ask whether there is a function of the form $J(t,i,j,P)$ depending on the current state of both the observed and unobserved process and the conditional probabilities of the unobserved process and a control of the form $u(t,i,P)$ such that

$$(52)\qquad J_{u^*}(t,X_n) = J(t,i,j,P_{u^*}(t,Y_k))$$

and

$$(53)\qquad u^*(t,Y_k) = u(t,i,P_{u^*}(t,Y_k))$$

In (17) $J_{u^*}(t,X_n t,\ell,m)$ occurs where

$$(54)\qquad X_{n+1} = (X_n,t,\ell,m) \ .$$

If $\ell = i$, that is if the observed state at time τ_n and τ_{n+1} are the same,

X_{n+1} has corresponding observed history Y_k and (52) gives the correspondence

(55) $$J_{u^*}(t,X_{n+1}) = J(t,\ell,m,P_{u^*}(t,Y_k))$$

If in (54), $\ell \neq i$, then X_{n+1} has corresponding observed history $Y_{k+1} = (Y_k,t,\ell)$ and (29) implies

$$P_{u^*}(t,Y_{k+1}) = P^+(t,\ell,i,P_{u^*}(t,Y_k),u^*(t,Y_k))$$

thus (52) gives the correspondence

(56) $$J_{u^*}(t,X_{n+1}) = J(t,\ell,m,P^+(t,\ell,i,P_{u^*}(t,Y_k)),u^*(t,Y_k))$$

Thus using the correspondences (52) (55) (56) define $H(t,i,j,P,u)$ analagous to (17) by

(57) $$H(t,i,j,P,u) = c(t,i,j,u) + q(t,i,j,u)\{\sum_{m\neq j} J(t,i,m,P)\pi[(i,m)|i,j,t,u] + \sum_{\substack{\ell m \\ \ell\neq i}} J(t,\ell,m,P^+(t,\ell,i,u))\pi[(\ell,m)|i,j,t,u] - J(t,i,j,P)\}$$

If

(58) $$H[(t,X_n,u^*(t,Y_k)] = H[t,i,j,P_{u^*}(t,Y_k),u^*(t,Y_k)]$$

then

(59) $$E[H[t,X_{n(t)},u^*(t,Y_k)]\,|\,k(t)=k,Y_k] = \sum_j H[t,i,j,P_{u^*}(t,Y_k),u^*(t,Y_k)]P_j(t,Y_k)$$

Notice that (57) and (59) imply that to determine $J(t,i,j,P)$ and $u(t,i,P)$ so that (52) and (53) satisfy the equations of the minimum principle, it suffices to determine functions $J(t,i,j,P)$ and $u(t,i,P)$ such that the following family of two point boundary valuc problems with supplementary minimum condition are satisfied.

The two point boundary value problems and the minimum condition are: Determine $J(s,i,j,P)$ and $u(s,i,P)$ so that if for each (t,P) for which $0 \leq t \leq T$ and $0 \leq P_j \leq 1$, $\sum_j P_j = 1$ if $P(s)$ is a solution of

(60) $$\frac{d}{ds} P(s) = \dot{P}(s,i,P(s),u(s,i,P(s)))$$

on $[t,T]$ with initial condition $P(t) = P$, then $J(s,i,j,P(s))$ is a solution of

(61) $$\frac{d}{dt} J(s,i,j,P(s)) = -H(s,i,j,P(s),u(s,i,P(s)))$$

on $[t,T]$ with terminal condition $J(T,i,j,P(T)) = 0$ and

(62) $$\underset{u\in U}{\text{Min}} \sum_j H(s,i,P,u)P_j = \sum_j H(s,i,j,P,u(s,i,P))P_j$$

To check to see that when this family of two point boundary value problems with supplementary minimum condition has a solution then (52) and (53) give a solution of the equations of the minimum principle, it suffices to notice that $P_{u^*}(s,Y_k)$ is a solution of (60) on $[\bar{\tau}_k,T]$ with initial condition given by (29). Thus (55), 56), (57), and (61) imply (52) will satisfy (18). By (55), (56), (57) and (59); (62) with $P = P_{u^*}(t,Y_k)$ is of the form (20). Thus we see that (52) and (53) satisfy the conditions (18) - (20) of the minimum principle.

The two point boundary value problem and minimum condition (60), (61), (62) is associated with the family of optimization problems with initial conditions (t,i,P). That is t rather than zero is the initial time and at this time initial conditions for $y(t)$, $z(t)$ are $y(t) = i$ and $P\{z(t)=j\} = P_j$. The cost criteria is given by

(63) $$E\{\int_t^T c(s,x(s)),u(s))ds\} .$$

Formulas (60), (61), (62) assert that $u(t,i,P)$ is a control which satisfies the minimum principle simultaneously for each of these optimization problems.

Next we shall show that if $u(t,i,P)$ is a control which is simultaneously optimal for each of these optimization problems that an additional necessary condition holds. Define controls u^* by

(64) $$u^*(s,Y_k) = u(s,i,P(s,Y_k))$$

where $P(s,Y_0)$ satisfies the initial condition $P(t,Y_0) = P$. $P(s,Y_k)$ satisfies (28) on $(\tau_k,T]$ and $P(s,Y_k)$ and $P(s,Y_{k+1})$ are related by (29).

Theorem VII-1: *If the conditional cost corresponding to the control* u^* *for the problem with initial conditions* (t,i,P) *has the form*

(65) $$E\{\int_t^T c(s,x(s),u^*(s))ds \mid z(t)=j\} = J(t,i,j,P)$$

and if $u(t,i,P)$ *is simultaneously optimal for each of these problems in the sense that for each of these problems* $u^*(s,Y_k)$ *described in* (64) *is an optimal control; then at each point at which it is differentiable with respect to* P, $J(t,i,j,P)$ *satisfies for each* r

(66) $$\sum_j J_{P_r}(t,i,j,P)P_j = 0 .$$

where J_{P_r} *denotes partial derivative of* J *with respect to the* r-th *component of* P.

Proof: Let P be a point at which $J(t,i,j,P)$ is differentiable. Let $\bar{P}$ be distinct from P. Let

(67) $$\bar{u}(s,Y_k) = u(s,i,\bar{P}(s,Y_k))$$

where $\bar{P}(s,Y_k)$ satisfies $\bar{P}(t,Y_0) = \bar{P}$, $\bar{P}(s,Y_k)$ satisfies (28) with control $\bar{u}$ on $(\bar{\tau}_k,T]$ and $\bar{P}(s,Y_k)$ and $\bar{P}(s,Y_{k+1})$ are related by (29). Then $J(t,i,j,\bar{P})$ is the value of (65) corresponding to the initial conditions $(t,i,\bar{P})$ and control $\bar{u}$.

Consider using the control $\bar{u}(s,Y_k)$ in the problem with initial conditions (t,i,P). That is using the optimal control but with the incorrect, initial estimate $\bar{P}$ of the initial probabilities rather than the correct one P. By our hypotheses

(68) $$J(t,i,j,\bar{P}) = E\{\int_t^T c(s,x(s),\bar{u}(s)ds \mid z(s)=j\}$$

Thus the expected cost when the control $\bar{u}$ is used is given by

(69) $$\sum_j J(t,i,j,\bar{P})P_j$$

Since this must be greater than or equal to the expected cost when the optimal control u^* is used we must have

(70) $$\sum_j J(t,i,j,\bar{P})P_j \geq \sum_j J(t,i,j,P)P_j$$

Thus the right hand side of (70) considered as a function of $\bar{P}$ takes its minimum at $\bar{P} = P$. Thus its gradient with respect to $\bar{P}$ evaluated at $\bar{P} = P$ must be zero, which is the relationship (66).

With these preliminary considerations carried out we now are in a position to begin our discussion of the correspondence between the conditions of the minimum principle and the separated dynamic programming partial differential equation. Formally differentiating (52) and using (18) leads to

(71) $$J_t(t,i,j,P) + \sum_r J_{P_r}(t,i,j,P))\dot{P}_r[t,i,P,u(t,i,P)] = -H[t,i,j,P,u(t,i,P)] .$$

Rewriting (20) using (55), (56), (57) and (59) leads to

(72) $$\underset{u\in U}{\text{Min}} \sum_j H(t,i,j,P,u)P_j = \sum_j H[t,i,j,P,u(t,i,P)]P_j$$

Notice also that if there is a solution of the family of two point boundary value problems (60), (61), (62) such that $J(t,i,j,P)$ is continuously differentiable in (t,P) that (71) follows from (61) and (72) is condition (62).

The theorem given below connects (71) and (72), two conditions which are a strengthened form of the minimum principle, with the separated dynamic programming partial differential equation and gives us our second comparison of optimality conditions.

Theorem VII-II: *If* $J(t,i,j,P)$ *and* $u(t,i,P)$ *satisfy* (71) *and* (72) *and the additional conditions* (66) *and if* $W(t,i,P)$ *is defined by*

(73) $$W(t,i,P) = \sum_j J(t,i,j,P)P_j$$

then $W(t,i,P)$ *and* $u(t,i,P)$ *satisfy the separated dynamic programming partial differential equation* (45).

Proof: First we shall show that

$$(74)\quad \sum_j J(t,i,j,P)\dot{P}_j(t,i,P,u) - \sum_j H(t,i,j,P,u)P_j =$$

$$- r(t,i,P,u)[\sum_{\substack{\ell \\ \ell\neq i}} W(t,\ell,P^+(t,\ell,i,P,u))\mu[\ell,t,i,P,u] - W(t,\ell,P,u)] - \sum_j C(t,i,j,u)P_j \ .$$

From (43) and (57)

$$(75)\quad \sum_j J(t,i,j,P)\dot{P}_j(t,i,P,u) - \sum_j H[t,i,j,P,u]P_j = \sum_j J(t,i,j,P)r(t,i,P,u)P_j$$

$$- \sum_j J(t,i,j,P)q(t,i,j,u)P_j + \sum_j J(t,i,j,P) \sum_{\substack{m \\ m\neq j}} q(t,i,m,u)\pi[(i,j)|i,m,t,u]P_m$$

$$- \sum_j q(t,i,j,u)\{\sum_{\substack{m \\ m\neq j}} J(t,i,m,P)\pi[(i,m)|i,j,t,u]P_j$$

$$+ \sum_{\substack{\ell m \\ \ell\neq i}}\sum J(t,\ell,m,P^+(t,\ell,i,u))\pi[(\ell,m)|i,j,t,u]P_j - J(t,i,j,P)P_j\} - \sum_j c(t,i,j,u)P_j \ .$$

An interchange of order of summation shows that the right side of (75) equals

$$(76)\quad r(t,i,P,u) \sum_j J(t,i,j,P)P_j - \sum_{\ell m} J(t,\ell,m,P^+(t,\ell,i,u))r[(\ell,m)|t,i,P,u] - \sum_j c(t,i,j,u)P_j$$

$$= r(t,i,P,u)\left[\sum_j J(t,i,j,P)P_j - \sum_{\ell m} J(t,\ell,m,P^+(t,\ell,i,u))\frac{r[(\ell,m)|t,i,P,u]}{r[\ell|t,i,P,u]}\,\frac{r[\ell|t,i,P,u]}{r(t,i,P,u)}\right]$$

$$- \sum_j c(t,i,j)P_j$$

$$= r(t,i,P,u)[W(t,i,P) - \sum_\ell W(t,\ell,P^+(t,\ell,i,u)]\mu[\ell|t,i,P,u]] - \sum_j c(t,i,j)P_j \ .$$

Thus (74) is demonstrated.

Now since $u(t,i,P)$ satisfies the minimum condition

$$\sum_j H(t,i,j,P,u)P_j \geq \sum_j H(t,i,j,P,u(t,i,P))P_j \ .$$

Since $\sum_j J_{P_r}(t,i,j,P,u)P_j = 0$ for each r and (71) holds we have that

$$(77)\quad \sum_j J_t(t,i,j,P)P_j + \sum_r\sum_j J_{P_r}(t,i,j,P)P_j\dot{P}_r(t,i,P,u) - \sum_j J(t,i,j,P)\dot{P}_j(t,i,P,u)$$

$$+ \sum_j J(t,i,j,P)P_j(t,i,P,u) + \sum_j H(t,i,j,P,u)P_j \geq \sum_j J_t(t,i,j,P)P_j$$

$$+ \sum_r\sum_j J_{P_r}(t,i,j,P)P_j\dot{P}_r(t,i,P,u(t,i,P)) - \sum_j J(t,i,j,P)\dot{P}_j(t,i,P,u(t,i,P))$$

$$+ \sum_j J(t,i,j,P)\dot{P}_j(t,i,P,u(t,i,P)) + \sum_j H(t,i,j,P,u(t,i,P))P_j = 0$$

From (73) and (74) we see that (77) is equivalent to (42) and (44). Since (42) and (44) are equivalent to (45) the theorem is proven.

VIII. CONCLUSIONS

For a partially observed controlled jump Markov process looking for a solution of the dynamic programming optimality conditions in terms of sufficient statistics lead through a heuristic argument to the separated dynamic programming partial differential equation. Conversely a smooth solution of the separated dynamic programming partial differential equation gave a solution of the dynamic programming optimality conditions. Thus the existence of a smooth solution of the separated dynamic programming partial differential equation gives a sufficient condition for there to be an optimal control.

Looking for a solution of the optimality conditions of the minimum principle in terms of sufficient statistics lead to a family of two point boundary value problems with minimum side condition. A smooth solution of this two point boundary value problem which satisfies an additional condition gives a solution of the separated dynamic programming partial differential equation. Thus a smooth solution of the family of two point boundary value problems which satisfies the additional condition gives a sufficient condition for there to be an optimal control.

The separated dynamic programming partial differential equation and the family of two point boundary value problems with minimum side conditions are expressed in terms of sufficient statistics and thus would be much easier to use in computations than the minimum principle or dynamic programming conditions because they have much "lower dimensional" arguments. For instance the arguments of the separated dynamic programming partial differential equation are (t,i,P) while those of the dynamic programming conditions are (t,Y_k) for all Y_k. Similarly the arguments of the two point boundary value problems are (t,i,j,P) while those of the minimum principle are (t,X_n) for all X_n. Thus it seems that the separated dynamic programming partial differential equation and family of two point boundary value problems with minimum side conditions will be much simpler to compute with than dynamic programming conditions or the minimum principle.

The separated dynamic programming partial differential equation resembles but is more complicated than the dynamic programming partial differential equation which arises in deterministic optimal control problems. Similarly the family of two point boundary value problems with minimum side condition resemble but are more complicated than the Pontryagin principle for deterministic control problems. Thus we should expect that difficulties which occur in computations for deterministic control problems for each method will continue to occur for the corresponding methods for the stochastic problems.

It would appear that imposition of the extra condition (66) which was needed to demonstrate the sufficiency of two point boundary value problem conditions for optimality would be difficult to implement in a numerical calculation. There is some evidence to suspect that (66) should automatically be satisfied by a smooth solution of the two point boundary value problem with minimum side condition. However the author has not been able to demonstrate this.

REFERENCES

[1] R. Boel and P. Varaiya, "Optimal Control of Jump Processes," SIAM J. Control and Optimization (1977), vol. 15.

[2] P. Bremaud and J. Jacod, "Point Processes and Martingales: Review of Recent results on Modeling and Filtering," Advances in Applied Probability, Vol. 9 (1977).

[3] R.W. Rishel, "A Minimum Principle for Controlled Jump Processes, in Springer Lecture Notes in Economics and Mathematics Systems, Vol. 107, "Control Theory, Numerical Methods and Computer Systems Modelling, (1975).

[4] R.W. Rishel, "Controls Optimal From Time t Onward and Dynamic Programming for Systems of Controlled Jump Processes," in Mathematical Programming study 6, Stochastic Systems, Modelling, Identification and Optimization II, North Holland (1976).

[5] R.W. Rishel, "State Estimation for Partially Observed Jump Processes," Journal of Mathematical Analysis and Applications, Vol. 66 (1978)

[6] R.W. Rishel, "The Minimum Principle, Separation Principle, and Dynamic Programmin for Partially Observed Jump Processes" IEEE Transactions on Automatic Contrc Vol. AC-23 (1978).

[7] Mats Rudemo, "State Estimation for Partially Observed Markov Chains," Journal of Mathematical Analysis and Applications, vol. 44 (1973).

[8] A. Segall, M.H.A. Davis, T. Kailath, "Nonlinear Filtering with Counting Observations," IEEE Transactions on Information Theory, IT 22 (1976).

[9] A. Segall, "Optimal Control of Finite State Markov Processes," IEEE Transactions on Automatic Control, Vol. AC-22 (1977).

[10] D.L. Synder, "Information Processing for Observed Jump Processes," Information and Control 22 (1973).

[11] D.L. Synder, "Random Point Processes," Wiley-Interscience (1975).

[12] W.M. Wonham, "On the Separation Theorem of Stochastic Control", SIAM Journal on Control, Vol. 5 (1968).

STOCHASTIC FILTERING THEORY: A DISCUSSION OF CONCEPTS, METHODS ,AND RESULTS

J.H. van Schuppen
Stichting Mathematisch Centrum
Tweede Boerhaavestraat 49
1091 AL Amsterdam, The Netherlands

1. INTRODUCTION

The purpose of this paper is to give an exposition of the problem, methods and results of stochastic filtering theory. The novelty of this paper is in the definition and application ot the concept of a stochastic dynamical system, and in the formulation that includes both sample continuous and jump process observations.

In this paper we restrict attention to observed processes on $\Omega \times T \Rightarrow R^k$. Due to space limitation we will not discuss stochastic filtering problems for infinite dimensional stochastic systems, for random fields, and quantum mechanical systems. Neither will we discuss the important practical issues of asymptotic analysis of filtering algorithms, filtering techniques, estimation bounds, and adaptive filtering. The reader is referred to the literature on these topics.

We briefly summarize the historical development of the stochastic filtering problem. Suppose given a stationary second order process specified by its mean and covariance function, that is considered to be observed. The linear observation prediction problem is to find a linear operation on the observations that yields a least squares estimate of the future observations. It has been the contribution of Wiener [44] and Kolmogorov to have reduced this problem to the problem of solving the Wiener-Hopf equation. The difficulty with this equation is that it seems impossible to solve it in its full generality.

It is the contribution of Kalman, and of Bucy, to have singled out a class of observed processes for which the linear observation prediction problem can be solved. The idea underlying their approach is the concept of a state and of a linear dynamical system, as developed by Kalman [17]. The model taken is a Gauss-Markov model, which class allows consideration of non-stationary processes. The linear stochastic filtering problem is then defined as the linear estimation of the state of this system given past observation. The resulting algorithms, known as the Kalman and the Kalman-Bucy filter for respectively discrete and continuous time processes, have found wide spread application [14, 15].

At about 1960 a generalization of the linear stochastic filtering problem has been formulated, in which the linear dynamical system is replaced by a nonlinear dynamic model driven by disturbances having Gaussian distribution. A precise definition of a stochastic dynamical system is not given. The filtering problem is then defined to be the estimation of the "state" of this model given past observations. For this problem a representation for the estimate has been derived known as the Kushner-Stratonovich formula [19, 39]. The filtering problem has only been resolved for two models.

Since about 1970 the filtering problem for counting and jump processes has received attention. A model similar to that in the proceeding paragraph has been adopted. A representation for the estimate of the "state" given past observations has been derived under various sets of assumptions [1, 2, 3, 4, 5, 32, 33, 37, 38, 42, 43, 47].

In this paper we propose a general framework for the stochastic filtering problem, based on the following principles. The objects we deal with are stochastic processes defined on a totally ordered parameter set, and, of course, specified by their distributions. At any time one has a past history that is assumed known with certainty, and an uncertain future about which one can only speak in terms of conditional distributions. Then we define a stochastic dynamical system in which the state transition function and the read-out function map into the distribution of the state and the observation respectively. The stochastic filtering problem is then defined to be the determination of the conditional distribution of the state given past observations.

The emphasis in this paper is on conceptual ideas. Therefore no proofs will be given. In section two we define the concept of a stochastic dynamical system and the filtering problem . In section three we present two methods to analyze filtering problems. Some examples are presented in section four. We close with some miscellaneous comments in section five. For a comprehensive survey of the literature up to 1974 on filtering theory the reader is referred to [12].

We assume that the reader is familiar with the concepts and results of the modern theory of stochastic processes, in particular on σ-algebra families, martingales, stochastic integrals and stochastic differential equations. We refer the reader to the references [6, 7, 10, 23, 27, 28, 50] for further details.

2. THE PROBLEM FORMULATION

2.1. The set-up. The objects that we will deal with are stochastic processes defined on some probability space and a totally ordered parameter set. We take as specification of these processes their distribution. Estimation will be understood to mean the determination of the conditional distribution given information.

DEFINITION 2.1 An *observed process* will be a collection

$$\{\{\Omega, F, P\}, \{T, B_T\}, \{R^k, B_k\}, \{F_t, t \in T\}, y\}$$

where $\{\Omega, F, P\}$ is a complete probability space, $T \subset R$ is an interval, B_T the Borel σ-algebra of subsets of T, $\{R^k, B_k\}$ the k-dimensional Euclidean space with its Borel σ-algebra, $\{F_t, t \in T\}$ an increasing and complete family of σ-algebras, $y: \Omega \times T \to R^k$ a separable and measurable stochastic process such that $\{y_t, F_t, t \in T\}$ is adapted. Usually the distribution of y is specified by $E[\exp(iv'y_t)|F_s]$ for all $s, t \in T$, $s < t$, $v \in R^k$. For short we call $\{y_t, F_t, t \in T\}$ an observed process.

Historically the filtering problem has been motivated by the stochastic observation prediction problem, which is to determine $E[\exp(iv'y_t)|F^y_s]$ for all $s, t \in T$, $s < t$, $v \in R^k$. This problem can be embedded in the stochastic filtering problem. To define the stochastic filtering problem we need the definition of a stochastic dynamical system.

2.2. Conditional Independence. In this subsection we define a relation for a triple of σ-algebras, that will be used in the sequel.

DEFINITION 2.2. The σ-algebras F_1, F_2 are said to be *conditionally independent* given the σ-algebra G iff

$$E[x_1 \, x_2|G] = E[x_1|G] \, E\,[x_2|G]$$

for any $x_1 \in L_{1b}(F_1)$, $x_2 \in L_{1b}(F_2)$. Notation $\{F_1, F_2, G\} \in CI$.

PROPOSITION 2.3. The following are equivalent:

a. $\{F_1, F_2, G\} \in CI$;

b. $E[x_1|F_2 \vee G] = E[x_1|G]$ for all $x_1 \in L_1(F_1)$;

c. $\{F_2, F_1, G\} \in CI$;

d. $\{F_1 \vee G, F_2 \vee G, G\} \in CI$.

PROOF. Omitted.

The concept of conditional independence is known in the literature [27], and is used in the study of Markov processes. The equivalent property 2.3.b. expresses that conditioning F_1 on $F_2 \vee G$, it is sufficient to know G only. Thus conditional independence is seen to be equivalent to a sufficiency property for σ-algebras. Sufficient σ-algebras in the Bayesian formulation of statistics have been considered in [36]. The concept of a splitting σ-algebra, as introduced by McKean [26], is also seen to be the same concept of conditional independence. The equivalence between these concepts seems to us to be particularly important for a stochastic system theory.

A publication on certain problems related to the conditional independence relation is in preparation.

2.3. Stochastic Dynamical Systems. In this subsection we propose a definition for a stochastic dynamical system. So as not to overburden the paper we consider here only systems without input.

Briefly, a dynamical system, that we will here call a deterministic dynamical system, without input is a collection

$$\Sigma = \{T, Y, \underline{Y}, X, f, g\}$$

where the state transition function $f: T\times T\times X \to X$, $x(t) = f(t, s, x(s))$, and the read-read-out map $g: T\times X \to Y$, $y(t) = g(t, x(t))$ satisfy certain conditions [17, p. 5].

With this definition in mind one way define a stochastic dynamical system as a collection

$$S\Sigma = \{\Omega, F, P, T, Y, \underline{Y}, X, f, g\}$$

such that the maps $f(t, s, x(s)) \longmapsto$ distribution of $x(t)$, and $g(t, x(t)) \longmapsto$ distribution of $y(t)$ satisfy certain conditions. This definition has been suggested by Kalman [17, p. 5]. However this definition presupposes a "finite dimensional" state space. Below we present a definition of a stochastic dynamical system that incorporates this idea.

Because we want to work with stochastic integrals and stochastic differential equations it is necessary to consider the increments of the observation process as the output of the stochastic dynamical system. The alternative is to work with the observation as the output but then one must use white noise processes in the representations. For discrete time processes this issue does not arise.

We introduce a somewhat different viewpoint on stochastic dynamical systems. Let $\{y_t, F_t, t \in T\}$ be an observed process, where F_t represents past information at time $t \in T$. With the above intuitive definition of a stochastic dynamical system in mind a state process $\{x_t, t \in T\}$ based on the past $\{F_t, t \in T\}$ should be adapted $\{x_t, F_t, t \in T\}$ and such that

$$E[\exp(iu'x_\tau + iv'(y_t-y_s))|F_s] = E[\exp(iu'x_\tau + iv'(y_t-y_s))|F^{x_s}]$$

for all $s, t \in T$, $s < t$, $u \in R^n$, $v \in R^k$. This statement is equivalent to $\{{}_tF^{\Delta y} \vee {}_tF^x, F_t, F^{x_t}\} \in CI$ and $F^{x_t} \subset F_t$ for all $t \in T$, where ${}_tF^{\Delta y} = \sigma(\{y_s-y_t, \forall s > t\})$, ${}_tF^x = \sigma(\{x_s, \forall s > t\})$, $F^{x_t} = \sigma(\{x_t\})$.
We will take this last statement as our definition of a stochastic dynamical system.

To obtain a general formulation for stochastic dynamical systems we will work with σ-algebra families rather then with stochastic processes. Thus let $\{F_t, t \in T\}$ and $\{G_t, t \in T\}$ be σ-algebra families, F_t representing past information and G_t representing future information at time $t \in T$.

DEFINITION 2.4. A *stochastic dynamical system* is a collection

$$\{\{\Omega, F, P\}, T, \{G_t, t \in T\}, \{F_t, t \in T\}, \{H_t, t \in T\}\}$$

where $\{\Omega, F, P\}$ is a complete probability space, T a totally ordered set, $\{G_t, t \in T\}$, $\{F_t, t \in T\}$, $\{H_t, t \in T\}$ are complete sub-σ-algebra families of F, such that for all $t \in T$

$$\{G_t \vee (\vee_{s\geq t} H_s),\ F_t \vee (\vee_{\tau\leq t} H_\tau),\ H_t\} \in CI.$$

Then we call $\{H_t,\ t \in T\}$ the *state σ-algebra* at $t \in T$.
Notation $\{G_t, F_t, H_t, t\in T\} \in \Sigma S$.
b. If in addition there exists a stochastic process $x : \Omega \times T \to R^n$ such that $H_t = F^{x_t}$ for all $t \in T$, then we call $\{G_t, F_t, F^{x_t}, t \in T\}$ a *finite dimensional stochastic dynamical system* and x the *state process*. Notation $\{G_t, F_t, F^{x_t}\} \in \Sigma SF$.

DEFINITION 2.5. Given the observed process $\{y_t, F_t, t \in T\}$.
a. If there exists a complete σ-algebra family $\{H_t, t \in T\}$ with $H_t \subset F_t$ for all $t \in T$ and $\{{}_tF^{\Delta y}, F_t, H_t, t \in T\} \in \Sigma S$, then we call this collection a *forward stochastic dynamical system for y*. Here ${}_tF^{\Delta V} = \sigma(\{y_s - y_t, \forall s>t\})$.
b. If in addition there exists a process $x : \Omega \times T \to R^n$ with $\{x_t, F_t, t \in T\}$ adapted such that $\{{}_tF^{\Delta y}, F_t, F^{x_t}, t \in T\} \in \Sigma SF$ then we call this collection a *finite dimensional forward stochastic dynamical system for y*. In this case we call

$$E[\exp(iv'(y_t-y_s))|F^{x_s}]:\Omega\times T\times T\times R^n \to \underline{C}_k,\quad E[\exp(iu'x_t)|F^{x_s}]:\Omega\times T\times T\times R^n \to \underline{C}_n$$

respectively the *stochastic read-out function* and the *stochastic state-transition function* of this stochastic dynamical system, where $\underline{C}_k$ is the set of characteristic functions $\underline{C}_k$: $R^k \to C$.
c. A *stochastic dynamical system representation* is a specification of the stochastic state transition function and the stochastic read out function of a stochastic dynamical system.
d. A *stochastic differential stochastic dynamical system representation* is a stochastic dynamical system representation in the form of a pair of stochastic differential equations driven by independent increment processes for the state process and the observed process.

The justification for calling the collection $\{G_t, F_t, H_t, t \in T\}$ a stochastic dynamical system is in the interpretation of the defining property, namely that $\{G_t \vee (\vee_{s\geq t} H_s),\ F_t \vee (\vee_{\tau\leq t} H_\tau),\ H_t\} \in CI$ for all $t \in T$, or, equivalently, that for all $t \in T$, $A \in G_t \vee (\vee_{s\geq t} H_s)$ we have

$$E[I_A \mid F_t \vee (\vee_{\tau\leq t} H_\tau) \vee H_t] = E[I_A \mid H_t].$$

In words this says that any event in the future information or the future states conditioned on past information and past states, depends only on the current state. Thus the two properties of a dynamical system, namely sufficiency of the state for the output and recursiveness of the state, are captured by the above definition.

The definition of a stochastic dynamical system also implies that $\{\vee_{s\geq t} H_s,\ \vee_{\tau\leq t} H_\tau,\ H_t\} \in CI$ for all $t \in T$, hence $\{H_t, t \in T\}$ may be called a Markovian σ-algebra family. If in addition there exists a process $x : \Omega \times T \to R^n$ such that $H_t = F^{x_t}$ for all $t \in T$, then we can conclude that $\{x_t, F_t, t \in T\}$ is a Markov process.

Note that in definition 2.4 no restriction is given on the σ-algebra family $\{H_t, t \in T\}$. The term forward in definition 2.5 is now to be understood in connection with the condition $F^{x_t} \subset F_t$; thus the state is constructed on the basis of past information. A corresponding definition can be given for a backward stochastic dynamical system, reminiscent of backward Markov models. This topic will not be elaborated here.

Having given a definition of a stochastic dynamical system the following problems arise, the stochastic realization problem, the definition of stochastic observability, and related issues. We will leave these problems to future publications, except for stating the following problem.

DEFINITION 2.6. The *stochastic realization problem*. Given an observed process $\{y_t, F_t, t \in T\}$.

a. Find, if possible, a σ-algebra family $\{H_t, t \in T\}$ with $H_t \subset F_t$ for all $t \in T$, such that $\{_tF^{\Delta y}, F_t, H_t, t \in T\} \in \Sigma S$.

b. Find, if possible, a stochastic process $x : \Omega \times T \to R^n$ with $\{x_t, F_t, t \in T\}$ adapted, such that $\{_tF^{\Delta y}, F_t, F^{x_t}, t \in T\} \in \Sigma SF$.

c. Given $\{_tF^{\Delta y}, F_t, F^{x_t}, t \in T\} \in \Sigma SF$. Find, if possible, a stochastic differential stochastic dynamical system representation for x, y.

Some examples of stochastic dynamical systems are given in section four.

We point out that the above approach to stochastic cynamical systems differs essentially from what should be called linear stochastic dynamical systems. There the objects are second order stochastic processes, specified by their first and second moment; the spaces are the Hilbert spaces generated by linear operations on these processes; and the conditioning operation is the Hilbert space projection operation. This formulation is more or less implicit in Kalman's work [16], and has been formalized in the work by Faurre, Akaike, Picci, Lindquist and Ruckebush. For references see [20, 21, 22, 29]. The definitions given here have been inspired by these publications, in particular by the work by Picci [29].

2.4. The Filtering Problem. With the concept of a stochastic dynamical system defined, we can now present the definition of the stochastic filtering problem.

DEFINITION 2.7. Given the observed process $\{y_t, F_t, t \in T\}$ and suppose that $\{_tF^{\Delta y}, F_t, F^{x_t}, t \in T\} \in \Sigma SF$.

a. The *stochastic filtering problem* is to determine the conditional characteristic function

$$E[\exp(iu'x\ ) \mid F^y_t]$$

for all $t \in T$, $u \in R^n$.

b. If there exists a process $z : \Omega \times T \to R^m$ with $\{z_t, F^y_t, t \in T\}$ adapted, such that

$\{F^{x_t}, F_t^y, F^{z_t}, t \in T\} \in \Sigma SF$, then we call this collection a *finite dimensional stochastic dynamical filter system* for the above defined stochastic filtering problem. For short, we call this collection a *filter system*, and z the *filter state*.

To determine the conditional characteristic function in 2.7.a. will be understood as to exhibit the function from the past of the observations to the characteristic function. We will use the term stochastic filtering problem rather than the term stochastic reconstruction problem, which term is suggested by the analogy with deterministic dynamical system theory [17].

A filter system has the two properties

$$E[\exp(iu'x_t)|F_t^y] = E[\exp(iu'x_t)|F^{z_t}],$$

$$E[\exp(iw'z_t)|F_s^y] = E[\exp(iw'z_t)|F^{z_s}],$$

or z_t is a sufficient variable in estimating x_t given F_t^y, and $\{z_t, F_t^y, t \in T\}$ is a Markov process. The last statement implies intuitively that z can be computed recursively, but this aspect we have been unable to clarify yet. Clearly the existence of a finite dimensional filter system is important for the practical application of this theory. It is not at all clear that the filter state will be $E[x_t|F_t^y]$.

It can be shown that the stochastic observation prediction problem can be embedded in the stochastic filtering problem. Here we will not consider the stochastic prediction and the stochastic smoothing problem, which are to determine

$$E[\exp(iu'x_t)|F_s^y]$$

for $t > s$ and $t < s$ respectively.

A method to solve the stochastic filtering problem is to reduce it to the problem of solving an equation for the conditional characteristic function.

3. METHODS

In this section we present two methods for the stochastic filtering problem, both of which yield equations for the conditional characteristic function.

3.1. *The Semi-Martingale Representation Method.* We start by defining two concepts from the theory of stochastic process.

DEFINITION 3.1. The process $\{x_t, F_t, t \in T\}$ is called an *uniformly integrable semi-martingale* iff x has a decomposition as $x = x_0+a+m$ where $x_0 \in L_1(F_0)$, $\{a_t, F_t, t \in T\} \in V_1$ is of integrable variation, $a_0 = 0$, $\{m_t, F_t, t \in T\} \in M_{1u}$ is an uniformly integrable martingale, $m_0 = 0$. Notation $\{x_t, F_t, t \in T\} \in SM_{1u}$.

The above class of semi-martingales is a sub-class of those introduced in [28], to which the reader is referred for further details. The class of semi-martingales has proven to be an extremely general class of processes, that is closed under a large number of operations.

DEFINITION 3.2. Let $\{y_t, F_t, t \in T\}$ be an observed process. We say that the *martingale representation condition* holds for the class $M_{1uloc}\{F_t^y, t \in T\}$ if there exists a sample continuous local martingale m^c and a positive integer valued random measure p such that if $m \in M_{1uloc}\{F_t^y, t \in T\}$ then m has a representation as

$$m = m_0+(h.m^c)+(\phi.(p-\bar{p}))+(\psi.p),$$

for certain predictable processes h, ϕ, ψ.

Here the expressions on the right hand side are stochastic integrals, we refer to [10, 28] for details. It is a rather deep and important result in stochastic integration theory that the martingale representation condition is satisfied for a large number of observed processes.

We formulate a sub-problem of the stochastic filtering problem.

DEFINITION 3.3. Given the observed process $\{y_t, F_t, t \in T\}$ and assume that the martingale representation condition is satisfied for $M_{1uloc}\{F_t^y, t \in T\}$.
Let $\{x_t, F_t, t \in T\} \in SM_{1u}$. The *semi-martingale representation problem* is to give a decomposition for the projection of x on $\{F_t^y, t \in T\}$.

The solution to this problem is provided by the following ideas. The projection of x on $\{F_t^y, t \in T\}$ is defined to be $\hat{x} = \{E[x_t|F_t^y], F_t^y, t \in T\}$ which is again a semi-martingale, say with decomposition $\hat{x} = \hat{x}_0+\bar{a}+\bar{m}$. A relation between a and $\bar{a}$ can be given. Then the martingale representation condition is invoked to obtain a repre-sentation for $\bar{m}$. Finally the processes in this martingale representation can be determined. The above method has been proposed in [9]. Note the analogy with linear stochastic filtering theory.

We will not attempt to solve the above problem here. Below we present two canonical cases. Special cases and generalizations may be found in [1, 3, 4, 9, 23, 32, 33, 40, 41, 42, 43, 48].

THEOREM 3.4. Let the observed process $\{y_t, F_t\ t \in T\}$ and $x : \Omega \times T \to R^n$ satisfy

$$dx_t = f_t dt+dm_t,\ x_0,$$
$$dy_t = h_t dt+dw_t,\ y_0,$$

where $w : \Omega \times T \to R^k$, $\{w_t, F_t, t \in T\}$ is a standard Brownian motion process, $h : \Omega \times T \to R^k$, $\{h_t, F_t, t \in T\} \in SM_{1u}$ with $E[\int_T \|h_s\|^2 ds] < \infty$, $m : \Omega \times T \to R^n$, $\{m_t, F_t, t \in T\} \in M_2$, $f : \Omega \times T \to R^n$, $\{f_t, F_t, t \in T\} \in SM_{1u}$ with $E[\int_T \|f_s\|^2 ds] < \infty$, and that $\|x_t(\omega)\| \le 1$ for all $(\omega, t) \in \Omega \times T$.

a. Then the martingale representation condition holds for the class $M_{1uloc}\{F_t^y, t \in T\}$.

b. There exists a process $\phi : \Omega \times T \to R^{n+k}$, $\{\phi_t, F_t, t \in T\} \in L_1(t) \cap SM_{1u}$ such that $<m, w>_t = \int_0^t \phi_s ds$.

c. The solution to the semi-martingale representation problem is given by

$$d\hat{x}_t = \hat{f}_t dt + [\hat{\Sigma}_t^{xh} + \hat{\phi}_t]\ (dy_t - \hat{h}_t dt),\ \hat{x}_0 = E[x_0 | F_0^y],$$

$$\hat{\Sigma}_t^{xh} = E[(x_t - \hat{x}_t)(h_t - \hat{h}_t)' | F_t^y],$$

where the hat symbol denotes the projection of a semi-martingale on the σ-algebra $\{F_t^y,\ t \in T\}$.

PROOF [9, 23]

The formula of 3.4.c. is known in the literature as the Kushner-Stratonovich formula.

THEOREM 3.5. Let the observed process $\{y_t,\ F_t,\ t \in T\}$ and $x : \Omega \times T \to R^n$ satisfy

$$x_t = x_0 + a_t + m_t,$$
$$p(w,\ dt \times dv) = h(t,\ v)\ \mu(dt,\ dv) + q(w,\ dt \times dv)$$

where y is a pure jump process, p its associated jump measure, $\{h(t,\ v),\ F_t,\ t \in T,\ v \in R^k\}$ predictable, $\{\mu((0,\ t]xA),\ F_t^y,\ t \in T,\ A \in B_k\}$ predictable, $\{q(w,\ (0,\ t]xA),\ F_t,\ t \in T,\ A \in B_k\} \in M_{1uloc}$, $x \in SM_{1u}$ with $m \in M_2$.

a. Then the martingale representation condition holds for $M_{1uloc}\{F_t^y,\ t \in T\}$.
b. There exists a predictable process $\{\psi(t,v),\ F_t,\ t \in T,\ v \in R^k\}$ such that

$$\langle m,\ q(w,\ (0,\ t]xA)\ \rangle_t = \int_0^t \int_A \psi(s,\ v)\ h(s,\ v)\ \mu(ds,\ dv).$$

c. The solution to the semi-martingale representation problem is given by

$$\hat{x}_t = \hat{x}_0 + \bar{a}_t + \int_0^t \int_{R^k} k(s,\ v)\ \bar{q}(w,\ ds \times dv),$$

$$\bar{q}(w,\ dt \times dv) = (p(w,\ dt \times dv) - \hat{h}(t,\ v)\ \mu(dt,\ dv),$$

$$k(t,v) = \left(E[(x_t - \hat{x}_t)(h(t,\ v) - \hat{h}(t,\ v))' | F_t^y] + E[\psi(t,\ v) h(t,\ v) | F_t^y]\right) \hat{h}(t,\ v)^{-1},$$

of which a predictable version is taken.

PROOF [1, section 5].

We return to the stochastic filtering problem. Let $\{{}_tF^{\Delta y},\ F_t,\ F^{xt},\ t \in T\} \in \Sigma SF$, and suppose that the state process x is a semi-martingale. Then it can be shown that for all $u \in R^n$ the process $\{\exp(\ iu'xt),\ F_t,\ t \in T\} \in SM_{1u}$ is a semi-martingale. Depending on the availability of the solution to the semi-martingale representation problem for the stochastic system under consideration, one obtains the semi-martingale decomposition for the process $\hat{c}(u) = \{E[\exp(iu'x_t) | F_t^y],\ F_t^y,\ t \in T\}$. In general one can express the processes in the decomposition as operations on $\hat{c}(u)$, so that this representation becomes a genuine equation for the conditional characteristic function. One is then faced with the question how to obtain a solution for this equation.

There are few results on this equation for the conditional characteristic function. To be specific, one would want conditions for the existence and uniqueness of the solution, and methods to determine the solution. We mention a few cases in which the equation can be resolved. The first case is where the state process is a finite state Markov process. The second case is where the state process is a discrete state Markov process, see [31]. The third case is for the linear Gaussian, Gauss-Markov model that underlies the Kalman-Bucy filter. The method consists of converting the equation to an equation for the conditional moments, which may then be solved by using properties of the Gaussian distribution; see [13] for details. Yet another method is to extent the results for the discrete time case by a limiting argument, but one would hope for a more direct approach.

3.2. *The Measure Transformation Method.* A second method to obtain an equation for the conditional characteristic function is the measure transformation method introduced by Zakai [49].

The idea of this approach is to perform a measure transformation, such that under the new measure the processes x and y are independent. An equation for the operator of conditioning on F_t^y then readily follows, which equation has to be solved. The advantage of the method is that the independence of x and y under the new measure makes the calculations involved easier.

The only assumption necessary for the application of this method is the absolute continuity, for which conditions are available in the literature. The generator for the state process, which is a Markov process by the stochastic dynamical system assumption, is not needed.

The resulting equation obtained by this method can be converted into a semimartingale representation as obtained in section 3.1.

The application of this method to sample continuous observed processes may be found in [45, 49] of which we give a summary below. For jump processes the method can be found in [1, 2, 5, 6].

THEOREM 3.6. Given the observed process $\{y_t, F_t, t \in T\}$ and the process $x : \Omega \times T \to R^n$ satisfying

1. $E[\exp(iv'(y_t-y_s))|F_s \vee_s F^x] = \exp(iv'\int_s^t C(\tau)x_\tau d\tau - \frac{1}{2}v' I_k(t-s)v)$ where $s, t \in T$, $s < t$, $v \in R^k$, $C : T \to R^{k\times n}$;
2. $\{x_t, F_t, t \in T\}$ is a Markov process such that

$$E[\int_T \| C(\tau)x_\tau \|^2 d\tau] < \infty.$$

a. Then $\{_tF^{\Delta y}, F_t, F^{xt}, t \in T\} \in \Sigma SF$.

b. There exists a probability measure $P_0 : F \to [0,1]$ such that

1. $P \ll P_0$ on F with $\rho_t = E_0[dP/\,dP_0|F_t]$,

$$\rho_t = \exp(\int_0^t x_s' C'(s)\, dy_s - \tfrac{1}{2}\int_0^t x_s' C'(s)\, C(s)\, x_s ds);$$

2. under P_0 $\{y_t, F_t, t \in T\}$ is standard Brownian motion;
3. under P_0 F_T^x, F_T^y are independent;
4. $P = P_0$ on F_T^x.

Then $E[\exp(iu'x_t)|F_t^y] = E_0[\exp(iu'x_t)\rho_t|F_t^y]/E_0[\rho_t|F_t^y]$ a.s.

c. We have the equation

$$E_0[\exp(iu'x_t)\ \rho_t|F_t^y] = E[\exp(iu'x_t)]$$

$$+\int_0^t E_0[\rho_s\ E_0[\exp(iu'x_t)|F^{x_s}]x_s'|F_s^y]C'(s)\ dy_s.$$

PROOF [45, 6.5].

4. EXAMPLES

In this section we indicate some stochastic dynamical systems for which the stochastic filtering problem has been resolved. In the list below we summarize the stochastic dynamical system by the conditional distribution for the observed process and the character of the state process.

The stochastic filtering problem has been resolved for the following stochastic dynamical systems.

1. The Gaussian, Gauss-Markov system, yielding the Kalman-Bucy filter [15, 23].
2. The Gaussian, Finite State Markov process system, Wonham [46].
3. The Poisson, Finite State Markov process system, Segall [34], Rudemo [30].
4. The Poisson, Gamma system, Frost [51], see theorem 4.3. below.
5. The jump process with Gaussian kernel in its dual predictable measure, with Gauss-Markov state process. Reference Fishman, Snyder [8].
6. The observed process is a function of the state process, while the state process is a Markov process with a discrete state space, Rudemo [31].
7. The Gaussian, Bilinear system, as presented by Marcus, Willsky [25].

We remind the reader that we have excluded stochastic filtering problems on geometric structures, algebraic structures, and partially ordered sets. No claim is made that the above list is complete.

Below we present the solutions to the stochastic filtering problem for three stochastic dynamical systems.

THEOREM 4.1. The linear Gaussian - Gauss Markov system.
Given the observed process $\{y_t, F_t, t \in T\}$, $x : \Omega \times T \to R^n$, and assume that

1. $E[\exp(iv'(y_t - y_s))|F_s \vee F_s^x] = \exp(iv'\int_s^t C(\tau)x_\tau d\tau - \tfrac{1}{2}v'I_k(t-s)v)$

   for $s, t \in T$, $s < t$, $v \in R^k$, $C : T \to R^{k\times n}$, $I_n \in R^{k\times k}$ the unit matrix, $y_0 = 0$;

2. $\{x_t, F_t, t \in T\}$ a Gauss-Markov process such that $E(x_t) = 0$, $Q(t, s) = E[x_t x_s'] > 0$ for all $s, t \in T$, x is almost surely sample continuous, $Q : T \times T \to R^{n\times n}$ is differentiable and

$$dQ(t, s)/dt = A(t)Q(t, s),$$

$$A(t)Q(t, t)+Q(t, t)A'(t) \le -dQ(t, t)/dt.$$

<u>a</u>. Then $\{{}_tF^{\Delta y}, F_t, F^{x_t}, t \in T\} \in \Sigma SF$.

<u>b</u>. There exists $m \in Z_+$ and independent standard Brownian motion processes $v : \Omega \times T \to R^m$, $w : \Omega \times T \to R^k$ such that we have the representation

$$dx_t = A(t)\, x_t dt+Q(t, 0)B(t)dv_t,\ x_0,$$

$$dy_t = C(t)\, x_t dt+dw_t,\ y_0 = 0,$$

where $B : T \to R^{n\times m}$ is a full rank solution to

$$B(t)B'(t) = Q(t,0)^{-1}[dQ(t, t)/dt-A(t)Q(t, t)-Q(t, t)A'(t)]Q^{-1}(t, 0).$$

<u>c</u>. The solution to the stochastic filtering problem for the stochastic system of <u>a</u>. is given by

$$E[\exp(iu'x_t)|F_t^y] = \exp(iu'\hat{x}_t-\tfrac{1}{2}u'\Sigma(t)u),$$

$$d\hat{x}_t = A(t)\hat{x}_t dt+\Sigma(t)C\ (t)(dy_t-C(t)\hat{x}_t dt),\ \hat{x}_0 = E(x_0),$$

$$d\Sigma(t)/dt = A(t)\Sigma(t)+\Sigma(t)A'(t)+Q(t,0)B(t)B'(t)Q'(t,0)-\Sigma(t)C(t)C'(t)\Sigma(t),$$

$$\Sigma(0) = E[(x_0-E(x_0))(x_0-E(x_0))'].$$

<u>d</u>. $\{F^{x_t}, F_t^y, F^{\hat{x}_t}, t \in T\}$ is a finite dimensional filter system, known as the Kalman-Bucy filter system.

PROOF. The results of <u>a</u>. and <u>b</u>. are easily established. For <u>c</u>. see [23]. Then <u>d</u>. follows.

THEOREM 4.2. The *Poisson-FSMP system*. Given the observed process $\{y_t, F_t, t \in T\}$, $y : \Omega \times T \to R$ and $x : \Omega \times T \to R^n$ and assume that

1. $E[\exp(iv'(y_t-y_s))|F_s \vee_s F^x] = \exp(\int_s^t C(\tau)x_\tau dt(e^{iv}-1))$ for $s, t \in T$, $s < t$, $v \in R$, $y_0 = 0$, $C : T \to R^{1\times n}$;
2. $\{x_t, F_t, t \in T\}$ is a finite state Markov process, say with state space $X = \{x_1, x_2, \ldots x_m\} \subset (0,\infty)^n$; let $z : \Omega \times T \to R^m$, $z_t^i = I_{\{x_t = x_i\}}$, $\phi : T \times T \to R^{m\times m}$

$$\phi^{ij}(t, s) = E[z_t^i z_s^j]/E[z_s^j] \quad \text{if} \quad E[z_s^j] > 0,\ s \le t,$$
$$= 0 \qquad \text{otherwise;}$$

assume that $\phi(t, s) > 0$ for all $s, t \in T$, and that $\phi(\cdot,0) : T \to R^{m\times m}$ is differentiable, say with

$$d\phi(t, 0)/dt = A(t)\phi(t,0)$$

for $A : T \to R^{m\times m}$; let $D = (x_1, x_2, \ldots x_m)$.

a. Then $\{{}_tF^{\Delta y}, F_t, F^{x_t}, t \in T\} \in \Sigma SF$.

b. There exist processes m, m' such that we have the representation

$$dz_t = A(t)z_t dt + \phi(t, 0)dm'_t, \; z_0,$$

$$dy_t = C(t)Dz(t)dt + dm_t, \; y_0 = 0$$

where $\{m_t, F_t, t \in T\} \in M_1$, $\{m'_t, F_t, t \in T\} \in M_1$.

c. The solution to the stochastic filtering problem for the stochastic system of definition a. is

$$E[\exp(iu'x_t)|F_t^y] = \sum_{i=1}^{m} \exp(iu'x_i)\,\hat{z}_t^i,$$

$$d\hat{z}_t = A(t)\hat{z}_t dt + \hat{k}_{t-}(D\hat{z}_{t-})^{-1}(dy_t - C(t)D\hat{z}_t dt), \; \hat{z}_0 = E(z_0),$$

$$\hat{k}_t = [\text{diagonal}(\hat{z}_t) - \hat{z}_t\hat{z}'_t]D'C'(t).$$

PROOF. The results of a. and b. follow from the theory for stochastic dynamical systems. For c. see [30, 34].

THEOREM 4.3. Let the observed process $\{y_t, F_t, t \in T\}$ with $k = 1$, and $x : \Omega \times T \to R_+$ satisfy

1. $E[\exp(iv(y_t - y_s))|F_s \vee_s F^x] = \exp(\int_s^t x_\tau d\tau\,(e^{iv} - 1))$
   for $s, t \in T$, $s < t$, $v \in R$, $y_0 = 0$;
2. $\{x_t, F_t, t \in T\}$ is a Markov process of the form $x_t = e^{\alpha t}x_0$
   where $x_0 : \Omega \to R_+$ has a Gamma distribution with parameters $r, \beta \in (0, \infty)$, and $\alpha \in R_-$.

   a. Then $\{{}_tF^{\Delta y}, F_t, F^{x_t}, t \in T\} \in \Sigma SF$, and we have the representation

$$dx_t = \alpha x_t dt, \; x_0$$
$$dy_t = x_t dt + dm_t, \; y_o = 0,$$

   where $\{m_t, F_t, t \in T\} \in M_1$. Also y is a counting process.

   b. The solution to the stochastic filtering problem is given by

$$E[\exp(iux_t)|F_t^y] = (1 - iu\beta(t))^{-(y_t + r)},$$

$$d\beta(r)/dt = \alpha\beta(t) - \beta^2(t), \; \beta(0) = \beta.$$

   Then $\hat{x}_t = \beta(t)(y_t + r)$.

   c. A recursive equation for $\hat{x}$ is given by

$$d\hat{x}_t = \alpha\hat{x}_t dt + \beta(t)(dy_t - \hat{x}_t dt), \; \hat{x}_0 = r\beta,$$

$$d\beta(t)/dt = \alpha\beta(t) - \beta^2(t), \; \beta(0) = \beta.$$

PROOF. The solution in b. can be found in [51] for the case $\alpha = 0$. See also [32]. Attempts to generalize the above solution to a larger class of stochastic dynamical systems have proven futile.

5. COMMENTS

5.1. *Research on the Stochastic Filtering Problem.* Here we give a few remarks on the stochastic filtering problem that may be relevant to future research efforts in this area.

The practical application of this theory seems to demand finite dimensional filter systems as solutions to stochastic filtering problems. It seems extremely unlikely that the solution to the stochastic filtering problem for arbitrary stochastic dynamical systems will be a finite dimensional filter system. The question should therefore be posed: find all stochastic dynamical systems that yield finite dimensional filter systems. One would hope that a resolution of this question also would yield structural information that may be used in filtering techniques.

We mention a few ideas that may be used to resolve the above question. It seems worthwile to require that the conditional distribution $E[\exp(iu'x_t)|F_t^y]$ is invariant in time, in other words is of the same type for all $t \in T$. If the underlying dynamics are linear, this probably will lead to the class of infinitely divisible distributions. One way the distribution may be made invariant is to choose a pair of conjugate distributions [52] for the stochastic dynamical system.

5.2. *Open Problems.* We mention a few issues that are relevant to the future development of a stochastic filtering theory.

1. The formulation of a general theory for stochastic dynamical systems. The issues here are general definitions, the stochastic realization problem, the formulation of the concepts of stochastic observability and stochastic controllability, etc.
2. The question of which classes of stochastic dynamical systems yield finite dimensional stochastic dynamical filter systems.
3. The investigation of equations for the conditional characteristic function. The issues here are the existence and uniqueness of solutions, and techniques to solve these equations.
4. The extension of the ideas presented in this paper to infinite dimensional stochastic systems, to systems defined on geometric structures, and stochastic systems on partially ordered sets.

5.3. *On Stochastic Filtering and Stochastic Control.* Since this paper is presented at a stochastic control oriented meeting we briefly indicate the relation between stochastic filtering and stochastic control.

Suppose given $\{\Omega, F, P\}$, $\{F_t, t \in T\}$, an observed process $\{y_t, F_t, t \in T\}$, and an input process $\{u_t, F_t, t \in T\}$ belonging to a class U of admissable input processes. If there exists a process $\{x_t, F_t, t \in T\}$ such that for all $t \in T$

$$\{{}_tF^{\Delta y} V {}_tF^x, F_t, F^{x_t} V {}_tF^u\} \in CI$$

then we call the collection $\{{}_tF^{\Delta y}, F_t, F^{x_t} V {}_tF^u, t \in T\}$, a stochastic dynamical system, with input.

The stochastic filtering problem in the context of control is to determine $E[\exp(iw'x_t)|F_t^y V F_t^u]$ for all $t \in T$, $w \in R^n$; if there exists a process $\{z_t, F_t^y V F_t^u, t \in T\}$ such that $\{F^{x_t}, F_t^y V F_t^u, F^{z_t} V_t F^u, t \in T\}$ is a stochastic dynamical system, then we call this collection a filter system.
The filter separation property is said to hold iff
$E[\exp(iw'x_t)|F_t^y V F_t^u] = E[\exp(iw'x_t)|F_t^y]$ for all $t \in T$, $w \in R^n$.

Given a cost function $C : \Omega \times U \to R_+$. The stochastic control problem is to find $u^* \in U$ such that

$$E[c(u^*)|F_t^y V F_t^{u^*}] \leq E[c(u)|F_t^y V F_t^u]$$

for all $u \in U$ such that $u_s^* = u_s$ for $s \in [0, t]$, and all $t \in T$.
The control separation property is said to hold iff there is no loss in cost in restricting attention to controls adapted to the σ-algebra generated by $\{E[\exp(iw'x_t)|F_t^y V F_t^u], t \in T\}$. If both separation properties hold, then the control process will be a function of the filter state.

The above remark should be considered to be a first sketch of a general formulation.

ACKNOWLEDGEMENT

We acknowledge Professor R.E. Kalman for his ideas on dynamical systems and stochastic filtering theory.

We acknowkedge Professor J.C. Willems and Mr. C. van Putten for helpful discussions.

REFERENCES

[1] R. BOEL, P. VARAIYA, E. WONG, Martingales on Jump Processes. I. Representation Results. II. Applications, SIAM J. Control, 13, (1975), pp. 999-1061.

[2] P.M. BRÉMAUD, A martingale approach to point processes, Electronics Research Lab., Memo M-345, University of California, Berkeley, Cal., 1972.

[3] P.M. BRÉMAUD, The martingale theory of point processes over the real half line admitting an intensity, Control Theory, Numerical Methods and Computer Systems Modelling, Lect. Notes in Econ. and Math. Systems Th., vol. 107, Springer-Verlag, Berlin, 1974, pp. 519-542.

[4] P.M. BRÊMAUD, La méthode des semi-martingales en filtrage lorsque l'observation est un processus ponctuel marqué,Séminaire de Probilités, Lect. Notes in Math., 511, Springer-Verlag, Berlin, 1975, pp 1-18.

[5] P.M. BRÊMAUD, M. YOR, Changes of filtration and of probability measures, report IRIA.

[6] P. BREMAUD, J. JACOD, Processus Ponctuels et Martingales: Résultats récents sur la modélisation et le filtrage, Advances in Appl. Probability, 9, (1977), pp. 362-416.

[7] C. DELLACHERIE, P.A. MEYER, Probabilités et Potentiel, Hermann, Paris, 1975.

[8] P. FISHMAN, D. SNYDER, How to track a swarm of fireflies by observing their flashes, IEEE Trans. Information Theory, 21, (1975), pp. 692-694.

[9] M. FUJISAKI, G. KALLIANPUR, H. KUNITA, Stochastic Differential Equations for the non-linear filtering problem, Osaka J. Math., 9, (1972). pp. 19-40.

[10] J. JACOD, Un théorème de représentation pour les martingales discontinues, Z. Wahrscheinlichkeitstheorie und verw. Gebiete, 34, (1976), pp. 225-244.

[11] T. KAILATH, The innovations approach to detection and estimation theory, Proc. IEEE, 58, (1970), pp. 680-695.

[12] T. KAILATH, A view of three decades of linear filtering theory, IEEE Trans. Information Theory, 20, (1974), pp. 146-181.

[13] G. KALLIANPUR, Non linear filtering, in Optimizing methods in Statistics, J.S. Rustagi ed., Acad. Press, N.Y., 1971, pp. 211-232.

[14] R.E. KALMAN, A new approach to linear filtering and prediction problems, Trans. ASME, series D., Journal of Basic Engineering, 82, (1960), pp. 35-45.

[15] R.E. KALMAN, R.S. BUCY, New results in linear filtering and prediction theory, Trans. ASME, series D., Journal of Basic Engineering, 83, (1961), pp. 95-108.

[16] R.E. KALMAN, Linear stochastic filtering theory - reappraisal and outlook, Proc. Symp. System Theory, J. Fox ed., Polytechnic Press, N.Y., 1965, pp. 197-205.

[17] R.E. KALMAN, P.L. FALB, M.A. ARBIB, Topics in Mathematical System Theory, McGraw-Hill, N.Y., 1969.

[18] H. KUNITA, Asymptotic behaviour of the non-linear filtering errors of Markov processes, J. Multivariate Anal., 1, (1971), pp. 365-393.

[19] H.J. KUSHNER, Dynamical equations for optimal nonlinear filtering, J. Differential Equations, 3, (1967), pp. 179-190.

[20] A. LINDQUIST, G. PICCI, On the stochastic realization problem, SIAM J. Control, to appear.

[21] A. LINDQUIST, G. PICCI, A state-space theory for stationary stochastic processes, Proc. 21st Midwest Symposium on Circuits and Systems, August 1978.

[22] A. LINDQUIST, G. PICCI, G. RUCKEBUSCH, On minimal splitting subspaces and Markovian representations, preprint.

[23] R.S. LIPTSER, A.N. SHIRYAYEV, Statistics of random processes. I. General Theory, II. Applications, Springer-Verlag, Berlin, 1977, 1978.

[24] J.T. LO, A.S. WILLSKY, Estimation for rotational processes with one degree of freedom, IEEE Tans. Automatic Control, 20, (1975), pp. 10-33.

[25] S.I. MARCUS, A.S. WILLSKY, Algebraic structure and finite dimensional nonlinear estimation, SIAM J. Math. Anal., 9, (1978), pp. 312-327.

[26] H.P. McKEAN, Brownian motion with a several dimensional time, Theory Prob. Appl., 8, (1963), pp. 335-354.

[27] P.A. MEYER, Probabilités et Potentiel, Hermann, Paris, 1965; english translation, Probability and Potential, Blaisdell, Waltham, Mass., 1966.

[28] P.A. MEYER, un cours sur les intégrales stochastiques, in Séminaire de Probabilités X, Lecture Notes in Math., 511, Springer-Verlag, Berlin, 1975.

[29] G. PICCI, Stochastic Realization of Gaussian processes, Proc. IEEE, 64, (1976), pp. 112-122.

[30] M. RUDEMO, Doubly stochastic Poisson processes and process control, Acvances in Appl. Probability, 4, (1972), pp. 318-338.

[31] M. RUDEMO, State estimation for partially observed Markov chains, J. Math. Anal. Appl., 44, (1973), pp. 581-611.

[32] A. SEGALL, A martingale approach to modelling, estimation, and detection of jump processes, Ph. D. thesis, Stanford University, 1973.

[33] A. SEGALL, M.H.A. DAVIS, T. KAILATH, Nonlinear filtering with counting observations, IEEE Trans. Information Theory, 21, (1975), pp. 143-149.

[34] A. SEGALL, Dynamic file assignment in a computer network, IEEE Trans. Automatic Control, 21, (1976), pp. 161-173.

[35] A.N. SHIRYAYEV, Stochastic equations of nonlinear filtering of Markovian jump processes, Problems of Information Transmission, 2, (1966), pp. 1-18.

[36] M. SKIBINSKY, Adequate subfields and sufficiency, Ann. Math. Stat., 38, (1967), pp. 155-161.

[37] D.L. SNYDER, Filtering and detection for doubly stochastic Poisson processes, IEEE Trans. Information Theory, 18, (1972), pp. 97-102.

[38] D.L. SNYDER, Random Point processes, Wiley, N.Y., 1975.

[39] R.L. STRATONOVICH, Conditional Markov processes, Theor. Probability Appl., 5, (1960), pp. 156-178.

[40] J. SZPIRGLAS, G. MAZZIOTTO, Modèle général de filtrage non linéaire et équations différentielles stochastiques associées, C.R. Acad. Sc. Paris, Série A, 286, (1978), pp. 1067-1070.

[41] M.V. VACA, D.L. SNYDER, Estimation and Decision for observations derived from martingales: Part 1, Representations, IEEE Trans. Information Theory, 22, (1976), pp. 691-707.

[42] J.H. VAN SCHUPPEN, Estimation Theory for continuous-time processes, a martingale approach, Ph.D. thesis, University of California, Berkeley, Memo ERL M-405, 1973.

[43] J.H. VAN SCHUPPEN, Filtering, prediction, and smoothing for counting process observations, a martingale approach, SIAM J. Appl. Math., 32, (1977), pp. 552-570.

[44] N. WIENER, The extrapolation, interpolation, and smoothing of stationary time series with engineering applications, Wiley, N.Y., 1949.

[45] E. WONG, Stochastic Processes in Information and Dynamical Systems, McCraw-Hill, N.Y., 1971.

[46] W.M. WONHAM, Some applications of stochastic differential equations to optimal nonlinear filtering, SIAM J. Control, 2, (1965), pp.347-369.

[47] A.I. YASHIN, Filtering of jump processes, Automat. Remote Control, 31, (1970), pp. pp. 725-730.

[48] M. YOR, Sur les théories du filtrage et de la prédiction, in Séminaire de Probabilités XI, Lecture Notes in Math., 581, Springer-Verlag, Berlin, 1977, pp. 257-297.

[49] M. ZAKAI, On the optimal filtering of diffusion processes, Z. Wahrscheinlichkeitstheorie verw. Gebiete, 11, (1969), pp.230-243.

[50] C. DOLÉANS-DADE, P.A. MEYER, Equations différentielles stochastiques, in Séminaire de Probabilités XI, Lecture Notes in Math., 581, Springer-Verlag, Berlin, 1977, pp. 376-382.

[51] P.A. FROST, Examples of linear solutions to nonlinear estimation problems, Proc. 5th Princeton Conf. on Info. Sc. and Systems, 1971, pp. 20-24.

[52] H. RAIFFA, R. SCHLAIFER, Applied Statistical Decision Theory, Division of Research, Harvard University, Boston, Mass., 1961.

INTRODUCTION TO THE THEORY OF OPTIMAL STOPPING

J. Zabczyk
Institute of Mathematics, Polish Academy of Sciences
Sniadeckich 8, 00-950 Warsaw, Poland

1. PRELIMINARIES. To stop optimally a stochastic process is one of the simplest examples of a stochastic control problem. Such problems were first formulated in connection with the sequential analysis in statistics and can be found in the classical book by Wald [29]. In sequential analysis the number of experiments made by an experimenter is not fixed in advance but can depend on the results of experiments. The natural question here is "when is it optimal to stop". It is not desirable to repeat an experiment a large number of times, on the other hand if the number of experiments is too small the basis for a right statistical decision is not sufficient.

A general theory of optimal stopping was first developped for stochastic sequences around 1960 although the classical supermartingale characterization of the "value process" was formulated and proved by Snell in 1952, [27]. Recently the literature devoted to this topic is very extensive. We refer to the book [7] by Chow Y.S., Robbins and Siegmund D. and to the first part of Shiryaev's book [26].

First general results for continuous-time processes were obtained by Dynkin [10] and independently, in a less general setting, by Mc Kean [17]. Both Dynkin and Mc Kean considered only the so called "Markov case" and their approaches were influenced by the probabilistic potential theory. In his paper [17], Mc Kean discovered also a connection between optimal stopping and some free boundary problems. This connection was studied in 1966 by Griegelionis and Shiryaev [15]. Continuous time version of the Snell's characterization was first obtained by Fakeev [13] and Mertens [18]. The idea to apply variational parabolic or elliptic inequalities to stopping time problems was introduced by Fleming [14], Bensoussan and Lions [2] and by Tobias [28]. This approach was important not only from the theoretical point of view but also from the point of view of numerical computations.

The theory of optimal stopping is a starting point to more

complicated stochastic control problems like control of alternating processes and impulse control. It is still an active area of research. Let us mention, for instance, recent papers by Bismut [4] , Bismut and Skalli [5] , Nisio [21] , Robin [23] and monographs [3] by Bensoussan and Lions and [26] by Shiryaev.

In this survey paper we are only concerned with the theory of optimal stopping for continuous-time processes and with results which are valid for general classes of processes. We present only some results and examples which seem to be typical, to show the variety of possible approaches. Our aim is also to emphasize the probabilistic meaning of some analytical techniques used to solve optimal stopping problems, for instance, the penalty method. For more details and references we refer to [1] , [3] and [26] .

The content of the paper is as follows:

1. Preliminaries. 2. Examples. 3. Supermartingale characterization of solutions of optimal stopping problems. 4. Markov case. 5. Free boundary problems and optimal stoppings. 6. Examples. Continuation. 7. The penalty method. 8. Optimal stopping and non-linear semigroups. 9. Stochastic control of alternating processes. 10. References.

2. EXAMPLES. We describe here two specific optimal stopping problems to make the subsequent material more intuitive.

Example 1. A correction problem. Let (x_t) be the trajectory of a particle in 3-dimensional space R^3 which uniform movement towards the origin is perturbed by a "white noise" process. Mathematically

$$(1) \qquad x_t = x_o - \frac{x_o}{|x_o|} t + w_t \quad , \qquad t \geqslant 0$$

where (w_t) is a Brownian motion.

Let $p(|x_o|)$ be the probability that the process (x_t) hits the ball $K = \{x \in R^3 \ ; \ |x| \leq r\}$. If $|x_o| > r$ then, due to disturbances, $p(|x_o|) < 1$. Let us assume now that it is possible, but only once, to correct the movement with the aim to maximize the probability of hitting the ball K. The correction made at a state $\hat{x} = x_t$, $|\hat{x}| > r$, consists in changing the initial velocity $-\frac{x_o}{|x_o|}$ by : $-\frac{\hat{x}}{|\hat{x}|}$. One would like to know how much one can gain by making correction and find the optimal switching surface. More precisely one would like to find a stopping time T, relative to the process (x_t), which maximizes the expectation:

$$E\{p(|x_T|)\} .$$

Example 2. This example has an important interpretation in economics, see [4], [17] and [32], and can be described as a game. To play the game a gambler must put down stake $c > 0$ and the outcome of the game depends on the behaviour of a non-negative process (x_t) in a fixed time interval $[0,s]$, $s \leq +\infty$. The gambler can stop the process at any instant $T \leq s$ and then he receives immediately the discounted reward $e^{-bT}(x_T - 1)$. If he does not stop it then his reward is zero. Therefore the problem he wants to solve is to find a stopping rule T which maximizes the expectation:

$$E^x\{e^{-bT}(x_T - 1)^+\} \tag{2}$$

where x denotes the starting point of the process (x_t) : $x = x_0$. If the game is fair then

$$R(x,s) = \sup_{T \leq s} E^x\{e^{-bT}(x_T - 1)^+\} = c \tag{3}$$

In the case when x_t is the price, at moment t, of 1 share of a common stock then the function R is exactly Samuelson's rational price of warrant and if $s = +\infty$, the rational price of the perpetual warrant.

3. SUPERMARTINGALE CHARACTERIZATION OF SOLUTIONS OF OPTIMAL STOPPING PROBLEMS.

Let (Ω, F, P) be a fixed probability space and $(F_t)_{t \geq 0}$ an increasing family of, (complete, right-continuous), σ-fields contained in F. For instance F_t can be the family of all events associated with the behaviour of a stochastic process (x_t) up to time t; equivalently F_t can be interpreted as the set of all statements which can be a priori made about the behavoiur of (x_t) up to time t. Markov time is any non-anticipating stopping rule. Formally a real valued function $T : \Omega \to [0, +\infty]$ is a Markov time relative to (F_t) if for any $t < +\infty$:

$$(4) \qquad \{\omega : T(\omega) \leqslant t\} \in F_t$$

Inclusion (4) means that any non-anticipating decision to stop befor or at instant t should depend only on the information available at t. It is intuitively clear that the first hitting time of K:

$$(5) \qquad T_K = \inf\{t > 0 \; ; \; x_t \in K\} \quad ,$$

where the process (x_t) and ball K were introduced in Example 1, is a Markov time but not the moment

$$T = \sup\{t > 0 \; ; \; x_t \in K\} \quad ,$$

of leaving the set K for ever.
The set of all Markov times and all Markov times $T \geqslant t$ will be denoted by $\overline{M}$ and $\overline{M}_t$. Whereas M and M_t will be subsets of $\overline{M}$ and $\overline{M}_t$ composed only of finite Markov times.

Let now (z_t) be a right-continuous, real valued stochastic process adapted to (F_t) and for simplicity, such that

$$(6) \qquad E\{\sup_{t \geqslant 0} |z_t|\} < +\infty \quad .$$

The optimal stopping problem consists in finding $T \in M(\overline{M})$ for which the expectation

$$E\{z_T\}$$

has the maximal possible value. (If $T = +\infty$ we define $z_T = \overline{\lim}_{t \uparrow +\infty} z_t$). Let us consider the following more general problem:

For each $t \geqslant 0$ find $T \in M_t$ which maximizes the conditional expectation:

$$E\{z_T \mid F_t\}$$

Let us introduce the following notations:

$$v_t = \operatorname*{essup}_{T \in M_t} E\{z_T | F_t\} \quad , \qquad V_t = \sup_{T \in M_t} E\{z_T\} \quad ,$$

$$\bar{v}_t = \operatorname*{essup}_{T \in \bar{M}_t} E\{z_T | F_t\} \quad , \qquad \bar{V}_t = \sup_{T \in \bar{M}_t} E\{z_T\} \quad .$$

There is an important class of processes (z_t), for which the formulated general problem has a trivial solution $T \equiv t$, namely so called supermartingales. A process (z_t) is a supermartingale if for $s \geqslant t$

$$(7) \qquad E\{z_s | F_t\} \leqslant z_t \qquad \text{a.e.}$$

It is a fundamental result of Doob that inequalities (7) imply

$$(8) \qquad E\{z_T | F_t\} \leqslant z_t \qquad \text{a.e.}$$

for all $T \in M$, if, for instance, (6) is satisfied. It turns out that the class of supermartingales is rich enough to allow a useful characterization of the process (v_t). The following result first proved by Fakeev [13] is an extension to continuous time processes of the Snell's characterization [27].

<u>Theorem 1.</u> The process (v_t) is the smallest supermartingale which majorizes process (z_t). Moreover for each $t \geqslant 0$

$$(9) \qquad v_t = \bar{v}_t \quad , \qquad P - \text{a.e.}$$

and

$$V_t = \bar{V}_t \quad .$$

It is instructive to sketch the proof of the supermartingale and minimality properties of the process (v_t). Let $s \geqslant t$ and let (T_n) be an increasing sequence, (which always exists), of stopping times from M_s such that

$$E\{z_{T_n} | F_s\} \uparrow v_s \quad , \qquad P - \text{a.e.}$$

Then

$$(10) \qquad E\{E\{z_{T_n} | F_s\} | F_t\} \uparrow E\{v_s | F_t\} \quad .$$

But the left hand side of (10) is equal to $E\{z_{T_n} | F_t\}$ and consequently is majorized by v_t. Therefore

$$E\{v_s | F_t\} \leq v_t \quad .$$

If $(\tilde{v}_t)$ is a supermartingale such that $\tilde{v}_t \geq z_t$ a.e., then for $T \in M_t$

$$\tilde{v}_t \geq E\{\tilde{v}_T | F_t\} \geq E\{z_T | F_t\}$$

and thus

$$\tilde{v}_t \geq \operatorname*{essup}_{T \in M_t} E\{z_T | F_t\} = v_t \quad .$$

The next theorem, also due to Fakeev [13], shows that in terms of the process (v_t) one can construct optimal or ε-optimal Markov times.

<u>Theorem 2.</u> Let us define for $\varepsilon \geq 0$

$$T_t^{\varepsilon} = \inf\{s \geq t \; ; \; v_s \leq z_s + \varepsilon\} \quad ,$$

$$S_t^{\varepsilon} = \inf\{s > t \; ; \; v_s \leq z_s + \varepsilon\} \quad , \quad \inf \phi = +\infty \quad ,$$

Then $T_t^{\varepsilon}, S_t^{\varepsilon} \in \overline{M}_t$ and for $\varepsilon > 0$

$$\overline{V}_t \leq E\{z_{T_t^{\varepsilon}}\} + \varepsilon \quad ,$$

$$\leq E\{z_{S_t^{\varepsilon}}\} + \varepsilon \quad .$$

Moreover if (z_t) is a continuous process, T_t^{o} is optimal Markov time.

The supermartingale (v_t) is sometimes called Snell's envelope of the process (v_t). There exist still more general theorems characterizing the process (v_t) or giving weaker conditions under which T_t^{o} is the optimal Markov time. For those extensions we refer the reader to paper [18] by Mertens and [5] by Bismut and Skalli.

4. MARKOV CASE. Let now (z_t) be a stochastic process of a special form

$$z_t = e^{-\alpha t} h(x_t) , \qquad t \geqslant 0 , \tag{11}$$

where $X = (x_t, F_t, P^x)$ is a (standard) Markov process, see [6], on a state space E, h a non-negative measurable function on E and $\alpha \geqslant 0$. According to the general theory the solution of the optimal stopping problem can be expressed in terms of the smallest supermartingale which majorizes (z_t). Due to the Markov nature of the process X the Snell's envelope can be found in the class of supermartingales of the special form $(e^{-\alpha t} f(x_t))$, where f are some measurable functions. Those functions h for which the process (z_t) given by (11) is a supermartingale are called in probabilistic potential theory, see [6], α-excessive. More precisely a (nearly) Borel function $f \geqslant 0$ is α-excessive for the Markov process X if and only if

$$e^{-\alpha t} P_t f(x) \leqslant f(x) , \qquad \text{for all } x \in E , \quad t \geqslant 0 \tag{12}$$

$$\lim_{t \downarrow 0} e^{-\alpha t} P_t f(x) = f(x) , \qquad \text{for all } x \in E . \tag{13}$$

In (12) and (13), $P_t f$ denotes the basic semigroup associated with the process X :

$$P_t f(x) = E^x \{ f(x_t) \} . \tag{14}$$

The following characterization of the Snell's envelope of the process $(e^{-\alpha t} h(x_t))$ is due to Dynkin [10]. Similar characterizations were independently discussed by Mc Kean [17].

<u>Theorem 3.</u> Let us assume that the process (11) has continuous, or lower semicontinuous trajectories, (for process (x_t) starting from any initial point $x \in E$), then Snell's envelop of (z_t) is of the form:

$$v_t = e^{-\alpha t} \hat{h}(x_t) , \qquad t \geqslant 0 \tag{15}$$

where $\hat{h}$ is the smallest α-excessive function majorizing h.

From Theorem 2 we know that if, for all $x \in E$,

$E^x\left\{\sup_{t\geq 0} e^{-\alpha t} h(x_t)\right\} < +\infty$, then hitting times:

(16) $$T^{\varepsilon} = \inf\left\{t \geq 0 \ ; \ e^{-\alpha t}\hat{h}(x_t) \leq e^{-\alpha t} h(x_t) + \varepsilon\right\}$$

are $\varepsilon > 0$ optimal. Under more restrictive assumption the hitting time T^0:

(17) $$T^0 = \inf\left\{ t \geq 0 : x_t \in \Gamma \right\} \quad , \text{ where}$$

$$\Gamma = \left\{ x \in E \ ; \ \hat{h}(x) = h(x) \right\}$$

is the optimal Markov time.

The above theorem was subsequently extended by many authors including, Engelbert G, [11] , Engelbert A. [12] , Shiryaev [26] , Mertens [19] and Bismut [4] .

Let us sketch now the proof that the moment T^{ε} is ε-optimal. For simplicity we assume that $\alpha = 0$, h is a bounded function, and for all $x \in E$

(18) $$P^x\left\{x_{T^{\varepsilon}} \in \Gamma^{\varepsilon}\right\} = 1 \quad ,$$

$$\Gamma^{\varepsilon} = \left\{ x \in E : \hat{h}(x) \leq h(x) + \varepsilon \right\} .$$

Then

$$E^x\left\{h(x_{T^{\varepsilon}})\right\} \geq E^x\left\{\hat{h}(x_{T^{\varepsilon}})\right\} - \varepsilon$$

and it is sufficient to show that the function f :

$$f(x) = E^x\left\{\hat{h}(x_{T^{\varepsilon}})\right\} \quad , \qquad x \in E \ ,$$

majorizes function $\hat{h}$. It is easy to check that the function f satisfies property (12) and we additionally assume that it satisfies a technical condition (13). Therefore f is an excessive function and, because of Theorem 3, it majorizes $\hat{h}$ if, for all $x \in E$, $f(x) \geq h(x)$. Let, on the contrary, $\sup\{h(x) - f(x)\} = c > 0$, then for some $\bar{x} \in E$, $h(\bar{x}) - f(\bar{x}) > 0$ and $h(\bar{x}) - f(\bar{x}) > c - \varepsilon$. But $f + c \geq h$ and consequently $f + c \geq \hat{h}$. Therefore:

$$h(\bar{x}) = (h(\bar{x}) - f(\bar{x})) + f(\bar{x})$$

$$\geqslant (c - \varepsilon) + \hat{h}(\bar{x}) - c$$

$$\geqslant \hat{h}(\bar{x}) - \varepsilon$$

and we see that $\bar{x} \in \Gamma^{\varepsilon}$. But then $f(\bar{x}) = E^{\bar{x}}\{\hat{h}(x_{T^{\varepsilon}})\} = \hat{h}(\bar{x})$, what contradicts the inequality $h(\bar{x}) > f(\bar{x})$.

It is appropriate now to comment on Theorem 3 from the point of view of the probabilistic potential theory for which excessive functions and excessive envelopes are basic objects. First, excessive functions are natural generalizations of the so called non-negative super-harmonic functions. In fact excessive functions for the Brownian motion process are exactly those non-negative functions f which satisfy inequality $\Delta f \leqslant 0$, where Δ denotes the Laplace operator. In particular all non-negative concave functions on an interval $[a,b]$ are exactly excessive functions for the Brownian motion on $[a,b]$ with absorption at boundary points. In general all α-potentials:

$$R_\alpha g(x) = E^x\left\{\int_0^{+\infty} e^{-\alpha t} g(x_t)dt\right\}, \qquad g \geqslant 0$$

are α-excessive and any α-excessive function is a limit of an increasing sequence of α-potentials.

Let now $A \subset E$ be a Borel set, regular in the following sense: if process X starts from $x \in A$ then it stays in the set A for a positive interval of time $[0,t)$, $t > 0$. The following theorem is a special case of the fundamental Hunt's theorem, see [6].

<u>Theorem 4.</u> For each α-excessive function f, $\alpha > 0$, there exists the smallest α-excessive function $Q_A^\alpha f$ which majorizes f on the set A. Moreover for all $x \in E$,

$$(19) \qquad Q_A^\alpha f(x) = E^x\left\{e^{-\alpha T_A} f(x_{T_A})\,;\; T_A < +\infty\right\},$$

where T_A is the first hitting time of A:

$$(20) \qquad T_A = \inf\{t > 0\,;\; x_t \in A\}.$$

The function $Q_A^\alpha f$ is called the balayage of f on A. Under additional assumptions the theorem holds for $\alpha = 0$. In particular if $f \equiv 1$, then

(21) $$Q_A 1(x) = P_x\{T_A < +\infty\} ,$$

is the capacitory potential of the set A.

The Hunt theorem can be "derived" from the Dynkin Theorem 3. Namely let us consider the optimal stopping problem for the function

$$h = I_A f$$

where f is a given α-excessive function. It is clear that the optimal rule, in this case is to stop the process X at the first hitting time of A, but then Theorem 3 implies (19). Let us notice that the lower semicontinuity of the process $e^{-\alpha t}h(x_t)$ is exactly the regularity property of the set A. Without this property the smallest envelope of the function $I_A f$ does not exist in the class of α-excessive functions and one needs the concept of strongly supermedian functions introduced by Mertens [19]. The interplay between probabilistic potential theory and optimal stopping is still an area of intense research, see recent paper by Bismut [4].

5. FREE BOUNDARY PROBLEMS AND OPTIMAL STOPPING. Characteristic operator $\tilde{A}$ of a Markov process $X = (x_t, F_t, P^x)$ is defined by the formula, see [9],

(22) $$\tilde{A}h(x) = \lim_{U \downarrow x} \frac{E^x\{h(x_{T(U)})\} - h(x)}{E^x\, T(U)}$$

The limit (22) is taken with respect to all sequences of open neighbourhoods of the point x converging to x, and T(U) denotes the first hitting time of the complement of U. The operator $\tilde{A}$ is an extension of the infinitesimal generator A of the process X, see [9].

If $h \geq 0$ then, as we know, function v :

(23) $$v(x) = \sup_T E^x\{h(x_T)\} , \qquad x \in E$$

is the smallest excessive function majorizing h. Since v is

excessive therefore, from the definition of A :

$$(24) \qquad \tilde{A}v(x) \leqslant 0 \quad , \qquad x \in E \quad ,$$

provided that $\tilde{A}v(x)$ is well defined. Let Γ be the set which defines the optimal stopping rule, then

$$(25) \qquad v(x) = h(x) \quad , \quad \text{for} \quad x \in \Gamma$$

and, it is intuitively clear, that

$$(26) \qquad \tilde{A}v(x) = 0 \quad , \quad \text{for} \quad x \in E \setminus \Gamma \quad .$$

(If a neighbourhood U of x is contained in $E \setminus \Gamma$ then $T(U) \leqslant T_{\Gamma} = \inf \{t \geqslant 0 \ ; \ x_t \in \Gamma\}$ and the strong Markov property implies $v(x) = E^x\{v(x_{T(U)})\}$). Consequently, in a sense, the optimal stopping problem is a problem of finding a set Γ and a function $v \geqslant 0$ such that conditions (24) - (26) are satisfied. This is exactly the so called, a free boundary problem. Problems of this type, for parabolic operators A, were first considered by Stefan in connection with phase transitions and are sometimes called Stefan's problems, see [24] .

In many important situations, if for instance A is an elliptic operator, function v can characterized as an element from a cone $\{u \in H \ ; \ u \geqslant h\}$ contained in a Hilbert space H, at which, an "energy" functional $J(v)$, attains its minimum. Necessary conditions for minimum have then the form of the so called variational inequality, see [20] . Literature devoted to such an approach is very extensive. For details and references concerning process with continuous trajectories, mainly diffusions we refer to the monograph [3] and to the survey [1] . Some results for a mixture of diffusion type processes and continuous-time Markov chains are available in Robin's dissertation [23] , (see also references there).

6. EXAMPLES. CONTINUATION. In this section we show how the general theory can be applied to specific problems. We start from Example 1 and sketch the proof of the following proposition, see [30]. Let (x_t) be a stochastic process satisfying:

(27) $$dx_t = (1,0,0)dt + dw_t$$

and let $Q_K 1$ be the capacitory potential corresponding to the ball K. Then

(28) $$p(R) = Q_K 1(-R,0,0)$$ and the correction

problem is equivalent to finding

$$q(R) = v(-R,0,0) = \sup_T E^{(-R,0,0)}\{p(|x_T|)\}, \qquad R > r.$$

<u>Proposition 1.</u> For each $R > r$

(29) $$q(R) \leq e^{2r}\sqrt{\frac{\pi}{2R}}\left(1 + \sqrt{\frac{2}{\pi R}}\right)$$

and, as $R \to +\infty$,

(30) $$q(R) \geqslant \sqrt{\frac{\pi}{2R}}\,(1 + o(R)).$$

Proof. The potential kernel for the process (27), see [6] is:

(31) $$G(x,y) = \frac{1}{2\pi}\,\frac{1}{|x-y|}\,e^{-(y_1-x_1)}\,e^{-|x-y|},$$

and therefore all functions $G\mu$:

$$G\mu(x) = \int G(x,y)\mu(dy), \qquad x \in R^3,$$

where μ is a non-negative measure, are excessive. Taking $\mu = \gamma\,\delta_{\{0\}}$, and $\gamma > 0$ such that $G\mu \geqslant 1$ on K, we obtain

$$p(R) = Q_K 1(-R,0,0) \leqslant G\mu(-R,0,0) \leqslant \frac{r}{R}\,e^{2r}.$$

In a similar way it is possible to show that

$$p(R) \geqslant \frac{r}{R}$$

To obtain an estimate for

$$q(R) \leqslant re^{2r}\sup_T E^{(-R,0,0)}\{|x_T|^{-1}\}$$

it is enough to find a good excessive majorant for $h : h(x) = |x|^{-1}$, $x \in R^3$. Since $(\frac{1}{2}\Delta + \frac{\partial}{\partial x_1})h(x) = -2\pi\delta_{\{0\}} - \frac{x_1}{|x|^3}$, therefore

$$\frac{1}{|x|} = 2\pi G(x,0) + \int_{y_1 \geq 0} G(x,y)\frac{y_1}{|y|^3}\,dy + \int_{y_1 < 0} G(x,y)\frac{y_1}{|y|^3}\,dy$$

and the function f :

$$f(x) = re^{2r}\left(\frac{1}{|x|} + \int_{y_1 \geq 0} G(x,y)\frac{y_1}{|y|^3}\,dy\right), \qquad x \in R^3$$

is the required majorant. As a result of straightforward estimations we obtain (29). The estimation (30) was obtained by considering a correction on the hyperplane $\{x \in R^3 \;;\; x_1 = 0\}$.

In some, rather exceptional cases, it is possible to find value function in a closed form. This can be done for Example 2 if, for instance, the process (x_t) is multiplicative and increasing, with possible jumps to 0, where it is absorbed. For such a process there exists an increasing process with stationary independent increments (y_t) and an exponentially distributed random variable Y, independent of (y_t), such that:

$$x_t = x_0\, e^{y_t} \qquad \text{for } t < Y$$

$$x_t = 0 \qquad \text{for } t \geq Y \quad .$$

Then there exists a number a such that

$$E^x\{x_t\} = e^{at}\, x \;, \qquad t \geq 0 \quad .$$

We assume that the discounting factor $b > a$ and that $a \geq 0$, see [17] .

<u>Proposition 2</u> (see [32]). For each $s \leq +\infty$, the rational price of a warrant:

$$R(x,s) = \sup_{T \leq s} E^x\{e^{-bT}(x_T - 1)^+\} \quad ,$$

is given by the formula

$$(32) \qquad R(x,s) = E^x\{e^{-bS}(x_S - 1)^+\}$$

where $\qquad S = \inf\{0 \leq t \leq s,\ x_t \geq \frac{b}{b-a}\}$.

A special case of this proposition corresponding to the multiplicative translation with absorption was obtained in [17] .

Proof. By changing appropriately the random variable Y we can always assume that $E^x\{x_t\} = e^{-(b-a)t}x$ and that we are maximizing $E^x(x_T - 1)^+$. Let the state space E be $E = \{0\} \cup [1, +\infty)$ and let us assume first that $s = +\infty$. If $h(x) = x - 1$, for $x \geq 1$ and $h(0) = 1$, then

$$Ah(x) = \lim_{t \downarrow 0} \frac{1}{t}(E^x\{h(x_t)\} - h(x)$$

$$= x(a - b) + b \qquad \text{if } x \geq 1$$

$$= 0 \qquad \text{if } x = 0 \ .$$

Define $\Gamma = \{x \in E\ ;\ Ah(x) \leq 0\}$, then $\Gamma = \{0\} \cup [\frac{b}{b-a}, +\infty)$, and to prove the proposition it is sufficient to show that the function $f : f(x) = E^x\{h(x_S)\}$, $x \in E$, majorizes h and is excessive. By direct computation we check that the process

$$h(x_t) - \int_0^t Ah(x_s)ds \qquad , \qquad t \geq 0$$

is (F_t) martingale. Thus for all initial points $x \leq \frac{b}{b-a}$, process $(h(x_{t \wedge S}))$ is a submartingale. Moreover

$$h(x_{t \wedge S}) \leq x_0 \exp(y_Y)$$

and since $E\{x_0 \exp(y_Y)\} < +\infty$ therefore

$$\lim_{t \uparrow +\infty} E^x h(x_{t \wedge S}) = f(x) \qquad .$$

Consequently, the submartingale property implies, for $x \leq \frac{b}{b-a}$,

$$h(x) \leq E^x\{h(x_{t \wedge S})\} \leq f(x) \qquad .$$

Since $f(x) = h(x)$ for $x \geqslant \frac{b}{b-a}$, therefore f majorizes h. One can also chack directly excessivity of f. This way the proof for the case $s = +\infty$ is complete. If $s < +\infty$ then the first part of the proof applied to the following space-time process $\widetilde{X}$ and function $\widetilde{h}(x,t) = h(x)$ gives the required result in general. The process $\widetilde{X}$ is defined on the state space $\widetilde{E} = E \times [0,s]$ and for any initial point (x_o,u):

$$\begin{aligned}\widetilde{x}_t &= (x_t\ ;\ u+t)\ , \quad \text{if} \quad t \leqslant s-u \\ &= (x_{s-u},\ s)\ , \quad \text{if} \quad t > s-u\ .\end{aligned}$$

7. THE PENALTY METHOD. Penalty method is an important, from theoretical and computational point of view, approach to optimal stopping problems, see [2]. Due to its probabilistic interpretation it is also called the method of randomized stopping, see [16]. Suppose that we have to find

$$v(x) = \sup_{T} E^x\{ e^{-\alpha T} h(x_T)\}\ , \qquad x \in E$$

where $\alpha > 0$ and h is a bounded function. Then the function v can be obtained as a limit of solutions v_r, $r \uparrow +\infty$ of the following randomized stopping problems:

(33) Find a stopping intensity (u_t) adapted to (F_t), satisfying inequalities

$$0 \leqslant u_t \leqslant r \quad , \qquad t \geqslant 0\ ,$$

which maximizes the functional

$$(34) \qquad J(u)(x) = E^x\left\{ \int_0^{+\infty} u_t h(x_t)\, e^{-\int_0^t (u_s+\alpha)ds} \right\}\ .$$

Functions v_r are defined as maximal values of $J(u)$. The adjective "randomized" is justified by the fact that it is possible to define, for each stopping intensity (u_t), a new Markov process $\widetilde{X} = (\widetilde{x}_t, \widetilde{F}_t, \widetilde{P}^x)$ equivalent to X and a Markov time T, (relative to the new process $\widetilde{X}$), such that

$$\tilde{E}^x\{e^{-\alpha T}h(\tilde{x}_T)\} = J(u)(x) \quad .$$

For each $r > 0$ the formulated problem (33) is a simple stochastic control problem and the corresponding Bellman equation for v_r is of the form:

(35) $$Av_r - \alpha v_r + r(h - v_r)^+ = 0 \quad .$$

In the equation (35), A denotes the infinitesimal generator of the process X. Using the resolvent operator R_α it is possible to replace (35) by a simpler equation, with a well defined meaning:

(36) $$v_r = rR_\alpha(h - v_r)^+ \quad .$$

Let us assume, for simplicity, that the following strong Feller property is satisfied:

(37) For each $\alpha > 0$ the resolvent operator transforms bounded Borel functions onto continuous functions,

Then the following theorem holds, (see [23] where a more general theorem is proved).

<u>Theorem 5.</u> If h is a continuous function then functions v_r, $r > 0$ are unique continuous solutions of (36). The optimal stopping density (u_t^r) is given by:

$$u_t^r = r \quad , \text{ if } \; v_r(x_t) \leq h(x_t)$$

$$= 0 \quad , \quad \text{otherwise} \quad .$$

Moreover for each $x \in E$, $v_r(x) \uparrow v(x)$, $r \to +\infty$.

Under more restrictive assumptions function v is also continuous and the first hitting time of the set $\{ x \in E \; ; \; h(x) = v(x) \}$ is the optimal one, see [23].

Let us remark that if we let $r \uparrow +\infty$ in the equation (35) then we formally obtain Bellman equation:

(38) $$Av - \alpha v + \sup_{r \geq 0}(h - v) = 0$$

which can be made rigorous as a differential (variational) inequality, see [2] .

8. <u>OPTIMAL STOPPING AND NON-LINEAR SEMIGROUPS</u>. We start from the following result due to M.Nisio [21] . Let C denotes the space of all uniformly continuous functions on R^n and let the Markov process $X = (x_t, F_t, P^x)$ be such that for any positive $t > 0$ there exists λ such that for all $s \leqslant t$ and functions $h \in C$ satisfying

$$\|h\| \leqslant 1 \quad \text{and} \quad |h(x) - h(y)| \leqslant |x-y| \qquad x,y \in R^n$$

it holds

$$|P_s h(x) - P_s h(y)| \leqslant e^{\lambda s}|x - y| \quad , \qquad x,y \in R^n \ ,$$

where $\quad P_s h(x) = E^x\{h(x_s)\} \quad , \qquad x \in R^n, \qquad s \geqslant 0 \ .$

For a fixed, bounded and satisfying Lipschitz condition function g and for all $h \in C$ we define

$$V_t h\,(x) = \sup_{T \leqslant t} E^x\Big\{\int_0^T e^{-\alpha s} g(x_s)ds + e^{-\alpha T} h(x_T)\Big\} \quad ,$$

then the following theorem holds [21] :

<u>Theorem 6.</u> The family of operators (V_t) is a strongly continuous semigroup on C with the following properties:

(39) $\qquad \|V_t h - V_t \bar{h}\| \leqslant \|h - \bar{h}\| \quad , \qquad\qquad h, \bar{h} \in C$

(40) $\qquad V_t h \leqslant V_t \bar{h} \qquad \text{if} \quad h \leqslant \bar{h}$

(41) $e^{-\alpha t} P_t h + \int_0^t e^{-\alpha s} P_s g\, ds \leqslant V_t h \ , \qquad h \leqslant V_t h \ , \qquad t \geqslant 0$

(42) If $\widetilde{V}_t$ is a strongly continuous semigroup satisfying (40) and (41) then

$$V_t h \leqslant \widetilde{V}_t h \quad , \qquad h \in C \ , \qquad t \geqslant 0 \ .$$

(43) If h belongs to the domain $D(A)$ of the generator A of the semigroup (P_t) then h belongs to the domain $D(G)$ of the generator G of the semigroup (V_t) and

$$(44) \qquad Gh = (Ah - \alpha h + g)^+ \quad .$$

The important property (42) can be formulated as follows: the optimal stopping semigroup $(V_t h)$ is the smallest semigroup which majorizes the affine semigroup $\left(e^{-\alpha t}P_t h + \int_0^t e^{-\alpha s}P_s g ds\right)$ and the identity transformation $Ih = h$.

The way the semigroup (V_t) was constructed in [21] differed significantly from the penalty scheme. Let first, t be a dyadic number $t = \frac{k}{2^n}$, $d = \frac{1}{2^m}$ and define for every $m \geqslant n$

$$Q_m h(x) = \max(h(x), \quad e^{-\alpha d}P_d h(x) + \int_0^d e^{-\alpha s}P_s g(x)ds)$$

$$V_t^m h(x) = (Q_m)^{k.2^{m-n}} h(x) \quad .$$

Then $V_t^m h(x)$ is exactly the maximum one can achieve stopping process X only at dyadic instances of time: $0, d, 2d, \ldots$. Therefore it is clear that the sequence $(V_t^m h(x))$ increases and assumptions of Theorem 6 imply that

$$(45) \qquad V_t h(x) = \lim_{m \uparrow +\infty} V_t^m h(x) \quad .$$

Extension to all $t \geqslant 0$ follows from the fact that for all $h \in D(A)$, function $t \to V_t h$ is Lipschitz continuous on the set of dyadic numbers.

Let us remark that if for all $t \geqslant 0$, $V_t h \in D(G)$ then the following Bellman equation is satisfied:

$$\frac{d}{dt^+} V_t h = G(V_t h) \quad , \qquad t \geqslant 0$$

$$V_o h = h \quad .$$

Unfortunately the general theory of non-linear semigroups does not imply the crucial property $V_t h \in D(G)$, even if $h \in D(A) \subset D(G)$, (the main reason being that C is not a reflexive space). The situation is different for contraction semigroups on convex subsets of Hilbert spaces. Such semigroups possess many properties of linear semigroups: denseness of the domain, differentiability for almost all $t \geq 0$ and initial conditions from $D(G)$, etc. It turns out that modifying sligtly the definition of the semigroup (V_t) one obtains a contraction semigroup on a Hilbert space H. Suppose that, for a measure $\mu \geq 0$ on R^n, semigroup (P_t) is a contraction on $H = L^2(R^n, \mu)$. (Such measures are exactly excessive measures for X : $\int P(t,x,\Gamma)\mu(dx) \leq \mu(\Gamma)$ for all Borel sets $\Gamma \subset R^n$. In particular any invariant measure is excessive, see e.g. [33]). Let moreover h be a continuous function on R^n such that the transformation $t \to |h|_t$:

$$|h|_t = \sup_{T \leq t} E^x\{|h(x_T)|\} \quad , \quad t \geq 0 \, , \quad x \in R^n$$

acts from $[0, +\infty)$ into H. Then for all $f \in K = \{ f \in H \, ; \ f \geq h \}$ and $t \geq 0$ the value function:

$$(46) \qquad V_t f(x) = \sup_{T \leq t} E^x\{h(x_T)_{\,T<t} + f(x_t)_{\,T=t}\}$$

is a well defined element of K.
The following theorem holds [33].

<u>Theorem 7.</u> If the set $D(A) \cap K$ is dense in K, then the family (V_t) given by (46) has the following properties:

(47) V_t is a continuous and contraction semigroup on K

(48) If $(\tilde{V}_t)$ is a semigroup on K such that $\tilde{V}_t f \geq P_t f$ for all $t \geq 0$ and $f \in K$, then $V_t f \leq \tilde{V}_t f$.

(49) If $f \in D(A) \cap K$ then the function $t \to V_t f$ is almost everywhere differentiable.

As a corollary we obtain that if G is the generator of (V_t) then for all $f \in D(A) \cap K$

$$(50) \qquad \frac{d}{dt} V_t f = G(V_t f) \qquad t \ \text{a.e.}$$

In some particular cases, if $f \in D(A) \cap K$ then $f \in D(G)$ and

$$Gf(x) = Af(x) \qquad \text{if} \quad f(x) > h(x)$$

$$= (Af)^{+}(x) \qquad \text{if} \quad f(x) = h(x) \quad ,$$

see [33], and we conjecture that a result of this type should be true in general.

The evolution equation (50) is an equivalent formulation of parabolic variational inequalities associated with optimal stopping. For a different application of the theory of non-linear semigroups to optimal stopping we refer to [22].

9. STOCHASTIC CONTROL OF ALTERNATING PROCESSES. Closely related to optimal stopping are more complicated stochastic control problems. We describe here briefly one of them namely control of alternating processes. A different type - impulse control-will be discussed in the lecture by Professor A. Bensoussan.

Let $X^i = (x^i_t, F_t, P^x_i)$, $i = 1,2,\dots,N$, be a family of Markov processes on a state space E. At any instant of time a control system evolves like a process X^i chosen by a controller. The controller can switch, in an arbitrary way, from one process to another, and his aim is to maximize profit. Let the infinitesimal profit $g(x)$ depends only on the current state x and let $c(j,j')$ denotes the cost of switching from the j-process to j'-process.
In this situation, a strategy π is a sequence $\pi = (T_n, Y_n)$ of Markov times T_n of consecutive switches and numbers Y_n of processes chosen at T_n. Let $(x^{\pi}_t, F_t, P^x_{\pi})$ denotes the stochastic process corresponding to the strategy π, then the corresponding total profit will be given by:

$$J_i(\pi)(x) = E^x_{\pi}\left\{ \int_0^{+\infty} e^{-\alpha t}\, g(x^{\pi}_t)dt - \sum_{n=1}^{+\infty} e^{-\alpha T_n}\, c(Y_{n-1}, Y_n)\right\}$$

where $\alpha > 0$ is a discounting factor and $Y_0 \equiv i$, is the number of the initial process. If $u_1,\dots,u_N$ denote maximal profits

$$u_i(x) = \sup_{\pi} J_i(\pi)(x) \quad , \qquad i = 1,\dots,N \; , \quad x \in E$$

then a dynamic programming argument leads to the following system of equations (see [23] and [31]) :

(51) $$u_i(x) = \sup_T E_i^x\left\{\int_0^T e^{-\alpha t} g(x_t)dt + e^{-\alpha T}(Mu)_i(x_T)\right\}$$

where

$$(Mu)_i(x) = \max_{1\leqslant k\leqslant N}(u_k(x) - c(i,k)) \qquad i = 1,2,\dots,N .$$

It is possible to deduce from equations (51), the following excessive characterizations of the functions $u_1,\dots,u_N$, see [23].

<u>Theorem 8.</u> Let g be a bounded continuous function $c(i,j)$ positive numbers, and X^i satisfy (37) , then function $u = (u_1,u_2,\dots,u_n)$ is the minimal function satisfying the following conditions:

(52) u_i are continuous functions,

(53) $$u_i(x) \geqslant (Mu)_i(x) ,$$

(54) $$u_i(x) \geqslant e^{-\alpha t} P_t^i u_i(x) + \int_0^t e^{-\alpha s} P_s^i g(x)ds \qquad i=1,2,\dots,N,\ t\geqslant 0 ,$$

where (P_t^i) are semigroups corresponding to X^i.

The solution $u = (u_1,\dots,u_N)$ can be obtained by the following approximating scheme, see [23] and [31] . Let $u^n = (u_1^n,\dots,u_N^n)$ denote maximal profits when the number of corrections is bounded by n. Then $u_i^o(x) = R^i g(x) \qquad i = 1,2,\dots,N$

and

$$u_i^{n+1}(x) = \sup_T E_i^x\left(\int_0^T e^{-\alpha t} g(x_t)dt + e^{-\alpha T}(Mu^n)_i(x_T)\right)$$

Thus functions (u^n) are solutions of some stopping time problems and therefore all types of approaches described in previous sections can be applied. It is also intuitively clear that $u^n \uparrow u$.

REFERENCES

[1] A.Bensoussan, Introduction to the theory of impulse control, in Control Theory and Topics in Functional Analysis, vol.3, International Atomic Energy Agency, Vienna, 1976.

[2] A.Bensoussan, J.L.Lions, Problèmes de temps d'arret optimal et inéquations variationnelles paraboliques, Applicable Anal. 3(1973), 267-294.

[3] A.Bensoussan and J.L.Lions, Temps d'Arret et Controle Impulsionnel, Herman , Paris, to appear.

[4] J.M.Bismut, Dualité convexe, tmeps d'arret optimal et controle stochastique, Z. Wahrscheinlichkeitstheorie verw.Gebiete, 38(1977), 169-198.

[5] J.M.Bismut and B.Skalli, Temps d'arret optimal, théorie générale des processus et processus de Markov, Z. Wahrscheinlichkeitstheorie verw.Gebiete, 39(1977), 301-314.

[6] R.M.Blumenthal and R.K.Getoor, Markov Processes and Potential Theory, New York and London, Academic Press 1968.

[7] Y.S.Chow, H.Robbins and D.Siegmund, Great Expectations: The Theory of Optimal Stopping, Houghton Mifflin Comp., Boston, 1971.

[8] H.Chernoff, Optimal stochastic control, Sankhya, ser.A, 30(1968), 221-252.

[9] E.B.Dynkin, Markov Processes, Springer Verlag, 1965.

[10] E.B.Dynkin, Optimal choice of a stopping time for a Markov process , Dokl.Akad.Nauk USSR, 150(1963), No.2, 238-240.

[11] G.Engelbert, On optimal stopping rules for Markov processes with continuous time, Theory of Prob. and Appl., 19(1974), No.2, 289-307.

[12] A.Engelbert, On ε-optimal Markov times for Markov processes with continuous time, Mathematische Nachrichten 70(1975), 251-257.

[13] A.G.Fakeev, Optimal stopping rules for stochastic processes with continuous parameter, Theory of Prob. and Appl., 18(1973), No.2, 304-311.

[14] W.Fleming, Optimal continuous parameter stochastic control, SIAM Review, 11(1969), No.4.

[15] B.I.Griegelionis and A.N.Shiryaev, On controlled Markov processes and the Stefan problem, Problemy Peredachi Informacii, 4(1968), 60-72.

[16] N.B.Krylov, Controlled Processes of Diffusion Type,

Nauka, Moscow, 1977.

[17] M.P.Mc Kean, A free boundary problem for the heat equation arising from a problem in Mathematical Economics, Industrial Management Review, 6(1965), 32-39.

[18] J.F.Mertens, Processus stochastiques généraux et surmartingales, Z. Wahrscheinlichkeitstheorie verw.Gebiete, 22(1972), 45-48.

[19] J.F.Mertens, Strongly supermedian functions and optimal stopping, Z. Wahrscheinlichkeitstheorie verw. Gebiete, 26(1973), 119-139.

[20] U.Mosco, Introduction to variational and quasi-variational inequalities, in Control Theory and Topics in Functional Analysis, vol.3, International Atomic Energy Agency, Vienna, 1976.

[21] M.Nisio, On nonlinear semigroups for Markov processes associated with optimal stopping, Appl. Math. and Optimization 4(1978) No.2, 143-169.

[22] S.R.Pliska, A semigroup representation of the maximum expected reward vector in continuous parameter Markov decision theory, SIAM J. on Control 13(1975), No.6, 1115-1129.

[23] M.Robin, Contrôle impulsionnel des processus de Markov, Thèse de Doctorat, l'Université Paris IX, 1978.

[24] L.I.Rubinstein, Stefan's Problem, Riga, 1967.

[25] P.A.Samuelson, Mathematics of speculative prices, SIAM Review, 15(1973), No.1, 1-42.

[26] A.N.Shiryaev, Statistical Sequential Analysis, Nauka, Moscow, 1976, (in Russian).

[27] I.L.Snell, Applications of martingale system theory, Trans. Amer. Math. Soc. 73(1953), 293-312.

[28] T.Tobias, Optimal stopping of diffusion processes and parabolic variational inequalities, Diff. Equations, 9(1973), No.4, 702-708.

[29] A.Wald, Sequential Analysis, Wiley, New York, 1947.

[30] J.Zabczyk, A mathematical correction problem, Kybernetika, 8(1972), No.4, 317-322.

[31] J.Zabczyk, Optimal control by means of switching, Studia Math. XLV(1973), 161-171.

[32] J.Zabczyk, Stochastic control on Stock Exchange, CRM-803, Université de Montreal, 1978.

[33] J.Zabczyk, Semigroup methods in stochastic control theory, CRM-821, Université de Montreal, 1978.

P A R T II :

R E S E A R C H   R E P O R T S

Lecturers : T.Basar , E.O.Bertsch , J.M.Bismut , N.Christopeit , M.Deistler , G.de Mey , B.Doshi , T.E.Duncan , T.Eisele , R.J.Elliott , T.Gasser , B.Grigelionis , M.Hazewinkel , K.Helmes , J.Jacod , A.Kistner , W.Kliemann , M.Kohlmann , A.J.Krener , H.Kunita , A.Moro , E.Pardoux , D.Plachky , M.M.Rao , B.Rustem , G.Sawitzki , A.Segall , R.Sentis , S.E.Shreve , J.Szpirglas , R.Tarres , R.Theoduresc u , P.Varaiya , H.Walk , M.P.Yershov

WEAK MARTINGALES ASSOCIATED WITH A TWO PARAMETER JUMP PROCESS

Ata Al-Hussaini
University of Alberta, Canada
and
Robert J. Elliott
University of Hull, England

1. INTRODUCTION

Jump processes and their related martingales have been studied in the papers of Chou and Meyer [4] , Boel, Varaiya and Wong [1], Davis [5], Elliott [6],[7] and Jacod [8]. On the other hand, continuous martingales, whose time parameter is two dimensional, have been studied by Cairoli and Walsh [2],[3], Wong [9] and Wong and Zakai [10].

In this paper we consider the basic situation of a process which has just one jump, and whose time parameter set is the positive quadrant of the plane. If $p(t)$is the process which becomes one after the jump time, we define a process $\tilde{p}(t)$ such that $q(t) = p(t) - \tilde{p}(t)$ is a weak martingale. That is, if $s = (s_1, s_2)$, $t = (t_1, t_2)$, $s_1 \le t_1$, $s_2 \le t_2$, and F_s denotes the σ - field generated up to time s, then $E[\Delta q(s,t) | F_s] = 0$, where $\Delta q(s,t) = q(s) + q(t) - q(s_1,t_2) - q(t_1,s_2)$.Stochastic integrals $\int g dq$ are defined and are shown to be weak martingales. The martingale representation problem is discussed in the weak sense of determining the integrand in such a stochastic integral if the random variable, which is its value at 'time' (∞,∞), is given. Finally it is shown that if the two components T_1 and T_2 of the jump time are independent the related strong martingales are just products of one dimensional martingales of the kind discussed by Chou and Meyer [4] and Davis [5].

This work was commenced during a visit of the second author to the University of Alberta. Professor Elliott would like to thank Professor Ghurye and the Department of Mathematics for making that visit possible.

2. THE BASIC MARTINGALE

We suppose that our 'time' parameter set is the quadrant $R^+ \times R^+$. Consider a process that has one jump at the 'time' $T = (T_1, T_2) \in R^+ \times R^+$. We can take $\Omega = R^+ \times R^+$ as our probability space.

Write, for $s = (s_1, s_2)$, $t = (t_1, t_2)$:

$$p_t(\omega) = I_{t_1 \geq T_1} I_{t_2 \geq T_2}$$

$$F_s = \sigma \{ I_{t_1 \geq T_1} : t_1 \leq s_1 \} \otimes \{ I_{t_2 \geq T_2} : t_2 \leq s_2 \} ,$$

$$F = \bigvee_{s \in \Omega} F_s .$$

Suppose a probability measure μ describing the jump processes is given on (Ω, F) and put $F_t = \mu\{s \in \Omega : s_1 > t_1, s_2 > t_2\}$. Then F_t is right continuous, and the left hand limits $F_{t-}, F_{t_1-,t_2}, F_{t_1,t_2-}$ exist. Further suppose that $\mu\{(o, s_2) \cup (s_1, o) : (s_1, s_2) \in \Omega\} = 0$, so that the jump occurs on neither axis, and take the σ - fields completed in the usual way.

Write $$\tilde{p}_t(\omega) = \int_o^{t \wedge T} \frac{dF_u}{F_{u-}}$$

$$= \int_{\substack{o < u_1 \leq t_1 \wedge T_1 \\ o < u_2 \geq t_2 \wedge T_2}} \frac{dF_u}{F_{u-}}$$

, the integral being interpreted as a two dimensional Lebesgue - Stieltjes integral.

THEOREM 2.1. The process $q_t = p_t - \tilde{p}_t$ is a weak martingale on (Ω, F_t, μ).

PROOF. Consider 'times' $s, t \in \Omega$ where $s_1 \leq t_1$ and $s_2 \leq t_2$. Then the increment in p over the rectangle formed by s and t is $\Delta p(s,t) = p_{t_1 t_2} + p_{s_1 s_2} - p_{t_1 s_2} - p_{s_1 t_2}$, and $E[\Delta p(s,t) | F_s]$ is the probability that the jump T occurs in this rectangle, given F_s.

So $$E\,[\Delta p(s,t) | F] = I_{T>s}\, (F_{t_1,t_2} + F_{s_1,s_2} - F_{t_1,s_2} - F_{s_1,t_2})\, F^{-1}_{s_1,s_2}. \qquad (2.1)$$

(Here $T>s$ means that $T_1 > s_1$ and $T_2 > s_2$). Again writing

$\Delta\tilde{p}(s,t) = \tilde{p}_{t_1,t_2} + \tilde{p}_{s_1,s_2} - \tilde{p}_{t_1,s_2} - \tilde{p}_{s_1,t_2}$ we see immediately that

$\Delta\tilde{p}(s,t) = 0$ if $T_1 \leq s_1$ or $T_2 \leq s_2$. There remain four further cases for relative positions of T, s and t.

Case 1: $s_1 < T_1 \leq t_1$ and $s_2 < T_2 \leq t_2$.

In this case the conditional expectation of $\Delta\tilde{p}(s,t)$, given F_s, is

$$F_s^{-1} \int_s^t \int_s^T \frac{dF_u}{F_{u-}} \, dF_T = F_s^{-1} \int_{\substack{s_1 < T_1 \leq t_1 \\ s_2 < T_2 \leq t_2}} \int_{\substack{s_1 < u_1 \leq T_1 \\ s_2 < u_2 \leq T_2}} \frac{dF_u}{F_{u-}} \, dF_T .$$

Interchanging the order of integration this is:

$$= F_s^{-1} \int_{\substack{s_1 < u_1 \leq t_1 \\ s_2 < u_2 \leq t_2}} \Big(\int_{\substack{u_1 \leq T_1 \leq t_1 \\ u_2 \leq T_2 \leq t_2}} dF_T \Big) \frac{dF_u}{F_{u-}}$$

$$= F_s^{-1} \int_s^t (F_{t_1,t_2} + F_{u_1-,u_2-} - F_{u_1-,t_2} - F_{t_1,u_2-})\, F_{u-}\, dF_{u-}.$$

Case 2: $s_1<T_1\le t_1$ and $T_2>t_2$

In this case the conditional expectation of $\Delta\tilde{p}(s,t)$, given F_s, is

$$F_s^{-1} \int_{s_1<T_1\le t_1} \int_{\substack{s_1<u_1\le T_1\\ s_2<u_2\le t_2}} \frac{dF_u}{F_{u-}} (-d^1F_{T_1,t_2})$$

where d^1F_{r,t_2} is the Stieltjes measure given by the decreasing function of r F_{r,t_2}.

Again, interchanging the order of integration, and integrating with respect to T_1 first, this is :

$$F_s^{-1} \int_s^t (F_{u_1-,t_2} - F_{t_1,t_2}) F_{u-} dF_u.$$

Case 3: $T_1>t_1$ and $s_2<T_2\le t_2$

In this case the conditional expectation of $\Delta\tilde{p}(s,t)$, given F_s, is

$$F_s^{-1} \int_{s_2<T_2\le t_2} \int_{\substack{s_1<u_1\le t_1\\ s_2<u_2\le T_2}} \frac{dF_u}{F_{u-}} (-d^2F_{t_1,T_2})$$

where $d^2F_{t_1,r}$ is the Stieltjes measure given by the decreasing function of r $F_{t_1,r}$.

Interchanging the order of integration, the above is:

$$F_s^{-1} \int_s^t (F_{t_1,u_2-} - F_{t_1,t_2}) F_{u-} dF_u.$$

Case 4: $T_1>t_1$ and $T_2>t_2$.

In this case the conditional expectation of $\Delta\tilde{p}(s,t)$, given F_s, is

$$F_{t_1,t_2} (F_s)^{-1} \int_s^t F_{u-} dF_u .$$

Adding the contributions from cases 1 to 4 we see that

$$E\,[\Delta\tilde{p}(s,t)|\,F_s] = I_{T>s} (F_s)^{-1} \int_s^t F_{u_1-,u_2-} F^{-1}_{u_1-,u_2-} dF_u$$

$$= I_{T>s} (F_{t_1,t_2} + F_{s_1,s_2} - F_{t_1,s_2} - F_{s_1,t_2}) F^{-1}_{s_1,s_2} \qquad (2.2)$$

From equations (2.1) and (2.2), therefore, we see that

$$E\,[\Delta q(s,t)|F_s] = E\,[\Delta p(s,t) - \Delta\tilde{p}(s,t)|F_s] = 0 ,$$

and so q_t is a weak martingale on (Ω, F_t, μ).

3. STOCHASTIC INTEGRALS

For suitable measurable functions $g: \Omega \to R$ we can consider Stieltjes integrals with respect to the processes p and $\tilde{p}$. In fact

$$\int_\Omega g(t)p(dt) = g(T_1,T_2) \text{ and } \int_\Omega g(t)\tilde{p}(dt) = \int_o^T \frac{g(t)}{F_{t-}}\, dF_t .$$

LEMMA 3.1 For $g \in L^1(\Omega,\mu)$,

$$E\,[\int_\Omega g dp] = E\,[g] = E\,[\int_\Omega g d\tilde{p}].$$

PROOF. The first identity is immediate from the definition. For the second, consider

$$E\,[\int_\Omega g d\tilde{p}] = E\,[\int_\Omega \frac{g(t)}{F_{t-}}\, dF_t] = \int_{\substack{o<T_1\le\infty \\ o<T_2\le\infty}} \int_{\substack{o<t_1\le T_1 \\ o<t_2<T_2}} \frac{g(t)}{F_{t-}}\, dF_t\, dF_T$$

$$= \int_{\substack{o<t_1\le\infty \\ o<t_2\le\infty}} \Big(\int_{\substack{t_1\le T_1\le\infty \\ t_2\le T_2\le\infty}} dF_T \Big) \frac{g(t)}{F_{t-}}\, dF_t = \int_{\substack{o<t_1\le\infty \\ o<t_2\le\infty}} (F_{t_1-,t_2-}) \frac{g(t)}{F_{t-}}\, dF_t$$

$$= \int_\Omega g(t)\, dF_t.$$

DEFINITION 3.2. For $g \in L^1(\Omega,\mu)$ we define the stochastic integral with respect to the basic martingale q by.

$$\int_\Omega g(t)q(dt) = \int_\Omega g(t)p(dt) - \int_\Omega g(t)\tilde{p}(dt).$$

THEOREM 3.3 For $g \in L^1(\Omega,\mu)$ the process $M_t^g = \int_\Omega I_{s\le t}\, g(s)q(ds)$

$$= I_{t_1\ge T_1,\, t_2\ge T_2}\, g(T_1, T_2) - \int_o^{t\wedge T} \frac{g(s)dF_s}{F_{s-}}$$ is an F_t martingale.

PROOF. The proof is similar to that of Theorem 2.1. Again consider two times $s, t \in \Omega$, $s_1\le t_1$, $s_2\le t_2$, and write Δ for the increment around the rectangle with opposite vertices s and t, so

$$\Delta M^g(s,t) = M^g_{t_1,t_2} + M^g_{s_1,s_2} - M^g_{t_1,s_2} - M^g_{s_1,t_2}$$

Now if $T_1\le s_1$ or $T_2\le s_2$, $\Delta M^g(s,t) = 0$. Again there are four further cases.

Case 1. $s_1<T_1\le t_1$ and $s_2<T_2\le t_2$.

Then

$$\Delta M^g(s,t) = g(T_1,T_2) - \int_{\substack{s_1<u_1\le T_1 \\ s_2<u_2\le T_2}} \frac{g(u)dF_u}{F_{u-}}$$, and in this case

$$E\,[\Delta M^g(s,t)\,|\,F_s] = F_s^{-1} \int_{\substack{s_1<u_1\le t_1\\ s_2<u_2\le t_2}} g(u)\,dF_u$$

$$- F_s^{-1} \int_{\substack{s_1<T_1\le t_1\\ s_2<T_2\le t_2}} \Big(\int_{\substack{s_1<u_1\le T_1\\ s_2<u_2\le T_2}} \frac{g(u)dF_u}{F_{u-}} \Big)\, dF_T$$

$$= F_s^{-1} \int_{\substack{s_1<u_1\le t_1\\ s_2<u_2\le t_2}} (F_{u_1-,t_2} + F_{t_1,u_2-} - F_{t_1,t_2})\, F_{u-}^{-1}\, dF_u,$$

after interchanging the order of integration.

Case 2: $s_1<T_1\le t_1$ and $T_2>t_2$.

Then

$$\Delta M^g(s,t) = - \int_{\substack{s_1<u_1\le T_1\\ s_2<u_2\le t_2}} \frac{g(u)dF_u}{F_{u-}} .$$

If d^1F_{r,t_2} is the Stieltjes measure given by the decreasing function of r, F_{r,t_2},

$$E\,[\Delta M^g(s,t)\,|\,F_s] = - F_s^{-1} \int_{s_1<T_1\le t_1} \int_{\substack{s_1<u_1\le T_1\\ s_2<u_2\le t_2}} \frac{g(u)dF_u}{F_{u-}} (-d^1F_{r},t_2)$$

$$= F_s^{-1} \int_{\substack{s_1<u_1\le t_1\\ s_2<u_2\le t_2}} (F_{t_1,t_2} - F_{u_1-,t_2})\, F_u^{-1}\, dF_u .$$

after interchanging the order of integration.

Case 3. $T_1>t_1$ and $s_2<T_2\le t_2$

Then

$$\Delta M^g(s,t) = -\int_{\substack{s_1<u_1\le t_1\\ s_2<u_2\le T_2}} \frac{g(u)}{F_{u-}}\, dF_u ,$$ and by a similar calculation to

Case 2:

$$E\,[\Delta M^g(s,t)\,|\,F_s] = F_s^{-1} \int_{\substack{s_1<u_1\le t_1\\ s_2<u_2\le t_2}} (F_{t_1,t_2} - F_{t_1,u_2-})\, F_{u-}^{-1}\, dF_u .$$

Case 4: $T_1>t_1$ and $T_2>t_2$.

Then

$$\Delta M^g(s,t) = \int_{\substack{s_1<u_1\le t_1\\ s_2<u_2\le t_2}} \frac{g(u)}{F_{u-}}\, dF_u ,$$

and $$E\,[\Delta M^g(s,t)|F_s] = F_s^{-1}\,F_t \int_{\substack{s_1<u_1\le t_1\\ s_2<u_2\le t_2}} g(u)F_{u-}^{-1}\,dFu.$$

Adding the contributions from Cases, 1, 2, 3 and 4 we see that

$E\,[\Delta M^g(s,t)|F_s] = 0$, so M_t^g is a weak F_s martingale.

4. MARTINGALE REPRESENTATION

Unfortunately , no analog for the martingale convergence theorem is yet available, which will apply to weak martingales in two dimensional time. At this stage, therefore, we consider the martingale representation question as an inversion problem for weak martingales of the form M_t^g . That is, we suppose the random variable $M_{\infty,\infty}^g$ is given, and investigate what additional information is required to determine the integrand g. We show that g can be calculated if, as well as $M_{\infty,\infty}^g$, certain expectations of the 'boundary value' random variables $M_{t_1,\infty}^g$ and M_{∞,t_2}^g are given.

REMARK 4.1 Note that if either $M_{t_1,\infty}^g$ or M_{∞,t_2}^g , is given then g is immediately obtained because

$$M_{t_1,\infty}^g = g(T_1,T_2)\,I_{t_1\ge T_1} - \int_{\substack{0<u_1\le T_1\wedge t_1\\ 0<u_2\le T_2}} \frac{g(u)dF_u}{F_{u-}}\,.$$

Considering $T_1>t_1$ determines the integral for arbitrary upper limits, so g itself is easily computed.

THEOREM 4.2. Consider a weak martingale of the form M_t^g , $t\in\Omega$, and suppose the random variable $M_{\infty,\infty}^g$ and the expectations $E\,[M_{t_1,\infty}^g|\,T_2>t_2]$, $E\,[M_{\infty,t_2}^g|T_1>t_1]$ are given.

Then

$$g(T_1,T_2) = M_{\infty,\infty}^g - F_T^{-1}\,\{\textstyle\int_0^T M_{\infty,\infty}^g\,dF - E\,[M_{t_1,\infty}^g\,|T_2>t_2]-E[M_{\infty,\infty}^g|\,T_1>t_1]\,\}\,.$$

PROOF. Write:

$$M_{\infty,\infty}^g = g(T_1,T_2) - \int_0^T \frac{g(u)}{F_{u-}}\,dF_u = H(T_1,T_2),$$

$$M_{t_1,\infty}^g = g(T_1,T_2)\,I_{t_1\ge T_1} - \int_{\substack{0<u_1\le T_1\wedge t_1\\ 0<u_2\le T_2}} \frac{g(u)dF_u}{F_{u-}} = H^1(T_1,T_2,t_1),$$

$$M_{\infty,t_2}^g = g(T_1,T_2)\,I_{t_2\ge T_2} - \int_{\substack{0<u_1\le T_1\\ 0<u_2\le T_2\wedge t_2}} \frac{g(u)dF_u}{F_{u-}} = H^2(T_1,T_2,t_2).$$

Then, by changing the order of integration,

$$\int_{\substack{0<T_1\le t_1\\ 0<T_2\le t_2}} H(T_1,T_2)dF_T = \int_{\substack{0<T_1\le t_1\\ 0<T_2\le t_2}} g(T)dF_T - \int_{\substack{0<T_1\le t_1\\ 0<T_2\le t_2}} \int_{\substack{0<u_1\le T_1\\ 0<u_2\le T_2}} \frac{g(u)dF_u}{F_{u-}} dF_T$$

$$= \int_0^t g(T)dF_T - \int_0^t (F_{u_1-,u_2-} + F_{t_1,t_2} - F_{u_1-,t_2} - F_{t_1,u_2-})\, g(u)F_{u-}^{-1}\, dF_u$$

$$= \int_0^t (F_{u_1-,t_2} + F_{t_1,u_2-})g(u)F_{u-}^{-1}\, dF_u - F_t \int_0^t g(u)F_{u-}^{-1}\, dF_u\,. \tag{4.1}$$

Now

$$E\,[M^g_{t_1,\infty}|T_2\le t_2] = \int_{\substack{0<T_1\le\infty\\ 0<T_2\le t_2}} H^1(T_1,T_2,t_1)\, dF_T$$

$$= \int_{\substack{0<T_1\le t_1\\ 0<T_2\le t_2}} g(T)dF_T - \int_{\substack{0<T_1\le t_1\\ 0<T_2\le t_2}} \Big(\int_{\substack{0<u_1\le T_1\\ 0<u_2\le T_2}} g(u)F_{u-}^{-1}\, dF_u \Big)dF_T$$

$$+ \int_{0<T_2\le t_2} \Big(\int_{\substack{0<u_1\le t_1\\ 0<u_2\le T_2}} g(u)\, F_{u-}^{-1}\, dF_u \Big)\, d^2F_{t_1,T_2},$$

where the measure $d^2F_{t_1,T_2}$ is defined in Theorem 2.1.

Interchanging the order of integration the final double integral above is

$$\int_{\substack{0<u_1\le t_1\\ 0<u_2\le t_2}} (F_{t_1,t_2} - F_{t_1,u_2-})\, g(u)\, F_{u-}^{-1}\, dF_u$$

so, as the first two integrals are evaluated in (4.1),

$$E\,[M^g_{t_1,\infty}|T_2\le t_2] = -\int_{\substack{0<u_1\le t_1\\ 0<u_2\le t_2}} F_{u_1-,t_2}\, g(u)F_{u-}^{-1}\, dF_u\,.$$

In particular, as $F_{u_1-,\infty} = 0$ $\quad E[M^g_{t_1,\infty}] = 0$

so
$$E\,[M^g_{t_1,\infty}|T_2>t_2] = \int_{\substack{0<u_1\le t_1\\ 0<u_2\le t_2}} F_{u_1-,t_2}\, g(u)F_{u-}^{-1}\, dF_u\,. \tag{4.2}$$

Similarly

$$E\,[M^g_{\infty,t_2}|T_1>t_1] = \int_{\substack{0<u_1\le t_1\\ 0<u_2\le t_2}} F_{t_1,u_2-}\, g(u)F_{u-}^{-1}\, dF_u. \tag{4.3}$$

From (4.1), (4.2) and (4.3), therefore,

$$- F_t \int_0^t g(u)\, F_{u-}^{-1}\, dF_u = \int_0^t M^g_{\infty,\infty}\, dF - E\,[M^g_{t_1,\infty} \mid T_2 > t_2]$$

$$- E\,[M^g_{\infty,t_2} \mid T_1 > t_1]$$

and the result is immediate.

5. INDEPENDENT JUMP TIMES

In this final section we discuss the particularly simple situation that arises when the components T_1, T_2 of the jump time are independent. We again take $\Omega = R^+ \times R^+$ with the product σ - fields F_s, but the probability measure μ of the jump now factors into a probability measure μ^1, describing T_1 and a probability measure μ^2, describing T^2.

If $F^1_{t_1} = \mu^1\{s_1 \in R^+ : s_1 > t_1\}$

and $F^2_{t_2} = \mu^2\{s_2 \in R^+ : s_2 > t_2\}$

then $F_t = F^t_{t_1} F^2_{t_2}$

Writing

$$p_{t_i} = I_{t_i \geq T_i} ,$$

$$\tilde{p}_{t_i} = -\int_{]0,t_i \wedge T_i]} (F^i_{u_i -})^{-1}\, dF^i_{u_i} ,$$

and $q_{t_i} = p_{t_i} - \tilde{p}_{t_i}$, for $i = 1,2$,

we have the following result:

LEMMA 5.1. $\hat{q}_t = q_{t_1} q_{t_2}$

is an F_t martingale. (Note that $\hat{q}_t$ is different from the q_t of section 2.)

PROOF. Suppose $s = (s_1,s_2)$, $t = (t_1,t_2)$ and $s_1 \leq t_1$, $s_2 \leq t_2$. We are to show that $\hat{q}_t$ is a martingale, that is show $E\,[\hat{q}_t - \hat{q}_s \mid F_s] = 0$.

However,

$$\hat{q}_t - \hat{q}_s = q_{t_1} q_{t_2} - q_{t_1} q_{s_2} + q_{t_1} q_{s_2} - q_{s_1} q_{s_2}$$

so, because $F_s = F_{s_1} \otimes F_{s_2}$ and $\mu = \mu^1 \times \mu^2$,

$$E\,[\hat{q}_t - \hat{q}_s \mid F_s] = E^1\,[E^2\,[q_{t_1}(q_{t_2} - q_{s_2}) \mid F_{s_2} \mid F_{s_1}]$$

$$+ E^2\,[E^1[q_{s_2}(q_{t_1} - q_{s_1}) \mid F_{s_1} \mid F_{s_2}] = 0,$$

where E^i denotes the expectation with respect to measure μ^i.

DEFINITION 5.2 For $g \in L^1(\Omega,\mu)$ we can define the stochastic integral

$$\int_\Omega g d\hat{q} = \int_{R^+ \times R^+} g(s_1,s_2)\, dq_{s_1}\, dq_{s_2}$$

$$= g(T_1, T_2) - \int_{]o,T_1]} g(T_1,s_2)\,(F^2_{s_2-})^{-1} dF^2_{s_2}$$

$$- \int_{]o,T_2]} g(s_1,T_2)(F^1_{s_1-})^{-1} dF^1_{s_1} + \int_{\substack{o<s_1\leq T_1\\ o<s_2\leq T_2}} g(s_1,s_2) F^{-1}_{s_1,s_2-}\, dF_s\,,$$

and it is easy to see that

$$\int_{\substack{o<s_1\leq t_1\\ o<s_2\leq t_2}} g(s_1,s_2)\, d\hat{q}(s_1,s_2) \text{ is an } F_s \text{ martingale.}$$

<u>LEMMA 5.3</u> Suppose M_{t_1,t_2} is a uniformly integrable , F_t martingale such that $M_{o,t_2} = 0$ a.s and $M_{t_1,o} = 0$ a.s. for all t_1,t_2. Then there is an $H \in L^1(\Omega,\mu)$ such that

$$M_{t_1,t_2} = H(T_1,T_2) I_{t_1\geq T_1} I_{t_2\geq T_2}$$

$$- I_{t_2\geq T_2} I_{T_1>t_1} F^1(t_1)^{-1} \int_{]o,t_1]} H(u_1,T_2)\, dF^1_{u_1}$$

$$- I_{t_1\geq T_1} I_{T_2>t_2} F^2(t_2)^{-1} \int_{]o,t_2]} H(T_1,u_2)\, dF^2_{u_2}$$

$$+ I_{T_1>t_1} I_{T_2>t_2} F(t)^{-1} \int_{\substack{o<u_1\leq t_1\\ o<u_2\leq t_2}} H(u_1,u_2)\, dF_u.$$

<u>PROOF.</u> Because M_{t_1,t_2} is uniformly integrable it is of the form

$$M_{t_1,t_2} = E\,[H \mid F_t] \text{ for some } H \in L^1(\Omega,F,\mu).$$

Now

$$E\,[H \mid F_t] = H(T_1,T_2) I_{t_1\geq T_1} I_{t_2\geq T_2}$$

$$+ I_{t_2\geq T_2} I_{T_1>t_1} F^1(t_1)^{-1} \int_{]t_1,\infty]} H(u_1,T_2) dF^1_{u_1}$$

$$+ I_{t_1\geq T_1} I_{T_2>t_2} F^2(t_2)^{-1} \int_{]t_2,\infty]} H(T_1,u_2) dF^2_{u_2}$$

$$+ I_{T_1>t_1} I_{T_2>t_2} F(t)^{-1} \int_{\substack{t_1<u_1\le\infty \\ t_2<u_2\le\infty}} H(u_1,u_2)dF_u \ .$$

However, $M_{o,t_2} = 0$ *a.s.* and $M_{t_1,o} = 0$ *a.s.* imply that, for almost every t_1(resp. t_2),

$$\int_{]o,\infty]} H(t_1,u_2)dF^2_{u_2} = \int_{]o,\infty]} H(u_1,t_2)dF^1_{u_1} = 0,$$

and the result follows.

<u>THEOREM 5.4</u> Suppose M_{t_1,t_2} is a uniformly integrable, strong F_t martingale such that $M_{o,t_2} = 0$ *a.s.* and $M_{t_1,o} = 0$ *a.s.* for all t_1,t_2.

Then

$$M_{t_1,t_2} = \int_{\substack{o<s_1\le t_1 \\ o<s_2\le t_2}} g(s_1,s_2)d\hat{q}(s_1,s_2)$$

where

$$g(s_1,s_2) = H(s_1,s_2) + I_{s_1<c_1}(F^1_{s_1})^{-1} \int_o^{s_1} H(u_1,s_2)dF^1_{u_1}$$

$$+ I_{s_2<c_2}(F^2_{s_2})^{-1} \int_o^{s_2} H(s_1,u_2)dF^2_{u_2}$$

$$+ I_{s_1<c_1} I_{s_2<c_2} F_s^{-1} \int_{\substack{o<u_1\le s_1 \\ o<u_2\le s_2}} H(u_1,u_2)dF_u.$$

Here $H = M_{\infty,\infty}$ and $c_i = \inf\{t_i : F^i_{t_i} = 0\}$, $i = 1,2$.

<u>PROOF.</u> Write:

$$G^1(s_1,s_2) = H(s_1,s_2) + I_{s_1<c_1}(F^1_{s_1})^{-1} \int_o^{s_1} H(u_1,s_2)dF^1_{u_1}$$

So

$$g(s_1,s_2) = G^1(s_1,s_2) + I_{s_2<c_2}(F^2_{s_2})^{-1} \int_o^{s_2} G^1(s_1,u_2)dF^2_{u_2} \ .$$

As shown in Theorem 1 of Davis [5] :

$$\int_o^{t_2} (F^2_{u_2-})^{-1} g(s_1,u_2)dF^2_{u_2} = (F^2_{t_2})^{-1} \int_o^{t_2} G^1(s_1,u_2)dF^2_{u_2} \text{ for each } s_1.$$

Therefore, by Fubini's Theorem,

$$\int_{\substack{o<u_1\le t_1\\ o<u_2\le t_2}} F^{-1}_{u_1-,u_2-}\, g(u_1,u_2)dF_u = \int_{o<u_1\le t_1}\int_{o<u_2\le t_2} (F^1_{u_1-})^{-1}(F^2_{u_2-})^{-1}\, g(u_1,u_2)dF^1_{u_1}dF^2_{u_2}$$

$$= (F_{t_1,t_2})^{-1} \int_{\substack{o<u_1\le t_1\\ o<u_2\le t_2}} H(u_1,u_2)dF_u .$$

From Definition 5.2 we see after some calculation that $\int_{\substack{o<s_1\le t_1\\ o<s_2\le t_2}} g(s_1,s_2)d\hat{q}(s_1,s_2)$

$$= H(T_1,T_2)\, I_{t_1\ge T_1}\, I_{t_2\ge T_2}$$

$$- I_{t_2\ge T_2}\, I_{T_1>t_1}\, F^1(t_1)^{-1} \int_{]o,t_1]} H(s_1,T_2)dF^1_{s_1}$$

$$- I_{t_1\ge T_1}\, I_{T_2>t_2}\, F^2(t_2)^{-1} \int_{]o,t_2]} H(T_1,s_2)dF^2_{s_2}$$

$$+ I_{T_1>t_1}\, I_{T_2>t_2}\, F(t)^{-1} \int_{\substack{o<s_1\le t_1\\ o<s_2\le t_2}} H(s_1,s_2)dF_s .$$

$$= E\,[H|F_t] = M_{t_1 t_2} ,$$

so establishing the martingale representation result.

REFERENCES

1. Boel R. Varaiya P. and Wong E.
Martingales on jump processes, Part 1:Representation results. S.I.A.M. J. Control and Optimization, 13, 999-1061 (1975).

2. Cairoli, R. and Walsh, J.B.
Stochastic integrals in the plane. Acta Math. 134,111-183 (1975)

3. Cairoli, R. and Walsh, J.B.
Martingale representations and holomorphic processes Ann.Prob. 5, 511-521 (1977)

4. Chou, C. S. and Meyer, P. A.
Sur la représentation des martingales comme intégrales stochastiques dans les processus ponctuels. Séminaire de Probabilités IX, Lecture Notes in Math; vol 465, Springer Verlag, Berlin, (1975).

5. Davis M. H. A.
The representation of martingales of jump processes. S.I.A.M. J. Control and

Optimization 14, 623-638 (1976).

6. Elliott, R. J.
Innovation projections of a jump process and local martingales. Proc. Camb. Phil. Soc. 81, 77-90 (1977).

7. Elliott, R. J.
Stochastic Integrals for martingales of a jump process with partially accessible jump times. Zeits für Wahrs. 36, 213-226 (1976).

8. Jacod, J.
Multivariate point processes: Predictable projection, Radon-Nikodym derivatives representation of martingales. Zeits für Wahrs. 31, 235-253 (1975).

9. Wong, E.
A likelihood ratio formula for two dimensional random fields. I.E.E.E. Trans. Info. Theory I.T. - 20, 418-422,(1974).

10. Wong, E. and Zakai, M.
Martingales and stochastic integrals for processes with a multidimensional parameter. Zeits für Wahrs 29, 109-122 (1974).

STOCHASTIC STAGEWISE STACKLEBERG STRATEGIES FOR LINEAR QUADRATIC SYSTEMS

Tamer Basar*
Departement of Applied Mathematics
Twente University of Technology
P.O. Box 217, 7500 AE Enschede
The Netherlands

ABSTRACT

This paper obtains a set of stagewise Stackelberg strategies for discrete-time linear stochastic systems that involve two controllers, two quadratic objective functionals and the one-step-delay information sharing pattern. The optimal strategies are linear and they can be implemented recursively, with the off-line computations requiring the solution of a Liapunov-type equation, at each stage, and appropriate updating.

1. INTRODUCTION AND PROBLEM FORMULATION

In the optimum hierarchical control and coordination of multilevel systems, the "Stackelberg Equilibrium" concept provides an appropriate and rational approach toward obtaining the desired control strategies [1]. This solution concept is especially suited to situations in which there are at least two separate controllers, with one of them — called the leader — being in a position to enforce his strategy on the other(s), the follower(s). Depending on the nature of this enforcement, two different types of Stackelberg equilibria can be defined under dynamic information, and when time is discrete [2]. In the first one, which is called "Global Stackelberg Equilibrium", the leader announces his entire sequence of strategies at the very beginning, whereas in the second one — the so-called "Stagewise Stackelberg Equilibrium" (SSE) — the leader announces his strategy at the beginning of every stage.

In this paper, a set of SSE strategies are obtained for a class of stochastic systems that involve two controllers, with each controller having his own (quadratic) objective functional to optimize, and dynamic information. The problem is formulated in discrete time, with the state dynamics described by a linear difference equation,

---

* On leave from Marmara Research Institute, Applied Mathematics Division, Gebze-Kocaeli, Turkey

$$x(n+1) = Fx(n) + G_1u_1(n) + G_2u_2(n) + v(n), \; x(0) = x_0, \tag{1}$$

where $x(.)$ denotes the p-dimensional state vector, $u_1(.)$ denotes the r_1-dimensional control of the first controller, the leader, and $u_2(.)$ stands for the r_2-dimensional control of the second controller, the follower. n is the discrete time variable taking values in $\theta = \{0,1, \ldots, N-1\}$, $\{v(n), n \in \theta\}$ is a Gaussian white noise process with statistics $v(.) \sim N(0,\phi)$ and independent of the initial state $x_0 \sim N(\bar{x}_0,\Sigma)$. Matrices F, G_1, G_2 and ϕ are taken to be constant for simplicity in notation, but the results of this paper can easily be generalized to the case when these matrices vary with n.

At each stage n, the leader and the follower have access, respectively, to the observations $z_1(n)$ and $z_2(n)$, defined by

$$z_i(n) = H_ix(n) + w_i(n), \quad i = 1,2, \tag{2}$$

where $\dim(z_i) = m_i$, $\{w_1(n), n \in \theta\}$ and $\{w_2(n), n \in \theta\}$ are statistically independent Gaussian white noise processes with statistics $w_i(.) \sim N(0,R_i)$, $R_i > 0$, $i = 1,2$. Furthermore, these discrete time processes are statistically independent of x_0 and $\{v(n), n \in \theta\}$. It is assumed that these observations, as well as the past control values, are exchanged between the leader and the follower with a one-step delay. Such an information pattern is known, in the literature, as the "one-step delay information sharing pattern" [3]. Denoting the information available to the leader and the follower at stage n by η_1^n and η_2^n, respectively, we note that, under the adopted information pattern, they can be written as

$$\eta_i^n = \{Z_{n-1}, U_{n-1}, z_i(n)\}, \quad i = 1,2, \tag{3a}$$

where

$$Z_n \triangleq \{z_1(0), z_2(0), \ldots, z_1(n), z_2(n)\} \tag{3b}$$

$$U_n \triangleq \{u_1(0), u_2(0), \ldots, u_1(n), u_2(n)\}. \tag{3c}$$

Admissible strategies for the leader, at stage n, will be measurable mappings from the appropriate dimensional Euclidean space (and its Borel sets) generated by η_1^n into the r_1-dimensional Euclidean space. They are also required to satisfy a finite norm property. (For a mathematically precise definition of admissible strategies, the reader is referred to [4].) Let us denote such strategies by γ_1^n and the space they belong to by Γ_1^n. The class of admissible strategies for the follower can analogously be defined at stage n, with only η_2^n replacing η_1^n, and r_2 replacing r_1 in the preceding statement. It should be noted that the followers control, at stage n, depends not only on η_2^n, but also on γ_1^n as a consequence of the SSE concept. However, this latter dependence can be handled separately in the derivation of the solution, without treating it as a part of the information structure. We now finally denote the class of admissible strategies for the follower by Γ_2^n, at stage n, and its typical element by γ_2^n.

Let $\bar{\gamma}_i$ denote the entire sequence $\{\gamma_i^n, n \in \theta\}$ for each i = 1,2. Then, for a given admissible pair $\{\bar{\gamma}_1,\bar{\gamma}_2\}$, the quadratic expected cost of the leader is given by $\bar{J}_1(\bar{\gamma}_1,\bar{\gamma}_2)$, and that of the follower by $\bar{J}_2(\bar{\gamma}_1,\bar{\gamma}_2)$, where

$$\bar{J}_i(\bar{\gamma}_1,\bar{\gamma}_2) = E[J_i^0(\underline{u}_1^0,\underline{u}_2^0) \mid \underline{u}_j^0 = \bar{\gamma}_j(.),\ j=1,2], \qquad i=1,2, \tag{4a}$$

and

$$J_i^m(\underline{u}_1^m,\underline{u}_2^m) = x'(N)\tilde{Q}_i x(N) + \sum_{n=m}^{N-1} x'(n)\tilde{C}_i x(n) + u_1'(n)\tilde{D}_{i1}u_1(n) + u_2'(n)\tilde{D}_{i2}u_2(n), i=1,2. \tag{4b}$$

Here, $\tilde{Q}_i \geq 0$, $\tilde{C}_i \geq 0$, $\tilde{D}_{ii} > 0$, $\tilde{D}_{ij} \geq 0$, $i \neq j$, i,j = 1,2, are appropriate dimensional constant matrices, $\underline{u}_i^m$ is defined as the sequence $\underline{u}_i^m = \{u_i(m), \ldots, u_i(N-1)\}$, and E[.] denotes the expectation operation taken over the statistics of all the random variables involved. We should remark again that taking all the weighting matrices in the cost function (4b) as constants results in considerable simplification (notationwise) in some of the expressions to be derived in the sequel, while bringing in not so much loss of generality as far as the method of derivation of SSE strategies is concerned.

Definition of a Stagewise Stackelberg Equilibrium Solution.

Stagewise Stackelberg Equilibrium (SSE) strategies have the property that they are in static Stackelberg equilibrium at every stage of the decision problem, that is, at every stage the leader minimezes his expected cost on the reaction set of the follower. In order to give a mathematically precise definition of SSE strategies, let us first introduce the notation γ_{in}, to imply the entire sequence $\bar{\gamma}_i$ but with only γ_i^n missing, i.e.,

$$\gamma_{in} \triangleq \{\gamma_i^0, \ldots, \gamma_i^{n-1}, \gamma_i^{n+1}, \ldots, \gamma_i^{N-1}\}, \qquad i=1,2. \tag{5}$$

Furthermore, let $\{\bar{\gamma}_1^*,\bar{\gamma}_2^*\}$ be a given pair of admissible strategy sequences, and define

$$\overset{*}{\hat{J}}{}_i^n(\gamma_1^n,\gamma_2^n) \triangleq \bar{J}_i(\gamma_{1n}^*,\gamma_1^n,\gamma_{2n}^*,\gamma_2^n), \qquad i=1,2,\ n \in \theta. \tag{6}$$

That is, $\overset{*}{\hat{J}}{}_i^n$ is a function of the pair $\{\gamma_1^n,\gamma_2^n\}$, obtained by evaluating $\bar{J}_i$ at the other components of $\{\bar{\gamma}_1^*,\bar{\gamma}_2^*\}$.Then, we say that <u>the pair of strategies $\{\bar{\gamma}_1^*,\bar{\gamma}_2^*\}$ is in</u>

SSE if (i) $\bar{\gamma}_1^*$ satisfies the set of inequalities

$$\sup_{\gamma_2^n \in R_n({}^*\gamma_1^n)} {}^*\hat{J}_1^n({}^*\gamma_1^n,\gamma_2^n) \leq \sup_{\gamma_2^n \in R_n(\gamma_1^n)} {}^*\hat{J}_1^n(\gamma_1^n,\gamma_2^n), \quad n \in \theta, \tag{7}$$

and (ii) ${}^*\gamma_2^n \in R_n({}^*\gamma_1^n)$, $n \in \Theta$, where $R_n(\gamma_1^n)$ is called the rational reaction set of the follower, at stage n, to the strategy γ_1^n announced by the leader, and it is defined by

$$R_n(\gamma_1^n) = \{\hat{\gamma}_2^n \in \Gamma_2^n : {}^*\hat{J}_2^n(\gamma_1^n,\hat{\gamma}_2^n) \leq {}^*\hat{J}_2^n(\gamma_1^n,\gamma_2^n),\ \forall \gamma_2^n \in \Gamma_2^n\}. \tag{8}$$

Remark: If $R_n(\gamma_1^n)$ is a singleton for each $\gamma_1^n \in \Gamma_1^n$, $n \in \theta$, then the supremum operation can be dropped out in (7).

It should be noted that the definition given above enables one to obtain the SSE solution recursively, by starting at stage N-1, and moving iteratively backwards in time, while computing static Stackelberg strategies at every stage. The details of this procedure will become clear in section 3 of the paper. In the next section, we first present the Stackelberg solution of the single stage version of this problem, a result that will be utilized in the derivation of the SSE strategies in section 3. Section 2 contains one other auxiliary result that involves the conditional mean of the state x(.) given the common information available to the leader and the follower.

2. PRELIMINARY RESULTS

Consider now the static version of the Stackelberg problem formulated above. There is a single r_1-dimensional control u_1 for the leader, and an r_2-dimensional control u_2 for the follower, with the cost functions (4b) replaced by

$$J_1(u_1,u_2) = u_1'\hat{D}_{11}u_1 + u_2'\hat{D}_{12}u_2 + 2u_1'\hat{D}_{13}u_2 + 2u_1'\hat{C}_{11}x + 2u_2'\hat{C}_{12}x, \tag{9a}$$

$$J_2(u_1,u_2) = u_2'\hat{D}_{22}u_2 + u_1'\hat{D}_{21}u_1 + 2u_2'\hat{D}_{23}u_1 + 2u_1'\hat{C}_{21}x + 2u_2'\hat{C}_{22}x, \tag{9b}$$

and the observation equations (2) replaced by

$$z_i = H_i x + W_i \quad , i = 1,2, \tag{10}$$

where $x \sim N(\bar{x},\Sigma)$, $w_i \sim N(0,R_i)$ and these random vectors are statistically independent. Furtermore, the control u_i is assumed to be a function of only z_i, i.e., $u_i = \gamma_i(z_i)$, $i = 1,2$.

The Stackelberg solution of this problem has been obtained in [5], with a rigorous proof of existence given in [6]. The essential steps of the derivation are as follows: First determine the unique reaction of the follower to every strategy γ_1 of the leader, which is

$$\gamma_2(z_2) = -\hat{D}_{22}^{-1}\hat{C}_{22}E[x|z_2] - \hat{D}_{22}^{-1}\hat{D}_{23}E[\gamma_1(z_1)|z_2]. \tag{11}$$

Then, substitute this expression into (9a) for u_2, and consider the first and second Gateaux variations of the resulting expression around a candidate optimizing solution $\gamma_1^*(.)$; and finally solve for $\gamma_1^*(.)$ from the first order conditions. This gives rise to the unique Stackelberg solution given below the Theorem 1.

<u>Theorem 1</u> [5]

Let the condition

$$0 < \hat{D}_{11}^{-\frac{1}{2}} M \hat{D}_{11}^{-\frac{1}{2}} < 2I \tag{12}$$

be satisfied ; where

$$M \triangleq \hat{D}_{11} + \hat{D}_{23}'\hat{D}_{22}^{-1}\hat{D}_{12}\hat{D}_{22}^{-1}\hat{D}_{23} - \hat{D}_{13}\hat{D}_{22}^{-1}\hat{D}_{23} - \hat{D}_{23}'\hat{D}_{22}^{-1}\hat{D}_{13}'. \tag{13}$$

Then, the static Stackelberg problem defined above admits a unique solution given by

$$\gamma_1^{*}(z_1) = A_1(z_1 - H_1\bar{x}) + B_1\bar{x} \quad , \tag{14a}$$

$$\gamma_2^{*}(z_2) = -\hat{D}_{22}^{-1}\hat{C}_{22}[\Sigma_2(z_2 - H_2\bar{x}) + \bar{x}] - \hat{D}_{22}^{-1}\hat{D}_{23}E[\gamma_1^{*}(z_1)|z_2] \tag{14b}$$

$$\equiv A_2(z_2 - H_2\bar{x}) + B_2\bar{x} \quad , \tag{14c}$$

where

$$\Sigma_i \triangleq \Sigma H_i' (H_i \Sigma H_i' + R_i)^{-1} \quad , \; i = 1,2 \quad , \tag{15}$$

$$B_1 \triangleq M^{-1} [\hat{D}_{13}\hat{D}_{22}^{-1}\hat{C}_{22} + \hat{D}_{23}'\hat{D}_{22}^{-1}\hat{C}_{12} - \hat{C}_{11} - \hat{D}_{23}'\hat{D}_{22}^{-1}\hat{D}_{12}\hat{D}_{22}^{-1}\hat{C}_{22}] \; , \tag{16}$$

and A_1 is defined as the unique solution of

$$\hat{D}_{11}A_1 + (M - \hat{D}_{11})A_1\Sigma_2H_2\Sigma_1 = [(\hat{D}_{13} - \hat{D}_{23}'\hat{D}_{22}^{-1}\hat{D}_{12})\hat{D}_{22}^{-1}\hat{C}_{22} + \hat{D}_{23}'\hat{D}_{22}^{-1}\hat{C}_{12}]\Sigma_2H_2\Sigma_1 - \hat{C}_{11}\Sigma_1 . \square$$

The second auxiliary result that we shall need in the sequel is an expression for

$$\xi(n) \triangleq E[\, x(n) |\, Z_{n-1} \, , U_{n-1}] \; , \tag{18}$$

where x(.) is given by (1). To this end, we first note that

$$\xi(n) = F\hat{x}(n-1) + e(n-1), \tag{19a}$$

where

$$e(n) \triangleq G_1u_1(n) + G_2u_2(n), \tag{19b}$$

and

$$\hat{x}(n) \triangleq E[x(n) |\, Z_n, U_{n-1}], \tag{19c}$$

which is given recursively by the Kalman filter equations:

$$\hat{x}(n+1) = [I - K(n+1)H]F\hat{x}(n) + K(n+1)z(n+1) + [I - K(n+1)H]e(n) \; ; \; \hat{x}(-1) = \bar{x}_o \tag{20a}$$

$$K(n+1) = L(n)H'[H\,L(n)H' + R]^{-1} \tag{20b}$$

$$L(n) = F\,P(n)F' + \phi \ ; \ L(-1) = \Sigma \tag{20c}$$

$$P(n) = FP(n-1)F' - K(n)[HL(n-1)H' + R]K'(n) + \phi \ ; \ P(-1) = \Sigma , \tag{20d}$$

$$H \overset{\Delta}{=} [H_1', H_2']' \tag{21a}$$

$$z(.) \overset{\Delta}{=} [z_1'(.), z_2'(.)]' \tag{21b}$$

$$R \overset{\Delta}{=} \text{diag } [R_1, R_2] . \tag{21c}$$

Thus, a recursive equation for $\xi(.)$ is

$$\xi(n+1) = F[I - K(n)H]\xi(n) + e(n) + FK(n)z(n);\xi(0) = \bar{x}_0. \tag{22}$$

3. MAIN RESULTS

In this section, we outline derivation of a set of liner SSE strategies, by going through a dynamic programming type of argument, and by making repeated use of the solution of the static problem at each stage. The complete solution to the problem is provided in Theorem 2, whose proof is outlined below.

Let us first, consider inequality (7) and the reaction set (8) for n = N-1. Under the given information structure, they define a static Stackelberg problem with the relevant average cost expressions being $E[J_1^{N-1}]$ and $E[J_2^{N-1}]$, where J_i^{N-1} is defined by (4b). It should be noted that J_i^{N-1} is quadratic in $u_1(N-1)$ and $u_2(N-1)$; and when compared with (9), it is easy to see that the corresponding expressions are structurally alike, with only x(N-1) replacing x in J_i^{N-1}. Furthermore, under the given past information, i.e. $\{Z_{N-2}, U_{N-2}\}$, x(N-1) becomes a Gaussian random vector with mean $\xi(N-1)$ and covariance L(N-2), quantities which were already defined in the last section. Hence, the Stackelberg problem to be solved at stage N-1 is no different than the static problem of section 2, and consequently, it will admit a unique solution in the form (14), with ${}^{*}\gamma_i^{N-1}(\eta_i^{N-1})$ being linear in $z_i(N-1) - H_i\xi(N-1)$ and $\xi(N-1)$, say given by

$$ {}^{*}\gamma_i^{N-1}(\eta_i^{N-1}) = A_i(N-1)[z_i(N-1) - H_i\xi(N-1)] + B_i(N-1)\xi(N-1), \; i = 1,2, $$

where $A_i(N-1)$ and $B_i(N-1)$ are matrices that depend on the parameters of the problem. To determine te SSE strategies at stage n=N-2, we then consider inequality (7) together with the reaction set (8) for n=N-2. The relevant average cost expressions are now $E[J_1^{N-2}]$ and $E[J_2^{N-2}]$, but since they also depend on $u_i(N-1)$, i = 1,2, the optimal choice (23) has to be substituted in. In this process, we should express $z_i(N-1)$ as

$$ z_i(n-1) = H_i x(n-1) + W_i(N-1) = H_i Fx(N-2) + H_i e(N-2) + H_i v(N-2) + W_i(N-1) $$

$$ \equiv H_i Fx(N-2) + H_i e(N-2) + q_i(N-2) \quad , \; i = 1,2, $$

and $\xi(N-1)$ as

$$ \xi(N-1) = F\hat{x}(N-2) + e(N-2) \; , $$

where $q_i(N-2)$ is a zero-mean random vector which is statistically independent of the information sets η_i^{N-2} and η_2^{N-2}; consequently it does not affect the solution of the problem. The implication, then, is that the resulting average cost at stage n= N-2 can be written as a quadratic function of $u_1(N-2)$, $u_2(N-2)$, $x(N-2)$ and $\varepsilon(N-2)$, where $\varepsilon(N-2) = x(N-2) - \hat{x}(N-2)$, a quantity which does not depend on the past controls, and which has the property $E[\varepsilon(N-2)|\eta_i^{N-2}] = 0$, $i = 1,2$. Hence, as far as the solution at stage $n = N-2$, and also the derivation of past controls are concerned, the linear terms in $\varepsilon(N-2)$ can be dropped out, and the quadratic term in $\varepsilon(N-2)$ can be considered just as a constant. The problem, then, becomes essentially equivalent to the one considered at stage n=N-1, and its solution can likewise be obtained. Now, it should be apparent from the preceding discussion that a of . SSE strategies can be derived by following this sequential procedure up to the initial stage, or equivalently, by an inductive argument. The resulting expressions are given in Theorem 2, below:

Preliminary notation. New terms and notation used in Theorem 2 (unless otherwise stated, $i \neq j$ and $i,j = 1,2$):

$$D_{ii}(n) = G_i' S_i(n+1) G_i + \tilde{D}_{ii}(n) , \tag{24a}$$

$$D_{ij}(n) = G_j' S_i(n+1) G_j + \tilde{D}_{ij}(n) \tag{24b}$$

$$D_{i3}(n) = G_i' S_i(n+1) G_j \tag{24c}$$

$$C_{ii}(n) = G_i' S_i(n+1) F \tag{24d}$$

$$C_{ij}(n) = G_j' S_i(n+1) F \tag{24f}$$

$S_i(.)$: a (pxp) matrix determined recursively from

$$S_i(n) = [F + G_1B_1(n) + G_2B_2(n)]' S_i(n+1)[F + G_1B_1(n) + G_2B_2(n)]$$
$$+ B_i'(n)\tilde{D}_{ii}(n)B_i(n) + B_j'(n)\tilde{D}_{ij}(n)B_j(n)+\tilde{C}_i; S_i(N) = \tilde{Q}_i. \tag{25}$$

$$B_1(n) \triangleq M^{-1}(n)[D_{13}(n) D_{22}^{-1}(n)C_{22}(n) + D_{23}'(n)D_{22}^{-1}(n)C_{12}(n)-C_{11}(n)$$
$$-D_{23}'(n)D_{22}^{-1}(n)D_{12}(n)D_{22}^{-1}(n)C_{22}(n)] \tag{26}$$

$$M(n) \triangleq D_{11}(n) + D_{23}'(n)D_{22}^{-1}(n)D_{12}(n)D_{22}^{-1}(n)D_{23}(n)-D_{13}(n)D_{22}^{-1}(n)D_{23}(n)$$
$$-D_{23}'(n)D_{22}^{-1}(n)D_{13}'(n) \tag{27}$$

$$A_2(n) \triangleq -D_{22}^{-1}(n)[C_{22}(n) + D_{23}(n)A_1(n)H_1]K_2(n) \tag{28}$$

$$B_2(n) = - D_{22}^{-1}(n)[C_{22}(n) + D_{23}(n)B_1(n)] \tag{29}$$

$$K_i(n) = L(n-1)\ H_i'[H_i\ L(n-1)H_i' + R_i\ ]^{-1}. \tag{30}$$

Finally, $A_1(n)$ is determined as a solution of

$$D_{11}(n)A_1(n) + [M(n)-D_{11}(n)]\,A_1(n)K_2(n)H_2(n)K_1(n)$$

$$= [(D_{13}(n)-D_{23}'(n)D_{22}^{-1}(n)D_{12}(n))D_{22}^{-1}(n)C_{22}(n) + D_{23}'\ (n)D_{22}^{-1}(n) \tag{31}$$

$$\cdot\ C_{12}(n)]K_2(n)H_2K_1(n) - C_{11}(n)K_1(n).$$

Theorem 2.

Let the condition

$$0 < D_{11}^{-\frac{1}{2}}(n)M(n)D_{11}^{-\frac{1}{2}}(n) < 2\ I \tag{32}$$

be satisfied for every $n \in \Theta$. Then,

(i) There exists a unique solution $A_1(n)$ of the Liapunov-type equation (31) for each $n\ \in \Theta$.

(ii) The strategies

$$^{*}\gamma_i^n(\eta_i^n) = A_i(n)[z_i(n) - H_i\ \xi(n)] + B_i(n)\xi(n),\ i = 1,2;\ n\ \in \Theta, \tag{33}$$

constitute a *stagewise Stackelberg equilibrium solution* for the problem formulated in section 1, where $\xi(.)$ is defined recursively by (22).

Proof. Essential steps of the derivation of (33) have already been outlined. Since the information structure is of the "one-step delay sharing" type, an induction argument (and a dynamic programming type of approach) is applicable here, and one solves a static stochastic Stackelberg problem at every stage of this induction process. Details of this will not be provided here because of limited space. Part (i) of Theorem 2, on the other hand, follows by direct application of the result of Theorem 1, since condition (32) is analogous to (12). □

Remark: It has been shown earlier in [2] that the deterministic SSE solution is not in general unique under dynamic information. Similar, if not indentical, reasoning applies here to yield the conclusion that the solution presented in Theorem 2 is not unique. In other words, it is possible to obtain other (in general more complex) strategies that also satisfy inequalities (7) and property (ii) that just follows (7). But it seems that the SSE solution obtained in this paper is the only one that is amenable to iterative implementation, and further that, it is a robust solution under the "delayed commitment" point of view. □

4. SOME REMARKS ON THE GSE SOLUTION

In hierarchical optimization and control, an alternative to the stagewise Stackelberg equilibrium concept is the global Stackelberg equilibrium (GSE) concept, as it has already been mentioned in section 1. This latter one puts the leader in a relatively more powerful position, since he can then enforce his entire sequence of strategies on the follower at the very beginning of the decision process. To obtain the GSE solution, even under the one-step-delay sharing pattern, however, is a nontrivial problem, since for every announced strategy sequence of the leader, it is not in general possible to determine the rational reaction set of the follower explicitly. The follower's reaction can only be expressed implicitly in terms of certain functional relationships. This, evidently, makes the stochastic optimization problem faced by the leader a nonstandard one that involves implicit constraints. One way to circumvent this difficulty, if at all, is to investigate those class of problems in which the leader, by announcing an appropriate strategy, could achieve the best he can possibly do. To extend somewhat further on this idea, let $\bar{J}_1(\bar{\gamma}_1,\bar{\gamma}_2)$ denote the expected cost function of the leader, when he picks a strategy sequence $\bar{\gamma}_1 \in \Gamma_1$ and the follower picks $\bar{\gamma}_2 \in \Gamma_2$. Then, the lowest possible value for $\bar{J}_1$ is definitely $\min_{\bar{\gamma}_1 \in \Gamma_1} \min_{\bar{\gamma}_2 \in \Gamma_2} \bar{J}_1(\bar{\gamma}_1,\bar{\gamma}_2)$ assuming the minima exist. Denote a minimizing set of control strategies for this problem by $\bar{\gamma}_1^*$ and $\bar{\gamma}_2^*$. In general, $\bar{\gamma}_1^*$ is not the only element of Γ_1 that achieves this. There exists a nontrivial subset of Γ_1, say Γ_1^*, such that $\bar{J}_1(\bar{\gamma}_1,\bar{\gamma}_2^*) = \bar{J}_1(\bar{\gamma}_1^*,\bar{\gamma}_2^*)$ for all $\bar{\gamma}_1 \in \Gamma_1^*$. For the LQG systems of section 1, for example, Γ_1^* is comprised of infinitely many elements. Now, if there exists a $\bar{\gamma}_1^0 \in \Gamma_1^*$ such that $\min_{\gamma_2 \in \Gamma_2} \bar{J}_2(\bar{\gamma}_1^0,\bar{\gamma}_2) = \bar{J}_2(\bar{\gamma}_1^0,\gamma_2^*)$ then $\bar{\gamma}_1^0$ will definitely be considered as a GSE strategy for the leader, since by enforcing this particular strategy on the follower, he can achieve the lowest possible average cost on his behalf. It has actually been shown in [5], within the context of a 2-stage version of the problem treated in this paper, that such a powerful strategy could exist for the leader, under the one-step-delay sharing pattern. Extension of this result to the general LQ problem of section 1, however, still stands out as a challenging endeavour.

REFERENCES

[1] CRUZ, Jr., J.B., "Stackelberg Strategies in Multi-level Systems", in *Directions in large-Scale Systems*, edt. Y.C.Ho and S.K. Mitter, Plenum Press 1975.

[2] BASAR, T., "Information Structures and Equilibria in Dynamic Games", *Technical report No. 40, Marmera Research Institute*, Gebze-Kocaeli, Turkey, September 1977. Also in *New trends in Dynamic Systems Theory and Economics*, edt. M.Aoki and A. Marzollo, Academic Press, 1978.

[3] WITSENHAUSEN, H., "Separation of Estimation and Control For Dicrete Time Systems", *Proc. IEEE*, vol.59, no. 11, 1557-1566, 1971.

[4] BASAR, T., "Two-Criteria LQG Decision Problems with One-Step Delay Observation Sharing Pattern", *Information and Control*, Vol.38. No. 1, 21-50, 1978.

[5] BASAR, T., "Hierarchical Decision Making Under Uncertainty", *Proceedings of the 1978 Kingston Conferende on Differential Games and Control Theory*, edt. P.T. Liu, Plenum Press, 1979.

[6] BASAR, T., "Noncooperative Equilibrium Solutions in 2-Person Hierarchical Decision Problems", submitted for publication, 1978.

SOME REMARKS CONCERNING ATTAINABLE SETS OF STOCHASTIC OPTIMAL CONTROL SYSTEMS

E.O. Bertsch

TU Berlin

0. INTRODUCTION

This work contains an analogon of the existence result for time - optimal control in [1] , using no longer Girsanov solutions but Itô solutions. It is derived for the type of control system introduced in [2].
After some notations are fixed, this system is described. The main part contains then results about the attainable sets of this system and the existence theorem for optimal control.

1. NOTATIONS

1.1. Let us fix a probability space $(\Omega, \mathcal{A}, P)$.
Given a stochastic process $X(t)$, $t \in \mathbb{R}$, $\mathcal{B}_{uv}(X)$ denotes the least σ- Algebra generated by $\{X(t),\ t \in [u,v]\}$, and $\mathcal{B}_{uv}(dX)$ denotes the least σ- Algebra generated by $\{X(t)-X(s)\ ,\ u \leq s \leq t \leq v\}$.
The least σ-Algebra that contains $\mathcal{A}_1$, $\mathcal{A}_2$, ... is denoted by $\mathcal{A}_1 \vee \mathcal{A}_2 \vee \ldots$.
The past of X up to the time $s \geq 0$ is expressed by the process $p_s X$ which is defined by

$$(p_s X)(t) = X(s+t) \quad , \quad -\infty < t \leq 0 \quad .$$

The space C^l_- of $\mathbb{R}^l$ - valued continuous functions , defined on $(-\infty,0]$, is a separable complete metric space with the metric

$$\rho_-(f,g) = \sum_{n=1}^{\infty} 2^{-n} \cdot \frac{\|f-g\|_n}{1 + \|f-g\|_n} \quad , \quad \text{where}$$

$$\|h\|_n = \sum_{i=1}^{l} \max_{-n \leq t \leq 0} |h_i(t)| \quad .$$

ρ_- is a metric for the topology of uniform convergence on compact subintervalls of $(-\infty,0]$.
The modifications for C^l_+ and C^l are obvious.

1.2. Let Σ be a separable complete metric space with the metric ϱ and $\mathcal{B}(\Sigma)$ the Borel -σ- Algebra on Σ. For probability measures μ_1, μ_2 on $\mathcal{B}(\Sigma)$ the Prohorov distance $L(\mu_1, \mu_2)$ is a metric which metrizes the weak convergence of measures :

$$\mu_n \xrightarrow[n\to\infty]{} \mu \iff \int_\Sigma f\, d\mu_n \xrightarrow[n\to\infty]{} \int_\Sigma f\, d\mu$$ for all continuous bounded functionals on Σ.

With the metric $L(.,.)$ the set of all probability measures on $\mathcal{B}(\Sigma)$ is a separable complete metric space $\Sigma(\mathcal{B}(\Sigma))$.

1.3. Let Σ be any metric space with metric ϱ. We shall use the following Hausdorff metric on the set of compact subsets of Σ:

$$d(A,B) = \max\{d_o(A,B), d_o(B,A)\} \quad \text{where}$$

$$d_o(A,B) = \sup\{d_o(x,B) : x \in A\} \quad \text{and} \quad d_o(x,B) = \inf\{\varrho(x,y) : y \in B\}.$$

2. THE CONTROL PROBLEM

2.1. Definition : We call (X_-,U,B) admissible system , if

(i) $X_-(t)$, $t \in (-\infty, 0]$ is an n-dim. stochastic process with continuous paths

(ii) $(B(t))_{t\in\mathbb{R}}$ is k-dim. Brownian motion , $B(0) = \mathcal{O}$

(iii) $P(U(0) = \mathcal{O}$ and $|U_i(t)-U_i(s)| \leq |t-s|$, $0 \leq t,s < \infty$, $i=1,\dots,k) = 1$

(iv) $\sigma(X_-) \vee \mathcal{B}_{ot}(U) \vee \mathcal{B}_{-\infty t}(B)$ is independent of $\mathcal{B}_{t\infty}(dB)$ for all $t \geq 0$.

2.2. Definition : Let $\alpha(.,.)$ and $\beta(.,.,.)$, defined on $[0,\infty) \times C^n_-$ resp. $[0,\infty) \times C^n_- \times C^k_-$, be continuous $(n \times k)$ - matrix valued functions.

A stochastic process $X(t)$ with continuous paths is a solution of

$$(\ast) \quad dX(t) = \alpha(t, p_t X)dU(t) + \beta(t, p_t X, p_t B)dB(t)$$

for the admissible system (X_-,U,B) , if

(i) $X(t) = X(0) + \int_0^t \alpha(s, p_s X)dU(s) + \int_0^t \beta(s, p_s X, p_s B)dB(s)$, $t \geq 0$

$X(t) = X_-(t)$, $t \leq 0$ w. pr. 1

(ii) $\mathcal{B}_{-\infty t}(X) \vee \mathcal{B}_{ot}(U) \vee \mathcal{B}_{-\infty t}(B)$ is independent of $\mathcal{B}_{t\infty}(dB)$ for all $t \geq 0$.

$\int \alpha(\ )dU$ in (i) can be regarded as ordinary Riemann-Stieltjes-integral for almost all paths , $\int \beta(\ )dB$ can be defined as Itô - integral.

2.3. Theorem (Fleming, Nisio) : For every admissible system (X_-,U,B) under the assumptions A1 , A2 , A3 below there exists one and only one solution of (*) with locally bounded second moment.

A1 (Lipschitz condition) :
There exists a bounded measure Γ_1 on $(-\infty,0]$ such that

$$\sum_{i,j} [|\alpha_{ij}(t,f)-\alpha_{ij}(t,\tilde{f})|^2 + |\beta_{ij}(t,f,g)-\beta_{ij}(t,\tilde{f},g)|^2]$$
$$\leq \sum_{l=1}^{n} \int_{-\infty}^{o} |f_l(s)-\tilde{f}_l(s)|^2 \, d\Gamma_1(s) \text{ for all } t \in [0,\infty)$$
$$\text{and } f,\tilde{f} \in C_-^n \text{ , } g \in C_-^k \text{ .}$$

A2 (Boundedness condition) :
There exist an integer M, two bounded measures Γ_2 and Γ_3 on $(-\infty,0]$ and two increasing functions M_1 , M_2 such that

$$\sum_{i,j} |\beta_{ij}(t,f,g)|^4 \leq M_1(t) + \sum_{l=1}^{n} \int_{-\infty}^{o} f_l^4(s)d\Gamma_2(s)$$
$$+ \sum_{l=1}^{k} \int_{-\infty}^{o} g_l^{2M}(s)d\Gamma_3(s)$$

$$\text{and } \quad k \cdot \sup_{o \leq \tau \leq t} \int_{-\infty}^{o} |s+\tau|^M \, d\Gamma_3(s) \leq M_2(t)$$

A3 : $E\, X_-^4(t) \leq c < \infty$ for all $t \leq 0$.

Proof: see [2] .

2.4. Remark concerning the cost criterion :
In deterministic optimal control theory the following time-optimal problem is standard : Given a closed set B , the first entrance-time $\tau_X u$ into B of the system state X using control u has to be minimal. This problem can be stochastisized by looking for $\min_u E\, \tau_X u$, and the existence of optimal controls in this sense for our system (*) can be established by specializing the optimality result in [2]. Now [1] has pointed out that for some purposes criteria e.g of the

form

$$\min \{t : P(\tau_X u > t) < \alpha\}$$

might be more interesting , and they have noticed that the optimal time t for such problems might be finite even if $E\,\tau_X u = \infty$.

More generally : [1] considers the (infinite dimensional) problem of driving the attainable probability distributions of the system state to a given set of distributions in minimal time. In analogy to the existence result in [1] , where Girsanov solutions are used , we shall derive a result for the system (*) .

3. ATTAINABLE SETS

3.1. Definition : Let $\tilde{X}_-(t)$, $t \leq 0$, be fixed.

$\mathfrak{M} := \{ (X_-,U,B) : (X_-,U,B)$ is admissible, defined on the probability space $\Omega = [0,1]$ (Lebesgue - interval) and $\mu_{X_-} = \mu_{\tilde{X}_-} \}$, where μ_X is the distribution of X.

$A := \{\mu_{X_S} : S \in \mathfrak{M}\}$, where X_S is the unique solution of (*) with locally bounded 2. moment for the admissible system S, restricted to $[0,\infty)$.

3.2. Theorem : A is a compact subset of $\Sigma(\mathcal{B}(C^n_+))$.

Proof: [2] proves essentially the closedness and sequentially compactness of this set.

Now we are interested in sets which are attainable at a fixed time.

3.3. Definition : Let $t \in [0,\infty)$ be fixed.

$$A_t := \{ \mu_{X_S(t)} : S \in \mathfrak{M} \}$$

As we now evaluate the processes at time t , we need the following lemmata :

3.4. Lemma : Let $(X_m)_{m\in\mathbb{N}}$ and X be stochastic processes (Parameter $t\in\mathbb{R}_+$) with continuous paths and let $\mu_{X_m} \xrightarrow[m\to\infty]{} \mu_X$ in $\Sigma(\mathcal{B}(C^n_+))$.

Then $\mu_{X_m(t)} \xrightarrow[m\to\infty]{} \mu_{X(t)}$ in $\Sigma(\mathcal{B}(\mathbb{R}^n))$ for all $t \geq 0$.

Proof :

1) Set $h:=e_t$ where $e_t(f) = f(t)$. Then $h:C_+^n \longrightarrow \mathbb{R}^n$ is continuous, if the topology in C_+^n is the topology of uniform convergence on compact subintervalls (see [3]).

2) $\mu_{X_m} \longrightarrow \mu_X$ and $h:C_+^n \longrightarrow \mathbb{R}^n$ continuous $\Rightarrow$ $\mu_{h \circ X_m} \longrightarrow \mu_{h \circ X}$ (see [4]).

3.5. Lemma : For $t_n \longrightarrow t$ in $[0,\infty)$, every sequence $\mu_{X_{S_n}}(t_n) \in A_{t_n}$ contains some convergent subsequence with limit in A_t .

Proof :

As A is compact , the sequence $\mu_{X_{S_n}}$ in A contains some convergent subsequence , named again $\mu_{X_{S_n}}$, which converges to some μ_{X_S} in A. But then $\mu_{X_{S_n}}(t_n) \longrightarrow \mu_{X_S}(t) \in A_t$, which is a consequence of the following result in [4] :

Let $P_n \longrightarrow P$, h_n measurable and let $P(E) = 0$ for

$$E := \{ x : \exists \; x_n \longrightarrow x \text{ such that } h_n(x_n) \not\longrightarrow h(x)\} .$$

Then $P_n h_n^{-1} \longrightarrow Ph^{-1}$.

If we set $P_n = \mu_{X_{S_n}}$, $P = \mu_{X_S}$, $h_n := e_{t_n} : C_+^n \longrightarrow \mathbb{R}^n$, $f \longmapsto f(t_n)$, $h := e_t$,

then we get $E = \emptyset$, because the map

$$e : C_+^n \times [0,\infty) \longrightarrow \mathbb{R}^n$$
$$(f,t) \longmapsto f(t)$$

is continuous (see [3]). So we get our result.

Now we can prove

3.6. Theorem :

(i) A_t is a compact subset of $\Sigma(\mathcal{B}(\mathbb{R}^n))$ for every $t \geq 0$.

(ii) The map $t \longmapsto A_t$ is a continuous map from $[0,\infty)$ to the set of compact subsets of $\Sigma(\mathcal{B}(\mathbb{R}^n))$ if the Hausdorff metric is used.

Proof :

(i) sequentially compactness of A_t :

For $(\mu_{X_m(t)})_{m\in\mathbb{N}}$ in A_t the sequence μ_{X_m} in A contains a convergent subsequence $\mu_{X_{mk}}$ and by Lemma 3.4. the sequence $\mu_{X_{mk}(t)}$ is convergent in $\Sigma(\mathcal{B}(\mathbb{R}^n))$.

closedness of A_t :

Let $\mu_{X_m(t)} \in A_t$ for all m and $\mu_{X_m(t)} \xrightarrow[m\to\infty]{} \mu \in \Sigma(\mathcal{B}(\mathbb{R}^n))$.

The sequence μ_{X_m} in A contains some subsequence $\mu_{X_{mk}}$ which is convergent to some $\mu_X \in A$. By Lemma 3.4. $\mu_{X_{mk}(t)} \longrightarrow \mu_{X(t)} \in A_t$.

So $\mu = \mu_{X(t)} \in A_t$.

(ii) (by contradiction) :

Let $t_n \longrightarrow t$ in $[0,\infty)$. Assume :

$\exists\ \varepsilon > 0$ such that there exists some subsequence, again denoted by t_n , such that $d(A_t, A_{t_n}) > \varepsilon \quad \forall n$

i.e. $\forall n$
$$\begin{cases} \sup \{ d_o(x, A_{t_n}) : x \in A_t \} > \varepsilon \\ \text{or} \\ \sup \{ d_o(x, A_t) : x \in A_{t_n} \} > \varepsilon \end{cases}$$

First case:

There is some subsequence , again named t_n , such that
$$\sup \{ d_o(x, A_{t_n}) : x \in A_t \} > \varepsilon \quad \forall n ,$$

i.e. for all $n \in \mathbb{N}$ there is some $S_n \in \mathfrak{M}$ such that
$$d_o(\mu_{X_{S_n}(t)}, A_{t_n}) > \varepsilon .$$

As A_t is compact , for some subsequence - again denoted S_n - we have for some $S \in \mathfrak{M}$: $\mu_{X_{S_n}(t)} \xrightarrow[n\to\infty]{} \mu_{X_S(t)}$, and especially for this S we get $L(\mu_{X_{S_n}(t)}, \mu_{X_S(t_n)}) > \varepsilon \quad \forall n.$

But now $\mu_{X_{S_n}(t)} \longrightarrow \mu_{X_S(t)}$ and $\mu_{X_S(t_n)} \longrightarrow \mu_{X_S(t)}$, and this contradicts the last inequality .

Second case:

There is some subsequence , again denoted by t_n , such that

$$\sup \{ d_o(x,A_t) : x \in A_{t_n} \} > \varepsilon \quad \forall n ,$$

i.e. for all $n \in \mathbb{N}$ there is some $S_n \in \mathfrak{M}$ such that

$$d_o(\mu X_{S_n}(t_n) , A_t) > \varepsilon .$$

But this contradicts Lemma 3.5. .

4. EXISTENCE THEOREM FOR TIME OPTIMAL CONTROL

4.1. Theorem : Assume A1, A2, A3 and additionally

$$A4 : \lim_{s \downarrow t} d_o(K(s) \cap A_s , K(t)) = 0 \quad \text{for all } t \geq 0 ,$$

where the target set K(t) is a closed subset of $\Sigma(\mathfrak{B}(\mathbb{R}^n))$.

If $K(T) \cap A_T \neq \emptyset$ for some $T > 0$ then there is a smallest $t \in [0,T]$ such that $K(t) \cap A_t \neq \emptyset$.

Proof:

Set $Q := \{ t \geq 0 : K(t) \cap A_t \neq \emptyset \}$ .This implies $T \in Q$, $Q \neq \emptyset$.

For $t^* := \inf Q \leq T$ we show : $t^* \in Q$.

There exists some sequence $t_n \downarrow t^*$, such that all $t_n \in Q$,

i.e. there are solutions X_{S_n} of (*) such that $\mu X_{S_n}(t_n) \in K(t_n) \cap A_{t_n}$.

Lemma 3.5. says that this sequence contains some convergent subsequence denoted equally , such that $\mu X_{S_n}(t_n) \longrightarrow \mu \in A_{t^*}$.

We still have to show: $\mu \in K(t^*)$. Now

$$\inf_{\tilde{\mu} \in K(t^*)} L(\mu,\tilde{\mu}) \leq \underbrace{L(\mu,\mu X_{S_n}(t_n))}_{\xrightarrow[n\to\infty]{} 0} + \underbrace{\inf_{\tilde{\mu} \in K(t^*)} L(\mu X_{S_n}(t_n),\tilde{\mu})}_{\xrightarrow[n\to\infty]{} 0}$$

since $\inf_{\tilde{\mu} \in K(t^*)} L(\mu X_{S_n}(t_n),\tilde{\mu}) = d_o(\mu X_{S_n}(t_n),K(t^*))$

$$\leq d_o(K(t_n) \cap A_{t_n},K(t^*)) \xrightarrow[A4]{n\to\infty} 0.$$

As K(t*) is closed , this implies $\mu \in K(t^*)$.

4.2. Remarks :

- Right-continuity of $t \longmapsto K(t)$ in the Hausdorff metric implies A4 , because $d_o(K(s) \cap A_s , K(t)) \leqslant d_o(K(s) , K(t))$.
- For applications of the theorem see the examples of right-continuous K(t) in [1] .

REFERENCES

[1] Haussmann,U.G., Anderson,W.J., Boyarsky,A.:
A new stochastic time optimal control problem
SIAM J. Control Optimization, 16, 1978

[2] Fleming,W.H., Nisio,M.:
On the existence of optimal stochastic controls
J. Math. Mech., 15, 1966

[3] Dugundji,J.:
Topology
Allyn and Bacon, Boston, 1966

[4] Billingsley,P.:
Convergence of probability measures
John Wiley, New York, 1968

POTENTIAL THEORY IN OPTIMAL STOPPING AND ALTERNATINC PROCESSES

Jean-Michel Bismut
Université Paris-Sud
Département de Mathématiques
91405 Orsay

The purpose of this paper is to give a brief account of a series of results on optimal Stopping, Control of stopped diffusions, and control of alternating processes obtained in [3]-[12]. Special attention will be given to the duality arguments used in these papers.

1. OPTIMAL STOPPING

Let $(\Omega, \mathcal{F}_t, P)$ be a probability space verifying the "conditions habituelles" of [13].

X_t is an optional process defined on $\Omega \times [0, +\infty]$ with values in R.

$\mathcal{C}$ is the set of stopping times with values in $[0, +\infty]$.

The problem of optimal stopping is the search of $T \in \mathcal{C}$ maximizing $T' \longrightarrow E(X_{T'})$ on $\mathcal{C}$.

To ensure existence of an optimal stopping time, we make the following assumptions :

H1 : . X_t is of class (D) (i.e. the random variables $(X_T)_{T \in \mathcal{C}}$ are uniformly integrable).

H2 : . For any increasing or decreasing sequence of stopping times $T_n \longrightarrow T$, then

$$E(X_T) \geqslant \limsup E(X_{T_n}). \tag{1}$$

The following is proved in [3].

PROPOSITION 1. *If X verifies H1, for X to verify H2, it is necessary and sufficient that :*

a) X *is right u.s.c. on* $[0,+\infty[$

b) *If* ${}^3X$ *is the predictable projection of* X, *then on* $]0,+\infty]$,

$$ {}^3X_t \geqslant \limsup_{s \uparrow\uparrow t} X_s \tag{2}$$

If there is equality in (1), a) *and* b) *are replaced by*

a') X *is right-continuous on* $[0,+\infty[$, *with left-hand limits in* $]0,+\infty]$

b') *On* $]0,+\infty]$, ${}^3X = X^-$

Let Z be the Snell envelop of X, i.e the smallest strong supermartingale $\geqslant X$, which exists by a result of Mertens in [15].

THEOREM 1. *Z is a regular supermartingale (i.e. if $T_n \uparrow T$, $E(Z_{T_n}) \downarrow E(Z_T)$). If there is equality in (1), Z is right continuous. If $Z = M - B$ is the Mertens decomposition of Z into a difference of a martingale and of a predictable increasing process B, B is left-continuous. B is continuous if there is equality in (1).*

Let A be the optional set $(Z = X)$. Then A is closed on the right. Moreover B increases only on A. Let D' be the stopping time :

$$D' = \inf\{t \geqslant 0\ ; B_t > 0\}.$$

Then for a stopping time T to maximize $T' \longrightarrow E(X_{T'})$ it is necessary and sufficient that $X_T \in A$ a.s. and that $T \leqslant D'$. In particular D_A and $D' \wedge \{+\infty\}$ are optimal stopping times.

The existence result on optimal stopping times is probably the best it is possible to obtain in general. It had been partly obtained by Fakeev in [14].

This result is applied in [3] to general Markov processes. It has been extended in [7] - [9] by introducing the notion of quasi-stopping time, and an interpretation of potential theory results using optimal stopping on reversed Markov processes has been given in [7] - [10].

While proved in [3] by elementary methods using Zorn's lemma, it may be interpreted using fonctional analysis techniques : $\mathcal{C}$ may be imbedded in a convex weakly compact set B of linear fonctions, in which $\mathcal{C}$ is the set of extremal points and such that X defines a weakly continuous linear function.

Incidently, these techniques are helpful to derive the following result :

THEOREM 2. If X is an optional process of class (D) verifying a'), b') there is a continuous (non adapted) process Y with $E(\sup_{0\leq t\leq +\infty} |Y_t|) < +\infty$ such that X is the optional projection of Y.

Proof. This is Theorem 3 of [11]. The proof is based on optimal stopping techniques and a Theorem of Krein- Smulian. □

2. STOPPING MEASURES

Let x_t be a Markov right process with values in a metrisable Lusin space $E \cup \{\delta\}$ with finite life-time ζ, and cemetery δ.

Rost has given in [7] the following result.

THEOREM 3. Let λ be a finite ≥ 0 measure on E. Then if a ≥ 0 measure μ on E is such that for any excessive function f, $<\mu, f> \leq <\lambda. f>$ there exists a randomized stopping time T such that for any bounded Borel h, $<\mu, h> = E^{P_\lambda} h(\hat{x}_T)$.

If λ and μ verify the conditions of Theorem 3, we write $\lambda < \mu$.

Let g be a bounded Borel function on E. Rg is the smallest strongly supermedian function $\geq g$, which exists by [16]. By [16] we know that $Rg(x_t)$ is the Snell envelop of $g(x_t)$ for any P_λ.

We may then write

$$(3) \qquad <\lambda, Rg> = \sup_{\substack{\mu\geq 0\\ \lambda<\mu}} <\mu, g>$$

and in particular

$$(4) \qquad Rg(x) = \sup_{\substack{\mu \geq 0 \\ \varepsilon_x < \mu}} < \mu, g >$$

E is now taken to be locally compact, countable at infinity and metrizable.

x is a Hunt process with finite life-time ζ, and cemetery δ. Then :

PROPOSITION 2. For any finite ≥ 0 measure λ ,$\{\mu \geq 0 ; \lambda < \mu\}$ is tightly compact.

Proof. This is Proposition 1 of Appendix of [8].

We assume now x to be also Feller, and moreover that it verifies the following assumptions.

H3 : If g is bounded continuous, Rg is bounded continuous.

In the Appendix of [8], H3 is prove to be equivalent to the uniform tightness of $\{\mu \geq 0 ; \exists x \in L ; \varepsilon_x < \mu\}$ when L is a compact set of E, and also to the fact that the speed at which x gets away from a compact set must be bounded in probability.

These assumptions are verified in particular by killed diffusions [4].

If $\bar{K}$ is the cone of bounded continuous excessive function, then it is proved in [4] for the diffusion case, and in [8]-Appendix in general, that if g is bounded and u.s.c., for $x \in E$, the two problems

$$(5) \qquad (p) \quad \inf_{f \in \bar{K} \geq g} f(x) \qquad (p') \quad \sup_{\mu \geq 0, \varepsilon_x < \mu} < \mu, g >$$

are dual to each other in the sense of convex analysis.

This very fact is very useful in any of the subsequent optimal stopping problems.

The optimal μ is then a Lagrange multiplier for problem (p).

Let us note that (5) are standard convex linear programs.

Remark. In the case of diffusions, when g is sufficiently regular, the minimal f is founded by Bensoussan-Lions in [1] as a solution of a variational inequality, related to the minimization of I on $\{f \in H^1, f \geq g\}$ where I is a quadratic Dirichlet form associated to the considered diffusion. The Lagrange multiplier $\tilde{\mu}$ associated to the constraint $f \geq g$ is the measure $\tilde{\mu}$ such that if G is the Green function associated to the diffusion, $f = G\tilde{\mu}$.

It is interesting to note that two apparently different convex minimization problems have the same solution;however it seems that the probabilistic approach is simpler and more direct, as long as we are not interested in differentiable regularity of f.

3. CONTROL AND OPTIMAL STOPPING

Let x be a controlled diffusion.

$$(6) \qquad \begin{cases} dx = b(s,x,u)dt + \sigma(t,x)dw \\ x(0) = x. \end{cases}$$

If $T \in \mathcal{C}$, we want to minimize

$$(7) \qquad E_x\{\int_0^T e^{-pt}L(x,u)dt + (e^{-pt}g(x_T)\}$$

in u and T.

By using uniform tightness results on the stopping measures μ when the drift of a diffusion is taken to vary boundedly, existence and characterization of optimums are given in [4] by using elementary compactness arguments.

4. ALTERNATING PROCESSES

Let x and x' be two Markov right processes with values in E, finite life-time, and cemetery δ. Order relations $<$ and $'<$ on bounded measures are defined for x and x' as previously.

If λ is a ≥ 0 measure on E, and $T_1,\ldots,T_n$ is an increasing sequence of stopping times, we consider the process which starts like process x with entrance measure λ up to time T_1, then like x' up to time T_2, then like x up to T_3, etc...

If g and g' are bounded Borel functions, we want to maximize

$$(8) \qquad E_\lambda \left[\sum_1^{+\infty} (g(x_{T_{2i-1}}) + g(x_{T_{2i}})\right]$$

Let μ_i the law of X_{T_i}. (μ,μ') are defined by :

$$(9) \quad \begin{cases} \mu = \sum_1^{+\infty} \mu_{2i-1} \\ \mu' = \sum_1^{+\infty} \mu_{2i} \end{cases}$$

We have then the following :

THEOREM 4. If μ and μ' are finite, then, $\lambda < \mu - \mu' \nmid 0$. Conversely if two $\geqslant 0$ measures μ and μ' are such that $\lambda < \mu - \mu' \nmid 0$, there exists a family $\{\mu_i\}$ of $\geqslant 0$ measures such that $\lambda < \mu_1 ' < \mu_2 < \mu_3 \ldots$ and two $\geqslant 0$ measures m and m' such that

$$(10) \quad \begin{aligned} \mu &= \sum_1^{+\infty} \mu_{2i-1} + m \\ \mu &= \sum_1^{+\infty} \mu_{2i} + m' \\ &0 < m - m' \nmid 0. \end{aligned}$$

Proof : This is Proposition 2.3 and 2.4 of [8].

We assume now there exists $\tilde{f}$ bounded and strongly supermedian for x, and $\tilde{f}'$ bounded and strongly supermedian for x' such that

$$g \leqslant \tilde{f} - \tilde{f}' \leqslant -g'$$

We define a sequence of functions (f_i, f_i') by :

$$(11) \quad \begin{aligned} f_1 &= Rg & f_1' &= R'g' \\ f_{i+1} &= R(f_i' + g) & f_{i+1}' &= R'(f_i + g'). \end{aligned}$$

We have then the following :

THEOREM 5. The sequences $\{f_i\}, \{f_i'\}$ are increasing and converge to (f,f') which are respectively strongly supermedian for x and x' and $\leqslant \tilde{f}$ and $\leqslant \tilde{f}'$.

Moreover, (f,f') is the minimal solution of

$$(12) \quad \begin{cases} f = R(f' + g) \\ f' = R'(f + g'). \end{cases}$$

Finally

$$(13) \quad \begin{aligned} f(x) &= \sup_{\varepsilon_x < \mu - \mu' \not< 0} \langle \mu, g \rangle + \langle \mu', g' \rangle \\ f'(x) &= \sup_{\varepsilon_x \not< \mu' - \mu < 0} \langle \mu, g \rangle + \langle \mu', g' \rangle \end{aligned}$$

Proof. This is Theorem 2.1 and 2.2 of [8].

If x, x' are Feller process as in 2, verify assumption H3, if g and g' are bounded and u.s.c., and if there is $\beta > 0$, $\tilde{f} \in \bar{K}$, $\tilde{f}' \in \bar{K}'$ such that

$$(14) \quad g + \beta \leqslant \tilde{f} - \tilde{f}' \leqslant -g' - \beta$$

then the following may be proved :

THEOREM 6. The problems

$$(15) \quad (P) \quad \begin{array}{l} \inf \langle \lambda, \bar{f} \rangle \\ \bar{f} \in \bar{K} \,;\, \exists\, \bar{f}' \in \bar{K}' \\ g \leqslant \bar{f} - \bar{f}' \leqslant -g' \end{array} \qquad (P') \quad \begin{array}{l} \sup \langle \mu, g \rangle + \langle \mu', g' \rangle \\ \mu, \mu' \geqslant 0 \\ \varepsilon_x < \mu - \mu' \not< 0 \end{array}$$

are dual to each other.

Moreover $(f.f')$ defined in Theorem 5 are u.s.c., and equal to the inf of the couples $(\bar{f}, \bar{f}') \in \bar{K} \times \bar{K}'$ such that $g \leqslant \bar{f} - \bar{f}' \leqslant -g'$. There exists $\mu, \mu' \geqslant 0$ maximizing the programm (P'). If g and g' are continuous, f and f' are continuous.

Proof. This is Theorem 2.4 of [8]. □

This result is useful to solve the maximization of (8). By this way two domains A and B are defined : the T_{2i-1} are the hitting times of A, and T_{2i} the hitting times of B.

Remark. The existence of $\beta > 0$ such that (14) holds is interpreted in [8] as a qualification condition in convex programming.

This result is applied in [8] to the case of two diffusions and of impulse control. In fact, an impulsion in a given direction in R^n may be interpreted as a uniform translation process with speed 1. Some problems of impulse control may be solved as a problem of alternating optimally a diffusion process and a uniform translation process. It gives a very simple solution to "quasi-variational inequalities". [2].

The case of more than two processes is more difficult to study. It necessitates the careful study of trees of measures [18].

In [8], the control of alternating processes is also studied, as well as various types of constraints. Game situations are studied in [5]-[6].

REFERENCES

(1) BENSOUSSAN A., LIONS J.L. : Problèmes de temps d'arrêt optimal et inéquations variationnelles paraboliques. Applicable Anal. 3, 267-294 (1973).

(2) BENSOUSSAN A., LIONS J.L. : Temps d'arrêt optimaux et contrôle impulsionnel. Livre en préparation.

(3) BISMUT J.M., SKALLI B. : Temps d'arrêt optimal, théorie générale des processus et processus de Markov. Z. Wahrscheinlichkeitstheorie verw. Gebiete, 39, 301-313 (1977).

(4) BISMUT J.M. : Dualité convexe, temps d'arrêt optimal et contrôle stochastique. Z. Wahrscheinlichkeitstheorie werw. Gebiete, 38, 169-198 (1977).

(5) BISMUT J.M. : Sur un problème de Dynkin. Z. Wahrscheinlichkeitstheorie verw. Gebiete. 39, 31-53 (1977).

(6) BISMUT J.M. : Contrôle stochastique, jeux et temps d'arrêt. Applications de la Théorie probabiliste du potentiel. Z. Wahrscheinlichkeitstheorie verw. Gebiete, 39, 315-338 (1977).

(7) BISMUT J.M. : Temps d'arrêt optimal, quasi-temps d'arrêt et retournement du temps. (A paraître aux Ann. Probability).

(8) BISMUT J.M. : Contrôle des processus alternants et applications. Z. Wahrscheinlichkeitstheorie verw. Gebiete. A paraître (1979).

(9) BISMUT J.M. : Temps d'arrêt optimal et quasi-temps d'arrêt. C.R. Acad. Sci. 284, serie A, 1519-1521 (1977).

(10) BISMUT J.M. : Temps d'arrêt optimal et retournement du temps. C.R. Acad. Sci. 285, serie A, 71-72 (1977).

(11) BISMUT J.M. : Régularité et continuité des processus. Z. Wahrscheinlichkeitstheorie verw. Gebiete. 44, 261-268 (1978).

(12) BISMUT J.M. : Application de la théorie du potentiel à des problèmes de contrôle. Séminaire de Theorie du potentiel n° 3, 7-17. Lecture Notes in Mathematics n° 681. Berlin-Heidelberg-New-York : Springer 1978.

(13) DELLACHERIE C., MEYER P.A. : Probabilités et Potentiels, 2° edition, Paris : Hermann 1975.

(14) FAKEEV A.G. : Optimal stopping rules for stochastic processes with continuous parameters. Theory prob. Appl. 15, 324-331 (1970).

(15) MERTENS J.F. : Théorie des processus stochastiques généraux. Application aux surmartingales. Z. Wahrscheinlichkeitstheorie verw. Gebiete. 22, 45-68 (1972).

(16) MERTENS J.F. : Strongly Supermedian functions and optimal stopping. Z. Wahrscheinlichkeitstheorie verw. Gebiete. 26, 119-139 (1973).

(17) ROST M. : The stopping distribution of a Markov process. Inventiones Math., 14, 1-16 (1971).

(18) BISMUT J.M. : Problèmes à frontière libre et arbres de mesures. Séminaire de probabilité n° 13. Lecture Notes in Mathematics. Berlin-Heidelberg-New-York. A paraître (1979).

ADAPTIVE CONTROL OF MARKOV CHAINS

Vivek Borkar and Pravin Varaiya
Departement of Electrical Engineering and Computer Sciences
and the Electronics Research Laboratory
University of California, Berkeley, CA 94720

ABSTRACT

Consider a controlled Markov chain whose transition probabilities are parameterized by α known to be in a finite set A. To each α is associated a prespecified control law $\phi(\alpha)$. The adaptive controller selects at each time t the control action indicated by $\phi(\alpha_t)$, where α_t is the maximum likelihood estimate of α. The asymptotic behavior of α_t is studied.

INTRODUCTION

We consider a controlled Markov chain x_t, $t = 0,1,\ldots$ taking values in $I = \{1,\ldots,I\}$. The transition probability at time t depends upon the control action u_t and a parameter α,

$$\text{Prob}\{x_{t+1}=j \mid x_t=i\} = p(i,j;u_t,\alpha).$$

At each t, x_t is observed and based upon its value u_t is selected from a prespecified set U. The parameter α has the constant but unknown value α^0; it is known, however, that α^0 belongs to a finite known set A.

The selection of u_t is to be made so as to guarantee that the resulting state process is satisfactory. A classical way of formulating this is to specify a cost function and then seek to determine the control policy $u_t = \phi_t(x_0,\ldots,x_t)$ which minimizes the expected value of the cost. The cost-minimizing policy can be formally expressed as the solution of the usual equations of dynamic programming. Unfortunately, even for some of the simplest such formulation, for example for the so-called "Two-armed Bandit" problem where A contains just two parameter values, the solution of the dynamic programming problem is extremely complex [1]. We may conclude that it is impractical to formulate the selection of satisfactory control actions as an optimal stochastic control problem. It is natural to simplify the search for a satisfactory control policy by limiting the class of functions $\{\phi_t\}$, $u_t = \phi_t(x_0,\ldots,x_t)$, over which the search is carried out. By adopting the point of view of the so-called "dual control" function, one can propose a sequence of such classes of increasing complexity [2]. The simplest of such classes is the one customarily labelled "enforced separation." The idea here is to estimate at each t the parameter value α_t. Many different estimation schemes are possible; however, here we suppose that α_t is the maximum likelihood estimate, i.e., α_t satisfies

$$\text{Prob}\{x_0,\ldots,x_t \mid x_0,u_0,\ldots,u_{t-1},\alpha_t\} = \prod_{s=0}^{t-1} p(x_s,x_{s+1};u_s,\alpha_t)$$

$$\geq \prod_{s=0}^{t-1} p(x_s,x_{s+1};u_s,\alpha), \qquad \text{for } \alpha \in A.$$

Having obtained α_t we select $u_t \in U$ according to some rule pretending that α_t is the true parameter value. One popular rule is to take $u_t = \phi(\alpha_t,x_t)$ where $\phi(\alpha,\cdot)$ is the optimal policy when the parameter is α [3]. However this is not really necessary, and $\phi(\alpha,\cdot)$ may be chosen, for instance, on the basis of ease of implementation. Be that as it may, we shall assume that there is prespecified a rule $\phi(\alpha,\cdot)$ for each α in A. The resulting control policy is often called an "Adaptive Control" law. The behavior of the closed loop system is therefore governed by,

$$\text{Prob}\{x_{t+1}=j \mid x_t=i\} = p(i,j;u_t,\alpha^0),$$

$$u_t = \phi(\alpha_t,i) \quad ,$$

$$\alpha_t = g_t(x_0,\ldots,x_t),$$

where $g_t(\cdot)$ is the maximum likelihood estimator.

MAIN RESULTS

The behavior of the adaptive control law is critically determined by the asymptotic properties of the estimator α_t. The study of these properties is complicated in part by the fact that the closed loop system has non-stationary transition probabilities (since α_t is no longer constant), and by a more subtle difficulty concerned with identifiability of closed loop systems. To appreciate this point consider the following condition introduced by Mandl:

for each $\alpha \neq \alpha'$, there exists $i \in I$ so that $[p(i,1;u,\alpha),\ldots,p(i,I;u,\alpha)] \neq [p(i,1;u,\alpha'),\ldots,p(i,I;u,\alpha')]$ for all u in U.

Under this condition Mandl has shown that α_t converges almost surely to the true parameter value α^0. Unfortunately, in many practical situations the control law $\phi(\alpha,\cdot)$ is such that it can make certain parameters indistinguishable so that the preceding condition does not hold. As an example consider the familiar Markovian

$$x_{t+1} = ax_t + bu_t + v_t, \qquad t = 0,1,\ldots$$

where x_t is a real-valued variable and the v_t are i.i.d. disturbance variables. The unknown parameter is $\alpha = (a,b)$. Then, for the linear control law $u_t = -gx_t$ and two parameter values $\alpha = (a,b)$, $\alpha' = (a',b')$ such that $a/b = a'/b' = g$,

$$p(x_t,x_{t+1};u_t=-gx_t,\alpha) = p(x_t,x_{t+1};u_t=-gx_t,\alpha')$$

for all x_t, x_{t+1}, and so the identifiability condition cannot hold. It is known moreover that for this example α_t need not converge to the true value [4].

We report here our results on the asymptotic behavior of α_t in the absence of the above-mentioned condition. We assume that

(i) There is $\varepsilon > 0$ such that for all i, j either $p(i,j;u,\alpha) > \varepsilon$ for all u, α, or $p(i,j;u,\alpha) = 0$ for all u, α.

(ii) For every i, j there is a sequence $i_1,\ldots,i_r$ such that for all u, α, $p(i_{s-1},i_s;u,\alpha) > 0$, $s = 1,\ldots,r+1$, where $i_0 = i$ and $i_{r+1} = j$.

Assumption (i) guarantees mutual absolute continuity of the probability measures induced by the various α; it is not at all essential. Assumption (ii) guarantees ergodicity; some such mixing condition is clearly required for identifiability.

The main result, which we give without proof, is this.

Theorem. There is a set N of zero probability, a random variable α^* with values in A, and a finite random time T such that if $\omega \notin N$, $t > T(\omega)$,

$$\alpha_t(\omega) = \alpha^*(\omega),\ u_t(\omega) = \phi(\alpha^*(\omega),x_t(\omega))$$

$$p(i,j;\phi(\alpha^*(\omega),i),\alpha^*(\omega)) = p(i,j;\phi(\alpha^*(\omega),i),\alpha^0),\ \text{all } i,\ j. \tag{1}$$

(Here ω denotes sample points.)

Condition (1) says that the estimate α_t converges to those values α^* which, in the closed loop system, cannot be distinguished from α^0. It is easy to check that if Mandl's identifiability condition holds, then $\alpha^* \equiv \alpha^0$. Also, examples can be given such that (1) implies $\alpha^* \equiv \alpha^0$ even when this condition cannot hold. Unfortunately, examples can also be given for which $\alpha^* \neq \alpha^0$ with probability one. Nevertheless, (1) can be used as a guide in the choice of the rules $\phi(\alpha,\cdot)$.

ACKNOWLEDGEMENT

The authors are grateful to Han-Shing Liu and Jean Walrand for discussions, and for research support to the National Science Foundation under Grant ENG76-16816 and Joint Services Electronics Program Contract F44620-76-C-0100.

REFERENCES

[1] M.H. Degroot, Optimal Statistical Decisions, McGraw-Hill, New York, 1970.

[2] Y. Bar-Shalom and E. Tse, Dual effect, certainty equivalence, and separation in stochastic control, IEEE Trans. Aut. Cont. AC-19(5), 494-500, 1974.

[3] P. Mandl, Estimation and control in Markov chains, Adv. Appl. Prob. 6, 40-60, 1974.

[4] K.J. Astrom and B. Wittenmark, On self-tuning regulators, Automatica 9, 185-199, 1973.

SOLUTION OF THE LIMITED RISK PROBLEM WITHOUT RANK CONDITIONS

N. Christopeit

Institut für Ökonometrie
und Operations Research
University of Bonn

1. INTRODUCTION

Consider a system whose dynamics are governed by the linear stochastic differential equation

(1.1) $$dz = A(t)z(t)dt + B(t)u(t)dt + C(t)dw, \qquad 0 \le t \le T,$$

with initial condition

(1.2) $$z(0) = z_o.$$

z is the n-dimensional state variable, u the m-dimensional control and w is a d-dimensional standard Brownian motion defined on some probability space $(\Omega, \mathcal{F}, P)$.

Instead of maximizing the expected value of some functional $g(z(T))$ of the final state in some class of feasible controls – which is a standard problem in stochastic control theory – it is proposed in [2] to choose a control action so as to maximize the upper allowable limit γ that is exceeded by $g(z(T))$ with a prescribed probability $1-\alpha$, $0<\alpha<1$, i.e. to maximize the $(1-\alpha)$-quantile of the distribution of $g(z(T))$. This model takes into account the fact that a control dominating others in the expected value of $g(z(T))$ may nevertheless be more risky in that the probability of actually getting a very low value is higher than for other controls because of a large dispersion of the corresponding state variable.

As feasible control laws we admit linear feedback controls of the form

(1.3) $u(t) = U(t)z(t) + v(t)$, where $U(\cdot)$, $v(\cdot)$ are nonstochastic measurable functions satisfying $(U(t),v(t)) \in \mathcal{U}(t)$ a.e. on $[0,T]$, $\mathcal{U}(t)$ being subsets of $\mathbb{R}^{m\times n} \times \mathbb{R}^m$.

It should be noted that the case where only partial observation is available can be treated within this framework. Suppose for instance that the state decomposes as $z = (x',y')'$, where only the y-component is observable or can be computed from observations. (E.g., y may be the filtered linear estimate of x based on the past of some observation process.) Then we obtain a class of linear Markov controls in y by choosing $\mathcal{W}(t) = \{(U,v)=(U_1,U_2,v)/U_1=0,\ U_2 \in \mathcal{U}(t),\ v \in \mathcal{V}(t)\}$, where the subdivision of U corresponds to the decomposition of z.

Now the problem to be investigated can be stated as

$$(P)\qquad \begin{cases} \gamma = \max! \\ \text{subject to } (1.1)-(1.3) \\ \text{and} \\ P(g(z(T)) \geq \gamma) \geq 1-\alpha\,. \end{cases}$$

Inserting (1.3) into (1.1) we obtain

$$dz = [A(t)+B(t)U(t)]z(t)dt + B(t)v(t) + C(t)dw. \tag{1.4}$$

Assume that

(A) the matrix functions $A(\cdot)$, $B(\cdot)$ and $C(\cdot)$ are nonstochastic, measurable and bounded;

(B) z_o is normally distributed (possibly degenerate) and independent of $w(t)$, $0 \leq t \leq T$;

(C) the sets $\mathcal{W}(t)$, $0 \leq t \leq T$, are convex, compact and all contained in some bounded set.

Then the solution of (1.4) with initial condition (1.2) is a Gaussian process whose mean μ and covariance Σ satisfy the ordinary differential equations

$$\dot{\mu}(t) = [A(t)+B(t)U(t)]\mu(t) + B(t)v(t), \tag{1.5}$$

$$\dot{\Sigma}(t) = [A(t)+B(t)U(t)]\Sigma(t) + \Sigma(t)[A(t)'+U(t)'B(t)'] + C(t)C(t)' \tag{1.6}$$

with initial conditions

$$\mu(0) = \mu_o = E(z_o), \tag{1.7}$$

$$\Sigma(0) = \Sigma_o = E(z_o-\mu_o)(z_o-\mu_o)'. \tag{1.8}$$

The chance constraints in (P) takes the form

$$P(g(z(T)) \geq \gamma) = P(z(T) \in g^{-1}([\gamma,\infty)) = \int_{g^{-1}([\gamma,\infty))} N(\mu(T),\Sigma(T);d\zeta)$$

$$= G(\mu(T),\Sigma(T),\gamma) \geq 1-\alpha. \tag{1.9}$$

Here $N(\mu,\Sigma;d\zeta)$ is the n-variate normal distribution with mean μ and covariance Σ.

Introducing the class of feasible deterministic control laws

$$\mathcal{F} = \{(U,v):[0,T] \to \mathbb{R}^{m\times n}\times\mathbb{R}^m \;/\; (U,v) \text{ measurable}, \\ (U(t),v(t)) \in \mathcal{U}(t) \text{ a.e.}\}$$

we arrive at the deterministic problem

$$(P')\qquad \begin{cases} \gamma = \underset{(U,v)\in\mathcal{F}}{\max!} \\ \text{subject to } (1.5)-(1.9), \end{cases}$$

which is equivalent to (P) in the following sense: If $(\bar{U},\bar{v})$ is optimal for (P') then $\bar{u}=\overline{Uz}+\bar{v}$ is optimal for (P), with $\bar{z}$ being the solution of (1.4), (1.2) corresponding to $(\bar{U},\bar{v})$, and vice versa.

In [2] existence of a solution of (P') has been shown under the assumption that the initial distribution (1.2) is nondegenerate or C(t) has rank n a.e. The first assumption is not appopriate for the subsystem of (1.1) describing the observation process, where usually $y_o=0$ is a realistic specification. The second assumption excludes the case of definitorial equations as they naturally arise when the system (1.1) is the first order reduction of a higher order differential equation; moreover, it does not allow for some linear combinations of components of x to be observable without noise, thus producing a singular diffusion matrix.

Here it will be shown that these rank conditions can be dispensed with if only the functional g is continuous.

2. EXISTENCE OF OPTIMAL CONTROLS

Under the assumptions made above the system (1.5)-(1.8) has a unique solution $(\mu_{U,v},\Sigma_{U,v})$ for every $(U,v) \in \mathcal{F}$.

Define the attainable set

$$\mathcal{A}(T) = \{(\mu_{U,v}(T),\Sigma_{U,v}(T)) \;/\; (U,v) \in \mathcal{F}\}.$$

In [3] it is proved that under assumptions (A)-(C) $\mathcal{A}(T)$ is compact. Problem (P'') can now be written in the equivalent form

$$(P'')\qquad \begin{cases} \gamma = \underset{(\mu,\Sigma,\gamma)}{\max!} \\ \text{subject to } (\mu,\Sigma) \in \mathcal{A}(T), \\ G(\mu,\Sigma,\gamma) \geq 1-\alpha. \end{cases}$$

Let us first show that (P'') possesses a finite value. This will follow from the next lemma, observing that $G(\mu,\Sigma,\gamma)$ is monotonically decreasing in γ.

Lemma 1. Assume that g is continuous and assumptions (A)-(C) hold. Then there exists a number γ^* such that

$$G(\mu,\Sigma,\gamma^*) < 1-\alpha$$

for all $(\mu,\Sigma) \in \mathcal{A}(T)$.

Proof. For every Borel set A in $\mathbb{R}^n$ put

$$P_{\mu,\Sigma}(A) = \int_A N(\mu,\Sigma;d\zeta).$$

Then $\mathcal{P} = \{P_{\mu,\Sigma} \,/\, (\mu,\Sigma) \in \mathcal{A}(T)\}$ is a family of probability measures on $\mathbb{R}^n$ which is compact in the topology of weak convergence of measures. To see this, take a sequence (μ_k,Σ_k), $k=1,2,\ldots$, in $\mathcal{A}(T)$. Since $\mathcal{A}(T)$ is compact there exists a subsequence – also indexed by k – converging to some $(\mu_o,\Sigma_o) \in \mathcal{A}(T)$. The characteristic functions of P_{μ_k,Σ_k} are given by

$$\phi_k(\lambda) = \exp[i\lambda'\mu_k - \tfrac{1}{2}\lambda'\Sigma_k\lambda], \quad k=0,1,2,\ldots,$$

hence $\phi_k(\lambda) \to \phi_o(\lambda)$ as $k\to\infty$ for every $\lambda\in\mathbb{R}^n$. Consequently,

$$P_{\mu_k,\Sigma_k} \to P_{\mu_o,\Sigma_o}$$

weakly. By Prohorov's theorem (cf. [1]) the family $\mathcal{P}$ is tight; this means in particular that there exists a compact set A^* in $\mathbb{R}^n$ such that

$$P_{\mu,\Sigma}(\overline{A^*}) < 1-\alpha$$

for all $(\mu,\Sigma) \in \mathcal{A}(T)$ ($\overline{A}$ denotes the complement of A). By continuity of g, $g(A^*)$ is compact. Take $\gamma^* > \max g(A^*)$. Then

$$g^{-1}([\gamma^*,\infty)) \subset g^{-1}(\overline{g(A^*)}) = \overline{g^{-1}(g(A^*))} \subset \overline{A^*},$$

hence

$$P_{\mu,\Sigma}(g^{-1}([\gamma^*,\infty))) < 1-\alpha$$

uniformly in $(\mu,\Sigma) \in \mathcal{A}(T)$. ∎

Let $\overline{\gamma}$ denote the value of (P''):

$$\overline{\gamma} = \sup\{\gamma \,/\, (\mu,\Sigma) \in \mathcal{A}(T),\ G(\mu,\Sigma,\gamma) \geq 1-\alpha\}.$$

We can now prove

Theorem 1. Under the assumptions of lemma 1 the problem (P'') (and hence (P)) possesses an optimal solution.

Proof. Take a maximizing sequence $(\mu_k,\Sigma_k,\gamma_k)$, where $\gamma_k \nearrow \bar{\gamma}$, $(\mu_k,\Sigma_k) \in \mathcal{A}(T)$ and $G(\mu_k,\Sigma_k,\gamma_k) \geq 1-\alpha$ for all k. Since $\mathcal{A}(T)$ is compact we can extract a subsequence – denoted by the same index k – such that (μ_k,Σ_k) converges to some $(\bar{\mu},\bar{\Sigma}) \in \mathcal{A}(T)$. It remains to show that

$$G(\bar{\mu},\bar{\Sigma},\bar{\gamma}) \geq 1-\alpha. \tag{2.1}$$

To this end, put

$$P_k = P_{\mu_k,\Sigma_k}, \qquad \bar{P} = P_{\bar{\mu},\bar{\Sigma}},$$

(with the notation as in the proof of lemma 1) and

$$S_k = g^{-1}([\gamma_k,\infty)), \quad \bar{S} = g^{-1}([\bar{\gamma},\infty)).$$

Then

$$P_k \to \bar{P} \tag{2.2}$$

weakly and

$$P_k(S_k) = G(\mu_k,\Sigma_k,\gamma_k) \geq 1-\alpha.$$

Fix k*. Then, since

$$S_1 \supset S_2 \supset \cdots\cdots \supset \bar{S},$$

$$P_k(S_{k^*}) \geq P_k(S_k) \quad \text{for all } k \geq k^*.$$

Consequently,

$$\limsup_{k\to\infty} P_k(S_{k^*}) \geq \limsup_{k\to\infty} P_k(S_k)$$
$$\geq 1-\alpha$$

and, since S_{k^*} is closed,

$$\bar{P}(S_{k^*}) \geq \limsup_{k\to\infty} P_k(S_{k^*}) \geq 1-\alpha$$

for every fixed k* by virtue of (2.2) (cf. [1]). But

$$\bar{S} = \bigcap_{k=1}^{\infty} S_k,$$

from which

$$\bar{P}(\bar{S}) = G(\bar{\mu},\bar{\Sigma},\bar{\gamma}) \geq 1-\alpha. \quad \blacksquare$$

REFERENCES

[1] P. Billingsley, Convergence of Probability Measures, Wiley, New York, 1968.

[2] N. Christopeit, A Limited Risk Model in Stochastic Control, Oper. Res. Verfahren XXVIII (1978), 145-152.

[3] N. Christopeit, A Stochastic Control Model with Chance Constraints, SIAM J. Control and Optimization 16 (1978), 702-714.

THE PARAMETERIZATION OF RATIONAL TRANSFERFUNCTION LINEAR SYSTEMS

M. Deistler

Institute of Econometrics

Technical University of Vienna

0. ABSTRACT

The paper deals with discrete time, multivariable linear systems in difference equation form with observed inputs and errors in the equations (ARMAX systems).
Structural Identifiability of ARMAX systems is considered and the topological properties of the parameterization relevant for consistency are examined.

1. INTRODUCTION

A question preceding estimation of linear, dynamic, stochastic systems is the question of appropriate parameterization. The importance as well as the difficulties of this problem, especially in the multivariable case has been fully realized only quite recently.
We restrict ourselves to linear systems with rational transferfunctions (finite dimensional systems) which can be described by a finite number of parameters. There are two different ways to describe such systems, namely by state space models and by difference equations (in the discrete-time case we consider here).

The latter type of models we restrict to, is also called ARMAX models; they are of the form:

$$(1) \quad \sum_{s=o}^{h} A_s y_{t-s} = \sum_{s=o}^{k} B_s x_{t-s} + \sum_{s=o}^{1} C_s \varepsilon_{t-s}$$

where A_s, $C_s \in \mathbb{R}^{nxn}$, $B_s \in \mathbb{R}^{nxm}$, where $(y_t)_{t\in\mathbb{Z}}$ and $(x_t)_{t\in\mathbb{Z}}$ are the observed (stochastic) output and input processes respectively (with dimensions n and m respectively) and where the nonobserved errors $u_t = \sum_{s=o}^{1} C_s \varepsilon_{t-s}$ are of MA type, i. e. (ε_t) is white noise:

$$E\varepsilon_s \varepsilon_t' = \delta_{st} \cdot \Sigma$$

Let us define:

$$A(z) := \sum_{s=o}^{h} A_s z^s \; ; \; B(z) := \sum_{s=o}^{k} B_s z^s \; ; \; C(z) := \sum_{s=o}^{1} C_s z^s$$

The following assumptions are maintained throughout the paper:

(I) $\det A(z) \neq o \quad \forall z : |z| \leq 1$

(thus we restrict ourselves to stable systems).

Without restriction of generality we assume:

(II) $\det C(z) \neq o \quad \forall z : |z| < 1$

such that (ε_t) are the linear innovations of y_t given $y_{t-1}, y_{t-2}, \ldots$ and $x_t, x_{t-1}, \ldots$

Furthermore we postulate:

$$E x_t \varepsilon_s' = o \quad \forall t \in \mathbb{Z} \;, \quad s \leq t$$

and that the process (x_t) uniquely determines the input (-to output) transferfunction

$K(z) := A^{-1}(z).B(z)$

The last requirement would hold, if in the stationary case, (x_t) has a spectral density being nonsingular on a set of Lebesgue--measure unequal to zero. For more general conditions see [4].

Finally we assume:

$\det \Sigma \neq 0$

and

(III) $C_0 = A_0$

Thus the error (-to output) transferfuncion

$J(z) := A^{-1}(z).C(z)$

is identifiable too. For short let us write

$D(z) := (B(z), C(z))$ and $H(z) := A^{-1}(z).D(z) = (K(z), J(z))$

As well known, the parameters $A(z)$, $B(z)$, $C(z)$, cannot be uniquely determined in general by an infinite data record. However, under our assumptions Σ is identifiable and thus we can restrict ourselves on the mapping π defined by $(A(z), D(z)) \mapsto H(z)$ and its equivalence kernel, called observational equivalence. A model is called identifiable if the equivalence classes contain at most one element. A pair $(A(z), D(z))$ (of polynomical matrices) such that $H(z) = A^{-1}(z)D(z)$ is known as (left) matrix fraction description (MFD) of $H(z)$.

One problem in parameterization is to decribe each equivalence class by suitable parameters. We will do this by picking a suitable representative out of every equivalence class. There are two different situations where this is done. The first is to obtain structural identifiability by a priori restrictions [7]

[2] [9] . In this case the parameters in (1) have a direct physical interpretation and the question is whether we have enough a priori restrictions to detect these parameters. This is the case we are considering here.

The second case is when we have no (further) a priori restrictions on the parametermatrices and when this matrices have no direct physical interpretation, so that we can pick out an arbitrary, convenient members from every equivalence class - a socalled canonical form - by a suitable prescription. Whereas in the first case, the set of all parameters is described by one coordinate system, in this second case the set all systems of prescribed order has to be described by a finite number of local coordinates. However results analogous to those in this paper can be shown [8] .

2. STRUCTURAL IDENTIFIABILITY

It seems reasonable to exclude a priori redundant MFD's (A(z), D(z)) which contain nonunimodular common left factors (a square polynomical matrix U(z) is called unimodular if det U(z) = const $\neq$ 0). Thus We assume:

(III) Only left coprime MFD's are feasible

(or equivalently only MFD's for which (A(z), D(z)) has full row for all $z \in \mathbb{C}$ are feasible [11]).

Then we have:

Lemma 1: Two left coprime MFD's, say $(\bar{A}(z), \bar{D}(z))$ and (A(z), D(z)) are observationally equivalent iff there exists a unimodular matrix U(z) such that:

(2) $(\bar{A}(z), \bar{D}(z)) = U(z).(A(z), D(z))$

If only (A(z), D(z)) is left coprime, then the two MFD's are observationally equivalent iff a relation (2) holds, where now U(z) is a polynomial matrix.

This important lemma has been shown independently by Hannan [6] [7], Popov [10] and Rosenbrock [11].

We prescribe the maximum lag lenghts h, k and 1 in (1). By (2), the degree of U (z) cannot exceed g : = min (hn, 1n) and thus we can write (2) as:

$$(3)\quad (\bar{A}_o,..\bar{A}_h,\ 0,..0,\ \bar{B}_o,..\bar{B}_k,\ 0,..0,\ \bar{C}_o,..\bar{C}_1,\ 0,..0) = (U_o..U_g).\hat{A}$$

where

$$\hat{A} := \begin{pmatrix} A_o, & A_1 \cdots & A_h & 0 \cdots & 0 & B_o \cdots & B_k & 0 \cdots & 0 & C_o \cdots & C_1 & 0 \cdots & 0 \\ 0 & A_o & A_1 & \ddots & \vdots & 0 & \ddots & \ddots & \vdots & 0 & \ddots & \ddots & \vdots \\ \vdots & \ddots & \ddots & \ddots & 0 & \vdots & \ddots & \ddots & 0 & \vdots & \ddots & \ddots & 0 \\ 0 \cdots & 0 & A_o \cdots A_1 & & A_h & 0 \cdots & 0 & B_o \cdots & B_k & 0 \cdots & 0 & C_o \cdots & C_1 \end{pmatrix}$$

has dimension n. (g+1)x n.(h+1+g)+m(k+1+g)+n(1+1+g). Defining the "vec"-operation rowwise , (3) can be written as:

$$\bar{\tau} := \mathrm{vec}\ (\bar{A}_o,\ldots\bar{A}_h,\ 0,\ldots 0,\ \bar{B}_o,\ldots\bar{B}_h,\ 0,\ldots 0,\ \bar{C}_o,\ldots\ \bar{C}_1,\ 0\ldots 0) = \mathrm{vec}\ (U_o,\ldots U_g).(I \otimes \hat{A})$$

with $\tau \in \mathbb{R}^{1xN}$, $N := n^2\ (h+1+g) + nm(k+1+g) + n^2(1+1+g)$

and:

$$(I \otimes \hat{A}) := \begin{pmatrix} \hat{A}, & 0 & \ldots. & 0 \\ 0, & \hat{A} & \ldots. & 0 \\ 0, & \ldots. & 0, & \hat{A} \end{pmatrix} \in \mathbb{R}^{MxN}$$

$M := n^2\ .(g+1)$

Now, let us assume that the a priori restrictions on the parameters τ additional to (I), (II), (III) are in the form of affine ("cross equation") restrictions:

(5) $R\tau' = r$

where $R \in \mathbb{R}^{p\times N}$ and $r \in \mathbb{R}^{p\times 1}$ are known. The restrictions (5) especially include the knowledge about the "trivial" zeromatrices in $(A_0, \ldots A_h, 0\ldots 0, B_0, \ldots B_k, 0\ldots 0, C_0, \ldots C_1, 0\ldots 0)$ and about $A_0 = C_0$

Then we can show [2]:

Theorem 1: Under our assumptions the model is identifiable if

(6) $D.\ (I \otimes \hat{A})' \in \mathbb{R}^{p\times M}$ has rank M

3. THE TOPOLOGICAL PROPERTIES OF THE IDENTIFYING FUNCTION

Let us denote by S the set of all feasible τ in the case of an identifiable model, thus the function $\pi^{-1}: \pi(S) \rightarrow S$ is well defined. This function π^{-1} is called identifying function, as it attaches to the transferfunctions the "internal" parameters τ. The likelihood function only depends on the transferfunction H(z) (and on Σ) (and not explicitely on τ). Dunsmuir and Hannan [5] (see also [8]) showed that the (Gaussian) maximum likelihood estimator of H (z) isstrongly consistent in the sense of (pointwise) convergence of the coefficients in the power series expansion of H (z). This convergence gives a natural topology on $\pi(S)$, say T_{pt}. On the other hand, when we are interested in the parameters themselves, the natural topology for S is the relative Euclidian topology. If we can prove π^{-1} to be continuous w.r.t. these topologies, of course, the strong consistency of the maximum likelihood estimator follows from what was stated above. The next theorem is a slight generalisation of a theorem given in [3]

Theorem 2: Under the assumptions of theorem 1, $\pi^{-1}: \pi(S) \rightarrow S$ is (T_{pt}-) continous.

<u>Proof</u>: It is easily seen [3] that

$$A(z).H(z)=D(z)$$

is equivalent to:

(7) $$\sum_{r=0}^{s} A_r H_{s-r} = D_s \;, \qquad s=0, \ldots, \max\,(k,l)+n.h$$

(7) can be rewritten as:

(8) $$T\,\tau' = t$$

where the elements of the matrix T and of the vector t are determined by H(z). Writing (8) and (5) together we have:

(9) $$\begin{pmatrix} T \\ R \end{pmatrix} \tau' = \begin{pmatrix} t \\ r \end{pmatrix}$$

For given $H(z)\,\epsilon\,\pi(S)$, (9) has at least one solution satisfying in addition (I)-(III) and (6). By lemma 1, every solution of (9) is related to a feasible one by a polynominal matrix U (z) (non necessarely unimodular) such that (4) holds. But then (6) implies ((2)) U (z)=I, thus (9) has only one solution at all and therefore $\begin{pmatrix} T \\ R \end{pmatrix}$ must have full columm rank and then (9) immediately implies the continuity of π^{-1}.

REFERENCES

[1] Deistler, M.: "The Identifiability of Linear Econometric Models with Autocorelated Errors"Int.Ec.Rev. 17 (1976), 26-46.

[2] Deistler,M: "The Structural Identifiability of Linear Models with Autocorrelated Errors in the Case of Cross-Equations Restrictions". J. of Econometrics 8 (1978), 23-31.

[3] Deistler, M., W. Dunsmuir and E.J. Hannan:"Vector Linear Time Series Models: Corrections and Extensions". Adv. Appl. Prob. 10 (1978), 360-372.

[4] Deistler, M. and J. Schrader: "Identifiability of Transfer Functions of Linear Systems". Mimeo, Bonn 1977.

[5] Dunsmuir, W. and E.J. Hannan: " Vector Linear Time Series Models". Adv.Appl.Prob. 8 (1976), 339-364.

[6] Hannan, E.J.: " The Identification of Vector Mixed Autoregressive Moving Average Systems". Biometrika 57 (1969), 223-225.

[7] Hannan, E.J.: " The Identification Problem for Multiple Equation Systems with Moving Average Errors". Econometrica 39 (1971), 751-765.

[8] Hannan, E.J., Deistler M. and W. Dunsmuir: "Estimation of Vector ARMAX Models". Mimeo, Bonn 1978.

[9] Kohn, R.: " Local and Global Identification and Strong Consistency in Time Series Models" J. of Econometrics 8 (1978), 269 - 293.

[10] Popov, V.M.: " Some Properties of the Control Systems with Irreducible Matrix-Transfer Functions", in: Seminar on Differential Equations and Dynamical Systems. Springer Lecture Notes in Mathematics, No. 144, Berlin 1966.

[11] Rosenbrock, H.H. " State Space and Multivariable Theory", Nelson, London 1970.

A STOCHASTIC MODEL FOR THE ELECTRICAL CONDUCTION IN NON HOMOGENEOUS LAYERS

G. De Mey

Laboratory of Electronics
Ghent State University
Sint Pietersnieuwstraat 41
9000 Ghent, Belgium

SUMMARY

The equation for the potential in a non homogeneous conducting layer is derived. If the conductivity is represented by a stochastic process, the potential ϕ becomes a stochastic quantity. For a simple rectangular geometry an analytic treatment will be presented to calculate the expectation value and mean square deviation of the potential. At last an integral equation technique will be put forward.

1. INTRODUCTION

The potential distribution in a non homogeneous layer has been the subject of several contributions. Most authors consider a given deterministic function $\sigma(\bar{r})$ in order to represent the non homogeneous conductivity [1]. This function $\sigma(\bar{r})$ is often chosen in such a way that the resulting potential equation can still be solved, rather than looking for a function $\sigma(\bar{r})$ fitting the actual state as good as possible. By investigating conducting layers experimentally, one generally observes a statistical nature of the conductivity. Due to corn boundaries, distributed at random in the layer, it is clear that a realistic approach to the problem can only be done by representing $\sigma(\bar{r})$ as a two dimensional stochastic process [2][3][4].

In this contribution the basic equations will be derived, after which a perturbation method will be introduced. It is also interesting to note that similar techniques have been used to calculate related problems such as the resonance frequency in cavities with rough walls [5].

2. BASIC EQUATIONS

Denoting $\overline{J}$ as the current density, $\overline{E}$ as the electric field and ϕ as the potential, one has the following basic equations:

$$\overline{J} = \sigma\overline{E} \ , \ \overline{E} = - \nabla\phi \ , \ \nabla.\overline{J} = 0 \tag{1}$$

which give rise to:

$$0 = \nabla.(\sigma \nabla\phi) = \sigma \nabla^2\phi + \nabla\sigma.\nabla\phi \tag{2}$$

or:

$$\nabla^2\phi + \nabla\ln\sigma.\nabla\phi = 0 \tag{3}$$

If the sheet conductivity σ is a stochastic process, the potential becomes a stochastic process too.

In order to solve the equation (3), a perturbation method will be used. One assumes the conductivity $\underline{\sigma}$ being given by:

$$\underline{\sigma}(\overline{r}) = \sigma_0 + \underline{\sigma}_1(\overline{r}) \tag{4}$$

where $\sigma_0 = <\underline{\sigma}(\overline{r})>$ is the mean conductivity and $\underline{\sigma}_1$ the smaller stochastic component. Writing the potential $\underline{\phi}$ in a similar fashion:

$$\underline{\phi}(\overline{r}) = \phi_0(\overline{r}) + \underline{\phi}_1(\overline{r}) \tag{5}$$

one obtains the equations:

$$\nabla^2\phi_0(\overline{r}) = 0 \tag{6}$$

$$\nabla^2\underline{\phi}_1(\overline{r}) = - \frac{1}{\sigma_0} \nabla\underline{\sigma}_1.\nabla\phi_0 \tag{7}$$

The equation (6) is nothing else than the potential equation for a homogeneous layer with conductivity σ_0. The equation (7) shows the given stochastic process $\underline{\sigma}_1$ only in the right hand member, which will faciliate the solution.

Similar expressions as (4) and (5) can be found for the current density $\underline{\overline{J}} = \overline{J}_0 + \underline{\overline{J}}_1$:

$$\overline{J}_0 = \sigma_0\overline{E}_0 \tag{8}$$

$$\underline{\overline{J}}_1 = \underline{\sigma}_1\overline{E}_0 + \sigma_0\underline{\overline{E}}_1 \tag{9}$$

In the next section an analytic solution of the equations (6) and (7) for a simple rectangular resistor will be given. The mean square deviation on the current for a given constant voltage is then evaluated. The subsequent section will give us a general numerical method based on an integral equation formulation of the problem [6]. Integral equations have proved to be extremely suited to solve potential problems numerically as they only involve the boundary of the given geometry [7][8][9].

3. ANALYTIC SOLUTION FOR A RECTANGULAR RESISTOR

We consider a rectangular resistor as shown on fig.1. The boundary conditions for ϕ_0 and $\underline{\phi}_1$ are found to be:

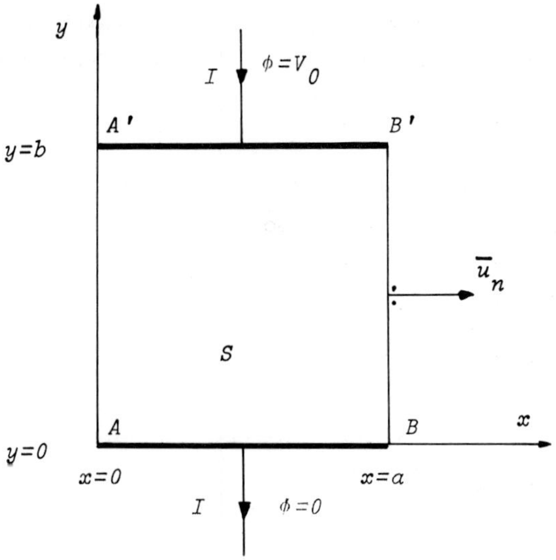

Fig.1: Rectangular resistor supplied with a constant voltage V_0.

$$\phi_0 = \underline{\phi}_1 = 0 \quad \text{on AB}$$

$$\phi_0 = V_0 \;;\; \underline{\phi}_1 = 0 \quad \text{on A'B'}$$

$$\nabla\phi_0 \cdot \bar{u}_n = \nabla\underline{\phi}_1 \cdot \bar{u}_n = 0 \quad \text{on AA' and BB'} \tag{10}$$

The zeroth order component can be easily calculated:

$$\phi_0 = \frac{V_0}{b} y \qquad \bar{E}_0 = -\frac{V_0}{b}\bar{u}_y$$

$$I_0 = \sigma_0 E_0 ad \tag{11}$$

where I_0 is the zeroth order component of the current supplied through the contacts and d the thickness of the layer.

The equation (7) for $\underline{\phi}_1$ turns out to be:

$$\nabla^2 \underline{\phi}_1 = -\frac{\nabla\underline{\sigma}_1 \cdot \bar{E}_0}{\sigma_0} = \frac{V_0}{b\sigma_0}\frac{\partial \underline{\sigma}_1}{\partial y} \tag{12}$$

By using the Green's function $G(\bar{r}|\bar{r}')$ satisfying the boundary conditions (10), the solution of (12) can be written as:

$$\underline{\phi}_1(\bar{r}) = \frac{V_0}{b\sigma_0} \iint_S \frac{\partial \underline{\sigma}_1}{\partial y} G(\bar{r}|\bar{r}')\, dS' \tag{13}$$

For the calculation of the Green's function in (13) one is referred to the literature [3]. After some lengthly calculations the current component $\underline{I}_1$ is found to be:

$$\underline{I}_1 = -d \int_{A'}^{B'} \underline{\bar{J}}_1 \cdot \bar{u}_y\, dx = \frac{dE_0}{b} \iint_S \underline{\sigma}_1\, dS' \tag{14}$$

As $<\underline{\sigma}_1>=0$ one gets immediatly $<\underline{I}_1>=0$, which is an obvious result of the first order perturbation method used here. A more physical interesting quantity is then the mean square deviation on the current $\underline{I}$:

$$\sigma_I^2 = \frac{<\underline{I}_1^2>}{I_0^2} = \iint_S dS' \iint_S dS'' \;<\underline{\sigma}_1(\bar{r}')\underline{\sigma}_1(\bar{r}'')> \tag{15}$$

In order to find σ_I^2 one has to integrate the correlation function $<\underline{\sigma}_1(\bar{r}')\underline{\sigma}_1(\bar{r}'')>$ twice over the surface S. The determination of this correlation function from the actual state or a model of a conducting layer is a much more difficult problem than performing the integration (15). Therefore a rude approximation will be used here. It is quite evident to everyone that the correlation between the conductivities $\underline{\sigma}_1(\bar{r}')$ and $\underline{\sigma}_1(\bar{r}'')$ will decrease if the distance $|\bar{r}'-\bar{r}''|$ increases.

We therefore use the following function:

$$\langle \underline{\sigma}_1(r')\underline{\sigma}_1(r'')\rangle = R\exp\left(-\frac{|\bar{r}'-\bar{r}''|^2}{2\rho^2}\right) \tag{16}$$

This function also offers the advantage that the integration (15) can be easily performed. The result is:

$$\sigma_I^2 = \frac{R}{\sigma_0^2}\, f\left(\frac{a}{\rho}\right)\, f\left(\frac{b}{\rho}\right) \tag{17}$$

where:

$$f(x) = -\frac{2}{x^2} + \frac{\sqrt{2\pi}}{x}\,\mathrm{erf}\left(\frac{x}{\sqrt{2}}\right) + \frac{2}{x^2}\exp\left(-\frac{x^2}{2}\right) \tag{18}$$

The function f(x) is plotted in fig.2. Note that $f(x)\approx 1$ for $x=1$. This means that σ_I^2 is practically constant when the correlation

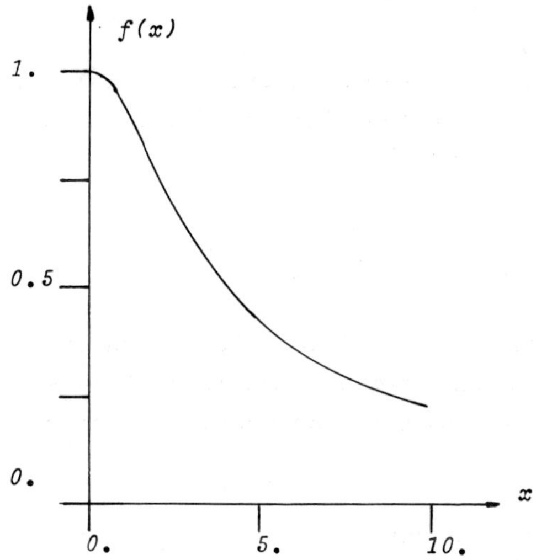

Fig.2: Plot of f(x) as a function of x.

distance ρ is greater than or comparable to the dimensions of the conducting layer. Only when ρ is much smaller than the sample's dimensions, a decrease of σ_I^2 will follow.

From the physical point of view, a conducting layer contains many microcrystallites and hence corn boundaries. The correlation distance ρ can be seen as the average corn diameter. Electrical resistance measurements will give a mean square deviation if the corn diameter is comparable to the sample's dimensions.

4. NUMERICAL INTEGRAL EQUATION METHOD

The solution of the equation (6) for ϕ_0 can be done by an integral equation described elsewhere [7][8][9]. $\nabla\phi_0$ is thus known and can be put in the rigth hand member of (7). However, $\underline{\sigma}_1$ is generally not known as a function of $\bar{r}$ as a stochastic process is usually described by the mean value, correlation function and other statistical parameters. Therefore we have not to calculate $\underline{\phi}_1$ but our purpose will be to determine e.g. $\langle\underline{\phi}_1^2\rangle$ in a given point as a function of $\langle\underline{\sigma}_1(\bar{r}')\underline{\sigma}_1(\bar{r}'')\rangle$.

Let us consider an arbitrary geometry S with boundary C. The potential $\phi_0=f(\bar{r})$ is known along the boundary. Therefore, the boundary condition for $\underline{\phi}_1$ reads:

$$\underline{\phi}_1 = 0 \quad \text{along C} \tag{19}$$

In order to solve (7) by an integral equation method the solution is written as:

$$\underline{\phi}_1 = \oint_C \underline{\rho}(\bar{r}')\, G(\bar{r}|\bar{r}')\, dC' - \iint_S \frac{\nabla\underline{\sigma}_1}{\sigma_0}\cdot\nabla\phi_0\, G(\bar{r}|\bar{r}')\, dS' \tag{20}$$

where:

$$G(\bar{r}|\bar{r}') = \frac{1}{2\pi}\ln|\bar{r}-\bar{r}'| \tag{21}$$

denotes the Green's function. $\underline{\rho}$ is still an unknown stochastic function defined on the boundary C. Imposing the boundary condition (19) on the proposed solution (20), one obtains:

$$\oint_C \rho(\bar{r}')\, G(\bar{r}|\bar{r}')\, dC' = \iint_S \frac{\nabla\underline{\sigma}_1}{\sigma_0}\cdot\nabla\phi_0\, G(\bar{r}|\bar{r}')\, dS' \tag{22}$$

$$\bar{r} \in C$$

(22) is an integral equation in the unknown function $\underline{\rho}$.

In order to solve (22) numerically, the boundary C is divided in n elements ΔC_i (i=1,...n). In each element (centre point $\bar{r}_i$) the function $\underline{\rho}$ is replaced by a stochastic variable $\underline{\rho}_i$. The integral equation reads:

$$\sum_{j=1}^{n} \underline{\rho}_j \int_{\Delta C_j} G(\bar{r}_i | \bar{r}')\, dC' = \iint_S \frac{\nabla \underline{\sigma}_1}{\sigma_0} \cdot \nabla\phi_0 \; G(\bar{r}_i | \bar{r}')\, dS' \tag{23}$$

and similarly, (20) is replaced by:

$$\underline{\phi}_1(\bar{r}) = \sum_{j=1}^{n} \underline{\rho}_j \int_{\Delta C_j} G(\bar{r} | \bar{r}')\, dC' \tag{24}$$

Rewriting (23) in a condensed form:

$$\sum_{j=1}^{n} A_{ij}\underline{\rho}_j = \underline{b}_i \qquad i=1,\ldots n$$

The solution $\underline{\rho}$ is found by inverting the matrix A:

$$\underline{\rho}_i = \sum_{j=1}^{n} (A^{-1})_{ij}\, \underline{b}_j \tag{25}$$

Only $\underline{b}$ and $\underline{\rho}$ contain stochastic variables, so there is no problem to calculate A^{-1}. Due to (25) all stochastic quantities such as $<\underline{\rho}_i\underline{\rho}_j>$ can be calculated as $\underline{b}_j$ depends linearly upon $\underline{\sigma}_1$. The mean square deviation on the potential in a given point:

$$<\underline{\phi}_1^2(\bar{r})> = \sum_{i=1}^{n} \sum_{j=1}^{n} <\underline{\rho}_i\underline{\rho}_j> \int_{\Delta C_i} G(\bar{r}|\bar{r}')dC' \int_{\Delta C_j} G(\bar{r}|\bar{r}'')dC'' \tag{26}$$

is then also a known quantity.

5. CONCLUSION

The potential equation in a non homogeneous semiconductor sample has been derived. By using a perturbation method it is possible to evaluate mean square deviations, ... of the potential inside the layer. An example has been calculated analytically and a numerical method for arbitrary shapes was presented. However, actual calculations still remain very complicated.

Another interesting problem which has not been treated yet in the literature is how to determine the statistical parameters of $\underline{\sigma}$

starting from an actual conducting layer. Nevertheless, by using a rather intuitive correlation function (16), it was possible to obtain physical interesting results.

REFERENCES

1) *S. Amer:*
"Van der Pauw's method of measuring resistivities on lamellae of non uniform resistivity"
Solid State Electronics, 1963, vol.6, p.141-146.

2) *W. M. G. Van Bokhoven:*
"Calculation of noise in distributed conductive elements, due to stochastic conductivity fluctuations"
Archiv für Elektronik und Uebertragungstechnik, 1978, vol.32, p.349-352.

3) *G. De Mey:*
"Specific conductivity measurements on non homogeneous semiconductor samples"
Applied Physics, 1975, vol.6, p.189-197.

4) *G. De Mey:*
"A second order perturbation method for potential calculations in non homogeneous semiconducting layers"
Applied Physics, 1977, vol.12, p.213-215.

5) *G. De Mey:*
"Frequency shift in cavities with rough walls"
Applied Physics, 1977, vol.12, p.83-86.

6) *G. De Mey:*
"An integral equation method to solve Poisson's equation for stochastic charge densities and boundary potential"
Lettere al Nuovo Cimento, 1975, vol.12, p.470-472.

7) *G. De Mey:*
"Integral equation for the potential distribution in a Hall generator"
Electronics Letters, 1973, vol.9, p.264-266.

8) *G. De Mey:*
"Potential calculations in thin conducting films by integral equation techniques"
Invited talk presented at the International Symposium on Solid State Physics, Calcutta, 10-14 january 1977.

9) *G. De Mey:*
"Numerical applications of integral equations in semiconductor physics"
Colloquium Numerical Treatment of Integral Equations, Mathematisch Centrum Amsterdam, 13 october 1978.

POLICY IMPROVEMENT ALGORITHM FOR CONTINUOUS TIME MARKOV DECISION PROCESSES WITH SWITCHING COSTS

Bharat Doshi
Departement of Statistics
Rutgers University
New Brunswick, N.J. 08903
U.S.A.

ABSTRACT

This paper deals with computation of an optimal policy for Markov decision processes involving continuous movement as well as switching costs. Recently the author derived conditions for the optimality of a policy in such decision processes. These conditions can be used to verify the optimality of a given stationary policy but cannot be used to obtain one directly. Some computational procedure is needed to arrive at a stationary optimal policy. In this paper we develop an algorithm which generates a sequence of successively improving policies converging (at least along a subsequence) to an optimal stationary policy. Two special cases are considered. The first one is a general continuous-time Markov decision process with a countable state space. In this case the sufficient conditions for optimality suggest an algorithm procedure. It is shown that this algorithm either terminates at a stationary optimal policy or converges to one (at least along a subsequence). The second special case is the case of controlled one dimensional diffusion process. In this case the simple algorithm suggested by the sufficient conditions does give a sequence of successively improving policies. However, this may terminate at or converge to a suboptimal policy. An additional step in the algorithm is proposed. It is shown that this modified algorithm does work. That is, it either terminates at a stationary optimal policy or converges to one along a subsequence. Similarly modified algorithms can be developed for the Markov decision processes in which the underlying process is compound Poisson with a drift. Such processes frequently occur in controlled queues and inventory systems.

1. INTRODUCTION

Recently (4,5] the author investigated conditions for optimality of a policy in a continuous-time Markov decision process with continuous movement as well as switching costs. These conditions can be used to verify the optimality of a given stationary policy (see [1,6,7]) but cannot be used to obtain a stationary optimal policy if its form cannot be guessed in advance. Thus there is a need for a computational procedure for arriving at a stationary policy directly. In this paper we develop an algorithmic procedure for this purpose. Two special cases will be considered: The first one is a general Markov decision process with countable state space and the second is a controlled one dimensional diffusion process with reflecting boundaries. The sufficient conditions for optimality derived in [4,5] suggest a natural algorithmic procedure to compute a stationary optimal policy. It is shown that for countable state space case this algorithm either terminates at a stationary optimal policy or converges to one (at least along a subsequence). For controlled diffusions this algorithm may terminate at a suboptimal policy or converge to a suboptimal policy. An additional step is proposed in the algorithm. It is shown that this modified algorithm does have the desired properties. That is, it either terminates at an optimal policy or converges to one. It will be clear from these results that similarly modified algorithms can be developed for other decision processes (such as a compound Poisson process with a drift arising in queueing and inventory control models). Algorithms in this paper are developed for discounted cost criterion. Similar algorithms can be developed for average cost case (see [2,3] for such an algorithm for general decision processes. Because this algorithm is for general decision process, the results are not as explicit as ours).

Section 2 briefly describes the decision model (see [4,5] for details) and states the sufficient conditions for optimality as proved in [4]. Section 3 concerns with a policy improvement algorithm for the Markov decision process with a countable state space. Section 4 discusses the modification of this algorithm to make it suitable for controlled diffusion processes with reflecting boundaries.

2. MODEL AND CONDITIONS FOR OPTIMALITY

The decision model to be investigated can be described by the following components:

The state space $\mathcal{X}$ is a Polish space with the usual topology $C_{\mathcal{X}}$ and the Borel σ-algebra $\beta_{\mathcal{X}}$.

The action space $\mathcal{A}$ is a finite set. For each $a \in \mathcal{A}$, there exists a conservative, strongly measurable, strong Markov process $\{X_t^a; t \geq 0\}$ on the state space $\mathcal{X}$.

Let $\mathcal{B}$ be the set of bounded measurable functions on $\mathcal{X}$. For $x \in \mathcal{X}$ let $\mathcal{B}_a(x)$ be the subset of $\mathcal{B}$ such that for $g \in \mathcal{B}_a(x)$

$$(2.1) \qquad \lim_{t \downarrow 0^+} E_x g(X_t^a) = g(x).$$

For $\Lambda \subset \mathcal{X}$ let $\mathcal{B}_a(\Lambda) = \bigcap_{x\in\Lambda} \mathcal{B}_a(x)$ and let $\mathcal{B}_a = \mathcal{B}_a(\mathcal{X})$. For $x \in \mathcal{X}$, let $\mathcal{D}_a(x)$ be the subset of $\mathcal{B}_a(x)$ such that for $g \in \mathcal{D}_a(x)$

$$(2.2) \qquad A_a g(x) = \lim_{t \downarrow 0^+} \frac{E_x[g(X_t^a)] - g(x)}{t}$$

exists. For $\Lambda \subset \mathcal{X}$ let $\mathcal{D}_a(\Lambda) = \bigcap_{x\in\Lambda} \mathcal{D}_a(x)$. Denote $\mathcal{D}_a(\mathcal{X})$ by $\mathcal{D}_a$. Finally, let

$$(2.3) \qquad \mathcal{B}_o = \bigcap_{a\in\mathcal{A}} \mathcal{B}_a \quad \text{and} \quad \mathcal{D} = \bigcap_{a\in\mathcal{A}} \mathcal{D}_a.$$

Policies. Since the algorithm generates only stationary policies we will only define stationary policies here. For the definition of a general policy see [4,5]. It was shown in [4,5] that if an optimal policy exists among stationary policies, then it is optimal among all policies.

A stationary policy is characterized by a function $f = \mathcal{X} \times \mathcal{A} \to \mathcal{A}$ with the interpretation that the action $f(x,a)$ is used at time t if the state at time t is x and the action in use at time t^- is a. So as long as $X_t \in \Lambda_a = \{x\in\mathcal{X}; f(x,a)=a\}$ we continue to use action a, and at the first instant at which $X_t \notin \Lambda_a$, we change the action from a to $f(X_t,a)$. We will restrict to those f for which

(i) Λ_a is open for each $a\in\mathcal{A}$, and

(ii) if a_t denote the action in use at time t, then with probability 1, $\{a_t; t \geq 0\}$ is right continuous, piecewise constant with only a finite number of jumps in any finite interval of time.

Such a policy f is called a stationary admissible policy. Let D denote the set of all stationary admissible policies.

Cost structure. Let $C_a(x)$ be the rate at which cost is incurred when the current state is x and the current action is a, $x\in\mathcal{X}$, $a\in\mathcal{A}$. Moreover, let $R(a,a')$ be the non-negative lump cost incurred when the action is changed from a to a'. We assume the following:

(i) For $a\in\mathcal{A}$, $C_a \in \mathcal{B}_o$.

(ii) $R(a,a'') \leq R(a,a') + R(a',a'')$ for all $a, a', a'' \in \mathcal{A}$. Also $R(a,a) = 0$ for $a \in \mathcal{A}$, and $R(a,a') > 0$ for $a \neq a'$.

Economic criterion. Let $\alpha > 0$ be the fixed discount rate. For the initial state x, the initial action a and a policy $f\in D$ define the discounted cost by

$$(2.4) \qquad V(f;a,x) = E_{f,x,a}\left[\int_0^\infty e^{-\alpha t} C_{a_t}(X_t)dt + \sum_1^\infty e^{-\alpha\tau_k} R(a_{k-1},a_k)\right]$$

$$= E_{f,x,a}\left[\sum_{n=1}^\infty \int_{\tau_{n-1}}^{\tau_n} e^{-\alpha t} C_{a_{n-1}}(X_t)dt + \sum_1^\infty e^{-\alpha\tau_k} R(a_{k-1},a_k)\right],$$

where τ_k is the time of kth change in action, $a_o = a$ and a_k, $k \geq 1$ is the action used in the time interval $[\tau_k, \tau_{k+1})$.

A policy f^* is optimal if

$$V(f^*;a,x) = \min_{f \in D} V(f;a,x) \qquad (x \in \mathcal{X}, a \in \mathcal{A}).$$

Value determination and conditions for optimality

Lemma 1. Let $f \in D$. Then $\{V(f;a,\cdot); a \in \mathcal{A}\}$ is the unique family of functions satisfying

(2.5) $$V(f;a,\cdot) \in \mathcal{D}_a(\Lambda_a) \quad \text{for all } a \in \mathcal{A},$$

(2.6) $$\alpha V(f;a,x) = C_a(x) + A_a V(f;a,x) \quad x \in \Lambda_a,$$

and

(2.7) $$V(f;a,x) = R(a,f(x,a)) + V(f;f(x,a),x) \quad x \notin \Lambda_a.$$

Theorem 1. Suppose there exists a policy $f^* \in D$ such that $V(f^*;a,\cdot) \in \mathcal{D}$ for all $a \in \mathcal{A}$,

(2.8) $$\alpha V(f^*;a,x) \leq C_a(x) + A_a V(f;a,x) \quad (x \in \mathcal{X}, a \in \mathcal{A}),$$

and

(2.9) $$V(f^*;a,x) \leq \min_{a' \in \mathcal{A}} \{R(a,a') + V(f^*;a',x)\} \quad (x \in \mathcal{X}, a \in \mathcal{A}),$$

then f^* is an optimal policy.

3. COUNTABLE STATE SPACE CASE

In this section we assume that $\mathcal{X}$ is countable. That is, $\mathcal{X} = \{1,2,\ldots.\}$. In this case the infinitesimal operator A_a corresponds to a matrix (A_{aij}). We assume that $\sum_{j \neq i} A_{aij} \leq N < \infty$ for all $i \in \mathcal{X}$ and $a \in \mathcal{A}$, and $\sum_j A_{aij} = 0$ for all $i \in \mathcal{X}$ and $a \in \mathcal{A}$. Then $\mathcal{D} = \mathcal{B}_o = \mathcal{B}$ = set of all bounded measurable functions on $\mathcal{X}$, and

(3.1) $$A_a g(x) = \sum_y A_{axy}\, g(y)$$

for all $x \in \mathcal{X}$ and $g \in \mathcal{D}$. Moreover,

(3.2) $$V(f;a,\cdot) \in \mathcal{D}$$

for all $a \in \mathcal{A}$ and $f \in D$. Thus the condition $V(f^*;a,\cdot) \in \mathcal{D}$ in Theorem 1 is automatically satisfied. The set D corresponds to all functions $f:\mathcal{X} \times \mathcal{A} \to \mathcal{A}$ such that $f(x,a) = a'$ implies $f(x,a') = a'$.

The sufficient conditions of Theorem 1 suggests the following algorithmic procedure:

Let f_1 be an arbitrary stationary policy in D. Use the following iterative procedure to generate $\{f_n; n \geq 2\}$ starting with f_1.

Step 1. Value determination: given the policy f_n calculate $V(f_n;\cdot,\cdot)$ using Lemma 1.

Step 2. Define a policy f_n' by taking $f_n'(x,a)$ to be the action minimizing $R(a,a') + V(f_n;a',x)$ over all $a' \in \mathcal{A}$. The ties are broken in favor of the a' with the largest $R(a,a')$ (This, in particular, guarantees that $f_n' \in D$). Let $\Lambda_{n,a}' = \{x \in \mathcal{X}; f_n'(x,a) = a\}$ be the continuation set for action a in policy f_n', $a \in \mathcal{A}$. Calculate $V(f_n';\cdot,\cdot)$ using Lemma 1.

Step 3. For $a \in \mathcal{A}$, let

$$\Lambda_{n+1,a} = \Lambda_{n,a}' \cup \{x \in \mathcal{X}; \alpha V(f_n';a,x) > C_a(x) + A_a V(f_n';a,x)\}, \tag{3.3}$$

and define $f_{n+1} \in D$ by

$$f_{n+1}(x,a) = a \qquad \text{if } x \in \Lambda_{n+1,a} \tag{3.4}$$

$$= f_n'(x,a) \qquad \text{otherwise.}$$

If $f_{n+1} \equiv f_n$, then stop. Otherwise go back to step 1.

The following lemmas and theorem show that the above algorithm has desirable properties.

Lemma 2. For $n \geq 1$,

$$V(f_{n+1};a,x) \leq V(f_n';a,x) \leq V(f_n;a,x) \qquad (x \in \mathcal{X}, a \in \mathcal{A}). \tag{3.5}$$

Proof. For $x \notin \Lambda_{n,a}$, $a \in \mathcal{A}$

$$V(f_n;a,x) = R(a,f_n(x,a)) + V(f_n;f_n(x,a),x)$$

$$\geq \min_{a' \in \mathcal{A}-\{a\}} \{R(a,a') + V(f_n;a',x)\}.$$

So $\Lambda_{n,a}' \subset \Lambda_{n,a}$ for all $a \in \mathcal{A}$. Let $U: \mathcal{A} \times \mathcal{X} \to R$ be defined by

$$U(a,x) = V(f_n;a,x) - V(f_n';a,x) \qquad (x \in \mathcal{X}, a \in \mathcal{A}).$$

Then $\Lambda_{n,a}' \subset \Lambda_{n,a}$ implies that

$$\alpha U(a,x) = A_a U(a,x) \qquad x \in \Lambda_{n,a}' \tag{3.6}$$

The definition of f_n' implies

(3.7) $$U(a,x) \geq U(f_n'(x,a),x) \qquad x \notin \Lambda_{n,a}'.$$

Now from (3.6), (3.7) and Lemma 1 we get

$$U(a,x) \geq 0,$$

which implies the second inequality in (3.5).

Next, we have $\Lambda_{n,a}' \subset \Lambda_{n+1,a}$ for all $a \in \mathcal{A}$. The definition of f_{n+1} and $\Lambda_{n+1,a}$ implies that

(3.8) $$\alpha W(a,x) = A_a W(a,x) \qquad x \in \Lambda_{n,a}'$$

(3.9) $$\alpha W(a,x) \geq A_a W(a,x) \qquad x \in \Lambda_{n+1,a} - \Lambda_{n,a}'$$

and

(3.10) $$W(a,x) = W(f_{n+1}(x,a),x) \qquad x \notin \Lambda_{n+1,a},$$

where $W(a,x) = V(f_{n+1};a,x) - V(f_n';a,x)$ $(x \in \mathcal{X}, a \in \mathcal{A})$. Now (3.8)-(3.10) and Lemma 1 imply that $W \geq 0$ thus proving the first inequality in (3.5).

Remark 1. It is clear from the proof of Lemma 2 that countability of $\mathcal{X}$ is not necessary for (3.5) to be true. In fact, (3.5) is true for any Markov decision process for which $f_n \in D$ implies $f_n' \in D$ and $f_{n+1} \in D$. This is true, in particular, for the controlled one dimensional diffusion to be studied in Section 4.

Lemma 3. If, for some n,

(3.11) $$f_{n+1} \equiv f_n' \equiv f_n,$$

then f_n is optimal.

Proof. Clearly, (3.11) implies that

$$V(f_{n+1};a,x) = V(f_n';a,x) = V(f_n;a,x) \qquad (x \in \mathcal{X}, a \in \mathcal{A}).$$

From the definition of f_n' and f_{n+1}, we get

(3.12) $$\alpha V(f_n;a,x) \leq C_a(x) + A_a V(f_n;a,x)$$

for all $a \in \mathcal{A}$, $x \in \mathcal{X}$ with equality on $x \in \Lambda_{n,a}$, and

(3.13) $$V(f_n;a,x) \leq \min_{a' \in \mathcal{A}} \{R(a,a') + V(f_n;a',x)\}$$

for all $x \in \mathcal{X}$, $a \in \mathcal{A}$ with equality on $x \notin \Lambda_{n,a}$. Moreover, $V(f_n;a,\cdot) \in \mathcal{D}$ for all $a \in \mathcal{A}$.

So, by Theorem 1, f_n is an optimal policy.

Theorem 2. Let $\{f_n; n \geq 1\}$ be the sequence of stationary policies in D generated by the above algorithm. Then there exists an $f \in D$ and a subsequence $\{f_{n'}\}$ such that

(i) $f_{n'}$ converges to f pointwise, and

(ii) f is an optimal policy.

Proof. Since $\mathcal{A}$ is finite $\mathcal{A}^{\mathcal{X} \times \mathcal{A}}$ is compact with respect to the topology of pointwise convergence. Clearly, D is a bounded closed subset of $\mathcal{A}^{\mathcal{X} \times \mathcal{A}}$. So D is compact with respect to the topology of pointwise convergence. This implies (i).

The functions C_a are bounded and $\sum_{j \neq i} A_{aij} \leq N < \infty$ for all $i \in \mathcal{X}$, $a \in \mathcal{A}$. Using these facts and the arguments of Whitt [[10], Section 10] we conclude that $V(\cdot; a, x)$ is continuous on D for each $a \in \mathcal{A}$, $x \in \mathcal{X}$. So

$$V(f;a,x) = \lim_{n' \to \infty} V(f_{n'};a,x) \qquad (x \in \mathcal{X},\ a \in \mathcal{A}). \tag{3.14}$$

Finally, by the definition of the steps in the algorithm we conclude that f satisfies the hypotheses of Theorem 1 and hence is optimal.

4. CONTROLLED ONE DIMENSIONAL DIFFUSION WITH REFLECTING BOUNDARIES

Let $-\infty < r_0 < r_1 < \infty$ and for each $a \in \mathcal{A}$, let $\{X_t^a; t \geq 0\}$ be a diffusion process on the state space $\mathcal{X} = [r_0, r_1]$ with drift coefficient $b(x,a)$ and diffusion coefficient $d(x,a)$ and reflecting boundaries at r_0 and r_1. We assume that $b(\cdot,a)$ and $d(\cdot,a)$ are continuous in $x \in \mathcal{X}$ for each $a \in \mathcal{A}$, and there exist $0 < M_1 < M_2 < \infty$ and $M_3 < \infty$ such that $M_1 \leq d(x,a) \leq M_2$, $|b(x,a)| \leq M_3$ for all $x \in \mathcal{X}$ and $a \in \mathcal{A}$. Also assume that $C_a(\cdot)$ is continuous on $\mathcal{X}$ for each $a \in \mathcal{A}$.

In this case D corresponds to all $f: \mathcal{X} \times \mathcal{A} \to \mathcal{A}$ such that

(i) $f(\cdot,a)$ is piecewise constant with only finite number of jumps for each $a \in \mathcal{A}$, and

(ii) If $f(x,a) = a'$, then $f(y,a') = a'$ for all y in some neighborhood of x.

Then each $\Lambda_{f,a}$ is the union of finite number of disjoint open intervals (note that r_0 and r_1 are interior points of $[r_0, r_1]$). Thus

$$\Lambda_{f,a} = \bigcup_{i=1}^{n_a} \lambda(f;i,a) = \bigcup_{i=1}^{n_a} (A(f;i,a), B(f;i,a)) \tag{4.1}$$

where n_a denotes the number of intervals in $\Lambda_{f,a}$.

For any open $\Lambda \subset \mathcal{X}$ and $a \in \mathcal{A}$, $\mathcal{D}_a(\Lambda)$ is the set of all functions g on $\mathcal{X}$ with the following properties:

(i) g is continuously differentiable on Λ.

(ii) $g''(x^-)$ and $g''(x^+)$ exist at all $x \in \Lambda$ and for all but a finite number of points $g''(x^-) = g''(x) = g''(x^+)$.

(iii) If $r_i \in \Lambda$, $i=0,1$, then $g'(r_i) = 0$.

Then $\mathcal{D}$ is the set of all continuously differentiable functions on $\mathcal{X}$ with continuous second derivative at all but a finite number of points. Moreover, for any $g \in \mathcal{D}$, $g'(r_0) = g'(r_1) = 0$.

The infinitesimal operator A_a is defined by

$$(4.2) \qquad A_a g(x) = b(x,a)g'(x) + \frac{d(x,a)}{2}\,[g''(x^-) + g''(x^+)]$$

at all $x\in\mathcal{X}$ at which g' is continuous. The function $A_a g$ is not defined at $x\in\mathcal{X}$ at which g' is not continuous.

Suppose we use the algorithm of Section 3 for this problem. Then the Remark 1 implies that

$$V(f_{n+1};a,x) \le V(f_n;a,x) \quad (n \ge 1,\ x\in\mathcal{X},\ a\in\mathcal{A}).$$

Thus the improvement property is valid. Also, as in Lemma 3, $f_{n+1} \equiv f'_n \equiv f_n$ for some $n \ge 1$ implies that (2.8) and (2.9) hold with $f^* \equiv f_n$. However, the function $V(f_n;a,\cdot)$ may not have continuous derivative at the boundary points of $\Lambda_{n,a}$ (In fact, we have a numerical example showing that this does happen). So $V(f_n;a,\cdot)$ may not belong to $\mathcal{D}$ as required in Theorem 1. Chernoff and Petkau [1] showed that the continuity of $V'(f_n;a,\cdot)$ is not only sufficient but also necessary for f_n to be optimal. This implies that the terminal policy f_n may be suboptimal. By the same argument it can be shown that if $f_{n'} \to f$ for some subsequence $\{f_{n'}\}$ of $\{f_n\}$, then f may be suboptimal. To overcome this difficulty we add an extra step in the algorithm. The modified iteration can be described as follows:

Step 1. Given policy $f_n \in D$ calculate $V(f_n;\cdot,\cdot)$ using Lemma 1.

Step 2. Let $f'_n \in D$ be defined by taking $f'_n(x,a)$ to be the action that minimizes $R(a,a') + V(f_n;a',x)$ over all $a'\in\mathcal{A}$ with ties broken in favor of an a' with the largest value of $R(a,a')$. Calculate $V(f'_n;\cdot,\cdot)$ using Lemma 1.

Step 3. For each of the $N' = \sum_{a\in\mathcal{A}} n'_a$ subintervals corresponding to the continuation sets of policy f'_n, select one of the two boundary points. Suppose that for the interval $\lambda(f'_n;i,a) = (A(f'_n;i,a),\ B(f'_n;i,a))$ we select $B(f'_n;i,a)$. Let Γ be the set of all open intervals $\Lambda = (A'',B'')$ such that

$$A'' \le A(f'_n;i,a) < B(f'_n;i,a) \le B''$$

$$A'' \notin \Lambda'_{n,a},\ B'' \notin \Lambda'_{f_n,a}.$$

Let $T(\Lambda) = \inf\{t \geq 0;\ X_t \notin \Lambda\}$. For $x \in \Lambda$ define

(4.3) $$V(\Lambda \cdot f_n';a,x) = E_{x,a}\left[\int_0^{T(\Lambda)} e^{-\alpha t} C_a(X_t)dt + e^{-\alpha T(\Lambda)} V(f_n';a,X_{T(\Lambda)})\right]$$

$$= g_1(\Lambda;a,x) + g_2(\Lambda;a,x),$$

where $g_1(\Lambda;a,x) = E_{x,a}\left[\int_0^{T(\Lambda)} e^{-\alpha t} C_a(X_t)dt\right]$, and $g_2(\Lambda;a,x) = E_{x,a}\left[e^{-\alpha T(\Lambda)} V(f_n';a,X_{T(\Lambda)})\right]$.

Find $\Lambda = (A''(i,a),B''(i,a))$ such that Λ minimizes $V(\Lambda \cdot f_n';a,B(f_n;i,a))$ over all $\Lambda \in \Gamma$. Let $\lambda''(i,a) = (A''(i,a),B''(i,a))$. Repeat this for each of the N' subintervals of f_n'.

Let $\Lambda''_{n,a} = \bigcup_{i=1}^{n'_a} \lambda''(i,a)$ and define $f''_n \in D$ by

(4.4) $$f''_n(x,a) = a \quad \text{if} \quad x \in \Lambda''_{n,a}$$
$$= f'_n(x,a) \quad \text{otherwise.}$$

(Note that $\Lambda''_{n,a} \supset \Lambda'_{n,a}$ be each $a \in \mathcal{A}$.

Step 4. For $a \in \mathcal{A}$, let

(4.5) $$\Lambda_{n+1,a} = \Lambda''_{n,a} \cup \{x \notin \Lambda_{f''_n,a};\ \alpha V(f'_n;a,x) > C_a(x) + A_a V(f'_n;a,x)\},$$

and define f_{n+1} by

(4.6) $$f_{n+1}(x,a) = a \quad \text{if} \quad x \in \Lambda_{n+1,a}$$
$$= f'_n(x,a) \quad \text{otherwise.}$$

If $f_{n+1} \equiv f_n$, then stop. Otherwise go back to Step 1.

Remark 2. The functions $g_1(\Lambda;\cdot,\cdot)$ and $g_2(\Lambda;\cdot,\cdot)$ can be calculated using the following sets of equations:

(4.7) $$\alpha g_1(\Lambda;a,x) = C_a(x) + A_a g_1(\Lambda;a,x) \quad x \in \Lambda = (A'',B'')$$
$$g_1(\Lambda;a,A'') = g_1(\Lambda;a,B'') = 0,$$

where $g_1(\Lambda;a,\cdot)$ is defined at A'' and B'' as the limit of $g_1(\Lambda;a,x)$ as $x \in \Lambda$ approaches A'' and B'', respectively.

(4.8) $$\alpha g_2(\Lambda;a,x) = A_a g_2(\Lambda;a,x) \quad x \in \Lambda$$

(4.9) $$g_2(\Lambda;a,A'') = V(f'_n;a,A''),$$

and

(4.10) $$g_2(\Lambda;a,B'') = V(f'_n;a,B'').$$

Remark 3. Since $0 < M_1 \le d(x,a) \le M_2 < \infty$ and $|b(x,a)| \le M_3 < \infty$, any $y\epsilon\Lambda$ is accessible from any $x\epsilon\Lambda$ with positive probability. This implies the following:

(i) If Λ minimizes $V(\Lambda\cdot f_n';a,B(f_n';i,a))$ over all $\Lambda\epsilon\Gamma$, then Λ also minimizes $V(\Lambda\cdot f_n';a,x)$ for all $x\epsilon\Lambda$. In particular, Λ minimizes $V(\Lambda\cdot f_n';a,A(f_n';i,a))$ over all $\Lambda\epsilon\Gamma$. This justifies considering only one of the boundary points for each continuation subinterval.

(ii) For $i \neq j$, $\lambda''(i,a) = \lambda''(j,a)$ or $\lambda''(i,a)$ and $\lambda''(j,a)$ are disjoint.

Remark 4. Suppose $\lambda''(i,a) = (A'',B'')$ minimizes $V(\lambda''(i,a);a,B(f_n';i,a))$ over all $\Lambda\epsilon\Gamma$. Now suppose $A \le B(f_n';i,a) \le B(A \le A'(i,a)$ need not hold), and $\Lambda = (A,B)$. Then by Lemma 1.2 of De Leve and Tijms [2] we have

$$V(\Lambda\cdot f_n';a,B(f_n';i,a)) \ge V(\lambda''(i,a)\cdot f_n';a,B(f_n';i,a)). \tag{4.11}$$

We now show that the modified algorithm described above has the desired properties. That is, if $f_n \equiv f_n' \equiv f_n'' \equiv f_{n+1}$ for some $n \ge 1$, then f_n is optimal. When $f_n \equiv f_n' \equiv f_n'' \equiv f_{n+1}$, the arguments in the proof of Lemma 3 implies that $V(f_n;\cdot,\cdot)$ satisfies (2.8) and (2.9) of Theorem 1. So we only need to verify that $V(f_n;a,\cdot)\epsilon\mathcal{D}$ for each $a\epsilon\mathcal{A}$. This amounts to showing that $V'(f_n;a,\cdot)$ is continuous at the boundary points of the continuation subintervals of f_n.

Theorem 3. If $f_n \equiv f_n' \equiv f_n'' \equiv f_{n+1}$, then $V'(f_n;a,\cdot)$ is continuous at boundary points of $\Lambda_{f_n,a}$ for each $a\epsilon\mathcal{A}$ and hence f_n is an optimal policy.

Proof. It suffices to prove the continuity of $V'(f_n;a,\cdot)$ at the boundary point $B(f_n;i,a) = B(f_n';i,a)$ of $\Lambda_{f_n,a}$. The proofs for other boundary points are similar. To simplify notations let $B = B(f_n';i,a)$. For some $\delta > 0$ let $A' = B-\delta$ and $B' = B+\delta$ and $\Lambda = (A',B')$. Then by Remark 4

$$V(\Lambda\cdot f_n;a,B) \ge V(\lambda(i,a)\cdot f_n;a,B) = V(f_n;a,B), \tag{4.12}$$

or, equivalently

$$V(\Lambda\cdot f_n;a,B) - V(f_n;a,B) \ge 0 \tag{4.13}$$

Let $d = d(B,a)$, $b = b(B,a)$ and $C = C(B,a)$. Since $d(\cdot,a)$, $b(\cdot,a)$ and $C_a(\cdot)$ are continuous in x, $d(x,a) = d + O(\delta)$, $b(x,a) = b+O(\delta)$ and $C_a(x) = C+O(\delta)$ for all $x\epsilon\Lambda$. So for small $\delta > 0$ the diffusion process in the interval Λ behaves approximately like a Brownian motion with drift b, diffusion coefficient d and cost rate C. Using this fact and equations (4.7) and (4.8) we get

$$0 \le V(\Lambda\cdot f_n;a,B) - V(f_n;a,B) \tag{4.14}$$

$$= \frac{-\alpha\delta^2}{2d} V(f_n;a,B) + \frac{\delta}{2}(V'(f_n;a,B^+) - V'(f_n;a,B^-))$$

$$+ \frac{b\delta^2}{4d} [V'(f_n;a,B^+) + V'(f_n;a,B^-)]$$

$$+ \frac{\delta^2}{4} [V''(f_n;a,B^+) + V''(f_n;a,B^-)] + o(\delta^2]$$

as $\delta \downarrow o^+$. (4.14) implies that

$$(4.15) \qquad V'(f_n;a,B^+) \geq V'(f_n;a,B^-).$$

But by Step 2 of the algorithm we have

$$(4.16) \qquad V(f_n;a,B) = R(a,f_n(B,a)) + V(f_n;f_n(B,a),B),$$

and

$$(4.17) \qquad V(f_n;a,x) \leq R(a,f_n(B,a)) + V(f_n;f_n(B,a),x)$$

for $x < B$. From (4.16) and (4.17) we get

$$(4.18) \qquad V'(f_n;a,B^-) \geq V'(f_n;f_n(B,a),B) = V'(f_n;a,B^+).$$

Inequalities (4.15) and (4.18) now imply continuity of $V'(f_n;a,\bullet)$ at B. This proves the theorem.

If the sequence $\{f_n\}$ generated by the algorithm has a converging subsequence $\{f_{n'}\}$ such that $f_{n'} \to f \in D$ in some topology, and if $V(\bullet;a,x)$ is continuous on D, then the results of Theorems 2 and 3 will imply that f is an optimal policy. In future we plan to investigate conditions under which this is true.

REFERENCES

[1] Chernoff, H. and Petkau, J. (1977). Optimal Control of a Brownian Motion. Tech. Rpt. Univ. of British Columbia.

[2] De Leve, G. and Tijms, H. D. (1974). A General Markov Lecision Method, with Applications to Controlled Queueing System. Mathematisch Centrum, Amsterdam.

[3] De Leve, G., Fodergruen, A., and Tijms, H. C. (1976). A General Markov Decision Mathod I:Model and Techniques. Mathematisch Centrum.

[4] Doshi, B. T. (1976). Markov Decision Processes with Both Continuous and Lump Costs. Tech. Rpt. Rutgers University.

[5] Doshi, B. T. (1978). Optimal Control of a Diffusion Process with Relecting Boundaries and Both Continuous and Lump Costs. To appear in Dynamic Programming and its Applications. Ed. M. Puterman.

[6] Doshi, B. T. (1978). Two Mode Control of a Brownian Motion with Quadratic Loss and Switching Costs. Stochastic Processes and Their Applications 6, 277-289.

[7] Doshi, B. T. (1978). Production Inventory Control Models with Average Cost Criterion. Submitted for publication.

[8] Dynkin, E. (1965). Markov Processes I-II. Academic Press.

[9] Mandl, P. (1968). Analytical Treatment of One-Dimensional Markov Processes. Springer-Verlag, New York.

[10] Whitt, W. (1975). Continuity of Markov Processes and Dynamic Programs. Tech. Rpt. Yale University.

AN ALGEBRO-GEOMETRIC APPROACH TO ESTIMATION AND STOCHASTIC CONTROL FOR LINEAR PURE DELAY TIME SYSTEMS*

T.E. Duncan**

1. INTRODUCTION

In this paper an algebro-geometric proof of the equations for the optimal estimator and the error covariance for linear Gaussian systems with pure delays only in the state matrix will be given. The corresponding equations for linear Gaussian systems with delays in both the state and the observation matrices will be given without proof and some sufficient conditions will be described for the existence of the infinite time estimation problem. The methods that are used here interpret a linear system with pure delays as a system over a ring of polynomials formed from the delays. This local description of the system describes a finitely generated, projective module (Byrnes [4]) and this description can be viewed geometrically as a vector bundle using some results of Serre [24]. The fact that this vector bundle is always globally trivial ([22,26]) provides the natural geometric setting for the rigorous approach to the formal view of these linear systems with pure delays as systems with parameters.

In addition to the estimation problem, the problems of stochastic optimization for complete and partial observations are solved by these geometric techniques and the principle of separation of control and estimation is verified. The duality of deterministic control and stochastic estimation for systems with pure delays only in the state matrix follows immediately by the geometric techniques that are described here. These problems have been studied previously by various authors (e.g. [16,17-19,21]). However, none of these authors used

* Research supported by AFOSR Grant 77-3177 and as a guest of the SFB 72 of the Deutsche Forschungsgemeinschaft, Bonn.
** Institute of Applied Mathematics, University of Bonn, FRG and Department of Mathematics, University of Kansas, Lawrence, Kansas, 66045 USA.

an algebro-geometric approach.

One reason for the relative simplicity of the optimization and estimation problems when the pure delays occur only in the state matrix will be briefly described. Considering the Hamiltonian equations and the Lagrangian Grassmannian, one can imagine for the case of delays only in the state matrix that there is an infinite dimensional (trivial) vector bundle that is over the Lagrangian n-plane. In the solution of the Hamiltonian equations a computation has to be made in these fibers, but then this is projected down to the Lagrangian plane. The evolution of the planes in the Lagrangian Grassmannian is determined by the connection between the χ-plane and the ξ-plane which are finite dimensional objects. Thus, it is to be expected that the results are simpler in this case than for the case of delays in both the state and observation matrices.

2. ESTIMATION

For the estimation problem consider the stochastic process (X_t, Y_t) defined by the linear pure delay time stochastic differential equations

$$dX_t = FX_t\, dt + G\, dB_t \tag{1}$$

$$dY_t = HX_t\, dt + d\tilde{B}_t \tag{2}$$

where $X(0)=X_0$ is a Gaussian random variable with mean zero and covariance P_0, $X(s)\equiv 0$ for $s<0$ and (B_t) and $(\tilde{B}_t)$ are independent $\mathbb{R}^m$ and $\mathbb{R}^p$ dimensional standard Brownian motions, respectively, that are independent of X_0, $G\in \mathrm{Hom}\,(\mathbb{R}^p,\mathbb{R}^n)$, $H\in \mathrm{Hom}\,(\mathbb{R}^n,\mathbb{R}^m)$ and F is the state transition matrix that contains linear pure delay operators.

The stochastic system (1-2) can be interpreted as a system over a ring ([4,14-15,25,27]). The ring is formed from the polynomial ring $\mathbb{R}[z_1,\dots,z_k]$ where the family (z_i) correspond to delays such that there are no relations among the monomials of the form

$$\prod_{i=1}^{l} z_i^{n_i} = \prod_{j=1}^{l} z_j^{m_j} \tag{3}$$

To verify (3) it suffices to show that if $n_i\in\mathbb{Z}$ then $\prod_{i=1}^{l} n_i a_i=0$ implies $n_i=0$ for all i where the family (a_i) are the pure delays and $z_i X(t) = X(t-a_i)$.

This description of a linear system over a ring is not merely formal because Kamen [15] has shown that this ring of polynomials can be naturally identified with the elements of the convolution ring of Schwartz distributions and that the solution of a linear pure delay time differential equation can be given in terms of this latter ring in a manner that is formally similar to the Laplace transform. This technique provides existence and uniqueness for the solutions to the linear, constant coefficient, pure delay time differential equations where the initial conditions are allowed to be pointwise and functional. Delfour-Mitter [8-10] have demonstrated existence and uniqueness for solutions of linear, pure delay time differential equations with time varying coefficients. From these results of Kamen [15] and Delfour-Mitter [8-10] all the linear pure delay time equations that appear in this paper will have solutions that exist and are unique (almost surely) where the usual probabilistic method is used to extend the interpretation from deterministic to stochastic equations.

The geometric approach to systems over rings that has been successfully used by Byrnes [4] in the study of realization and coefficient assignability of the characteristic polynomial will be briefly described. Serre [24] showed that a finitely generated, projective A-module can be viewed geometrically as a vector bundle over the algebraic variety Spec (A) where A is a ring of polynomials $k[Z_1,\ldots,Z_j]$ and k is a field. This picture appears naturally for the system described by (1-2) as a system over the ring of polynomials $\mathbb{R}[Z_1,\ldots,Z_k]$.

The fibres of the bundle are obtained by the formal procedure of evaluation of the "parameters" $Z_1,\ldots,Z_k$. Quillen [22] and Suslin [26] have shown that such a vector bundle is always globally trivial which provides a positive answer to the Serre problem. The global triviality of the bundle ensures that the formal operation of evaluation of parameters can be given a precise geometrical description.

For the estimation problem an equation is sought for $E[X_t|Y_s,\ 0\le s\le t]$ which is the conditional mean of X_t given the observations $\sigma(Y_s,\ 0\le s\le t)$. The solution to this problem is given in the following result.

Theorem 1. Consider the estimation problem described by (1-2). The stochastic equation for the evolution of the conditional mean is

$$d\hat{X}_t^t = F\hat{X}_t^t\, dt - P(t,t)H'H\hat{X}_t^t\, dt + PH'dY_t \tag{4}$$

where

$$\hat{X}_t^t = E[X_t | Y_s,\ 0 \le s \le t]$$

and if Z_i is the operator corresponding to the delay a_i, then

$$Z_i \hat{X}_t^t = \hat{X}_{t-a_i}^t = E[X_{t-a_i} | Y_s,\ 0 \le s \le t]$$

and $\hat{X}_0^0 \equiv 0$

The equation for the evolution of the error covariance is

$$\frac{dP}{dt} = FP + PF' - PH'HP + GG' \tag{5}$$

where $P(0,0) = P_0$, $Z_i P(t,t) = P(t-a_i,t)$ and $P(t,t)Z_i = P(t,t-a_i)$.

Proof. Viewing the linear pure delay time system geometrically as a system over a ring we can also obtain the Hamiltonian equations

$$\frac{d\chi}{dt} = -F'\chi + H'H\xi \tag{6}$$

$$\frac{d\xi}{dt} = GG'\chi + F\xi \tag{7}$$

where $\xi(0) = P_0\chi(0)$. These Hamiltonian equations describe an algebraic vector bundle over the algebraic variety determined by the ring of polynomials formed from the delays in the same manner that the linear system (1-2) determines a vector bundle. This vector bundle has fibers that are $\mathbb{R}^{2n}$ and it preserves a skew symmetric form so that it is called a symplectic (algebraic) vector bundle. As Bass [2] has shown, the global triviality of this bundle follows from the solution of the Serre problem. The existence and the uniqueness of the solution of these Hamiltonian equations follows from the results of Kamen [15].

From the properties of the Hamiltonian equations and the Lagrangian Grassmannian (e.g. [1,12]) there is a symmetric, linear transformation that relates $\chi(t)$ and $\xi(t)$ which will be denoted $P(t,t)$. Recall that for the Lagrangian Grassmannian, there is a generating function $s(q)$ such that

$$p = \frac{\partial s}{\partial q}$$

where the canonical coordinates (p,q) are used ([1,12]). This representation is determined from the integral $s(q)=\int_{q_0}^{q} \tilde{p}(\tilde{q})d\tilde{q}$ which gives $s(q) = \frac{1}{2}\langle Sq,q\rangle$ where S is a symmetric linear transformation. For the estimation problem, the delays can act on both χ and ξ so that P must be a function of two time variables to allow for these two actions.

From the Hamiltonian equations and the symmetric transformation, P, between χ and ξ the equation

$$\frac{dz}{dt} = Fz - P(t,t)H'Hz \tag{8}$$

follows immediately for the homogeneous part of the equation for the conditional mean.

The observations appear as an inhomogeneous term in the equation (8) in a manner identical to the equation for the conditional mean for systems without delays by viewing the equation (8) geometrically. Thus, the stochastic equation for the conditional mean is

$$d\hat{X}_t^t = (F\hat{X}_t^t - P(t,t)H'H\hat{X}_t^t)dt + P(t,t)H'dY_t \tag{9}$$

where $\hat{X}_0^0 \equiv 0$.

Using the same techniques as in the derivation of the optimal filter for systems without delays ([12]) it follows that P(t,t) is the error covariance $E[\tilde{X}_t^t\tilde{X}_t^{t'}]$ where the error $\tilde{X}_t^t$ satisfies the equation

$$d\tilde{X}_t^t = F\tilde{X}_t^t dt - PH'H\tilde{X}_t^t dt + GdB_t - PH'd\tilde{B}_t \tag{10}$$

$$\tilde{X}_0^0 = X_0 \quad .$$

Since the global triviality of the algebraic vector bundle with the skew form, the symplectic algebraic vector bundle, means that the Hamiltonian equations can be described globally in one coordinate system (χ,ξ), it also follows that the Riccati equation is globally defined. If a family of symplectic transformations $(\beta(t))$ that are generated by

$$B = \begin{bmatrix} B_{11} & B_{12} \\ B_{21} & B_{22} \end{bmatrix}$$

in the Lie algebra of the symplectic group act on a Lagrangian plane then the corresponding family of symmetric transformations satisfy the Riccati equation (cf. [12])

$$\frac{dX}{dt} = B_{21} + B_{22}X - XB_{11} - XB_{12}X \tag{11}$$

Performing a local computation from the Hamiltonian equations (6-7) it follows that the relation between χ and ξ ($\xi = P\chi$) is given by the Riccati equation

$$\frac{dP}{dt} = FP + PF' - PH'HP + GG' \tag{12}$$

$$P(o) = P_0$$

To verify the proper action of the delay operators on P it suffices to note that in (11) B_{22} is clearly an action on ξ so that F in (12) acts on the left time variable of P and in (11) B_{11} is an action on χ so that F' in (12) acts on the right time variable of P. ∎

Remark. It is important to note that the equation for P does not completely specify it as is the case for linear systems without delays. To obtain a complete system of equations it is necessary to enlarge the Lagrangian Grassmannian or equivalently the Hamiltonian equations from the pure delay time data. A geometric treatment of the equations for a complete description of the Riccati equation (12) requires that the smoothing problem also be solved and this would exceed the spatial limitations of this paper and introduce a topic that was not intended for discussion in this paper.

For completeness of the presentation, the solution of the estimation problem for linear, pure delay time differentiable equations where the delays occur in both F and H will be presented without proof. The equations are the following

$$d\hat{X}_t^t = F\hat{X}_t^t dt - (PH')(H\hat{X}_t^t)dt + (PH')dY_t \tag{13}$$

$$\frac{dP}{dt} = FP + PF' - (PH')(HP) + GG' \tag{14}$$

$$\hat{X}_0^0 \equiv 0$$

$$P(o,o) = P_0$$

where the parentheses ($\cdot$) are used to indicate where the actions of the delays occur when there is a product of terms.

3. STOCHASTIC OPTIMIZATION

Two stochastic optimization problems will be solved. In the first problem it will be assumed that there are complete observations of the state, while in the second problem it will be assumed that there are only partial, noisy observations of the state.

Initially, the stochastic system is described by the following linear, pure delay time stochastic differential equation

$$dX_t = FX_t dt + GdB_t + CU_t dt \tag{15}$$

where the assumptions are the same as for (1) for the similar terms, $C \in \mathrm{Hom}(\mathbb{R}^1, \mathbb{R}^n)$ and U_t is a stochastic process called the control. The family of admissible controls are all maps $U: [o,T] \times \Omega \to \mathbb{R}^1$ that are square integrable functions of time for fixed $\omega \in \Omega$ and (U_t) is predictable with respect to (the completion of) the sub-σ-algebras $(\sigma(X_s, 0 \le s \le t))$. An admissible control is sought that minimizes the cost functional

$$J(u) = \frac{1}{2} E\left[\int_o^T \langle QX_t, X_t\rangle + \langle U_t, U_t\rangle dt + \langle AX_T, X_T\rangle\right] \tag{16}$$

where A and Q are nonnegative definite, symmetric elements of $\mathrm{Hom}(\mathbb{R}^n, \mathbb{R}^n)$.

For a fairly general class of stochastic optimization problems there is a Hamilton-Jacobi (or so-called dynamic programming) condition that has been obtained in different settings by various authors (e.g. [7,11,23]). It states that for the stochastic control problem described by (15-16) the optimal control must satisfy the equation

$$V_t + \frac{1}{2}\mathrm{tr}(G'V_{\chi\chi}G) + \min_u \left(\langle V_\chi, F\chi + Cu\rangle + \frac{1}{2}\langle Q\chi,\chi\rangle + \frac{1}{2}\langle u,u\rangle\right) = 0 \tag{17}$$

$$V(T,\chi) = \langle A\chi,\chi\rangle$$

A necessary condition for the minimization in (17) is clearly computed in terms of the partial derivative with respect to u. Thus, it suffices to solve the Hamilton-Jacobi equation

$$V_t + \frac{1}{2}\mathrm{tr}(G'V_{\chi\chi}G) + H(\chi, V_\chi, t) = 0 \tag{18}$$

where

$$H(\chi,\xi,t) = \frac{1}{2}\left[\langle Q\chi,\chi\rangle + 2\langle F\chi,\xi\rangle - \langle C'\xi, C'\xi\rangle\right] \tag{19}$$

This Hamilton-Jacobi equation can be obtained by a fairly straightforward generalization of the Hamilton-Jacobi equation for deterministic systems where it is only necessary to have the notion of an infinitesimal generator of a semigroup.

From the definition of the Hamiltonian manifolds it is known that the Hamiltonian is only determined up to a function of t alone ([12]). Thus, if it is assumed that the term $\frac{1}{2}$ tr $(G'V_{\chi\chi}G)$ in (18) is only a function of t, then we have the same problem as for the deterministic control problem with the Hamiltonian equations

$$\frac{d\chi}{dt} = F\chi - CC'\xi \tag{20}$$

$$\frac{d\xi}{dt} = - Q\chi - F'\xi \tag{21}$$

From the estimation results that were given in Theorem 1 and the usual duality notion, which is valid from our geometric approach, the generating function for the Hamiltonian equations (20-21) is obtained from the solution of the Riccati equation

$$\frac{-dS}{dt} = F'S + SF - SCC'S + Q \tag{22}$$

$$S(T) = A$$

where S is a function of two time variables and some other equations are necessary for its solution. Thus the solution of the Hamilton-Jacobi equation (18) is

$$V(t,\chi) = \frac{1}{2} \langle S(t,t)\chi,\chi\rangle + \frac{1}{2} s(t) \tag{23}$$

where S is given by (22) and

$$\frac{ds}{dt} = - \mathrm{tr}\ (G'S(t,t)G) \tag{24}$$

$$s(T) = 0$$

The second stochastic optimization problem is a problem with noisy, partial observations. The stochastic system is described by the following equations

$$dX_t = FX_t dt + CU_t dt + GdB_t \tag{25}$$

$$dY_t = HX_t dt + d\tilde{B}_t \tag{26}$$

where the assumptions are the same as in the equations (1,2,15) except that the family of admissible controls are the maps

$U: [o,T] \times \Omega \to \mathbb{R}^1$ that are square integrable functions of time for each $\omega \varepsilon \Omega$ and (U_t) is predictable with respect to (the completion of) the sub-σ-algebras $(\sigma(Y_s, 0 \le s \le t))$. The cost functional is given by (16).

The equation for the conditional mean is

$$d\hat{X}_t^t = F\hat{X}_t^t dt + CU_t dt + P(t,t)H'H\hat{X}_t^t dt + PH'dY_t \tag{27}$$

and the cost functional can be expressed as

$$\begin{aligned} J(u) = \frac{1}{2} E\Big[\int_o^T & <H\hat{X}_t^t, H\hat{X}_t^t> + <U_t, U_t> dt \\ & + <A\hat{X}_T^T, \hat{X}_T^T>\Big] + \frac{1}{2} \int_o^T tr(PH'H) \\ & + \frac{1}{2} tr\ (P(T,T)A) \end{aligned} \tag{28}$$

The verification of these equations is the same as for systems without delays ([12]).

Since this problem is now formally similar to the problem with complete observations, the optimal control is the same. Thus the problems of estimation and control satisfy the separation principle as is the case for linear systems without delays.

4. INFINITE TIME PROBLEMS

A brief discussion will now be given of the infinite time problems of control and estimation. In this case we can consider the estimation problem where the delays occur in both F and H or dually the control problem where the delays occur in both F and G.
The infinite time results will be described only for the control problem. Wonham [28] showed that for linear systems without delays reachability is equivalent to the property of pole placement or coefficient assignability of the characteristic polynomial of the system.
This latter problem is the following: given a monic polynomial, p, of degree n with coefficients in R, where n is the state space dimension, find a $K \varepsilon \mathrm{Hom}_R(Q,U)$ such that $\chi_{F+GK}(\lambda) = p(\lambda)$ where χ is the characteristic polynomial and Q is the state module. If p splits into linear factors over the ring R, then this problem is called pole placement instead of coefficient assignability.

Unfortunately, for linear systems with pure delays the conditions for coefficient assignability of the characteristic polynomial are incomplete. A.S. Morse [20] proved that reachability implies pole placement over a principal ideal domain. This is the case for commensurate delays. If the system σ is reachable over R and the pointwise Kronecker indices are locally constant, then σ is coefficient assignable ([4,5]). The Kronecker indices can be determined by the action of the feedback group (cf. Brunovsky [3], Kalman [13]). From this result we have the equivalence of reachability and pole placement for scalar input linear, pure delay time systems. Some other specialized results exist, for example, if $\mathrm{rk}G(\chi)=1$ for all $\chi \varepsilon X$ then reachability is equivalent to coefficient assignability and there are also some results for small n([4]).

Geometrically the problem of coefficient assignability can be posed as follows: there is a vector bundle $(\pi, \mathrm{Hom}_R(V,\mathbb{R}^m), X)$ where V is the state module and X is the variety determined by R and there is a variety Y in this bundle defined by the equation

$$\chi_{F+GK}(\lambda) = p(\lambda)$$

Wonham's proof [28] implies that given reachability $\pi: Y \to X$ is surjective and locally algebraic. It is only necessary to show that this map has a global section. For the stability of the optimal estimator it is only necessary to show that there is a global section for some p that gives a stable system. The ring can be any one that contains $\mathbb{R}[z_1,...,z_k]$.

REFERENCES

1 V.I. Arnold, Characteristic classes entering in quantization conditions, Funct. Anal. Appl. 1 (1967) 1-13.

2 H. Bass, Quadratic modules over polynomial rings, Contributions to Algebra, (H. Bass, P. Cassidy, J. Kovacic, eds.), 1-23, Academic Press, New York, 1977.

3 P. Brunovsky, A classification of linear controllable systems, Kybernetika 3 (1970)

4 C. Byrnes, On the control of certain deterministic infinite dimensional systems by algebro-geometric techniques, to appear in Amer. J. Math.

5 C.I. Byrnes, Feedback invariants for linear systems defined over rings, preprint.

6 C.I. Byrnes and T.E. Duncan, Topological and geometric invariants arising in control theory, to appear.

7 M.H.A. Davis and P. Varaiya, Dynamic programming conditions for partially observable stochastic systems, SIAM J. Control 11 (1973), 226-261.

8 M.C. Delfour and S.K. Mitter, Controllability, observability and optimal feedback control of affine hereditary differential systems, SIAM J. Control 10 (1972), 298-328.

9 M.C. Delfour and S.K. Mitter, Hereditary differential systems with constant delays I. General case, J. Differential Equations, 12 (1972), 213-235.

10 M.C. Delfour and S.K. Mitter, Hereditary systems with constant delays II. A class of affine systems and the adjoint problem, J. Differential Equations 18 (1975), 18-28.

11 T.E. Duncan, Dynamic programming optimality criteria for stochastic systems in Riemannian manifolds, Appl. Math. Optim. 3 (1977), 191-208.

12 T.E. Duncan, A geometric approach to linear control and estimation, this volume

13 R.E. Kalman, Kronecker invariants and feedback, Ordinary Differential Equations, (L. Weiss, ed.) Academic Press, New York, 1972.

14 E.W. Kamen, On an algebraic theory of systems defined by convolution operators, Math. Systems Theory 9 (1975) 57-74.

15 E.W. Kamen, An operator theory of linear functional differential equations, J. Differential Equations 27 (1978) 274-297.

16 R. Kwong and A. Willsky, Optimal filtering and filter stability of linear stochastic delay systems, IEEE Trans. Auto. Contr. AC-22 (1977), 196-201.

17 A. Lindquist, A theorem on duality between estimation and control for linear stochastic systems with time delay, J. Math. Anal. Appl. 37 (1972) 516-536.

18 A. Lindquist, Optimal control of linear stochastic systems with applications to time lag systems, Inform. Sci. 5 (1973), 81-126.

19 A. Lindquist, On feedback control of linear stochastic systems, SIAM J. Control, 11 (1973), 323-343.

20 A.S. Morse, Ring models for delay differential systems, Automatica 12 (1976), 529-531.

21 S.K. Mitter and R.B. Vintner, Filtering for linear stochastic hereditary differential systems, Intern. Symp. Control Theory, Numerical Methods, and Computer Systems Modelling, IRIA, Rocquencourt, France, June 1974.

22 D. Quillen, Projective modules over polynomial rings, Invent. Math. 36 (1976), 167-171.

23 R. Rishel, Necessary and sufficient dynamic programming conditions for continuous-time stochastic optimal control, SIAM J. Control 8 (1970), 559-571.

24 J.-P. Serre, Modules projectifs et espaces fibrés à fibre vectorielle, Sém. Dubreil-Pisot, no. 23, 1957/58.

25 E. Sontag, Linear systems over commutative rings: A survey, Ricerche Automatica 7 (1976), 1-34.

26 A.A. Suslin, Projective modules over a polynomial ring are free, Dokl. Akad. Nauk. S.S.S.R. 229 (1976) (Soviet Math. Dokl. 17 (1976), 1160-1164).

27 N.S. Williams and V. Zakian, A ring of delay operators with applications to delay-differential systems, SIAM J. Control and Optim. 15 (1977), 247-255.

28 W.M. Wonham, On pole assignment in multi-input controllable linear systems, IEEE Trans. Auto. Contr. AC-12 (1967), 660-665.

A NON-LINEAR MARTINGALE PROBLEM

Th. Eisele

Institut für Angewandte Mathematik
Im Neuenheimer Feld 294
D - 6900 Heidelberg

O. INTRODUCTION

In the present paper we give a proof for the existence and uniqueness of the solution of a martingale problem whose infinitesimal operator is non-linear on the basic space $\mathbb{R}^d$. In fact we treat the case of a non-degenerate diffusion process which has temporally Poisson distributed branching points. At these points the particles die out, creating simultanously a random number n=o,1,2,... of new particles which are again independently submitted to diffusion.
There is no other interaction between the particles.
Branching processes of that kind have been regarded since several years (cf. [3], [8]; [7] and [6]). So far the investigations were more concerned with the associated integral equations (called (S)- and (M)-equations in [3]), but not so much with a direct treatment of the infinitesimal operator, which is non-linear on the basic space $\mathbb{R}^d$, but - as is well known - may be "linearized" by using higher dimensional spaces.
The martingale approach, as presented here, is especially useful when one has to do with multiplicative transformations of these processes as it is the case in stochastic control theory. Actually, in a second paper we shall treat the control problem for branching diffusions in the spirit of [1] and [2].

1. NOTATIONS

Our basic space is $\mathbb{R}^d$. To regard several indiscernible particles in that space, we introduce in $(\mathbb{R}^d)^n$ the equivalence relation $\wedge$:

$(x_i)_{i<n} \wedge (x'_i)_{i<n}$ iff there is a permutation π of $n = \{o,1,2,\dots, n-1\}$ such that $x_i = x'_{\pi_i}$ for $i<n$.

Let $\hat{\mathbb{R}}^{d\,n} = (R^d)^n/_\wedge$ and

$$E = \{\gamma\} \cup \bigcup_{n=1}^{\infty} \hat{\mathbb{R}}^{dn} \cup \{\Gamma\} ,$$

where γ corresponds to extinction of the system and Γ to its explosion. $\langle x_i \rangle$ denotes the equivalence class of $(x_i)_{i<n} \in (\mathbb{R}^d)^n$ under $\wedge$.

If D is any topological space, then $\tilde{D} = D \cup \{\Delta_D\}$ where Δ_D is an extra, isolated point. For $h: D \to \mathbb{R}$ we set $h(\Delta_D) = 0$ without further comment.

If $f: \mathbb{R}^d \to \mathbb{R}$ is a real function, then define $\hat{f}: E \to \mathbb{R}$ and $\overline{f}: E \to \mathbb{R}$ by

$$\hat{f}(e) = \begin{cases} 1 & \text{if } e = \gamma \\ \prod_{i<n} f(x_i) & \text{if } e = \langle x_i \rangle_{i<n} \\ 0 & \text{if } e = \Gamma \end{cases}$$

and

$$\overline{f}(e) = \begin{cases} 0 & \text{if } e = \gamma \text{ or } \Gamma \\ \sum_{i<n} f(x_i) & \text{if } e = \langle x_i \rangle_{i<n} \end{cases}$$

If H_t is an operator on some functions $f: \mathbb{R}^d \to \mathbb{R}$, then let $\overline{H}_t$ be the operator on $\hat{f}: E \to \mathbb{R}$, defined by

$$\overline{H}_t \hat{f}(e) = \begin{cases} 0 & \text{if } e = \gamma \text{ or } \Gamma \\ \sum_{i<n} H_t f(x_i) \prod_{\substack{j<n \\ j \neq i}} f(x_j) & \text{if } e = \langle x_i \rangle_{i<n} \end{cases}$$

and $\operatorname{dom}(\overline{H}_t) = \{\hat{f}: E \to \mathbb{R},\ f \in \operatorname{dom}(H_t)\}$.

As usual let $\mathcal{D}(\mathbb{R}^+, E)$ denote the space of right continuous functions from $\mathbb{R}^+$ to E with left-hand limits, endowed with the Skorokhod metric.

Let

$$\Omega = \mathcal{C}(\mathbb{R}^+, \mathbb{R}^d) \quad , \quad M_s = \sigma\{x_r, r \geq s\}$$

where $x_t: \Omega \to \mathbb{R}^d$ is the usual projection, and

$$\hat{\Omega} = \{\hat{\omega} \in \mathcal{D}(\mathbb{R}^+, E);\ \text{if } \hat{x}_s(\hat{\omega}) \in \{\gamma, \Gamma\}, \text{ then } \hat{x}_t(\hat{\omega}) = \hat{x}_s(\hat{\omega}) \text{ for all } t \geq s\}$$

$$\hat{M}_s = \sigma\{\hat{x}_r;\ s \leq r\} \quad , \quad \hat{M}_s^t = \sigma\{\hat{x}_r,\ s \leq r \leq t\}$$

where $\hat{x}_t: \hat{\Omega} \to E$ is the projection on $\hat{\Omega}$.

Definition

We say that a family $(P_{s,e})_{(s,e)\in\mathbb{R}^+\times E}$ of probability measures on $\hat\Omega$ solves the martingale problem for the infinitesimal operator $(\bar H_t)_{t\in\mathbb{R}^+}$ if

(i) $(s,e) \longmapsto P_{s,e}(A)$ is Borel measurable on $\mathbb{R}^+\times E$ for all $A\in\hat{M}_s$

(ii) $P_{s,e}\{\hat\omega,\ \hat x(\hat\omega,s) = e\} = 1$

(iii) for all $\hat f \in \mathrm{dom}(\bar H_t)$

$$\hat f(\hat x_t) - \int_s^t \bar H_r \hat f(\hat x_r)\,dr \qquad \text{is a } P_{s,e}\text{-martingale}$$

with respect to $(\hat M_s^r)_{s,r\in\mathbb{R}^+}$.

2. EXISTENCE

Let us state the following assumptions:

(A_1) Let $0 \le \rho(s,x) \le M$ be a bounded, Borel measurable function on $\mathbb{R}^+\times\mathbb{R}^d$ and

$0 \le q_n(s,x) \le 1$ positive, Borel measurable functions for $n=0,2,3\ldots$

with

$$\sum_{n=0,2,3..} q_n(s,x) \equiv 1 \quad .$$

(A_2) Assume moreover, that $\sum_{n'\neq 1} q_{n'}(s,x)\cdot(n'-1) \le M' < \infty, (s,x)\in\mathbb{R}^+\times\mathbb{R}^d$.

Then we have the probability generating functional

$$F(s,x,z) = \sum_{n\neq 1} q_n(s,x)z^n$$

which for fixed (s,x) converges uniformly on $|z| \le 1$.

Let

$$q_1(s,x) \equiv -1$$

and $$G(s,x,z) = \rho(s,x)\sum_{n\geq 0} q_n(s,x)z^n \quad .$$

According to our notation we have for $e = \langle x_i\rangle_{i<n} \in E$, $f:\mathbb{R}^d \to [-1,+1]$.

$$\bar G_s \hat f(e) = \sum_{i<n} G(s,x_i,f(x_i))\cdot\prod_{\substack{j<n\\ j\neq i}} f(x_j) = \sum_{i<n}\left[\sum_{n'\geq 0}^{n'} \rho(s,x_i)q_{n'}(s,x_i)f(x_i)^{n'} \prod_{\substack{j<n\\ j\neq i}} f(x_j)\right] .$$

Theorem 1

Let $H = (H_t)$ be an infinitesimal operator, defined on some functions $f: \mathbb{R}^d \to \mathbb{R}$, $f \in \operatorname{dom}(H) \subseteq C_b(\mathbb{R}^d, \mathbb{R})$.

Let $(Q_{s,x})_{(s,x)\in\mathbb{R}^+\times\mathbb{R}^d}$ be a family of probability measures on (Ω, M_s), defining a Markov process, which solves the martingale problem for (H_t). Then, under the assumptions (A_1, A_2), there is a family of probability measures $(P_{s,e})_{(s,e)\in\mathbb{R}^+\times E}$ on $(\hat{\Omega}, \hat{M}_s)$, solving the martingale problem for $(\overline{H_t+G_t})$ with

$$\operatorname{dom}(\overline{H_t+G_t}) = \{\hat{f},\ f \in \operatorname{dom}(H_t);\ \|f\| \leq 1\} .$$

Proof:

For each $n \in \mathbb{N}$ we have the natural embedding $< >: \Omega^n \to \hat{\Omega}$ by

$$<\omega_i>_{i<n} = \left[t \longmapsto <x_t(\omega_i)>_{i<n}\right].$$

This allows us to define measures $(P^{(o)}_{s,e})_{(s,e)\in\mathbb{R}^+\times E}$ on $\mathcal{D}(\mathbb{R}^+, E)$ by

$$P^{(o)}_{s,\gamma} = \delta_{\underline{\gamma}} \quad , \quad P^{(o)}_{s,\Gamma} = \delta_{\underline{\Gamma}}$$

where $\underline{\gamma}$ (resp. $\underline{\Gamma}$) is the constant function with value γ (resp. Γ), and for $e = <x_i>_{i<n}$ let $P^{(o)}_{s,e}$ be the image measure of $\prod_{i<n} Q_{s,x_i}$ on Ω^n under $< >$.

Now define the perturbation measure $C_{s,e}$ on E by

$$C_{s,e} = \delta_e \quad \text{if} \quad e = \gamma \text{ or } \Gamma \quad \text{and for} \quad e = <x_i>_{i<n}$$

$$C_{s,e} = \sum_{i<n} \sum_{n'\neq 1} \rho(s,x_i)\, q_{n'}(s,x_i)\, \delta_{<e,n',x_i>}$$

where for $e = <x, x_1', \ldots, x_{n-1}'>$ we set $<e,n',x> = <\underbrace{x,\ldots,x}_{n'\text{-times}}, x_1', \ldots, x_{n-1}'>$.

Recursively we now get

$$P^{(k+1)}_{s,e}(A) = \int_{\hat{\Omega}} P^{(o)}_{s,e}(d\hat{\omega}) \int_s^\infty dr \exp\{-\int_s^r \overline{\rho}(r',\hat{x}_{r'}(\hat{\omega}))dr'\} \int_E C_{r,\hat{x}_{r-o}(\hat{\omega})}(de') \cdot$$

$$\cdot \left[\delta_{\hat{\omega}} \overset{r}{\otimes} P^{(k)}_{r,e'}(A) \right] ,$$

where $\delta_{\hat\omega} \overset{r}{\otimes} P^{(k)}_{r,e}$ is the unique measure on $\hat\Omega$ satisfying

$\delta_{\hat\omega} \overset{r}{\otimes} P^{(k)}_{r,e'}(A' \cap A'') = \delta_{\hat\omega}(A')\, P^{(k)}_{r,e'}(A'')$ for $A' \in \sigma\{\hat x_{r'}, r'<r\}, A'' \in \hat M_r$.

It is clear that $(s,e) \mapsto P^{(k)}_{s,e}(A)$ is $\mathcal{B}(\mathbb{R}^+ \times E)$-measurable for $A \in \hat M_s$.

Set $\tau_o \equiv s$ and

$$\tau^{(\hat\omega)}_{k+1} = \inf\{t > \tau_k(\hat\omega)\ ,\ \hat x_t(\hat\omega) \neq \hat x_{t-o}(\hat\omega)\}\ .$$

We shall show now that for $s \le t_1 < t_2$, $A \in \hat M_s^{t_1} = \sigma\{\hat x_r, s \le r \le t_1\}$ and $f \in \operatorname{dom} H$, $\|f\| \le 1$, $k \geq 1$ we have

$$E^{(k)}_{s,e}\left[1_A\Big(\hat f(\hat x_{t_2}) - \int_s^{t_2} \overline{(H_r + 1_{\{r<\tau_k\}} G_r)}\ \hat f(\hat x_r)dr \Big) \right] =$$

(1)

$$= E^{(k)}_{s,e}\left[1_A\Big(\hat f(\hat x_{t_1}) - \int_s^{t_1} \overline{(H_r + 1_{\{r<\tau_k\}} G_r)}\ \hat f(\hat x_r)dr\Big)\right]$$

where clearly $E^{(k)}_{s,e}$ means expectation with respect to $P^{(k)}_{s,e}$.

(1) is trivially satisfied if $e = \gamma$ or Γ . For $e \in E \setminus \{\gamma,\Gamma\}$ we first prove by induction $(k \geq 1)$

$$E^{(k)}_{s,e}\left[1_A\Big(1_{\{\tau_k > t_2\}} \hat f(\hat x_{t_2}) - \int_{t_1}^{t_2} 1_{\{\tau_k > r\}} \overline{(H_r + 1_{\{\tau_{k-1}>r\}} \rho(r)\cdot F_r)} \hat f(\hat x_r)dr\right]$$

(2)

$$= E^{(k)}_{s,e}\left[1_A\Big(1_{\{\tau_k > t_1\}} \cdot \hat f(\hat x_{t_1}) - \int_{t_2}^{t_2} 1_{\{\tau_k > r\}} \overline{\rho}(r,\hat x_r)\cdot \hat f(\hat x_r)dr\Big) \right] .$$

But first we need the following assertion: for $f \in \operatorname{dom} H \subseteq C_b(\mathbb{R}^d,\mathbb{R})$

(3) $\hat f(\hat x_t) - \int_s^t \overline{H_r}\ \hat f(\hat x_r)\ dr$ is a $P^o_{s,e}$ - martingale.

This follows with $a = t_2 - t_1$, $e = \langle x_i \rangle_{i<n}$ from:

$$E^{(o)}_{s,e}\left[1_A\Big(\int_{t_1}^{t_2} \overline{H_r}\ \hat f(\hat x_r)dr\Big)\right] = E^{(o)}_{s,e}\left[1_A\Big(\sum_{j=o}^{m-1} \int_{t_1+j\frac{\alpha}{m}}^{t_1+(j+1)\frac{\alpha}{m}} \overline{H_r}\ \hat f(\hat x_r)dr\Big)\right] =$$

$$= \lim_{m\to\infty} E_{s,e}^{(o)}\Big[1_A\Big(\sum_{j=o}^{m-1} \sum_{i<n} \big(\prod_{\ell<i} f(x_{\ell,t_1+j\frac{\alpha}{m}}) \prod_{\ell>i} f(x_{\ell,t_1+(j+1)\frac{\alpha}{m}}) \cdot \int_{t_1+j\frac{\alpha}{m}}^{t_1+(j+1)\frac{\alpha}{m}} H_r\, f(x_{i,r})dr\big)\Big)\Big] =$$

$$= \lim_{m\to\infty} E_{s,e}^{(o)}\Big[1_A\Big(\sum_{j=o}^{m-1} \sum_{i<n} \big(\prod_{\ell<i} f(x_{\ell,t_1+j\frac{\alpha}{m}})\cdot \prod_{\ell>i} f(x_{\ell,t_1+(j+1)\frac{\alpha}{m}})(f(x_{i,t_1+(j+1)\frac{\alpha}{m}}) - f(x_{i,t_1+j\frac{\alpha}{m}}))\big)\Big)\Big]$$

$$= E_{s,e}^{(o)}\Big[1_A\big(\hat{f}(\hat{x}_{t_2}) - \hat{f}(\hat{x}_{t_1})\big)\Big] \quad .$$

This shows (3).

Moreover, by the Feynman-Kac formula (see Lemma 2.1 in [9]) for

$$\varphi(t) = \hat{f}(\hat{x}_t) - \int_s^t \overline{H_r}\, \hat{f}(\hat{x}_r)dr \qquad \text{and}$$

$$\psi(t) = \exp\{- \int_s^t \overline{\rho}(r,\hat{x}_r)dr\}$$

we know that

(4) $\qquad \varphi(t)\cdot\psi(t) + \int_s^t \varphi(r)\cdot\psi(r)\cdot\overline{\rho}(r,\hat{x}_r)dr \qquad$ is a $P_{s,e}^{o}$-martingale.

Calculating this last expression yields

$$E_{s,e}^{(1)}\Big[1_{A\cap\{\tau_1>t_2\}}\big(\hat{f}(\hat{x}_{t_2})\big)\Big] = E_{s,e}^{(o)}\Big[1_{A\cap\{\tau_1>t_1\}}\cdot\exp\{- \int_{t_1}^{t_2} \overline{\rho}(r,\hat{x}_r)dr\}\cdot\hat{f}(\hat{x}_{t_2})\Big]$$

(5)

$$\underset{(4)}{=} E_{s,e}^{(1)}\Big[1_A\cdot\Big(1_{\{\tau_1>t_1\}}\hat{f}(\hat{x}_{t_1}) + \int_{t_1}^{t_2} 1_{\{\tau_1>r\}}\, \overline{H_r}\, \hat{f}(\hat{x}_r)dr - \int_{t_1}^{t_2} 1_{\{\tau_1>r\}}\, \overline{\rho}(r,\hat{x}_r)\, \hat{f}(\hat{x}_r)dr\Big)\Big]$$

which is (2) for $k = 1$.

For the induction step of (2) we note first

$$E_{s,e}^{(k+1)}\big(1_{A\cap\{\tau_{k+1}>t_2\}}\, \hat{f}(\hat{x}(t_2))\big) = E_{s,e}^{(k)}\Big[1_{A\cap\{\tau_k>t_2\}}\, \hat{f}(\hat{x}(t_2))\Big] +$$

$$+\ E_{s,e}^{(k+1)}\left[1_{A\cap\{\tau_k\le t_2<\tau_{k+1}\}}\,\hat f(\hat x(t_2))\right].$$

But

$$E_{s,e}^{(k+1)}\left[1_{A\cap\{\tau_k\le t_2<\tau_{k+1}\}}\,\hat f(\hat x(t_2))\right]=E_{s,e}^{(k)}\left[1_{A\cap\{\tau_k\le t_2\}}\exp\{-\int_{\tau_k}^{t_2}\bar\rho(r,\hat x_r)dr\}\hat f(\hat x_{t_2})\right]$$

$$=E_{s,e}^{(k)}\left[1_{A\cap\{\tau_k\le t_1\}}\cdot\exp\{-\int_{\tau_k}^{t_1}\bar\rho(r,\hat x_r)dr\}\,E_{t_1,\hat x_{t_1}}^{(o)}\left[\exp\{-\int_{t_1}^{t_2}\bar\rho(r,\hat x_r)dr\}\hat f(\hat x_{t_2})\right]\right]$$

$$+\ E_{s,e}^{(k)}\left[1_{A\cap\{t_1<\tau_k\le t_2\}}\,E_{\tau_k,\hat x_{\tau_k}}^{(o)}\left[\exp\{-\int_{\tau_k}^{t_2}\bar\rho(r,\hat x_r)dr\}\,\hat f(\hat x_{t_2})\right]\right]$$

$$\overset{(5)}{=}\ E_{s,e}^{(k+1)}\left[1_{A\cap\{\tau_k\le t_1\}}\left(1_{\{\tau_{k+1}>t_1\}}\hat f(\hat x_{t_1})+\int_{t_1}^{t_2}1_{\{\tau_{k+1}>r\}}\left(\bar H_r-\bar\rho(r,\hat x_r)\right)\hat f(\hat x_r)dr\right)\right]+$$

$$+\ E_{s,e}^{(k+1)}\left[1_{A\cap\{t_1<\tau_k\le t_2\}}\left(\hat f(\hat x_{\tau_k})+\int_{\tau_k}^{t_2}1_{\{\tau_{k+1}>r\}}(\bar H_r-\bar\rho(r,\hat x_r))\,\hat f(\hat x_r)dr\right)\right]$$

$$=E_{s,e}^{(k+1)}\left[1_{A\cap\{\tau_k\le t_1<\tau_{k+1}\}}\,\hat f(\hat x_{t_1})+1_{A\cap\{\tau_k\le t_1\}}\int_{t_1}^{t_2}1_{\{\tau_{k+1}>r\}}(\bar H_r-\bar\rho(r,\hat x_r))\hat f(\hat x_r)dr\right]$$

$$+\ E_{s,e}^{(k+1)}\left[1_{A\cap\{t_1<\tau_k\le t_2\}}\overline{(\rho_{\tau_k}\cdot F_{\tau_k})\hat f}(\hat x_{\tau_k-o})+1_{A\cap\{t_1\le\tau_k\le t_2\}}\int_{t_1}^{t_2}1_{\{\tau_{k+1}>r\ge\tau_k\}}\cdot\right.$$
$$\left.(\bar H_r-\bar\rho(r,\hat x_r))\hat f(\hat x_r)dr\right]$$

$$=E_{s,e}^{(k+1)}\left[1_{A\cap\{\tau_k\le t_1<\tau_{k+1}\}}\hat f(\hat x_{t_1})+1_A\int_{t_1}^{t_2}1_{\{\tau_{k+1}>r\ge\tau_k\}}(\bar H_r-\bar\rho(r,\hat x_r))\hat f(\hat x_r)dr\ +\right.$$

$$\left.+\ 1_A\int_{t_1}^{t_2}1_{\{\tau_k>r\ge\tau_{k-1}\}}\overline{(\rho_r\ F_r)}\,\hat f(\hat x_r)dr\right].$$

By induction hypothesis we have also

$$E_{s,e}^{(k)}\left[1_{A\cap\{\tau_k>t_2\}}\,\hat f(\hat x(t_2))\right]=E_{s,e}^{(k)}\left[1_{A\cap\{\tau_k>t_1\}}\,\hat f(\hat x_{t_1})\ +\right.$$

$$\left.+\ 1_A\int_{t_1}^{t_2}1_{\{\tau_k>r\}}\overline{(H_r+1_{\{\tau_{k-1}>r\}}\rho_rF_r)}\,\hat f(\hat x_r)dr-1_A\int_{t_1}^{t_2}1_{\{\tau_k>r\}}\bar\rho(r,\hat x_r)\hat f(\hat x_r)dr\right]$$

where we can replace $E^{(k)}_{s,e}$ by $E^{(k+1)}_{s,e}$. The last three equations together yield just equation (2) for $k+1$ instead of k, and thus the induction is complete. Furthermore we have for all $k \geq 1$

$$E^{(k)}_{s,e}\left[1_{A\cap\{t_1<\tau_k\leq t_2\}}\hat{f}(\hat{x}(t_2))\right] = E^{(k)}_{s,e}\left[1_{A\cap\{t_1<\tau_k\leq t_2\}}\left(\hat{f}(\hat{x}_{\tau_k}) + \int_{\tau_k}^{t_2} \overline{H}_r\hat{f}(\hat{x}_r)dr\right)\right]$$

(6)

$$= E^{(k)}_{s,e}\left[1_A \int_{t_1}^{t_2} 1_{\{\tau_k>r\geq\tau_{k-1}\}}\overline{(\rho_r F_r)\hat{f}}(\hat{x}_r)dr + 1_A \int_{t_1}^{t_2} 1_{\{r\geq\tau_k>t_1\}}\overline{H}_r\hat{f}(\hat{x}_r)dr\right]$$

as well as

(7) $$E^{(k)}_{s,e}\left[1_{A\cap\{\tau_k\leq t_1\}}\hat{f}(\hat{x}_{t_2})\right] \underset{(3)}{=} E^{(k)}_{s,e}\left[1_{A\cap\{\tau_k\leq t_1\}}\left(\hat{f}(\hat{x}_{t_1}) + \int_{t_1}^{t_2} \overline{H}_r\hat{f}(\hat{x}_r)dr\right)\right] .$$

Adding (2),(6) and (7) we receive (1).

Since by construction $P^{(k)}_{s,e}$ and $P^{(k+1)}_{s,e}$ agree on $M_s^{\tau_k}$ we have with $P^{(\infty)}_{s,e} = \lim_{k\to\infty} P^{(k)}_{s,e}$ a probability measure, well defined on $M_s^{<\tau_\infty} = \sigma\{\hat{x}_r,\ s \leq r < \tau_\infty\}$ where $\tau_\infty = \lim_{k\to\infty} \tau_k$. We set

$$P_{s,e} = \int_{\hat{\Omega}} \left(\delta_{\hat{\omega}} \overset{\tau_\infty}{\otimes} P_{\tau_\infty,\Gamma}\right) P^{(\infty)}_{s,e}(d\hat{\omega}) .$$

Now let us change $(q_n(s,x))_{n\neq 1}$ to $(q'_n(s,x))_{n\neq 1}$ by

$$q'_o = o\ ,\ q'_2 = q_o + q_2 \quad \text{and} \quad q'_j = q_j \quad \text{for } j \geq 3 .$$

We find by our assumption (A_2)

$$\sum_{n\neq 1} (n-1)\, q'_n(s,x) = \sum_{n\geq 2} (n-1)\, q_n(s,x) + q_o(s,x) \leq M .$$

In the same way as above we construct with respect to $(Q_{s,x},\rho(s,x),q'_n(s,x))$ a new probability measure $P'_{s,e}$ on $\hat{\Omega}$. But with probability 1 $P'_{s,e}$ does not have extinction of a particle without the generation of new ones, so

(8) $$P'_{s,e}\left(\#\hat{x}_{t_2} \geq \#\hat{x}_{t_1} \quad \text{for all } t_2 \geq t_1 \geq s\right) = 1$$

where $\#\hat{x}_t$ denotes the number of particles at time t . Moreover

(9) $P_{s,e}(\# \hat{x}_t \geq N) \leq P'_{s,e}(\# \hat{x}_t \geq N)$ for all $N \geq o$.

We now claim that for all $k \geq 1$

(10) $\# \hat{x}_t - \int_s^t M^2 \# \hat{x}_r \, dr$ is a $P'^{(k)}_{s,e}$- supermartingale.

This follows immediately from

$$E'^{(k)}_{s,e} \left(\# \hat{x}_{t+\Delta t} - \# \hat{x}_t \,\middle|\, \# \hat{x}_t = \ell \right) \leq \int_t^{t+\Delta t} \ell \cdot M \cdot \exp\{-\ell M(r-t)\} \cdot \left(\sum_{n \neq 1} E'^{(k)}_{s,e}(q'_n(s,\hat{x}_r)) \cdot (n-1) \right) dr + o(\Delta t)$$

$$\leq \ell M^2 \Delta t + o(\Delta t) .$$

But then we have

(11) $E'_{s,e}(\# \hat{x}_t) \leq \# e \exp(M^2(t-s))$.

From (8),(9) and (11) we deduce

$$P_{s,e}\left(\sup_{s \leq r \leq t} \# \hat{x}_r \geq N \right) \leq P'_{s,e}\left(\sup_{s \leq r \leq t} \# \hat{x}_r \geq N \right) = P'_{s,e}(\# \hat{x}_t \geq N)$$

$$\leq \# e \exp(M^2(t-s))/N .$$

Choose N_ε such that $\# e \exp(M^2(t-s))/N_\varepsilon \leq \varepsilon$. Then with $A = \{ \sup_{s \leq r \leq t} \# \hat{x}_r < N_\varepsilon \}$ we find

$$P_{s,e}(\{\tau_k \geq t\} \cap A) \geq (1-\varepsilon) \exp(-N_\varepsilon \cdot M(t-s)) \left(\sum_{j=o}^{k-1} \frac{(N_\varepsilon M (t-s))^j}{j!} \right) .$$

Hence for all k

$$P_{s,e}(\{\tau_k < t\}) \leq 1 - (1-\varepsilon) \exp(-N_\varepsilon M(t-s)) \left(\sum_{j=o}^{k-1} \frac{(N_\varepsilon M(t-s))^j}{j!} \right)$$

or $P_{s,e}(\{\tau_\infty < t\}) \leq \varepsilon$.

This shows $\tau_\infty = \infty$ $P_{s,e}$ - a.e. and thus $P_{s,e}$ solves the martingale problem for all t .

Remark:

Even without the assumption (A_2) the above constructed probability measure $P_{s,e}$ solves the martingale problem for functions $f \in \operatorname{dom} H$ with $\|f\| < 1$. But then we can not guarantee that the explosion time

τ_∞ is a.s. infinite.

Let us state furthermore the following assumption:

$$(A_3)\quad \begin{cases} \text{Let} \quad L_t = \sum_{i=o}^{d-1} b_i(t,x)\frac{\partial}{\partial x_i} + \sum_{i,j=o}^{d-1} d_{ij}(t,x)\frac{\partial^2}{\partial x_i \partial x_j} \\ \text{where} \quad b(t,x) = (b_i(t,x)) \in \mathbb{R}^d \quad \text{is measurable and bounded} \\ \text{and} \quad d(t,x) = (d_{ij}(t,x)) \quad \text{is a continuous and positive definite} \\ \qquad\qquad \text{function on } \mathbb{R}^+ \times \mathbb{R}^d . \end{cases}$$

Then the above theorem, together with the well-known results of Stroock-Varadhan [10] yields

Corollary.

Under the assumption (A_1-A_3) there exists a measurable family of probability measures $(P_{s,e})_{(s,e)\in\mathbb{R}^+\times E}$ which solves the martingale problem for the operator $\overline{L_t + G_t}$ and

$$\text{dom}\,(\overline{L_t + G_t}) = \{\hat{f},\ f \in C^2(\mathbb{R}^d),\ \|f\| \leq 1\} .$$

3. UNIQUENESS

We continue with the definitions and assumptions of the last section. Especially, $(Q_{s,x})_{(s,x)\in\mathbb{R}^+\times\mathbb{R}^d}$ is the family of probability measures on $\Omega = C(\mathbb{R}^+,\mathbb{R}^d)$, solving the martingale problem for the infinitesimal operator

$$L_t = \sum_{i=o}^{d-1} b_i(t,x)\frac{\partial}{\partial x_i} + \sum_{i,j=o}^{d-1} d_{ij}(t,x)\frac{\partial^2}{\partial x_i \partial x_j}$$

on $C^2(\mathbb{R}^d)$. By [10] we know that under the assumption (A_3) $(Q_{s,x})$ is the unique solution of the martingale problem for L_t .

Let $(R_{s,x})_{(s,x)\in\mathbb{R}^+\times\mathbb{R}^d}$ be the subprocess of the Markov process $(Q_{s,x})$ with respect to the multiplicate functional

$$\alpha_s^t(\omega) = \exp\left\{-\int_s^t \rho(r, x(\omega, r))dr\right\}$$

i.e.

$$R_{s,x}(f(x_t)) = \int_\Omega \alpha_s^t(\omega)\cdot f(x(\omega,t))\; Q_{s,x}(d\omega) \quad .$$

It is well known, that $(R_{s,x})$ solves the martingale problem for

$$M_t\; f(x) = L_t\; f(x) - \rho(t,x)\; f(x) \qquad , \; f \in C^2(\mathbb{R}^d) \; ,$$

which follows also by the Feynman-Kac formula.
Applying the multiplicate functional $(\alpha_s^t)^{-1}$ to $(R_{s,x})$ yields a solution of the martingale problem for L_t , hence $(Q_{s,x})$ by the uniqueness theorem. This shows, that

$(R_{s,x})$ is the unique solution of the martingale problem for M_t .

We regard the same operators in higher dimensions. Let for $n \geq 1$ the operator

$$\tilde{L}_t f(x_o,\ldots,x_{n-1}) = \sum_{\ell=o}^{n-1} \Big(\sum_{i=o}^{d-1} b_i(t,x_\ell)\frac{\partial}{\partial x_{\ell i}} f(x_o,\ldots,x_{n-1}) + \sum_{i,j=o}^{d-1} d_{ij}(t,x_\ell)\frac{\partial^2}{\partial x_{\ell i}\partial x_{\ell j}} f(x_o,\ldots,x_{n-1})\Big)$$

and

$$\tilde{M}_t\; f(x_o,\ldots,x_{n-1}) = \tilde{L}_t\; f(x_o,\ldots,x_{n-1}) - \Big(\sum_{\ell=o}^{n-1} \rho(t,x_\ell)\Big) f(x_o,\ldots,x_{n-1}) .$$

Again we have

<u>Lemma 1</u>

(i) The family $\Big(\prod_{\ell=o}^{n-1} Q_{s,x_\ell}\Big)_{(s,(x_o,\ldots,x_{n-1}))\in\mathbb{R}^+\times\mathbb{R}^{d\cdot n}}$ of probability measures on $\Omega^n = C(\mathbb{R}^+,\mathbb{R}^{d\cdot n})$ in the unique solution of the martingale problem for $\tilde{L}_t$.

(ii) The family $\Big(\prod_{\ell=o}^{n-1} R_{s,x_\ell}\Big)_{(s,(x_o,\ldots,x_{n-1}))\in\mathbb{R}^+\times\mathbb{R}^{d\cdot n}}$ of submeasures on Ω^n is the unique solution of the martingale problem for $\tilde{M}_t$.

We want to deduce the same uniqueness result also for the factorized space $\hat{\mathbb{R}}^{d\cdot n}$ and the infinitesimal operators $\bar{L}_t$ and

$$\overline{M}_t \hat{f}<x_0,\ldots,x_{n-1}> = \overline{L}_t \hat{f}<x_0,\ldots,x_{n-1}> + \Big(\sum_{\ell=0}^{n-1} \rho(t,x_\ell)\Big)\cdot \hat{f}<x_0,\ldots,x_{n-1}> ,$$

$f \in C_b^2(\mathbb{R}^{d\cdot n})$.

Let us first remark that both $C(\mathbb{R}^+,\mathbb{R}^{d\cdot n})$ and $C(\mathbb{R}^+,\hat{\mathbb{R}}^{d\cdot n})$, endowed with the topology of uniform convergence on compact sets, are polish and the mapping

$$< > : \Omega^n = C(\mathbb{R}^+,\mathbb{R}^{d\cdot n}) \longrightarrow C(\mathbb{R}^+,\hat{\mathbb{R}}^{d\cdot n})$$

with $<\omega_0,\ldots,\omega_{n-1}> = [t \mapsto <x(\omega_0,t),\ldots,x(\omega_{n-1},t)>]$

is continuous.

For $(s,e) = (s,<x_0,\ldots,x_{n-1}>) \in \mathbb{R}^+ \times \hat{\mathbb{R}}^{d\cdot n}$ let

$Q_{s,e}$ be the image measure of $\big(\prod_{\ell<n} Q_{s,x_\ell}\big)$ on Ω^n under $< >$

and $R_{s,e}$ the image measure of $\big(\prod_{\ell<n} R_{s,x_\ell}\big)$.

<u>Lemma 2</u>

(i) The family $(Q_{s,e})_{(s,e)\in\mathbb{R}^+\times\hat{\mathbb{R}}^{d\cdot n}}$ of probability measures on $C(\mathbb{R}^+,\hat{\mathbb{R}}^{d\cdot n})$ is the unique solution of the martingale problem for $\overline{L}_t$.

(ii) The family $(R_{s,e})_{(s,e)\in\mathbb{R}^+\times\hat{\mathbb{R}}^{dn}}$ of submeasures on $C(\mathbb{R}^+,\hat{\mathbb{R}}^{d\cdot n})$ is the unique solution of the martingale problem for $\overline{M}_t$.

<u>Proof:</u> As above (ii) follows from (i) by an argument about multiplicative functionals. For (i), we restrict ourselves to the case $n=2$.

Starting from any solution $(Q'_{s,<x_0,x_1>})$ of the martingale problem for $\overline{L}_t$ on $C(\mathbb{R}^+,\hat{\mathbb{R}}^{d\cdot 2})$ we can construct a solution $(Q_{s,(x_0,x_1)})$ of martingale problem for $\tilde{L}_t$ on Ω^2 .

Set $\tau_s<\omega_0,\omega_1> = \inf\{t\geq s;\ <x(\omega_0,t),x(\omega_1,t)> = <x(\omega_0,t),x(\omega_0,t)>\}$, $<\omega_0,\omega_1>\in C(\mathbb{R}^+,\hat{\mathbb{R}}^{d2})$.

Now for $(x_0,x_1) \in \mathbb{R}^{d2}$, $x_0 \neq x_1$, there is a unique and bijective function

(x_o,x_1): $\hat{C}_{<x_o,x_1>} := \{<\omega_o,\omega_1> \upharpoonright [s,\ \tau_s<\omega_o,\omega_1>],\ <x(\omega_o,s),x(\omega_1,s)> = <x_o,x_1>\}$

$$\longrightarrow\ C_{(x_o,x_1)} := \{(\omega_o,\omega_1) \upharpoonright [s,\tau_s<\omega_o,\omega_1>],(\omega_o,\omega_1) \in \Omega^2,(x(\omega_o,s),x(\omega_1,s))=(x_o,x_1)\}$$

with $^{(x_o,x_1)}<\omega_o,\omega_1> = (\omega_o,\omega_1)$ for $(\omega_o,\omega_1) \in C_{(x_o,x_1)}$

and $^{(x_o,x_1)}<x(\omega_o,s),x(\omega_1,s)> = (x_o,x_1)$.

By that, we define $(Q_{s,(x_o,x_1)})$ by the following formula*), where $s=t_o<t_1<..<t_{k-1}<t_k=\infty$ and f_i,g_i $(i\leq k)$ are bounded measurable functions on $\mathbb{R}^d$ with $f_k=g_k=1$:

$$E_{Q_{s,(x_o,x_1)}}\Big(\prod_{j<k}(f_j,g_j)(x(\omega_o,t_j),x(\omega_1,t_j))\Big) =$$

$$\int_{(\mathbb{R}^+,\hat{\mathbb{R}}^{d2})}\sum_{j<k}\Big(1_{\{t_j\leq\tau_s<t_{j+1}\}}<\omega_o,\omega_1>\prod_{i<j}(f_i,g_i)\ ^{(x_o,x_1)}<x(\omega_o,t_i),x(\omega_1,t_i)> \cdot$$

$$\cdot\ \prod_{i\geq j}\frac{(f_i,g_i)+(g_i,f_i)}{2}<x(\omega_o,t_i),x(\omega_1,t_i)>\Big)\ Q'_{s,<x_o,x_1>}(d<\omega_o,\omega_1>).$$

We first remark that

$$E_{Q_{s,(x_o,x_1)}}\Big(\prod_{j<k}(f_j,f_j)(x(\omega_o,t_j),x(\omega_1,t_j))\Big)=E_{Q'_{s,<x_o,x_1>}}\Big(\prod_{j<k}(f_j,f_j)<x(\omega_o,t_j),x(\omega_1,t_j)>\Big).$$

Thus $Q'_{s,<x_o,x_1>}$ is the image of $Q_{s,(x_o,x_1)}$ under $<\ >$.

To show that $Q_{s,(x_o,x_1)}$ is a solution of the martingale problem for $\tilde{L}_t$, let $s\leq t_1\leq t_2, f,g \in C_b^2(\mathbb{R}^+,\mathbb{R}^d)$ and $A \in \sigma\{(x(\omega_o,r),x(\omega_1,r));\ r\leq t_1\}$. Then

$$E_{Q_{s,(x_o,x_1)}}\Big(1_A\Big[(f,g)(x(\omega_o,t_2),x(\omega_1,t_2))-\int_{t_1}^{t_2}\tilde{L}_r(f,g)(x(\omega_o,r),x(\omega_1,r))dr\Big]\Big) =$$

$$= E_{Q_{s,(x_o,x_1)}}\Big(1_{A\cap\{\tau_s\leq t_2\}}\Big[\frac{(f,g)+(g,f)}{2}<x(\omega_o,t_2),x(\omega_1,t_2)> -$$

$$-\int_{\tau_s\vee t_1}^{t_2}\bar{L}_r\Big(\frac{(f,g)+(g,f)}{2}\Big)<x(\omega_o,r),x(\omega_1,r)>dr\Big] +$$

*) For $f:A\to\mathbb{R}$ and $g:B\to\mathbb{R}$ we set $(f,g):A\times B\to\mathbb{R}$: $(f,g)(a,b) = f(a)\cdot g(b)$.

$$+ \ 1_{A\cap\{\tau_s\le t_2\}}\left[\int_{t_1}^{\tau_1\vee t_1}\tilde{L}_r(f,g)^{(x_o,x_1)}<x(\omega_o,r),x(\omega_1,r)>dr\right]$$

$$+ \ 1_{A\cap\{\tau_s>t_2\}}\left[(f,g)^{(x_o,x_1)}<x(\omega_o,t_2),x(\omega_1,t_2)> - \int_{t_1}^{t_2}\tilde{L}_r(f,g)^{(x_o,x_1)}<x(\omega_o,r),x(\omega_1,r)>dr\right]\Big)$$

$$= E_{Q_s,(x_o,x_1)}\Big(1_A\Big[(f,g)^{(x_o,x_1)}<x(\omega_o,t_2\wedge(\tau_s<\omega_o,\omega_1>\vee t_1)),x(\omega_1,t_2\wedge(\tau_s<\omega_o,\omega_1>\vee t_1))> +$$

$$+ \int_{t_1}^{t_2\wedge(\tau_s<\omega_o,\omega_1>\vee t_1)}\tilde{L}_r(f,g)^{(x_o,x_1)}<x(\omega_o,r),x(\omega_1,r)>dr\Big]\Big) \ .$$

Now for every point $(y_o,y_1)\in\mathbb{R}^{d2}$, $y_o\neq y_1$ there exists a symmetric function $h\in C_b^2(\mathbb{R}^+,\mathbb{R}^{d2})$ with $h=(f,g)$ in a neighborhood of (y_o,y_1). But then

$$\tilde{L}_r(f,g)(y_o,y_1) = \overline{L}_t\ h<y_o,y_1> \ .$$

By that, the martingale problem for $\overline{L}_t$, solved by $Q'_{s,<x_o,x_1>}$, the equality of $Q_{s,(x_o,x_1)}$ and $Q'_{s,<x_o,x_1>}$ on symmetric events and by the fact, that τ_1 is a predictable stopping time, the last expression above is equal to

$$E_{Q_{s,(x_o,x_1)}}\Big(1_A\Big[(f,g)^{(x_o,x_1)}<x(\omega_o,t_1),\ x(\omega_1,t_1)>\Big]\Big) \ .$$

Thus $(Q_{s,(x_o,x_1)})$ solves the martingale problem for $\tilde{L}_t$ and by lemma 1 $Q_{s,(x_o,x_1)} = \prod_{i=o,1} Q_{s,x_i}$ on Ω^2. Therefore $Q'_{s,<x_o,x_1>} = Q_{s,<x_o.x_1>}$ and the proof is complete.

We now come to the main result of this section.

<u>Theorem 2</u>

Under the assumption (A_1), (A_3) and:

(A_4) there exists m_o such that $q_\ell(s,x)=o$ for all $\ell>m_o,(s,x)\in\mathbb{R}^+\times\mathbb{R}^d$, the martingale problem on $\hat{\Omega}$ for the infinitesimal operator

$$\overline{L_t+G_t} \quad \text{with} \quad \mathrm{dom}(\overline{L_t+G_t}) = \{\hat{f}:E\to\mathbb{R},\ f\in C^2(\mathbb{R}^d),\ \|f\|\le 1\}$$

has a unique solution.

Proof:

Let $(P'_{s,e})$ and $(P''_{s,e})$ $((s,e) \in \mathbb{R}^+ \times E)$ be two solutions of the above martingale problem.

For $e = \langle x_0,\dots,x_{n-1}\rangle \in \hat{\mathbb{R}}^{dn}$, $s \leq t$, and $f \in \mathrm{dom}(\overline{L_t+G_t})$ we first want to show that $E^{P'_{s,e}}(\hat{f}(\hat{x}_t)) = E^{P''_{s,e}}(\hat{f}(\hat{x}_t))$.

Let $\tau_{s,e}(\hat{\omega}) = \inf\{t > s;\ \hat{x}(\hat{\omega},t) \notin \hat{\mathbb{R}}^{dn}\}$ and we shall suppress the subscript s,e. Then

$$\left(1_{\hat{\mathbb{R}}^{dn}}\cdot\hat{f}\right)(\hat{x}_{t\wedge\tau}) - \int_s^{t\wedge\tau} 1_{\hat{\mathbb{R}}^{dn}}(\hat{x}_r)\left(\overline{L}_r\ \hat{f}(\hat{x}_r) - \overline{\rho}(r,\hat{x}_r)\hat{f}(\hat{x}_r)\right)dr$$

is a martingale w.r.t. $P'_{s,e}$ and $P''_{s,e}$. With the equality

$$\left(1_{\hat{\mathbb{R}}^{dn}}\cdot\hat{f}\right)(\hat{x}_{t\wedge\tau}) = \hat{f}(\hat{x}_t)\cdot 1_{\{t<\tau\}}$$

we receive by lemma 2 for $s \leq t_0 < t_1 < \dots < t_{k-1}$ and bounded measurable functions $f_i\,(i<k)$

$$(1)\quad E^{P'_{s,e}}\left[\prod_{i<k}\hat{f}_i(\hat{x}_{t_i})\cdot 1_{\{t_{k-1}<\tau\}}\right] = E^{P''_{s,e}}\left[\prod_{i<k}\hat{f}_i(\hat{x}_{t_i})\cdot 1_{\{t_{k-1}<\tau\}}\right] =$$

$$= E^{R_{s,e}}\left[\prod_{i<k}\hat{f}_i(\hat{x}_{t_i})\right] = E^{Q_{s,e}}\left[\exp\left\{-\int_s^{t_{k-1}}\overline{\rho}(r,\hat{x}(r))dr\right\}\cdot\prod_{i<k}\hat{f}_i(\hat{x}_{t_i})\right]$$

where the last two equalities can also be regarded as the definition of a submeasure on $\hat{M}_s^{<\tau}$.

On the other hand for measurable f with $\|f\| \leq 1$

$$\left(1_{E\setminus\hat{\mathbb{R}}^{dn}}\cdot\hat{f}\right)(\hat{x}_{t\wedge\tau}) - \int_s^{t\wedge\tau}\sum_{\substack{i<n\\ n'\neq 1}}\left(\rho(r,x_i(r))\,q_{n'}(r,x_i(r))\,f^{n'}(x_i(r))\prod_{\substack{j<n\\ j\neq i}}f(x_j(r))\right)dr$$

is a martingale w.r.t. $P'_{s,e}$ and $P''_{s,e}$. Hence

$$(2)\quad E^{P'_{s,e}}\left(1_{\{t\geq\tau\}}\hat{f}(\hat{x}_\tau)\right) \underset{(1)}{=} \int_s^t E^{Q_{s,e}}\left[\exp\left\{-\int_s^r\overline{\rho}(r',\hat{x}(r'))dr'\right\}\cdot\right.$$

$$\left.\cdot\left[\sum_{\substack{i<n\\ n'\neq 1}}\rho(r,x_i(r))q_{n'}(r,x_i(r))f^{n'}(x_i(r))\prod_{\substack{j<n\\ j\neq i}}f(x_j(r))\right]\right]dr$$

$$\underset{(1)}{=} E^{P''_{s,e}}\left(1_{\{t\geq\tau\}}\hat{f}(\hat{x}_\tau)\right) \quad .$$

Regarding the regular conditional probability $P'_{s,e}(\ |M_s^\tau)(\hat{\omega})$ as a function of $\hat{\omega}\restriction[s,\tau]$ we get from (2)

$$(3)\quad E^{P'_{s,e}}\left(1_{\{t\geq\tau\}}\hat{f}(\hat{x}_t)\right) = E^{P'_{s,e}}\left(1_{\{t\geq\tau\}}E^{P'_{s,e}}\left(\hat{f}(\hat{x}_t)|M_s^\tau\right)(\hat{\omega}\restriction[s,\tau])\right)$$

$$\underset{(2)}{=} \int_s^t \int_{C(\mathbb{R}^+,\hat{\mathbb{R}}^{dn})} \exp\{-\int_s^r \bar{\rho}(r',\hat{x}(\tilde{\omega},r'))dr'\}\cdot\Big[\sum_{\substack{i<n\\ n'\neq 1}} \rho(r,x_i(\tilde{\omega},r))\cdot q_{n'}(r,x_i(\tilde{\omega},r))$$

$$\cdot E^{P'_{s,e}}\left[\hat{f}(\hat{x}_t)|M_s^\tau\right](\tilde{\omega}\restriction[s,r]\cup(r,\langle x_o(\tilde{\omega},r),..,\underbrace{x_i(\tilde{\omega},r),..,x_i(\tilde{\omega},r)}_{n'\text{ times}},..,x_{n-1}(\tilde{\omega},r)\rangle))\Big] Q_{s,e}(d\tilde{\omega})dr \; .$$

The same for $P''_{s,e}$. For $s\leq t$, we define

$$u(s,n,t) = \sup \left| E^{P'_{s,e}}\left(\hat{f}(\hat{x}_t)\right) - E^{P''_{s,e}}\left(f(x_t)\right)\right|$$

where the supremum runs over all $(P'_{s,e}),(P''_{s,e})$, solutions of the martingale problem for $\overline{L_t+G_t}$ on $\hat{\Omega}$ starting from (s,e), and $e\in\hat{\mathbb{R}}^{d\cdot n}$.

Of course $o\leq u(s,n,t)\leq 1$ and $u(s,o,t)\equiv o$.

Reflecting, that $P'_{s,e}(\ |M_s^\tau)(\hat{\omega}\restriction[s,\tau])$ is a solution of the martingale problem for $\overline{L_t+G_t}$ on $\hat{\Omega}$ starting from $(\tau(\hat{\omega}),x(\hat{\omega},\tau(\hat{\omega})))$, we receive from (1) and (3)

$$(4)\quad u(s,n,t)\leq \int_s^t \int_{C(\mathbb{R}^+,\hat{\mathbb{R}}^{dn})} \exp\{-\int_s^r \bar{\rho}(r',\hat{x}(\tilde{\omega},r'))dr'\}\cdot$$

$$\cdot\Big[\sum_{i<n}\rho(r,x_i(\tilde{\omega},r))\sum_{h'\neq 1} q_{n'}(r,x_i(\tilde{\omega},r))\cdot u(r,h+n'-1,t)\Big]Q_{s,e}(d\tilde{\omega})dr \quad .$$

We define $u^{(o)}(s,n,m,t)\equiv 1$ and for $k\geq 1$

$$(5)\quad u^{(k)}(s,n,m,t) = 1 - e^{-Mn(t-s)}\sum_{i=o}^{k-1}\frac{1}{i!}\frac{n}{m}\cdot\ldots\cdot\left(\frac{n}{m}+i-1\right)\left(1-e^{-nM(t-s)}\right)^i$$

Since

$$e^{nM(t-s)} = \left(1-(1-e^{-mM(t-s)})\right)^{-\frac{n}{m}} = 1+\sum_{i=1}^{\infty}\frac{1}{i!}\frac{n}{m}\left(\frac{n}{m}+1\right)\cdot\ldots\cdot\left(\frac{n}{m}+i-1\right)\left(1-e^{-mM(t-s)}\right)^i$$

we have

$$(6)\qquad u^{(k)}(s,n,m,t)\searrow o \qquad \text{for } k\to\infty \; .$$

Next we claim for $k \geq o$

(7) $$u^{(k+1)}(s,n,m,t) = \int_s^t e^{-Mn(r-s)} \, Mn \, u^{(k)}(r,n+m,m,t)\,dr \quad .$$

But this is easily shown by induction. Now, it is not difficult to check that $u^{(k)}(s,n,m,t)$ is decreasing in k and s and increasing in n and m. This gives us together with (A_4)

(8) $$\int_s^t \int_{C(\mathbb{R}^+,\mathbb{R}^{dn})} \exp\{-\int_s^r \rho(r',\hat{x}(\tilde{\omega},r'))dr'\} \Big[\sum_{i<n} \rho(r,x_i(\tilde{\omega},r)) \sum_{n \neq 1} q_n(r,x_i(\tilde{\omega},r)) \, u^{(k)}(r,n+n-1,m_o,t) \Big] \, Q_{s,e}(d\tilde{\omega})dr$$

$$\leq \int_s^t e^{-M\,n(r-s)} \, Mn \, u^{(k)}(r,n+m_o,m_o,t)\,dr$$

$$\underset{(7)}{=} \quad u^{(k+1)}(s,\, n,\, m_o,\, t) \quad .$$

Since $u(s,n,t) \leq u^{(o)}(s,n,m_o,t) \equiv 1$ ist follows from (8) that

$$u(s,n,t) \leq u^{(k)}(s,n,m_o,t) \quad \text{for all } k \text{ , hence by (6)}$$

$$u(s,n,t) \equiv o \; .$$

This shows $E^{P'_{s,e}}(\hat{f}(\hat{x}_t)) = E^{P''_{s,e}}(\hat{f}(\hat{x}_t))$.

By the same argument we can show that the regular conditional expectations are equal:

$$E^{P'_{s,e}}(\hat{f}(\hat{x}_{t_2})|\hat{M}_s^{t_1}) = E^{P''_{s,e}}(\hat{f}(\hat{x}_{t_2})|\hat{M}_s^{t_1}) \qquad (P'_{s,e}+P''_{s,e}) \text{ - a.s.}.$$

Hence $$E^{P'_{s,e}}\Big(\prod_{i<k} \hat{f}_i(\hat{x}_{t_i}) \Big) = E^{P''_{s,e}}\Big(\prod_{i<k} \hat{f}_i(\hat{x}_{t_i}) \Big)$$

for $s \leq t_o < t_1 < \ldots < t_{k-1}$ and $\|f_i\| \leq 1$ $(i<k)$.

This completes the proof of theorem 2.

As a direct consequence of theorem 2 we have

Corollary.

Under the assumptions (A_1)-(A_4) the unique solution $(P_{s,e})_{(s,e)\in\mathbb{R}^+\times E}$ of the martingale problem for $\overline{L_t+G_t}$ is a strong Markov process.

REFERENCES

1. Bismut, J.-M.: Théorie probabiliste du contrôle des diffusions. Mem.Amer.math.Soc. 163, Providence, 1976.

2. Bismut, J.-M.: Control of Jump Processes and Applications. Bull.Soc.math.France 106, 25-60, (1978).

3. Ikeda, N., Nagasawa, M. and Watanabe, S.: Branching Marcov Processes I - III. J.Math.Kyoto Univ. 8, 233-278 and 365-410, (1968); 9, 95-160 (1969).

4. Jacod, J.: Multivariate Point Processes: Predictable Projection, Radon-Nikodym Derivatives, Representation of Martingales. Z.Wahrscheinlichkeitstheorie verw.Gebiete 31, 235-253 (1975).

5. Jacod, J.: Calcul Stochastique et Problèmes de Martingales. (to appear in Lecture Notes in Mathematics, Berlin, Heidelberg, New-York: Springer).

6. Nagasawa, M.: Basic Models of Branching Processes. ISI NewDelhi(1977).

7. Silverstein, M.L.: Markov Processes with Creation of Particles. Z.Wahrscheinlichkeitstheorie verw.Gebiete 9, 235-257 (1968).

8. Skorokhod, A.V.: Branching Diffusion Processes. Theory Prob.Appl. 8, 492-497 (1964).

9. Stroock, D.W.: Diffusion Processes Associated with Lévy Generators. Z.Wahrscheinlichkeitstheorie verw.Gebiete 32, 209-244 (1975).

10. Stroock, D.W. and Varadhan, S.R.S.: Diffusion Processes with Continuous Coefficients I,II. Commun. Pure Appl. Math. XXII, 345-400 and 479-530 (1969).

PATHWISE CONSTRUCTION OF RANDOM VARIABLES AND FUNCTION SPACE INTEGRALS

A Ferroni, G S. Goodman, A. Moro

Istituto Matematico "U. Dini"

Florence - Italy

1) Introductory remarks, notation, and statement of results.

Consider the initial value problem

(1) $$\dot{x} = f(t, x, u(t)) \qquad t \geq 0$$

(2) $$x(0) = x^o$$

where the "state" variable x ranges over the real line $\mathbb{R}$, the "input" u is a real valued function defined on some interval $[0, T]$ and f is a real valued function defined on $[0, T] \times \mathbb{R} \times \mathbb{R}$.

The most obvious stochastic version of the initial value problem (1), (2) is obtained by assuming that the input u is a random function and that the initial state x^o is a random variable. The solution should then be a random process.

Following Loève ([1] pp. 163 ff) we can define a random function in different ways. More precisely a random function y in $[0, T]$ is

(i) a function on $[0, T]$ to a space R of random variables $y_t(\omega)$ on some probability space $(\Omega, \mathfrak{F}, P)$;

(ii) a measurable function on $(\Omega, \mathfrak{F}, P)$ to a space of sample paths, i. e. of functions $y_\omega(t)$ of $[0, T]$;

(iii) a function on $[0, T] \times \Omega$ to $\mathbb{R}$ whose sections $y(\cdot) = (y(t, \omega), \omega \in \Omega)$ at every t are random variables.

We define y to be almost surely (a. s.) continuous at t iff

(3) $$\mathbb{P}(\{\omega : \lim_{s \to t} y_s(\omega) = y_t(\omega)\}) = 1$$

y is stochastically continuous at t iff

(4) $$\lim_{s \to t} \mathbb{P}(\{\omega: y_t(\omega) - y_s(\omega) > \varepsilon\}) = 0$$

When y_s does not converge a. s. to y_t as $s \to t$, we say that t is fixed discontinuity point of y. Remark that a. s. continuity of y means no fixed discontinuity points.

Now suppose that we insert the random function u into (1) and decide to integrate the resulting differential equation along sample paths. This means that we fix ω and consider the initial value problem

(5) $$\dot{x}_\omega(t) = f(t, x_\omega(t), u_\omega(t))$$

(6) $$x_\omega(0) = x_\omega^o.$$

Notice that, even for a continuous function f, the right-hand side of (5) is only going to be measurable in t. We therefore must decide what we mean by a solution to (5). If we follow Carathéodory [2], we shall say that $x_\omega(t)$ is a solution to (5) if it is absolutely continuous in t and satisfies (5) a. e..

Under what conditions on f will a Carathéodory solution of (5), (6) exist? Carathéodory made the following assumptions

1. f is measurable in t for every fixed x;
2. f is continuous in x for every fixed t in $0, T$;
3. f is dominated in modulus by a summable function M of t in $0, T$

(7) $$|f(t, x, u(t))| \leq M(t) \in \mathcal{L}_1([0, T])$$

He then proved that under these conditions, the initial value problem (5), (6) can be transformed into the integral equation

$$x_\omega(t) = x_\omega^o + \int_0^t f(s, x_\omega(s), u_\omega(s))\, ds$$

and that the equation (8) possesses at least one solution. Therefore, by differentiation, the initial value problem (3), (4) always possesses a Carathéodory solution.

It was observed later on that the same conclusion holds when (7) is weakened to

(9) $$|f(t, x, u(t))| \leq M(t)|x| + N(t)$$

where M(t) and N(t) are $\mathcal{L}_1$ - functions ([3] p 94).

In this paper we shall adopt Carathéodory's approach and prove the following theorem.

Theorem Suppose that, for each fixed $\omega \in \Omega$, x_ω is a Carathéodory solution of the initial value problem

(5) $$\dot{x}_\omega(t) = f(t, x_\omega(t), u_\omega(t)) \quad \text{a. e.}$$

(6) $$x_\omega(0) = x_\omega^o$$

where f is measurable in t, uniformly continuous in (x, u) and satisfies the bound

(9) $$|f(t, x, u)| \leq M(t)|x| + N(t)$$

where M, N are non negative $\mathcal{L}_1$ - functions Suppose further that the random function $u_\omega(t)$ is stochastically continuous. Then there is a set of t of full measure for which $\dot{x}$ exists in probability and satisfies (5). Moreover, if u has no fixed points of discontinuity, the derivative exists and satisfies (5) a. s. for each such t.

We remark that even under Carathéodory hypotheses, point continuity is no totally lacking We have in fact the following theorem, which in an equivalent formulation, was proved by Scorza - Dragoni in 1948 [4], v;. Goodman [5].

Scorza - Dragoni's theorem

If f is measurable in t and continuous in (x, u) on the strip $[0, T] \times \mathbb{R} \times \mathbb{R}$, then there can be found a sequence of disjoint, perfect subsets of $[0, T]$, whose union has measure T, with the property that f is continuous in (t, x, u) when t is restricted to any set in the sequence.

Scorza-Dragoni used this theorem to establish the remarkable result that the exceptional set in Carathéodory's existence theorem does not depend on the solution x(t) nor even on the initial value.

2. Proof of the theorem

In what follows, we shall need the following lemma

Lemma. Suppose that for each fixed ω, $\dot{x}_\omega$ satisfies

$$\dot{x}_\omega(t) = f(t, x_\omega, u_\omega) \qquad t \geq 0$$

and

$$|f(t, x, u)| \leq M(t)\, x + N(t)$$

where M, N are non-negative $\mathcal{L}_1$ functions. Then for each ω

$$|x_\omega(t)| \leq A(t)|x_\omega(0)| + B(t)$$

where

$$A(t) = \exp \int_0^t M(s)\,ds$$

$$B(t) = \left[\exp \int_0^t M(s)\,ds\right]\left[\int_0^t N(s)\left(\exp - \int_0^s M(r)\,dr\right) ds\right]$$

To prove this lemma, observe that the absolute continuity of $x(t)$ implies the absolute continuity of $|x(t)|$. Hence $\frac{d}{dt}|x(t)|$ exists a. e. and is Lebesgue integrable. By looking at the difference quotients, we see that

$$\frac{d}{dt}|x(t)| \leq |\dot{x}(t)| \qquad \text{a. e.}$$

The lemma then follows by Gronwall's inequality ([6], p 15) applied to $x(t)$

According to a mild extension of Scorza-Dragoni theorem, there is a countable family of disjoint compact sets of t, whose union has full measure, such that when t is restricted to any set F of sequence, the function (t, x, u) is uniformly continuous in (t, x, u)

The subset of F consisting of points of density 1, which, at the same time are Lebesgue points of the functions $M(\cdot)\,1_{F^c}(\cdot)$ and $N(\cdot)\,1_{F^c}(\cdot)$, where F^c denotes the complement of F, has the same measure as F. Hence the union of these subsets again has full measure. By an abuse of notation, we shall henceforth denote by F any one of these subsets.

Now take any t belonging to a set F and define, for $h \neq 0$,

$$F_h(t) = F \cap [t, t+h]$$

$$G_h(t) = F^c \cap [t, t+h]$$

Then we have

$$\left| \frac{x_\omega(t+h) - x_\omega(t)}{h} - f(t, x_\omega(t)\ n_\omega(t)) \right| =$$

$$= \left| \frac{1}{h} \int_t^{t+h} [f(s, x_\omega(s), u_\omega(s)) - f(t\ x_\omega(t), u_\omega(t)] \, ds \right| \leq \frac{1}{|h|} \int_{F_h(t)} |f(s\ x_\omega(s), u_\omega(s) -$$

$$- f(t, x_\omega(t), u_\omega(t)| \, ds + \frac{1}{|h|} \int_{G_h(t)} |f(s, x_\omega(s), u_\omega(s))| \, ds + f(t, x_\omega(t), u_\omega(t) \frac{mG_h(t)}{h}$$

In each of the last two terms we make use of the inequality, following from the Lemma,

$$|f(\cdot, x_\omega(\cdot), u_\omega(\cdot))| \leq [A(\cdot)|x_\omega(0)| + B(\cdot)] \, M(\cdot) + N(\cdot)$$

where A and B are non-negative and continuous and so have upper bounds $\bar{A}$ and $\bar{B}$ respectively on $[t, t+h]$ Then the integral over $G_h(t)$ is dominated by

$$[\bar{A} \, |x_\omega(0)| + \bar{B}] \frac{1}{|h|} \int_{G_h(t)} M(s) \, ds + \frac{1}{|h|} \int_{G_h(t)} N(s) \, ds \tag{10}$$

while the term involving $m\,G_h(t)$ is dominated by

$$\{[\bar{A} \, |x_\omega(0)| + \bar{B}] \, M(t) + N(t)\} \frac{m\,G_h(t)}{|h|} . \tag{11}$$

Now suppose that the input u is stochastically continuous at t and that $x_\omega(0)$ is measurable Let $\varepsilon > 0$ be given. Then, by the measurability of $|x_\omega(0)|$, there will be a measurable set of ω, call it K_ε, and a positive real number R such that $\mathbb{P}(K_\varepsilon) > 1 - \varepsilon/2$ and $|x_\omega(0)| \leq R$ for $\omega \in K_\varepsilon$.

Now f is uniformly continuous on $F_h(t) \times \mathbb{R} \times \mathbb{R}$; hence for $\eta > 0$ given, there is a δ such that the integral satisfies

(12) $$| f(s, x_\omega(s), u_\omega(s)) - f(t, x_\omega(t), u_\omega(t)) | < \eta$$

whenever $|s-t| < \delta$, $s \in F_h(t)$, and $|x_\omega(s) - x_\omega(t)| < \delta, |u_\omega(s) - u_\omega(t)| < \delta$

By the stochastic continuity of u, there is a measurable set of ω, J_ε^δ with $$\mathbb{P}(J_\varepsilon^\delta) > 1 - \varepsilon/2$$
and a $\sigma > 0$ such that the final inequality on u holds throughout J_ε^δ provided that $|t - s| < \sigma$ Then is no loss of generality in **our** taking $\sigma < \varepsilon$

If follows from the Lemma that

$$|x_\omega(t)| \leq |x_\omega(0)| \; M(t) A(t) + M(t) B(t) + N(t)$$

Hence

$$|x_\omega(t) - x_\omega(s)| \leq |x_\omega(0)| \int_s^t M(u) A(u) \, du + \int_s^t M(u) B(u) + N(u) \, du$$

Now, for $\omega \in K_\varepsilon$, $|x_\omega(0)| \leq R$, so by taking $|t - s| < q$ for some $q > 0$ we can achieve that

$$|x_\omega(t) - x_\omega(s)| < \delta \qquad \text{for } \omega \in K_\varepsilon \; |t - s| < \; .$$

There is no loss of generality in taking $q < \sigma$. If then follows that (12) will be valid for $|s - t| < q$ $s \in F_h(t)$ and $\omega \in K_\varepsilon \cap J_\varepsilon^\delta$. The latter set has measure greater than $1-\varepsilon$. Because of assumption 1. - 3. we shall have for ω in this set

$$\frac{1}{|h|} \; F_h(t) \; | f(s, x_\omega(s), u_\omega(s)) - f(t, x_\omega(t), u_\omega(t) | \; ds < \eta$$

It is clear that by taking q sufficiently small, we can achieve that the contributions coming from the terms bounded by (10) and (11) will each be less than η, for $\omega \in K_\varepsilon \cap J_\varepsilon^\delta$.

This proves that the stochastic continuity of u and the measurability of $x(0)$ imply that $\frac{x.(t+h) - x(t)}{h}$ converges to $f(t, x.(t), u.(t))$ in probability for almost all t.

If, in place of the stochastic continuity of u, we assume that it has no fixed points of discontinuity, then the sets J_ε^δ can be closen, by Egorov's theorem, to be independent of δ. In this case, the foregoing reasoning shows that at each value of t considered above the pointwise derivative $\dot{x}_\omega(t)$ esists a. s. and equals $f(t, x_\omega(t), u_\omega(t))$ Here the set of ω where the equality holds depends upon t, but whenever any sample path $u_\omega(\cdot)$ is continuous at one of the above values of t, the correspon-ding solution $x_\omega(\cdot)$ is differentiable and satisfies the differential equation at that value t.

Note that in the foregoing proof, we did not require $x_\omega(t)$ to be measurable in ω. In the case of non-uniqueness of the solution of the initial value problem, it is enough that we choose, for each ω, any fixed solution $x_\omega(\cdot)$. If, however, $x_\omega(t)$ has been chosen in such a way that it is measurable in ω, we can say more. Suppose that $x.(0) \in \mathcal{L}_p(\Omega)$ for some p, $1 \leq p \leq \infty$. Then when x and u. are measurable the estimate

$$| f(t, x.(t), u.(t) | \leq [A(t) \, | x.(0) | + B(t)] \, M(t) + N(t)$$

shows that $f \in \mathcal{L}$. If u has no fixed points of discontinuity, then, for almost all t

$$\dot{x}_\omega(t) = f(t, x_\omega(t), u_\omega(t)) \quad \text{a. s.}$$

so that $\dot{x}.(t) \in \mathcal{L}_p$ As shown below, the right side of this equation, considered as a map of t into $\mathcal{L}_p$, is measurable, hence $\dot{x}.(\cdot)$, considered as a map of t into $\mathcal{L}_p$ is measurable Since $A(\cdot)$ and $B(\cdot)$ are continuous, and $M(\cdot)$ and $N(\cdot)$ are in $\mathcal{L}^1$ it follows that $\dot{x}.(\cdot) \in \mathcal{L}^1_{L_p}(\Omega)$. Hence $x.(\cdot)$ can be recovered from $\dot{x}.(\cdot)$ by Bochner integration. Since the Fundamental Theorem of Calculus holds for the Bochner in-tegral, we find that

$$\left\| \frac{x(t+h) - x(t)}{h} - \dot{x}(t) \right\| \to 0 \qquad \text{as } h \to 0$$

Hence the solution x(t) found by integrating along sample paths actually solves the initial value (Peano) problem

$$\dot{x}.(t) = f(t, x, u) \qquad \text{a. e. } t \geq 0$$

$$x.(0) = x^o.$$

in $\mathcal{L}_p(\Omega)$

3) Remarks on the $\mathcal{L}_p$ problem

We have seen that the procedure of integrating the differential equation for each fixed ω will give rise to solutions of the differential equation in $\mathcal{L}_p$ spaces, whenever the initial values belong to $\mathcal{L}_p$ and the input process u has no fixed points of discontinuity.

Could we arrive at the same result by considering the equation

$$\dot{x} = f(t, x, u(t)), \; t \geq 0,$$

with initial conditions $x(0) = \overset{o}{x}$, as a Peano problem in $\mathcal{L}_p$?

The answer is disappointing. Set $g(t, x) = f(t, x, u(t))$. Then g is measurable in t for each fixed real value x and uniformly continuous in such x for each fixed t.

Replacing x by any $\mathcal{L}_p$ function $x_.$, $g(t, \cdot)$ becomes a nonlinear operator from $\mathcal{L}_p$ to $\mathcal{L}_p$: $\quad g(t, x)(\omega) = g(t, x_\omega)$.

Our first question is: is $g(t, \cdot)$ strongly continuous in x ?

The answer is no. The original hypotheses imply only that $g(t, \cdot)$ is strongly continuous when restricted to the subspace made up of functions in $\mathcal{L}_p$ which are constant a. e., but this does not imply strong continuity throughout the rest of $\mathcal{L}_p$.

Our next question is: is $g(\cdot, x_.)$ measurable in t? Since $g(t, \cdot)$ is continuous with respect to a. s. convergence we can establish measurability in t by first observing that for any simple function $x_.$ in $\mathcal{L}_p$ $g(\cdot, x_.)$ is measurable (use Lusin's theorem for ω fixed) and then remarking that every function in $\mathcal{L}_p$ is the a. s. limit of simple functions. Hence we do get the measurability in t of g

As the Carathéodory bounds

(i) $$|g(t, x)| \leq M(t) |x| + N(t),$$

with M, N in $\mathcal{L}_1([0, T])$ we get, immediately

(ii) $$\|g(t, x.)\|_p \leq M(t)\ \|x\|_p + N(t)$$

so that these bounds remain valid in the $\mathcal{L}_p$ norm.

Summarizing then, the reduction of the initial value problem to a Peano problem in $\mathcal{L}_p$ brings to light that the resulting operator $g(t,\cdot)$ is not strongly continuous in $\mathcal{L}_p$ and therefore any attempt to solve the problem in $\mathcal{L}_p$ must deal with this deficiency.

Moreover it should be pointed out that even for strongly continuous operators g the Peano problem may not possess a solution in $\mathcal{L}_p$ Thus even the reduction of our problem to one in $\mathcal{L}_p$ would not give us automatically an existence theorem The situation improves if we impose a Lipschitz condition on f (and, therefore, on g) as a function of x, with a Lipschitz constant which is an $\mathcal{L}_1$ function of t It is easily seen that the Lipschitz condition then carries over to $\mathcal{L}_p$ with the same Lipschitz constant This is fortunate, because now the Peano problem in $\mathcal{L}_p$ is known to have a unique solution.

Moreover, the Lipschitz condition in $\mathcal{L}_p$ implies in turn the Lipschitz condition on f and g when x is real, so that the original sample path problem has a unique solution.

Since, as we have seen, the sample path solution also solves the Peano problem in $\mathcal{L}_p$, there is a complete equivalence and we can say that we are able to construct the $\mathcal{L}_p$ solution by sample path integration.

This leads to the following question: is it always possible to generate the $\mathcal{L}_p$ solution of any Peano problem in $\mathcal{L}_p$ by sample path integration when the Lipschitz condition is satisfied ?

In this case we start off with a family $g(t,\cdot)$ of Lipschitz operators in $\mathcal{L}_p$ and we want to regard then as giving rise to velocity vectors along sample paths.

If we insert an a. s. constant function x, into $g(t,\cdot)$ we get, for each ω,a real valued function

$$h(t, x, \omega) = g(t, x_\bullet)(\omega)$$

which is Lipschitzian in x, measurable in t and in ω, and which satisfies a growth condition of the from (1) whenever g satisfies (ii).

But notice that now ω appears explicity on the left-hand side. What we get, in terms of sample paths, is a random evolution which does not correspond to the original type of sample path problem considered in this paper, since h would not be continuous in ω.

The situation would not be improved by using f in place of g This would give rise to an input variable u in h, but the ω would still remain as an extra variable.

The only case in which ω disappears is when the operator g (or f) has the property of carrying a. s. constant functions into a. s. constant functions in

This is exactly the case that arises when the original sample path problem is put into $\mathcal{L}_p$ space form.

In this way we see that our original problem gives rise only to subclass of operators on $\mathcal{L}_p$ and it is for this reason that we can solve the Peano problem in space by sample path integration.

References

1 Loève, M. "Probability Theory" II 4 th Edition - Springer- Verlag (1978)

2 Carathéodory, C. "Vorlesungen uber reelle funktionen" 2 Aufl. Leipzig (1927)

3 Reid, W. T "Ordinary Differential Equations" Wiley, New York (1971)

4 Scorza- Dragoni G. " Un teorema sulle funzioni continue rispetto ad un'altra

variabile.''Rend. Sem Mat Univ Padova 17, 102 -106 (1948)

5 Goodman, G. S. ''On a theorem of Scorza Dragoni and its application to optimal control'', in Mathematical Theory of Control, Balakrishnan and Neustadt eds. Academic Press. N. Y. 222-233 (1967)

6 Walter W. ''Differential and Integral Inequalities,'' Ergebnisse der Mathematik und Ihrer Grenzgzbiete - B. d. 55 - Springer - Verlag (1970)

NON-GAUSSIANITY AND NON-LINEARITY IN ELECTROENCEPHALOGRAPHIC TIME SERIES

Th. Gasser[1)] & G. Dumermuth
Universitäts-Kinderklinik
Steinwiesstr. 75
CH-8032 Zürich

SUMMARY

In this interdisciplinary contribution we discuss a number of problems related to stochastic models and statistical methods used in electroencephalography. The main part of the paper is devoted to the assumption of a Gaussian process. We present a variety of methods to check empirically such an assumption, together with examples. The deviations from a Gaussian process which occur in EEG analysis are interpreted in terms of non-linear dynamics; the input-output-map is assumed to be well represented by a Volterra series.

1. INTRODUCTION

In this paper we want to discuss an interdisciplinary topic, i.e. how mathematical concepts and statistical methods - mainly time series analysis - can fruitfully be applied to human neurophysiology and how problems in this field lead to mathematical problems and (hopefully) solutions. Many of our methods and arguments are not restricted to electroencephalography, but the concentration on one field of application could help to prevent an undue abstraction and the use of unrealistic models.

---

1) Now at the Central Institute of Mental Health, J5, D-6800 Mannheim 1

The methodological issues in electrophysiological research are tackled by two groups of scientists: Statisticians and engineers from communication and control theory. The different background is reflected in the diversity of the literature. In this contribution we will focus on spontaneous electroencephalographic activity without designed exterior stimulation, and include steady state light flicker input as the only stimulated activity. The estimation of event-related potentials is of high interest from a methodological point of view, but this topic would go beyond the scope of this contribution. Let us summarize some of the difficulties that we face in EEG analysis:

1) The wide variety of stochastic patterns encountered, and a lack of knowledge about their biophysical generation, make it difficult to propose valid and general stochastic models for EEG activity.

2) Important sources of input to the brain are autonomous and are not measurable.

3) There are important and not infrequent phenomena which are hardly compatible with a linear model (compare § 3,4).

4) The mass of data is enormous, which limits both the number and complexity of the methods we can realistically apply. (An example: A study with 20 patients with just 2 min of EEG, taken at 8 locations on the skull, leads to 1'920'000 data points.

An additive decomposition of the observed EEG time series in signal and noise may not be quite realistic, but this is nevertheless a useful working hypothesis. Sources of noise are technical and extracerberal biological influences: Instrumental noise, quantizing noise, muscle activity, movement artefacts, etc.

In the next chapter we start with a brief review of the methods that are presently the main tools in EEG research, with a discussion of their shortcomings and merits. In the following two chapters we take a look at the model assumption of Gaussianity - our main theme - non-linear dynamical relations, and in particular the Volterra representation for the input-output-map enable a qualitative insight and a solution to some quantitative problems.

2. METHODS OF QUANTITATIVE EEG ANALYSIS

The interest in quantitative EEG analysis stems from two differing objectives:

1) To replace or assist the clinician's eyeball analysis in clinical routine.

2) In the analysis of planned experiments, involving neurophysiological data. (We will concentrate on this aspect.)

Between 8 and 12 electrodes are placed on the skull, leading to a 8-12 dimensional vector time series (Gevins et al, 1975, give an excellent introduction into techniques). Fig. 1 shows examples of EEG activity of a 14 year old girl (diagnosis: generalized epilepsy) at four placements; note the high diversity of patterns within one individual occurring at the same time.

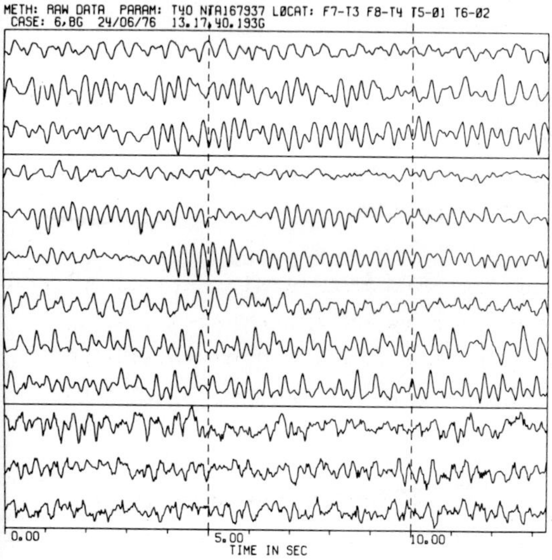

Fig.1: EEG tracings of one proband at four locations

Let us assume an additive decomposition of the recordings $Y_i^T(t)$ into cerebral activity $X_i^T(t)$ and noise $\varepsilon_i^T(t)$:

$$X_i^T(t) = X_i^T(t) + \varepsilon_i^T(t)$$

$$i = 1,\ldots,K \text{ (no.of placements)}$$
$$t \varepsilon [0,T]$$

There is strong non-stationary noise which often lies in a distinct frequency band different from cerebral activity; we will in the following assume that a preprocessing (bandpass-filtering or rejection of artefacts) has led to a realtively "clean" record. The latter is assumed to be a realization of a stochastic process ($\underline{X}(t) = (X_1(t),\ldots,X_K(t))$ characterized by its finite-dimensional multivariate distributions:

$$F_{t_1,\dots,t_i}^{j_1,\dots,j_i}(x_1,\dots,x_i) = P(X_{j_1}(t_1)<x_1,\dots,X_{j_i}(t_i)<x_i)$$

for all i, for all $t_1,\dots,t_i$; $\{j_1,\dots,j_i\} \subset \{1,\dots,K\}$

For various reasons, and with doubtful validity, the K-dimensional vector process is usually assumed to be stationary, ergodic and Gaussian. We might approach the problem of the violations of these basic assumptions from two sides:

A) Is the statistical methodology used for the analysis of the data robust to mild deviations from the model assumed?

B) We would like to quantify the deviation, e.g. the time dynamics involved in the violation of stationarity.

When outlining the statistical concepts in this chapter, we focus on A); when treating the validity and the implications of the Gaussian assumption in the sequel, we are interested in aspect B). Stationary processes are defined by invariance to time shifts:

$$F_{t_1,\dots,t_i}^{j_1,\dots,j_i}(x_1,\dots,x_i) = F_{t_1+\tau,\dots,t_i+\tau}^{j_1,\dots,j_i}(x_1,\dots,x_i),$$

for all τ, for all i

and this leads to the spectral decomposition of the process with orthogonal components $d\underline{Z}(\nu)$ (Rozanov, 1967).

$$\underline{X}(t) = \int_I e^{2\pi i\nu t}\, d\underline{Z}(\nu), \quad I = (-\tfrac{1}{2}, +\tfrac{1}{2}) \text{ t discrete}$$
$$(-\infty, +\infty) \text{ t continuous}$$

$$E(dZ_i(\nu_1)\,\overline{dZ_j(\nu_2)}) = \begin{cases} f_{ij}(\nu_1)\,d\nu_1, & \nu_1 = \nu_2 \\ 0, & \nu_1 \neq \nu_2 \end{cases}$$

for i=j, f_{ij} is the spectrum of channel i
for i≠j, f_{ij} is the cross-spectrum between channel i and channel j

For Gaussian processes we obtain not only uncorrelated but independent components dZ_i. The orthogonalization is the basic reason for going from the time to the fequency domain in time series analysis. The Fourier-transformation of finite stretches of data $X_i^T(t)$ leads to asymptotically (as $T \to \infty$) independent and Gaussian spectral components; this holds given a mixing condition, without assuming Gaussianity of the X_i^T (Brillinger, 1975).

Multivariate distributions are statistically untractable, and one therefore concentrates on second moments, preferably the spectrum matrix $(f_{ij}(\nu)/i,j = 1,\ldots,K)$. For a Gaussian process this summarizes the whole probabilistic information, but the most relevant information about EEG time series is contained in this matrix even without a Gaussian assumption. The diagonal terms, the power-spectra, give the distribution of energy on frequency bands and provide information about the existence and the shape of generators of brain activity (compare fig.3) uppermost trace, and fig.4). The off-diagonal terms, properly normalized (= coherence), give the degree of coupling of rhythmic generators and of brain noise at different locations of the skull.

The statistical theory of spectrum and cross-spectrum estimation is well developed (Brillinger, 1975), and the speed of Fourier algorithms allows the analysis of large data sets (Cooley & Tukey, 1965). It is not necessary to assume Gaussianity of the underlying process; stationarity and a condition related to asymptotic independence (stronger than ergodicity) are essential to obtain rigorous results. If stationarity is violated, the interpretation of spectra and cross-spectra becomes difficult, due to the fact that they are computed via averaging over the time rather than the ensemble. The interested reader may find a more extensive discussion of this topic in a paper by the first author, 1977.

Spectrum analysis is a non-parametric method, well suited for exploratory purposes. To obtain parameters - in order to make comparisons over groups, or for purposes of discrimination and classification - Zetterberg (1969) has suggested the use of linear parametric models (for K=1):

$$\sum_{i=0}^{P} \alpha_i X_{t-i} = \sum_{i=0}^{Q} \beta_i Z_{t-i}, \quad Z = \text{White noise}$$

We call X a mixed autoregressive-moving-average process of order (P,Q) (if $P,Q \neq 0$) and an autoregressive process of order P if $Q = 0$. The determination of $\{\alpha_i, \beta_i\}$ is equivalent to fitting a rational function of order (Q,P) to the spectrum of X. Such a difference equation should not be regarded as a biophysical model but rather as a method for spectral shaping. Since the incorporation of the $\{\beta_i\}$ is not crucial, but poses computational problems, a pure autoregressive model ("all pole model") is advantageous. For stationarity (and stability) the polynomial

$$A(z) = \alpha_o z^P + \ldots + \alpha_{p-1} z + \alpha_p$$

has to have all its zeroes in the interior of the unit circle. The parameters α_i do not have an interpretation in EEG terms, and Zetterberg (1969) proposed to use an equivalent, more redundant set of "SPA-parameters" $\left\{F_i, a_i, b_i, \nu_i, H_i, G_i\right\}$, based on the decomposition of the autocorrelation function r_K in resonances:

$$r_K = \sum_{i=1}^{p_1} F_i \exp(-|K|a_i) + \sum_{i=1}^{p_2} \exp(-|K|b_i)(G_i \cos K2\Pi\nu_i - H_i \sin|K|2\Pi\nu_i),$$

$$p = p_1 + 2p_2$$

where: $\exp(-a_j)$, $j=1,\ldots,p_1$ (real roots of A)
$\exp(-b_j \pm i\, 2\Pi\nu_j)$, $j=1,\ldots,p_2$ (complex roots of A)

It is essential to determine the order p of the model from the data; this can be done by Akaike's criterion (Akaike, 1970), or by some other method based on residuals. The following statistical problems are yet to be solved and will be tackled within project B1 of the Sonderforschungsbereich 123 (University of Heidelberg):

1) Bias and Variability (asymptotically) of SPA-parameters, based on the estimation by autoregression

2) Extension of the method to multidimensional time series.

The parametric method has a methodologically appealing and practically relevant application for the detection of epileptic spikes in a EEG-tracing (Lopes da Silva, 1975): Let us assume that these spikes are superposed transients on the normal EEG; by using the autoregressive coefficients as an inverse filter, we obtain the residuals, where the spikes should stand out as a deviation from the stationary, Gaussian model.

3. DEVIATIONS FROM A GAUSSIAN MODEL

In the proceeding chapter, we have discussed the problem of quantitative EEG analysis at a descriptive level. Here we aim at a better understanding of the phenomenology of the EEG. The diversity of EEG pattern is large, even within one individual over different pharmacological, metabolic or vigilance states. To go beyond the spectrum matrix, i.e. to study deviations from a Gaussian model could lead to a better understanding of the multitude of patterns (a parametric approach is not in sight; compare chap.4). The first step is to check the empirical basis of the mentioned hypothesis; we will present the respective methodology and give some interpretations.

Cumulants of order higher than p = 2 are zero for normal distributions; spectral components dZ( ), dZ( ) (≠) are independent for Gaussian processes, and uncorrelated for stationary processes in general. Both statements lead us to consider polyspectra (Brillinger & Rosenblatt, 1967):

Definition: The polyspectrum $F_{i_1,\ldots,i_p}$ of order p of

$$\left\{X_{i_1}(t),\ldots,X_{i_p}(t) \mid t \in \mathbb{Z},\ (i_1,\ldots,i_p) \subset (1,\ldots,K)\right\}$$

is given by: $\mathcal{C}_p\,(dZ_{i_j}(\nu_j);\ j = 1,\ldots p) = \eta(\nu_1+\ldots+\nu_p)\,dF_{i_1,\ldots,i_p}(\nu_1,\ldots,\nu_p)$

where: $\mathcal{C}_p$ = p-th order cumulant; $\eta(\lambda) = \sum_{i=-\infty}^{\infty} \delta(\lambda+i)$

In the following, we assume the existence of a density for F:

$$dF_{i_1,\ldots,i_p}(\nu_1,\ldots,\nu_p)\eta(\nu_1+\ldots+\nu_p) = f_{i_1,\ldots,i_p}(\nu_1,\ldots,\nu_p)\eta(\nu_1+\ldots+\nu_p)\,d\nu_1\ldots d\nu_p$$

Note that the time domain concept of stationarity translates into the fact that the p-th order spectral cumulant is located on the manifold

$$\sum_{i=1}^{p} \nu_i = 0 \text{ (modulo 1)}$$

Examples

1) For p = 2, $f_{i_1 i_2}(\nu_1,\nu_2) = f_{i_1 i_2}(\nu)\ (\nu_1 = -\nu_2 = \nu)$

becomes the ordinary spectrum (if $i_1 = i_2$) resp. cross-spectrum (if $i_1 \neq i_2$).

2) The bispectrum (p=3) is the only higher order spectrum which has gained some popularity. We replace $\nu_3 = -\nu_1 - \nu_2$:

$$b_{i_1 i_2 i_3}(\nu_1, \nu_2, -\nu_1 - \nu_2) = \text{auto-bispectrum if } i_1 = i_2 = i_3$$

$$b_{i_1 i_2 i_3}(\nu_1, \nu_2, -\nu_1 - \nu_2) = \text{cross-bispectrum if } i_1 = i_2 \neq i_3$$

The quantity of data needed and the computations involved limit us to bispectrum (p=3) and perhaps trispectrum (p=4) analysis for practical reasons; the important deviations from Gaussianity should, however, turn up for p = 3,4. Polyspectra give a measure of coupling between different frequency bands; as a special case, they allow the identification of spectral peaks as higher harmonics or subharmonics. In order to have a quantity independent of scale ("polycoherencies"), we divide by the respective spectra:

$$C_{i_1,\ldots,i_p}(\nu_1,\ldots,\nu_p) = \frac{|f_{i_1,\ldots,i_p}(\nu_1,\ldots,\nu_p)|^2}{\prod_{i=1}^{p} f_{ii}(\nu_i)}$$

To obtain an estimate for polyspectra, we replace the spectral component in the definition by finite Fourier transforms and smooth the result by convoluting with a (p-1)-dimensional kernel. This estimate is asymptotically unbiased and normally distributed, with a variance depending on the smoothing procedure. The estimated polycoherencies provide thus a test for Gaussianity, but also a detailed information regarding the deviation found. Fig. 2 shows an auto-bicoherence 3-22 Hz, same proband as in fig. 1 (40 sec of activity corresponding to the three lowest traces of fig. 1). Significant values are put in classes 1-7, corresponding from 10^{-2} to 10^{-5} error probability. Those bicoherence peaks which confirm the aharmonic pattern of two brain generators with fundamentals at 6 and 10 Hz are encircled; the peak at approximately (10,6,-16) Hz may indicate a coupling between the two generators (more examples are given in Dumermuth et al 1971, Dumermuth et al 1975).

Polyspectra are statistically delicate and computationally expensive tools; we have explored the following simplifications (Gasser, 1972):

1. a) S-polyspectra) directly related to polyspectra
   b) skewness and kurtosis)
2. Complex Demodulation

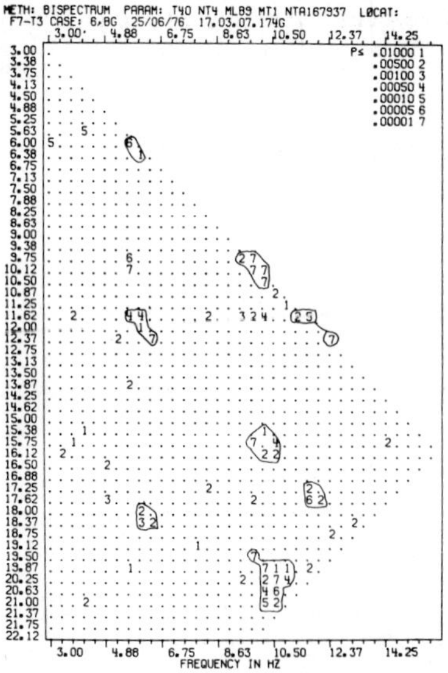

Fig.2: Discrete auto-bispectrum, 3.0-22.12 Hz

S-polyspectra of order $p(=f_X p_Y)$ of X(t) and Y(t) are defined as the ordinary cross-spectrum between $X(t)^p$ and Y(t); a straightforward calculation relates them to polyspectra:

$$f_X p_Y(\nu) = \int \ldots \int_{\nu_1 + \ldots + \nu_{p-1} = \nu} f_{x \ldots xy}(\nu_1, \ldots, \nu_{p-1}, -\nu)\, d\nu_1 \ldots d\nu_{p-1}$$

There are two potential sources of loss of information on the coupling of bands:

(i) Due to the summation over $\nu_1 + \ldots + \nu_{p-1} = \nu$, we can only postulate that a frequency band ν is affected by an interaction, but not which bands contribute to this. (Not so serious in most practical situations).

(ii) Since complex-valued functions are integrated, cancelling of polyspectrum peaks may occur.

Fig. 3 shows a logarithmic spectrum of the proband of fig. 1 + 2 in the uppermost trace and the S-autobicoherence in the middle trace. The peak at about 20 Hz proves that the weak energy concentration around 20 Hz in the spectrum is harmonically related to the 10 Hz α-activity and that the harmonic energy is at least 2/3 of the energy of that band. Using the S-bicoherence we cannot find a (6,6,-12) Hz coupling, indicated in the bispectrum (for $\nu_1 = \nu_2$) in the lowest trace.

Complex demodulation allows us to estimate band-specific envelopes (Bingham et al. 1967). When plotting the demodulates of possibly coupled bands one over the other, one has a heuristic measure of coupling and particularly one giving information about evolutionary aspects.

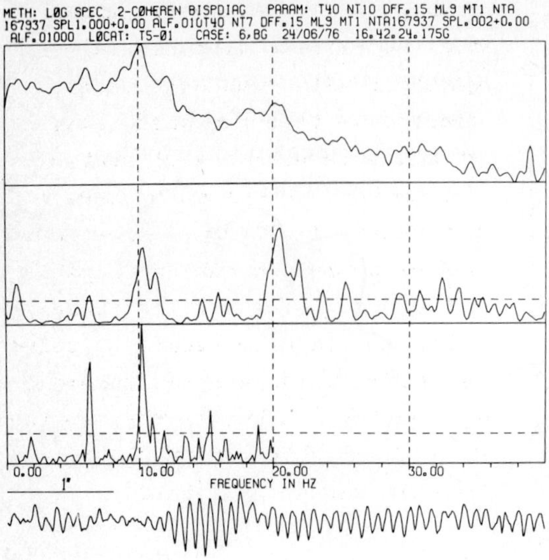

Fig.3: Logarithmic spectrum, S-auto-bicoherence and auto-bicoherence for $\nu_1 = \nu_2$ (top to bottom)

The distinction between Gaussian and non-Gaussian processes yields some additional statistical characteristica; what we also need is a qualitative understanding of the deviations measured by polyspectra in physical and engineering concepts. A linear dynamical system maps a Gaussian process into a Gaussian process, whereas a non-linear system in general produces non-Gaussian processes even with Gaussian input. From this we postulate an association between non-Gaussian EEG time series and a non-linear generation or transfer of brain activity. This leads to the following questions:

1) Can we find non-linear mechanisms when an input to the brain is recorded?
2) How can we model such a transfer with a minimum of assumptions?

Fig. 4 is an example of a non-linear response to a visual stimulation by repetitive flashes: To the left are logarithmic spectra of the input, with a fundamental ranging from 5 to 29 Hz (40 sec each piece); a linear reaction of the brain would lead to spectral peaks at the input frequencies, whereas we find additional peaks at 1/2, 3/2 and 5/2 of the fundamental when stimulating from 15 to 19 Hz (spectra to the right). This gives an empirical basis to regard the coupling of frequency bands in spontaneous activity as a non-linear reaction to internal stimuli.

A basic structural condition that we require is the time-invariance of the response of the brain to a stimulus; for the input-output-map $\mathcal{f}$ we have therefore:

$$\text{If } X_u(t) = X(t+u),\ Y(t) = \mathcal{f}(X(t))$$
$$\text{then } Y(t+u) = \mathcal{f}(X_u(t)).$$

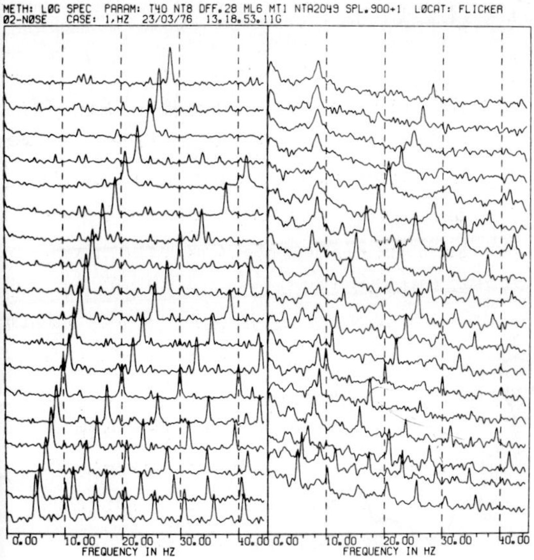

Fig.4: Spectra of flashes (left), spectra brain activity (right); logarithmic

When going to parametric models, i.e. non-linear differential equations with constant coefficients, we face two difficulties: Firstly the scarcity of statistical methods to estimate these parameters in the non-linear case and secondly the choice of plausible structures for the brain activity. To circumvent the second difficulty, a non-parametric approach via a kernel representation (= impulse response) may be used in linear analysis.

This approach can be generalized to N-th order Volterra expansions (introduced into stochastics by Wiener, 1958):

$$Y(t) = s(t) + \varepsilon(t)$$

$$= \sum_{i=1}^{n} \frac{1}{i!} \int_{\tau_1} \cdots \int_{\tau_i} h_i(t-\tau_1, \ldots, t-\tau_i) \prod_{k=1}^{i} X(\tau_k)\, d\tau_k + \varepsilon(t)$$

(X = input, ε = independent noise)

In the following we discuss the validity of the model as well as the determination of the i-th order impulse response h_i or of its Fourier transform, the i-th order transfer function H_i (compare Brillinger, 1970, and the first author's thesis, 1972):

<u>Theorem 1</u>

Let us assume:

(i) $E(X^k(t)) < \infty$ (for finite k)

(ii) $E(\prod_{i=1}^{k} X(t_i+\tau)) = E(\prod_{i=1}^{k} X(t_i))$ (k-th order stationary)

(iii) $E(\prod_{i=1}^{k} X(t_i))$ is continuous in (k-1) of its arguments

(iv) h_i is Lebesgue-measurable and in $L_1(R^i, L^i, dt^i)$

(v) The Fourier transforms of the moments are finite complex measures.

Then the following holds:

(a) The Volterra-expansion exists with probability one.
(b) The moments of (X,Y) of finite order exist.
(c) (X,Y) are k-th order stationary.
(d) Y(t) is mean-square continuous.
(e) The spectral decomposition of s(t) has the following form:

$$s(t) = \sum_{k=1}^{n} \frac{1}{k!} e^{2\pi i \nu t} \int_{\nu_1+\ldots+\nu_k=\nu} \ldots \int H_k(\nu_1,\ldots,\nu_k)\, dZ(\nu_1)\ldots dZ(\nu_k)$$

The proof which is given in Gasser (1972) is routine. Note that the assumptions become simpler when X is Gaussian. The next question is the validity of the Volterra expansion as an approximation for a time-invariant input-output map S:

Theorem 2

If the input-output map S is unique and continuous on a compact subset $A \subset L_p(\Omega, \mathcal{A}, P)$, it can be uniformly approximated on A by a Volterra expansion with kernels $a_i \in L_1(R^i, L^i, dt^i)$.

Since the Volterra expansion is polynomial, we need an analogon of Weierstrass' theorem for operators; to prove theorem 2 we have to verify the assumption of such a theorem given by Marti (1971). It is not always empirically justified to assume uniqueness of S, as demonstrated by hysteresis phenomena of non-linear oscillators.

For a linear input-output map S(n=1), the kernel is given by the cross-spectrum f_{xy}:

$$f_{xy}(\nu) = H_1(\nu)\, f_{xx}(\nu)$$

The generalization to n > 1 necessitates some modifications.

Definition: Define G_i as

$$G_i(X(t_1),\ldots,X(t_i)) = \sum_{s=0}^{i} \int_{t_1}\ldots\int_{t_s} c_s(t_1,\ldots,t_s) \prod_{k=0}^{s} X(t_k)\, dt_k$$

The Volterra-expansion is called orthogonal if G_{i+1} is orthogonal to G_i with respect to the scalar product E(XY).

Theorem 3

Let X be a stationary Gaussian process, mean square continuous and linearly regular. The kernels of an orthogonal Volterra-expansion $HO_i\ (\nu_1, \ldots, \nu_i)$ are given by the cross-polyspectra

$$f_{x\ldots xy}\ (\nu_1, \ldots, \nu_i) = HO_i\ (\nu_1, \ldots, \nu_i) \prod_{l=1}^{i} f_{xx}\ (\nu_k)$$

The relation to the kernels of the non-orthogonal expansion is as follows:

$$HO_{2m-1}(\nu_1, \ldots, \nu_{2m-1}) = \sum_{k=m}^{[\frac{n+1}{2}]} \frac{1}{2^{k-m}\ (k-m)!} \int_{\Omega_1} \ldots \int_{\Omega_{k-m}} \prod_{s=1}^{k-m} d\Omega_s\ f_{xx}\ (\Omega_s)$$

$$H_{2k-1}(\nu_1, \ldots, \nu_{2m-1}, \Omega_1, -\Omega_1, \ldots, \Omega_{k-m}, -\Omega_{k-m})$$

$$HO_{2m}\ (\nu_1, \ldots, \nu_{2m}) = \sum_{k=m}^{[\frac{n}{2}]} \frac{1}{2^{k-m}\ (k-m)!} \int_{\Omega_1} \ldots \int_{\Omega_{k-m}} \prod_{s=1}^{k-m} d\Omega_s\ f_{xx}\ (\Omega_s)$$

$$H_{2k}(\nu_1, \ldots, \nu_{2m}, \Omega_1, -\Omega_1, \ldots, \Omega_{k-m}, -\Omega_{k-m})$$

Similarly, we can obtain an expression for the spectrum of Y(t). The proof is based on the frequency domain representation of the orthogonal development, where $\nu_i \pm \nu_j \neq 0$ for any pair of frequencies and on the decomposition of higher order moments in second order moments which is valid for Gaussian random variables.

The Volterra-expansion has been useful in engineering and in science to treat non-linear problems; a note of caution is, however, appropriate at this place. The relation of Volterra-expansions to differential equations is to a great extent an open problem. The fact that non-linear oscillators can have more than one (stable and unstable) equilibrium state indicates that this relation is far from simple. We would conjecture that it is e.g. adequate for subresonant states of non-linear oscillators; we do, however, not foresee a possibility to represent a subharmonic with a Volterra-expansion.

ACKNOWLEDGEMENT

This work was supported by the Schweiz. Nationalfonds zur Förderung der wissenschaftlichen Forschung (No. 3.433.70).

REFERENCES

Akaike, H. (1970). Statistical predictor identification. Ann. Inst. Statist. Math. 22, 203-17

Bingham, C., M.D. Godfrey, J.W. Tukey (1967). Modern techniques of power spectrum estimation. IEEE Trans. Audio Electroac. AU-15, 56-66

Brillinger, D.R. (1970). The identification of polynomial systems by means of higher order spectra. J. Sound Vib. 12, 301-313

Brillinger, D.R. (1975). Time series analysis. Holden-Day, San Francisco

Brillinger, D.R., M. Rosenblatt (1967). Asymptotic theory of estimates of k-th order spectra. Spectral Analysis of Time Series, 153-186, ed. B. Harris, J. Wiley, New York

Cooley, J.S., J.W. Tukey (1965). An algorithm for the machine calculation of complex Fourier series. Math. Comput. 19, 267-301

Dumermuth, G., P.J. Huber, B. Kleiner, T. Gasser (1971). Analysis of the interrelations between frequency bands of the EEG by means of the bispectrum. Electroenceph. Clin. Neurophysiol. 31, 137-148

Dumermuth, G., Th. Gasser, B. Lange (1975). Aspects of EEG analysis in the frequency domain, CEAN, ed. G. Dolce & H. Künkel, 429-457, G.Fischer Stuttgart

Gasser, Th. (1977). General characteristics of the EEG as a signal. EEG-Informatics, ed. A. Rémond, 37-52, Elsevier/North Holland, Amsterdam.

Gevins, A.S., Ch.L. Yeager, S.L. Diamond, J.P. Spire, G.M. Zeitlin, A.H. Gevins (1975). Automated analysis of the electrical activity of the human brain. Proc. IEEE, 63, 1382-1399

Lopes da Silva, F.H., A. Dijk, H. Smits (1975). Detection of non-stationarities in EEG using the autoregressive model. CEAN, ed. G. Dolce & H. Künkel, 180-199, G. Fischer, Stuttgart

Marti, J.T. (1971). On the approximation of continuous non-linear operators in normed spaces by polynomial operators, ZAMP 22, 991-996

Rozanov, Y. (1967). Stationary stochastic processes. Holden-Day, San Francisco.

Wiener, N. (1958). Non-linear problems in random theory. Cambridge, MIT-Press

Zetterberg, L.H. (1969). Estimation of parameters for a linear difference equation with application to EEG-analysis. Math. Biosci.5,227-275

CANONICAL FORM AND LOCAL CHARACTERISTICS OF SEMIMARTINGALES

B. Grigelionis
Lietuvos TSR
Mokslu Akademija
Vilnius, CCCP

1. INTRODUCTION. It is the classical problem of considering the structure of the paths of stochastic processes with given finite dimensional distributions. From rather different points of view (absolute continuity of probability measures, structure of the functionals of stochastic processes, weak convergence of probability measures, criteria of sufficiency and markovity of statistics in sequential analysis, etc.) the inverse problem is considered: Under given structure of the path and some quantitative characteristics, which can play the analogous role as the infinitesimal operator for the Markov processes, to describe properties of finite dimensional distributions of the given stochastic process. The aim of this report is the review of some results in this direction obtained for multidimensional semimartingales using the techniques of stochastic calculus.

2. CANONICAL FORM OF SEMIMARTINGALES

Let us consider a measurable space (Ω,F) with the right continuous families $\mathbb{F} = (F_t, t \geq 0)$ of increasing sub-σ-algebras. Denote by $\mathbb{P}(\mathbb{F})$ the σ-algebra of $\mathbb{F}$-predictable subsets of $[0,\infty) \times \Omega$, and let $E = \mathbb{R}^m \setminus \{0\}$, $\mathcal{E} = \mathcal{B}(\mathbb{R}^m \setminus \{0\})$, $\tilde{\mathbb{P}}(\mathbb{F}) = \mathbb{P} \otimes \mathcal{E}$. Let P be a probability measure on F and denote by $M_{loc}(P, \mathbb{F})$ a class of $(P, \mathbb{F})$-local martingales.

We shall consider a right-continuous m-dimensional stochastic process with left limits $X = (X_t = (X_t^1, \ldots, X_t^m), t \geq 0)$. X is said to be a $(P, \mathbb{F})$-*semimartingale* if it is adapted to the family $\mathbb{F}$ and the paths of X can be decomposed as a sum

$$(1) \qquad X_t = X_o + A_t + L_t \quad , \; t \geq 0,$$

where A has a P - a.e. finite variation on every finite time interval and $L = (L^1,\dots,L^m)$, $L^j \in M_{loc}(P, \mathbb{F})$, $j = 1,\dots,m$. The representation (1) is not unique in the general case. Nevertheless, every semimartingale X can be represented in the following canonical form (see [1],[2]):

$$X_t = X_o + \alpha_t + X_t^c + \int_0^t \int_{|x|\le 1} x\, q(ds,dx) + \int_0^t \int_{|x|>1} x\, p(ds,dx) \ , \ t \ge 0 \ ,$$

where p(ds,dx) is the measure of jumps of the process X, q(ds,dx) = = p(ds,dx) - π(ds,dx), π(ds,dx) is the dual predictable projection of p, α is the predictable process having P - a.e. finite variation on every finite time interval,

$$\alpha_t - \alpha_{t-} = \int_{|x|\le 1} x\, \pi(\{t\} \times dx) \ , \ t \ge 0 \ ,$$

X^{cj}, $j = 1,\dots,m$, are continuous local martingales. The triplet (α,B,π), where $B_t = \|\beta_{i,k}(t)\|_1^m$, $\beta_{i,k}(t) = \langle X^{cj},X^{ck}\rangle_t$, $t \ge 0$, is called *the characteristics of the (P, $\mathbb{F}$) - semimartingale X* and is defined uniquely up to the modification.

The general theorems on integral representation for local martingales [3] and on absolute continuity and singularity of probability measures, corresponding to semimartingales [4], contain assumptions that in some sense the initial distribution and the triplet of characteristics (α,B,π) uniquely define the finite dimensional distribution of a semimartingale, so that the problem of characterization those triplets (α,B,π) which are triplets of a semimartingale, and the uniqueness problem are important ones. As we shall see later on these problems are too general to be settled without any additional assumptions, and we must restrict ourselves necessarily to some subclasses of semimartingales in order to receive reasonable results.

Before turning to the special classes of semimartingales let us consider two important types of transformations of semimartingales which play a fundamental role in non-linear filtering and stochastic control theory.

Denote

$$\mathbb{F}^X = (F_t^X = \bigcap_{\varepsilon>0} \sigma(X_s,\ s \le t + \varepsilon) \ , \ t \ge 0).$$

Using C. Stricker's result [5], it is not difficult to prove the following statement.

Theorem 1 ([6]): *If X is a $(P, \mathbb{F})$-semimartingale with characteristics (α, B, π), then X is a $(P, \mathbb{F}^X)$-semimartingale with characteristics (α^X, B, π^X), where α^X (π^X) is the dual predictable projection of α (π) w.r.t. P and $\mathbb{F}^X$.* ◊

The analogous statement is evidently true in the more general situations for filtrations $\mathbb{G} = (G_t, t \geq 0)$, such that

$$F_t \supseteq G_t \supseteq F_t^X \quad \text{for every } t \geq 0.$$

Let us now consider a $(P,\mathbb{F})$-semimartingale X with characteristics (α,B,π). Denote (cf [1],[4])

$$\beta(t) = \sum_{j=1}^{m} \beta_{j,j}(t) \quad , \quad \bar{\beta}_{j,k}(t) = \frac{d\beta_{j,k}}{d\beta}(t) \quad , \quad j,k = 1,\dots,m,$$

$$\bar{\beta}(t) = \| \beta_{j,k}(t) \|_1^m \quad , \quad a(t) = \pi(\{t\} \times E)$$

$$\hat{\psi}(t) = \int_E \psi(t,x)\, \pi(\{t\} \times dx) \quad , \quad t \geq 0,$$

$$L^2_{loc}(B,P,\mathbb{F}) = \{g = (g_1,\dots,g_m) \,/\, g \text{ is } \mathbb{P}(\mathbb{F})\text{-measurable and for all } t \geq 0$$
$$\int_0^t (g(s), g(s)\bar{B}(s))\, d\beta(s) < \infty \}$$

$$G_{loc}(\pi,P,\mathbb{F}) = \{\psi = \psi(t,x)/\psi \text{ is } \tilde{\mathbb{P}}(\mathbb{F})\text{-measurable and for all } t \geq 0$$
$$\int_0^t \int_E \frac{(\psi(s,x) - \hat{\psi}(s))^2}{1 + |\psi(s,x) - \hat{\psi}(s)|^2}\, \pi(ds,dx) +$$
$$+ \sum_{s \leq t} \frac{(\hat{\psi}(s))^2}{1 + |\hat{\psi}(s)|} (1 - a(s)) < \infty \} \quad .$$

Stochastic integrals

$$X_t^c(g) = \sum_{j=1}^{m} \int_0^t g_i(s)\, dX_s^{cj} \quad , \quad t \geq 0, \quad g \in L^2_{loc}(B,P,\mathbb{F})$$

and

$$Q_t(\psi) = \int_0^t \int_E \psi(s,x)\, q(ds,dx) \quad , \quad t \geq 0, \quad \psi \in G_{loc}(\pi,P,\mathbb{F})$$

can be well defined. The following subspaces of local martingales

$$M_{loc}(X^c,P,\mathbb{F}) = \{X^c(g) \,/\, g \in L^2_{loc}(B,P,\mathbb{F})\}$$

and

$$M_{loc}(q,P,\mathbb{F}) = \{Q(\psi)\ /\ \psi \in G_{loc}(\pi,P,\mathbb{F})\}$$

are stable and orthogonal (see [4], [7], [8]).

Let us now have the probability measure P' on F such that $P_t' \ll P_t$ for all $t \geq 0$, where P_t' (P_t) is the restriction of P' (P) on F_t. Denote

$$Z_t = \frac{dP_t'}{dP_t}, \quad t \geq 0 .$$

We shall have a unique decomposition

$$Z_t = Z_o + X_t^c(g^Z) + Q_t(\psi^Z) + Z_t' \quad , t \geq 0,$$

where $g^Z \in L^2_{loc}(B,P,\mathbb{F})$, $\psi^Z \in G_{loc}(\pi,P,\mathbb{F})$, $Z' \in M_{loc}(P,\mathbb{F})$, and Z' is orthogonal to the subspaces $M_{loc}(X^c,P,\mathbb{F})$ and $M_{loc}(q,P,\mathbb{F})$. Let

$$g(t) = Z^{\oplus}_{t-}\, g^Z(t)\ ,\ \psi(t,x) = Z^{\oplus}_{t-}(\psi^Z(t,x) - \hat{\psi}^Z(t)\,\chi_{\{a<1\}}(t)),\ t \geq 0,\ x \in E,$$

where $Z^{\oplus} = Z^{-1}$ if $Z \neq 0$, and $Z^{\oplus} = 0$ if $Z = 0$.

<u>Theorem 2</u> (cf. [1],[4],[9],[10]): *If X is a (P, $\mathbb{F}$)-semimartingale with characteristics (α,B,π), then X is a (P', $\mathbb{F}$)-semimartingale with characteristics (α',B,π'), where*

$$\alpha'(t) = \alpha(t) + \int_0^t g(s)\bar{B}(s)\, d\beta(s) + \int_0^t \int_{|x|\leq 1} x\, \psi(s,x)\ \pi(ds,dx)$$

$$\pi'(dt,dx) = (\psi(t,x) + 1)\ \pi(dt,dx) \quad , \quad t \geq 0,\ x \in E.\ \Diamond$$

3. PROCESSES WITH CONDITIONALLY INDEPENDENT INCREMENTS

Let G be the sub - σ - algebra of F. We say that the m-dimensional process X, adapted to $\mathbb{F}$, has *conditionally independent increments* with respect to G, if for all $\Gamma \in \mathcal{B}(\mathbb{R}^m)$ and $0 \leq s < t$ P-a.e.

$$P(X_t - X_s \in \Gamma\ /\ F_s \vee G) = P(X_t - X_s \in \Gamma\ /\ G)$$

Denote $\mathbb{F}(G) := (F_t \vee G\ ,\ t \geq 0)$.

The following theorem is true:

Theorem 3 ([11],[12]): *The process X has conditionally independent increments with respect to G iff $X = X' + X''$, where X'' is a $(P, \mathbb{F}(G))$-semimartingale, the triplet of characteristics of which and X' are G-measurable. An explicit formula holds for*

$$E\left[\exp(i(z,X_t - X_s)) \mid F_s \quad G\right]$$

in terms of X' and the characteristics of X''. ◇

Applying this theorem to the case $G = \{\emptyset, \Omega\}$, we have a characterization of all semimartingales with the non-random triplet of characteristics.

Corollary 1 ([2]): *A semimartingale X has a non-random triplet of characteristics iff it has independent increments. Under this assumption for all $z \in \mathbb{R}^m$, $0 \le s < t$, P-a.e.*

$$E\left[e^{i(z,X_t - X_s)} \mid F_s\right] = \exp\{i(z,\alpha_t^c - \alpha_s^c) - \frac{1}{2}(z,z(B_t - B_s))\} + \\ + \int_s^t \int_E \left[e^{i(z,x)} - 1 - i(z,x)\chi_{\{|x|\le 1\}}(x)\right]\pi^c(du,dx) \cdot \\ \cdot \prod_{s<u\le t}\left[1 + \int_E (e^{i(z,x)} - 1)\,\pi(\{u\}\times dx)\right],$$

where

$$\alpha_t^c = \alpha_t - \sum_{s\le t} \int_{|x|\le 1} x\,\pi(\{s\}\times dx),$$

and

$$\pi^c([0,t]\times\Gamma) = \pi([0,t]\times\Gamma) - \sum_{s\le t} \pi(\{s\}\times\Gamma). \; ◇$$

Well known theorems of P. Lévy and S. Watanabe are special cases of this statement.

Now let us apply theorem 3 to the case of *Markov additive processes*. Let $(W,\mathcal{W})$ be a measurable space. Recall that a stochastic process $(X,Y) = ((X_t,Y_t), t \ge 0)$, adapted to $\mathbb{F}$, such that X is m-dimensional and Y takes values in $(W,\mathcal{W})$, is a Markov additive process if for all $\Gamma \in \mathcal{B}(\mathbb{R}^m)$, $B \in \mathcal{W}$, and $u \le s < t$ P-a.e.

(2) $$P(X_t - X_s \in \Gamma, Y_t \in B \mid F_s) = P(X_t - X_s \in \Gamma, Y_t \in B \mid Y_s).$$

Denote

$$G_s^t(Y) = \sigma(Y_u \ , \ u\in[s,t]) \ , \ G = G_0^\infty(Y)$$

$$\alpha_s^t(z) = E[\exp(i(z,X_t - X_s)) \mid G_s^t(Y)] \ , \ 0 \le s < t \ , \ z \in \mathbb{R}^m \ .$$

From (2) we obtain that for all $z \in \mathbb{R}^m$ and $0 \le s < t$, P-a.e.

$$(3) \qquad E[\exp(i(z,X_t - X_s)) \mid F_s \vee G] = \alpha_t^s(z) \ .$$

Using (3) we have that the component X has conditionally independent increments w.r.t. the σ-algebra G and for all $z \in \mathbb{R}^m$, $s < u < t$, P-a.e.

$$\alpha_s^t(z) = \alpha_s^u(z) \ \alpha_u^t(z) \ .$$

We say that a process $Z = (Z_t \ , \ t \ge 0)$ is an *additive functional of Y* if for every $0 \le s < t$, $Z_t - Z_s$ is $G_s^t(Y)$ - measurable.

Theorem 4 ([12]): *A process (X,Y) is a Markov additive process iff*

(i) $X = X' + X''$, X'' is a $(P, \mathbb{F}(G))$ - semimartingale, the triplet of characteristics of which and X' are additive functionals of Y;

(ii) Y has the Markov property w.r.t. $\mathbb{F}$, i.e. for all $B \in W$ and $0 \le s < t$, P-a.e.

$$P(Y_t \in B / F_s) = P(Y_t \in B / Y_s) \ . \quad \diamond$$

The examples of semimartingales connected with processes having conditionally independent increments show us evidently the possible complexity of the triplets of semimartingales.

The following class of semimartingales includes the important models of stochastic systems defined by Itô's stochastic equations.

4. LOCALLY INFINITELY DIVISIBLE PROCESSES

A semimartingale X is called *locally infinitely divisible* if its characteristics are absolute continuous in t w.r.t. the Lebesgue measure, i.e. for all $t \ge 0$, $\Gamma \in \mathcal{B}(\mathbb{R}^m)$

$$\alpha_t = \int_0^t a(s)\,ds \quad , \quad B_t = \int_0^t A(s)\,ds \quad , \quad \pi([u,t] \times \Gamma) = \int_u^t \pi(s,\Gamma)\,ds \ .$$

The functions (a,A,π) are called the local characteristics of the process X.

Theorem 5 ([13]): *A process X adapted to $\mathbb{F}$ is locally infinitely divisible iff on some extension of the probability space (Ω,F,P) the independent standard Wiener process $W = (W_t = (w_t^1,\dots,w_t^m),\ t \geq 0)$ and Poisson measure $\tilde{p}(dt,dx)$ can be constructed such that the following representation holds:*

$$X_t = X_0 + \int_0^t \tilde{a}(s)\,ds + \sum_{k=1}^m \int_0^t \sigma_k(s)\,dw_s^k + \int_0^t \int_{|x|\le 1} f(s,x)\,\tilde{q}(ds,dx) + \tag{4}$$
$$+ \int_0^t \int_{|x|>1} f(s,x)\,\tilde{p}(ds,dx)\ ,$$

where $\tilde{q}(dt,dx) = \tilde{p}(dt,dx) - \dfrac{dt\,dx}{|x|^{m+1}}$, *the functions $\tilde{a}$, f and σ_k, $k = 1,\dots,m$, have explicit expressions by means of the local characteristics (a,A,π). (for a more detailed formulation see [13])* ◊

It is important to note that in the case when $a(t,\omega) = a(X_{t-}(\omega))$, $A(t,\omega) = A(t,X_{t-}(\omega))$ and $\pi(t,\omega,\Gamma) = \pi(t,X_{t-}(\omega),\Gamma)$, $t \geq 0$, $\omega \in \Omega$, $\Gamma \in \mathcal{E}$, from (4) we obtain Itô's stochastic equation for a semimartingale X and in this way we can characterize a wide class of Markov processes. A martingale characterization of one-dimensional diffusion processes was given by J.L. Doob (see also [14],[15]).

5. STOCHASTIC PROCESSES WITH PENETRABLE BOUNDARIES

Denote

$$G = \{x \mid x \in \mathbb{R}^m,\ x_1 \neq 0\}$$
$$G_+ = \{x \mid x \in \mathbb{R}^m,\ x_1 > 0\}\ , \qquad G_- = \{x \mid x \in \mathbb{R}^m,\ x_1 < 0\}$$
$$\partial G = \{x \mid x \in \mathbb{R}^m,\ x_1 = 0\}\ ,$$

$\hat{C}^2(\mathbb{R}^m)$ a class of continuous functions f such that

$$D_j f\ ,\ D_{jk}^2 f\ ,\quad j,k = 2,\dots,m$$

exist and are continuous; $D_1 f$, $D_{1j}^2 f$, $j = 1,\dots,m$ exist and are continuous on the sets $G_+ \cup \partial G$ and $G_- \cup \partial G$, where these derivatives for $x \in \partial G$ are considered as one sided. Let $\hat{C}_b^2(\mathbb{R}^m)$ be a class of bounded functions $f \in \hat{C}^2(\mathbb{R}^m)$ with bounded first and second derivatives.

We are going to define a general class of stochastic processes satisfying the two-sided *Wentzell's type boundary conditions* on ∂G, which for the first time was considered by S. Watanabe [16] in a special case (see also [17], [18]). Let us start with the following example. Consider the sequence of diffusion processes $\{X_n\}$ such that

$$dX_n(t) = a_n \chi_{\left[-\frac{1}{n},\frac{1}{n}\right]} X_n(t)\, dt + dW_t ,$$

where a_n are nonnegative constants, and W is a standard Wiener process. Following N.I. Portenko [17], it is easy to check that the sequence $\{P_n\}$ of measures corresponding to X_n on the space of continuous functions $C(\mathbb{R}^m)$ with the topology of uniform convergence on compacts, converges weakly to the limiting measure $P^{(a)}$, if

$$\frac{2a_n}{n} \to a \quad , \text{ as } n \to \infty \quad .$$

The measure $P^{(a)}$ can be characterized as a measure corresponding to the time homogenous diffusion process the transition probability function of which is a fundamental solution to the following equation:

$$\frac{\partial u(t,x)}{\partial t} = \frac{1}{2} \Delta u(t,x) \quad , \ x \neq 0$$

$$\gamma_+ \frac{\partial u^+(t,0)}{\partial x} = \gamma_- \frac{\partial u^-(t,0)}{\partial x} \quad , \ t > 0,$$

where $\gamma_+ = \dfrac{e^a}{e^a + e^{-a}}$, $\gamma_- = \dfrac{e^{-a}}{e^a + e^{-a}}$ if $0 \le a < \infty$

and $\gamma_+ = 1$, $\gamma_- = 0$ if $a = \infty$.

This equation can be solved explicitly.

We have that $P^{(0)}$ is a Wiener measure and $P^{(\infty)}$ is a measure corresponding to the Wiener process for which the point $X = 0$ is a reflection boundary to $\mathbb{R}^1_+$.
In the case $0 < a < \infty$ the point $x = 0$ is a penetrable boundary for the limiting diffusion.
Denote $X_t(\omega) = \omega(t)$ for $\omega \in C(\mathbb{R}^m)$, $t \ge 0$, and consider the standard system $\mathcal{C} = (\mathcal{C}_t , t \ge 0)$ of σ-algebras on $C(\mathbb{R}^m)$. The measures $P^{(a)}$ can also be characterized in the terms of martingales as the measures for

which there exists an increasing continuous process ϕ, such that $P^{(a)}$-a.e.

$$\phi_t = \int_0^t \chi_{\{0\}}(X_s)\,ds \quad , \quad \int_0^t \chi_{\{0\}}(X_s)\,ds = 0 \ , \ t \geq 0,$$

and for all $f \in \hat{C}_b^2(\mathbb{R}^1)$

$$M_t(f) = f(X_t) - \frac{1}{2}\int_0^t \Delta f(X_s)\,ds - \int_0^t [\gamma_+ D_1^+ f(x_s) - \gamma_- D_1^- f(X_s)]\,d\phi_s \ , \quad t \geq 0$$

is a $(P^{(a)}, \mathcal{C})$ - martingale.

Let us now return to the case of the general probability space and consider $\mathbb{P}(\mathbb{F})$ - measurable functions

$$\gamma_+(t) \geq 0 \quad , \quad \gamma_-(t) \geq 0$$

$$\delta(t) \geq 0, \ \hat{\alpha}(t) = (\hat{\alpha}_1(t), \ldots, \hat{\alpha}_m(t)), \ \hat{B}(t) = \|\hat{\beta}_{jm}(t)\|_1^m ,$$

$$\hat{\pi}(t,\Gamma) \quad , \ \tilde{\alpha}(t) = (\tilde{\alpha}_2(t), \ldots, \tilde{\alpha}_m(t)), \ \tilde{B}(t) = \|\tilde{\beta}_{jm}(t)\|_2^m ,$$

$\hat{\pi}(t,\Gamma)$, $t \geq 0$, $\Gamma \in \mathcal{E}$, and for all $f \in \hat{C}_b^2(\mathbb{R}^m)$ denote

$$\hat{A}(t)\,f(x) = \frac{1}{2}\sum_{j,k=1}^m \hat{\alpha}_{jk}(t)\,D_{jk}^2\,f(x) + \sum_{j=1}^m \hat{\beta}_j(t)\,D_j\,f(x) +$$

$$+ \int_E (f(y+x) - f(x) - \sum_{j=1}^m y_j\,D_j\,f(x)\chi_{\{|y|\leq 1\}}(y))\,\hat{\pi}(t,dy),$$

$$\tilde{A}(t)\,f(x) = \frac{1}{2}\sum_{j,k=2}^m \tilde{\alpha}_{jk}(t)\,D_{jk}^2\,f(x) + \sum_{j=2}^m \tilde{\beta}_j(t)\,D_j\,f(x) +$$

$$+ \int_E (f(y+x) - f(x) - \sum_{j=1}^m y_j\,D_j\,f(x)\chi_{\{|y|\leq 1\}}(y))\,\tilde{\pi}(t,dy)$$

$$+ \gamma_+(t)\,D_1^+\,f(x) - \gamma_-(t)\,D_1^-\,f(x) \ .$$

We say that the functions $(\hat{\alpha}, \hat{B}, \hat{\pi}, \gamma_+, \gamma_-, \delta, \tilde{\alpha}, \tilde{B}, \tilde{\pi})$ are local characteristics of the process X with respect to the measure **P** and the system $\mathbb{F}$, if there exists an increasing continuous process ϕ, such that P-a.e.

$$\phi_t = \int_0^t \chi_{\partial G}(X_{s-})\,d\phi_s \ , \quad \int_0^t \chi_{\partial G}(X_{s-})\,ds = \int_0^t \delta(s)\,d\phi_s \ , \ t \geq 0,$$

and for all $f \in \hat{C}_b^2(\mathbb{R}^m)$

$$M_t(f) = f(X_t) - \int_0^t \chi_G(X_s)\, \hat{A}(s)\, f(X_s)\, ds - \int_0^t \tilde{A}(s)\, f(X_s)\, d\phi_s \;, \; t \geq 0,$$

are $(P, \mathbb{F})$-local martingales.

<u>Lemma 1</u> ([6]): *If for all $t \geq 0$ P-a.e.*

$$\gamma_+(t) + \gamma_-(t) + \delta(t) + \mathrm{sp}\, \tilde{B}(t) + \int_E (|x|^2 \wedge 1)\, \tilde{\pi}(t,dx) > 0,$$

then ϕ is determined uniquely. ◇

The process ϕ is called the local time of X on the boundary ∂G.

<u>Lemma 2</u> ([6]): *If the functions γ_+, γ_-, δ, and $\tilde{B}$ are adapted to $\mathbb{F}^X$ and for all $t \geq 0$, P-a.e.*

$$\gamma_+(t) + \gamma_-(t) + \delta(t) + \mathrm{sp}\, \tilde{B}(t) > 0$$

then ϕ is also adapted to $\mathbb{F}^X$. ◇

A more detailed discussion of measurability properties of ϕ is given in [6].

<u>Theorem 6</u> ([6]): *If the process X has local characteristics $(\hat{\alpha}, \hat{B}, \hat{\pi}, \gamma_+, \gamma_-, \delta, \tilde{\alpha}, \tilde{B}, \tilde{\pi})$ w.r.t. P and $\mathbb{F}$, then X is a $(P, \mathbb{F})$-semimartingale, the triplet of characteristics of which has the form:*

$$\alpha_1(t) = \int_0^t \chi_G(X_s)\, \hat{\alpha}_1(s)\, ds + \int_0^t (\gamma_+(s) - \gamma_-(s))\, d\phi_s + \int_0^t \int_{|x|\leq 1} x_1\, \tilde{\pi}(s,dx)\, d\phi_s \;,$$

$$\alpha_j(t) = \int_0^t \chi_G(X_s)\, \hat{\alpha}_j(s)\, ds + \int_0^t \tilde{\alpha}_j(s)\, d\phi_s \qquad , \; j = 2,\ldots,m \;,$$

$$\beta_{1j}(t) = \int_0^t \chi_G(X_s)\, \hat{\beta}_{1j}(s)\, ds \qquad , \; j = 1,\ldots,m \;,$$

$$\beta_{jk}(t) = \int_0^t \chi_G(X_s)\, \hat{\beta}_{jk}(s)\, ds + \int_0^t \tilde{\beta}_{jk}(s)\, d\phi_s \qquad , \; j,k = 2,\ldots,m \;,$$

$$\pi([0,t] \times \Gamma) = \int_0^t \chi_G(X_s)\, \hat{\pi}(s,\Gamma)\, ds + \int_0^t \tilde{\pi}(s,\Gamma)\, d\phi_s \quad ;$$

$$\int_0^t \int_E \chi_G(X_s)(|x|^2 \wedge 1)\, \hat{\pi}(s,dx)\, ds < \infty, \quad \int_0^t \int_E (x_1 \wedge 1 + |x|^2 \wedge 1)\, \tilde{\pi}(s,dx)\, d\phi_s < \infty$$

for $t \geq 0$. ◇

Remark: Using the results of P.A. Meyer [19] on semimartingales and convex functions it is not difficult to prove that a process has the local characteristics $(\hat{\alpha},\hat{B},\hat{\pi},\gamma_+,\gamma_-,\delta,\tilde{\alpha},\tilde{B},\tilde{\pi})$ w.r.t. P and $\mathbb{F}$ iff X is a quasi left continuous (P, $\mathbb{F}$)-semimartingale and the process

$$X_o(t) = X(t) - \int_0^t \chi_{\partial G}(X_{s-})\, dX_s \quad , t \geq 0,$$

is locally infinitely divisible. ◇

From theorems 1 and 6 it follows:

Corollary 3 ([6]): *Under the assumptions of lemma 2, if the process X has local characteristics* $(\hat{\alpha},\hat{B},\hat{\pi},\gamma_+,\gamma_-,\delta,\tilde{\alpha},\tilde{B},\tilde{\pi})$ *and a local time* ϕ *w.r.t. P and* $\mathbb{F}$, *then X has local characteristics* $(\hat{\alpha}^X,\hat{B},\hat{\pi}^X,\gamma_+,\gamma_-,\delta,\tilde{\alpha}^X,\tilde{B},\tilde{\pi}^X)$ *and a local time* ϕ *w.r.t. P and* $\mathbb{F}^X$, *where* $\hat{\alpha}^X$, $\hat{\pi}^X$, $\tilde{\alpha}^X$ *and* $\tilde{\pi}^X$ *are predictable projections of* $\hat{\alpha}$, $\hat{\pi}$, $\tilde{\alpha}$ *and* $\tilde{\pi}$, *correspondingly, w.r.t. P and* $\mathbb{F}^X$. ◇

Applying theorems 2 and 6 we have:

Corollary 4: *If the process X has local characteristics* $(\hat{\alpha},\hat{B},\hat{\pi},\gamma_+,\gamma_-,\delta,\tilde{\alpha},\tilde{B},\tilde{\pi})$ *and a local time* ϕ *w.r.t. P and* $\mathbb{F}$, *then X has the local characteristics* $(\hat{\alpha}',\hat{B},\hat{\pi}',\gamma_+,\gamma_-,\delta,\tilde{\alpha}',\tilde{B},\tilde{\pi}')$ *and the local time* ϕ *w.r.t. P' and* $\mathbb{F}$, *where*

$$\hat{\alpha}'(t) = \hat{\alpha}(t) + g(t)\,\hat{B}(t) + \int_{|x|\leq 1} x\,\psi(t,x)\,\hat{\pi}(t,dx) \,,$$

$$\tilde{\alpha}_j(t) = \tilde{\alpha}_j(t) + \sum_{k=2}^{m} g_k(t)\,\tilde{\beta}_{kj}(t) + \int_{|x|\leq 1} x_j\,\psi(t,x)\,\tilde{\pi}(t,dx) \,, \; j = 2,\dots,m,$$

$$\hat{\pi}'(t,\Gamma) = \int_\Gamma (\psi(t,x) + 1)\,\hat{\pi}(t,dx)$$

$$\tilde{\pi}(t,\Gamma) = \int_\Gamma (\psi(t,x) + 1)\,\tilde{\pi}(t,dx) \,. \quad ◇$$

In order to find conditions of absolute continuity of measures corresponding to stochastic processes with penetrable boundaries in terms of local characteristics besides the corollaries 3 and 4 we shall need conditions of existence of exponential moments for a local time. Such conditions are found in [6] and [20], but we shall not go into the details. We also can derive general non-linear filtering equations in the case, when the observable process X is a process with penetrable boundary. Let us remark only that the similar notions of local characteristics and their properties are also investigated for semimartingales taking values in $\mathbb{R}_+^m$ or in the one-dimensional space interval (see [20] - [23]).

REFERENCES

[1] Jacod,J.;Memin,J.,Characteristiques locales et conditions de continuite absolue pour les semimartingales,Z.Wahrscheinlichkeits theorie verw.Gebiete,1976,B.35, p. 1-35 .

[2] Grigelionis,B.,On the martingale characterization of random processes with independent increments,Liet.matem.rink.,1977,t.XVII, Nr.4,p.53-60.

[3] Jacod,J.,A general theorem of representation of martingales, Proc.Symp.Pure Math.,vol.31,1977,p.37-53.

[4] Kabanov,Y.M.;Liptser,R.S.;Shiryaev,A.N.,Absolute continuity and singularity of locally absolute continuous probability distributions I, Math.Sb.,107,p.364-415,1978.

[5] Stricker,C.,Quasimartingales,martingales locales,semimartingales et filtrations,Z.Wahrscheinlichkeitstheorie verw.Gebiete,B.39, p.55-63,1977.

[6] Grigelionis,B.;Mikulevicius,R.,On stochastic processes with penetrable boundaries,Liet.matem.rink.,1980,t.XX,Nr.1.

[7] Jacod,J.,Un theoreme de representation pour les martingales discontinues,Z.Wahrscheinlichkeitstheorie verw.Gebiete,1976,B.35, p.1-37

[8] Jacod,J.,Sur la construction des integrales stochastiques et les sous-espaces stables de martingales,Seminaire de Prob. Strasbourg XI,Lect.N.in Math.,581,390-410,Springer Verlag:Berlin-Heidelberg New-York,1977.

[9] Girsanov,I.V.,On transforming a certain class of stochastic processes by absolutely continuous substitution of measures,Theory Probab.Appl.,1960,vol.5,p.285-301.

[10] Grigelionis,B.,On absolutely continuous substitution of measures and Markov property of stochastic processes,Liet.matem.rink., 1969,t.IX,Nr.1,p.57-71.

[11] Grigelionis,B.,The characterization of stochastic processes with conditionally independant increments,Liet.matem.rink.,1977, t.XVIII,Nr.1,p.75-86.

[12] Grigelionis,B.,On Markov additive processes,Liet.matem.rink., 1978,t.XVIII,Nr.3,p.43-47.

[13] Grigelionis,B.,On representation of integer valued random measures by mean of stochastic integrals with respect to the Poisson measure,Liet.matem.rink.,1971,t.XI,Nr.1,p.93-108.

[14] Grigelionis,B.,On Markov property of stochastic processes,Liet. matem.rink.,1968,t.VIII,Nr.3,p.489-502.

[15] Stroock,D.W.;Varadhan,S.R.S.,Diffusion processes with continuous coefficients I,II,Comm.Pure Appl.Math.,1969,Vol.22,p.345-400, 479-530.

[16] Watanabe,S.,Applications of Poisson point process to the construction of diffusions,Abstracts of Comm.,Internat.Conf. on Probab. and Math.Stat.,1973,Vilnius.

[17] Portenko,N.J.,Generalized diffusion processes,Dissertation,1978, Kiev.

[18] Anulova,S.V.,Diffusion processes with singular characteristics, Abstracts of Comm.,Internat.Symp. on Stoch.Different.Equations, 1978,Vilnius.

[19] Meyer,P.A.,Un cours sur les integrales stochastiques,Seminaire de Prob. Strasbourg X,Lect.N. in Math.,511,245-400,Springer Verlag,Berlin-Heidelberg-New York,1976.

[20] Grigelionis,B.;Mikulevicius,R.,On semimartingales with values in R_+^m,Liet.matem.rink.,1979,t.XIX,Nr.2.

[21] Grigelionis,B.,On statistical problems of stochastic processes with boundary conditions,Liet.matem.rink.,1976,t.XVI,Nr.1 , p.63-87.

[22] Grigelionis,B.,On stochastic processes in the finite space interval,Liet.matem.rink.,1976,t.XVI,Nr.2,p.51-63.

[23] Grigelionis,B.,On the reduced stochastic equations for non linear filtering of random processes,Liet.matem.rink.,1976,t.XVI,Nr.3, p.51-63.

ON IDENTIFICATION AND THE GEOMETRY OF THE SPACE OF LINEAR SYSTEMS

Michiel Hazewinkel
Dept. Math. Econometric Inst.
Erasmus Univ. Rotterdam
50, Burg. Oudlaan
ROTTERDAM, The Netherlands

1. INTRODUCTION AND MOTIVATION

Let

$$\dot{x} = Fx + Gu \qquad\qquad x_{t+1} = Fx_t + Gu_t$$

(1.1)

$$y = Hx \qquad\qquad y_t = Hx_t$$

be a continuous time or discrete time linear dynamical system of state space dimension n, with m inputs and with p outputs. (So that $x \in \mathbb{R}^n$, $u \in \mathbb{R}^m$, $y \in \mathbb{R}^p$). Here the matrices F,G,H are supposed to be independant of time. We use $L_{m,n,p} = \mathbb{R}^{mn+np+n^2}$ to denote the space of all such systems, and we let $L^{co}_{m,n,p}$ (resp. $L^{cr}_{m,n,p}$, resp. $L^{co,cr}_{m,n,p}$) denote the open and dense subspaces of all completely observable (resp. completely reachable, resp. completely observable and completely reachable) systems. Base change in state space induces an action of GL_n, the group of real invertible n × n matrices on $L_{m,n,p}$, viz. $(F,G,H)^S = (SFS^{-1},SG,HS^{-1})$, and two systems in $L_{m,n,p}$ which are related in this way are indistinguisable from the point of view of their input-output behaviour. Inversely, if (F,G,H), $(\bar{F},\bar{G},\bar{H})$ are two systems in $L_{m,n,p}$ with the same input-output behaviour and at least one of them is cr and co then they are GL_n-equivalent (i.e. there is an $S \in GL_n$ such that $(\bar{F},\bar{G},\bar{H}) = (F,G,H)^S$). This makes the space of orbits $M^{co,cr}_{m,n,p} = L^{co,cr}_{m,n,p}/GL_n$ important in identification of systems theory, essentially because the input-output data of a given black box give zero information concerning a basis for state space. More precisely suppose we have given a black-box which is to be modelled by means of a linear dynamical system. Then the input-output data give us (hopefully) a point of $M^{co,cr}_{m,n,p}$ (for some more remarks concerning this cf. below in 1.10). As more and more input-output data come in we find a sequence of points in $M^{co,cr}_{m,n,p}$ representing better and better n-dimensional linear dynamical system approximations of the given black box. If this sequence approaches a limit we have found the best linear dynamical system model (of dimension n) of our black box. We have then "identified" the black box. The same picture is relevant if we are dealing with a slowly time varying linear dynamical system. (In practice of course it is often desirable to have a concrete representation in terms of triples of matrices of our sequence of systems; this is where the matter of continuous canonical forms comes in). Unfortunately the space $M^{co,cr}_{m,n,p}$ is never compact; i.e. a sequence of points in $M^{co,cr}_{m,n,p}$ may fail to converge. There are holes in $M^{co,cr}_{m,n,p}$. To illustrate what kinds of holes there are we offer the following three 2-dimensional, 1 input-1 output examples.

1.2. Example.

$g_a = \binom{1}{1}$, $F_a = \begin{pmatrix}1 & 1\\ 0 & 1\end{pmatrix}$, $h_a = (a,0)$. The result of starting in $x_o = 0$ at time $t = 0$ with the input function $u(t)$ is then

$$y(t) = \int_o^t (1+t-\tau)ae^{t-\tau}u(\tau)d\tau \tag{1.3}$$

Taking e.g. $u(t) = 1$ for $0 \leq t \leq T$ and $u(t) = 0$ for $t > T$ we see that the family of systems $(F_a,g_a,h_a)_a$ does not have any reasonable limiting input-output behaviour as $a \to \infty$. Such a family can hardly represent a sequence of better and better approximations to any (physical or economical) black box.

1.4. Example.

$g_a = \binom{a}{1}$, $F_a = \begin{pmatrix}1 & 1\\ 0 & 1\end{pmatrix}$, $h_a = (a^{-1},0)$, $0 < a \in \mathbb{R}$. In this example the result of input $u(t)$, starting in $x_o = 0$ at $t = 0$, is the output

$$y(t) = \int_o^t h_a e^{(t-\tau)F_a} g_a u(\tau)d\tau = \int_o^t e^{t-\tau}u(\tau)d\tau + \int_o^t a^{-1}e^{t-\tau}(t-\tau)u(\tau)d\tau \tag{1.5}$$

We see that the limiting input/output behaviour of this family of systems as $a \to \infty$ is the same as that of the 1-dimensional system $g = 1$, $F = 1$, $h = 1$. This kind of hole is of course expected. Obviously a family of systems (g_a,F_a,h_a) may "suddenly" have zero-pole cancellation as $a \to \infty$. The example also illustrates that the family of systems itself $(g_a,F_a,h_a)_a$ may not converge to anything as $a \to \infty$, while the family of input-output operators

$$U_a\colon u(t) \mapsto y_a(t) = \int_o^t h_a e^{(t-\tau)F_a} g_a u(\tau)d\tau \tag{1.6}$$

does converge as $a \to \infty$ (In the pointwise, i.e. weak topology, sense that

$\lim_{a\to\infty} U_a(u(t))$ exists for each sufficiently nice u(t)). This type of phenomenon is of course expected if one takes quotients with respect to the action of a noncompact group.

1.7. Example. $g_a = \binom{1}{1}$, $F_a = \begin{pmatrix} -a & -a \\ 0 & -a \end{pmatrix}$, $h_a = (a^2,0)$, $a \in \mathbb{R}$. In this case the limit

$$\lim_{a\to\infty} y_a(t) = \lim_{a\to\infty} \int_o^t e^{-a(t-\tau)}(a^2-a^3(t-\tau))u(\tau)d\tau \tag{1.8}$$

does exist for all reasonable input functions u(t). (E.g. continuously differentiable input functions). The limit operator is in fact the differentiation operator D: $u(t) \mapsto y(t) = \frac{du(t)}{dt}$. But this operator is not the input-output operator of any system of the form (1.1). E.g. because D is unbounded, while the input-output operators of systems of the form 1.1 are necessarily bounded.

1.9. The Example 1.7 also shows that an obvious first thing to try: "just add in some nice way the lower dimensional systems" will not be sufficient at least for continuous time systems. However, even for discrete time systems, where as we shall see, the phenomenon of example 1.7 cannot occur, "adding in the lower dimensional systems" is of doubtful utility. To see this we turn our attention to a second bit of motivation for studying possible compactifications of $M^{co,cr}_{m,n,p}$. This has to do with finding a point in $M^{co,cr}_{m,n,p}$ which approximates, in some to be specified sense, a given set of input-output data, a point which was skipped over somewhat lightly in the first paragraph of this introduction. Incidentally it is reasonable to try to limit one's attention to co and cr systems because only the co and cr part of a system is deducible from its input-output behaviour. Also the quotient $L_{m,n,p}/GL_n$ is not Hausdorff, while $L^{co,cr}_{m,n,p}/GL_n$ is a nice smooth manifold (cf. [1]), so that the abstract mathematics and the more physical interpretation agree rather well.

1.10. On finding best $\leq$ n-dimensional linear system approximations to given input-output data. To avoid a number of far from trivial extra difficulties which adhere to the continuous time case we here concentrate on discrete time systems. Suppose therefore that we have input-output data relating inputs u(t), t = 0,1, ..., T-1 to outputs y(t), t = 1, ..., T and that, for various reasons, e.g. economy of data storage, we wish to model this relationship by means of a discrete time system (1.1). Here n is supposed to be small comparent to T. One straightforward way to approach this in the 1 input-1 output case is as follows. Every cr triple $(F,g,h) \in L_{1,n,1}$ is GL_n equivalent to one of the form

$$(1.11) \qquad g = \begin{pmatrix} 0 \\ \cdot \\ \cdot \\ \cdot \\ 0 \\ 1 \end{pmatrix}, \quad F = \begin{pmatrix} 0 & 1 & 0 & \cdots & 0 \\ 0 & 0 & \cdot & \ddots & \vdots \\ \vdots & & \ddots & \ddots & 0 \\ 0 & \cdot & \cdot & 0 & 1 \\ -a_o & \cdot & \cdot & \cdot & -a_{n-1} \end{pmatrix}, \quad h = (b_o, \ldots, b_{n-1})$$

This results in the following ARMA relationship between inputs and outputs

$$(1.12) \qquad y_{N+n} + a_{n-1}y_{N+n-1} + \ldots + a_1 y_{N+1} + a_o y_N = b_{n-1}u_{N+n-1} + \ldots + b_1 u_{N+1} + b_o u_N$$

for all $N \geq 0$, $N \leq T-n$. And, inversely, an ARMA model like (1.12) implies that the input-output relationship can be thought of as generated by an underlying discrete dynamical system (1.1) which is GL_n-equivalent to one with its matrices as in (1.11).

Our input-output data give a collection of vectors $d = (z_n, \ldots, z_o; v_{n-1}, \ldots, v_o) \in \mathbb{R}^{2n+1}$ and it remains to find that hyperplane defined by an equation of the form $Z_n + a_{n-1}Z_{n-1} + \ldots + a_o Z_o = b_{n-1}V_{n-1} + \ldots + b_1 V_1 + b_o V_o$ in $\mathbb{R}^{2n+1}$ which passes best through the collection of data points $\{d\}$. This seems straightforward enough and moreover an essentially linear procedure. There is only a small hint of trouble in that the hyperplane through zero such that e.g. the sums of the squares of the distances of the data points d to this hyperplane is minimal, may very well make only a very small angle with the hyperplane $Z_n = 0$. The problem of finding the best hyperplane is linear in the sense of projective geometry rather then affine geometry. A related difficulty is reflected by the fact that the natural limit of e.g. the family of ARMA schemes

$$(1.13) \qquad y_{N+2} + y_{N+1} + ay_N = au_{N+1} + u_N$$

as $a \to \infty$ is the relation $y_N = u_{N+1}$. But there is no discrete time linear dynamical system which can generate this relation, and it is also not true that the family of discrete time systems given by

$$(1.14) \qquad g = \binom{0}{1}, \quad F = \begin{pmatrix} 0 & 1 \\ -a & -1 \end{pmatrix}, \quad h = (1,a)$$

converges in input-output behaviour as $a \to \infty$. There is finally a hint of more possible trouble in the more inputs-more outputs case because in the one input-one output case the matrices of the form (1.11) induce a global continuous canonical form on $M^{co,cr}_{1,n,1}$ but in the case of $m > 1$ and $p > 1$ such global continuous canonical forms do not exist (and cannot exist) on all of $M^{cr,co}_{m,n,p}$, [1-4].

As it turns out the linearization carried out by (1.11) and (1.12) is rather more suspect that would be suggested by the remarks above, To see this we describe the situation as follows. There are natural bases of the space of all input functions and the space of all output functions, viz. the functions ε_i, $i = 0, \ldots, T-1$, $\varepsilon_i(t) = 0$ if $t \neq i$, $\varepsilon_i(i) = 1$ and η_i, $i = 1, \ldots, T$, $\eta_i(t) = 0$ if $t \neq i$, $\eta_i(i) = 1$.

Incidentally, in the discrete time, finite horizon case a different choice of basis does not essentially affect the picture to be described below. In the continuous time case, or in the discrete time case with infinite horizon the choice of bases in input- and output function space is much more consequential.

The space of all possible linear input-output relations (causal or not) is the space of all matrices

$$\begin{pmatrix} A_0 & \cdots & A_{0,T-1} \\ \vdots & & \vdots \\ A_{T-1,0} & \cdots & A_{T-1,T-1} \end{pmatrix}$$

(The causal input-output relations form a linear subspace). The space of input-output relations generated by a linear discrete time system of dimension $\leq$ n is an open dense subspace of the space of all matrices of Hankel form

$$H(A) = \begin{pmatrix} A_o & A_1 & \cdots & A_{T-1} \\ A_1 & & \cdot^{\cdot^{\cdot}} & \vdots \\ \vdots & \cdot^{\cdot^{\cdot}} & & \vdots \\ A_{T-1} & & \cdots & A_{2T-2} \end{pmatrix}$$

which moreover satisfy the condition rank $H(A) \leq n$. This is a highly nonlinear subspace, as is illistrated by the picture below which shows the closure of the subspace of input-output operators generated by a system of dimension ≤ 1 as a subspace of A_o, A_1, A_2 - space. The subspace is the cone with top in 0 through the hyperbola $A_1 = 1, A_0A_2 = 1$. The origin in the picture is the zero system and the points $A_o = 0$, $A_1 = 0$, $A_2 \neq 0$ are the points in the surface which are not realizable as ≤ 1 dimensional systems.

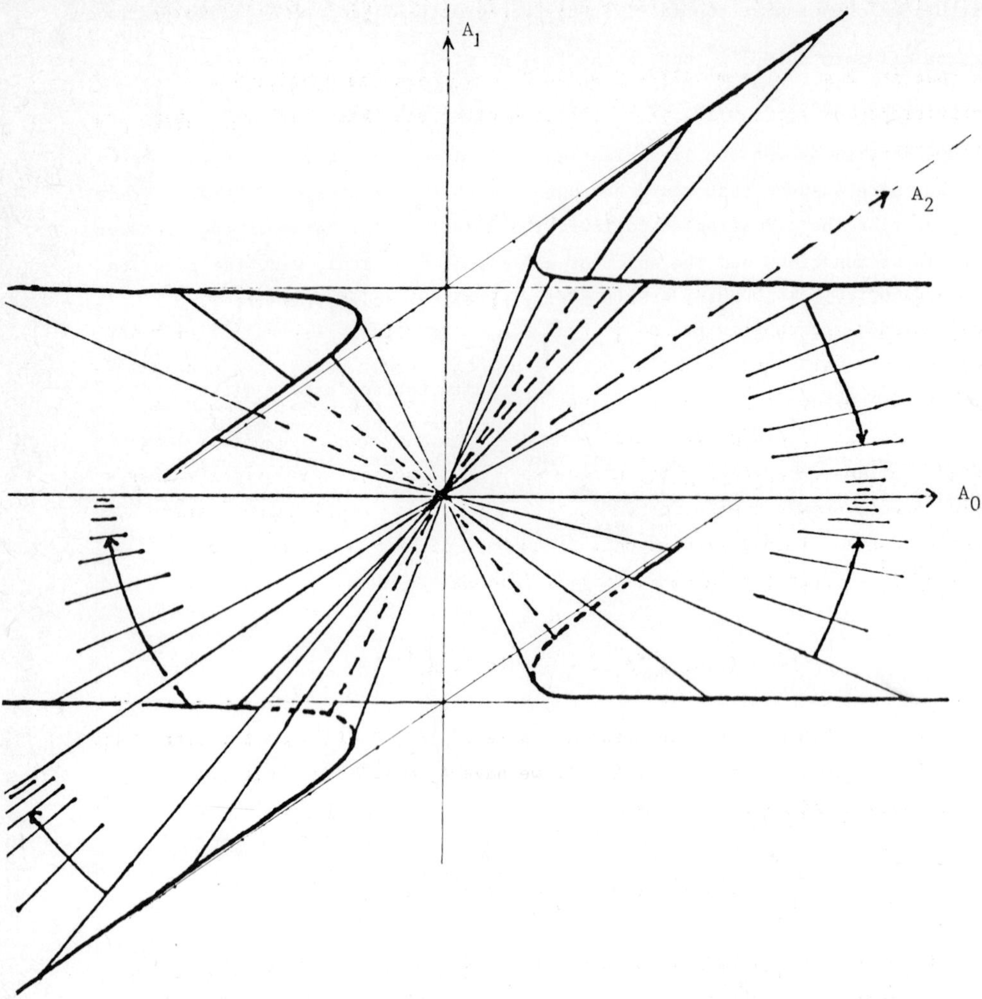

The nonlinearity of the picture is such as to suggest that it may will be impossible to linearize this surface without losing all a priori guarantees concerning the quality of our identification in terms of the noise in our data. This is indeed the case and to see this we calculate the sensitivity coefficients of the outputs y(1), y(2), y(3), .. with respect to the ARMA model parameters $a_o, \ldots, a_{n-1}, b_o, \ldots, b_{n-1}$. For simplicity we take n = 1. We write $a_o = -f$ and $b_o = h$. We then have of course

$$y(1) = hu(o),\ y(2) = hfu(0) + hu(1),\ y(3) = hf^2u(0) + hfu(1) + hu(2)$$

So that if, e.g., $u(1) = u(2) = 0$ and $u(0) = 1$, then the sensitivity coefficients of $y(1)$, $y(2)$, $y(3)$ with respect to the ARMA model parameters are respectively

$$\frac{\partial y}{\partial h} = (1,f,f^2),\quad \frac{\partial y}{\partial f} = (0,h,2hf)$$

which do not remain bounded independent of h and f. These sensitivity coefficients are especially had if both f and h are large. This fits with the remark made just above (1.13) above, because this corresponds to a hyperplane of best fit which is very close to the hyperplane $Z_n = 0$. On the other hand it is possible to divide the surface into a number of pieces and find local linearizations on each of these pieces such that the sensitivity coefficients calculated everywhere with respect to the appropriate local linearization do remain bounded. Indeed with respect to the coordinates A_o, A_1 we have $A_2 = A_o^{-1}A_1^2$ so that the sensitivity coefficients become

$$\frac{\partial y}{\partial A_o} = (1,0,-A_o^{-2}A_1^2),\ \frac{\partial y}{\partial A_1} = (0,1,2A_o^{-1}A_1)$$

and these are bounded by 2 in absolute value if $|A_o| \geq |A_1|$. On the other hand with respect to the coordinates A_1, A_2 we have $A_o = A_2^{-1}A_1^2$ so that the sensitivity coefficients become.

$$\frac{\partial y}{\partial A_1} = (2A_1A_2^{-1},1,0),\quad \frac{\partial y}{\partial A_2} = (-A_2^{-2}A_1^2,0,1)$$

and these are bounded by 2 in absolute value in the region where $|A_2| \geq |A_1|$. Now the surface has the equation $A_oA_2 = A_1^2$, so that for every point on the surface we must have $|A_o| \geq |A_1|$ or $|A_2| \geq |A_1|$ (or both). So we see that for this example two pieces suffice to find a piecewise linearization with uniformly bounded sensitivity coefficients. The picture incidentally suggests that to avoid trouble where both A_o and A_2 are small it would be good to introduce a third neighbourhood with coordinates A_1 and $\frac{1}{2}(A_o-A_2)$ in the intersection of the surface with, say, the solid cylinder $A_o^2 + A_2^2 \leq \frac{1}{2}$. The original coordinates h,f also work well in this region. It is perhaps also worth remarking that while the sensitivity coefficients $\frac{\partial y(n)}{\partial f}$, $\frac{\partial y(n)}{\partial h}$ get very rapidly worse if $f > 1$ and $n \to \infty$ this is much less so the case for the sensitivity coefficients $\frac{\partial y(n)}{\partial A_o}$, $\frac{\partial y(n)}{\partial A_1}$ and $\frac{\partial y(n)}{\partial A_1}$, $\frac{\partial y(n)}{\partial A_2}$ in their appropriate regions. Indeed in A_o, A_1 coordinates one has $A_n = A_o^{-n+1}A_1^n$ and in A_1, A_2 coordinates $A_n = A_1^{-n+2}A_2^{n-1}$ and the remark follows.

In the continuous time case we find instead of 1.12 a model

$$(1.15)\quad D^n y(t) + b_{n-1}D^{n-1}y(t) + \ldots + b_o y(t) =$$

$$= a_{n-1}D^{n-1}u(t) + \ldots + a_1 Du(t) + a_o u(t)$$

where D is again the differential operator. This model is already a priori more suspect than its discrete counterpart (1.12), simply because D is not a bounded operator.

1.16. The example suggests that it may be possible to construct the following sort of set up for identification procedures (discrete time case). There is a large open neighbourhood U of $\bar{\bar{M}}_{m,n,p}$, the closure in the space of all linear input-output relations of the space of those input-output matrices which are realizable by means of $\leq$ n dimensional linear systems. This neighbourhood U comes equipped with a finite covering U_i and coordinate maps $\phi_i: U_i \to \mathbb{R}^q$, $q = mpT^2$ such that $\phi_i(U_i \cap \bar{\bar{M}}_{m,n,p}) \subset \mathbb{R}^{mn+np} \subset \mathbb{R}^q$ (canonical embedding) and such that the Jacobian of ϕ_i is bounded on all of U_i for all i. The identification procedure would then roughly work as follows. Our input-output data give as a point in $\mathbb{R}^q$ the space of all linear input-output relations. If $x \notin U$, this input-output relation cannot be well approximated by a linear dynamical system of dimension $\leq$ n (and there should be an explicit number stating how badly the best approximation would still be). If $x \in U$, find an i such that $x \in U_i$. Apply ϕ_i to x and find the point $y \in \mathbb{R}^{mn+np} \subset \mathbb{R}^q$ closest to $\phi_i(x)$ (linear projection). Then take $\phi_i^{-1}(y)$ and this will be a good linear dynamical system approximation of the input-output operator x. The boundedness of the Jacobian of the ϕ_i guarantees that this procedure will have bounded sensitivity coefficients. In all this one can of course assume that x is already of Hankel form (if not first project on to the linear subspace of all input-output operators of Hankel form), so that the essential problem really is how curved $\bar{\bar{M}}_{m,n,p}$ lies in the space of all Hankel type matrices.

1.17. When can we expect that such a procedure can be constructed. Obviously this will be the case if we can find a suitable smooth Riemannian compactification of $M_{m,n,p}^{co,cr}$. Of course not every smooth compactification will do. The associated metric must fit with the topology on the space of the input-output operators belonging to the points of $M_{m,n,p}^{co,cr}$. The relevant topology on the space of operators appears to be the weak or pointwise-convergence topology. This is suggested by the results to be discussed below and also fits in well with (infinite dimensional) realization theory (Schwartz kernel theorem).

For instance the space of all cr systems of dimension n with one input and one output is $\mathbb{R}^{2n}$ and a nice smooth Riemannian compactification is the 2n-sphere S^{2n}, giving us also a nice smooth Riemannian compactification of $M_{1,n,1}$. Of course the same lower dimensional systems occur several times in the boundary of $M_{1,n,1}$ in S^{2n}; this, however, is not particularly bad for our purposes, and is a small pricc to pay for smoothness (and also appears to be unavoidable if one wants a smooth compactification). Much worse is that the one point compactification S^{2n} of $\mathbb{R}^{2n}$ brings systems very close together (in the Riemannian metric) which are very far from each other in input-output behaviour.

All this then is a second bit of motivation for studying (partial) compactifications of $M^{co,cr}_{m,n,p}$ which are system theoretically meaningful and for studying the degeneration possibilities of families of systems. Possibly, as is suggested by the results below, it is too much to hope for a total smooth Riemannian compactification. In that case one would try to find a smooth Riemannian partial compactification $\hat{M}_{m,n,p}$ which is system theoretically meaningful in the sense that a family of points in $\hat{M}_{m,n,p}$ converges to a point in $\hat{M}_{m,n,p}$ if the associated family of input-output operators converges in the weak topology (to some linear operator) and which has moreover the property that $\hat{M}_{m,n,p}$ is flat enough everywhere where it is not closed. This is precisely the situation one obtains if in the example above one adds to $M^{co,cr}_{1,1,1}$ the origin and the nonsystem points $A_o = 0$, $A_1 = 0$, $A_2 \neq 0$ and then resolves the singularity at the origin.

The remainder of this paper (sections 2-4) discusses some partial compactification results, these sections are essentially a somewhat revised version of the corresponding sections of [2].

2. DIFFERENTIAL OPERATORS OF ORDER ≤ n-1 AS LIMITS OF $L^{co,cr}_{1,n,1}$.

In this and the following section we consider continuous time systems only.

2.1. Definition. A differential operator of order n - 1 is (for the purposes of this paper) an input-output map of the form

$$(2.2) \qquad y(t) = a_o u(t) + a_1 Du(t) + \dots + a_{n-1} D^{n-1} u(t)$$

where the $a_o, \dots, a_{n-1}$ are real constants and $a_{n-1} \neq 0$. The zero operator $u(t) \mapsto 0$ is, by definition, the unique differential operator of order -1. In this and the following section we shall always suppose that u(t) is as often continuously differentiable as is necessary.

2.3. Theorem. Let L be a differential operator of order $\leq$ n-1. Then there exists a family of (continuous time) linear dynamical systems $(F_a,g_a,h_a)_a \subset L^{co,cr}_{1,n,1}$ such that (F_a,g_a,h_a) converges in input-output behaviour to L as $a \to \infty$. Here this last phrase means that for every smooth input function u(t) of compact support

$$\lim_{a\to\infty} \int_0^t h_a e^{(t-\tau)F_a} g_a u(\tau)d\tau = Lu(t) \tag{2.4}$$

uniformly in t on every bounded t-interval in $[0,\infty)$.

2.5. To prove theorem 2.3 we do first some preliminary exercises concerning differentiation, partial integration and determinants. The determinant exercise is the following. Let $k = \mathbb{N} \cup \{0,-1\}$ and let $n \in \mathbb{N}$. Let B(n,k) be the n $\times$ n matrix with the binomial coefficient entries $B(n,k)_{i,j} = \binom{i+j+k}{i+1+k}$, i,j = 1, ..., n. Then $\det(B(n,k)) = 1$ for all n,k. The combined differentiation/partial integration exercise says that

$$\int_0^t e^{-a(t-\tau)} a^n (t-\tau)^m u(\tau)d\tau = (-1)^m m! \sum_{i=m+1}^{n} (-1)^{i+1} a^{n-i} \binom{i-1}{m} u^{(i-1-m)}(t) + O(a^{-1}) \tag{2.6}$$

where $u^{(j)}(t)$ is short for $\frac{d^j u}{dt^j}(t) = D^j u(t)$.

2.7. Proof of theorem 2.3. Let $1 \leq m \leq n$ and consider the following family of n-dimensional 1 input-1 output linear dynamical systems.

$$g_a = \begin{pmatrix} 0 \\ \vdots \\ 0 \\ a^m \end{pmatrix}, \quad F_a = \begin{pmatrix} -a & a & 0 & \cdots & 0 \\ 0 & \ddots & \ddots & \ddots & \vdots \\ \vdots & & \ddots & \ddots & 0 \\ \vdots & & & \ddots & a \\ 0 & \cdots & \cdots & 0 & -a \end{pmatrix}, \quad h_a = (0,\ldots,0,b_m,\ldots,b_1) \tag{2.8}$$

where the b_1, ..., b_m are still to be determined real numbers independant of the parameter a. Now sF_a is the sum of the diagonal matrix $-saI_n$ and the matrix with superdiagonal elements sa and zero's elsewhere. These matrices commute making it easy to write down e^{sF_a} explicitly and using this and (2.6) one finds without difficulty that

$$\int_0^t h_a e^{(t-\tau)F_a} g_a u(\tau)d\tau = \sum_{\ell=0}^{m-1} (-1)^{m-\ +1} a^{\ell} \left(\sum_{i=1}^{m} b_i \binom{m+i-\ell-1}{i}\right) u^{(m-\ell-1)}(t) + O(a^{-1}) \tag{2.9}$$

Using the determinant result of 2.5 above it follows that we can choose $b_1, \ldots, b_m$ in such a way that

$$\int_o^t h_a e^{(t-\tau)F_a} g_a u(\tau)d\tau = bu^{(m-1)}(t) + O(a^{-1}) \tag{2.10}$$

where b is any pregiven real number. Now let L be any differential operator of order $\leq$ n-1, say $L = b_o + b_1 D + \ldots + b_{n-1}D^{n-1}$. For each $i = 0, \ldots, n-1$ let $(F_a(i), g_a(i), h_a(i))$ be a family of dynamical systems such that (2.10) holds with $m - 1 = i$ and $b = b_i$. Now let (F'_a, g'_a, h'_a) be the n^2-dimensional system which is the direct sum of the n n-dimensional systems $(F_a(i), g_a(i), h_a(i))$. I.e.

$$g'_a = \begin{pmatrix} g_a(0) \\ \vdots \\ g_a(n-1) \end{pmatrix}, \quad F'_a = \begin{pmatrix} F_a(0) & & 0 \\ & \ddots & \\ 0 & & F_a(n-1) \end{pmatrix}, \quad h'_a = (h_a(0), \ldots, h_a(n-1)) \tag{2.11}$$

The transfer function of (F'_a, g'_a, h'_a) is then $T_a(s) = \sum_{i=o}^{n-1} h_a(i)(s-F_a(i))^{-1}g_a(i)$ and because $F_a(i)$ is the same matrix for all i it follows that the degree of the denominator of $T_a(s)$ can be taken to be $\leq$ n. By realization theory or decomposition theory, cf. [5], [6], it follows that there exists for all $a \in \mathbb{R}$ an n-dimensional system (F''_a, g''_a, h''_a) with transfer function $T_a(s)$, and the same input-output behaviour as (F'_a, g'_a, h'_a).

Finally because $L^{co,cr}_{1,n,1}$ is open and dense in $L_{1,n,1}$ we can find for all $a \in \mathbb{R}$ a cr and co system (F_a, g_a, h_a) such that

$$|h''_a e^{(t-\tau)F''_a} g''_a - h_a e^{(t-\tau)F_a} g_a| \leq \varepsilon_a |t-\tau| e^{|t-\tau|M_a}$$

where M_a is 1 plus the maximum of the absolute values of the entries of F''_a.

Taking e.g. $\varepsilon_a = e^{-aM_a}$ we see that the families (F''_a, g''_a, h''_a) and (F_a, g_a, h_a) have the same limiting input-output behaviour. This concludes the proof of theorem 2.3

3. LIMITS OF TRANSFER FUNCTIONS

Let $(F,g,h) \in L^{co,cr}_{1,n,1}$. Its transfer function is $T(s) = h(s-F)^{-1}g$, which is a rational function of the form

$$T(s) = \frac{b_{n-1}s^{n-1}+\ldots+b_1 s+b_o}{s^n+a_{n-1}s^{n-1}+\ldots+a_1 s+a_o} \tag{3.1}$$

such that numerator and denominator have no factors in common. The system (F,g,h) is up to GL_n equivalence uniquely determined by $T(s)$ so that we can and shall identify $M^{co,cr}_{1,n,1}$ with the space of all such rational functions (3.1). There is an obvious smooth compactification of this space of all rational functions, viz. $\mathbb{P}^{2n}$, real projective space of dimension 2n, which consists of all ratios $(x_o:\ldots:x_{2n})$, $x_i \in \mathbb{R}$, such that at least one x_i is nonzero. We embed $M^{co,cr}_{1,n,1}$ in $\mathbb{P}^{2n}$ by mapping (F,g,h) to $(b_o:\ldots:b_{n-1}:a_o,\ldots,a_{n-1}:1)$, where the b_i and a_i are the transfer coefficients as in (3.1). The image of this mapping ψ is clearly open and dense.

Now let $\bar{M}_{1,n,1}$ be the subspace of $\mathbb{P}^{2n}$ consisting of those points $(x_o:\ldots:x_{2n}) \in \mathbb{P}^{2n}$ for which at least one of the $x_n, \ldots, x_{2n}$ is non-zero. To each $x \in \bar{M}_{1,n,1}$ we associate a (generalized) transfer function

$$(3.2)\qquad T_x(s) = \frac{x_{n-1}s^{n-1}+\ldots+x_1s+x_o}{x_{2n}s^n+\ldots+x_n} = c_{k-1}s^{k-1} + \ldots + c_o + \frac{b_{n-k-1}s^{n-k-1}+\ldots+b_o}{s^{n-k}+\ldots+a_1s+a_o}$$

where $k = 2n - m$ if m is the index of the last coordinate of x which is nonzero. We write $L_x(s) = c_o + c_1s + \ldots + c_{k-1}s^{k-1}$ and $T^r_x(s) = T_x(s) - L_x(s)$.

3.3. Lemma. Let $T_\alpha(s)$ be a family of transfer functions (3.1) of systems $(F_\alpha,g_\alpha,h_\alpha) \in L^{co,cr}_{1,n,1}$ indexed by a parameter α. Then $\lim_{\alpha\to\infty} T_\alpha(s)$ exists pointwise for infinitely many values of s iff (i) all limit points of the sequence $(x_\alpha)_\alpha$, $x_\alpha = \psi(F_\alpha,g_\alpha,h_\alpha)$, are in $\bar{M}_{1,n,1} \subset \mathbb{P}^{2n}$ and (ii) if x and x' are two limit points of this sequence then $T_x(s) = T_{x'}(s)$. Moreover if these conditions are fulfilled then $\lim_{\alpha\to\infty} T_\alpha(s) = T_x(s)$ for all limit points x of $(x_\alpha)_\alpha$.

The proof is elementary. Clearly if $(x_{\alpha'})_{\alpha'}$ is a subsequence of $(x_\alpha)_\alpha$ which converges to $x \in \bar{M}_{1,n,1}$ then $\lim_{\alpha'\to\infty} T_{\alpha'}(s) = T_x(s)$. Now suppose $(x_{\alpha'})_{\alpha'}$ is a subsequence which converges to some point in $\mathbb{P}^{2n}_x \setminus \bar{M}_{1,n,1}$, then $\lim_{\alpha'\to\infty} T_{\alpha'}(s) = \pm\infty$ for all but finitely many s. Finally if $(x_\alpha)_\alpha$ has all its limit points in $\bar{M}_{1,n,1}$ and there are limit points x, x' such that $T_x(s) \neq T_{x'}(s)$, then $\lim_{\alpha\to\infty} T_\alpha(s)$ cannot exist for infinitely many values of s because then we would have two unequal rational functions which are equal for infinitely many values of their argument.

3.4. Theorem. Let $x \in \overline{M}_{1,n,1}$ and let (F,g,h) be any $(n-k)$-dimensional system with transfer function equal to $T_x^r(s)$, and such that $\det(s-F) = s^{n-k} + x_m^{-1}x_{m-1} + \ldots + x_m^{-1}x_{2n}$, where $m = 2n-k$ is the index of the last non zero coordinate of x. Then there exists a family of systems $(F_a,g_a,h_a) \subset L_{1,n,1}^{co,cr}$ such that

$$(3.5) \qquad \lim_{a\to\infty} \int_0^t h_a e^{(t-\tau)F_a} g_a u(\tau)d\tau = L_x(D)u(t) + \int_0^t he^{(t-\tau)F} gu(\tau)d\tau$$

and such that moreover

$$(3.6) \qquad \lim_{a\to\infty} T_a(s) = T_x(s), \qquad \lim_{a\to\infty} \psi(F_a,g_a,h_a) = x$$

where $T_a(s)$ is the transfer function of (F_a,g_a,h_a).

Proof. Let (F'_a,g'_a,h'_a) be a family of k-dimensional systems in $L_{1,k,1}$ whose input-output behaviour converges to the differential operator $L_x(D)$. Let (F''_a,g''_a,h''_a) be the direct sum of (F'_a,g'_a,h'_a) and (F,g,h). As in the proof of theorem 2.3 we can change the family (F''_a,g''_a,h''_a) to a family (F_a,g_a,h_a) of co and cr systems with the same limit input-output behaviour. Then (3.5) holds. The first part of (3.6) follows by taking u(t) to be smooth of bounded support. Then the integrals and $L_x(D)u(t)$ in (3.5) are all Laplace transformable and the first part of (3.6) follows by the continuity of the Laplace transform (cf. [7], theorems 8.3.3 and 4.3.1). The second part of (3.6) follows from the first part together with the condition on det(s-F).

3.7. Theorem. Let (F_a,g_a,h_a) be a family of n-dimensional systems such that

$$\lim_{a\to\infty} \int_0^t h_a e^{(t-\tau)F_a} g_a u(\tau)d\tau$$

converges uniformly in t on bounded t intervals. Then there exists a $k \geq 0$, a differentail operator L of degree $\leq k-1$ and an $(n-k)$-dimensional system (F,g,h) such that

$$(3.8) \qquad \lim_{a\to\infty} \int_0^t h_a e^{(t-\tau)F_a} g_a u(\tau)d\tau = Lu(t) + \int_0^t he^{(t-\tau)F} gu(\tau)d\tau$$

Proof. By changing the (F_a,g_a,h_a) slightly if necessary (as in the proof of theorem 2.3) we can assume that $(F_a,g_a,h_a) \in L_{1,n,1}^{co,cr}$ for all a. Let u(t) be a given smooth input function of bounded support and let U(s) be its Laplace transform. The Laplace transform of the expresion under the limit sign in (3.8) is then $T_a(s)U(s)$, where $T_a(s)$ is the transfer function of (F_a,g_a,h_a). The continuity of the Laplace transform ([7], theorem 8.3.3) and lemma 3.3 above together then imply that there is an $x \in \overline{M}_{1,n,1}$ such that $\lim_{a\to\infty} T_a(s) = T_x(s)$. Take $L = L_x(D)$ and let (F,g,h) be any $(n-k)$-dimensional system with transfer function $T_x^r(s)$. Then the statement of the theorem follows because the Laplace transform is injective.

3.9. Theorems 3.4 and 3.7 together say that $\overline{M}_{1,n,1}$ is a maximal partial compactification in the sense that if a family of systems (F_a,g_a,h_a) converges in input-output behaviour then their associated points in $\overline{M}_{1,n,1}$ converge in $\overline{M}_{1,n,1}$, and inversely every point of $\overline{M}_{1,n,1}$ arises as a limit of a family $(x_a)_a$ which comes from a family of systems (F_a,g_a,h_a) which converges in input-output behaviour. It is not true, however, that a family (F_a,g_a,h_a) converges in input-output behaviour iff the sequence of associated points converges; cf. 3.10 below.

3.10. One cannot use realization theory directly to prove theorem 2.3. For instance the family of rational functions $(s-a)^{-1}a$ converges to -1 as $a \to \infty$ and -1 is the Laplace transform of the operator $u(t) \mapsto y(t) = -u(t)$. The transfer functions $(s-a)^{-1}a$ are realized by the systems $F = 1$, $g = 1$, $h = a$. But the limit $\lim_{a\to\infty} \int_0^t ae^{t-\tau}u(\tau)d\tau$ does not exist for almost all $u(t)$.

On the other hand the following is true. Let (F_a,g_a,h_a) be a family of systems with transfer functions $T_a(s)$. Suppose that there is a $c \in R$ such that $T_a(s)$ has no poles with real part $\geq c$ for all a. Then the limit of the $T_a(s)$ exists for $a \to \infty$ iff the family (F_a,g_a,h_a) converges in input-output behaviour. Half of this was proved in theorem 3.7 above. The other half is proved by using a continuity property of the inverse Laplace transform when applied to a converging sequence of rational functions with the extra property just mentioned.

This can be used to give another proof of theorem 2.3 as well as its obvious more input - more output generalization. The other theorems above generalize immediately to this case.

4. LIMITS OF DISCRETE TIME SYSTEMS

4.1. First let (F_a,g_a,h_a) be a family of co and cr continuous time systems of dimension n which converges in input-output behaviour. Let $A_i(a) = h_aF_a^ig_a$. Suppose in addition that for every i the $A_i(a)$ remain bounded. Then for every i there is a subsequence of $(A_i(a))_a$ which converges to some matrix A_i. Consider the block Hankel matrices

$$\mathcal{H}_{r,r}(a) = \begin{pmatrix} A_0(a) & \cdots & A_r(a) \\ \vdots & \cdot^{\cdot^{\cdot}} & \vdots \\ A_r(a) & \cdots & A_{2r}(a) \end{pmatrix} \qquad \mathcal{H}_{r,r} = \begin{pmatrix} A_0 & \cdots & A_r \\ \vdots & \cdot^{\cdot^{\cdot}} & \vdots \\ A_r & \cdots & A_{2r} \end{pmatrix}$$

By choosing the subsequences inductively we can see to it that a subsequence of $\mathcal{H}_{r,r}(a)$ converges to $\mathcal{H}_{r,r}$. It follows that $\mathrm{rank}(\mathcal{H}_{r,r}) \leq n$ for all r, which in turn (cf. [5], chapter 10) means that $A_0, A_1, A_2, \ldots$ is realizable by a $\leq n$ dimensional system. From this we see that the limit input-output behaviour of the family (F_a,g_a,h_a) is necessarily the input-output behaviour of a $\leq n$ dimensional system. I.e. the extra boundedness assuption on the $A_i(a)$ sees to it that the limit differential operator L occurring in (3.8) is always zero.

4.2. Now let (F_a, g_a, h_a) be a family of discrete time systems. The input-output operator of (F_a, g_a, h_a) is the matrix $(A_0(a) \,\vdots\, A_1(a) \,\vdots\, \dots\ )$. Now assume that the (F_a, g_a, h_a) are n-dimensional and that the family converges in input-output behaviour. Then the $A_i(a)$ remain bounded for all i, and argueing exactly as in 4.1 above we find that the limit input-output behaviour is that of a linear discrete time system, possibly of lower dimension. In other words, in the discrete time time case a maximal partial compactification of $M^{co,cr}_{1,n,1}$ is the space $\hat{M}_{1,n,1}$ consisting of all $(x_0 : x_1 : x_2 : \dots : x_{2n}) \in P^{2n}$ such that the polynomial part of the associated rational function, $L_x(s)$, is zero. That is, the smooth partial compactification $\hat{M}_{1,n,1}$ is obtained by adding in (several times) all lower dimensional systems and nothing else.

REFERENCES

1.M.Hazewinkel, Moduli and canonical forms for linear dynamical systems.II: the topological case, J. Math. System Theory 10 (1977), 363-385.

2.M.Hazewinkel, Degenerating families of linear dynamical systems I, Proc. 1977 IEEE CDC (New Orleans, Dec. 1977),258-264.

3.M.Hazewinkel, R.E.Kalman, Moduli and canonical forms for linear dynamical systems, Report 7504, Econometric Inst.,Erasmus Univ. Rotterdam, 1975.

4.M.Hazewinkel, R.E.Kalman, On invariants, canonical forms and moduli for linear, constant, finite dimensional, dynamical systems, Lect. Notes in Economics and Math. Systems 131 (1976), Springer, 48-60.

5.R.E.Kalman, P.L.Falb, M.A.Arbib, Topics in system theory, McGraw-Hill,1969.

6.L.M.Silverman, Realization of linear dynamical systems, IEEE Trans. AC 16 (1971), 554-567.

7.A.H.Zemanian, Distribution theory and transform analysis, McGraw-Hill, 1965.

A NUMERICAL COMPARISON OF NON-LINEAR WITH LINEAR PREDICTION FOR THE TRANSFORMED ORNSTEIN-UHLENBECK PROCESS

K. Helmes
Institut für Angewandte Mathematik
Universität Bonn

Abstract.

For a class of stationary processes which are defined by polynomial functions of the Ornstein-Uhlenbeck process we investigate what advantage can be expected in passing from optimal linear prediction to non-linear prediction. By "optimal" we mean the square error of prediction to be minimized. Using the SUMT algorithm as well as the VF02AD program of the Harwell Subroutine Library we computed the maximum relative error difference between both kinds of prediction. It turned out that it may be possible to achieve an improvement of up to 20% by using the best non-linear predictor.

1. Introduction

Let $(X_t)_t$, $t \in R$, denote the Ornstein-Uhlenbeck process i.e. the strictly stationary Gaussian Markov process with covariance function

(1) $$E\{X_t X_s\} = \exp[-|s-t|].$$

In Yaglom's paper [3] it was shown that the best non-linear predictors for the processes X_t^3 and X_t^5 give less than 2% error improvements over the optimal (minimum mean square) linear predictors. In Ref.[1], Maltz and Donelson looked at the same question for a larger class of stationary processes. They studied what advantages can be expected in passing from optimal linear prediction to non-linear prediction for polynomial functions of X_t of the form

(2) $$Y_t = p_M(X_t) = a_1 H_1(X_t) + \cdots + a_M H_M(X_t), \; t \in R, \; a_k \in R,$$

where $H_k(x)$, $k \in N$, denotes the k-th Hermite polynomial defined by the recurrence relation

(3) $\quad H_{k+1}(x) - xH_k(x) + kH_{k-1}(x) = 0,$

(4) $\quad H_0(x) = 1$ and $H_1(x) = x.$

These Hermite polynomials are associated with the weight function $w(x) = (1/\sqrt{2\pi})\exp[-x^2/2]$ (in contrast to $\tilde{w}(x) = (1/\sqrt{\pi})\exp[-x^2])$ over the interval $(-\infty,+\infty)$ and are standardized by the relation

(5) $$\int_{-\infty}^{+\infty} H_n(x)H_m(x)dw(x) = n!\delta_{n,m}.$$

Here, $\delta_{n,m}$ denotes the Kronecker symbol (cf. Ref.[2], p.249 ff, but observe that there these polynomials are denoted by $He_k(x)$. The constant term $H_0(x)$ is omitted in (2) in order that the resulting process Y_t has expectation zero (see Prop. 1, below). In general, this process is non Markovian except when $p_M(x)$ is 1-1. Therefore it is difficult to determine the best non-linear predictor. But Donelson and Maltz were able to derive an upper bound for the relative error difference for non-linear prediction compared with optimal linear prediction. This expression is obtained as the ratio of two quadratic forms (see (13)-(18), below).

For small values of M they computed the maximum relative error difference by solving a constrained maximization problem and compared these values to the exact ones which can be rather easily evaluated analytically for M = 2,3,4.

Using a slightly modified version of the SUMT algorithm and alternatively the VF02AD program we looked at the same problem for values of M up to 9. Since the matrices which appear in both quadratic forms are ill conditioned we had numerical difficulties for larger M's. It turns out that for prediction lead times $\tau > \tau_M$, the error improvement is always less than ~10% (M=9). Since for lead times $\tau \leq \tau_M$ (τ_M decreasing in M) the most unfavorable parameter set $a = (a_k)_k$, $1 \leq k \leq M$, satisfies the equations $a_2 = \cdots a_{M-1} = 0$, the numerical computations indicate that for values of M around 50 and $\tau \leq 0.05$ it may be possible to achieve a relative improvement of 20% by using the best non-linear predictor for the process (2) as opposed to the optimal linear one.

2. Mean and Covariance of Y_t

In order to evaluate the mean value and covariance function of Y_t we have to prove two propositions about the relationship between Hermite polynomials and Gaussian random variables. These two lemmata were proved in Ref.[1] by direct computation. We shall show that the results follow rather quickly using the generating function of the Hermite polynomials.

Proposition 1. Let X be a random variable with a normal distribution having mean μ *and variance* $\sigma^2>0$. *Then for* $n\geq 0$ *we have*

$$(6)\qquad E\{H_n(X)\} = \begin{cases} (1-\sigma^2)^{n/2}H_n(\mu/\sqrt{1-\sigma^2}) & \text{if } \sigma^2 < 1 \\ \mu^n & \text{if } \sigma^2 = 1 \\ (-i)^n(\sigma^2-1)^{n/2}H_n(i\mu/\sqrt{\sigma^2-1}) & \text{if } \sigma^2 > 1. \end{cases}$$

Proof. The generating function of the Hermite polynomials (3) is (cf. Ref.[2])

$$(7)\qquad \exp[\gamma x-\gamma^2/2] = \sum_0^\infty H_n(x)\gamma^n/n!\ .$$

Hence, if $X \sim N(\mu,\sigma^2)$,

$$\sum_0^\infty E\{H_n(X)\}\gamma^n/n! = E\{\exp[\gamma X-\gamma^2/2]\} = \exp[\gamma\mu-(1-\sigma^2)\gamma^2/2].$$

Now, if $\sigma^2 = 1$ the second term of the sum vanishes and the relation (5) is obvious. If $0<\sigma^2<1$ we rewrite the right hand side as follows,

$$\exp[\gamma\mu\sqrt{1-\sigma^2}/\sqrt{1-\sigma^2} - (\gamma\sqrt{1-\sigma^2})^2/2].$$

By using equation (6) and comparing the coefficients of the two power series we get the desired result. If $\sigma^2>1$ we set $\gamma = i\tilde{\gamma}$ and conclude as before.

The next proposition will enable us to compute the covariance function of Y_t.

Proposition 2. Let (X,Y) *be a 2-dimensional normally distributed random variable, each component having mean zero and variance one. If their correlation is* ρ *then we have*

$$(8)\qquad E\{H_n(X)H_m(Y)\} = \rho^n n!\,\delta_{n,m}\ .$$

Proof. Inserting the random variable Y into equation (7) and taking the conditional expectation with respect to X on both sides yields

$$\sum_0^\infty E\{H_m(Y)|X\}\gamma^m/m! = E\{\exp[\gamma Y-\gamma^2/2]|X\}.$$

Since the conditional density of Y given X is $N(\rho X,1-\rho^2)$ it follows that

$$E\{\exp[\gamma Y-\gamma^2/2]|X\} = \exp[\gamma\rho X-(\gamma\rho)^2/2] = \sum_0^\infty \rho^m H_m(X)\gamma^m/m!\ .$$

Hence,

(9) $$E\{H_m(Y)|X\} = \rho^m H_m(X).$$

Summarizing and remembering equation (5) we find

$$E\{H_n(X)H_m(Y)\} = E\{H_n(X)E\{H_M(Y)|X\}\} = E\{H_n(X)\rho^m H_m(X)\}$$
$$= \rho^n n!\delta_{n,m} .$$

From now on we assume the Ornstein-Uhlenbeck process X_t to be normalized in such a way that for any $t\in R$, $X_t \sim N(0,1)$. Then its covariance function is given by

(10) $$K(\tau) = E\{X_t X_{t+\tau}\} = \exp[-|\tau|], \tau\in R,$$

and we get from the equations (6) and (8)

(11) $$E\{Y_t\} = 0 \text{ and } E\{Y_t^2\} = \sum_1^M a_k^2 k! .$$

Since the joint distribution of X_t and $X_{t+\tau}$ is normal with correlation given by (8) it follows by Prop. 2 that the strictly stationary process Y_t has the covariance function

(12) $$Q(\tau) = \sum_1^M a_k^2 k! \exp[-k|\tau|].$$

3. An upper bound for the relative error difference

The following notation will be used throughout this section.

F_t ≃ $\sigma(X_s, s\leq t)$, the past of the process X_t up to time t.
G_t ≃ $\sigma(Y_s, s\ t)$, the past of the process Y_t up to time t.
$\hat{Y}(t,\tau)$ ≃ the best *non-linear* predictor of $Y_{t+\tau}$, $\tau>0$, *based upon* G_t,
$\hat{\sigma}^2(\tau,M)$ ≃ the corresponding mean square error.
$\tilde{Y}(t,\tau)$ ≃ the best *non-linear* predictor of $Y_{t+\tau}$, $\tau>0$, *based upon* F_t,
$\tilde{\sigma}^2(\tau,M)$ ≃ the corresponding mean square error.
$Y^*(t,\tau)$ ≃ the best *linear* predictor of $Y_{t+\tau}$, $\tau>0$, *based upon* G_t,
$\sigma_*^2(\tau,M)$ ≃ the corresponding mean square error.
$D^*(\tau,M)$ = $[1-\hat{\sigma}^2(\tau,M)/\sigma_*^2(\tau,M)]$, relative error difference of the best non-linear predictor compared with the optimal linear predictor.
$D(\tau,M)$ = $[1-\tilde{\sigma}^2(\tau,M)/\sigma_*^2(\tau,M)]$, relative error difference of the best non-linear predictor *based upon* F_t compared with the optimal linear predictor.

Remark. Since G_t is contained in F_t, $D(\tau,M)$ is an upper bound for $D^*(\tau,M)$, for which we now derive an explicit expression.

Observing that equation (9) holds we obtain

$$(14) \qquad \tilde{Y}(t,\tau) = \sum_1^M a_k H_k(X_t)\exp[-k\tau],\tau>0,$$

and hence

$$(15) \qquad \tilde{\sigma}^2(\tau,M) = E\{|\tilde{Y}(t,\tau)-Y_{t+\tau}|^2\} = \sum_1^M a_k^2 k!(1-\exp[-2k\tau]).$$

Evaluating the spectral density of the covariance function $Q(\tau)$ (cf.(12)) it is shown in Ref.[1] that

$$(16) \qquad \sigma_*^2(\tau,M) = \sum_{j=1}^M \sum_{k=1}^M c_j c_k(1-\exp[-(j+k)\tau])/(j+k),$$

where the *non-negative* parameters $(c_k)_k$ are related to the $(a_k)_k$ by the equations

$$(17) \qquad a_k^2 k! = c_k \sum_{j=1}^M c_j/(j+k), \; k = 1,\cdots,M.$$

Substituting (17) into (15) we obtain

$$(18) \qquad \tilde{\sigma}^2(\tau,M) = \sum_{j=1}^M \sum_{k=1}^M c_j c_k(1-\exp[-2k\tau])/(j+k),$$

and both quadratic forms (16) as well as (18) are positive definite. Inserting the formulae (16) and (18) into the expression for $D(\tau,M)$ we recognize that an upper bound for the maximum relative error difference for all processes of the form (2) (M fixed) is determined by the minimum of $\sigma_*^2(\tau,M)$ (see (16)) where the *non-negative* vector $c = (c_k)_k$ is restricted to $\tilde{\sigma}^2(\tau,M) = 1$.

Table 1 compares the computations done using the SUMT algorithm with those obtained in Ref.[1] as well as the numerical results obtained by evaluating analytically the constrained minimum of $\sigma_*^2(\tau,4)$.

Figure 1 shows the graph of the upper bound $D(\tau,M)$ as a function of $\tau = 0.105$ and $\tau = 0.0503$. As mentioned in the introduction for lead times below a given threshold τ_M the M-dimensional minimazation program is reduced to a 2-dimensional one, which causes no computational difficulties. Even for larger values of τ (e.g. $\tau = 2.303$) the numerical programs work well when we start with a "good" initial vector c.
But in contrast to the case of small values of τ $D(\tau,M)$ does not change very much for different values of M, e.g.

$$D(2.303,4) = 0.0022805628866 \text{ and } D(2.303,20) = 0.0022805623373.$$

TABLE 1

Results of numerical computations for M=4
(the numbers in the second line are those obtained in Ref.[1]; the numbers in the third line are those obtained analytically)

τ	c_1	c_2	c_3	c_4	c_4/c_1	$D(\tau,M)$
2.303	0.734898	0.000000	1.266500	0.000000	-	0.002281
	0.740587	0.000000	0.326015	1.117507	-	0.002241
	-	-	-	-	-	-
1.609	0.757318	0.000000	0.000000	1.484036	1.959594	0.008848
	0.756179	0.000001	0.000000	1.486246	1.965468	0.008848
	0.757318	0.000000	0.000000	1.484036	1.959594	0.008848
1.204	0.773517	0.000000	0.000000	1.475825	1.907941	0.019454
	0.799122	0.000000	0.000000	1.475890	1.908154	0.019454
	0.773517	0.000000	0.000000	1.475825	1.907941	0.019454
0.916	0.799120	0.000000	0.000000	1.465292	1.833631	0.032828
	0.799122	0.000001	0.000001	1.465298	1.833634	0.032827
	0.799120	0.000000	0.000000	1.465292	1.833631	0.032828
0.693	0.838448	0.000000	0.000000	1.455080	1.735443	0.046703
	0.838440	0.000000	0.000000	1.455072	1.735451	0.046703
	0.838448	0.000000	0.000000	1.455080	1.735444	0.046703
0.511	0.899750	0.000000	0.000000	1.451845	1.613608	0.057810
	0.899772	0.000007	0.000004	1.451857	1.613583	0.057810
	0.899750	0.000000	0.000000	1.451844	1.613609	0.057810
0.357	1.000192	0.000000	0.000000	1.471608	1.471324	0.062263
	1.000234	0.000005	0.000005	1.471624	1.471279	0.062263
	1.000192	0.000000	0.000000	1.471607	1.471325	0.062263
0.223	1.183660	0.000000	0.000000	1.556995	1.315407	0.056178
	1.183582	0.000021	0.000010	1.557139	1.315615	0.056177
	1.183660	0.000000	0.000000	1.556995	1.315407	0,056178
0.105	1.623877	0.000000	0.000000	1.875861	1.155173	0.036242
	1.623936	0.000021	0.000016	1.875870	1.155137	0.036241
	1.623876	0.000000	0.000000	1.875860	1.155174	0.036242

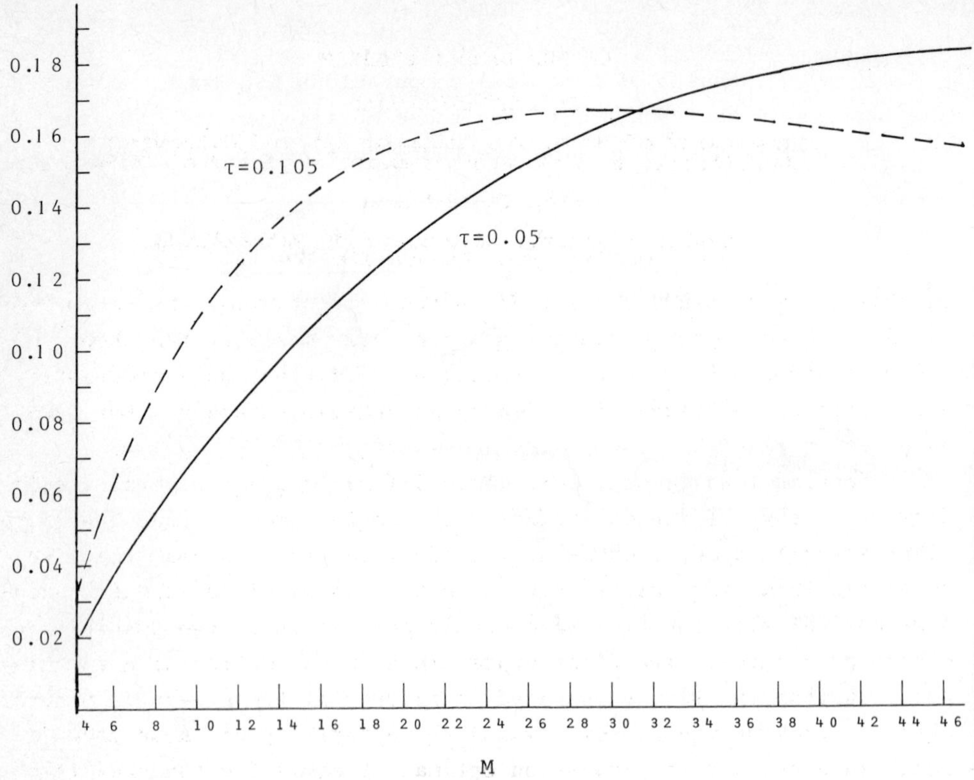

Figure 1

D(τ,M) as a function of M for two values of τ

References

[1] *Donelson, J. and Maltz, F.:* A comparison of linear versus non-linear prediction for polynomial functions of the Ornstein-Uhlenbeck process, J. Appl. Prob. 9, 725-744 (1972).

[2] *Magnus, W., Oberhettinger, F. and Soni, R.P.:* Formulas and theorems for the special functions of mathematical physics, 3. ed., Berlin, Heidelberg: Springer Verlag 1966.

[3] *Yaglom, A.M.:* Optimal non-linear extrapolation, Selected Translation in Mathematical Statistics and Probability, 273-298, Amer. Math. Soc., Providence, R.I. 1971.

ON THE BANDIT PROBLEM

Ulrich Herkenrath

University of Bonn, Institute of Applied Mathematics
Wegelerstr. 6, 5300 Bonn, Federal Republic of Germany

Radu Theodurescu

Laval University, Department of Mathematics
Quebec, Que. Canada G1K 7P4

In this paper we propose first an approach of studying the so-called two-armed bandit problem which is essentially based on the theory of random systems with complete connections. Next we apply stochastic approximation techniques for finding an optimal strategy. For detailed proofs, see [2-5].

In Section 1 we present some basic definitions and several results from the theory of random systems with complete connections. Next we adapt several concepts concerning general control systems, which we developed in a previous paper [2], to the actual circumstances. Further we deal with the two-armed bandit problem under two possible decision procedures. The first procedure is based on learning techniques, whereas the latter is based on sequential techniques. In both cases we examine the expediency and the optimality of these procedures. In Section 2 we propose an optimal strategy for the two-armed bandit problem by making use of the Kiefer-Wolfowitz stochastic approximation procedure. We further apply the same technique to a market pricing problem.

1. EXPEDIENCY AND OPTIMALITY

1.1. Random systems with complete connections

1.1.1. A random system with complete connections (abbreviated to RSCC) S is a quadruple $\{W,X,u,P\}$ where: (RSCC1) $(W,\mathcal{W})$ and $(X,\mathcal{X})$ are measurable spaces; (RSCC2) u is a mesurable function from $W\times X$ to W; (RSCC3) P is a stochastic kernel from W to $\mathcal{X}$. An RSCC induces for each $w\in W$ a probability space $(\Omega,\mathcal{K},\mathbb{P}_w)$ and two random processes

*Work supported by the Deutsche Forschungsgemeinschaft, by the Natural Sciences and Engeneering Research Council Canada grant A-7223, and by the Quebec Action Concertée grant 2662.

AMS 1970 subject classification: Primary 93A10, 62L20; Secondary 93C55, 90A15.

Key words and phrases: control systems, learning automata, learning algorithms, optimality, expediency, two-armed bandit problem, stochastic approximation.

$\{\zeta_n : n\geq 1\}$ and $\{\xi_n : n\geq 1\}$ with values in W and X respectively such that:

$$\mathbb{P}_w(\zeta_1 \in W') = 1_{W'}(w) = \begin{cases} 1 & \text{for } w\in W', \\ 0 & \text{for } w\notin W', \end{cases}$$

$$\mathbb{P}_w(\xi_1 \in X') = P(w,X'),$$

$$\mathbb{P}_w(\xi_n \in X' | \zeta_2,\ldots,\zeta_n, \xi_1,\ldots,\xi_{n-1}) = P(\zeta_n, X') \quad \mathbb{P}_w\text{-a.s.},$$

$$\mathbb{P}_w(\zeta_{n+1} \in W' | \zeta_2,\ldots,\zeta_n,\xi_1,\ldots,\xi_n) = 1_{W'}(u(\zeta_n,\xi_n)) \quad \mathbb{P}_w\text{-a.s.},$$

where $W'\in\mathcal{W}$ and $X'\in\mathcal{X}$ (here $\mathbb{P}_w$-a.s. stands for almost surely with respect to $\mathbb{P}_w$). Moreover $\{\zeta_n : n\geq 1\}$ is a Markov process and is called the <u>associated state process</u> of the RSCC: it has the transition probability function $Q(w,W') = P(w,\{x:u(w,x)\in W'\})$. $\{\xi_n : n\geq 1\}$ is in general not Markovian and is called the <u>associated event process</u> of the RSCC. For a proof of these facts and further results, see M. Iosifescu and R. Theodorescu [6], p. 63. We note that the concept of an RSCC is identical to that of learning model (see M. F. Norman [9], p. 25).

1.1.2. We shall next adapt certain definitions and results given previously by us in [2] for general control systems to the case of an RSCC.

We begin by evaluating the events $x\in X$ by means of a measurable function f from X into the real axis $\mathbb{R}$. We shall call f a <u>penalty function</u> and its values <u>penalties</u>; clearly negative penalties are interpreted as rewards. Suppose now that f is such that $\rho_n = \int_X f(x)P(\zeta_n,dx)$ exists for all $n\geq 1$. The quantity ρ_n represents the <u>conditional expected penalty</u> on trial n if the RSCC is in state ζ_n; obviously ρ_n is a random variable which can be written $\rho_n = r(\zeta_n)$, r being a measurable function from W into $\mathbb{R}$. Consequently $\mathbb{E}_w\rho_n$ represents the <u>expected penalty</u> on trial n, if the RSCC starts at w where $\mathbb{E}_w$ is the expectation with respect to $\mathbb{P}_w$. It seems natural that criteria for a good behaviour of an RSCC be based on the idea of reducing, in a certain sense, this expected penalty.

Suppose that $W_0\subset W$ and $\mathcal{P}_0\subset\mathcal{P}$ are nonempty given subsets, where $\mathcal{P}$ is the set of all stochastic kernels form W to $\mathcal{X}$. The transition function u is said to be <u>W_0-$\mathcal{P}_0$-expedient</u> if and only if $\limsup_{n\to\infty} \mathbb{E}_w\rho_n \leq \int_X f(x)P(w,dx)$ for all $w\in W_0$ and $P\in\mathcal{P}_0$. Further, u is said to be <u>absolutely W_0-$\mathcal{P}_0$-expedient</u> if and only if $\mathbb{E}_w(\rho_{n+1}|\zeta_n)\leq\rho_n$ $\mathbb{P}_w$-a.s. for all $n\geq 1$, $w\in W_0$, and $P\in\mathcal{P}_0$. Clearly absolute expediency implies expediency.

1.1.3. Now let us consider the optimality for RSCC's. Suppose that $\mathcal{F}_0\subset\mathcal{F}$, $\mathcal{F}_0\neq\emptyset$, is given, where $\mathcal{F}$ is the set of all transition functions from $W \times X$ into W. The family F_0 of transition functions u is said to W_0-P_0-ε-optimal if and only if for each $w \in W_0$ and $\varepsilon > 0$ there is $u_0 = u_{\varepsilon, w} \in F_0$ such that $\lim_{n\to\infty} \mathbb{E}_w^{u_0} \rho_n - \inf\{\mathbb{E}_{w'} \rho_1 : w' \in W\} < \varepsilon$ for all $P \in P_0$ (here $\mathbb{E}_w^{u_0}$ means that the expectation is computed using u_0). Further F_0 is said to be W_0-P_0-optimal if and only if for each $w \in W_0$ there is $u_0 = u_w \in F_0$ such that $\lim_{n\to\infty} \mathbb{E}_w^{u_0} \rho_n = \inf\{\mathbb{E}_{w'} \rho_1 : w' \in W\}$ for all $P \in P_0$. Clearly optimality implies ε-optimality and expediency.

1.2. The two-armed bandit problem

1.2.1. Let us describe the so-called two-armed bandit problem which we want to treat. Let two experiments (arms) A_0 and A_1 be given and let us restrict ourselves to the case of Bernoulli experiments (the outcomes being 0 = reward = R and 1 = nonreward = N). Let π_0 and π_1 be the probabilities of 0 in the first, respectively, the second experiment. On each trial $n \geq 1$ the controller is faced with the problem of choosing, dependently from the past outcomes between A_0 or A_1. He proceeds in such a way as to reduce the total number of units unaware of the values of π_0 and π_1.

In what follows we shall examine two possible procedures (strategies) of the controller. The first one is a randomized strategy which is based on learning techniques, whereas the latter, which is not randomized, leans on sequential techniques.

1.2.2. We begin with a strategy based on learning techniques. The controller starts at $n=1$ with a probability $p \in [0,1]$ for choosing A_0. If he chooses A_0 on trial n with probability p_n, his probability p_{n+1} for choosing A_0 on trial $n+1$ will be updated according to the following scheme, which depends on a learning parameter $\mu \in [0,1]$:

$$p_{n+1} = \begin{cases} \mu p_n + (1-\mu) & \text{if } A_0 \text{ and } 0 \text{ occured,} \\ \mu p_n & \text{if } A_1 \text{ and } 0 \text{ occured,} \\ p_n & \text{if } 1 \text{ occured.} \end{cases}$$

This situation can be described by an RSCC by setting: $W = [0,1]$, $X = \{ij : i,j \in \{0,1\}\}$, where i represents the arm A_i and j the outcome,

$$u(p,ij) = \alpha_{ij} p + (1 - \alpha_{ij}) \delta_{io} \tag{1.1}$$

with $\alpha_{00} = \alpha_{10} = \mu$, $\alpha_{01} = \alpha_{11} = 1$, where δ_{ij} is the Kronecker symbol, and

$$P(p,ij) = (p\delta_{i0} + (1-p)\delta_{i1})\pi_{ij} \tag{1.2}$$

with $\pi_{00} = 1-\pi_{01} = \pi_0$, $\pi_{10} = 1-\pi_{11} = \pi_1$. In this case for the associated event process $\{\xi_n : n\geq 1\}$ we can write $\xi_n = (\xi_{1n}, \xi_{2n})$ with $\xi_{1n}\in\{A_0, A_1\}$ and $\xi_{2n}\in\{0,1\}$ for all $n\geq 1$. Clearly ζ_n denotes the probability for choosing arm A_0 on trial n.

Further, the aim of the controller is to make the more expeditious choice between the arms. In order to tackle this problem, let us take as penalty function $f(ij) = j$, $ij\in X$, and let us examine whether the above updating scheme, i.e., the family F_0 of transition functions determined by (1.1), $u=u(\mu)$, $\mu\in[0,1]$, is absolutely expedient or optimal.

THEOREM 1.1. <u>The updating scheme</u> u <u>defined by</u> (1.1) <u>is absolutely</u> $[0,1]$ -P_0- <u>expedient for all</u> $\mu\in[0,1]$, <u>where</u> $P_0=\{P: P$ <u>given by</u> (1.2) $\}$.

CORROLLARY 1.2. Let $\pi_0\neq\pi_1$. <u>For all</u> $\mu, p\in[0,1]$: (i) ζ_n <u>converges</u> $\mathbb{P}_p$<u>-a.s. to a limit</u> ζ_∞ <u>as</u> $n\to\infty$; (ii) $P^n(p,A_0)$ <u>converges to a limit</u> $P^\infty(p,A_0)$ <u>as</u> $n\to\infty$.

Now we are able to characterize the ε-optimality of the family F_0 whose elements u are determined by (1.1) for $\mu\in[0,1]$. In what follows we shall use either a subscript of a superscript to indicate which u was used.

If A_k is the better action (i.e., $\pi_k>\pi_i$, $i\neq k$), let $\sigma_n = (1/n)\sum_{j=1}^{n} 1_{\{\xi_{1j} = A_k\}}$ be the proportion of right choices up to trial n, let $\tau_n = (1/n)\sum_{j=1}^{n} 1_{\{\xi_{2j} = R\}}$ be the proportion of rewards up to trial n. With respect to the family P_1 defined by $P_1=\{P: P\in\mathcal{P}_0$ and $\pi_0\neq\pi_1\}$ we get

THEOREM 1.3. <u>The following statements are equivalent</u>: (i) F_0 <u>is</u> $[0,1]$-P_1-ε-<u>optimal</u>; (ii) <u>for each</u> $p\in[0,1]$ <u>and</u> $\varepsilon>0$ <u>there is</u> $\mu_0 = \mu_{\varepsilon,p}\in[0,1)$ <u>such that</u> $(\pi_1-\pi_0)P^\infty_{\mu_0}(p,A_0)<\varepsilon$ <u>if</u> $\pi_0<\pi_1$ <u>and</u> $(\pi_0-\pi_1)P^\infty_{\mu_0}(p,A_1)<\varepsilon$ <u>if</u> $\pi_1<\pi_0$ <u>for all</u> $P\in P_1$; (iii) <u>for each</u> $p\in[0,1]$ <u>and</u> $\varepsilon>0$ <u>there is</u> $\mu_0 = \mu_{\varepsilon,p}\in[0,1)$ <u>such that</u> $(\pi_1-\pi_0)\lim_{n\to\infty}\mathbb{E}_p^{\mu_0}\sigma_n>(\pi_1-\pi_0)-\varepsilon$ <u>if</u> $\pi_0<\pi_1$ <u>and</u> $(\pi_0-\pi_1)\lim_{n\to\infty}\mathbb{E}_p^{\mu_0}\sigma_n>(\pi_0-\pi_1)-\varepsilon$ <u>if</u> $\pi_1<\pi_0$ <u>for all</u> $P\in P_1$; (iv) <u>for each</u> $p\in[0,1]$ <u>and</u> $\varepsilon>0$ <u>there is</u> $\mu_0 = \mu_{\varepsilon,p}\in[0,1)$ <u>such that</u> $\lim_{n\to\infty}\mathbb{E}_p^{\mu_0}\tau_n>\pi_1-\varepsilon$ <u>if</u> $\pi_0<\pi_1$ <u>and</u> $\lim_{n\to\infty}\mathbb{E}_p^{\mu_0}\tau_n>\pi_0-\varepsilon$ <u>if</u> $\pi_1<\pi_0$ <u>for all</u> $P\in P_1$. <u>Moreover if in</u> (ii) P_1 <u>is replaced by</u> $P_2=\{P\in P_0$ <u>and</u> $\pi_0,\pi_1\geq 0\}$, <u>then</u> (ii) <u>is equivalent to</u>: (v) <u>for each</u> $p\in[0,1]$ <u>and</u> $\varepsilon>0$ <u>there is</u> $\mu_0 = \mu_{\varepsilon,p}\in[0,1)$ <u>such that</u>

$(\pi_1 - \pi_0)\mathbb{P}_p^{\mu_0}(\zeta_\infty=0)>(\pi_1-\pi_0)-\varepsilon$ <u>if</u> $\pi_0<\pi_1$ <u>and</u> $(\pi_0-\pi_1)\mathbb{P}_p^{\mu_0}(\zeta_\infty=1)>(\pi_0-\pi_1)-\varepsilon$ <u>if</u> $\pi_1<\pi_0$ <u>for all</u> $P\in P_2$.

Roughly speaking (iv) means that the asymptotic expected proportion of successes (i.e., choices of the better arm) is 1 for an optimal family of transition functions. A similar concept of optimality was used by I.H. Witten in [14].

We note that ε-optimality of F_0 can be proven under additional conditions; for example, M.F. Norman [8] , p. 237, proves that F_0 is $[0,1)-P_1\cap P_2-\varepsilon$-optimal.

Finally, we can characterize the optimality of F_0 as we did it for the ε-optimality.

1.2.3. Let us examine now a procedure, as described by W. Vogel [11, 12] which is based on sequential techniques. Let A_{0k} and A_{1k} be the outcomes associated with the arms A_0 and A_1 , respectively, on trial k. Suppose now n be given. The controller proceeds as follows: Observe A_0 and A_1 on trial k , and then decide either to observe another pair, i.e., A_0 and A_1 or to continue exclusively with the experiment A_0 , or to continue exclusively with the experiment A_1 for the rest of the n-k trials. The decision is based upon $\eta_0=0$, $\eta_k = \sum_{j=1}^{k}(A_{0j}-A_{1j})$ and a given integer $\alpha>0$: if $|\eta_k|<\alpha$, another pair (A_0,A_1) is observed; if $|\eta_k|\geq\alpha$ for the first time the controller stops observing pairs (A_0, A_1) and chooses only pairs (A_0,A_0) and (A_1,A_1) according as $\eta_k\leq-\alpha$ or $\eta_k\geq\alpha$ for the rest of the n-k trials. Obviously this procedure makes sense only if $\alpha\leq n$. If κ represents the random number of observed pairs, then $0<\kappa\leq n$.

This situation can be described by an RSCC by setting:
$W = \{-\alpha,\ldots,0,\ldots,\alpha\}$, $X = \{ij: ij\in\{0,1\}\}$,

$$u(w,uj) = \begin{cases} w+i-j & \text{for } |w|<\alpha, \\ w & \text{for } |w|=\alpha, \end{cases} \tag{1.3}$$

and

$$P(w,00) = \begin{cases} \pi_0\pi_1 & \text{for } |w|<\alpha, \\ \pi_0^2 & \text{for } w=-\alpha, \\ \pi_1^2 & \text{for } w=\alpha, \end{cases} \quad P(w,01) = \begin{cases} \pi_0(1-\pi_1) & \text{for } |w|<\alpha, \\ \pi_0(1-\pi_0) & \text{for } w=-\alpha, \\ \pi_1(1-\pi_1) & \text{for } w=\alpha, \end{cases}$$

(1.4)

$$P(w,10) = \begin{cases} (1-\pi_0)\pi_1 & \text{for } |w|<\alpha, \\ (1-\pi_0)\pi_0 & \text{for } w=-\alpha, \\ (1-\pi_1)\pi_1 & \text{for } w=\alpha, \end{cases} \quad P(w,11) = \begin{cases} (1-\pi_0)(1-\pi_1) & \text{for } |w|<\alpha, \\ (1-\pi_0)^2 & \text{for } w=-\alpha, \\ (1-\pi_1)^2 & \text{for } w=\alpha. \end{cases}$$

$\{\zeta_n:n\geq 1\}$ and $\{\xi_n=(\xi_{0n},\xi_{1n}):n\geq 1\}$ are, respectively, the associated state and event processes of this RSCC. Then $\zeta_n=\eta_n$ as long as $\max\{|\eta_k|:1\leq k\leq n\}\leq\alpha$, otherwise $\zeta_{n+1}=\zeta_n$. Moreover $\xi_{0n}=A_{0n}$, $\xi_{1n}=A_{1n}$ as long as $\max\{|\eta_k|:1\leq k\leq n\}\leq\alpha$, otherwise ξ_n represents the outcome of the pair of identical experiments. Clearly the strategy of the controller corresponds to $\zeta_1=w=0$.

In order to examine the controller's procedure within our framework, let us introduce the following penalty function $f(ij)=i+j$, $ij\in X$, i.e., f assigns to the outcome of a pair of observed experiments its number of nonrewards. Further we have to examine the family F_0 of transition functions determined by (1.3), $u=u(\alpha)$, $\alpha\geq 1$. It is easily shown that absolute expediency fails. However we have

THEOREM 1.4. <u>The updating scheme</u> u <u>defined by</u> (1.3) <u>is</u> $\{0\}$-P_0- <u>expedient for all</u> $\alpha\geq 1$, <u>where</u> $P_0=\{P:P$ <u>given by</u> (1.4)$\}$.

Next, for the ε-optimality of the family F_0 we have

THEOREM 1.5. F_0 <u>is</u> $\{0\}$-P_1-ε-<u>optimal, where</u> $P_1=\{P:P\in P_0$ <u>and</u> $|\pi_0-\pi_1|\geq\beta>0\}$.

Note that since $\lim_{n\to\infty}\mathbb{E}_0\rho_n>2\min(1-\pi_0,1-\pi_1)$ for any finite $\alpha\geq 1$ and $\pi_0\neq\pi_1$, optimality is not possible except for the trivial case $\pi_0=\pi_1$.

Let us further consider the possibility of choosing a best possible α for a given n. Indeed, we need to introduce a loss function which will depend in fact on n, α, π_0 and π_1. In accordance with W. Vogel [11], p.435, we shall take as loss function the difference between the expected total number of nonrewards and the least possible expected total number of nonrewards, i.e.,

$$L_n(\alpha,\pi_0,\pi_1) = \mathbb{E}_0\left(\sum_{m=1}^{n}\xi_{0m}+\xi_{1m}\right)-2n\min(1-\pi_0,1-\pi_1).$$

This loss function can be written in the following form:

$$(1.5)\qquad L_n(\alpha,\pi_0,\pi_1)=(\pi_1-\pi_0)\left\{\sum_{m=1}^{n}Q^{m-1}(0,-\alpha)-\sum_{m=1}^{n}Q^{m-1}(0,\alpha)\right\}+$$

$$+\,n(2-\pi_0+\pi_1)-2n\min(1-\pi_0,1-\pi_1).$$

Suppose now that we already have some knowledge about π_0 and π_1, e.g., in the form of a discrete a priori distribution over (π_0, π_1). Then we can use (1.5) to calculate the exact value of the expected loss function $\bar{L}_n(\alpha)$ with respect to this a priori distribution, provided that n is not too large. Since $1 \le \alpha \le n$ we get an α_0 which minimizes $\bar{L}_n(\alpha)$.

If no a priori distribution is given or if n is large, we can approximate $L_n(\alpha, \pi_0, \pi_1)$ by another function $M_n(\alpha, \pi_0, \pi_1)$ such that $L_n \le M_n$ and $\lim_{n\to\infty}(M_n - L_n) = 0$; an example of such a function, M_n, is that proposed by W. Vogel [11], p.436. Next, given n, we can take as the best possible α that one evaluated by W. Vogel [11,12] by the application of the minimax principle to M_n.

2. STOCHASTIC APPROXIMATION PROCEDURES

2.1. Introduction

2.1.1. Let W and X be subsets of Euclidean multidimensional spaces, let P be an unknown stochastic kernel from W to the Borel sets of X, and let f be a measurable real-valued function defined on $W \times X$. Let the integral $M(w) = \int_X f(w,x) P(w,dx)$ exist for all $w \in W$ and let us assume that M has a maximum at the unknown point θ. Since P is unknown, M itself is unknown to the controller who often faces the problem of finding θ. In order to solve this problem, it is assumed that the controller can use the information provided by the outcomes occured according to $P(w,.)$ for any $w \in W$. In other words, finding θ reduces to finding an appropriate learning procedure.

A possible approach to such a problem is to make use of the theory of stochastic approximation techniques (which, incidentally, can be described as random systems with complete connections). In what follows we want to apply the Kiefer-Wolfowitz procedure [7] to two special situations: the two-armed bandit problem and a market pricing problem.

2.1.2. The Kiefer-Wolfowitz stochastic approximation procedure deals with the problem of finding the maximum of a regression function $R(w) = \int_{\mathbb{R}} y S(w,dy)$ which is supposed to be located at the unknown point $w = \theta$. It works as follows: given an initial value w_1, which, in general, can be the outcome of a random variable, one constructs a sequence $\{\zeta_n : n \ge 1\}$ of random variables by means of the algorithm

(2.1) $$\zeta_{n+1} = \zeta_n + (a_n/c_n)(\eta_{2n} - \eta_{2n-1}) , \quad n \ge 1 ,$$

where η_{2n-1} and η_{2n} are independent random variables distributed according to $S(\zeta_n - c_n,.)$ and $S(\zeta_n + c_n,.)$ respectively. $\{a_n : n \geq 1\}$ and $\{c_n : n \geq 1\}$ are given sequences of positive real numbers satisfying the conditions [1]:

$$(2.2) \qquad c_n \to 0 \quad (n \to \infty), \quad \sum_{n=1}^{\infty} a_n = \infty \ , \quad \sum_{n=1}^{\infty} (a_n/c_n)^2 < \infty \ .$$

Under certain regularity assumptions [1] on R, one being that R is increasing for $w<\theta$ and decreasing for $w>\theta$, then $\zeta_n \to \theta$ a.s. as $n \to \infty$, where $R(\theta)$ is the unique maximum of R. Since M can be written as a regression function R, the Kiefer-Wolfowitz procedure can be used for solving the problem stated at the beginning of this section for those cases satisfying the imposed regularity conditions (see, e.g., [1,7,13]).

2.2. The two-armed bandit problem

2.2.1. Consider the two-armed bandit problem under the following form. Let two experiments (arms) A_0 and A_1 be given and let us assume that A_0 and A_1 are characterized by the distribution functions F_0 and F_1 respectively. In what follows we assume that both F_0 and F_1 have finite variances. Let μ_0 and μ_1 be their expectations respectively. On each trial $n \geq 1$ the controller is faced with the problem of choosing dependent upon the past outcomes (=rewards), between A_0 and A_1. He proceeds in such a way that his expected reward per trial reaches its maximal value, i.e., $\max\{\mu_0, \mu_1\}$, being unaware of F_0 and F_1. Consequently he thus maximizes his asympototic averaged expected reward. A procedure (strategy) permitting the controller to achieve this goal is said to be optimal.

2.2.2. If we allow the controller to choose between A_0 and A_1 with a certain probability, we can propose an optimal strategy by making use of the Kiefer-Wolfowitz procedure. Therefore we have to find appropriate W, X, P, and f.

Take $W = [0,1]$ and let $w \in W$ be the probability of choosing the arm A_0. Next take $X = \{0,1\} \times \mathbb{R}$, where the first component of an $x = ir \in X$ represents the arm A_i and the second component represents its outcome. Further, take $P(w,iB) = w(1-i)\,F_0(B) + (1-w)iF_1(B)$ for any Borel set B of $\mathbb{R}$; here we use the same notations for the distribution functions F_0 and F_1 and the probability measures induced by them. Furthermore, for f we take $f(w,ir) = r$. With these elements, we get the expected reward $M(w) = \mu_0 w + \mu_1 (1-w)$. Thus the controller faces the problem of finding the maximum of M, i.e., $\max\{\mu_0, \mu_1\}$, being unaware of F_0 and F_1 : this maximum being attained either at $\theta=0$ or at $\theta=1$.

2.2.3. We now apply the Kiefer-Wolfowitz procedure under the conditions described in [1] for $W=\mathbb{R}$. The controller's strategy is described as follows. (δ) Given the starting point $\zeta_1=w_1\in[0,1]$ and the sequences $\{a_n:n\geq 1\}$ and $\{c_n:n\geq 1\}$ as required by (2.2) the controller performs his first trial according to w_1-c_1 and his second trial according to w_1+c_1 . This means that he chooses arm A_0 in the first trial (in the second trial) with probability w_1-c_1 (w_1+c_1) as long as $0\leq w_1-c_1\leq 1$ $(0\leq w_1+c_1\leq 1)$. If $w_1-c_1<0$ $(w_1+c_1<0)$, he chooses arm A_1 in the first trial (in the second trial) and, if $w_1-c_1>1$ $(w_1+c_1>1)$, he chooses arm A_0 in the first trial (in the second trial). As a result of this choice he will observe an outcome (= reward) r for each trial. This outcome may be regarded as a realization of the random variable η_1 (η_2) defined by

$$\eta_1 = \begin{cases} m_0(w_1-c_1)+r & \text{for } w_1-c_1<0, \\ r & \text{for } 0\leq w_1-c_1\leq 1, \\ m_1(1-w_1+c_1)+r & \text{for } 1<w_1-c_1, \end{cases}$$

$$\eta_2 = \begin{cases} m_0(w_1+c_1)+r & \text{for } w_1+c_1<0, \\ r & \text{for } 0\leq w_1+c_1\leq 1, \\ m_1(1-w_1-c_1)+r & \text{for } 1<w_1+c_1, \end{cases}$$

where m_0 and m_1 are arbitrary but given by the controller such that m_0 , $m_1>0$. According to the algorithm (2.1) the controller calculates $\zeta_2=w_1+(a_1/c_1)(\eta_2-\eta_1)$ and performs the third trial according to ζ_2-c_2 and the fourth trial according to ζ_2+c_2 as described above. He then calculates ζ_3 by means of η_3 and η_4 etc. In this way the controller gets from (2.1) a sequence $\{\zeta_n:n\geq 1\}$, which means that he chooses between A_0 and A_1 according to the sequence $\{\tau_n:n\geq 1\}$ defined as $\tau_{2n-1}=\zeta_n-c_n$ and $\tau_{2n}=\zeta_n+c_n$. From [1] we get that $\zeta_n\to\theta$ a.s. as $n\to\infty$. As a consequence we obtain $\tau_n\to\theta$ a.s. as $n\to\infty$. Thus we have

THEOREM 2.1. <u>Strategy</u> (δ) <u>is optimal</u>.

2.3. A market pricing problem

2.3.1. Let us consider the following model. A store is attempting to price a particular item in its inventory. It is assumed that potential customers arrive at a constant rate which is unaffected by the price $w\in W\subset[0,\infty)$ the store is charging for this item. By an appropriate choice of units this rate is taken to be one per period. Upon entering the store, a customer asks the price of the item and then decides whether to buy it or not. From the point of view of the store, each potential customer is a binomial random variable which will buy ("1") one unit with probability $\phi(w) = P(w,1)$ and not buy ("0") with probability $1-\phi(w) = P(w,0)$. The function ϕ depends on the price quoted to the customer and is unknown to the store. The store wants to maximize its expected profit per period $M(w) = (w-h)\phi(w)$, where h is the constant cost per item to the store owner assuming always that $w \geq h$. Each strategy permitting the store owner to maximize his asymptotic averaged expected profit is said to be <u>optimal</u>.

Such a model was discussed in [10] by means of dynamic programming methods when W contains only two elements and when an a priori distribution on the $\phi(w)$'s is given. Since the store owner has at his disposal only two prices, he is led in this case to a two-armed bandit problem. In what follows we apply stochastic approximation techniques to the case when W is an interval: such a situation leading to a multi-armed bandit problem.

2.3.2. In order to simplify the store owner's problem we shall assume that $w \leq H$, H being the maximal price he can quote to his customers. Next, it seems natural to assume that the probability of buying the item will be a nonincreasing function of $w \in W$.

With our previous notation, we have $W = [h,H]$, $X = \{0,1\}, P(w,1) = \phi(w)$ and $f(w,x) = (w-h)x$. Then the expected profit is $M(w) = \int_X f(w,x)P(x,dx) = (w-h)\phi(w)$. Again we have to make sure that the regularity assumptions required in [1] are satisfied. We mention here three special cases when this happens:

(a) $\phi(w) = e^{-\alpha w}$, where the parameter $\alpha > 0$ is unknown to the store owner. Then $M(w) = (w-h)\phi(w)$ attains its maximum either at $\theta = 1/\alpha + h$ (if $\alpha > 1/(H-h)$) or at $\theta = H$.

(b) $\phi(w) = Aw+B$, where the parameters $A<0$ and $B>0$ are unknown to the store owner. Then $M(w) = \alpha - \beta(w-\theta)^2$ with $\alpha = -(Ah+B)^2/4A$, $\beta = -A$: the maximum occurs either at $\theta = (Ah-B)/2A$ (if $B < A(h-2H)$) or at $\theta = H$.

(c) ϕ a continuously differentiable concave, positive function. Since in this case ϕ' is nonpositive and decreasing, $-\phi'(w)(w-h)$ is a nonnegative increasing function on $[h,H]$, whose graph can have at most one common point with the graph of the decreasing function ϕ. Therefore M' has at most one root w_0 so that the maximum of M is attained either at $\theta = w_0$ or at $\theta = H$.

The strategy of the store owner can be described as follows. (δ') Given the starting point $\zeta_1=w_1\in[h,H]$ and the sequences $\{a_n:n\geq 1\}$ and $\{c_n:n\geq 1\}$ as required by (2.2), the store owner quotes the price w_1-c_1 in the first period and the price w_1+c_1 in the second period as long as $h\leq w_1\pm c_1\leq H$ respectively. If $h\leq w_1-c_1\leq H$ and $w_1+c_1>H$, he quotes price H in the second period. If $w_1-c_1<h$ he quotes the price $\min\{w_1+c_1,H\}$ in the first period and the prices in the second and third period are quoted according to ζ_2, i.e., they are $\min\{\zeta_2-c_2,H\}$ and $\min\{\zeta_2+c_2,H\}$ respectively as long as $\zeta_2\pm c_2\geq h$. Taking into account the outcomes 1 or 0, i.e., whether the item was or was not bought for the quoted price, he calculates ζ_2 by means of (2.1). Therefore, the random variables η_1 and η_2 needed are given by

$$\eta_1 = \begin{cases} m_0(w_1-c_1-h) & \text{for } w_1-c_1<h, \\ 0 & \text{for } h\leq w_1-c_1\leq H \text{ and } 0 \text{ observed}, \\ w_1-c_1-h & \text{for } h\leq w_1-c_1\leq H \text{ and } 1 \text{ observed}, \\ m_1(H-w_1+c_1) & \text{for } H<w_1-c_1 \text{ and } 0 \text{ observed}, \\ m_1(H-w_1+c_1)+H-h & \text{for } H<w_1-c_1 \text{ and } 1 \text{ observed}, \end{cases}$$

$$\eta_2 = \begin{cases} m_0(w_1+c_1-h) & \text{for } w_1+c_1<h, \\ 0 & \text{for } h\leq w_1+c_1\leq H \text{ and } 0 \text{ observed}, \\ w_1+c_1-h & \text{for } h\leq w_1+c_1\leq H \text{ and } 1 \text{ observed}, \\ m_1(H-w_1-c_1) & \text{for } H<w_1+c_1 \text{ and } 0 \text{ observed}, \\ m_1(H-w_1-c_1)+H-h & \text{for } H<w_1+c_1 \text{ and } 1 \text{ observed}, \end{cases}$$

where $m_0,m_1>0$ are arbitrary chosen by the store owner. We calculate further ζ_n, $n\geq 2$, according to this scheme by means of η_3 and η_4 etc. Since the resulting sequence $\{\zeta_n:n\geq 1\}$ converges a.s. to the point where the maximum is attained, the algorithm produces values $\geq h$, which can be quoted as prices.

If we restrict ourselves to sequences $\{a_n:n\geq 1\}$ and $\{c_n:n\geq 1\}$ as required by (2.2) and having the special form $a_n=an^{-\alpha}$, $c_n=cn^{-\gamma}$, where $a<c$ (e.g., $a_n=an^{-1}$ and $c_n=cn^{-\frac{1}{4}}$), one easily shows that if $\zeta_1-c_1\geq h$, all possible values ζ_n-c_n, ζ_n+c_n are $\geq h$, i.e., all values produced by the algorithm can be quoted as prices.

Let $\{\tau_n:n\geq 1\}$ be the sequence of quoted prices. We get that $\tau_n\to\theta$ a.s. as $n\to\infty$, θ being the point where M reaches its maximum.

Using this strategy, the store owner will have at time n an expected profit $M(\tau_n)$ (which depends of course on the random variable τ_n). Since $\tau_n\to\theta$ a.s. as $n\to\infty$, the expected profit per period tends to its maximal value as $n \to \infty$. Thus we have

THEOREM 2.2. Strategy (δ') is optimal.

REFERENCES

[1] Blum, J.R., Approximation methods which converge with probability one. Ann. Math. Statist. 25 (1954), 382-386.

[2] Herkenrath, U., Theodorescu, R., General control systems. Information Sci. 14 (1978), 57-73.

[3] ———, On certain aspects of the two-armed bandit problem. Elektron. Informationsverarbeit. Kybernetik (1978).

[4] ———, Expediency and optimality for general control systems. Coll. Internat. C.N.R.S., Cachan, July 4-8, 1977.

[5] ———, On a stochastic approximation procedure applied to the bandit problem. (submitted to publication).

[6] Iosifescu, M., Theodorescu, R., Random processes and learning. Springer, New York 1969.

[7] Kiefer, J., Wolfowitz, J., Stochastic estimation of the maximum of a regression function. Ann. Math. Statist. 23 (1952), 462-466.

[8] Norman, M.F., On the linear model with two absorbing barriers. J. Math. Psychology 5 (1968), 225-241.

[9] ———, Markov processes and learning models. Academic Press, New York 1972.

[10] Rotschild, M., A two-armed bandit theory of market pricing. J. Econom. Theory 9 (1974), 430-443.

[11] Vogel, W., A sequential design for the two armed bandit. Ann. Math. Statist. 31 (1960), 430-443.

[12] ——— , An asympototic minimax theorem for the two armed bandit problem. Ann. Math. Statist. 31 (1960), 444-451.

[13] Wasan, M.T., Stochastic approximation. Cambridge University Press, Cambridge 1969.

[14] Witten, I.H., Finite-time performance of some two-armed bandit controllers. IEEE Trans. Syst., Man., Cybern. SMC-3 (1973), 194-197.

EXISTENCE AND UNIQUENESS FOR STOCHASTIC DIFFERENTIAL EQUATIONS

Jean Jacod (Université de Rennes, France)

1. INTRODUCTION

Throughout all the paper, a complete probability space $(\Omega, \underline{\underline{F}}, P)$ is fixed, and equipped with a right-continuous increasing family $\underline{F} = (\underline{\underline{F}}_t)_{t \geq 0}$ of sub-σ-fields of $\underline{\underline{F}}$, each of them containing all P-null sets of $\underline{\underline{F}}$. We are interested in strong solutions of stochastic differential equations (in short: s.d.f.).

The first s.d.f., as considered by K. Ito, was the next one

(1) $$X_t = x + \int_0^t \sigma_s \, dW_s + \int_0^t \beta_s \, ds$$

where the driving processes are a brownian motion W given on $(\Omega, \underline{\underline{F}}, \underline{F}, P)$ and the deterministic process t. Of course, here as well as in the sequel, the processes are possibly multi-dimensional and the coefficients (here: σ and β) have the appropriate dimensions. Then Skorokhod [14] introduced the following s.d.f.:

(2) $$X_t = x + \int_0^t \alpha_s \, ds + \int_0^t \beta_s \, dW_s + \int_0^t\int_E \gamma(s,x) I_{\{|\gamma(s,x)| \leq 1\}} (dp - dq)(s,x) + \int_0^t\int_E \gamma(s,x) I_{\{|\gamma(s,x)| > 1\}} dp(s,x)$$

where the driving processes are a brownian motion W, a Poisson random measure p on $E = \mathbb{R}^m$ and its compensator (intensity maesure) q, and the deterministic process t.

More recently, Galtchouk [4] introduced the equation

(3) $$X_t = H_t + \int_0^t \alpha_s \, dA_s + \int_0^t \beta_s \, dM_s + \int_0^t\int_{\{|x| \leq 1\}} \gamma(s,x)(d\mu - d\nu)(s,x) + \int_0^t\int_{\{|x| > 1\}} \gamma(s,x) d\mu(s,x)$$

where the driving processes are: a right-continuous and left-hand limited adapted process H, a multi-dimensional process A with finite variation, a multi-dimensional continuous local martingale M, an integer-valued random measure μ on $E = \mathbb{R}^m$ and its compensator ν. At last several authors (including Kazamaki [8], Doléans-Dade [2], Protter [13]) studied the following s.d.f.:

(4) $$X_t = H_t + \int_0^t g_s \, dY_s$$

where H is as above and Y is a multi-dimensional semimartingale.

Now in all these equations, three levels of generality are possible about the various coefficients:

(a) they depend on t and the left-hand limit X_{t-} of the solution at time t (or on X_t if the coefficient is to be integrated with respect to a continuous process)

(b) in addition, they depend on ω in a non-anticipating way

(c) in addition, they depend on the path $X_{\cdot}$ of the solution, strictly before time t .

Conditions of type (a) for equation (2) and of type (b) for equations (3) and (4) have been derived by the above-mentionned authors, in order to obtain one and only one solution. For the continuous case (equation (1)), type (c) hypothesis have also been investigated since a long time: cf. the book [5] of Gihman and Skorokhod. For equation (4), a decisive step in studying type (c) hypothesis was taken recently by Métivier and Pellaumail [9], [10].

Here we are concerned by the following s.d.f., at the level (c) of generality:

$$(5)\quad X_t = H_t + \int_0^t u_s dM_s + \int_0^t\int_E v(s,x)(d\mu - d\nu)(s,x) + \int_0^t\int_{E'} w(s,x)d\mu'(s,x) ,$$

where H, M, μ, ν are like in (3), and μ' is another random measure. We shall see in section 5 that all the above equations are particular cases of (5). Moreover, the conditions obtained here, when applied to the other equations, even at a lower level of generality, are weaker than the previously known conditions.

2. THE DRIVING PROCESSES

For the basic facts about σ-fields and stochastic integrals, we refer to Dellacherie [1] and Meyer [12]. Let us recall that the predictable (resp. optional) σ-field $\underline{\underline{P}}(\underline{\underline{F}})$ (resp. $\underline{\underline{O}}(\underline{\underline{F}})$) is the σ-field on $\Omega\times\mathbb{R}_+$ generated by all continuous (resp. right-continuous, left-hand limited) adapted processes, and the progressive σ-field $\underline{\underline{\Pi}}(\underline{\underline{F}})$ is the class of all subsets $A\subset\Omega\times\mathbb{R}_+$ such that $A\cap(\Omega\times[0,t])$ is $\underline{\underline{F}}_t\otimes\underline{\underline{B}}(\mathbb{R}_+)$-measurable for each t .

2.1 - The process H . This is an adapted, right-continuous, left-hand limited process $H=(H^i)_{i\leq m}$. It plays the role of the initial condition, and is often equal to a constant $x\in\mathbb{R}^m$.

2.2 - The process M . This is a m'-dimensional continuous local martingale $M=(M^i)_{i\leq m'}$. There exist an increasing continuous process C with $C_0=0$ and $C_t<\infty$ $\forall t<\infty$, and a predictable process $c=(c^{ij})_{i,j\leq m'}$ with values in the set of symetric nonnegative $m'\times m'$-matrices, such that with the usual notations:

$$<M^i,M^j>_t = \int_0^t c_s^{ij}\, dC_s$$

(for the brownian motion, take $C_t = t$ and $c_s^{ij} = \delta^{ij}$). Let $L(M)$ be the set of all progressive m'-dimensional processes $K = (K^i)_{i\le m'}$ such that

(6) $\quad \int_0^t (\sum_{i,j} K_s^i c_s^{ij} K_s^j) dC_s < \infty \qquad$ P-a.s. for all $t<\infty$.

This is exactly the class of processes which are stochastically integrable with respect to M, and the process in (6) is exactly the bracket $<\int_0^{\cdot} K_s dM_s, \int_0^{\cdot} K_s dM_s>_t$ (cf. for example Galtchouk [3] or Métivier and Pistone [11]). The class $L(M)$ does not depend on the particular choice of (C,c).

2.3 - The random measures μ and ν. For these questions we refer to [6] or [7], and content ourselves by just recalling some facts. E is an auxiliary Lusin space with its Borel σ-field $\underline{\underline{E}}$, and an extra point Δ. We consider an integer-valued random measure μ on E, that is a measure of the form

(7) $\quad \mu(\omega;dt,dx) = \sum_{s\ge 0} I_{\{\beta_s(\omega)\in E\}}\, \varepsilon_{(s,\beta_s(\omega))}(dt,dx)$

where $\varepsilon_{\bullet}$ denotes the Dirac measure, and β is an optional process with values in $E\cup\{\Delta\}$, such that the sets $\{t : \beta_t(\omega)\in E\}$ are at most countable. In addition we suppose that there exists a $\underline{\underline{P}}(\underline{F})\otimes\underline{\underline{E}}$-measurable partition (A_n) of $\Omega\times\mathbb{R}_+\times E$ such that

$$E[\int\mu(\omega;dt,dx) I_{A_n}(\omega,t,x)] < \infty \qquad \forall n\in\mathbb{N}.$$

A typical example of such a measure is the Poisson random measure.

Now we can define the dual predictable projection, or compensator, of μ: it is another positive random measure $\nu(\omega;dt,dx)$ such that for any $A\in \underline{\underline{P}}(\underline{F})\otimes\underline{\underline{E}}$,

$$\begin{cases} \int_0^t\int_E \nu(\omega;ds,dx) I_A(\omega,s,x) & \text{is predictable in } (\omega,t), \\ E[\int\nu(ds,dx)I_A(s,x)] = E[\int\mu(ds,dx)I_A(s,x)]. \end{cases}$$

If μ is Poisson, ν does not depend on ω and is equal to the (deterministic) intensity measure. We use the following notations:

$$(8) \quad \begin{cases} J = \{(\omega,t) : \nu(\omega;\{t\}\times E) > 0\} \\ \widehat{V}_t(\omega) = \int_E \nu(\omega;\{t\},dx)V(\omega,t,x) \quad \text{if this integral exists.} \end{cases}$$

Of course $\widehat{V} = 0$ outside J, and J is the "predictable support" of the set $\{(\omega,t) : \beta_t(\omega)\in E\}$.

Let us define the following increasing process:

$$(9) \quad C(V,\nu)_t = \begin{cases} \int_0^t\int_E V^2(s,x) I_{J^c}(s,x)\nu(ds,dx) + \sum_{0<s\le t}[\widehat{V^2_s} - (\widehat{V}_s)^2] \\ \qquad \text{if all those terms are well defined,} \\ +\infty \qquad \text{if not.} \end{cases}$$

We denote by $L(\mu)$ the set of all $\underline{\underline{P}}(\underline{F})\otimes\underline{\underline{E}}$-measurable functions V on

$\Omega\times\mathbb{R}_+\times E$ such that $C(V,\nu)_t<\infty$ P-a.s. $\forall t<\infty$. If $V\in L(\mu)$ we can define its stochastic integral $N_t = \int_0^t\int_E V(d\mu - d\nu)$, which is the only locally square integrable martingale with a vanishing continuous part and such that

$$\Delta N_t(\omega) = \int_E V(\omega,t,x)[\mu(\omega;\{t\},dx) - \nu(\omega;\{t\},dx)]$$

and $L(\mu)$ is the largest class for which we can define such a stochastic integral, and obtain a locally square integrable martingale.

2.4 - The random measure μ'. We consider another auxiliary Lusin space E' with its Borel σ-field $\underline{\underline{E}}'$. Then μ' is an optional random measure, that is for each ω we have a σ-finite measure $\mu'(\omega;dt,dx)$ on $\mathbb{R}_+\times E'$, and for each $\underline{\underline{O}}(\underline{\underline{F}})\otimes E'$-measurable function W on $\Omega\times\mathbb{R}_+\times E'$, the process $\int_0^t\int_{E'} W(\omega,s,x)\mu'(\omega;ds,dx)$ is optional in (ω,t), whenever it is well defined.

Notice that μ' is neither integer-valued, nor positive. For example (1) is a particular case of (5) if we take $E'=\{\delta\}$ to be a single point set, and

$$H_t(\omega) = x, \quad W = M, \quad \mu = \nu = 0, \quad \mu'(\omega;dt,\{\delta\}) = dt.$$

3. THE COEFFICIENTS

The solution will be a right-continuous and left-hand limited process $X=(X^i)_{i\leq m}$. Therefore it is convenient to introduce the canonical space $\check{\Omega}=D([0,\infty[;\mathbb{R}^m)$ equipped with the canonical process $\check{X}_t(\check{\omega})=\check{\omega}(t)$ and the canonical right-continuous filtration $\underline{\check{F}}=(\underline{\underline{\check{F}}}_t)_{t\geq 0}$. Let us consider the product

$$(10) \qquad \Omega' = \Omega\times\check{\Omega}, \qquad \underline{\underline{F}}'_t = \bigcap_{s>t} \underline{\underline{F}}_s\otimes\underline{\underline{\check{F}}}_s .$$

The notations $\underline{\underline{P}}(\underline{F}')$ and $\underline{\underline{\Pi}}(\underline{F}')$ denote the predictable and progressive σ-fields on $\Omega'\times\mathbb{R}_+$, relative to the right-continuous filtration $\underline{F}'=(\underline{\underline{F}}'_t)$.

DEFINITION 1 : The coefficients are

(i) a $\underline{\underline{\Pi}}(\underline{F}')$-measurable function $\check{u}=(\check{u}^{ij})_{i\leq m, j\leq m'}$ on $\Omega'\times\mathbb{R}_+$

(ii) a $\underline{\underline{P}}(\underline{F}')\otimes\underline{\underline{E}}$-measurable function $\check{v}=(\check{v}^i)_{i\leq m}$ on $\Omega'\times\mathbb{R}_+\times E$

(iii) a $\underline{\underline{P}}(\underline{F}')\otimes\underline{\underline{E}}'$-measurable function $\check{w}=(\check{w}^i)_{i\leq m}$ on $\Omega'\times\mathbb{R}_+\times E'$.

Remark: When μ' is "continuous", i.e. satisfies identically $\mu'(\{t\}\times E')=0$, then in (iii) above it is sufficient to take a $\underline{\underline{\Pi}}(\underline{F}')\otimes\underline{\underline{E}}'$-measurable function.

The symbol $|x|$ where x is a scalar, a vector, a matrix, denotes anyone of the usual norms. We define two right-continuous increasing functions by putting

$$(11)\qquad \begin{cases} \check{X}^*_t(\check{\omega}) = \sup_{s\leq t} |\check{X}_s(\check{\omega})| \\ \check{Z}_t(\check{\omega},\check{\omega}') = \sup_{s\leq t} |\check{X}_s(\check{\omega}) - \check{X}_s(\check{\omega}')| . \end{cases}$$

Now we shall give a number of various conditions on these three coefficients.

3.1 - The coefficient u . Let us begin by several Lipschitz-type conditions.

CONDITION A(u,1) : There exists a constant U such that

$$|\check{u}_t(\omega,\check{\omega}) - u_t(\omega,\check{\omega}')| \leq U\, \check{Z}_t(\check{\omega},\check{\omega}') \qquad \forall \omega, \check{\omega}, \check{\omega}', t .$$

CONDITION A(u,2) : There exists a progressive process U such that $\int_0^t U_s^2\, dC_s < \infty$ P-a.s. for each finite t and such that

$$(12)\quad |\check{u}_t(\omega,\check{\omega}) c_t(\omega)^\tau \check{u}_t(\omega,\check{\omega}) - \check{u}_t(\omega,\check{\omega}') c_t(\omega)^\tau \check{u}_t(\check{\omega},\check{\omega}')| \leq U_t^2(\omega) \check{Z}_t^2(\check{\omega},\check{\omega}')$$

($^\tau\check{u}$ denotes the transpose of the matrix $\check{u}$) $\forall \omega, \check{\omega}, \check{\omega}'$, t .

CONDITION A(u,3) : For each $n\in\mathbb{N}$ there exists a progressive process ^nU such that $\int_0^t (^nU)_s^2 dC_s < \infty$ P-a.s. for each finite t and such that (12) holds with ^nU instead of U , $\forall\omega, \check{\omega}, \check{\omega}'$, t such that $\check{X}^*_t(\check{\omega}) \leq n$ and $\check{X}^*_t(\check{\omega}') \leq n$.

CONDITION A(u,4) : The same as A(u,3), except that (12) is replaced by

$$\int_0^t |\check{u}_s(\omega,\check{\omega}) c_s(\omega)\, ^\tau\check{u}_s(\omega,\check{\omega}) - \check{u}_s(\omega,\check{\omega}') c_s(\omega)\, ^\tau\check{u}_s(\omega,\check{\omega}')|\, dC_s(\omega) \leq \int_0^t (^nU_s(\omega))^2\, \check{Z}^2_{s-}(\check{\omega},\check{\omega}') dC_s(\omega) .$$

These conditions are clearly less and less restrictive. The first one is strictly speaking the Lipschitz condition when $\check{\Omega}$ is endowed with the topology of uniform convergence on each compact set. A(u,2) is the same condition, adapted to the fact that u is to be integrated with respect to M , so the values of u on a set which is "M-negligible" do not matter at all. A(u,3) is a local Lipshitz condition, and A(u,4) is of "integral type": it is formally much weaker than A(u,3), but on concrete examples it is certainly easier to verify A(u,3) than A(u,4).

Now let us introduce some conditions implying that u is "not too big".

CONDITION A(u,5) : There exists a $\check{\omega}_0 \in \check{\Omega}$ such that

$$\int_0^t |\check{u}_s(\omega,\check{\omega}_0) c_s(\omega)\, ^\tau\check{u}_s(\omega,\check{\omega}_0)|\, dC_s(\omega) < \infty \quad \text{P-a.s. for all } t\in\mathbb{R}_+$$

(in other words, each vector-process $\check{u}^{i\cdot}(.,\check{\omega}_0)$ is in $L(M)$).

CONDITION A(u,6) : There exists a progressive process U' such that $\int_0^t U'^2_s\, dC_s < \infty$ P-a.s. for each finite t , and such that for all t , ω , $\check{\omega}$:

$$|\check{u}_t(\omega,\check{\omega})c_t(\omega)^{\tau}\check{u}_t(\omega,\check{\omega})| \leq U_t'^2(\omega)(1+\check{X}_t^{*2}(\check{\omega})) .$$

<u>3.2 - The coefficient</u> v . For notational purposes, we set

(13) $$K_{\check{\omega},\check{\omega}',i}(\omega,t,x) = \check{v}^i(\omega,\check{\omega},t,x) - \check{v}^i(\omega,\check{\omega}',t,x) .$$

CONDITION A(v,2) : There exist $\underline{\underline{P}}(\underline{F})\otimes\underline{\underline{E}}$-measurable functions V^i on $\Omega\times\mathbb{R}_+\times E$ which belong to $L(\mu)$ (this amounts to saying: $C(V^i,\nu)_t<\infty$ P-a.s. for each finite t) and such that

(14) $$\begin{cases} |K_{\check{\omega},\check{\omega}',i}(\omega,t,x)| \leq |V^i(\omega,t,x)|\,\check{Z}_t(\check{\omega},\check{\omega}') & \text{if } (\omega,t)\notin J \\ (\widehat{K^2_{\check{\omega},\check{\omega}',i}})_t(\omega) - (\widehat{K}_{\check{\omega},\check{\omega}',i})^2_t(\omega) \leq [\widehat{(V^i)^2_t}(\omega) - \widehat{V^i_t}(\omega)^2]\check{Z}^2_t(\check{\omega},\check{\omega}') & \text{if } (\omega,t)\in J , \end{cases}$$

$\forall\, \omega,\check{\omega},\check{\omega}', t$.

CONDITION A(v,3) : For each $n\in\mathbb{N}$ there exist elements ${}^nV^i$ of $L(\mu)$, such that (14) holds with ${}^nV^i$ instead of V^i , $\forall\,\omega,\check{\omega},\check{\omega}'$, t such that $\check{X}^*_t(\check{\omega})\leq n$ and $\check{X}^*_t(\check{\omega}')\leq n$.

CONDITION A(v,4) : The same as in A(v,3), except that (12) is replaced by

$$C(K_{\check{\omega},\check{\omega}',i},\nu)_t(\omega) \leq \int_0^t \check{Z}^2_{s-}(\check{\omega},\check{\omega}')\, dC({}^nV^i,\nu)_s(\omega) .$$

Here again we have: $A(v,2)\Longrightarrow A(v,3)\Longrightarrow A(v,4)$: the last implication is evident, after noticing that in (14) we may put $\check{Z}_{t-}$ instead of $\check{Z}_t$ without modifying the condition, because of the predictability of the coefficient. There is no such condition as A(u,1) here, because constants are usually not integrable with respect to $\mu-\nu$.

CONDITION A(v,5) : There exists a $\check{\omega}_0\in\check{\Omega}$ such that the functions $(\omega,t,x) \rightsquigarrow \check{v}^i(\omega,\check{\omega}_0,t,x)$ are in $L(\mu)$.

CONDITION A(v,6) : There exists elements V'^i of $L(\mu)$ such that for each $\omega,\check{\omega}$, t , x , i the functions $K_{\check{\omega},i}(\omega,t,x)=\check{v}^i(\omega,\check{\omega},t,x)$ satisfy:

$$\begin{cases} K_{\check{\omega},i}(\omega,t,x)^2 \leq V'^i(\omega,t,x)^2\,(1+\check{X}_t^{*2}(\check{\omega})) & \text{if } (\omega,t)\notin J \\ (\widehat{K^2_{\check{\omega},i}})_t(\omega) - (\widehat{K}_{\check{\omega},i})^2_t(\omega) \leq [\widehat{(V'^i)^2_t}(\omega) - \widehat{V'^i_t}(\omega)^2](1+\check{X}_t^{*2}(\check{\omega})) & \text{if } (\omega,t)\in J . \end{cases}$$

All those conditions are considerably simplified in the "quasi-left continuous case", that is when J is empty.

<u>3.3 - The coefficient</u> w . The positive random measure $|\mu'|$ is defined as usual as the "absolute value" of μ' . Here again we will not have a condition similar to A(u,1), because constants are not necessarily integrable with respect to $|\mu'|$.

CONDITION A(w,2) : There exists a $\underline{\underline{O}}(\underline{F})\otimes\underline{\underline{E}}'$-measurable nonnegative function W on $\Omega\times\mathbb{R}_+\times E'$ such that $\int_0^t\int_{E'} W(s,x)\,|\mu'|(ds,dx) < \infty$ P-a.s. for each finite t, and such that for all $\omega, \check{\omega}, \check{\omega}', t$:

$$(15)\qquad |\check{w}(\omega,\check{\omega},t,x) - \check{w}(\omega,\check{\omega}',t,x)| \leq W(\omega,t,x)\,\check{Z}_t(\check{\omega},\check{\omega}') .$$

CONDITION A(w,3) : For each $n\in\mathbb{N}$ there exists a $\underline{\underline{O}}(\underline{F})\otimes\underline{\underline{E}}'$-measurable nonnegative function ${}^nW$ on $\Omega\times\mathbb{R}_+\times E'$ such that $\int_0^t\int_{E'} {}^nW(s,x)\,|\mu'|(ds,dx) < \infty$ P-a.s. for each finite t, and such that (15) holds with ${}^nW$ instead of W, $\forall\omega, \check{\omega}, \check{\omega}', t$ with $\check{X}_t^*(\check{\omega})\leq n$ and $\check{X}_t^*(\check{\omega}')\leq n$.

CONDITION A(w,4) : The same as A(w,3), except that (15) is replaced by

$$\int_0^t\int_{E'} |w(\omega,\check{\omega},s,x) - \check{w}(\omega,\check{\omega}',s,x)|\,|\mu'|(\omega;ds,dx) \leq \int_0^t\int_{E'} {}^nW(\omega,s,x)\check{Z}_{s-}(\check{\omega},\check{\omega}')\,|\mu'|(\omega;ds,dx) .$$

For the same reasons as in the previous paragraph, we have again the implications: A(w,2) $\Longrightarrow$ A(w,3) $\Longrightarrow$ A(w,4) .

CONDITION A(w,5) : There exists a $\check{\omega}_0\in\check{\Omega}$ such that $\int_0^t\int_{E'} |\check{w}(\omega,\check{\omega}_0,s,x)|\,|\mu'|(\omega;ds,dx) < \infty$ P-a.s. for each finite t.

CONDITION A(w,6) : There exists a $\underline{\underline{O}}(\underline{F})\otimes\underline{\underline{E}}'$-measurable nonnegative function W' on $\Omega\times\mathbb{R}_+\times E'$ and a sequence (T_n) of stopping times increasing P-a.s. to $+\infty$, such that

$$\begin{cases} E[(\int_0^{T_n}\int_{E'} W'(s,x)\,|\mu'|(ds,dx))^2] < \infty & \forall n\in\mathbb{N}, \\ |w(\omega,\check{\omega},t,x)| \leq W'(\omega,t,x)(1+\check{X}_t^{*2}(\check{\omega}))^{1/2} & \forall\omega,\check{\omega},t,x . \end{cases}$$

In the sequel, we say "condition A(i)" instead of: "conditions A(u,i), A(v,i) and A(w,i)". We have: A(2) $\Longrightarrow$ A(3) $\Longrightarrow$ A(4). We also have the implication: A(4) <u>and</u> A(6) $\Longrightarrow$ A(5). Moreover, under A(4) and A(5), any $\check{\omega}\in\check{\Omega}$ satisfies the conditions imposed on a particular $\check{\omega}_0$ in A(u,5), A(v,5) and A(w,5).

4. THE MAIN RESULTS

At first we must make precise the concept of <u>solution</u> of the s.d.f. (5).

DEFINITION 2 : Let T be a $\underline{F}$-stopping time. A <u>solution on the stochastic interval</u> $[\![0,T]\!]$ is an adapted right-continuous and left-hand limited process $X=(X^i)_{i\leq m}$ defined on $(\Omega,\underline{\underline{F}},\underline{F},P)$, such that if

$$(16)\quad \begin{cases} \varphi:\ \Omega\longrightarrow\check{\Omega} \quad \text{is defined by}\quad \check{X}\circ\varphi = X \\ u_t(\omega) = \check{u}_t(\omega,\varphi(\omega)),\quad v(\omega,t,x) = \check{v}(\omega,\varphi(\omega),t,x),\quad w(\omega,t,x) = \check{w}(\omega,\varphi(\omega),t,x) \end{cases}$$

then for each $i \leq m$ we have $u^{i\cdot}I_{[\![0,T]\!]} \in L(M)$, $v^{i}I_{[\![0,T]\!]} \in L(\mu)$ and

$$(17) \quad X_t^i = H_{t\wedge T}^i + \int_0^{t\wedge T} u_s^{i\cdot}\, dM_s + \int_0^{t\wedge T}\int_E v^i(s,x)(d\mu - d\nu)(s,x) + \int_0^{t\wedge T}\int_{E'} w^i(s,x)\,d\mu'(s,x)\,.$$

Remarks: 1) u is progressive, v and w are predictable. Thus the random vectors $u^{i\cdot}I_{[\![0,T]\!]}$ belong to $L(M)$ if and only if they satisfy (6), while $v^{i}I_{[\![0,T]\!]}$ belongs to $L(\mu)$ if and only if $C(v^{i}I_{[\![0,T]\!]},\nu)_t < \infty$ P-a.s. for each finite t .

2) Of course formula (17) implies that $X_t = X_{t\wedge T}$; it also implies that the last (pathwise) integral in (17) makes sense.

We are now ready, at last ! , to state the results. As for all equations of this type (including the deterministic ones) we have a result on uniqueness, a result on the existence of a maximal solution, and criteria for non-explosion.

THEOREM 1 (Uniqueness): Under condition A(4), two solutions on the same stochastic interval $[\![0,T]\!]$ are P-indistinguishable.

THEOREM 2 (Existence of a maximal solution): Let us assume A(4) and A(5).

(a) There exists a predictable stopping time T such that for each stopping time S the following equivalence holds true:

$[\![0,S]\!] \subset [\![0,T[\![$ up to a P-evanescent set $\Longleftrightarrow$ there exists a solution on $[\![0,S]\!]$.

(b) There exists a process X such that $(X_{t\wedge S})_{t\geq 0}$ is a solution on $[\![0,S]\!]$ for each stopping time S such that $[\![0,S]\!] \subset [\![0,T[\![$.

(c) T is unique up to a P-null set; X is unique on $[\![0,T[\![$ up to a P-evanescent set; we have $X^*_{T-} = \infty$ P-a.s. on the set $\{T<\infty\}$.

As usual, X is called the maximal solution, and T is the explosion time.

THEOREM 3 (Non-explosion): Let us assume either A(4), A(6) and the local boundedness of the process H , or A(2) and A(5). Then there exists one and only one (up to a P-evanescent set) solution on $\mathbb{R}_+$ (which amounts to say: the explosion time is a.s. infinite).

We will not prove these theorems here, both because it would be too long, and because the proofs are in fact quite classical. Complete proofs of theorems 1 and 2, and of theorem 3 under the first set of assumptions, are displayed in the forthcoming "Lecture Notes" [7], while theorem 3 under the assumptions A(2) and A(5) may be proved in exactly the same way as the corresponding theorem for s.d.f. (4) by Métivier and Pellaumail [10, theorem 4].

Let us just say a few words about theorem 2. Let X be any adapted, right-continuous, left-hand limited process, to which we associate u, v, w by formula (16). Thus the right-hand side of (17) defines a new process denoted by γX (due to A(5) and to the fact that under A(4), any point $\check{\omega} \in \check{\Omega}$ satisfies the conditions required from the particular $\check{\omega}_0$ in A(5)). Now, it is not difficult to show the existence of a strictly positive stopping time S such that

$$E(\sup_{t<S} |(\gamma X)_t - (\gamma X')_t|^2) \leq \frac{1}{2} E(\sup_{t<S} |X_t - X'_t|^2) .$$

In fact, the delicate point is to get such a majoration strictly before S: here this difficulty is overcomed by using the fact that in (17) the two stochastic integrals give rise to locally square-integrable martingale, whose jumps may be "predictably controlled", whereas the last "pathwise" integral, as usual, does not bring any trouble.

So when we stop the processes strictly before S, we get a contraction; starting from $X_t(\omega) = \check{\omega}_0(t)$ where $\check{\omega}_0$ is the point in A(5), we are in good shape for using a successive approximation procedure: we obtain a process which is a "solution" on $[\![0,S[\![$ and due to the predictability of the coefficients v, w it is immediately extended into a solution on $[\![0,S]\!]$. Then, starting at time S, we repeat the procedure, thus getting the maximal solution by successive extensions in time.

5. APPLICATION TO OTHER S.D.F.

5.1 - Equation (4). Let us now consider equation (4), where the driving processes $H = (H^i)_{i \leq m}$ and $Y = (Y^i)_{i \leq m'}$ (a semimartingale) are given. The coefficient is a $\underline{P}(\underline{F}')$-measurable function $\check{g} = (\check{g}^{ij})_{i \leq m, j \leq m'}$ defined on the sapce $(\Omega', \underline{F}')$ given by (10). The definition of a solution follows closely the definition 2 for equation (5), so we will not repeat it here.

CONDITION B(1) : There exists a locally bounded predictable process G on $(\Omega, \underline{F}, \underline{\underline{F}}, P)$ such that for all $\omega, \check{\omega}, \check{\omega}', t$:

$$(18) \qquad |\check{g}_t(\omega,\check{\omega}) - \check{g}_t(\omega,\check{\omega}')| \leq G_t(\omega)\check{Z}_t(\check{\omega},\check{\omega}') .$$

CONDITION B(2) : For each $n \in \mathbb{N}$ there exists a locally bounded predictable process ${}^nG$ on $(\Omega, \underline{F}, \underline{\underline{F}}, P)$ such that (18) holds with ${}^nG$ instead of G, $\forall \omega, \check{\omega}, \check{\omega}', t$ such that $\check{X}^*_t(\check{\omega}) \leq n$ and $\check{X}^*_t(\check{\omega}') \leq n$.

CONDITION B(3) : There exists $\check{\omega}_0 \in \check{\Omega}$ such that the process: $(\omega,t) \rightsquigarrow \check{g}_t(\omega,\check{\omega}_0)$ is locally bounded.

CONDITION B(4) : There exists a locally bounded predictable process G' and a sequence (T_n) of stopping times increasing P-a.s. to $+\infty$, such that

$$\begin{cases} E[(\sum_{t\le T_n} |G'_t||\Delta Y_t| I_{\{|\Delta Y_t|>1\}})^2] < \infty & \forall n\in\mathbb{N} \\ |\check{g}_t(\omega,\check{\omega})| \le |G'_t(\omega)|(1+\check{X}^{*2}_t(\check{\omega}))^{1/2} & \forall\omega,\check{\omega},\ t. \end{cases}$$

Of course, $B(1)\Longrightarrow B(2)$.

THEOREM : For the s.d.f. (4) we obtain:

(a) The statement of theorem 1 is true under B(2).

(b) The statement of theorem 2 is true under B(2) and B(3).

(c) The statement of theorem 3 is true, either under B(2), B(4) and the local boundedness of the process H , or under B(1) and B(3).

This result is more general than the results of Doléans-Dade [2], Métivier and Pellaumail [10] for the finite-dimensional case, and Protter [13]. One may shown that it is slightly more general than those of Métivier and Pellaumail [9], again for the finite-dimensional case. However, these authors also consider the infinite-dimensional case, which we do not.

Sketch of the proof: The game consists in transforming the s.d.f. (4) into a s.d.f. (5), and then applying the previous theorems. Let μ be the integer-valued random measure on $E=\mathbb{R}^{m'}$ given by:

$$\mu(dt,dx) = \sum_{s>0} I_{\{\Delta Y_s\ne 0\}}\, \varepsilon_{(s,\Delta Y_s)}(dt,dx),$$

and ν its compensator. It is known [6] that Y admits the decomposition

$$Y_t = Y_0 + B_t + Y^c_t + \int_0^t\int_E x\, I_{\{|x|\le 1\}}(d\mu-d\nu)(s,x) + \int_0^t\int_E x\, I_{\{|x|>1\}}\, d\mu(s,x)$$

where Y^c is a m'-dimensional continuous local martingale, and where $B=(B^i)_{i\le m'}$ is a predictable m'-dimensional process with finite variation on each compact set and jumps bounded by 1 .

Let $E'=E\cup\{\delta_1,\ldots,\delta_{m'}\}$ and the random measure μ' on E' defined by

$$\begin{cases} \mu'(dt,\{\delta_i\}) = dB^i_t \\ \mu'(dt,dx)I_E(x) = \mu(dt,dx). \end{cases}$$

Now, to the original s.d.f. (4), we associate the s.d.f. (5) with the driving processes H , $M=Y^c$, μ , ν , μ' and with the following coefficients:

$$\check{u}_t(\omega,\check{\omega}) = \check{g}_t(\omega,\check{\omega})$$

$$\check{v}^i(\omega,\check{\omega},t,x) = \sum_{j\le m'} \check{g}^{ij}_t(\omega,\check{\omega})\, x^j\, I_{\{|x|\le 1\}}$$

$$\check{w}^i(\omega,\check{\omega},t,x) = \begin{cases} \check{g}^{ij}_t(\omega,\check{\omega}) & \text{if } x=\delta_j \\ \sum_{j\le m'} \check{g}^{ij}_t(\omega,\check{\omega})\, x^j\, I_{\{|x|>1\}} & \text{if } x\in E. \end{cases}$$

It is now easy to check that the set of solutions of the original s.d.f. (4)

is exactly the set of solutions of the s.d.f. (5) just defined.

It remains to notice that, for those equations, we have B(1) $\Longrightarrow$ A(2) (take $U_t(\omega) = |c_t(\omega)|\, G_t(\omega)$, $V^i(\omega,t,x) = G_t(\omega)\, x^i\, I_{\{|x|\leq 1\}}$, $W(\omega,t,x) = G_t(\omega)|x| I_{\{|x|>1\}}$ if $x \in E$ and $W(\omega,t,\delta_j) = G_t(\omega)$), we have B(2) $\Longrightarrow$ A(3) (same transformations, with index n), we have B(3) $\Longrightarrow$ A(5) (trivial), and finally we have B(4) $\Longrightarrow$ A(6) (again the same transformation of $|G'|$ in U', V'^i, W').

<u>Remark</u>: Actually, conditions B(1) - B(4) are much stronger than the corresponding conditions A(i) for the associated s.d.f. (5). The reader will be able to state more general conditions by himself.

<u>5.2 - Equation (3)</u>. As above, we will associate to the original s.d.f. (3) a new s.d.f. (5).

The driving processes of (3) are H, M, μ, ν, and an adapted process $A = (A^i)_{i\leq m''}$ with bounded variation on each compact set. The associated equation (5) will have the same driving processes H, M, μ, ν, and the random measure μ' on $E' = E \bigcup \{\delta_1, \ldots, \delta_{m''}\}$ defined by

$$\begin{cases} \mu'(dt, \{\delta_j\}) = dA_t^j \\ \mu'(dt,dx) I_E(x) = \mu(dt,dx) . \end{cases}$$

The coefficients $\check{\alpha}$, $\check{\beta}$, $\check{\gamma}$ of (3) are defined on the space Ω', in the same way as in definition 1, and the coefficients of the associated equation (5) will be:

$$\check{u} = \check{\beta}, \qquad \check{v}(\omega,\check{\omega},t,x) = \check{\gamma}(\omega,\check{\omega},t,x) I_{\{|x|\leq 1\}}$$

$$\check{w}^i(\omega,\check{\omega},t,x) = \begin{cases} \check{\alpha}_t^{ij}(\omega,\check{\omega}) & \text{if } x = \delta_j \\ \check{\gamma}^i(\omega,\check{\omega},t,x) I_{\{|x|>1\}} & \text{if } x \in E . \end{cases}$$

Here again, the set of solutions of the original s.d.f. (3) is exactly the set of solutions of its associated s.d.f. (5). Therefore it is quite straightforward (and left to the reader) to translate the conditions A(i) into conditions on the original coefficients $\check{\alpha}$, $\check{\beta}$, $\check{\gamma}$.

<u>Remark</u>: Of course (2) is a particular case of (3). However if the Lipschitz conditions A(2)-A(4) translate into Lipschitz conditions for the coefficients $\check{\alpha}$, $\check{\beta}$, $\check{\gamma}$, of (3), it is not at all the same for the coefficients of (2), because of the presence of the indicator functions $I_{\{|\gamma|\leq 1\}}$ and $I_{\{|\gamma|>1\}}$.

REFERENCES

1 C. DELLACHERIE: <u>Capacités et processus stochastiques</u>. Springer Verlag: Berlin, 1972.

2 C. DOLEANS-DADE: Existence and unicity of solution of stochastic differential equations. Z. für Wahr. 36, 93-102, 1976.

3 L. GALTCHOUK: The structure of a class of martingales. Proc. School-Seminar on random processes (Druskininkai), Vilnius, Acad. Sci. Lit. SSR, I, 7-32, 1975.

4 L. GALTCHOUK: Existence and uniqueness for stochastic differential equations with martingales and random measures. Proc. 2d Vilnius Conf. Proba. Math. Statist., 1977.

5 I.I. GIHMAN, A.V. SKOROKHOD: Stochastic differential equations. Springer Verlag: Berlin, 1972.

6 J. JACOD: Un théorème de représentation pour les martingales discontinues. Z. für Wahr. 34, 225-244, 1976.

7 J. JACOD: Calcul stochastique et problèmes de martingales. To appear.

8 N. KAZAMAKI: On a stochastic integral equation with respect to a weak martingale. Tôhoku Math. J. 26, 53-63, 1974.

9 M. METIVIER, J. PELLAUMAIL: A basic course on stochastic integration. Sém. Proba. Rennes 77, t. I, 1978.

10 M. METIVIER, J. PELLAUMAIL: On a stopped Doob's inequality and general stochastic equations. To appear (1978); cf. C.R.A.S. (A), 285, 685-688 and 921-923.

11 M. METIVIER, G. PISTONE: Une formule d'isométrie pour l'intégrale stochastique hilbertienne et équations d'évolution linéaires stochastiques. Z. für Wahr. 33, 1-18, 1975.

12 P.A. MEYER: Un cours sur les intégrales stochastiques. Sém. Proba. Strasbourg X, Lect. Notes Math. 581, Springer Verla: Berlin: 1976.

13 P.E. PROTTER: On the existence, uniqueness, convergence and explosions of solutions of systems of stochastic integral equations. Ann. Proba. 5, 243-261, 1977.

14 A.V. SKOROKHOD: Studies in the theory of random processes. Addison-Wesley: Reading, 1965.

ON THE SOLUTION AND THE MOMENTS OF LINEAR SYSTEMS WITH RANDOMLY DISTURBED PARAMETERS

A. Kistner

Institut A für Mechanik
Universität Stuttgart
Pfaffenwaldring 9
D-7000 Stuttgart 80

1. INTRODUCTION

The careful analysis of practical systems frequently leads to linear models the parameters of which are subject to steady variations. Mostly these are to be considered as random in nature. It is usually assumed then that the parameters are driven by Gaussian white noise. In this case the theory of stochastic differential equations is a powerful tool for computing the solution process of the model and its moments which are frequently used in practice for judging the behaviour of the system.

However, assuming white noise disturbances may be a very poor approximation. First of all white noise is not a physical process. Moreover in many cases more detailed information about the statistics of the driving processes is available. Thus real noise systems should be considered for appropriate modeling. But here considerable difficulties arise. Most of the results known are approximate results which differ from one another [1-4]. This fact gives rise to investigations what could be stated strictly about the solution process of a real noise system and its moments.

Let us consider a linear system

$$(1) \qquad \dot{x}_t = \{A + B\xi_t\}\cdot x_t \quad , \quad x_t \varepsilon R^n \quad , \quad \xi_t \varepsilon R^1 \quad , \quad t \geq 0 \quad ,$$

where the parameters in the real matrix A are disturbed according to the real matrix B by a single second order zero mean Gaussian process ξ_t the realizations of which are steady with probability one. The case of two or more driving processes may be treated just as described below without any difficulties in principle.

First a series expression of the solution process x_t is derived. It is used for computing relations of the important first and second moments of x_t. After some general discussion of these equations an illuminating comparison between the white noise idealization and the real noise case is given.

2. THE COMPUTATION OF THE SOLUTION PROCESS BY ITERATION

Let $\xi(t)$ be a steady realization of the process ξ_t. The corresponding realization of the solution process x_t of (1) with initial condition x_o may then be obtained as

$$(2)\qquad x(t)=\sum_{h=o}^{\infty}\omega_h(t)\cdot x_o \quad , \quad \omega_h(t)=\int_o^t\{A+B\xi(\tau)\}\omega_{h-1}(\tau)d\tau \ , \ h=1,2,..,\ \omega_o\equiv I \ .$$

This series converges absolutely and uniformly over every finite time interval [5].

Since the realizations of ξ_t are assumed to be steady with probability one the subsequent considerations may be restricted to the steady portion of ξ_t. Then almost all realizations of x_t may be computed evaluating (2). After some simple but nevertheless lengthy analysis based on the convergence properties of (2) this yields [6] the series expression

$$(3)\qquad x_t = e^{B\eta_t}\cdot e^{At}\cdot\sum_{j=o}^{\infty}G_j(t)\cdot x_o \qquad \text{almost surely} \quad , \quad t\geq 0 \quad ,$$

for the complete solution process x_t of system (1). Here

$$(4)\qquad \eta_t = \int_o^t \xi_\tau d\tau \qquad \text{almost surely} \quad , \quad t\geq 0 \quad ,$$

is a second order zero mean Gaussian process as well as ξ_t. The matrix-valued processes $G_j(t)$ may be obtained from the recursion system

$$G_j(t) = \sum_{g=o}^{j-1}\int_o^t \frac{1}{(j-g)!}\eta_\tau^{j-g}\cdot L_{j-g}(\tau)\cdot G_g(\tau)d\tau \quad \text{a.s.} \ , \ j=1,2,.., \quad G_o\equiv I \ ,$$

$$(5)\qquad L_h(\tau) = e^{-A\tau}\cdot K_h\cdot e^{A\tau} \quad ,$$

$$K_h = K_{h-1}B - BK_{h-1} \quad , \quad h=1,2,.. \quad , \quad K_o = A \quad .$$

By this procedure the process $G_j(t)$ becomes the sum of simple to j-fold iterated integrals of type

$$(6)\qquad \int_{t_1=o}^{t}\int_{t_2=o}^{t_1}\cdots\int_{t_p=o}^{t_{p-1}}\prod_{q=1}^{p}\frac{1}{(r_q)!}\eta_{t_q}^{r_q}\cdot e^{-At_q}\cdot K_{r_q}\cdot e^{At_q}\cdot dt_p\cdots dt_2 dt_1 \quad ,$$

$$1\leq r_q\leq j \quad , \quad \sum_{q=1}^{p}r_q=j \quad , \quad p=1,2,..,j \quad ,$$

over the process η_τ and the commutator products K_h , $j=1,2,...$.

3. THE FIRST AND SECOND MOMENTS OF THE SOLUTION PROCESS

The series (3) can easily be used to obtain an expression of the first moments $m(t)=Ex_t$ of x_t. Applying the expectation operator E and regarding that η_t is a zero mean Gaussian process yields [6]

$$(7)\quad m(t) = \left(e^{\frac{1}{2}B^2\sigma_\eta^2(t)} \cdot e^{At} + \sum_{g=o}^{\infty}\sum_{h=o}^{2g+1}\frac{1}{(2g+1-h)!}B^{2g+1-h}\cdot e^{At}\cdot E\left[\eta_t^{2g+1-h}G_{h+1}(t)\right]\right)\cdot m(0).$$

Here $\sigma_\eta^2(t)$ denotes the variance function of η_t. Furthermore it is assumed without any incisive restrictions that the initial state x_o is independent from ξ_t and thus η_t, $t\geq 0$.

Whereas (7) is useful for computing the evolution of the first moments $m(t)$ with increasing time the asymptotic behaviour of $m(t)$ is difficult to detect from (7). For this purpose it can be shown [6] that the first moments satisfy the inhomogeneous linear differential equation

$$(8)\quad \dot{m}(t) = \left(A + \frac{1}{2}\frac{d\sigma_\eta^2(t)}{dt}B^2\right)\cdot m(t) + B\cdot\Phi(t)$$

where

$$(9)\quad \begin{aligned} \Phi(t) &= \sum_{g=o}^{\infty}\sum_{h=o}^{2g}\frac{1}{(2g-h)!}B^{2g-h}\cdot e^{At}\cdot\varphi(\xi_t\eta_t^{2g-h}G_{h+1}(t))\cdot m(0) \\ \varphi(\xi_t\eta_t^pG_q(t)) &= E\left[\xi_t\eta_t^pG_q(t)\right] - p\cdot E\left[\xi_t\eta_t\right]\cdot E\left[\eta_t^{p-1}G_q(t)\right], \quad p=0,1,.., \; q=1,2,... \end{aligned}$$

For the second moments $M(t)=Ex_tx_t^*$ of x_t straightforward computation as above leads to a compound series expression [6] similar to (7). More revealing the second moments once again satisfy an inhomogeneous differential equation [6]

$$(10)\quad \begin{aligned} \dot{M}(t) = &\left(A + \frac{1}{2}\frac{d\sigma_\eta^2(t)}{dt}B^2\right)\cdot M(t) + M(t)\cdot\left(A + \frac{1}{2}\frac{d\sigma_\eta^2(t)}{dt}B^2\right)^* + \\ &+ \frac{d\sigma_\eta^2(t)}{dt}B\cdot M(t)\cdot B^* + B\cdot\left(\Psi(t)+\Psi^*(t)\right) + \left(\Psi(t)+\Psi^*(t)\right)\cdot B^*. \end{aligned}$$

Just as in (8) $A+\frac{1}{2}\frac{d\sigma_\eta^2(t)}{dt}B^2$ is one of the coefficient matrices. But now the inhomogeneous part is given by

---

* denotes transposition

$$\Psi(t) = \sum_{g=o}^{\infty}\sum_{h=o}^{2g}\sum_{j=o}^{\infty}\sum_{k=o}^{2j}\frac{1}{(2g-h)!(2j-k)!}B^{2g-h}\cdot e^{At}\cdot$$

$$\cdot\phi(\xi_t\eta_t^{2(g+j)-h-k}G_h(t)x_o x_o^* G_{k+1}^*(t))\cdot e^{A^*t}\cdot B^{*2j-k} +$$

$$+\sum_{g=o}^{\infty}\sum_{h=o}^{2g+1}\sum_{j=o}^{\infty}\sum_{k=o}^{2j+1}\frac{1}{(2g+1-h)!(2j+1-k)!}B^{2g+1-h}\cdot e^{At}\cdot$$

$$\cdot\phi(\xi_t\eta_t^{2(g+j+1)-h-k}G_h(t)x_o x_o^* G_{k+1}^*(t))\cdot e^{A^*t}\cdot B^{*2j+1-k}\,, \tag{11}$$

$$\phi(\xi_t\eta_t^p G_q(t)x_o x_o^* G_r^*(t)) = E\left[\xi_t\eta_t^p G_q(t)x_o x_o^* G_r^*(t)\right] -$$

$$- p\cdot E\left[\xi_t\eta_t\right]\cdot E\left[\eta_t^{p-1}G_q(t)x_o x_o^* G_r^*(t)\right]\,,$$

$$p,q=0,1,\ldots\;,\quad r=1,2,\ldots\;.$$

A more detailed discussion of the moments' equations (8) and (10) is given in the next sections.

Obviously the expressions of the first and second moments are not so easy to be used in general. But there are several classes of systems (1) which lead to simplifications. The most dramatic ones appear with commutative systems (1) which the matrices A and B commute for, i.e. $AB=BA$. It is readily seen from (5) that $G_o(t)\equiv I$ and $G_j(t)\equiv 0$, $j=1,2,..$, in this case. Thus in particular the moments' equations (8) and (10) reduce to the corresponding homogeneous ones [6].

Minor simplifications appear with the more extensive class of solvable systems (1) which the Lie algebra generated by the matrices A and B is solvable for [7], i.e. which A and B may be transformed to upper triangular, possibly complex matrices by means of the same nonsingular linear transformation for [6]. Here the outer form of (7)-(11) is not changed in general, but the structure of the processes $G_j(t)$ included is simplified: in case of a matrix A with simple eigenvalues $G_j(t)$ is the sum of simple to only $\hat{j}$-fold iterated integrals of type (6) where $\hat{j} = \min(j, n-1)$, $j=1,2,..$ [6].

By means of Lie algebra argumentation one can prove [6] that every commutative system (1) is solvable but not vice versa.

Further simplifications may be worked out for example for the class of systems (1) with $B^2 = 0$.

4. THE WHITE NOISE EXCITATION AS A LIMITING CASE

As already mentioned systems (1) are frequently assumed to be driven by Gaussian white noise. This idealization may be included into the considerations stated above as a limiting case.

Let us consider a family of second order zero mean stationary Gaussian processes $\xi_t^{(\alpha)}$, $\alpha\varepsilon R^+$, for which the realizations of each process $\xi_t^{(\alpha)}$ are steady with probability one and the autocorrelation functions $R_\xi^{(\alpha)}(t-s) = E\xi_t^{(\alpha)}\xi_s^{(\alpha)}$ satisfy

$$(12) \quad \lim_{\alpha\to\infty} R_\xi^{(\alpha)}(\tau) = \rho^2\cdot\delta(\tau)$$

where $\delta(\tau)$ denotes the Dirac delta distribution. Then the limiting process $\xi_t^{(\infty)}$ of the family is the Gaussian white noise of intensity ρ^2 . For example such a family is formed [8] by the zero mean stationary Ornstein-Uhlenbeck processes with $R_\xi^{(\alpha)}(\tau) = \rho^2\cdot\frac{\alpha}{2}\cdot\exp\{-\alpha|\tau|\}$.

For each pair of appropriate matrices A and B a family of systems

$$(13) \quad \dot{x}_t^{(\alpha)} = \{A + B\xi_t^{(\alpha)}\}\cdot x_t^{(\alpha)} \quad , \quad t\geq 0 \quad ,$$

is associated with the family of processes $\xi_t^{(\alpha)}$. The first and second moments of the solution processes $x_t^{(\alpha)}$ may be computed from the equations above for each finite α . As α goes to infinity the sequence of the processes $x_t^{(\alpha)}$ converges in the weak sense to the solution process y_t of the stochastic differential equation

$$(14) \quad dy_t = A\, y_t\, dt + B\, y_t\, dw_t \quad , \quad Ew_t\equiv 0 \quad , \quad Ew_t w_s=\rho^2\cdot\min(t,s) \; .$$

At the same time the sequences of the moments of $x_t^{(\alpha)}$ converge to the moments of y_t . Observing the limiting procedure with (8)-(11) in more detail it is readily seen [6] that

$$(15) \quad \lim_{\alpha\to\infty} \frac{d\sigma_\eta^{(\alpha)2}(t)}{dt} = \rho^2 \quad , \quad \lim_{\alpha\to\infty} \Phi^{(\alpha)}(t) \equiv 0 \quad , \quad \lim_{\alpha\to\infty} \Psi^{(\alpha)}(t) \equiv 0 \; .$$

Thus the first and second moments of y_t satisfy

$$(16) \quad \dot{m}(t) = \left(A+\tfrac{1}{2}\rho^2B^2\right)\cdot m(t) \quad ,$$

$$(17) \quad \dot{M}(t) = \left(A+\tfrac{1}{2}\rho^2B^2\right)\cdot M(t) + M(t)\cdot\left(A+\tfrac{1}{2}\rho^2B^2\right)^* + \rho^2B\cdot M(t)\cdot B^* \quad .$$

These are the well known equations belonging to (14) taken in the sense of Stratonovich. The derivation of these equations along the way described is rather natural and avoids complications with the definition of stochastic integrals. Since one starts from the real noise systems (13) the usual notion is emphasized that the Stratonovich approach to stochastic differential equations provides more realistic results than the Itô approach.

5. THE BEHAVIOUR OF THE MOMENTS AND THEIR STABILITY

The equations (8)-(11) admit general statements how the first and second moments of a system (1) with a stationary process ξ_t develop for small and for great values of time. Regarding (3) one obtains [6]

$$(18)\quad \frac{d\sigma_\eta^2(t)}{dt} = 2\cdot\int_0^t R_\xi(\tau)d\tau \quad , \quad \left.\frac{d\sigma_\eta^2(t)}{dt}\right|_{t=0} = 0 \quad , \quad \lim_{t\to\infty}\frac{d\sigma_\eta^2(t)}{dt} = S_\xi(0) = S_0$$

where $R_\xi(\tau)$ denotes the autocorrelation function of ξ_t and $S_\xi(\omega)$ its spectral density function. Moreover with $\eta_0=0$ and $G_j(0)=0$, $j=1,2,..$, (9) and (11) yield $\Phi(0)=0$ and $\Psi(0)=0$. Due to continuity considerations the behaviour of the first and second moments of (1) for rather small values of time therefore is governed by the equations

$$(19)\quad \dot{m}(t) \simeq A\cdot m(t) \qquad , \qquad \dot{M}(t) \simeq A\cdot M(t) + M(t)\cdot A^*$$

which correspond to the undisturbed system (1). This takes into account the clear notion that the excitation of the parameters of (1) affects the moments not instantaneously but only after a short while.

With increasing time the influence of the driving process ξ_t to the moments grows according to (8)-(11). At last as time goes to infinity one obtains formally

$$(20)\quad \dot{m}(t) \simeq \left(A+\tfrac{1}{2}S_0B^2\right)\cdot m(t) + B\cdot\Phi(\infty) \qquad ,$$

$$(21)\quad \begin{aligned}\dot{M}(t) \simeq &\left(A+\tfrac{1}{2}S_0B^2\right)\cdot M(t) + M(t)\cdot\left(A+\tfrac{1}{2}S_0B^2\right)^* + S_0B\cdot M(t)\cdot B^* + \\ &+ B\cdot\left(\Psi(\infty)+\Psi^*(\infty)\right) + \left(\Psi(\infty)+\Psi^*(\infty)\right)\cdot B^* \quad .\end{aligned}$$

These equations show that the value S_0 of the entire spectral density function of ξ_t plays a decisive part for the asymptotic behaviour of the moments. As is already proved by Willems and Aeyels [9] S_0 exclusively governs the asymptotic stability of the moments of commutative and solvable systems (1): necessary and sufficient for the first moments' stability is that all eigenvalues of the matrix $A+\frac{1}{2}S_0B^2$ have negative real parts; necessary and sufficient for the second moments' stability is [6] that all eigenvalues of the matrix $\tilde{A}+\frac{1}{2}S_o\tilde{B}$ have negative real parts where by means of Kronecker products [10] $\tilde{A} = A\times I + I\times A$ and $\tilde{B} = B^2\times I + I\times B^2 + 2B\times B$.

Using these stability conditions one can show [6] that even an unstable linear system may be stabilized in the sense of moments by exciting its parameters according to (1) with appropriate physical noise.

6. A COMPARISON BETWEEN THE REAL NOISE CASE AND THE WHITE NOISE CASE

The qualitative equations (19)-(21) of the first and second moments of a practical system (1) have constant coefficients. Thus they are suitable to be contrasted with the moments' equations which one obtains for the same system by means of the theory of stochastic differential equations if the parameters are ideally assumed to be driven by Gaussian white noise of intensity $\rho^2 = S_o$. It is readily seen then that with some reservation

a) the Stratonovich approach to the white noise modification provides good results concerning the behaviour of the first and second moments of a real noise system (1) for great values of time and concerning their stability,

b) the Itô approach to the white noise modification provides good results concerning the behaviour of the first moments of a real noise system (1) for small values of time,

c) neither the Itô nor the Stratonovich approach to the white noise modification provide good results concerning the behaviour of the second moments of a real noise system (1) for small values of time.

Consequently neither the Itô nor the Stratonovich approach to the white noise modification provide an over all approximation of the first and second moments of a real noise system (1). Actually a complicated transition occurs which can only be described by the general equations (8)-(11).

The latter turn out to be even more important. From simulations it is known [11] that the graphs of the moments of practical systems (1) may have huge humps for average values of time although the moments are asymptotically stable. First of all this means that the stability of the moments of a real noise system (1) does not always imply a moderate over all behaviour of the system and its moments. In this situation the equations (8)-(11) allow to quantify the moments and their humps analytically. The figure below which is computed for the simple second order system

$$(22)\quad \begin{pmatrix} x_1 \\ x_2 \end{pmatrix}_t^{\bullet} = \left\{ \begin{pmatrix} -20 & 0 \\ 0 & -5 \end{pmatrix} + \begin{pmatrix} 2 & 20 \\ 0 & 2 \end{pmatrix} \cdot \xi_t \right\} \cdot \begin{pmatrix} x_1 \\ x_2 \end{pmatrix}_t$$

shows that by means of the white noise approximation and the Stratonovich approach the first (and second) moments may sometimes be estimated satisfactorily if wide band noise ξ_t with a spectral density function of type $S_\xi(\omega) = 1/(1 + \omega^2)$ drives the parameters. But in case of narrow band excitation with a spectral density function of type $S_\xi(\omega) = 1/(1 + 2\lambda\omega^2 + \omega^4)$ neither the qualitative nor the quantitative behaviour of the moments might be met by the white noise idealization.

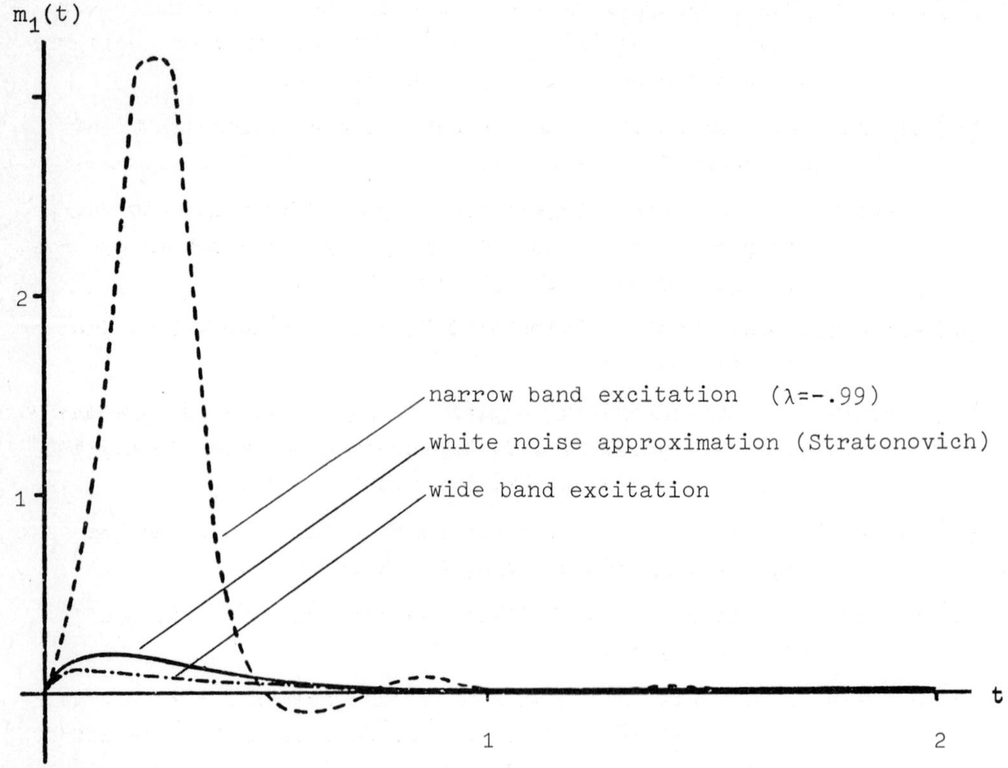

Fig.: First moments $m_1(t)=Ex_{1_t}$ of the system (22) with various types of exciting processes ξ_t .

CONCLUSION

By means of the considerations described above it was tried to contribute to the theory of systems the parameters of which are excited by real physical noise. It is obvious that even in the linear case many questions remain to be answered and that in most cases we are still far from methods which may be used with acceptable expense in practical applications. However the difficulties pointed out with the usual white noise approximations require further research on real noise systems.

REFERENCES

[1] Ariaratnam, S.T., Stability of Mechanical Systems under Stochastic Parameter Excitation. Lecture Notes Math. 294 (1972).

[2] Bolotin, V.V., Reliability Theory and Stochastic Stability. Study No.6 Stability, Solid Mechanics Division, University of Waterloo (Ontario, Canada) (1971).

[3] Zeman, J.L., Zur Lösung nichtlinearer stochastischer Probleme in der Mechanik. Acta mech. 14, 157-169 (1972).

[4] Kistner, A., Über die Güte von Näherungsverfahren zur Untersuchung der Momentenstabilität farbig verrauschter Systeme. Z. angew. Math. Mech. 57, T75-T77 (1977).

[5] Brockett, R.W., Finite Dimensional Linear Systems. Wiley, New York (1970).

[6] Kistner, A., Strenge Aussagen über Lösung, Momente und Stabilität linearer Systeme mit Parametererregung durch farbiges Rauschen. Dissertation, Stuttgart (1978).

[7] Sagle, A.A., Walde, R.E., Introduction to Lie Groups and Lie Algebras. Academic Press, New York (1973).

[8] Arnold, A., Stochastische Differentialgleichungen. Oldenbourg, München (1973).

[9] Willems, J.L., Aeyels, D., An Equivalence Result for Moment Stability Criteria for Parametric Stochastic Systems and Itô Equations. Internat. J. Systems Sci. 7, 577-590 (1976).

[10] Lancaster, P., Theory of Matrices. Academic Press, New York (1969).

[11] Mitchell, R.R., Kozin, F., Sample Stability of Second Order Linear Differential Equations with Wide Band Coefficients. SIAM J. appl. Math. 27, 571-605 (1974).

SOME EXACT RESULTS ON STABILITY AND GROWTH OF LINEAR PARAMETER EXCITED STOCHASTIC SYSTEMS

W. Kliemann
Forschungsgschwerpunkt "Dynamische Systeme"
Univerität Bremen

SUMMARY

We investigate the stability and growth of the linear parameter-excited stochastic system $\dot{x}_t = A_t x_t$, where A_t is a stationary diffusion process. The interplay between stochastic systems and associated deterministic control systems allows us to derive results on the ergodicity of $(x_t/|x_t|, A_t)$ and so on the growth of x_t. Using an effective computation procedure the 2-dimensional case is solved completely.

1. INTRODUCTION

In this paper we investigate the stability of the trivial solution of the linear parameter-excited stochastic system

(1) $\dot{x}_t = A_t x_t$.

The case where the noise process A_t is "white" was in principle completely solved by Chasminskii in [7] . In many problems in engineering and the natural sciences the noise can be considered as a Markov process. We are interested in continuous state Markov excitations, that is "coloured noise" which we model as stationary solutions of Ito equations

(2) $dA_t = \mathfrak{A}(A_t)\, dt + \mathfrak{B}(A_t)\, dW_t$.

Some work has been done in this direction by Blankenship [4] , Blankenship & Papanicolaou [5] and others. While these papers only derive sufficient conditions for stability, we are interested in characterizing the stability and instability regions exactly in terms of the coefficients of (2). The only known exact results are those of Rümelin in [19] for the undamped linear oszillator with positive restoring force.

Our method uses the well known projection idea of Chasminskii [7] and Infante [11] . We associate with the projected system on the sphere S^{n-1} a deterministic control system, whose controllability properties lead to results on the ergodicity of the projected system. From this we derive statements on the order of growth for (1). The use of the interplay between stochastic systems and associated deterministic control systems is related to the work of Stroock & Varadhan [20] , Kunita [15] and Brockett [6] .

As we assume the noise A_t to be Markov, the pair (x_t, A_t) is Markov, if the initial value x_o is independent of A_t. For Markov processes stationarity is equivalent to homogeneous transition probabilities and existence of an invariant measure. Since (1) and (2) do not depend explicitly on t we have homogeneous transition probabilities for (x_t, A_t). So we start discussing existence and uniqueness of invariant measures. These questions have been investigated with related techniques by Bhattacharya [3] (using the techniques of Stroock and Varadhan) and Brockett [6] (for some bilinear systems).

As our process A_t is stationary and Feller defined on a state space $Y \subset \mathbb{R}^{n \times n}$, Y can be decomposed into ergodic components Y_α, such that the process A_t is ergodic on each Y_α (see Yosida [22]). These ergodic components are the minimal invariant sets of the process in the state space Y, so we can consider them as connected. Therefore we can assume without loss of generality A_t to be ergodic on a minimal invariant set.

In section II we discuss the existence and uniqueness of invariant measures as well as a law of large numbers for general nonlinear stochastic systems with "coloured noise" in terms of the controllability properties of the associated deterministic control system. To give an effective computation procedure for the control sets of these systems, we introduce in section III the "no return sets" for the case of a one-dimensional state space X of x_t. Section IV contains our results on the stability problem including the complete solution for the 2-dimensional case.

2. INVARIANT MEASURES FOR NONLINEAR STOCHASTIC SYSTEMS

Existence and uniqueness of invariant measures for Markov systems is usually discussed under Doeblin-type conditions (see e.g. Maruyama & Tanaka [18]), or Lyapunov-type conditions (see e.g. Chasminskii [8]). While the first approach gives no explicit conditions in terms of the coefficients of the diffusion process, the second approach works only for nondegenerate or nearly nondegenerate systems (see e.g. Blankenship & Papanicolaou [5]).

To discuss invariant measures for the stochastic system

$$(S) \quad \dot{x}_t = f(x_t, \xi_t)$$

we associate with (S) the deterministic control system

$$(D) \quad \dot{x}(t) = f(x(t), u(t)) \quad .$$

We assume for (S) : (i) $x_t \in X \subset \mathbb{R}^n$

(ii) ξ_t is an ergodic diffusion process, i.e. a solution of an Ito equation (2) , with state space $Y \subset \mathbb{R}^m$

(iii) f is continuous in both variables and has a unique solution for every initial value $(x, \xi_0) \in X \times Y$ and all $t \in \mathbb{R}^+$

and for (D) : (i) $x(t) \in X \subset \mathbb{R}^n$

(ii) $u \in \mathcal{U} = \{v : [t_0, t_1] \longrightarrow Y \text{ continuous}, \ t_0 \leq t_1 \in \mathbb{R}^+\}$

(iii) f is continuous in both variables and (D) has a unique solution for every $(x,u) \in X \times Y$ and all $t \in \mathbb{R}^+$.

By $\varphi(t;x_o,t_o,u)$ we denote the solution of (D) at time $t \geq t_o$ with initial value $x(t_o) = x_o$ and control $u \in \mathcal{U}$.

Existence and uniqueness of invariant measures as well as a law of large numbers for (S) can be stated in terms of control sets for (D) :

Definition 1 : $G \subset X \times Y$ is a control set of (D), if for all $(x,u) \in G$ $\mathcal{O}^+(x,u) = G$.

$\mathcal{O}^+(x,u) = \{ (y,v) \in X \times Y$, there exists an $u \in \mathcal{U}$ such that $u(0) = u$, $u(t_1) = v$ and $\varphi(t_1;x,0,u) = y \}$

$G_\varepsilon \subset X \times Y$ is an ε-control set of (D), if for all $(x,u) \in G_\varepsilon$ $\mathcal{O}^+_\varepsilon(x,u) = \overline{G_\varepsilon}$.

$\mathcal{O}^+_\varepsilon(x,u) = \{ (y,v) \in X \times Y$, for all $\varepsilon' > 0$ there exists an $u_{\varepsilon'} \in \mathcal{U}$ such that $u_{\varepsilon'}(0) = u$, $u_{\varepsilon'}(t_1) = v$ and $|\varphi(t_1;x,o,u_{\varepsilon'}) - y| < \varepsilon' \}$

These notions differ from those of the usual control problem, as we define control sets not as subsets of X but of $X \times Y$. (See e.g. Lukes [17] for control with preassigned values $u(0)$, $u(t_1)$ and Dauer [9] for ε-control problems.) The common concept of reachability leads to the notion of weak control sets of (D) : $H \subset X \times Y$ is a weak control set, if every two points of H can be linked by applying a suitable control from $\mathcal{U}$, analogously the weak ε-control sets H_ε.

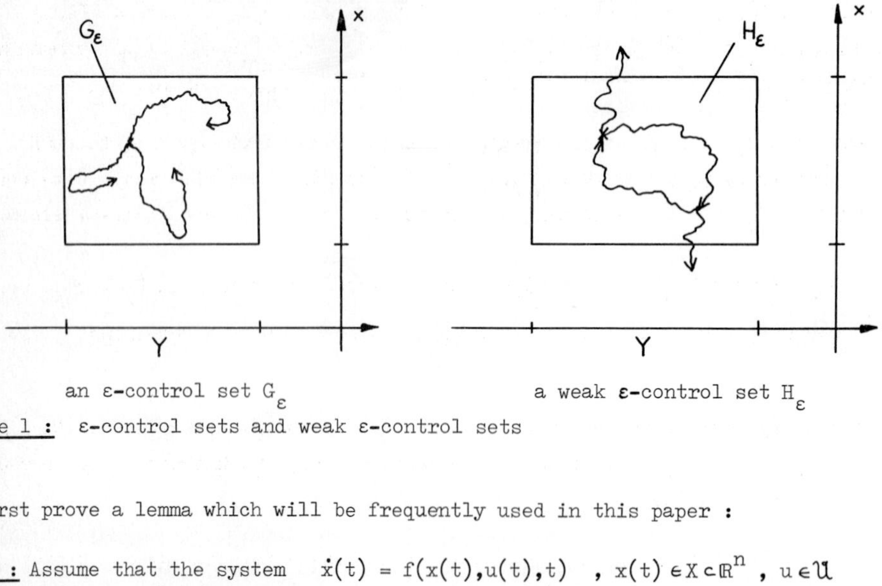

an ε-control set G_ε a weak ε-control set H_ε

Figure 1 : ε-control sets and weak ε-control sets

We first prove a lemma which will be frequently used in this paper :

Lemma : Assume that the system $\dot{x}(t) = f(x(t),u(t),t)$, $x(t) \in X \subset \mathbb{R}^n$, $u \in \mathcal{U}$ has a unique solution for every initial value (x_o,t_o) and every $u \in \mathcal{U}$, and that f is continuous in all variables.

If there exists a continuous control $u : [t_o,t_1] \longrightarrow Y$ such that $x(t_o) = x_o$ and $\varphi(t_1;x_o,t_o,u) = x_1$

then : for every $u_o, u_1 \in Y$ and every $\varepsilon > 0$ there exists a continuous control $u_\varepsilon : [t_o, t_1] \longrightarrow Y$ such that $u_\varepsilon(t_o) = u_o$, $u_\varepsilon(t_1) = u_1$, $x(t_o) = x_o$ and $|\varphi(t_1; x_o, t_o, u_\varepsilon) - x_1| < \varepsilon$.

Proof : Without loss of generality we adapt the initial value and take the time intervall $[0,1]$.

(i) Let Y be convex.

Define
$$u_n(t) := \begin{cases} (1-t\cdot n)u_o + t\cdot n\cdot u(\frac{1}{n}) & \text{for } t \in [0,1/n] \\ u(t) & \text{for } t \in [1/n,1] . \end{cases}$$

With the notations $x(t) = \varphi(t; x_o, 0, u)$ and $x_n(t) = \varphi(t; x_o, 0, u_n)$ we have

$$|x(1) - x_n(1)| = \left| \int_0^1 f(x(s),u(s),s)ds - \int_0^1 f(x_n(s),u_n(s),s)ds \right|$$

$$\leq \left| \int_0^{1/n} f(x(s),u(s),s)ds - \int_0^{1/n} f(x_n(s),u_n(s),s)ds \right| +$$

$$\left| \int_{1/n}^1 f(x(s),u(s),s)ds - \int_{1/n}^1 f(x_n(s),u_n(s),s)ds \right| .$$

Since f is bounded for all arguments the first summand tends to 0 for $n \longrightarrow \infty$ by the Lebesgue theorem. The second summand tends to 0 because of the continuous dependence on the initial value. So $\lim_{n\to\infty} |x(1) - x_n(1)| = 0$.

(ii) Let Y be connected.

There exist continuous $\alpha_n : [0,1/n] \longrightarrow Y$ with $\alpha_n(0) = u_o$, $\alpha_n(1/n) = u(1/n)$. We define $u_n(t)$ as in (i), but now with the help of α_n instead of the straight line between u_o and $u(1/n)$. Then the arguments of (i) can be repeated. □

By the lemma all G_ε sets are dense subsets of sets of the form $A \times Y$ with $A \subset X$, A connected. For every G_ε set K there exists an unique maximal (with respect to the set inclusion) G_ε set K^* containing K . In the following G_ε set always means maximal G_ε set.

We call a G_ε set open (closed, bounded) if its x-component is open (closed, bounded).

For convenience we list some results from [13] under the above assumptions on (S) and (D) :

Theorem 1 : Every minimal invariant set of (x_t, ξ_t) is contained in an ε-control set G_ε of (D). So every invariant measure of (x_t, ξ_t) has mass only on the G_ε sets of (D) .

Theorem 2 : If the state space X is compact, then there exists an invariant probability measure for (x_t, ξ_t) in $X \times Y$.

Remark 1 : If an ε-control set G_ε of (D) is

- compact, theorem 2 holds with $X \times Y$ replaced by G_ε ,

- open, a more detailed analysis of the interplay of f and ξ_t is necessary (see Kolmogoroff [14]) .

Theorem 3 : Suppose

(i) There exists an ε-control set G_ε for (D) ,

(ii) The solutions of (D) depend continuously on u ,

(iii) For every $\delta > 0$ and every $v : [0,t_1] \longrightarrow Y$ in $\mathfrak{U}$ the set $V_\delta = \{ w : [0,t_1] \longrightarrow Y \text{ in } \mathfrak{U}, \| v - w \| < \delta \}$ has positive P_ξ probability, where P_ξ is the measure induced by ξ in $C(\mathbb{R}^+, \mathbb{R}^n)$, the space of continuous functions from $\mathbb{R}^+$ to $\mathbb{R}^n$.

Then G_ε is a minimal invariant set for (x_t, ξ_t). This means : if there exists an invariant measure for (x_t, ξ_t) in G_ε, then it is unique.

Remark 2 : a) Condition (ii) is e.g. fulfilled, if f is lipschitz in x.

b) Condition (iii) is e.g. fulfilled, if ξ_t is an ergodic diffusion process with nonsingular diffusion matrix.

c) The existence of the invariant measure in G_ε implies the validity of the Birkhoff - Chinchin ergodic theorem for the (x_t, ξ_t) process, started with the invariant distribution.

These theorems clarify for a large class of noise processes existence and uniqueness of invariant measures for the (x_t, ξ_t) process in terms of ε-control sets for (D). The conditions are explicit conditions on the coefficients of the system. In order to apply those results to the stability problem, we have to show a law of large numbers.

Theorem 4 : a) Suppose on a G_ε set of (D) there exists an invariant measure μ and conditions (ii) and (iii) of theorem 3 hold.
Then we have a law of large numbers

$$P_{(x,u)} \left\{ \lim_{T\to\infty} \frac{1}{T} \int_0^T f(x_t, \xi_t) dt = \int_{G_\varepsilon} f(y,v) \; \mu d(y,v) \right\} = 1$$

for $(x,u) \in G_\varepsilon$ μ-a.s. .

b) Under the conditions of a) a law of large numbers holds for all (x,u) in a dense subset of G_ε .

Proof : a) Let

$$E := \left\{ \omega, \lim_{T\to\infty} \frac{1}{T} \int_0^T f(x_t, \xi_t) dt = \int_{G_\varepsilon} f(y,v) \; \mu d(y,v) \right\} .$$

From remark 2c) we have $P_\mu(E) = 1$ and so $P_\mu(E) = \int_{G_\varepsilon} P_{(x,u)}(E) \mu d(x,u) = 1$.

Since $\int_{G_\varepsilon} (1 - P_{(x,u)}(E)) \; \mu d(x,u) = 0$ and $1 - P_{(x,u)}(E) \geq 0$

$P_{(x,u)}(E) = 1$ μ-a.s.

b) is immediate from a), the fact that G_ε is a minimal invariant set (theorem 3) and the structure of G_ε sets. □

3. ε-CONTROL SETS IN ONE-DIMENSIONAL STATE SPACE

In the deterministic control literature the main subject is the local and global controllability of systems in the state space. Especially the results on global controllability of systems with compact state space (see e.g. Lobry [16] , Hermann & Krener [10]) can be used in our context, as ε-controllability of the system (D) in $X \times Y$ can be reduced to (ε-) controllability of (D) in X (see the lemma). Nevertheless it is necessary to determine the ε-control sets of (D) directly, as a system need not be globally controllable but may have several ε-control sets. In this section we introduce the notion of "no return sets". Using this notion we show, how all the ε-control sets for systems with one-dimensional state space can be computed from the dynamics f(x,u) of (D). We restrict ourselves in the present context of stability problems to bounded state space. The unbounded case can be handled with the obvious modifications (see [13]) .

Let $X \subset \mathbb{R}$ be bounded , $Y \subset \mathbb{R}^m$ connected.

Definition 2 : A hyperplane $a_+ \equiv$ const , $a_+ \in X$, in $X \times Y$ is a no return plane from above for the system (D), if $f(a_+,u) \leq 0$ for all $u \in Y$.
$a_- \equiv$ const is a no return plane from below , if $f(a_-,u) \geq 0$ f.a. $u \in Y$.

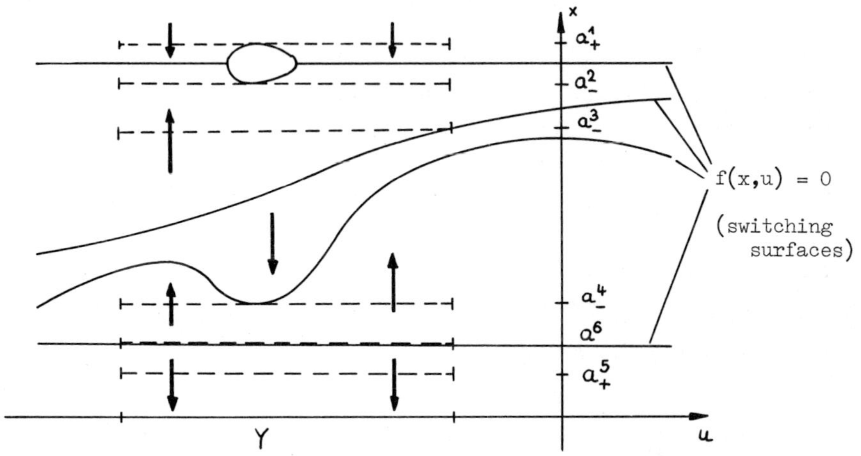

Figure 2 : State space of a 1×1 system with switching surfaces , the arrows indicate the sign of f .

Examples : In figure 2 : a_+^1 , a^6 , a_+^5 are no return planes from above ,
a_-^2 , a_-^3 , a_-^4 , a^6 are no return planes from below.

If a_+ is a no return plane from above, no trajectory of (D) with initial value (x,u), $x < a_+$ can cross this hyperplane. On the other hand, if

$(*)$ there exists an $u_+ \in Y$ such that $f(a_+,u_+) < 0$,

then for every (a_+,u) there is a control u such that $\varphi(t_1; a_+,0,u) < a_+$, $u(0)=u$: we find according to the lemma a control v with $v(0) = u$, $v(t_2) = u_+$ and $|\varphi(t_2;a_+,0,v) - a_+| < \varepsilon$. Then apply the constant control u_+. Because f is continuous there is a $t_3 \in \mathbb{R}^+$ such that $\varphi(t_3+t_2;a_+,0,u_+ \circ v) < a_+$.

A no return plane from above, for which $(*)$ is not valid, is also a no return plane from below. Analogous statements hold for no return planes from below, the condition now reads

$(**)$ there exists a $u_- \in Y$ such that $f(a_-,u_-) > 0$.

No return planes satisfying $(*)$ or $(**)$ are called strong.

<u>Definition 3 :</u> Let a_- be a no return plane from below, a_+ from above and $a_- < a_+$. Assume : for all $x \in (a_-,a_+)$ $x \equiv \text{const}$ is not a no return plane. Then the set $)a_-,a_+(= I \times Y$ is called a <u>no return set</u>, where I is defined as the interval between a_- and a_+, which we take closed at a_- (resp. at a_+), if a_- is strong from below (resp. a_+ strong from above), and open otherwise.

$)a_-,a_+($ is called open (closed), if I has this property.

The no return planes determining a no return set are called <u>extreme</u>.

If $a \equiv \text{const}$ is a no return plane from below and above, then the set $)a,a(= \{a\} \times Y$ is also called a no return set.

<u>Examples :</u> In figure 2 : $)a^2_-,a^1_+($ and $)a^6,a^6($ are (closed) no return sets.

We now characterize the G_ε sets for systems with bounded state space $X \subset \mathbb{R}$ using the notion of no return sets :

<u>Theorem 5 :</u> Let $f : X \times Y \longrightarrow \mathbb{R}$ satisfy :

for every $u \in Y$ there are only finitely many points $x \in X$ with $f(x,u)=0$.

Then for the system (D) :

a) $)a,a($ are exactly the closed G_ε sets having one point in the x-component.

b) The G_ε sets are exactly the no return sets.

c) The compact G_ε sets are exactly the closed no return sets.

<u>Proof :</u> a) follows directly from the lemma.

b) We first show that every no return set is a G_ε set.

Let $K = I \times Y \subset X \times Y$ be a no return set with more than one element in I. Then for all $x \in (a_-,a_+)$ there exists an $u_- \in Y$, $u_+ \in Y$ such that $f(x,u_+) < 0$ and

$f(x,u_-) > 0$. This is even true for the boundary points of I , if the corresponding no return planes are strong.

Now let (x,u) , $(y,v) \in K$. We show that there exists a continuous control from (x,u) to any neighbourhood of (y,v).

Case 1 : $x = y$:

The existence of a suitable control follows directly from the proof of the lemma.

Case 2 : $x < y$:

There exists an u_+^1 such that $f(x,u_+^1) > 0$.

Step 1 : By the lemma, there exists for every $\varepsilon > 0$ a control $u_1 : [0,t_1] \longrightarrow Y$ such that $u_1(0) = u$, $u_1(t_1) = u_+^1$ and $|\varphi(t_1;x,0,u_1) - x| < \varepsilon$.

Step 2 : If for all z , $y > z \geq x$, $f(z,u_+^1) > 0$, we apply the constant control $u_2 : [t_1,t_2] \longrightarrow Y$ with $u_2(t) \equiv u_+^1$ up to time t_2 so that $|\varphi(t_2;x,0,u_2 \circ u_1) - y| < \varepsilon'$ and again use the lemma to get a control with the preassigned terminal value v .

If there is x_1 , $y > x_1 > x$, with $f(x_1,u_+^1) = 0$, then for every $\varepsilon' > 0$ there is a control $u_2 : [t_1,t_2] \longrightarrow Y$, $u_2(t) = u_+^1$ such that $|\varphi(t_2;x,0,u_2 \circ u_1) - x_1| < \varepsilon'$. We call $\varphi(t_2;x,0,u_2 \circ u_1) =: x_1^{\varepsilon'}$.

Step 3 : By the assumption on K there exists an u_+^2 such that $f(x_1^{\varepsilon'},u_+^2) > 0$ and we proceed as in step 1 etc (see figure 3) .

By the assumption on f this procedure stops after a finite number of steps.

Case 3 : $x > y$:

Analogously.

So we can link (x,u) with every ε-neighbourhood of (y,v) applying a suitable control from $\mathcal{U}$. Since no trajectory of the system (D) can leave K , K is a G_ε set.

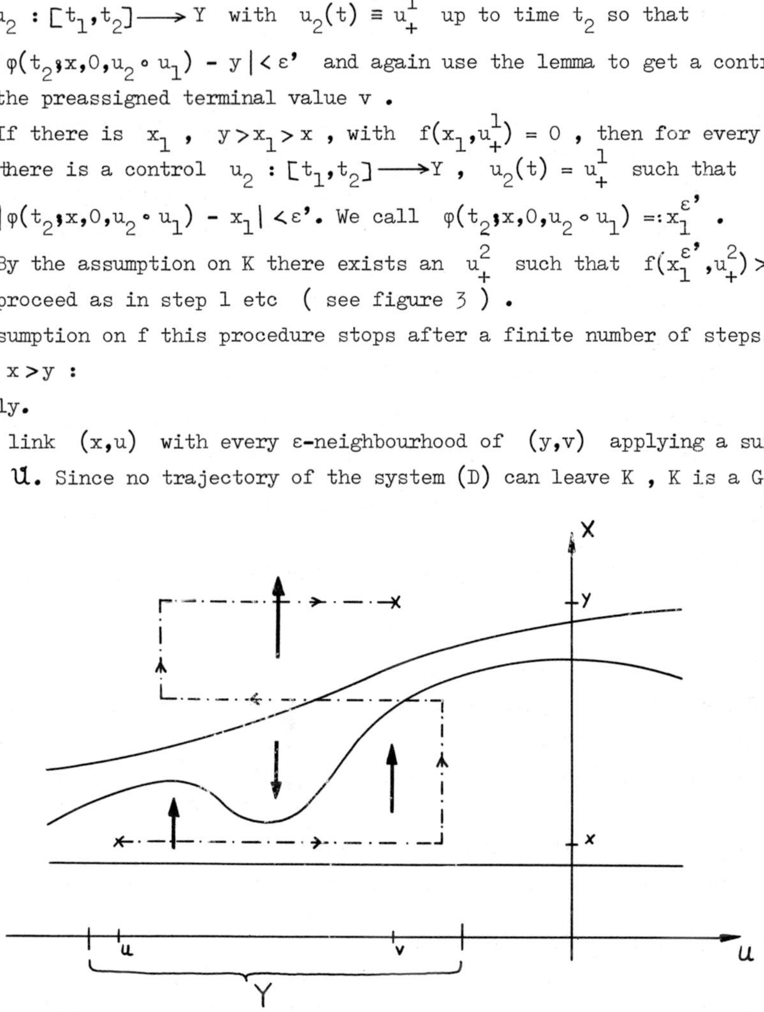

Figure 3 : A trajectory from (x,u) to a neighbourhood of (y,v).

Next suppose $)a,b(= I \times Y$ is a G_ε set. Then

1. if for a $x \in (a,b)$ $f(x,u) \geq 0$ (resp. $f(x,u) \leq 0$) for all $u \in Y$, we conclude that there is an $\varepsilon > 0$ such that the ε-neighbourhood of a (resp. of b) can not be reached from (x,u). So $)a,b($ is not a G_ε set, which is a contradiction. So for all $x \in (a,b)$ $x \equiv$ const is not a no return plane.
2. if b is not a no return plane from above, there exists an $u \in Y$ such that $f(b,u) > 0$. By the continuity of f this is true for a whole neighbourhood of (b,u). So there are trajectories leaving the set $)a,b($, which is again a contradiction. The analogous argument holds for a .

From 1. and 2. we conclude, that $)a,b($ is a no return set.

c) As we restrict ourselves to bounded state space, c) follows from b). □

<u>Remark 3 :</u> For a given $Y \subset \mathbb{R}^m$, the points $(x,u) \in X \times Y$ with $f(x,u) = 0$ define connected surfaces M_i in $X \times Y$, the switching surfaces. A large class of interesting systems is characterized by the fact that there are only finitel many of these surfaces. For these systems we give an effective computation procedure for the no return sets :

Compute for each of the surfaces the inf and the sup x-value , x_i^+ and x_i^- . (This is a well known deterministic optimization problem with constraints.) Arrange the surfaces according to the order of their inf values $x_1^- \leq x_2^- \leq \dots$. Then x_1^- is the "smallest" no return plane. Find that value x_i^+, such that i is the smallest index with $x_j^+ \leq x_i^+$ for all j , $1 \leq j$, with $x_j^- < x_i^+$. Then x_i^+ is a no return plane too. If x_1^- is from below and x_i^+ is from above, then $)x_1^-, x_i^+($ is a no return set. (Notice that if x_1^- is not from below or / and x_i^+ is not from above, the set $(x_1^-, x_i^+) \times Y$ still is a weak ε-control set H_ε.)

Now take the smallest $x_k^- \geq x_i^+$ and repeat this procedure.

<u>Example :</u> In figure 2 :

a^6 is the inf and the sup of M_1 , so $)a^6,a^6($ is a no return set.

a_-^4 is the inf of M_2 , a_-^3 is the "next" no return plane. But a_-^3 is not from above.

a_-^2 is the inf of M_4 , a_+^1 the sup of M_4. a_-^2 is from below, a_+^1 from above, so $)a_-^2, a_+^1($ is a no return set.

4. STABILITY

We now investigate the almost sure stability of the linear, parameter excited system

(1) $\dot{x}_t = A_t x_t$

where A_t is a $n \times n$ - matrix valued stationary stochastic process of diffusion type, i.e. A_t is the solution of an Ito equation

(2) $dA_t = \mathfrak{A}(A_t)dt + \mathfrak{B}(A_t)dW_t$

with appropriate initial value A_o in $Y \subset \mathbb{R}^{n \times n}$.
We call the trivial solution $x_t \equiv 0$ of (1) a.s. stable, if $\lim_{t\to\infty} x_t(c) = 0$ with probability 1 for all $c \in \mathbb{R}^n$, where $x_t(c)$ denotes the solution of (1) at time t starting in c at time 0. For systems of the form (1) this stability definition is equivalent to asymptotic stability w.p. 1 and asymptotic stability in probability (see Arnold & Wihstutz [1]).

Following Chasminskii [7] and Infante [11] we project the system (1) onto the unit sphere S^{n-1} and denoting $w_t = x_t / |x_t|$ we get

(3) $\dot{w}_t = h(w_t, A_t)$

$$h(w, A) = (A - q(w, A))w$$

$$q(w, A) = w^\tau (\tfrac{1}{2}(A^\tau + A))w ,$$

where $^\tau$ denotes the transpose. If we write the norm of x_t in the form

(4) $|x_t| = |x_o| \circ \exp\left(\int_0^t q(w_s, A_s)\,ds\right)$,

we see that the growth of x_t is completely determined by the time average behaviour of the pair (w_t, A_t) : Denote $R_t = \frac{1}{t}\int_0^t q(w_s, A_s)ds$ and suppose $R_t \longrightarrow R$ as $t \longrightarrow \infty$, then

(5) $|x_t| = |x_o| \cdot \exp(t \cdot (R + o(1)))$,

that is $\lim_{t\to\infty} \frac{1}{t} \log|x_t| = R$.
R is the order of growth of (1) and $R < 0$ means stability , $R > 0$ means instability and $R = 0$ separates points of stability and instability in the parameter space.

We aim at exact stability diagrams in the parameter space and so we are interested in
- R independent of ω, this is the case if (w_t, A_t) is ergodic ,
- R independent of x_o, this means a law of large numbers.

From now on we assume that A_t satisfies condition (iii) of theorem 3. By the remark at the end of section I we can assume that A_t is ergodic. So we have a connected state space $S^{n-1} \times Y$ for (w_t, A_t) .

From section II it follows :

If we know for the deterministic control system associated with (3) the G_ε and the closed G_ε sets, then

- every ergodic component of (w_t, A_t) is contained in a G_ε set,
- in each closed G_ε set there exists an invariant measure,
- if in a G_ε set there exists an invariant measure, this is unique and a law of large numbers holds in G_ε,
- every solution of (2) and (3) converges towards a G_ε set.

For the order of growth R this means :

- in the closed G_ε sets we have a.s. one constant order of growth.

The computation of R of course involves simulation procedures, which can be done using the law of large numbers. Some bounds on R are given by Benderski & Pastur [2] and Wihstutz [21] in special cases. Some direct results on R are obtained by Johnson [12].

For the computation of ε-control sets in $S^{n-1} \times Y$ a procedure is available, which we will describe in the case of 2×2 - systems using the no return sets of section III.

Put $A_t =: \begin{pmatrix} a_{11} & a_{12} \\ a_{21} & a_{22} \end{pmatrix}$, introduce polar coordinates for S^1. Then (3) becomes an equation for the angle φ_t :

(6) $$\dot{\varphi}_t = - a_{12}\sin^2\varphi_t + a_{21}\cos^2\varphi_t + (-a_{11} + a_{22})\sin\varphi_t\cos\varphi_t =: f(\varphi_t, A_t) \ .$$

With the transformation $z = \operatorname{tg}\varphi$, $\varphi \in [-\frac{\pi}{2}, \frac{\pi}{2}]$

(7) $$\dot{z}_t = - a_{12}z_t^2 + a_{21} + (- a_{11} + a_{22})\cdot z_t \ .$$

(7) completely describes the situation, since φ_t and $\varphi_t + \pi$ obey the same equation.

According to remark 3 we compute the roots of the right hand side of (7)

(8a) $$z_{1,2} = -\frac{1}{2}\frac{a_{11} - a_{22}}{a_{12}} \pm \sqrt{\frac{a_{21}}{a_{12}} + \left(\frac{1}{2}\frac{a_{11} - a_{22}}{a_{12}}\right)^2} \qquad \text{if } a_{12} \neq 0$$

(8b) $$z_3 = \frac{a_{21}}{a_{11} - a_{22}} \qquad \text{if } a_{12} = 0 \ , \ a_{11} \neq a_{22}$$

(8c) $$\dot{z}_t = a_{21} \qquad \text{if } a_{12} = 0 \ , \ a_{11} = a_{22} .$$

We have four cases for the number of switching surfaces :

Case 1 : two switching surfaces, if $a_{12} \neq 0$ and $(a_{11} - a_{22})^2 > - 4\, a_{21}a_{12}$,
(We call the surface defined by the positive root Z_1, the other one Z_2 .)

Case 2 : one switching surface, if (i) $a_{12} = 0$, $a_{11} \neq a_{22}$
(ii) $a_{12} \neq 0$, $(a_{11} - a_{22})^2 = - 4\, a_{21}a_{12}$,

Case 3 : no switching surface, if (i) $a_{12} \neq 0$, $(a_{11} - a_{22})^2 < -4\, a_{21}a_{12}$

(ii) $a_{12} = 0$, $a_{11} = a_{22}$, $a_{21} \neq 0$,

Case 4 : infinitely many switching surfaces, if $a_{12} = 0$, $a_{11} = a_{22}$, $a_{21} = 0$: then every $(z,A) \equiv$ const is a switching surface.

The surfaces are hyperplanes $z \equiv z_o$, if

Case 1 : $a_{12} = -\frac{1}{z_o}(a_{11} - a_{22}) + a_{21} \circ \frac{1}{z_o^2}$

Case 2 : (i) $a_{21} = z_o \circ (a_{11} - a_{22})$

(ii) $a_{12} = -\frac{1}{2}(a_{11} - a_{22}) \circ \frac{1}{z_o}$

Case 4 : every surface is a hyperplane .

For case 1 a lengthy but elementary calculation shows

(i) if a_{12} is constant, then $Z_1^- := \inf\{z \text{ , } (z,A) \in Z_1\} \geq \sup\{z \text{ , } (z,A) \in Z_2\} =: Z_2^+$ (this includes e.g. the damped linear oszillator, where $a_{12} = 1$) ,

(ii) if a_{12} lies in an intervall around 0, then $Z_1^- < Z_2^+$ is possible :
Take $a_{11} - a_{22} = -2$, $a_{21} = 1$, $a_{12} \in [-\frac{1}{2}, \frac{1}{2}]$

then $Z_1^- \leq -2 + \sqrt{2}$, $Z_1^+ \geq 2 + \sqrt{6}$

$Z_2^- \leq -2 - \sqrt{2}$, $Z_2^+ \geq 2 - \sqrt{6}$

thus $Z_1^- < Z_2^+$.

We summarize the 2×2 case in a tabulation :

Theorem 6 : Assume A_t is an ergodic diffusion process with minimal invariant set $Y \subset \mathbb{R}^{2\times 2}$ and condition (iii) of theorem 3 is satisfied. Then

	if	type of G_ε sets
1.	there is a $A \in Y$ such that (8a) has two complex roots	$S^1 \times Y$
2.	(8a) has only one real root for all $A \in Y$, or (8b)	
a	the switching surface is a plane $z \equiv z_o$	$\{w_o\} \times Y$, $\{-w_o\} \times Y$
b	the switching surface is not a plane	$S^1 \times Y$
3.	(8a) has real roots for all $A \in Y$, two real roots for one $A_o \in Y$	
a	the switching surfaces are planes $z \equiv z_o$, $z \equiv z_1$	$\{w_o\} \times Y$, $\{w_1\} \times Y$; $\{-w_o\} \times Y$, $\{-w_1\} \times Y$
b	the switching surfaces are not planes	
ba	$h(w,A)$ has the same sign f.a. $w \in S^1$, $A \in Y$	$S^1 \times Y$
bb	$h(w,A)$ takes different signs	
bba	a_{12} constant	two closed G_ε sets
bbb	a_{12} not constant and	
	$Z_1^- \geq Z_2^+$	two closed G_ε sets
	$Z_1^- < Z_2^+$	$S^1 \times Y$

(cont.)

4.	(8c) and	
a	a_{21} takes values $\neq 0$	$S^1 \times Y$
b	$a_{21} \equiv 0$	$\{w\} \times Y$ f.a. $w \in S^1$

For the closed G_ε sets we have a.s. one constant order of growth and a law of large numbers. If there is more than one G_ε set, the orders of growth coincide, exept for 3.a , where we have two orders of growth, $\alpha + \beta$ and $\alpha - \beta$. α depends on trace A_t , β depends on a_{12} and a_{21} .

Proof of theorem 6 : For the proof we use the angle φ, $\varphi \in [-\frac{\pi}{2}, \frac{\pi}{2}]$. Notice that $\varphi + \pi$ obeys the same equation as φ and S^1 is a closed circle.

1. If there is a matrix $A_o \in Y$ such that (8a) has two complex roots, then $f(\varphi, A_o) \geqslant \varepsilon > 0$ or $f(\varphi, A_o) \leqslant \varepsilon < 0$ for all φ . So we can apply the constant control A_o to reach all points $S^1 \times \{A_o\}$. By the lemma $S^1 \times Y$ then is a closed G_ε set.

2.a If the switching surface is $\varphi \equiv \varphi_o$, $\{w_o\} \times Y$ with w_o defined by φ_o is clearly a closed G_ε set. For all (φ, A) , $\varphi \not\equiv \varphi_o$, $A \in Y$, $f(\varphi, A)$ has the same sign. So there can not be another G_ε set.

2.b If the switching surface is not a plane, then $f(\varphi_1, A_1) = 0$ and $f(\varphi_2, A_2) = 0$ for some $\varphi_1 < \varphi_2$. We have $f(\varphi, A) \geqslant 0$ or $f(\varphi, A) \leqslant 0$ for all (φ, A). Piecing together the constant controls A_1 and A_2 continuously (by the lemma) we can reach any φ .

3.a (see 2.a)

3.ba (see 2.b)

3.bba If a_{12} is constant, then $Z_1^- \geqslant Z_2^+$, so by remark 3 we have two weak control sets of H_ε type. As the sign of f changes only twice on $[-\frac{\pi}{2}, \frac{\pi}{2}]$, one H_ε set is of the form $[a_-, a_+] \times Y$, where $_-$ indicates no return plane from below, $_+$ indicates no return plane from above. So we have one closed G_ε set.

3.bbb If a_{12} is not constant, we either have $Z_1^- \geqslant Z_2^+$, and so case 3.bba , or we have $Z_1^- < Z_2^+$. In this case the proof of theorem 5 b) shows, that $S^1 \times Y$ is a G_ε set.

4.a If a_{21} takes values $\neq 0$, there is a matrix A_o such that $f(\varphi, A_o) \geqslant \varepsilon > 0$ or $f(\varphi, A_o) \leqslant \varepsilon < 0$ for all φ and we proceed as in 1. .

4.b If $a_{21} \equiv 0$, $\dot{\varphi}_t = 0$ and every $\{w\} \times Y$ is a closed G_ε set. □

Example : Undamped linear oszillator

$$\ddot{y} + \xi_t y = 0$$

$$\dot{x}_t = \begin{pmatrix} 0 & 1 \\ -\xi_t & 0 \end{pmatrix} \cdot x_t$$

$$\dot{\varphi}_t = -\sin^2\varphi_t - \xi_t \cos^2\varphi_t =: f(\varphi_t, \xi_t)$$

$$\dot{z}_t = -z_t^2 - \xi_t$$

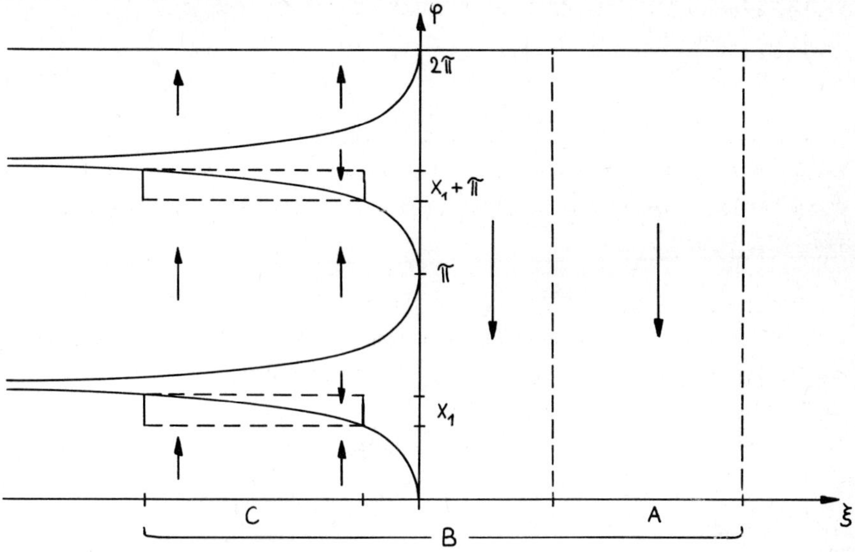

Figure 4 : State space of (φ_t, ξ_t) with switching curves, arrows indicating the sign of f.

Three cases are possible according to the choice of $Y = A, B, C$:

A : theorem 6 1. : $S^1 \times A$ is the closed G_ε set

B : theorem 6 1. : $S^1 \times B$ is the closed G_ε set

C : theorem 6 3.bba : $X_1 \times C$ and $(X_1 + \pi) \times C$ are the closed G_ε sets.

For the order of growth R this means :

A , B : we have a.s. one constant order of growth $R \geq 0$ and a law of large numbers

C : since ξ_t is an ergodic diffusion process, all solutions starting in $(\varphi_0, \xi_0) \in [0,2\pi] \times C$ enter into $X_1 \times C$ or $(X_1 + \pi) \times C$ in finite time. So we have a.s. one constant order of growth and a law of large numbers.
If $E|\xi_t| < \infty$, then $\sqrt{-b} \leq R \leq \sqrt{-E\xi_t}$, where $b = \sup C \leq 0$ (see Benderski & Pastur [2]) .

REFERENCES

[1] Arnold, L., Wihstutz, V. On the Stability and Growth of Real Noise Parameter-excited Linear Systems
in : Kölzow , Kallianpur (eds)
Proceedings of the Conference on Measure Theory and Stochastic Analysis, Oberwolfach July 1977
Springer Lecture Notes in Mathematics, to appear 1979

[2] Benderski, M.M., Pastur, L.A. On the Asymptotic Behaviour of the Solutions of a Second Order Equation with Random Coefficients (russ.)
Teor. Funkcii Funkcional. Anal. i Prilozen. Vyp 22 (1975) p. 3 - 14

[3] Bhattacharya, R.N. Criteria for Recurrence and Existence of Invariant Measures for Multidimensional Diffusions
Ann. Probability 6 (1978) p. 541 - 553

[4] Blankenship, G. Stability of Linear Differential Equations with Random Coefficients
IEEE Trans. AC 22 (1977) p. 834 - 838

[5] Blankenship, G., Papanicolaou, G.C. Stability and Control of Stochastic Systems with Wide - Band Noise Disturbances I
SIAM J. Appl. Math. 34 (1978) p. 437 - 476

[6] Brockett, R.W. Parametrically Stochastic Linear Differential Equations
Mathematical Programming Study 5 (1976) p. 8 - 21

[7] Chasminskii, R.Z. Necessary and Sufficient Conditions for the Asymptotic Stability of Linear Stochastic Systems
Theory Prob. Appl. 12 (1967) p. 167 - 172

[8] Chasminskii, R.Z. Stability of Systems of Differential Equations with Random Perturbation of their Parameters (russ.)
Nauka , Moscow (1969)

[9] Dauer, J.P. Approximate Controllability of Nonlinear Systems with Restrained Controls
J. Math. Ana. Appl. 46 (1974) p. 126 - 131

[10] Hermann, R., Krener, A.J. Nonlinear Controllability and Observability
IEEE Trans. AC 22 (1977) p. 728 - 740

[11] Infante, E.F. On the Stability of some Linear Nonautonomous Random Systems
ASME J. Appl. Math. 36 (1968) p. 7 - 12

[12] Johnson, R.A. Ergodic Theory and Linear Differential Equations
J. Diff. Equations 28 (1978) p. 23 - 34

[13] Kliemann, W. Stationäre nichtlineare stochastische Systeme
Ph. D. Thesis, Bremen (1979)

[14] Kolmogoroff, A.N. Zur Umkehrbarkeit der statistischen Naturgesetze
Math. Ann. 113 (1937) p. 766 - 772

[15] Kunita, H. Supports of Diffusion Processes and Controllability Problems
Proc. of Intern. Symp. SDE Kyoto (1976) p. 163 - 185

[16] Lobry, C. — Controllability of Nonlinear Systems on Compact Manifolds
SIAM J. Control 12 (1974) p. 1 - 4

[17] Lukes, D.L. — Global Controllability of Nonlinear Systems
SIAM J. Control 10 (1972) p. 112 - 126
11 (1973) p. 186

[18] Maruyama, G., Tanaka, H. — Ergodic Property of N-Dimensional Recurrent Markov Processes
Mem. Fac. Sci. Kyushu Univ. Ser. A 13 (1959) p. 157 - 172

[19] Rümelin, W. — Stability and Growth of the Solution of $\ddot{y} + f_t y = 0$ where f_t is a Positive Stationary Markov Process
Transactions of the Eighth Prague Conference Volume B (1978) p. 149 - 161

[20] Stroock, D.W., Varadhan, S.R.S. — On the Support of Diffusion Processes with Applications to the Strong Maximum Principle
Proc. Sixth Berkeley Symp. Mat. Stat. Prob. Vol 3 (1972) p. 333 - 359

[21] Wihstutz, V. — Ueber Stabilität und Wachstum von Lösungen linearer Differentialgleichungen mit stationären zufälligen Parametern
Ph. D. Thesis Bremen (1975)

[22] Yosida, K. — Functional Analysis
Springer, Berlin - Heidelberg - New York 4th Ed. (1974)

A VARIATIONAL INEQUALITY FOR A PARTIALLY OBSERVED STOPPING TIME PROBLEM

Michael Kohlmann
Institute for Applied Mathematics
University of Bonn, FRG

and

Raymond Rishel
University of Kentucky
Lexington, USA

1. INTRODUCTION

The paper gives an application of some representation results recently derived by the authors for conditional expectations of functionals on the past of a jump process. These representation results are shortly reviewed without giving the complete proofs and then used to derive a variational inequality for a partially observed stopping time problem with underlying jump Markov processes as dynamics.

1.1 Notations And Preliminaries

Let x be a continuous time process on $[0,T]$, resp. $[0,\infty)$ with values in an r-dimensional Euclidian space E^r, which with probability one has piecewise constant right continuous paths. The basic measure space (Ω,F) is assumed to be Blackwell just for technical reasons. There are different ways to get rid of this assumption [see e.g. 3]. The sequence

(1) $$x_0, \tau_1 x_1, \tau_2 x_2, \ldots$$

denotes the *successive states* x_i of the process *and times* τ_i at which the process jumps from x_{i-1} to x_i. With

(2) $$(X_n) := (x_0, \tau_1 x_1, \tau_2 x_2, \ldots, \tau_n x_n)$$

will be denoted *the vector of states and jump times*, and - if no confusion seems possible - also a vector in the range space of the random vector $X_n(\cdot)$.

The *probabilistic structure* of the process is given by

(3) $$P(\tau_{n+1} > t \mid X_n) = \exp\left(-\int_{\tau_n}^{t} q(s \mid X_n)\,ds\right)$$

and

(4) $P(x_{n+1} \in A | X_n, \tau_{n+1} = t) = \pi(A, X_n, t)$ for $A \in \mathcal{B}(E^r)$.

q will be referred to as the *conditional jump rate* and π as the *conditional state jump distribution.*

Now let us assume that q is bounded, so that the process x(t) only takes a finite number of different values in each finite interval, what implies that we get a one to one correspondence between x(t) and the associated sequence of states and jump times as given in (1). This allows us to think of x(t) as being defined by

(6)
$$\tau_0 \equiv 0$$
$$x(t) := x_n \quad \text{if} \quad \tau_n \leq t < \tau_{n+1} \quad .$$

The *history of the process* is as usual defined by the σ-algebra

(7) $$\sigma_t = \sigma(x_s | s \leq t)$$

and the history of events before some σ_t-stopping time s is denoted by σ_s. Furthermore we introduce the σ-algebra generated by the random vector X_n,

(8) $$\sigma_n = \sigma(X_n) \quad .$$

As the formulations of the announced representation theorems simplify a lot when we assume that henceforth any stopping time s only takes values in $[0,T)$ ($[0,\infty)$ resp.) we shall deal with this case only. This simplification comes from the fact that under this assumption

(9) $$P(\bigcup_{n=0}^{\infty} \{\tau_n \leq s < \tau_{n+1}\}) = 1.$$

In order to shorten our notation we introduce the abbreviation

(10) $$A_n^\tau := \{\tau_n \leq \tau < \tau_{n+1}\} \quad .$$

Using this notation we find from [6, Theorem 1 and Corollary 1] that any stopping time s may be written as

(11) $$s(\omega) = \sum_{n=0}^{\infty} I_{A_n^s} S(X_n(\omega)), \quad I_A = \text{indicator function of } A,$$

with Borel measurable functions $S(X_n)$ on the range space of the random vectors X_n. The functionals $S(X_n)$ will be called *respresentations of the stopping time* s. This is the special case of the representation of a functional on the past of the jump process x given in [6]. This allows us to cite the following results as special cases of [6, Theorem 3]:

The *strong conditioning formula* - called like this because of its analogy to the strong Markov property - shows that for an L_1-random variable $E(z|X_n,A_n^s)$ equals $E(z|X_n,A_n^t)$ considered as a function of t composed with $S(X_n)$, i.e.

$$(12) \qquad E(z|X_n,A_n^s) = E(z|X_n,A_n^t) \circ S(X_n).$$

Here $E(z|X_n)$ denotes the conditional expectation of z given the random vector X_n considered as a function on the range space of X_n.

The analogous formula for an integrable functional $\phi(t)$ on the past of x with representations $\phi(t,X_n)$ is given by

$$(13) \qquad \phi(s(\omega),\omega) = \sum_{n=0}^{\infty} I_{A_n^s}(\omega)\phi(t,X_n(\omega)) \circ S(X_n(\omega)) \quad .$$

A very special case of [6,14] which will be used in the following form in the derivation of the variational inequality will be referred to as the *integral formula for conditional expectations:*

$$(14) \qquad \begin{aligned} E(z|X_n) = {} & \exp\left(-\int_{\tau_n}^{S(X_n)} q(s|X_n)ds\right) E(z|X_n,A_n^s) \\ & + \int_{\tau_n}^{S(X_n)} \int_{E^r} E(z|X_{n-1})\pi(dx_{n+1}|X_n,\tau_{n+1})q(\tau_{n+1}|X_n) \\ & \qquad \exp\left(-\int_{\tau_n}^{\tau_n} q(s|X_n)ds\right) d\tau_{n+1} \quad . \end{aligned}$$

All these formulas can easily be derived from [6, Theorem 3]. The above special cases of [6, 14] suffice for deriving the desired variational inequality and we think that just giving these special cases instead of the general formula makes the following proofs more understandable.

2. A SUFFICIENT OPTIMALITY CONDITION FOR A PARTIALLY OBSERVED STOPPING TIME PROBLEM

Using the above results we shall prove that for a partially observed jump Markov process a certain variational inequality is a sufficient condition for optimality of a stopping rule. This variational inequality is similar to those given by Friedman [1,4,5], Bensoussan [2], and Rudemo [12].

2.1 The Optimal Stopping Problem.

Let x(t) be a *jump Markov process* defined on [0,T] the values of which are pairs of integers (i,j). Think of x(t) as given by the two component process

(15) $$x(t) = (y(t),z(t)) ,$$

where y(t) is the *observed component* and z(t) the *unobserved one*. Let $\mathfrak{M}_t = (y_s | s \leq t)$ be the *history of the observed process* and $\phi(t,i,j)$ be a *bounded pay off function*. Let Φ be a *family of* $\mathfrak{M}_t$*-stopping times* taking values in [0,T). The *problem* now is to maximize (or to minimize, then only invert all the following inequalities)

(16) $$E(\phi(s,x(s))) \quad \textit{with respect to } s \in \Phi.$$

We shall always use (i,j) to denote the current state, i.e.

(17) $$x_n = (y_n,z_n) = (i,j)$$

and the histories of the process are defined analogous to the definitions in the preceding section.

(18) $$X_n = (x_0,\tau_1 x_1,\tau_2 x_2, \ldots , \tau_n x_n)$$

and

(19) $$Y_k = (y_0,\tau_1 y_1,\tau_2 y_2, \ldots ,\tau_k y_k)$$

denote the successive states and jump times of the x-process resp. the y-process. Note here that the jump times of the x-process might not coincide with those of the observed process. Nevertheless we use the same notation for the jump times $(\tau_1,\ldots,\tau_n)$ of the x-process and for the jump times $(\tau_1,\ldots,\tau_k)$ of the y-process, as we think that no confusion will be possible.

Let the *probabilistic structure of the* x-*process* be given by

(20) $$P(\tau_{n+1} > t | X_n) = \exp\left(-\int_{\tau_n}^{t} q(s,i,j)ds\right)$$

and

(21) $$P((y_{n+1},z_{n+1}) = \pi(l,m) | X_n,\tau_{n+1}) = \pi(l,m | i,j,\tau_{n+1}).$$

Furthermore let $P(t,Y_k)$ be the vector given by

$$(22) \qquad P_j(t,Y_k) := P(z(t) = j \mid Y_k, \tau_k \leq t < \tau_{k+1}).$$

With this we find the *probabilistic structure of the observed process* y: The y-process is a jump process with conditional jump rate $\rho(t \mid Y_k)$ and conditional state jump distribution μ defined by

$$(23) \qquad P(\tau_{k+1} > t \mid Y_k) = \exp\left(-\int_{\tau_k}^{t} \rho(s \mid Y_k)ds\right)$$

and

$$(24) \qquad P(y_{k+1} = l \mid Y_k, \tau_{k+1}) = \mu(l \mid Y_k, \tau_{k+1})$$

where ρ and μ are computed from (20) and (21) using (22):

$$(25) \qquad \rho(t,Y_k) = \sum_j \sum_{\substack{l,m \\ l \neq i}} \pi[(l,m) \mid (i,j),t]q(t,i,j)P_j(t,Y_k)$$

$$(26) \qquad \mu(l \mid Y_k,t) = \frac{\sum_j \sum_m \pi[(l,m) \mid (i,j),t]q(t,i,j)\,P_j(t,Y_k)}{\rho(t,Y_k)} .$$

If now we know how to describe $P_j(t,Y_k)$ then ρ and μ are determined from (20) and (21). Now $P_j(t,Y_k)$ is given on the stochastic interval $[\tau_k,T]$ as the solution of the differential

$$(27) \qquad \frac{d}{dt}P_j(t,Y_k) = [\rho(t,Y_k) - q(t,i,j)]P_j(t,Y_k) + \\ + \sum_{\substack{m \\ m \neq j}} \pi[(i,j) \mid (i,m),t]q(t,i,m)P_m(t,Y_k) .$$

At the initial time τ_k of this interval - if $Y_k = (Y_{k-1},\tau_k,l)$ - $P(t,Y_k)$ and $P(t,Y_{k-1})$ are related by

$$(28) \qquad P_m(\tau_k,Y_k) = \frac{\sum_j \pi[(l,m) \mid (i,j),\tau_k]q(\tau_k,i,j)P_j(\tau_k,Y_{k-1})}{\sum_m \sum_j \pi[(l,m) \mid (i,j),\tau_k]q(\tau_k,i,j)P_j(\tau_k-Y_{k-1})} .$$

The right hand side of (28) will be denoted by $P_m^+(Y_{k-1},\tau_k,l)$ for abbreviation. (27) and (28) will be referred to as the *filtering equations* for obvious reasons. For details the reader is referred to [7,8,9].

2.2 The Variational Inequality.

We are now going to state and prove the announced variational inequality theorem for the stopping problem of section 2.1. Let Δ denote the set of probability vectors over $\mathcal{Z}$, i.e. the vectors P such that

$P \geq 0, \sum P_j = 1$.

Theorem: *Let there be a bounded function* $V(t,i,P)$ *defined on* $[0,T]\times Z\times\Delta$ *such that for each solution of (31), (32)* $V(t,i,P(t,Y_k))$ *is Lipschitzian in* t *on* $[\tau_k,T]$ *and satisfies on* $[\tau_k,T]$:

$$(29)\qquad 0 \geq \frac{d}{dt} V(t,i,P(t,Y_k)) - \rho(t,Y_k)V(t,i,P(t,Y_k) + + \rho(t,Y_k) \sum_l V(t,l\ P^+(Y_k,t,l)\mu(l|Y_k,t)$$

and

$$(30)\qquad V(t,i,P(t,Y_k)) \geq \sum_j \phi(t,i,j)P_j(t,Y_k)$$

If there is a stopping time s^* *with representation* $S^*(Y_k)$ *such that equality holds in (29) if* $\tau_k \leq t < S^*(Y_k)$ *and in (30) if* $S^*(Y_k) \leq t < T$, *then* s^* *is optimal.*

Proof: Let s be any stopping time of Φ with representation $S(Y_k)$ and let

$$(31)\qquad J(Y_k) := E(\phi(s,x(s))|Y_k)\ .$$

From the strong conditioning formula for functionals (13) and the integral formula as given in (14) we thus find

$$(32)\qquad J(Y_k) = \sum_j \phi(S(Y_k),i,j)P_j(S(Y_k),Y_k)e^{-\int_{\tau_k}^{S(Y_k)} \rho(s\ Y_k)ds} + \int_{\tau_k}^{S(Y_k)} \sum_l J(Y_k,\tau_{k+1},l)\mu(l|Y_k,\tau_{k+1})\rho(\tau_{k+1}|Y_k) \cdot e^{-\int_{\tau_k}^{\tau_{k+1}} \rho(s|Y_k)ds} d\tau_{k+1}\ .$$

Multiplying the variational inequality (29) by the integrating factor

$$(33)\qquad \exp\left(-\int_{\tau_k}^{t} \rho(s|Y_k)ds\right)$$

gives us

$$(34)\qquad 0 \geq \frac{d}{dt}\left[V(t,i,P(t,Y_k))e^{-\int_{\tau_k}^{t} \rho(s|Y_k)ds}\right] + \rho(t,Y_k)e^{-\int_{\tau_k}^{t} \rho(s|Y_k)ds}\ \cdot$$

$$\cdot\sum_{l} V(t,l,P^{+}(Y_k,t,l)\mu(l|Y_k,t).$$

Integrating this from τ_k to $S(Y_k)$ and using the filtering equations (27) and (28) yields

$$(35)\qquad V(\tau_k,i,P^{+}(Y_{k-1},\tau_k,i)) \geqq V(S(Y_k),i,P(S(Y_k),Y_k))e^{-\int_{\tau_k}^{S(Y_k)}\rho(s|Y_k)ds} + $$
$$+\int_{\tau_k}^{S(Y_k)}\rho(t,Y_k)e^{-\int_{\tau_k}^{t}\rho(S,Y_k)ds}\cdot\sum_{l}V(t,l,P^{+}(Y_k,t,l))\mu(l|Y_k,t)dt.$$

Now substract the formula given in (32) from the one given in (35) using (30) to find

$$(36)\qquad V(\tau_k,i,P^{+}(Y_{k-1},\tau_k,i)) - J(Y_k) \geqq \int_{\tau_k}^{S(Y_k)}\rho(\tau_{k+1}Y_k)e^{-\int_{\tau_k}^{\tau_{k+1}}\rho(s,Y_k)ds}\cdot$$
$$\cdot\sum_{l}[V(\tau_{k+1},l,P^{+}(Y_k,\tau_{k+1},l)) - J(Y_k,\tau_{k+1},l)]\mu(l|Y_k,\tau_{k+1})d\tau_{k+1}$$

what is valid for each k. So iterate this and find

$$(37)\qquad V(\tau_0,i,P^{+}(Y_0)) - J(Y_0) \geqq \int_{\tau_0}^{S(Y_0)}\rho(\tau_1|Y_0)e^{-\int_{\tau_0}^{\tau_1}\rho(s_1|Y_0)ds_1}\cdot$$
$$\cdot\sum_{l_1}\int_{\tau_1}^{S(Y_1)}\cdots\sum_{l_k}\int_{\tau_k}^{S(Y_k)}\rho(\tau_{k+1},Y_k)e^{-\int_{\tau_k}^{\tau_{k+1}}\rho(s_{k+1},Y_k)ds_{k+1}}\cdot$$
$$\cdot\sum_{l_{k+1}}[V(\tau_{k+1},l_{k+1},P^{+}(Y_{k+1})) - J(Y_{k+1})]\mu(l_{k+1}|Y_k,\tau_{k+1})d\tau_{k+1}\ \cdots$$
$$\cdots\ \mu(l_1|Y_0,\tau_1)d\tau_1\,.$$

Now it is easily seen that the absolute value of the right hand side of (37) is bounded by

$$(38)\qquad \frac{(CT)^k}{k!}\quad \text{for some C big enough,}$$

as any functional in (37) is bounded. (38) now tends to zero when k goes to infinity, so that

$$(39)\qquad V(\tau_0,i,P^{+}(Y_0)) - J(Y_0) \geqq 0.$$

Since $Y_0 = (i)$, where i is the value of the observed process, then

(40) $$E(\phi(s,x(s))) = \Sigma_i \, J(Y_0) \, \pi_i$$

where

(41) $\pi_i = \Sigma_j \, \pi_{ij}$ is the initial probability of having observed i.

The quantity $P^+(Y_0)$ is given in terms of the initial distribution by

(42) $$P_j^+(Y_0) = \frac{\pi_{ij}}{\Sigma_j \, \pi_{ij}} \quad .$$

Together with (39) this implies

(43) $$\Sigma_i \, V(0,i,P^+(Y_0))\pi_i \overset{(39)}{\geq} \Sigma_i J(Y_0)\pi_i \overset{(40)}{=} E(\phi(s,x(s))$$

for any $s \in \Phi$.

Repeating the preceding steps for s^* with equality replacing the inequalities gives

(44) $$\Sigma_i V(0,i,P^+(Y_0))\pi_i = E(\phi(s^*,x(s^*))) \overset{(43)}{\geq} E(\phi(s,x(s)))$$

for any $s \in \Phi$.

This finally proves that s^* is optimal.

Remark: After assuming sufficient conditions of differentiability on the function describing the remaining costs from some time t onwards it can be proved that this functional may be taken as the functional V the existence of which is assumed in the preceding theorem. But this is very lengthy to write down and seems not to be very interesting, so that this part as well as the proof of the necessity of the conditions of the theorem are left to the reader.

REFERENCES

[1] R. Anderson and A. Friedman, "A Quality Control Problem and Quasi-Variational Inequalities", Archive for Rational Mechanics and Analysis 63 (1973), pp. 205-252.

[2] A. Bensoussan and J.L. Lions, "Temps d'Arrêt et Contrôle" Impulsionel: Inéquations Variationelles et Quasi-Variationelles d'Évolutions", Cahier de Math. de la Décision, no. 7523, Univ. Paris IX.

[3] Ph. Courrège and P. Priouret, "Temps d'Arrêt d'une Fonction aléatoire:Relations d'Équivalence associées et Propriétés de Décompositions", Publications de l'Institut de Statistique de l'Université de Paris XIV (1965), pp. 245-274.

[4] A. Friedman, "Stochastic Differential Equations and Applications", Vol. 1, (1975), Academic Press.

[5] A. Friedman and M. Robin, " The Free Boundary for Variational Inequalities with Nonlocal Operators", SIAM J. Control and Optimization 16 (1978), pp. 347-362.

[6] M. Kohlmann and R. Rishel, "Strong Conditioning", preprint University of Bonn (1978), submitted.

[7] R. Rishel, "A Minimum Principle For Controlled Jump Processes", in Control Theory, Numerical Methods and Computer Systems Modelling, Springer Lecture Notes in Economics and Mathematical Systems 107 (1975), Springer Verlag.

[8] R. Rishel, "Controls Optimal From Time t onwards and Dynamic Programming For Systems of Controlled Jump Processes", Mathematical Programming Study 6 (1976), pp. 125-153.

[9] R. Rishel, "State Estimation for Partially Observed Jump Processes", to appear in J. Mathem. Analysis Appl.

[10] R. Rudemo, "State Estimation for Partially Observed Jump Markov Processes", J. Mathem. Analysis Appl. 44 (1973), pp. 581-611.

EQUATIONS DU FILTRAGE NON LINEAIRE POUR DES PROCESSUS A DEUX INDICES

H. KOREZLIOGLU* - G. MAZZIOTTO** - J. SZPIRGLAS**

* Ecole Nationale Supérieure des Télécommunications - 46 rue Barrault
75634 PARIS

**Centre National d'Etudes des Télécommunications - 196 rue de Paris
92220 BAGNEUX

RESUME : Un signal X, qui est représenté comme une semi-martingale d'un mouvement brownien B, est estimé à partir d'un processus d'observation Y, somme d'une fonctionnelle non anticipative de X et d'un mouvement brownien W, qui est indépendant de B et représente le bruit. Les équations récursives du filtrage, satisfaites par l'estimation de X, sont exprimées en fonction des innovations horizontale, verticale et diagonale.

SUMMARY : A signal X represented as a semi-martingale of a Brownian sheet B is estimated in terms of an observation process Y. Y is given as the sum of a non-anticipative functional of X and a Brownian sheet W which is independant of B and represents the noise. Recursive filtering equations satisfied by the estimation of X are expressed in terms of horizontal, vertical and diagonal innovations.

I - INTRODUCTION.

1 - Généralités : Le problème de filtrage consiste à estimer un signal X à partir d'une observation Y. Ici X et Y sont des processus réels, X(z) et Y(z) à paramètre z bidimensionnel, définis sur le rectangle R_{z_o} de $\mathbb{R}^2_+$: $R_{z_o} = \{z=(s,t) : 0 \leq s \leq s_o,\ 0 \leq t \leq t_o\}$. On munit R_{z_o} de la relation d'ordre partiel $z' \leq z$ si $z = (s,t)$, $z' = (s',t')$: $s' \leq s$ et $t' \leq t$. Le domaine R_z est formé des points z' "en dessous et à gauche de z" : $R_z = \{z' : z' \leq z\}$. Il représente le "passé" à l'instant z tandis que la frontière, $\partial R_z = \{(s',t') : s' = s \text{ ou } t' = t\}$, représente le "présent" à l'instant z. Une estimation $\bar{X}(z/z)$ de X(z) à l'instant z est dite causale si elle n'est fonction que de l'observation Y sur R_z. Le filtrage est dit récursif si le calcul de $\bar{X}$ sur $R_{z'}$, pour $z' > z$, ne dépend que des estimations sur ∂R_z et des observations Y comprises entre ∂R_z et $\partial R_{z'}$.

On définit, au paragraphe II, l'estimateur $\bar{X}(z/z)$ de $X(z)$ comme l'espérance conditionnelle de $X(z)$ par rapport à la tribu engendrée par les observations Y sur R_z et on exprime $\bar{X}(z/z)$ comme solution de plusieurs équations différentielles stochastiques. En considérant les différents processus sur un chemin croissant arbitraire, Γ, joignant O à z_o, on obtient au paragraphe III une équation du filtrage non récursive, formulation à deux paramètres de l'équation classique à un paramètre. L'équation récursive du filtrage non linéaire est obtenue au paragraphe IV en combinant les résultats obtenus sur des chemins horizontaux et verticaux. Cette équation fait intervenir trois types de processus d'innovation, les innovations diagonale, verticale et horizontale. Ces résultats généralisent ceux de Wong ([1]) et Korezlioglu ([2]) pour le cas linéaire et donnent une forme explicite de l'équation du filtrage non linéaire conjecturée par Wong ([3]). Le modèle de filtrage est construit par la méthode de la probabilité de référence de Zakaī ([4]) et l'articulation des calculs est en tout point analogue à celle de Szpirglas et Mazziotto ([5]) dans le cas à un paramètre.

2 - Notations - Préliminaires : On rappelle ici les règles de calcul stochastique à deux paramètres dues principalement à Wong et Zakaī ([6]), ([7]), Cairoli et Walsh ([8]) que l'on utilise dans la suite. Si $x = (s,t)$ et $y = (u,v)$ sont des points de R_{z_o}, on désigne par $x \boxtimes y$ le point (s,v), $x \vee y$ le point $(\max(s,u), \max(t,v))$ et par $x \wedge y$ la relation sur $R^2_{z_o}$ définie par $(s \leq u,\ t \geq v)$. L'indicatrice de l'ensemble $\{(x,y) \in R^2_{z_o}$ tel que $x \wedge y\}$ est notée $I(x,y)$. Si $x \wedge y$, on a : $y \boxtimes x = x \vee y$. Soit $\underline{\underline{R}}$ la tribu borélienne de R_{z_o}.

Sur un espace de probabilité $(\Omega, \underline{\underline{A}}, \mathbb{P})$, on considère une filtration $\underline{\underline{F}} = (\underline{\underline{F}}_z,\ z \in R_{z_o})$ de sous-tribus de $\underline{\underline{A}}$ satisfaisant aux propriétés de régularité F_1 à F_4 de ([6]) et ([8]) :

F_1) $z' > z \Rightarrow \underline{\underline{F}}_z \subset \underline{\underline{F}}_{z'}$

F_2) $\underline{\underline{F}}_o$ contient tous les ensembles $\mathbb{P}$-négligeables de $\underline{\underline{A}}$.

F_3) $\underline{\underline{F}}_z = \bigcap_{z' > z} \underline{\underline{F}}_{z'}$

F_4) $\underline{\underline{F}}_{z \boxtimes z_o}$ et $\underline{\underline{F}}_{z_o \boxtimes z}$ sont $\underline{\underline{F}}_z$-conditionnellement indépendantes.

On appelle $\underline{\underline{F}}$-brownien un processus continu, W, issu d'une mesure brownienne sur R_{z_o} et tel que $(W(z), \underline{\underline{F}}_z)$ soit une martingale forte. Pour les propriétés des divers types d'intégrales stochastiques relativement à un $\underline{\underline{F}}$-brownien, on se réferre à ([6]), on rappelle seulement les espaces fonctionnels sur lesquels elles sont définies. On définit l'intégrale simple relativement à W, ([6]) et ([8]), sur les ensembles $H_1(\underline{\underline{F}})$ des processus ϕ, pour i = o, 1, 2, vérifiant les conditions a), b), c_i) suivantes :

a) ϕ est une fonction mesurable relativement à $\underline{\underline{R}}\otimes\underline{\underline{F}}_{z_o}$

b) $\int_{R_{z_o}} E(\phi^2(z))dz < \infty$

c_o) (resp. c_1), c_2)) Pour tout z de R_{z_o}, $\phi(z)$ est mesurable par rapport à $\underline{\underline{F}}_z$ (resp. $\underline{\underline{F}}_{z\otimes z_o}$, $\underline{\underline{F}}_{z_o\otimes z}$).

On définit les différents types d'intégrales doubles par rapport à W et à la mesure de Lebesgue sur R_{z_o}, ([6]), ([8]) sur l'ensemble $H(\underline{\underline{F}})$ des fonctions Ψ sur $R^2_{z_o}$ qui vérifient les conditions d), e), f) :

d) Ψ est une fonction mesurable par rapport à $\underline{\underline{R}}\otimes\underline{\underline{R}}\otimes\underline{\underline{F}}_{z_o}$.

e) Pour tout (x,y) de $R^2_{z_o}$, $\Psi(x,y)$ est $\underline{\underline{F}}_{x\vee y}$-mesurable.

f) $\iint_{R_{z_o}\times R_{z_o}} I(x,y)\ E(\Psi^2(x,y))dx\ dy < \infty$

Pour Γ un chemin croissant de O à z_o, l'intégrale stochastique selon ce chemin est définie dans ([6]) sur l'ensemble $H_\Gamma(\underline{\underline{F}})$ des processus ϕ vérifiant a) et b) ci-dessus et c_Γ) suivante :

c_Γ) Pour tout $z\varepsilon R_{z_o}$, $\phi(z)$ est $\underline{\underline{F}}_{z_\Gamma}$-mesurable ; où z_Γ désigne le plus petit point de Γ supérieur à z.

3 - Modèle de filtrage - Hypothèses : Sur un espace de probabilité $(\Omega, \underline{\underline{A}}, \mathbb{P})$, on se donne deux mouvements browniens indépendants Y et B. Soit $\underline{\underline{F}} = (\underline{\underline{F}}_z, z\varepsilon R_{z_o})$, (resp. $\underline{\underline{G}}$), la filtration engendrée par (Y, B) (resp. Y) et les ensembles $\mathbb{P}$-négligeables. Les filtrations $\underline{\underline{F}}$ et $\underline{\underline{G}}$ satisfont aux propriétés de régularité F_1 à F_4 énoncées au paragraphe I - 2 qui permettent d'effectuer des calculs stochastiques relativement à $\underline{\underline{F}}$ ou à $\underline{\underline{G}}$. Grâce à l'indépendance des processus Y et B, l'ensemble $(\Omega, \underline{\underline{G}}, \underline{\underline{F}}, \mathbb{P})$ possède la propriété (K) suivante :

(K) $\forall z\varepsilon R_{z_o}$, $\forall U$ v.a. $\underline{\underline{F}}_z$-mesurable bornée

$E(U/\underline{\underline{G}}_z) = E(U/\underline{\underline{G}}_{z_o})$ $\mathbb{P}$-p.s.,

dont une formulation équivalente due à Brémaud et Yor ([9]) est :

(H) Toute $\underline{\underline{G}}$-martingale bornée est une $\underline{\underline{F}}$-martingale.

Dans le cas à un paramètre, ces propriétés sont particulièrement intéressantes pour la théorie du filtrage ([9]), ([5]), car elles permettent d'expliciter les projections de processus ([5]) et d'intégrales stochastiques ([9]) sur la filtration $\underline{\underline{G}}$. On montre au paragraphe II qu'il en est de même ici. D'autre part, le processus Y étant une martingale forte relativement aux filtrations $\underline{\underline{F}}$ ou $\underline{\underline{G}}$, on peut définir les intégrales stochastiques de processus de $H_i(\underline{\underline{G}})$ ou $H(\underline{\underline{G}})$ et de $H_i(\underline{\underline{F}})$ ou $H(\underline{\underline{F}})$. On montrerait comme dans ([9]) que, grâce à la propriété (H), les intégrales stochastiques de processus de $H_i(\underline{\underline{G}})$ ou $H(\underline{\underline{G}})$, évaluées relativement aux filtrations $\underline{\underline{G}}$ ou $\underline{\underline{F}}$ coïncident.

On définit une probabilité $\mathbb{Q}$ équivalente à $\mathbb{P}$ comme dans ([6]) par la formule $\mathbb{Q} = L(z_o)\mathbb{P}$. Pour H un processus borné de $H_o(\underline{\underline{F}})$, L est la martingale strictement positive, de puissance p-intégrable (p>1), définie par : $L(z) = \exp\{ \int_{R_z} H(x)Y(dx) - \frac{1}{2}\int_{R_z} H^2(x)dx \}$.

Le signal à filtrer X est une semi-martingale représentable, ([7]), par rapport à B et à sa filtration naturelle $\mathbb{P}$-complétée, $\underline{\underline{F}}^B$, de la forme suivante :

(1) $X(z)=\int_{R_z} [\Theta(x)dx+\phi(x)B(dx)]+\iint_{R_z x R_z} I(x,y)[f(x,y)dxB(dy)+g(x,y)B(dx)dy+\Psi(x,y)B(dx)B(dy)]$

On suppose que les processus Θ^2, ϕ^2 sont dans $H_o(\underline{\underline{F}}^B)$ et f^2, g^2, Ψ^2 dans $H(\underline{\underline{F}}^B)$. Ces hypothèses permettent d'appliquer le théorème de projection à la semi-martingale de carré intégrable LX dans les paragraphes III et IV. Dans ([6]), Wong et Zakaï montrent que sous la probabilité $\mathbb{Q}$, le processus $W(z) = Y(z) - \int_{R_z} H(x)dx$ est un mouvement brownien. On vérifie, en calculant les fonctions caractéristiques, que sous $\mathbb{Q}$, le processus B reste brownien et est indépendant de W. De plus, sur $\underline{\underline{F}}^B_{z_o}$, les probabilités $\mathbb{P}$ et $\mathbb{Q}$ coïncident.

En définitive, le modèle de filtrage étudié ici, où l'observation Y est la somme d'une fonctionnelle non anticipative de Y et X, $\int H(x)dx$, et d'un bruit brownien, W, indépendant de X, est décrit par le couple (Y, X) sur l'espace de probabilité $(\Omega, \underline{\underline{A}}, \mathbb{Q})$.

II - PROJECTIONS DE PROCESSUS ET D'INTEGRALES STOCHASTIQUES.

1 - ($\underline{\underline{G}}$-P)-projections de processus : Etant donné un processus H défini sur $(\Omega, \underline{\underline{A}}, \underline{\underline{G}}, \underline{\underline{F}}, \mathbb{P})$, adapté à la filtration $\underline{\underline{F}}$, on désire lui associer un processus $\hat{H}$, sa $\underline{\underline{G}}$-projection, adapté à la filtration $\underline{\underline{G}}$, aussi régulier que peut l'être H et tel que pour presque tout z, $\mathbb{P}$-p.s. : $\hat{H}(z/z) = E_{\mathbb{P}}(H(z)/\underline{\underline{G}}_z)$. Le procédé de construction employé ici est loin d'être général puisqu'il fait directement appel à la propriété (K).

a) Si H est une $\underline{\underline{F}}$-martingale de carré intégrable continue, on définit $\hat{H}$ comme la version continue de la $\underline{\underline{G}}$-martingale $\hat{H}(z/z) = E_{\mathbb{P}}(H(z)/\underline{\underline{G}}_z)$.

b) Soit H une fonction mesurable sur l'espace $(\Omega x R_{z_o}, \underline{\underline{A}}\otimes\underline{\underline{R}})$ (resp. $(\Omega x R^2_{z_o}, \underline{\underline{A}}\otimes\underline{\underline{R}}\otimes\underline{\underline{R}})$) et intégrable relativement à la mesure m, définie sur cet espace par $dm = d\mathbb{P}\otimes dz$ (resp. $dm = d\mathbb{P}\otimes dx\otimes dy$). On définit sa $\underline{\underline{G}}$-projection $\hat{H}$ comme l'espérance conditionnelle de H par rapport à la tribu $\underline{\underline{G}}_{z_o}\otimes\underline{\underline{R}}$ (resp. $\underline{\underline{G}}_{z_o}\otimes\underline{\underline{R}}\otimes\underline{\underline{R}}$) et la mesure m. Si pour z et y de R_{z_o}, H(z) est $\underline{\underline{F}}_y$-mesurable, le processus $\hat{H}$ considéré au point z coïncide p.s. grâce à la propriété (K) avec $E_{\mathbb{P}}(H(z)/\underline{\underline{G}}_y)$ que l'on note $\hat{H}(z/y)$. Cette définition permet d'associer à tout processus de $H_i(\underline{\underline{F}})$ ou $H_\Gamma(\underline{\underline{F}})$ (resp. $H(\underline{\underline{F}})$), un processus $\widehat{H}$ dans $H_i(\underline{\underline{G}})$ ou $H_\Gamma(\underline{\underline{G}})$ (resp. $H(\underline{\underline{G}})$). On note en particulier la $\underline{\underline{G}}$-projection d'un processus H de $H(\underline{\underline{F}})$ par : $\forall x,\ y \in R_{z_o}$: $\widehat{H}(x,y/x\vee y) = E(H(x,y)/\underline{\underline{G}}_{x\vee y})$ $\mathbb{P}$-p.s.. Bien évidemment, si H vérifie les conditions de a) et b), les deux définitions sont compatibles dans la mesure où $\widehat{H}$ au sens de a) appartient à la m-classe de processus $\widehat{H}$ au sens de b).

2 - <u>$(\underline{\underline{G}}, \mathbb{Q})$-projection de processus</u> : On définit maintenant la $\underline{\underline{G}}$-projection d'un processus X relativement à la probabilité $\mathbb{Q}$ par l'intermédiaire des $\underline{\underline{G}}$-projections précédentes. On note $\bar{X}$ la $(\underline{\underline{G}}, \mathbb{Q})$-projection d'un processus X, vérifiant les conditions des définitions a) ou b) avec la probabilité $\mathbb{Q}$. $\bar{X}(z/z)$ est défini par :

$$\bar{X}(z/z) = \widehat{LX}(z/z)/\widehat{L}(z/z).$$

On vérifie que pour tout z de R_{z_o} et $\mathbb{Q}$-p.s. : $\bar{X}(z/z) = E_{\mathbb{Q}}(X(z)/\underline{\underline{G}}_z)$.

3 - <u>Projection d'intégrales stochastiques</u> : Dans le cas à un paramètre, Brémaud et Yor (9) montrent un théorème de projection d'intégrales stochastiques sous l'hypothèse que l'espace $(\Omega, \underline{\underline{A}}, \underline{\underline{G}}, \underline{\underline{F}}, \mathbb{P})$ possède la propriété (H) ; ce résultat s'étend sans difficulté ici.

<u>Proposition 1</u> : Soit Y et B définis comme en (I - 3) sur l'ensemble $(\Omega, \underline{\underline{A}}, \underline{\underline{G}}, \underline{\underline{F}}, \mathbb{P})$ possédant la propriété (K).

a) Si $H \in H_i(\underline{\underline{F}})$ et $M(z) = \int_{R_z} H(x)Y(dx)$ resp. $i=0,1,2,\Gamma$ alors $\widehat{M}(z/z) = \int_{R_z} \widehat{H}(x/y_i)Y(dx)$ où resp. $y_i = x, x\boxtimes z, z\boxtimes x, x_\Gamma$

b) Si $H \in H(\underline{\underline{F}})$ et $M(z) = \iint_{R_z \times R_z} I(x,y)H(x,y)Y(dx)Y(dy)$ alors $\widehat{M}(z/z) = \iint_{R_z \times R_z} \widehat{H}(x,y/x\vee y)Y(dx)Y(dy)$

c) Si $H \in H_i(\underline{\underline{F}})$ et $M(z) = \int_{R_z} H(x)B(dx)$ alors $\widehat{M} = 0$.

La partie c) de la proposition résulte de l'indépendance des processus Y et B de la représentation des $(\underline{\underline{G}}, \mathbb{P})$-martingales en fonction de Y.

III - <u>EQUATIONS DU FILTRAGE SUR UN CHEMIN</u>.

Etant donné un chemin croissant Γ dans R_{z_o}, on cherche une équation vérifiée par $\bar{X}(z/z)$ quand z décrit Γ. En se restreignant à un chemin, on se ramène en fait à un problème de processus à un paramètre et il n'est donc pas étonnant de retrouver une équation du filtrage classique. Cependant, cette équation n'est pas causale, au sens défini dans l'introduction. Une semi-martingale du type de X (formule (1)) peut être représentée comme une Γ-semi-martingale (cf. ([6])), c'est-à-dire qu'il existe des processus u_Γ et v_Γ appartenant à $\underline{\underline{H}}_\Gamma(\underline{\underline{F}})$ tels que pour z décrivant Γ :

$$X(z) = \int_{R_z} [u(\Gamma,x)B(dx) + v(\Gamma,x)dx]$$

Pour $z\varepsilon\Gamma$ la martingale L s'écrit :

$$L(z) = 1 + \int_{R_z} L(x_\Gamma)H(x)Y(dx)$$

<u>Proposition 2</u> : Sur le chemin croissant Γ, le processus $\bar{X}(z/z)$ vérifie l'équation du filtrage suivante :

$$\bar{X}(z/z) = \int_{R_z} [\bar{v}(\Gamma,x/x_\Gamma)dx + \underline{\underline{R}}(X(x_\Gamma),H(x)/x_\Gamma)\nu(dx;x_\Gamma)]$$

où on a noté $\underline{\underline{R}}(X(x_\Gamma),H(x)/x_\Gamma)$ la valeur en x de la $(\underline{\underline{G}}, \mathbb{Q})$-projection du processus défini par le produit $(X(x_\Gamma)-\bar{X}(x_\Gamma/x_\Gamma))(H(x)-\bar{H}(x/x_\Gamma))$(qui est $\underline{\underline{F}}_{x_\Gamma}$-mesurable). L'innovation suivant le chemin Γ est définie par

$$\nu(z);\Gamma) = Y(z)-\int_{R_z} \bar{H}(x/x_\Gamma)dx.$$

<u>Démonstration</u> : Suivant ([6]), on montre que $\nu(z;\Gamma)$ est une Γ-martingale relativement à $(\underline{\underline{G}}, \mathbb{Q})$, ce qui justifie bien le nom d'innovation. Il s'agit d'évaluer $\bar{X}(z/z)$ en appliquant la formule de Ito au rapport $\widehat{LX}(z/z)/\widehat{L}(z/z)$ pour z décrivant Γ. On calcule d'abord le produit LX puis sa $\underline{\underline{G}}$-projection $\widehat{LX}$. Compte tenu du fait que le produit YB est une martingale sous $\mathbb{P}$ d'après l'hypothèse d'indépendance, on a :

$$L(z)X(z) = \int_{R_z} L(x_\Gamma)[v(\Gamma,x)dx+u(\Gamma,x)B(dx)]+\int_{R_z} L(x_\Gamma)X(x_\Gamma)H(x)Y(dx)$$

L'intégrale stochastique en B a une $\underline{\underline{G}}$-projection nulle en vertu de la proposition 2, $\widehat{LX}$ s'écrit donc :

$$\widehat{LX}(z/z) = \int_{R_z} \widehat{L}(x_\Gamma/x_\Gamma)\bar{v}(\Gamma,x/x_\Gamma)+\int_{R_z} \widehat{L}(x_\Gamma/x_\Gamma)\overline{XH}(x_\Gamma,x/x_\Gamma)Y(dx)$$

où $\overline{XH}(x_\Gamma,x/x_\Gamma)$ désigne la valeur en x de la $(\underline{\underline{G}}, \mathbb{Q})$-projection du processus U défini par $U(x) = X(x_\Gamma)H(x)$ (qui est $\underline{\underline{F}}_{x_\Gamma}$-mesurable). De même $\bar{v}(\Gamma,x/x_\Gamma)$ représente la valeur au point x de la $(\underline{\underline{G}}, \mathbb{Q})$-projection de $v(\Gamma,.)$. On obtient l'expression de $\widehat{L}$ en identifiant X à 1 dans le calcul précédent . La formule de Ito appliquée au rapport $\widehat{LX}/\widehat{L}$ conduit à l'équation du filtrage comme dans ([5]).

En choisissant des chemins Γ verticaux ou horizontaux, on obtient les équations du filtrage horizontal et vertical analogues à celles obtenues par Wong ([1]) et Korezlioglu ([2]) dans le cas linéaire.

<u>Proposition 3</u> - Equation du filtrage horizontal : Le processus X étant défini par la formule (1), on pose :

$$v(z,y) = \Theta(y)+\int_{R_z} I(x,y)g(x,y)B(dx).$$

L'équation vérifiée par $\bar{X}(z/z)$ est :

$$\bar{X}(z/z) = \int_{R_z}\bar{v}(z,y/y\boxtimes z)dy+\int_{R_z}\underline{\underline{R}}(X(y\boxtimes z),H(y)/y\boxtimes z)\nu(dy;y\boxtimes z)$$

où l'innovation horizontale associée au chemin horizontal passant par z' est définie pour $z \leqslant z\boxtimes z'$, par :

$$\nu(z;z\boxtimes z') = Y(z)-\int_{R_z}\bar{H}(y/y\boxtimes z')dy$$

Proposition 4 - Equation du filtrage vertical : Le processus X étant défini par la formule (1), on pose :

$$\tilde{v}(z,x) = \Theta(x)+\int_{R_z} I(x,y)f(x,y)B(dy).$$

L'équation vérifiée par $\bar{X}(z/z)$ est :

$$\bar{X}(z/z) = \int_{R_z}\bar{\tilde{v}}(z,x/z\boxtimes x)dx+\int_{R_z}\underline{\underline{R}}(X(z\boxtimes x),H(x)/z\boxtimes x)\nu(dx;z\boxtimes x)$$

où l'innovation verticale associée au chemin vertical passant par z' est définie pour $z \leqslant z'\boxtimes z$, par :

$$\nu(z;z'\boxtimes z) = Y(z)-\int_{R_z}\bar{H}(x/z'\boxtimes x)dx.$$

On remarque que ces équations ne peuvent être causales puisqu'à chaque instant y (resp. x), elles mettent en jeu des projections sur la tribu $\underline{\underline{G}}_{y\boxtimes z}$ (resp. $\underline{\underline{G}}_{z\boxtimes x}$) qui se situent dans le futur de y (resp. x).

IV - EQUATIONS RECURSIVES DU FILTRAGE.

L'équation du filtrage selon un chemin croissant du paragraphe III est unidimensionnelle dans son esprit et seule une formule de Ito à 1 paramètre est nécessaire pour l'obtenir. Les équations récursives suivantes sont essentiellement bidimensionnelles et leur démonstration utilise la formule de Ito de ([7]). On exprime d'abord $\widehat{LX}$ en tant que semi-martingale à deux paramètres. Au paragraphe précédent on a déjà écrit $\widehat{LX}$ en tant que 1-et 2-semi-martingale.

Proposition 5 - Equation non normalisée du filtrage :

$$\begin{aligned}\widehat{LX}(z/z) &= \int_{R_z}\widehat{L}(x/x)\{\overline{\Theta}(x/x)dx+\overline{XH}(x;x/x)Y(dx)\}\\ &+\iint_{R_z x R_z} I(x,y)\widehat{L}(y\boxtimes x/y\boxtimes x)\ \overline{XHH}(y\boxtimes x;x;y/y\boxtimes x)Y(dx)Y(dy)\\ &+\iint_{R_z x R_z} I(x,y)\widehat{L}(y\boxtimes x/y\boxtimes x)\ \overline{\tilde{v}H}(y\boxtimes x,x;y/y\boxtimes x)dxY(dy)\\ &+\iint_{R_z x R_z} I(x,y)\widehat{L}(y\boxtimes x/y\boxtimes x)\ \overline{vH}(y\boxtimes x,y;x/y\boxtimes x)Y(dx)dy\end{aligned}$$

avec $\overline{XHH}(y\boxtimes x;x;y/y\boxtimes x)$ (resp. $\overline{\tilde{v}H}(y\boxtimes x,x;y/y\boxtimes x)$, $(\overline{vH}(y\boxtimes x,y;x/y\boxtimes x))$ la valeur en (x,y) de la $(\underline{\underline{G}}, Q)$-projection du processus U défini par : $U(x,y) = X(x\vee y)H(x)H(y)$ (resp. $\tilde{v}(y\boxtimes x,x)H(y)$, $v(y\boxtimes x,y)H(x)$).

<u>Démonstration</u> : On exprime le produit LX à l'aide d'une formule de Ito où interviennent les deux browniens indépendants Y et B. Sa démonstration est analogue à celle de ([7]) et est omise ici. Le résultat s'en déduit en projetant les intégrales stochastiques sur $\underline{\underline{G}}$ selon la proposition 1.

L'expression de $\widehat{L}(z/z)$ figure dans ([6]) mais on peut l'obtenir ici directement en identifiant X à 1 dans la proposition 5 . Finalement, en appliquant la formule de Ito de ([7]) au rapport $\widehat{LX}/\widehat{L}$, on aboutit à l'équation récursive du filtrage vérifiée par $\bar{X}(z/z)$.

<u>Proposition 6</u> - Equation récursive du filtrage :

$$\bar{X}(z/z) = \int_{R_z} [\bar{\Theta}(x/x)dx + \underline{\underline{R}}(X(x),H(x)/x)\nu(dx;x)]$$
$$+\iint_{R_z \times R_z} [\underline{\underline{R}}(\tilde{v}(y\boxtimes x,x),H(y)/y\boxtimes x) - \underline{\underline{R}}(H(x),H(y)/y\boxtimes x)\underline{\underline{R}}(X(y\boxtimes x),H(x)/y\boxtimes x)]$$
$$I(x,y)\nu(dy;y\boxtimes x)dx$$
$$+\iint_{R_z \times R_z} [\underline{\underline{R}}(v(y\boxtimes x,y),H(x)/y\boxtimes x) - \underline{\underline{R}}(H(x),H(y)/y\boxtimes x)\underline{\underline{R}}(X(y\boxtimes x),H(y)/y\boxtimes x)]$$
$$I(x,y)\nu(dx;y\boxtimes x)dy$$
$$+\iint_{R_z \times R_z} I(x,y)\underline{\underline{R}}^2(X(y\boxtimes x),H(x),H(y)/y\boxtimes x)$$
$$[\nu(dx;y\boxtimes x)\nu(dy;y\boxtimes x) - \underline{\underline{R}}(H(x),H(y)/y\boxtimes x)dx\,dy]$$

où de façon générale on a noté, pour des processus $U_i(x,y)$, $i=1,2$ (resp. $i=1,2,3$), $\underline{\underline{R}}(U_1(x,y),\ U_2(x,y)/y\boxtimes x)$ (resp. $\underline{\underline{R}}^2(U_1(x,y),\ U_2(x,y),\ U_3(x,y)/y\boxtimes x)$) la valeur en (x,y) de la $(\underline{\underline{G}},\ Q)$-projection du processus défini en (x,y) par le produit $\prod_{i=1}^{2}(U_i(x,y) - \bar{U}_i(x,y/y\boxtimes x))$ (resp. $\prod_{i=1}^{3}$). Les innovations horizontales et verticales déjà définies et l'innovation diagonale est :

$$\nu(z/z) = Y(z) - \int_{R_z} \bar{H}(x/x)dx.$$

<u>Remarque</u> : Il est montré dans ([6]) que $\nu(z;z\boxtimes z')$ est une 1-$(\underline{\underline{G}},Q)$-martingale, $\nu(z;z'\boxtimes z)$ est une 2-$(\underline{\underline{G}},Q)$-martingale, $M(z) = \iint I(x,y)f(x,y)[\nu(dx;y\boxtimes x)\nu(dy;y\boxtimes x) - \underline{\underline{R}}(H(x),H(y)/y\boxtimes x)dx\,dy]$ est une $(\underline{\underline{G}},\ Q)$-martingale faible. On vérifie de même que $Y(z) - \int_{R_z}\bar{H}(x/x)dx$ est une $(\underline{\underline{G}},\ Q)$-martingale faible.

V - BIBLIOGRAPHIE.

(1) E. WONG : Recursive Causal Linear Filtering for Two-Dimensional Random Fields. IEEE, IT24, N°1, 50-59 (Jan. 1978).

(2) H. KOREZLIOGLU : Recursive Linear Filtering of Two Parameter Gaussian Markov Processes. Proceedings of the Eight Prague Conference on Information Theory, Statistical Decision Functions and Random Processes. Prague 28/8-1/9/1978.

(3) E. WONG : A Martingal Approach to Random Fields. N.A.T.O. Advanced Study Institute. Communication Systems and Random Process Theory. Darlington 8/8-20/8/1977.

(4) M. ZAKAI : On the Optimal Filtering of Diffusion Processes. Z. Wahr. V. Geb., 11, 230-249 (1969).

(5) J. SZPIRGLAS, G. MAZZIOTTO : Modèle général de filtrage non linéaire et équations différentielles stochastiques associées. C.R. Acad. Sc. Paris, t. 286 (5 juin 1978), Série A, pp. 1067-1070.

(6) E. WONG, M. ZAKAI : Likelihood Ratios and Transformation of Probability Associated with Two-parameter Wiener Processes. Z. Wahr. V. Geb., 40, 283-308 (1977).

(7) E. WONG, M. ZAKAI : Differentiation Formulas for Stochastic Integrals in the Plane. Stochastic Processes and their Applications. 6, 339-349 (1978).

(8) R. CAIROLI, J.B. WALSH : Stochastic Integrals in the Plane. Acta Mathematica. 134 (1975) 111-183.

(9) P. BREMAUD, M. YOR : Changes of Filtration and of Probability Measures. Z. Wahr. V. Geb. 45, 269-295 (1978).

MINIMUM COVARIANCE, MINIMAX AND MINIMUM ENERGY LINEAR ESTIMATORS

Arthur J. Krener
Department of Mathematics
University of California
Davis, CA 95616
USA

ABSTRACT. The estimators which minimize the error covariance for the filtering, prediction and smoothing of linear plants with Gaussian initial conditions and noises are well-known. We show that these same estimators arise when one seeks to minimize the maximum error assuming that initial conditions and noises are bounded in norm in an appropriate Hilbert space (minimax estimator). They also arise when one seeks the trajectory of least energy necessary to produce the given observations (minimum energy estimate).

1. INTRODUCTION.

Consider a linear plant with Gaussian initial condition, driven by Gaussian white noise and observed with additive Gaussian white noise. The problem of optimally estimating the state at time t, given observations up to time τ, is called filtering if $t = \tau$, prediction if $t > \tau$ and smoothing if $t < \tau$. A complete treatment of these problems can be found in [1].

In this paper, which is an extension of [2], we give two alternate characterizations of the minimum covariance filter, smoother and predictor for the linear Gaussian model. These characterizations employ the same linear model but they are nonstochastic, i.e., they do not assume that the unknown initial condition, driving noise and observation noise are stochastic. Instead they assume that these uncertainties lie in a Hilbert space, the norm of which measures the energy of the uncertainties. The norm is related to the covariances of the Gaussian model.

In minimax estimation we assume that the uncertainties are bounded in norm and we seek the estimate of the state which minimizes the maximum possible error given the observations.

The minimum energy estimate assumes that the state of the system is that which is achieved by the uncertainties of least energy necessary to produce the observations.

Both of the above estimators are identical with the minimum covariance estimate. This indicates the robustness of such estimators, and provides an alternative way of looking at the covariances. The latter is particularly desirable because frequently these covariances must be guesstimated when designing an estimator. Finally it is hoped that these the alternative characterizations of linear estimators might lead to computationally feasible nonlinear estimators.

2. THE MINIMUM COVARIANCE, MINIMAX, AND MINIMUM ENERGY ESTIMATORS. Throughout we consider the time-varying linear system

$$\begin{aligned} \dot{x}(t) &= A(t)x(t) + B(t)u(t) \\ x(0) &= x_0 \\ z(t) &= C(t)x(t) + v(t) \end{aligned} \tag{2.1}$$

where the state $x(t)$ is $n \times 1$, the driving noise $u(t)$ is $\ell \times 1$, the observation $z(t)$ and observation noise $v(t)$ are $m \times 1$. The matrices $A(t)$, $B(t)$ and $C(t)$ are $n \times n$, $n \times \ell$ and $m \times n$ respectively. We assume that (2.1) is a completely controllable system.

A. In minimum covariance estimation we assume that the initial condition x_0 is a Gaussian random vector of mean 0 and covariance

$$E(x_0 x_0') = P_0$$

The driving and observation noises are independent of each other and x_0. They are white Gaussian with zero mean and covariances

$$\begin{aligned} E(u(t)u'(s)) &= Q(t)\delta(t-s) \\ E(v(t)v'(s)) &= R(t)\delta(t-s) \end{aligned}$$

$R(t)$ is assumed to be positive definite but $Q(t)$ and P_0 need only be nonnegative definite. The estimation problem is to find for $t, \tau \in [0,T]$ the estimate $\hat{x}(t|\tau)$ based on the observations $z(s)$, $0 \leq s \leq \tau$ which minimizes the conditional covariance of the error $\tilde{x}(t|\tau) = x(t) - \hat{x}(t|\tau)$, i.e., $\hat{x}(t|\tau)$ minimizes

$$E(b\,\tilde{x}(t|\tau)\tilde{x}'(t|\tau)b' \,|\, z(s),\ 0 \leq s \leq \tau)$$

for any $1 \times n$ vector b. Standard statistical results imply that the minimum covariance estimate is the conditional mean

$$\hat{x}(t|\tau) = E(x(t)\,|\,z(s),\ 0 \leq s \leq \tau)$$

but one is interested in an efficient method of computing this from the observations.

B. In the minimax model we put a nonstochastic interpretation on the uncertainties x_0, $u(\cdot)$ and $v(\cdot)$. We assume $(x_0, u(\cdot), v(\cdot))$ is an element of a Hilbert space $\mathcal{H}$ and is bounded in norm. For convenience we take the bound to be 1; any bound results in the same estimate although not the same error. The norm is given by

$$\|x_0, u(\cdot), v(\cdot)\|^2 = x_0' P_0^{-1} x_0 + \int_0^T u'(s)Q^{-1}(s)u(s) + v'(s)R^{-1}(s)v(s)\,ds. \tag{2.2}$$

Since P_0 and $Q(t)$ are not necessarily invertible we adopt the following convention. If x_0 is the range of P_0, $x_0 = P_0 y$ then $x_0' P_0^{-1} x_0 = y' x_0$ and if x_0 is not in the range of P_0 then $x_0' P_0^{-1} x_0 = \infty$. This definition is independent of the choice of y since the null space of P_0 is orthogonal to the range of P_0. We adopt a similar convention for $u'(s)Q^{-1}(s)u(s)$. We define $\mathcal{H}$ as the space of triples $(x_0,u(\cdot),v(\cdot))$ satisfying $\|x_0,u(\cdot),v(\cdot)\| < \infty$.

The minimax estimation problem is to find for t, $\tau \in [0,T]$ the estimate $\hat{x}(t,\tau)$ based on the observations $z(s)$, $0 \leq s \leq \tau$ which minimizes the maximum of any linear functional of the error as $(x_0,u(\cdot),v(\cdot))$ ranges over those triples of norm less than or equal to 1 which give rise to the observations, $z(s)$, $0 \leq s \leq \tau$. In other words the minimax estimator $\hat{x}(t|\tau)$ minimizes the

$$\max \{b\tilde{x}(t|\tau) : \|x_0,u(\ ),v(\ )\| \leq 1 \text{ and produce } z(s),\ 0 \leq s \leq \tau\}$$

for any $1 \times n$ vector b.

If we fix the observations $z(s)$, $0 \leq s \leq \tau$, and require that $(x_0,u(\cdot),v(\cdot))$ produce these observations and be of norm ≤ 1 then the set of all possible $x(t)$ is convex because of the linear structure of the model. The minimax estimate is the centroid of this convex set.

The minimax estimator employs a worst case design philosophy and has a game-theoretic flavor. We assume that our opponent, Nature, chooses the uncertainties $(x_0,u(\cdot),v(\cdot))$ in order to hide the true state $x(t)$. Nature is restricted in the total amount of energy (as measured by $\|x_0,u(\cdot),v(\cdot)\|^2$) that she can use. We seek the estimate which minimizes our maximum loss as measured by any linear functional of the error.

C. The minimum energy estimate is characterized in the following fashion. Among all disturbance triples which give rise to the observations $z(s)$, $0 \leq s \leq \tau$, find the triple of minimum energy. This triple gives rise to a trajectory and the minimum energy estimate $\hat{x}(t|\tau)$ is defined to be the state of that trajectory at time t.

This approach is reminiscent of the variational characterization of certain physical laws, Nature generates the given observations in the most economical way possible and hence the estimate of the state at time t is the state of the minimum energy trajectory at time t.

3. THE EQUIVALENCE OF THE ESTIMATORS.

We begin by showing the minimum energy estimate is equivalent to the minimum covariance estimate. Let $P(t)$ be the solution of the matrix Riccati differential equation

$$\dot{P} = AP + PA + BQB' - PC'R^{-1}CP \qquad (3.1)$$
$$P(0) = P_0 .$$

The interpretation of P(t) it is well known; it is the conditional error covariance of the minimum covariance filter of Kalman and Bucy,

$$E(b\,\tilde{x}(t|t)\tilde{x}'(t|t)b' \,|z(s),\ 0 \le s \le t) = b\,P(t)\,b'$$

The minimum covariance filter $\hat{x}(t|t)$ satisfies

(3.3)
$$\frac{d}{dt}\hat{x}(t|t) = A(t)\hat{x}(t|t) + F(t)(z(t)-C(t)\hat{x}(t|t))$$
$$\hat{x}(0|0) = 0$$

where the feedback gain is given by

(3.3)
$$F(t) = P(t)C'(t)R^{-1}(t).$$

The minimum covariance predictor $\hat{x}(t|\tau)$, $t > \tau$, of Kalman and Bucy is simply the forward extrapolation of $\hat{x}(\tau|\tau)$ assuming no driving noise

(3.4)
$$\frac{d}{dt}\hat{x}(t|\tau) = A(t)\hat{x}(t|\tau).$$

Rauch, Tung and Striebel have shown that the minimum covariance smoother $\hat{x}(t|\tau)$, $t < \tau$, can be found by integrating backwards from $t = \tau$ the differential equation

(3.5)
$$\frac{d}{dt}\hat{x}(t|\tau) = A(t)x(t|\tau) + B(t)Q(t)B'(t)P^{-1}(t)(\hat{x}(t|\tau) - \hat{x}(t|t)).$$

Given the observations $z(s)$, $0 \le s \le \tau$, let $(\bar{x}_0, \bar{u}(\cdot|\tau)\ \bar{v}(\cdot|\tau))$ be the triple of minimum energy giving rise to these observations. Let $\bar{x}(\cdot|\tau)$ be the corresponding state trajectory then the minimum energy estimate at time t is $\bar{x}(t|\tau)$.

If $t > \tau$ neither $u(t)$ nor $v(t)$ affect the observations $z(s)$, $0 \le s \le \tau$ so clearly $\bar{u}(t|\tau) = 0$ and $\bar{v}(t|\tau) = 0$. Hence we seek to minimize

(3.6)
$$x_0' P_0^{-1} x_0 + \int_0^\tau u'(s)Q^{-1}(s)u(s) + v'(s)R^{-1}(s)v(s)\,ds$$

subject to (2.1).

Under the controllability assumption, P(t) is in invertible for all $t > 0$, and

(3.7)
$$\frac{d}{dt}P^{-1}(t) = -A'P^{-1} - P^{-1}A + C'R^{-1}C - P^{-1}BQB'P^{-1}.$$

Let $\xi(t)$ by a $1 \times n$ vector satisfying

(3.8)
$$\dot{\xi} = -\xi A - z'R^{-1}C - \xi BQB'P^{-1}$$
$$\xi(0) = 0$$

and let $\varphi(t)$ be a scalar satisfying

$$\dot{\varphi} = z' R^{-1} z - \xi BQB' \xi'$$

(3.9)

$$\varphi(0) = 0$$

If we add the zero quantity

$$(x' P^{-1} x + 2\xi x + \varphi)]_0^\tau - \int_0^\tau \frac{d}{ds} (x' P^{-1} x + 2\xi x + \varphi)\, ds = 0$$

to (3.6) we obtain

$$x'(\tau)P^{-1}(\tau)x(\tau) + 2\xi(\tau)x(\tau) + \varphi(\tau)$$
$$+ \int_0^\tau |Q^{-1/2}(s)u(s) - Q^{1/2'}(s)B'(s)P^{-1}(s)x(s) - Q^{1/2'}(s)B'(s)\xi'(s)|\, ds$$

where $|\cdot|$ is the standard Eculidean norm and $Q = Q^{1/2'} Q^{1/2}$. Clearly $\bar{x}(\tau|\tau)$ is the argument which minimizes

$$x' P^{-1}(\tau)x + 2\xi(\tau)x + \varphi(\tau)$$

i.e.

(3.10) $$\bar{x}(\tau|\tau) = -P(\tau)\xi'(\tau).$$

Furthermore for $t \leq \tau$,

(3.11) $$\bar{u}(t|\tau) = Q(t)B'(t)(P^{-1}(t)\bar{x}(t|\tau) + \xi'(t))$$

and for $t > \tau$

(3.12) $$\bar{u}(t|\tau) = 0.$$

If we differentiate the minimum energy filter (3.10) using (3.7) and (3.8) we see that it satisfies the same differential equation and initial conditions (3.3) as the Kalman-Bucy filter hence they are the same.

Using (2.1), (3.10), (3.11) and (3.12) we see that for $t > \tau$

$$\frac{d}{dt} \bar{x}(t|\tau) = A(t)x(t|\tau)$$

and for $t < \tau$

$$\frac{d}{dt} x(t|\tau) = A(t)\bar{x}(t|\tau) +$$
$$B(t)Q(t)B'(t)P^{-1}(t)(\bar{x}(t|\tau) - \bar{x}(t|t)).$$

These agree with (3.4) and (3.5) therefore the miniman energy estimate $\bar{x}(t|\tau)$ equals the Gaussian estimate $\hat{x}(t|\tau)$ for all t, $\tau \in [0,T]$.

Next we show that minimax and minimum energy estimates are equivalent. Let $(x_0, u(\cdot), v(\cdot))$ be any triple giving rise to the observations $z(s)$, $0 \leq s \leq \tau$ and let $(\bar{x}_0, \bar{u}(\cdot), \bar{v}(\cdot))$ be the minimum energy triple for the same observations.

Because it is the minimum energy triple $(\bar{x}_0, \bar{u}(\cdot), \bar{v}(\cdot))$ is orthogonal to any triple $(x_0-\bar{x}_0, u(\cdot)-\bar{u}(\cdot), v(\cdot)-\bar{v}(\cdot))$ giving rise to zero observations on $[0,T]$ with respect to the inner product corresponding to (2.2), i.e.

$$\bar{x}_0 P_0^{-1}(x_0-\bar{x}_0) + \int_0^T \bar{u}'(s)Q^{-1}(s)(u(s)-\bar{u}(s)) + \bar{v}'(s)R^{-1}(s)(v(s)-\bar{v}(s))\, ds = 0.$$

If not for some small $\epsilon \neq 0$ the triple

$$(\bar{x}_0, \bar{u}(\cdot), \bar{v}(\cdot)) + \epsilon(x_0-\bar{x}_0, u(\cdot)-\bar{u}(\cdot), v(\cdot)-\bar{v}(\cdot)) \tag{3.13}$$

gives rise to the same observations but is of less energy.

Therefore the norm of (3.13) depends only on $|\epsilon|$ and not on the sign of ϵ. Henceforth we assume $|\epsilon|$ is sufficiently small so that the norm of (3.13) is less than or equal to 1.

Let $x_\epsilon(t)$ be the solution of (2.1) for the triple (3.13), then for $\epsilon = 0$ we have the minimum energy estimate $\bar{x}(t|T)$. The linearity of (2.1) implies that

$$x_\epsilon(t) - \bar{x}(t|T) = -(x_{-\epsilon}(t) - x(t|T)),$$

i.e., the errors are symmetrically distributed around $\bar{x}(t|T)$. This shows that $\bar{x}(t|T)$ is the centroid of the set of all possible states reachable at time t by a triple of norm less than or equal to 1 which generates the observations $z(s)$, $0 \leq s \leq T$, i.e., $\bar{x}(t|T)$ is the minimax estimate.

REFERENCES

[1] A. Gelb, ed., Applied Optimal Estimation, M.I.T. Press, Cambridge, 1974.

[2] A. J. Krener, The Kalman-Bucy filter: an old answer to some new questions in linear filtering, 1978.

NON LINEAR FILTERING FOR THE SYSTEM WITH GENERAL NOISE

Hiroshi Kunita
Department of System Science
University of California, Los Angeles

1. INTRODUCTION

The stochastic differential equation (SDE) for non linear filter has been studied by many authors in case that the noise is "white" (e.g. [2], [4]). However, if the noise is not white, SDE mentioned above is not valid in general. In this paper, we shall show how the additional term is necessary for the filtering equation.

Let $(\Omega, \underline{\underline{F}}, P; \underline{\underline{F}}_t)$ be a probability space equipped with a reference family $\underline{\underline{F}}_t$, $t \geq 0$, i.e., a right continuous increasing family of complete sub σ-fields of $\underline{\underline{F}}$. Stochastic processes we will consider in this report are jointly measurable, $\underline{\underline{F}}_t$-adapted real valued process unless otherwise mentioned. Suppose that system process X_t, noise process $\int_0^t Z_s dW_s$ and observation process Y_t satisfy the following relations.

(i) W_t is a $\underline{\underline{F}}_t$-Wiener process.

(ii) X_t is a right continuous semimartingale represented as

$$X_t = X_0 + \int_0^t f_s ds + V_t, \tag{1.1}$$

where V_t is a square integrable $\underline{\underline{F}}_t$-martingale and $E(\int_0^t f_s^2 ds) < \infty$.

(iii) Z_t is a positive process such that $\int_0^t (Z_s^2 + Z_s^{-2}) ds < \infty$.

(iv) Y_t is represented as

$$Y_t = \int_0^t h_s ds + \int_0^t Z_s dW_s, \tag{1.2}$$

where h_s satisfies $E(\int_0^t h_s^2 Z_s^{-2} ds) < \infty$.

We set

$$(1.3) \qquad \underline{\underline{G}}_t = \bigwedge_{\varepsilon > 0} \sigma(Y_u ; u \leq t+\varepsilon)$$

The filter $\hat{X}_t$ is defined by $\hat{X}_t = E(X_t | \underline{\underline{G}}_t)$.

The SDE for the filter $\hat{X}_t$ is known in case that $Z_t = 1$ (white noise) or more generally Z_t is of the form $b(t, Y_s ; s \leq t)$, where $b(t,.)$ is a strictly positive Lipschitz continuous function. If the system X_t and the noise W_t are independent, SDE for $\hat{X}_t$ is written as

$$(1.4) \qquad \hat{X}_t = \hat{X}_0 + \int_0^t \hat{f}_s ds + \int_0^t Z_s^{-1} (\widehat{X_s h_s} - \hat{X}_s \hat{h}_s) dI_s$$

where

$$(1.5) \qquad I_t = \int_0^t Z_s^{-1} (dY_s - \hat{h}_s ds).$$

In this report, we shall obtain SDE when the process Z_t are of the following forms, (a) $\{Z_t\}$ and $\{W_t, X_t\}$ are independent, (b) Z_t is $\sigma(X_u ; u \leq t)$-measurable, (c) Z_t is $\sigma(W_s, X_s ; s \leq t)$-measurable. It turns out that SDE for the filter is given by (1.4) in case (a) and that additional terms are necessary in cases (b) and (c). (See Theorem 4.1.)

Our argument is based on the stochastic integral representation of $\underline{\underline{G}}_t$-martingales. It is known that if Z_t is deterministic or the form $b(t, Y_u ; u \leq t)$, any $\underline{\underline{G}}_t$-martingale is represented as stochastic integral by Wiener process I_t defined by (1.5). In our cases (a)$\sim$(c), this is not valid and more martingales are needed for the representation. This will be discussed in Section 3.

In the next section, we will discuss the space of square integrable martingales in general settings. Then it will be applied to the filtering problem in Sections 3 and 4.

2. BASE OF SQUARE INTEGRABLE MARTINGALES

Given a probability space $(\Omega, \underline{\underline{F}}, P; \underline{\underline{F}}_t)$, we denote by $\underline{\underline{M}}$ the set of all right continuous square integrable martingales M_t such that $M_0 = 0$. For detailed properties and associated notations concering the space $\underline{\underline{M}}$, we refer to Kunita-Watanabe [3] and Meyer [5].

2.1. EMBEDDING OF MARTINGALES

Suppose we are given another reference family $\underline{\underline{F}}'_t$, $t \geq 0$ on the same space $(\Omega, \underline{\underline{F}}, P)$ such that $\underline{\underline{F}}'_t \subset \underline{\underline{F}}_t$ for all t. We denote by $\underline{\underline{M}}(\underline{\underline{F}}'_t)$ the space of all square integrable $\underline{\underline{F}}'_t$-martingales with $M_0 = 0$. The space $\underline{\underline{M}}(\underline{\underline{F}}'_t)$ may not always be embedded in $\underline{\underline{M}}$ in general, i.e., $\underline{\underline{F}}'_t$-martingales are not always $\underline{\underline{F}}_t$-martingales. For example, the process I_t of (1.5) is known as a $\underline{\underline{G}}_t$-martingale, but it is not a $\underline{\underline{F}}_t$-martin-ale. In fact it is a $\underline{\underline{F}}_t$-semimartingale decomposed to sum of $\underline{\underline{F}}_t$-Wiener process W_t and $\underline{\underline{F}}_t$-adapted process of bounded variation $\int_0^t Z_s^{-1}(h_s - \hat{h}_s)ds$ We shall discuss the embedding problem connected with filtering in the next section. Here is given a simple cnodition for the embedding.

<u>Proposition 2.1</u>. The set $\underline{\underline{M}}(\underline{\underline{F}}'_t)$ is embedded into $\underline{\underline{M}}$ if and only if for each t, $\underline{\underline{F}}'$ and $\underline{\underline{F}}_t$ are conditionally independent given $\underline{\underline{F}}'_t$.

Proof is easy. It is left to the reader.

<u>Proposition 2.2</u>. Let $\underline{\underline{F}}'_t$, $t \geq 0$ and $\underline{\underline{F}}''_t$, $t \geq 0$ be reference families such that $\underline{\underline{F}} = \underline{\underline{F}}'_t \vee \underline{\underline{F}}''_t$ for each t. Suppose $\underline{\underline{F}}_0 = \{\phi, \Omega\}$. Then $\underline{\underline{F}}'_t$ and $\underline{\underline{F}}''_t$ are independent for all t if and only if the next two conditions are satisfied.

(i) $\underline{\underline{M}}(\underline{\underline{F}}'_t)$ and $\underline{\underline{M}}(\underline{\underline{F}}''_t)$ are embedded in $\underline{\underline{M}}$.

(ii) $\underline{\underline{M}}(\underline{\underline{F}}'_t)$ and $\underline{\underline{M}}(\underline{\underline{F}}''_t)$ are orthogonal.

<u>Proof.</u> Suppose $\mathbf{F}'_t$ and $\mathbf{F}''_t$ are independent. Let f and g be $\mathbf{F}'_\infty$ and $\mathbf{F}''_\infty$ measurable L^2-functions, respectively. Then it holds

$$(2.1) \qquad E(fg \mid \mathbf{F}'_t \vee \mathbf{F}''_t) = E(f \mid \mathbf{F}'_t) E(g \mid \mathbf{F}''_t)$$

If $g = 1$, we have $E(f \mid \mathbf{F}_t) = E(f \mid \mathbf{F}'_t)$. This proves that $\mathbf{M}(\mathbf{F}'_t)$ is embedded in $\mathbf{M}$. Similarly $\mathbf{M}(\mathbf{F}''_t)$ is embedded in $\mathbf{M}$. Now let $M \in \mathbf{M}(\mathbf{F}'_t)$ and $N \in \mathbf{M}(\mathbf{F}''_t)$. Then (2.1) shows

$$E(M_t N_t \mid \mathbf{F}_s) = E(M_t \mid \mathbf{F}'_s) E(N_t \mid \mathbf{F}''_s) = M_s N_s,$$

and they are orthogonal.

Conversely assume (i) and (ii) are satisfied. Choose any $A \in \mathbf{F}'_\infty$ and $B \in \mathbf{F}''_\infty$. Define $M_t = P(A \mid \mathbf{F}'_t)$ and $N_t = P(B \mid \mathbf{F}''_t)$. Since they are orhtogonal, it holds $E(M_\infty N_\infty) = E(M_0 N_0)$. This proves $P(A \cap B) = P(A)P(B)$. The proof is complete.

Now a subset $\mathbf{N}$ of $\mathbf{M}$ is said to generate $\mathbf{M}$ if there exists no nontrivial (except 0) element in $\mathbf{M}$, which is orthogonal to all of $\mathbf{N}$. In particular, if $\mathbf{N}$ consists of countable, mutually orthogonal elements, it is called a base of $\mathbf{M}$. If $\mathbf{N} = \{M^n_t\}$ is a base, then any element M of $\mathbf{M}$ is represented as

$$M_t = \sum_{i=1}^{\infty} \int_0^t g^i_s \, dM^i_s$$

making use of stochastic integral.

<u>Corollary</u>. Let $\{M^n_t\}$ and $\{N^n_t\}$ be bases of $\mathbf{M}(\mathbf{F}'_t)$ and $\mathbf{M}(\mathbf{F}''_t)$, respectively. If $\mathbf{F}'_t$ and $\mathbf{F}''_t$ are independent, then $\{M^n_t\} \cup \{N^n_t\}$ is a base of $\mathbf{M}$.

2.2. GIRSANOV'S THEOREM

We shall consider how the space $\mathbf{M}$ and its base are transformed when the probability measure is substituted by an absolute continuous one.

Let L_t be a local martingale satisfying $L_{T_n} \longrightarrow L_T$ for any increasing stopping times $T_n \uparrow T$. We denote by L_t^c the continuous part of L_t. Let R_t be the exponential martingale associated with L_t.

(2.2) $$R_t = 1 + \int_0^t R_{s-} dL_s .$$

Then by Doléans-Dade [1], R_t is represented as

(2.3) $$R_t = \exp(L_t - \tfrac{1}{2}\langle L^c \rangle_t) \prod_{s \leq t} (1 + \Delta L_s) e^{-\Delta L_s}$$

We assume $1 + \Delta L_s > 0$. Then R_t is a positive local martingale. If it is a martingale, we may define a probability measure $\tilde{P}$ on $(\Omega, \underline{\underline{F}}_t)$ such that

$$\tilde{P}(B) = \int_B R_t dP, \qquad B \in \underline{\underline{F}}_t .$$

The measure $\tilde{P}$ is called the Girsanov transformation of P. The space of martingales relative to $\tilde{P}$ is denoted by $\tilde{\underline{M}}$, and we use notations $\langle .,. \rangle^{\sim}$ and $[.,.]^{\sim}$ etc. relative to the measure $\tilde{P}$.

Now the set of all locally square integrable martingales with $M_0 = 0$ is denoted by $\underline{\underline{M}}^{loc}$ and the set of all elements in $\underline{\underline{M}}^{loc}$ whose size of jumps are bounded (independent of ω) is denoted by $\underline{\underline{M}}_b^{loc}$. If $M \in \underline{\underline{M}}_b^{loc}$, then $M_t L_t$ is locally integrable, so that there exists a continuous predictable process of bounded variation $\langle M, L \rangle_t$ such that $M_t L_t - \langle M, L \rangle_t$ is a local martingale. Define the map Φ by

(2.4) $$\Phi(M)_t = M_t - \langle M, L \rangle_t .$$

<u>Theorem 2.1</u>. The map Φ is an isomorphism from $\underline{\underline{M}}_b^{loc}$ onto $\tilde{\underline{\underline{M}}}_b^{loc}$, i.e. it is linear

$$(2.5)\qquad \Phi\left(\int f dM + \int g dN\right) = \int f d\,\Phi(M) + \int g d\,\Phi(N),$$

one to one, onto and isometric;

$$(2.6)\qquad [\Phi(M), \Phi(N)]^{\sim} = [M,N].$$

Proof. It was shown by van Schuppen and Wong [6] that $\Phi(M)$ is an element of $\underline{\underline{M}}_b^{loc}$. Clearly Φ is linear, one to one. We will prove that it is an onto map. Define a $(\underline{\underline{F}}_t, \tilde{P})$-martingale by $\tilde{L}_t = \tilde{L}_t^c + \tilde{L}_t^d$, where

$$\tilde{L}_t^c = -(L_t^c - \langle L^c \rangle_t), \qquad \Delta\tilde{L}_s^d = -\frac{\Delta L_s}{1 + \Delta L_s}$$

Then it holds

$$R_t^{-1} = \exp(\tilde{L}_t - \tfrac{1}{2}\langle L^c \rangle_t) \prod_{s \le t} (1 + \Delta\tilde{L}_s) e^{-\Delta\tilde{L}_s}.$$

Therefore R_t^{-1} is the exponential $(\underline{\underline{F}}_t, \tilde{P})$-martingale associated with $\tilde{L}_t$. Define the map Ψ by

$$\Psi(M) = \tilde{M} - \langle \tilde{M}, \tilde{L} \rangle^{\sim}, \qquad \tilde{M} \in \tilde{\underline{\underline{M}}}_b^{loc}.$$

It is a linear, one to one map from $\tilde{\underline{\underline{M}}}_b^{loc}$ into $\underline{\underline{M}}_b^{loc}$. It holds $\Phi\Psi(\tilde{M}) = \tilde{M}$ for all $\tilde{M}$ of $\tilde{\underline{\underline{M}}}_b^{loc}$. In fact,

$$\Phi\Psi(\tilde{M}) = \Psi(\tilde{M}) - \langle \Psi(\tilde{M}), L \rangle = \tilde{M} - \langle \tilde{M}, \tilde{L} \rangle^{\sim} - \langle \Psi(\tilde{M}), L \rangle.$$

Since $\Phi\Psi(\tilde{M})$ is a local martingale relative to $\tilde{P}$, we have $\Phi\Psi(\tilde{M}) = \tilde{M}$ and $\langle \tilde{M}, \tilde{L} \rangle^{\sim} + \langle \Psi(\tilde{M}), L \rangle = 0$ by the uniqueness of the Mayer decomposition of semimartingale. This proves that Φ is an onto map and $\Phi = \Psi^{-1}$. The isometric property follows from the relation

$$[M,M]_t = \lim_{|\Delta| \to 0} \sum_k (M_{t_{k+1}} - M_{t_k})^2 = \lim_{|\Delta| \to 0} \sum_k (\Phi(M)_{t_{k+1}} - \Phi(M)_{t_k})^2 =$$

$$= [\Phi(M), \Phi(M)]^{\sim}_t \qquad \text{a.s. } P \text{ and } \tilde{P}.$$

Here $\Delta = \{0=t_0 < \ldots < t_n = t\}$ and $|\Delta| = \max_k |t_{k+1} - t_k|$.

Corollary 1. If R_t is a continuous martingale, then it holds

$$(2.7) \qquad \langle M,N\rangle_t = \langle \Phi(M), \Phi(N)\rangle^{\sim}_t$$

Proof. It is enough to prove the assertion in case that M,N are both continuous or discontinuous martingales. If M and N are continuous, then $[M,N] = \langle M,N\rangle$. The same is true for $\Phi(M)$ and $\Phi(N)$. Hence (2.7) is a consequence of (2.6). If M and N are discontinuous martingales, then $[M,N] - \langle M,N\rangle$ is a local martingale which is orthogonal to L. Then it is a $(\underline{\underline{F}}_t, \tilde{P})$-martingale by the above theorem. On the otherhand, it holds $\Phi(M) = M$, $\Phi(N) = N$ so that $[M,N] - \langle \Phi(M), \Phi(N)\rangle^{\sim}$ is a $(\underline{\underline{F}}_t, \tilde{P})$-martingale. By the uniqueness of the Meyer decomposition, we have (2.7).

Corollary 2. Assume the same condition as the above corollary. A subset $\underline{\underline{N}}$ of $\underline{\underline{M}}_b^{loc}$ generates $\underline{\underline{M}}_b^{loc}$ if and only if $\Phi(\underline{\underline{N}})$ generates $\tilde{\underline{\underline{M}}}_b^{loc}$. Further, $\underline{\underline{N}}$ is a base of $\underline{\underline{M}}_b^{loc}$ if and only if $\Phi(\underline{\underline{N}})$ is a base of $\tilde{\underline{\underline{M}}}_b^{loc}$.

Proof is immediate from (2.7).

Remark. Theorem 2.1 can be extended to the case that R_t of (2.3) is not a martingale but a local martingale. Let $T_n \uparrow \infty$ be a sequence of stopping times such that $R_{t\wedge T_n}$, $n = 1,2,\ldots$ are martingales. Define $\tilde{P}^{(n)}$ by

$$\tilde{P}^{(n)}(B) = \int_B R_{t\wedge T_n} dP, \qquad B \in \underline{\underline{F}}_{t\wedge T_n}$$

Then $(\Omega, \underline{\underline{F}}_{t\wedge T_n}, \tilde{P}^{(n)})$ is a consistent family of probability measures so that it defines a (possibly finitely additive) measure $\tilde{P}$ on $\bigvee_n \underline{\underline{F}}_{t\wedge T_n}$. We may consider local martingales on this $\tilde{P}$. In fact we will call M_t as a local martingale, if there exists stopping times $S_n \leq T_n$, $S_n \uparrow \infty$ such that $M_{t\wedge S_n}$ is a $(\underline{\underline{F}}_{t\wedge T_n}, \tilde{P})$ martingale for each n. Then orthogonality and base of local martingales are also defined on $(\bigvee_n \underline{\underline{F}}_{t\wedge T_n}, \tilde{P})$. Theorem 2.1 and its corollary are valid in this case as is easily seen.

3. BASE OF $\underline{\underline{G}}_t$-MARTINGALES.

Let us return to the filtering problem stated in Section 1. We first remark that the process Z_t is $\underline{\underline{G}}_t$-measurable. In fact, we have $Z_t^2 = \lim_{|\Delta|\to 0} \sum (Y_{t_{k+1}} - Y_{t_k})^2$. Set

$$\underline{\underline{H}}_t = \bigwedge_{\varepsilon>0} \sigma(Z_u; u \leq t+\varepsilon).$$

Then $\underline{\underline{H}}_t$ is a sub σ-field of $\underline{\underline{G}}_t$.

Theorem 3.1. Suppose that Z_t satisfies condition (a) of Section 1 or condition (b').

(b'). Z_t is $\sigma(X_u; u \leq t)$-measurable, and for each t, $\sigma(Z_u; u \geq t)$ and $\sigma(X_u; u \leq t)$ are conditionaly independent given $\sigma(Z_u; u \leq t)$.

Then it holds

(i) $\underline{\underline{M}}(\underline{\underline{H}}_t)$ is embedded in $\underline{\underline{M}}(\underline{\underline{G}}_t)$.

(ii) $\underline{\underline{M}}(\underline{\underline{H}}_t)$ and I_t are orthogonal, or equivalently, $\underline{\underline{H}}_t$ and $\sigma(I_u; u \leq t)$ are independent.

(iii) If $\underline{\underline{N}}$ is a base of $\underline{\underline{M}}(\underline{\underline{H}}_t)$, then $\underline{\underline{N}} \cup \{I\}$ is a base of $\underline{\underline{M}}(\underline{\underline{G}}_t)$.

Proof. By Proposition 2.1 and assumption (a) or (b'), $\underline{\underline{M}}(\underline{\underline{H}}_t)$ is embedded in $\underline{\underline{M}}(\underline{\underline{F}}_t)$. Then $\underline{\underline{M}}(\underline{\underline{H}}_t)$ is embedded in $\underline{\underline{M}}(\underline{\underline{G}}_t)$. Now $\underline{\underline{M}}(\underline{\underline{H}}_t)$

and W_t are orthogonal in $\underline{\underline{M}}(\underline{\underline{F}}_t)$ because the corresponding σ-fields are independent. Then $\underline{\underline{M}}(\underline{\underline{H}}_t)$ and I_t are orthogonal in $\underline{\underline{M}}(\underline{\underline{G}}_t)$. In fact, it holds for $M \in \underline{\underline{M}}(\underline{\underline{H}}_t)$

$$\langle M, I\rangle_t = \lim_{|\Delta|\to 0} \sum_k (M_{t_{k+1}} - M_{t_k})(I_{t_{k+1}} - I_{t_k})$$

$$= \lim_{|\Delta|\to 0} \sum_k (M_{t_{k+1}} - M_{t_k})(W_{t_{k+1}} - W_{t_k}) = 0,$$

This proves (ii).

We shall prove (iii). Let $L_t = -\int_0^t Z_s^{-1}\hat{h}_s dI_s$ and R_t be the exponential local martingale associated with L_t. We shall apply Theorem 2.1 and its corollary to the present case. The map $\Phi(M) = M + \int Z^{-1}\hat{h}d\langle M, I\rangle$ defines the isomorphism from $\underline{\underline{M}}_b^{loc}(\underline{\underline{G}}_t)$ onto $\tilde{\underline{\underline{M}}}_b^{loc}(\underline{\underline{G}}_t)$. Set $\tilde{I} = \Phi(I)$. Then we have $\tilde{I} = \int Z^{-1}dY$ by (1.5). Therefore it holds

$$\underline{\underline{G}}_t = \underline{\underline{H}}_t \vee \sigma(\tilde{I}_u ; u \leq t).$$

Further it holds $\langle \tilde{I}\rangle_t = \langle I\rangle_t = t$, so that $\tilde{I}_{t\wedge T_n}$ is a $(\underline{\underline{G}}_{t\wedge T_n}, \tilde{P})$-Wiener process stopped at T_n. Then it is known that $\tilde{I}_t$ is a base of $(\sigma(\tilde{I}_u ; u \leq t), \tilde{P})$-martingales (e.g. Kunita-Watanabe [3]). Therefore, $\Phi(\underline{\underline{N}}) \cup \{\tilde{I}\}$ is a base of $\tilde{\underline{\underline{M}}}_b^{loc}(\underline{\underline{G}}_t)$ by corollary to Proposition 2.2. Then $\underline{\underline{N}} \cup \{I\}$ is a base of $\underline{\underline{M}}_b^{loc}(\underline{\underline{G}}_t)$ by Corollary 2 to Theorem 2.1. The proof is complete.

In case that Z_t depends on $\{X_t, W_t\}$, the space $\underline{\underline{M}}(\underline{\underline{H}}_t)$ might not be embedded into $\underline{\underline{M}}(\underline{\underline{G}}_t)$. As a typical example we shall consider the case that Z_t is a functional of a diffusion process governed by the SDE

$$Z'_t = Z'_0 + \int_0^t a(s, X_s, Y_s, Z'_s)ds + \int_0^t b_1(s, Y_s, Z'_s)dW_s \tag{3.1}$$

$$+ \int_0^t b_2(s,Y_s,Z'_s)d\tilde{W}_s ,$$

where a, b_1, b_2 are Lipschitz continuous functions , b_2 being strictly positive, and $\tilde{W}_t$ is a $\underline{\underline{F}}_t$-Wiener process independent of W_t. We assume $Z_t = f(t,Z'_u;u \leq t)$ and $\sigma(Z_u;u \leq t) = \sigma(Z'_u;u \leq t)$ for each t. We write $a(s,X_s,Y_s,Z_s)$ as a_s.

<u>Theorem 3.2</u>. Set

$$(3.2) \qquad \tilde{I}_t = \int_0^t b_2^{-1}(dZ'_s - b_1 dI_s - \hat{a}_s ds).$$

Then it is a $\underline{\underline{G}}_t$-Wiener process independent of I_t. Further, $\{I_t, \tilde{I}_t\}$ is a base of $\underline{\underline{M}}(\underline{\underline{G}}_t)$.

<u>Proof</u>. Clearly $\tilde{I}_t$ is a $\underline{\underline{G}}_t$-adapted process. Substitute

$$I_t = W_t + \int_0^t Z_s^{-1}(h_s - \hat{h}_s)ds$$

and (3.1) to (3.2), then

$$(3.3) \qquad \tilde{I}_t = \tilde{W}_t + \int_0^t b_2^{-1}((a_s - \hat{a}_s) - b_1 Z_s^{-1}(h_s - \hat{h}_s))ds$$

Then we see $E(\tilde{I}_t - \tilde{I}_s | \underline{\underline{G}}_s) = 0$ and $\langle \tilde{I} \rangle_t = \langle \tilde{W} \rangle_t = t$. Hence it is a $\underline{\underline{G}}_t$-Wiener process. Moreover it holds $\langle \tilde{I}, I \rangle = \langle \tilde{W}, W \rangle = 0$. Hence they are orthogonal.

It remains to prove that $\{I_t, \check{I}_t\}$ is a base. Set

$$L_t = - \int Z_s^{-1}\hat{h}_s dI_s - \int b_2^{-1}(\hat{a}_s - b_1 Z_s^{-1}\hat{h}_s)d\hat{I}_s$$

and let R_t be the exponential local martingale associated with L_t. Set $J_t = \Phi(I_t)$ and $\tilde{J}_t = \Phi(\check{I}_t)$. Then we have

$$(3.4) \qquad Y_t = \int_0^t f(s,Z'_u;u \leq s)dJ_s$$

$$Z'_t = Z'_0 + \int_0^t b_1 dJ + \int_0^t b_2 d\tilde{J}.$$

Since $(J_{t\wedge T_n}, \tilde{J}_{t\wedge T_n})$ is a $(\underline{\underline{G}}_{t\wedge T_n}, \tilde{P}^{(n)})$-Wiener process stopped at T_n, the SDE (3.4) has the unique solution up to time T_n. Then $(J_{t\wedge T_n}, \tilde{J}_{t\wedge T_n})$ is a base of $(\underline{\underline{G}}_{t\wedge T_n}, \tilde{P}^{(n)})$ martingale. Hence we see that $(J_t, \tilde{J}_t)$ is a base of $\tilde{\underline{\underline{M}}}_b^{loc}$, and Corollary 2 to Theorem 2.1 implies the assertion.

4. STOCHASTIC DIFFERENTIAL EQUATION FOR THE FILTERING

In the previous section, we have discussed the base of $\underline{\underline{G}}_t$-martingales. In any cases, $\underline{\underline{G}}_t$-martingales are $\underline{\underline{F}}_t$-martingales or at least $\underline{\underline{F}}_t$-semimartingales. So it seems natural to derive the stochastic differential equation for the filtering process when the base $\{J_t^n\} \vee \{I\}$ of $\underline{\underline{M}}(\underline{\underline{G}}_t)$ satisfies the following assumption.

<u>Assumption</u>. J_t^n, $n = 1,2,...$ are $\underline{\underline{F}}_t$-semimartingales decomposed as

$$J_t^i = \int_0^t g_s^i ds + \tilde{J}_t^i, \tag{4.1}$$

where $\tilde{J}_t^i$ are square integrable $\underline{\underline{F}}_t$-martingales such that $d\langle \tilde{J}^i\rangle$ are equivalent to dt a.s. and g_s^i are $\underline{\underline{F}}_s$-adapted processes with $E(\int_0^t |g_s^i|^2 ds) < \infty$.

We define processes c_s^i and d_s^i by

$$\langle \tilde{J}^i\rangle_t = \int_0^t c_s^i ds, \qquad \langle \tilde{J}^i, V\rangle_t = \int_0^t d_s^i ds. \tag{4.2}$$

<u>Remark</u>. It holds $\hat{g}_s^i = 0$. In fact, since $E(J_{s+h}^i - J_s^i | \underline{\underline{G}}_s) = E(\tilde{J}_{s+h}^i - \tilde{J}_s^i | \underline{\underline{G}}_s) = 0$, we have $\int_s^{s+h} E(g_u^i | \underline{\underline{G}}_s) du = 0$ from (4.1). Divide the left hand side by h and let h tend to 0. Then we see $\hat{g}_s^i = 0$.

<u>Theorem 4.1</u>. The filter $\hat{X}_t$ satisfies

$$\hat{X}_t = \hat{X}_0 + \int_0^t \hat{f}_s ds + \int_0^t Z_s^{-1}(\widehat{X_s h_s} - \hat{X}_s \hat{h}_s) dI_s \tag{4.3}$$
$$+ \sum_i \int_0^t (c_s^i)^{-1} (\widehat{X_s g_s^i} + \hat{d}_s^i) dJ_s^i .$$

Proof. Set $M_t = \hat{X}_t - \hat{X}_0 - \int_0^t \hat{f}_s ds$ and denote the sum of the second and third terms of the right hand side of the above as M_t^*. Since M_t and M_t^* are in $\underline{\underline{M}}(\underline{\underline{G}}_t)$, it is enough to show that $E(M_t N_t) = E(M_t^* N_t)$ holds for all $N_t \in \underline{\underline{M}}(\underline{\underline{G}}_t)$. For this purpose, rewrite M_t as

$$M_t = (\hat{X}_t - X_t) + V_t + \int_0^t (f_s - \hat{f}_s) ds + X_0 - \hat{X}_0$$
$$= (\hat{X}_t - X_t) + V_t + A_t,$$

where A_t is a $\underline{\underline{F}}_t$-adapted process of bounded variation. On the other hand, N_t is represented by stochastic integrals making use of base;

$$N_t = \sum \int \varphi^i dJ^i + \int \varphi dI$$
$$= \sum \int \varphi^i g^i ds + \int Z^{-1} \varphi (h - \hat{h}) ds + \sum \int \varphi^i d\tilde{J}^i + \int \varphi dW$$
$$= B_t + U_t,$$

where B_t is a $\underline{\underline{F}}_t$-adapted process of bounded variation and U_t is a $\underline{\underline{F}}_t$-martingale. Then we get

$$M_t N_t = (\hat{X}_t - X_t) N_t + V_t N_t + A_t N_t$$
$$= (\hat{X}_t - X_t) N_t + \int V_{s-} dU_s + \int V_{s-} dB_s + \int N_{s-} dV_s$$
$$+ \int A_{s-} dU_s + \int A_{s-} dB_s + \int N_s \, dA_s + \langle V, U \rangle_t$$

by Ito's formula. The first term is of mean 0, obviously. The second fourth, fifth terms are of mean 0, since they are martingales. The seventh term is also of mean 0, since it is written as $\int N_s (f_s - \hat{f}_s) ds$.

Hence

$$M_tN_t = \text{terms with mean } 0 + \int (V_{s-}+A_{s-})\,dB_s + \langle V,U\rangle_t$$

The middle term of the right hand side is equal to $\int M_s dB_s - \int (\hat{X}_s - X_s)\,dB_s$ where the first term is of mean 0. We have $\langle V,U\rangle_t = \sum_i \int \varphi^i d^i ds$. Therefore we obtain

$$M_tN_t = \text{terms with mean } 0 + \sum_i \int \varphi^i g^i (X - \hat{X})\,ds$$

$$+ \int Z^{-1} \varphi (h-\hat{h})(X-\hat{X})\,ds + \sum_i \int \varphi^i d^i ds.$$

Taking the expectation, we get

$$E(M_tN_t) = \int_0^t E(\varphi^i g^i (X-\hat{X}))\,ds + \int_0^t E(Z^{-1} \varphi (h-\hat{h})(X-\hat{X}))\,ds$$

$$+ \sum_i \int_0^t E(\varphi^i d^i)\,ds.$$

The right hand side of the above equals $E(M_t^* N_t)$. This proves $M_t = M_t^*$. The proof is complete.

<u>Corollary 1</u>. If Z_t is independent of $\{X_t, W_t\}$, then

$$\hat{X}_t = \hat{X}_0 + \int_0^t \hat{f}_s ds + \int_0^t Z_s^{-1} (\widehat{X_s h_s} - \hat{X}_s \hat{h}_s)\,dI_s \tag{4.4}$$

<u>Proof</u>. By Theorem 3.1, $\{J_t^i\}$ are $\underline{\underline{F}}_t$-martingales, so that $g_s^i = 0$, $i = 1,2,\ldots$ Moreover, J_t^i and V_t are independent, so that they are orthogonal. Therefore, $d_s^i = 0$, $i = 1,2,\ldots$ Then (4.3) implies (4.4).

<u>Corollary 2</u>. Suppose that Z_t is $\sigma(X_u; u \le t)$-measurable and $\sigma(Z_u; u \ge t)$ and $\sigma(X_u; u \le t)$ are conditionally independent given $\sigma(Z_u; u \le t)$. Then

$$\hat{X}_t = \hat{X}_0 + \int_0^t \hat{f}_s ds + \int_0^t Z_s^{-1} (\widehat{X_s h_s} - \hat{X}_s \hat{h}_s)\,dI_s + \sum_i \int_0^t (c_s^i)^{-1} \hat{d}_s^i dJ_s^i \tag{4.5}$$

Corollary 3. Suppose that Z_t is a functional of a diffusion process governed by (3.1). Then

$$\hat{X}_t = \hat{X}_0 + \int_0^t \hat{f}_s ds + \int_0^t (\widehat{X_s h_s} - \hat{X}_s \hat{h}_s) Z_s^{-1} dI_s + \int_0^t b_2^{-1} (\widehat{a_s X_s} - \hat{X}_s \hat{a}_s + \hat{d}_s) d\check{I}_s . \tag{4.6}$$

REFERENCES

[1] Doléans-Dade,C: Quelques applications de la formule de changement de variables pour les semi-martingales. Z. Wahrscheinlichkeitstheorie verw. Gebiete 16, 181-194(1970).

[2] Fuzisaki,M.-Kallianpur,G.-Kunita,H; Stochastic differential equations for non linear filtering problem. Osaka J. Math. 9, 19-40(1972)

[3] Kunita,H.-Watanabe,S: On square integrable martingales, Nagoya Math. J. 30, 209-245(1967)

[4] Liptzer,R.S.-Shiryaev,A.N: Statistics of stochastic processes. Nauka, 1974.

[5] Meyer,P.A; Integrals stochastiques, Séminaire de Probabilités I, Lecture Notes in Math, 39, Springer 1967.

[6] van Schuppen,J.H.-Wong,E: Transformations of local martingales under a change of law. Ann. Prob. 2, 879-888(1974).

FILTERING OF A DIFFUSION PROCESS
WITH POISSON-TYPE OBSERVATION

E. Pardoux
(C.N.R.S.)
IRIA-LABORIA
78150-Le Chesnay - France

We consider a filtering problem, where the signal X_t is a Markov diffusion process, and the observation is a marked point process (for instance a Poisson process), whose predictable projection (the stochastic intensity in the case of a point process) is a given function of the signal X_t.

We associate to this problem a backward stochastic PDE, whose solution is expressible in terms of the conditional law in the filtering problem. It then follows that the forward equation, adjoint to the backward one, governs the evolution of the "unnormalized conditional density".

Analogous results have been proved in the case of an observation corrupted by a Wiener noise in [5] and [6]. The proofs here are more direct.

§1. THE FILTERING PROBLEM

§.1.1. The signal Process.

We are given the following functions on $R_+ \times R^N$:

$\sigma_{i,j}(t,x)$ [resp. $b_i(t,x)$] continuous [resp. Borel measurable] and bounded on $[0,T] \times R^N$, $\forall T > 0$, $i,j = 1...N$.

Let $a = \sigma\sigma^*$. We suppose :

(1.1) $\quad \exists\alpha > 0$ s.t. $(a(t,x)\xi,\xi) \geq \alpha|\xi|^2$, $\forall\, \xi \in R^N$, $\quad \forall(t,x) \in R_+ \times R^N$

(1.2) $\quad \dfrac{\partial a_{ij}}{\partial x_j} \in L^\infty(]0,T[\times R^N)$, $\forall T > 0$, $\quad i,j = 1...N$

Let $\Omega_1 = C(R_+ ; R^N)$, $X_t(\omega_1) = \omega_1(t)$, $\mathcal{G}_t^s = \sigma\{X_\theta,\ s \leq \theta \leq t\}$, $\mathcal{G}^s = \bigvee_{t \geq s} \mathcal{G}_t^s$.

We consider the martingale problem, cf. STROOCK-VARADHAN [8], associated with the infinitesimal generator

$$L_t = \frac{1}{2} \sum_{i,j=1}^{N} a_{ij}(t,x) \frac{\partial^2}{\partial x_i\, \partial x_j} + \sum_{i=1}^{N} b_i\ (t,x) \frac{\partial}{\partial x_i}$$

Let P^1_{sx} denote the unique probability measure on $(\Omega_1, \mathcal{G}^s)$, solution of the martingale problem, with initial condition $P^1_{sx}(X_s = x) = 1$.

Let $p_o \in L^2(R^N)$ satisfy :

$$p_o(x) \geq 0 \quad \text{a.e.}, \quad \int_{R^N} p_o(x)\, dx = 1 ,$$

and let P_1 be the unique probability measure on $(\Omega_1, \mathcal{G}^o)$ satisfying :

$$P_1(X_t \in B) = \int_{R^N} p_o(x)\, P^1_{ox}(X_t \in B) dx ,$$

$\forall$ B Borel subset of R^N.

Then there exists a $P_1 - \mathcal{G}^o_t$ standard Wiener process W_t with values in R^N, such that, P_1 a.s. :

$$(1.3) \qquad dX_t = b(t,X_t)dt + \sigma(t,X_t)\, dW_t$$

$(W_t - W_s, t \geq s)$ is also a $P^1_{sx} - \mathcal{G}^s_t$ Wiener process.

§.1.2. <u>The observation process</u>

Let $(\Omega_2, \mathfrak{F}, P_2)$ be a probability space, on which we define a marked point process (cf. JACOD [3], BREMAUD-JACOD [2]). Let $(\bar{\mathfrak{F}}_t, t \geq 0)$ be an increasing and right continuous family of sub-σ-algebras of $\mathfrak{F}$. Let T_n be a strictly increasing family of $\bar{\mathfrak{F}}_t$ stopping times. We suppose :

$$\lim_{n \to \infty} T_n = +\infty \quad \text{a.s.}$$

Let z_n be a sequence of $\bar{\mathfrak{F}}_{T_n}$ measurable random variables with values in a measurable space $(Z, \mathbf{Z})$ (the set of "marks").

We define a transition measure from $(\Omega, \mathfrak{F})$ over $(R_+ \times Z, \mathcal{B} \otimes \mathbf{Z})$, where $\mathcal{B}$ is the Borel σ-field over R_+, by :

$$\mu(\omega ; A \times B) = \sum_{n>0} 1_{\{T_n \in A\}}\, 1_{\{z_n \in B\}}$$

where $A \in \mathcal{B}$, $B \in \mathbf{Z}$.

Let $\mathfrak{F}^\mu_t = \sigma\{\mu(]o,s] \times B), s \leq t, B \in \mathbf{Z}\}$ $\mathfrak{F}^\mu_t \subset \bar{\mathfrak{F}}_t$, and $\mathfrak{F}^\mu_t$ is increasing and right continuous (see COURREGE - PRIOURET [11], and [3]).

We suppose that there exists a positive finite measure ν on $(Z, \mathcal{Z})$ such that :

$$\mu(]o, t] \times B) - t\,\nu(B) \quad \text{is a } P_2 - \mathcal{F}_t^{\mu} \text{ martingale, } \forall B \in \mathcal{Z} .$$

It follows from WATANABE's result (see [9], [10]) that $\mu(]o, t] \times B)$ is a P_2- $\mathcal{F}_t^{\mu}$ Poisson process with intensity $\nu(B)$. In other words (JACOD [3]) , $dt \times \nu(dz)$ is the predictable projection of $\mu(dt \times dz)$.

Let now $(\Omega, \mathcal{F}^s) = (\Omega_1 \times \Omega_2, \mathcal{G}^s \otimes \mathcal{F})$. We will write $\mathcal{G}_t^s$ for $\mathcal{G}_t^s \otimes \{\Omega_2, \emptyset\}$ and $\mathcal{F}_t^{\mu}$ for $\{\Omega_1, \emptyset\} \otimes \mathcal{F}_t^{\mu}$. Define $\mathcal{F}_t = \mathcal{G}_{t+}^o \vee \mathcal{F}_t^{\mu}$.

Let $\tilde{P}_{sx} = P_{sx}^1 \times P_2$

$\tilde{P} = P_1 \times P_2$

Let $\Psi(t,x,z)$ be a measurable, non negative and bounded function defined on $R_+ \times R^N \times Z$. Consider the process :

$$\rho(t,z) = \Psi(t, X_t, z)$$

If $\mathcal{P}$ denotes the σ-field of $\mathcal{F}_t$-previsible subsets of $\Omega \times R_+$, ρ is $\mathcal{P} \otimes \mathcal{Z}$ measurable and bounded. We can define :

$$M_t^{\theta} = \prod_{\{n/\theta < T_n \leq t\}} \rho(T_n, z_n) \times \exp\left\{ - \int_{]\theta, t] \times Z} (\rho(s,z) - 1)\nu(dz)ds \right\}$$

We define the measure P on $(\Omega, \mathcal{F}_t)$ by :

$$\frac{dP}{d\tilde{P}} = M_t^o$$

can show (see BREMAUD [1]).

Lemma 1.1.

(i) P and $\tilde{P}$ coincide on $\mathcal{G}^o$

(ii) $\forall B \in \mathcal{Z}$, $\mu(]o,t] \times B) - \int_{]o,t] \times B} \rho(s,z)\,\nu(dz)ds$ is a $\mathcal{F}_t$ - P martingale. ∎

We will denote by E [resp. $\tilde{E}$, $\tilde{E}_{sx}$] the expectation with respect to P [resp. $\tilde{P}$, $\tilde{P}_{sx}$].

§.1.3. The filtering problem

Our aim is to caracterize the law of X_t, conditionned by $\mathcal{F}_t^{\mu}$, or equivalently quantities of the form : $E(f(X_t) / \mathcal{F}_t^{\mu})$.

We will see that this conditionnal law has a density with respect to Lebesgue measure, which we shall caracterize through the solution of a stochastic partial differential equation.

The following result is easy to prove :

Lemma 1.2.
Let f be a bounded Borel measurable function from R^N into R. Then $\forall t > 0$:

$$(1.4) \qquad E(f(X_t) / \mathcal{F}_t^{\mu}) = \frac{\tilde{E}(f(X_t)\, M_t^o / \mathcal{F}_t^{\mu})}{\tilde{E}(M_t^o / \mathcal{F}_t^{\mu})} \quad \text{a.s.}$$

2. STUDY OF A BACKWARD STOCHASTIC PDE

Define $H^1(R^N) = \{u \in L^2(R^N) ; \frac{\partial u}{\partial x_i} \in L^2(R^N), \ i = 1...N\}$,

and $H^{-1}(R^N)$ its dual space.

We will denote by $|.|$ and $||.||$ the norms in $L^2(R^N)$ and $H^1(R^N)$, $(.,.)$ the scalar product in $L^2(R^N)$, and $\langle .,. \rangle$ the duality between $H^1(R^N)$ and $H^{-1}(R^N)$.

L_t can be considered as a family of elements of $\mathcal{L}(H^1(R^N) ; H^{-1}(R^N))$, defined by :

$$\langle L_t u, v\rangle = -\frac{1}{2} \sum_{i,j=1}^{N} \int_{R^N} a_{ij}(t,x) \frac{\partial u}{\partial x_i} \frac{\partial v}{\partial x_j} dx - \\ - \sum_{i=1}^{N} \int_{R^N} a_i(t,x) \frac{\partial u}{\partial x_i} v \, dx$$

where $a_i = \frac{1}{2} \sum_{j=1}^{N} \frac{\partial a_{ij}}{\partial x_j} - b_i$.

We consider the following backward stochastic P.D.E. :

$$(2.1) \qquad \begin{cases} dv(t) + L_t v(t)dt + v(t) \int_{Z} h(t,z)(\mu(dt,dz) - \nu(dz)dt) = 0 \\ v(T) = f \end{cases}$$

where $h(t,x,z) = \Psi(t,x,z) - 1$ (we omit the variable x). We are looking for a solution v(t,x), which we will consider as a process with values in $L^2(R^N)$.

Write $\tilde{\Omega}$ for $(\Omega, \mathcal{F}_T, \tilde{P})$ and define :

$$D^2(0,T; H^1(R^N),L^2(R^N)) = \{v \in L^2(\tilde{\Omega}\times]0,T[; H^1(R^N)) , \\ \text{s.t. } v \text{ belongs a.s. to } \mathbb{D}(0,T ; L^2(R^N))\}$$

where $D(0,T\ ;\ L^2(R^N))$ denotes the space of right-continuous functions having left limits, in $L^2(R^N)$.

Theorem 2.1.

Suppose $f \in L^2(R^N)$, then equation (2.1) has a unique solution :

$$v \in D^2(0,T\ ;\ H^1(R^N),\ L^2(R^N))$$

Proof :

We solve equation (2.1) backward for each ω.

Suppose for instance that $T_n(\omega) = T$. Then :

$$(2.2) \qquad f - v(T_n^-) + f.\ h(T_n,z_n) = 0$$

(2.2) defines $v(T_n^-)$ as an element of $L^2(R^N)$.

We then solve equation (2.1) backward from T_n to T_{n-1}, i.e. :

$$(2.3) \qquad \begin{cases} v'(t) + L_t\ v(t) = \left(\int_Z h(t,z)d\nu(z)\right) v(t)\ , & T_{n-1} \leq t < T_n \\ v(T_n^-) = f(1+h(T_n,z_n)) \end{cases}$$

(2.3) defines a unique element of $L^2(T_{n-1}, T_n\ ;\ H^1(R^N)) \cap C([T_{n-1},T_n[;\ L^2(R^N))$.

Repeating this procedure, we define for each ω a unique element $v(\omega) \in L^2(0,T;H^1(R^N)) \cap D(0,T\ ;\ L^2(R^N))$. It is easy to check that $\omega \to v(\omega)$ is measurable.

Moreover,

$$|v(t)|^2 + 2\int_t^T \langle -Lv,v\rangle\, ds = |f|^2 + \int_t^T\int_Z |hv|^2\, \mu(ds \times dz) \ +$$

$$+ 2\int_t^T\int_Z \left(\int_{R^N} v^2\ h\ dx\right)(\mu(ds \times dz) - ds\ \nu(dz))$$

Let $t_n = \sup\{0 \leq t \leq T,\ |v(t)| > n\}$. Using backward martingale properties with respect to $\mathcal{F}_\mu^t = \sigma\{\mu([s,T]\times B), t\leq s\leq T, B\in\mathcal{Z}\}$, we get:

$$\tilde{E}(|v(t\vee t_n)|^2) + 2\tilde{E}\int_{t\vee t_n}^T \langle -Lv,v\rangle\, ds \leq |f|^2 + c\ \tilde{E}\int_{t\vee t_n}^T |v|^2\, ds$$

But from (1.1), it is easy to check that $\exists\ \lambda$, s.t. :

$$\langle -Lv,v\rangle + \lambda|v|^2 \geq \frac{\alpha}{2}\ ||v||^2$$

$$(2.4) \qquad \tilde{E}|v(t\vee t_n)|^2 + \alpha\, \tilde{E}\int_{t\vee t_n}^{T} ||v||^2 ds \le |f|^2 + c_1\, \tilde{E}\int_{t\vee t_n}^{T} |v|^2\, ds$$

One can take the limit in (2.4) when $n \to \infty$, yielding :

$$\tilde{E}\int_0^T ||v||^2\, dt \; < \; +\infty$$

We now prove our main result, which is a sort of generalization of the well-known FEYMAN-KAC formula.

Theorem 2.2.

Suppose f is Borel measurable and both bounded and square integrable, then, $\forall\theta \in [0,T]$,

$$(2.5) \qquad v(\theta,x) = \tilde{E}_{\theta x}\,(f(X_T)\, M_T^\theta \,/\, \mathcal{F}_T^\mu) \qquad \text{a.e. and a.s.}$$

Proof :

It suffices to prove (2.5) in the case of regular (in x) coefficients a, b, h and f. We can then take the limit of both sides of (2.5) when $a_n \to a$ uniformly on compact sets, b_n, h_n and f_n converge in measure on compact sets, as in [7].

But if a, b, h and f are regular-say C^∞ in x with compact support- then any partial derivative in x of v belongs to $D^2(0,T\,;\,H^1(R^N),L^2(R^N))$, because it is a solution of an equation similar to (2.1).

It then follows, by the properties of Sobolev spaces, that a.s. $v(\omega) \in C_b^{1,2}([T_k,T_{k+1}[\times R^N)$, $\forall k$ s.t. $[T_k(\omega),\, T_{k+1}(\omega)] \subset [0,T]$.

Define $V_t = v(t,\, X_t)$. It follows from Ito formula that between the jump times T_k :

$$d\, V_t = v'_t(t,X_t)dt + L_t\; v(t,X_t)dt + \nabla v(t,X_t).\; \sigma(t,X_t)d\, W_t$$

Then at any time t,

$$d\, V_t = dv(t,X_t) + L_t\; v(t,X_t)\; dt + \nabla v(t,X_t).\; \sigma(t,X_t)\; d\, W_t$$

On the other hand :

$$d\, M_t^\theta = M_{t^-}^\theta \times \int_Z h(t,X_t,z)(\mu(dt\times dz) - dt \times \nu(dz))$$

Define $\mathcal{H}_t = \mathcal{F}_t \vee \mathcal{F}_T^\mu$. V_t is a $\mathcal{H}_t$ semi-martingale, and M_t^θ is an $\mathcal{H}_t$-adapted process with finite variation. It then follows (see MEYER [4]) :

$$d\, V_t\, M_t^{\theta} = M_{t^-}^{\theta} \cdot d\, V_t + V_t \cdot d\, M_t^{\theta}$$

$$(2.6) \qquad d\, V_t\, M_t^{\theta} = M_{t^-}^{\theta} \cdot \nabla v(t,X_t).\ \sigma(t,X_t)d\, W_t$$

because v satisfies equation (2.1) at any point (t,x).

Integrating (2.6) from θ to T, and taking $E_{\theta x}\ (.\ /\ \mathcal{F}_T^{\mu})$ of both sides yield (2.5).

3. THE EQUATION FOR THE UNNORMALIZED CONDITIONAL DENSITY

Consider now equation :

$$(3.1) \qquad \begin{cases} du(t) - L_t^* u(t)dt = u(t^-) \displaystyle\int_Z h(t,z)(\mu(dt \times dz) - dt \times \nu(dz)) \\ \qquad u(o) = p_o \end{cases}$$

where p_o is the density of the law of X_o.

Again equation (3.1) has a unique solution in $D^2(0,T\ ;\ H^1(R^N),\ L^2(R^N))$.

The interesting fact is that (3.1) is the adjoint of (2.1) :

Theorem 3.1.

The following holds a.s. :

$$(3.2) \qquad (u(t),v(t)) = (u(s),v(s)),\quad \forall s,\ t \in [0,T]$$

Proof :

Between jump times,

$$\frac{d}{dt}\,(u(t),v(t)) = \langle L^* u,v\rangle - \langle u,\ Lv\rangle + (u \int h d\nu, v) - (v \int h d\nu, u) \quad = \quad 0$$

On the other hand,

$$u(T_n) = u(T_n^-)(1 + h(T_n,z_n))$$
$$v(T_n^-) = v(T_n)(1 + h(T_n,z_n))$$
$$(u(T_n),v(T_n)) = (u(T_n^-),\ v(T_n^-))$$

We now deduce from theorems 2.2 and 3.1 :

Corollary

(i) $\tilde{E}\,(f(X_T)M_T^o \,/\, \mathcal{F}_T^\mu) = (u(T),f)$

(ii) $E\,(f(X_T) \,/\, \mathcal{F}_T^\mu) = \dfrac{(u(T),f)}{(u(T),1)}$

Proof :

(2.5) and (3.2) yield :

$$\int_{R^N} p_o(x)\, \tilde{E}_{ox}(f(X_T)M_T^o \,/\, \mathcal{F}_T^\mu) = (u(T),f)$$

which proves (i), (ii) then follows from (1.4).

T is arbitrary. We have proved that equation (3.1) describes the evolution of the unnormalized conditional density.

CONCLUSION

Our method can be applied to more general filtering problems. Combining this result with that in [6], we can treat observation processes with both Wiener and Poisson noise, as in BREMAUD [1]. On the other hand, X_t could be in principle any Markov process - for instance a diffusion with jumps.

REFERENCES

[1] P. BREMAUD. Prédiction filtrage et détection pour une observation mixte par la méthode de la probabilité de référence. Thèse Doctorat U. Paris VI (1976).

[2] P. BREMAUD- J. JACOD. Processus Ponctuels et martingales : résultats récents sur la modélisation et le filtrage. Adv. Appl. Prob. 9, 362-416 (1977).

[3] J. JACOD. Multivariate Point Processes. Z. Wahrschein. verw. G. 31, 235-253, (1975).

[4] P.A. MEYER. Un cours sur les intégrales stochastiques. Sém. Proba. X Lect. Notes Math. 511, Springer.

[5] E. PARDOUX. Stochastic partial differential equation for the density of the conditional law of a diffusion process with boundary ; in "Stochastic Analysis", Ed. A. Friedman et M. Pinsky, 239-269, A.P. (1978).

[6] E. PARDOUX. Un résultat sur les équations aux dérivées partielles stochastiques et filtrage des processus de diffusion. Note CRAS Paris, Séance du 6.11.78.

[7] E. PARDOUX. Stochastic partial differential equations, and filtering of diffusion processes. To appear.

[8] D. STROOCK - S. VARADHAN. Diffusion processes with continuous coefficients. Comm. Pure and Appl. Math. 22, 345-400 et 479-530 (1969).

[9] S. WATANABE. On discontinuous additive functionals and Levy measures of a Markov process. Japanese J. Math. 34, 53-70, (1964).

[10] P. BREMAUD. An extension of Watanabe's theorem of characterization of Poisson processes. J. Appl. Prob. 12, 396-399, (1975).

[11] P. COURREGE - P. PRIOURET. Temps d'arrêt d'une fonction aléatoire. Publ. Inst. Stat. Univ. Paris, 245-274, (1965).

ON WEAK CLOSURES OF CONVEX AND SOLID SETS OF PROBABILITY MEASURES

D. Plachky

Institut für Mathematische Statistik

Roxeler Str. 64, 44 Münster

In the terminology of [2] let $ba(S, \Sigma)$ denote the family of bounded, additive set functions on the field Σ of subsets of the set S. An element $\mu \in ba(S, \Sigma)$ with $\mu \geqq 0$ will be called content and a content μ with $\mu(S) = 1$ is called in the following probability content. Furthermore $ca(S, \Sigma)$ denotes the subset of $ba(S, \Sigma)$ consisting of all countably additive set functions on Σ. If S is a metric space and Σ is the field generated by the closed subsets of S the subset of $ba(S, \Sigma)$ consisting of all regular, additive set functions is denoted by $rba(S)$. Finally we use the symbol $rca(S)$ for the subset of $rba(S)$ consisting of all countably additive set functions. If the underlying field Σ is a σ-field an element $\mu \in ca(S, \Sigma)$ is called measure and a measure μ with $\mu(S) = 1$ is called probability measure.

If C is a subset of $ba(S, \Sigma)$ consisting of contents, it is in many interesting cases possible, to decompose a content $\mu \in ba(S, \Sigma)$ according to $\mu = \mu_1 + \mu_2$ where μ_1 belongs to C and μ_2 is singular with respect to every content of C. Furthermore μ_1 and μ_2 is determined uniquely. One can choose for example C as the subset of all non negative and countably additive set functions of $ba(S, \Sigma)$, which leads to the Hewitt-Yosida decomposition. If one chooses for C the subset of all non negative elements of $rba(S)$, one yields the decomposition of any non negative element of ba(S) according to

$\mu = \mu_1 + \mu_2$ with $\mu_1 \in rba(S)$ and μ_2 being singular with respect to every $\upsilon \in rba(S)$, $\upsilon \geqq 0$. Besides it is interesting to point out - as my coworker Erpenbeck has observed - that the proof of IV. 6.2 in [2] yields the following description of μ_1:

$\mu_1(A) = \sup\{\inf\{\mu(O) \mid F \subset O,\ O \text{ open}\} \mid F \subset A,\ F \text{ closed}\}$ for any $A \in \Sigma$, where Σ is a field of subsets of a normal space S, lying between the field respectively σ-field generated by the closed subsets of S. A similar constructive description is well known for the Hewitt-Yosida decomposition.

If Σ' is a subfield of the field Σ and one chooses for C the subset of ba(S, Σ), consisting of all non negative elements $\mu \in ba(S, \Sigma)$ with the property that μ is uniquely determined by the restriction $\mu|\Sigma'$, then one yields the decomposition of any $\mu \in ba(S, \Sigma)$, $\mu \geqq 0$, according to $\mu = \mu_1 + \mu_2$, $\mu_1 \in C$ and μ_2 is singular with respect to any $\upsilon \in C$. As my coworker Ender has observed μ_1 can also be determined constructively according to

$$\mu_1(A) = \inf\{\mu_*(A_1) + \dots + \mu_*(A_n) \mid A_i \in \Sigma \text{ pairwise disjoint},\ i = 1,\dots,n,\ A_1 \cup \dots \cup A_n = A\}$$

for any $\Sigma \in A$, where μ_* denotes the inner content of μ.

Important for the following is the fact, that decompositions of the type described above imply immediately, that the corresponding C has the following property: If $\upsilon \in ba(S, \Sigma)$, $\upsilon \geqq 0$, is absolutely continuous with respect to some $\mu \in C$, then υ belongs to C. A subset C of non negative elements of ba(S, Σ) with this porperty will be called (measure theoretically) solid.

For application, for example with respect to optimization problems in statistics, it is important to know the weak closures of sets of probability contents or probility measures. With the help of the fact, that ba(S, Σ) respectively rba(S) is the dual of the space B(S, Σ) of all uniform limits of finite linear combinations of characteristic functions of sets belonging to Σ respectively the dual of C(S) of all bounded and continuous functions on S (see [2]), it is possible to give a simple measure theoretical description of the closures of convex and solid sets of probability contents or probability measures with respect to the $\sigma(ba(S, \Sigma), B(S, \Sigma))$-topology respectively $\sigma(rba(S), C(S))$-topology.

THEOREM

a) The closure of a convex and solid set P of probability contents on a field Σ of subsets of a set S with respect to the $\sigma(ba(S, \Sigma), B(S, \Sigma))$-topology is equal to $\{\mu \in ba(S, \Sigma) \mid \mu$ probability content with $\mu(A) = 0$ if $\upsilon(A) = 0$ for all $\upsilon \in P$, $A \in \Sigma\}$.

b) The closure of a convex and solid set P of regular probability contents on the field Σ generated by the closed subsets of a metric space S with respect to the $\sigma(rba(S), C(S))$-topology is equal to $\{\mu \in rba(S) \mid \mu$ probability content with $\mu(O) = 0$ if $\upsilon(O) = 0$ for all $\upsilon \in P$, O open$\}$.

Proof. a) Since a net μ_α of probability contents converges to a probability content μ with respect to the $\sigma(ba(S, \Sigma), B(S, \Sigma))$-topology if and only if $\mu_\alpha(A) \to \mu(A)$ for all $A \in \Sigma$, it is clear that a probability content μ belonging to the weak closure of P has the property that $\upsilon(A) = 0$ for all $\upsilon \in P$ implies $\mu(A) = 0$ for some $A \in \Sigma$. If in turn a probability content μ_o with this property would exist, which does not belong to the $B(S, \Sigma)$-closure of P, then a separation theorem (V. 2.10 of [2]) and the fact, that $B(S, \Sigma)$-continuous linear functionals are evaluation mappings (V. 3.9 and IV. 5.1 of [2]) imply the existence of an element $f_o \in B(S, \Sigma)$ and of a real number r such that

$$\int f_o \, d\mu_o < r < \int f_o \, d\mu$$

holds for any $\mu \in P$. If now for any natural number n the set $\{f_o - r < -\frac{1}{n}\} \in \Sigma$ is denoted by A_n, the assumption $\mu(A_n) > 0$ leads to the contradiction

$$-\frac{1}{n} \geq \int (f_o - r) \, d\mu_n > 0,$$

where $\mu_n \in P$ is defined by $\mu_n(A) = \mu_n(A \cap A_n)/\mu(A_n)$, $A \in \Sigma$. Hence the function $g_o = f_o - r$ on the set $\{f_o - r < 0\}$ and $g_o = 0$ on $\{f_o - r \geq 0\}$ is a μ-null function for all $\mu \in P$ and therefore also μ_o-function, which is a contradiction to

$$\int (f_o - r) \, d\mu_o < 0.$$

b) Observing, that a net μ_α of regular probability contents converging to a regular probability content μ satisfies the inequality $\limsup \mu_\alpha(O) \geq \mu(O)$ for any open set O (see [1], p. 13), the remaining part of the proof follows in a similar way as the proof of part a).

Considering that the set of probability measures on the Borel σ-field of a separable metric space is metrizable with respect to the $\sigma(ba(S), C(S))$-topology by the Prohorov distance (see [1], p. 236), the theorem above implies the following

COROLLARY

a) Let P be a convex and solid set of probability measures on a σ-field Σ. Then for any probability measure μ on Σ there exists a net $\mu_\alpha \in P$ such that $\mu_\alpha(A) \to \mu(A)$ for all $A \in \Sigma$ if and only if $\mu(A_o) = 0$ for all $\mu \in P$ and an $A_o \in \Sigma$ implies A_o is empty.

b) Let P be a convex and solid set of probability measures on the Borel σ-field Σ of a separable, metric space. Then for any probability measure μ on Σ there exists a sequence $\mu_n \in P$ such that $\mu_n(A) \to \mu(A)$ for all $A \in \Sigma$ with μ(boundary of A) = 0 if and only if $\mu(O) = 0$ for all $\mu \in P$ and an open set O implies O is empty.

Finally let us consider some examples of convex and solid sets P of probability measures with the property that the empty set is the only P-zero set respectively open P-zero set: If the σ-field Σ contains all one point sets and P denotes the set of all discrete probability measures on Σ, then clearly the empty set is the only P-zero set. The same is true for open P-zero sets if P is the set of all probability measures on the Borel σ-field of a (locally) compact, infinite and metrizable group, because the Haar measure has positive mass at all non empty and open sets. A further application of the theorem above yields the case, where P is the set of all countably additive probability contents on a field Σ. Here a P-zero set must be empty, which implies that any probability content on Σ can be approximated by a net of countably additive probability contents, i. e. the net converges for all sets belonging to Σ.

Since the theorem above remains true for the convex hull of a solid set P instead of a solid and convex set P, one gets with the help of Fubini's theorem the following

COROLLARY

a) Let P_i be a convex and solid set of probability measures on a σ-field Σ_i of subsets of a set S_i with the property that the empty set is the only P_i-zero set, i = 1, 2. Then the convex hull of $\{\mu_1 \otimes \mu_2 | \mu_i \in P_i, i = 1, 2\}$ is dense in the set of all probability measures on $\Sigma_1 \otimes \Sigma_2$ with respect to the $\sigma(ba(S_1 \times S_2, \Sigma_1 \otimes \Sigma_2), B(S_1 \times S_2, \Sigma_1 \otimes \Sigma_2))$-topology.

b) Let P_i be a convex and solid set of probability measures on the Borel σ-field Σ_i of a metric space S_i with the property that the empty set is the only open P_i-zero set, i = 1, 2. Then the convex hull of $\{\mu_1 \otimes \mu_2 | \mu_i \in P_i, i = 1, 2\}$ is dense in the set of all probability measures on $\Sigma_1 \otimes \Sigma_2$ with respect to the $\sigma(ba(S_1 \times S_2), B(S_1 \times S_2))$-topology.

Proof. It is enough to show that $\mu_1 \otimes \mu_2(A) = 0$ for all $\mu_i \in P_i$, i = 1, 2, and some $A \in \Sigma$ respectively some open set A implies that A is empty. From Fubini's theorem follows $\mu_1(\{s_1 \in S_1 | A_{s_1}$ non empty$\})$ = 0 for all $\mu_1 \in P_1$. This implies $\{s_1 \in S_1 | A_{s_1}$ non empty$\}$ is empty and hence A too.

REMARKS

1) It should be pointed out, that not every solid set P of contents or measures is convex respectively leads to a uniquely determined decomposition in the sense of the introduction of this paper. Consider for example the set of all finite measures μ on a σ-field Σ such that for any $A \in \Sigma$ there exists a $B \in \Sigma'$ with $\mu(A \Delta B) = 0$, where Σ' is a sub-σ-field of Σ. Such a probability measure μ is an extreme point in the set of all probability measures on Σ, which are equal to μ on Σ'. This implies that a decomposition as described in the introduction of this paper is impossible. Nevertheless the set P in this case is solid but not convex.

2) Let us remark that from the theorem above follows immediately the well known result (see [1], p. 239), that the set of all probability measures on the Borel-σ-field Σ of a metric space S is metrizable with respect to the $\sigma(ba(S), C(S))$-topology (if and) only if every probability measure on Σ has a separable support, since a sequence μ_n of discrete probability measures on Σ with finite supports S_n, converging to a probability measure μ on Σ in the $\sigma(ba(S), C(S))$-topology yields $\mu(\overline{\cup S_n}) \geq \limsup \mu_n(\cup S_n) = 1$.

3) From the theorem above we can conclude that every probability content on a field Σ of subsets of a set S can be approximated by a net of atomless probability contents on Σ in the $\sigma(ba(S, \Sigma), B(S, \Sigma))$-topology if and only if Σ is atomless (see [3]), because the approximation property is equivalent with the condition that the only P-zero set

is the empty set, if P denotes the set of all atomless probability contents on Σ.

I would like to thank Dr. Ch. Klein for pointing out [3] to me.

REFERENCES

[1] Billingsley, P.: Convergence of Probability Measures, John Wiley & Sons, New York, 1968.

[2] Dunford, N. and Schwartz, J.: Linear Operators, Part I, Interscience Publishers, New York, 1964.

[3] Rao, K. P. S. Bhaskara and Rao, M. Bhaskara: Existence Of Nonatomic Charges, J. Austral. Math. Soc. 25, 1 - 6, (1978).

NON L^1-BOUNDED MARTINGALES

M.M. Rao

1. INTRODUCTION. Let $(X, \underline{\underline{A}}, P)$ be a probability space and $\{f_n, \underline{\underline{F}}_n, n \geq 1\}$ be a (sub-)martingale in $L^1(P) = L^1(X, \underline{\underline{A}}, P)$. If the (sub-)martingale lies in a ball of $L^1(P)$, then it is L^1-bounded, and it is non L^1-bounded if there is no such ball containing all the f_n, $n \geq 1$. There exist several decompositions as well as convergence theorems for L^1-bounded (sub-) martingales. However in the non L^1-bounded case several peculiarities can be present. For instance, there exist martingales which converge in probability but not pointwise a.e., or those that converge in distribution but not in probability, and the like. (Cf., [1], [4] for such examples.)

The purpose of this note is to describe some positive results on non L^1-bounded (sub-) martingales. In the next section, conditions for pointwise a.e. convergence of submartingales with a directed index set are given. This will be utilized in section 3 to obtain an extension of Gundy's decomposition [5] for not necessarily L^1-bounded submartingales. The final section contains a brief account of the behaviour of non L^1-bounded (sub-) martingales indicating the sets on which convergence takes place (with finite limits), and some information on the pointwise approximation of measurable functions by a martingale. Since a martingale calculus plays a vital role in stochastic control and filtering, these structural results should be of importance in that work, as they are in other parts of analysis.

2. CONVERGENCE RESULTS

If $\{f_n, \underline{\underline{F}}_n, n \geq 1\} \subset L^1(P)$ is a (sub-) martingale, then (i) find conditions such that $f_n \longrightarrow f_\infty$ where f_∞ may take infinite values on a set of positive probability, and (ii) find the subset of X on which the submartingale (converges a.e. and) is finite a.e. Here the first problem is considered, and the second one will be treated in the last section. Since in some applications (e.g. in differentiation) directed index sets will also be of interest, the result is presented in this generality.

Recall that a set I is directed by a relation "<" if $(I, <)$ is partially ordered and if for each pair a, b in I, there is a $c \in I$ such that $a < c$, $b < c$. (In the applications below I will be countable.) If $\{\underline{\underline{F}}_i, i \in I\}$ is an increasing net of σ-algebras of $\underline{\underline{A}}$, and $T : X \longrightarrow I$ is a mapping, then T is a <u>stopping time</u> of the net if $[T \leq i] \in \underline{\underline{F}}_i$ and $[T \geq i] \in \underline{\underline{F}}_i$, $i \in I$. If I is linearly ordered and countable, then $[T = i] \in \underline{\underline{F}}_i$, $i \in I$ will be sufficient in this definition. If $\{f_i, \underline{\underline{F}}_i, i \in I\}$ is an adapted real process and T is a stopping time of $\{\underline{\underline{F}}_i, i \in I\}$, then f_T, defined as $(f_T)(.) = f(T(.), .)$, is a random variable. A family $\{T_j, j \in J\}$ is a <u>stopping time</u> process if J is directed, T_j is a stopping time and $T_{j_1} \leq T_{j_2}$ for $j_1 \leq j_2$ in J. If T is a stopping time of $\{\underline{\underline{F}}_i, i \in I\}$, then the σ-algebra of "events prior to T" is given as

$$\underline{\underline{B}}_T = \{B \in \underline{\underline{A}} : B \cap [T \leq i] \in \underline{\underline{F}}_i, \ i \in I\}.$$

The following concept will be needed to state the convergence results: Let $\{\underline{\underline{F}}_i, i \in I\}$ be an increasing net as before. If $B \in \underline{\underline{A}}$, $K_i \in \underline{\underline{F}}_i$, then $\{K_i, i \in I\}$ is called an <u>essential fine</u> covering of B if for each $i_o \in I$, $B \subset \bigcup_{i \geq i_o} K_i$ a.e. The net satisfies the <u>Vitali condition</u> V_o, if for each $B \in \underline{\underline{A}}$, each essential fine covering $\{K_i, i \in I\}$ of B, and $\varepsilon > 0$, there is a finite set $\{i_1, \ldots, i_{n_\varepsilon}\}$ in I and a.e. disjoint sets $L_j \in \underline{\underline{F}}_{i_j}$, $L_j \subset K_{i_j}$

a.e. such that $P(B - \bigcup_{j=1}^{n_\varepsilon} L_j) < \varepsilon$.

It can be verified quickly that, if I is countable and linearly ordered, then the Vitali condition V_o is always satisfied by a net $\{\underline{\underline{F}}_i , i \in I\}$ for any probability measure P on $\underline{\underline{A}}$. Only in the more general cases, this becomes important.

Now the desired result can be presented as follows :

THEOREM 1. *Let $\{f_i , \underline{\underline{F}}_i , i \in I\}$ be a submartingale on a complete probability space $(X , \underline{\underline{A}} , P)$, with I as a directed set. Suppose the net $\{\underline{\underline{F}}_i , i \in I\}$ satisfies the Vitali condition V_o . For each pair of finite stopping times T_1 , T_2 such that $T_1 \leq T_2$ assume that $\{g_i , \underline{\underline{B}}_{T_i}\}_1^2$, is again a submartingale where $g_i = f_{T_i}$ and $\underline{\underline{B}}_{T_i}$ is the σ-algebra of events prior to T_i . Suppose that for each $i_o \in I$ and each subsequence $J = \{i_{n+1} \geq i_n \geq i_o , n \geq 1\}$ of I , and stopping time T of $\{\underline{\underline{F}}_j , j \in J\}$, one has*

$$(1) \qquad \int_\Omega f_T^+ \, dP < \infty .$$

Then $f_i \longrightarrow f_\infty$ a.e., and f_∞ is P-measurable. In particular, if I is linearly ordered, countable, and (1) is true, then the conclusion holds. Here f_∞ may take infinite values on sets of positive probability.

It will be useful to make some explanatory remarks on this (somewhat general) result. In case the process is a martingale, then the condition that $\{g_i , \underline{\underline{B}}_{T_i}\}_1^2$ be a martingale for each pair of finite stopping times T_1 , T_2 with $T_1 \leq T_2$ is automatic and it may be dropped. If the given process is L^1-bounded, then it can be checked that (1) is satisfied. On the other hand, one can construct simple examples to show that there are martingales satisfying (1), but not L^1-bounded. (A trivial submartingale example is $\{f_n , \underline{\underline{F}}_n , n \geq 1\}$ where $f_n = n$, $\underline{\underline{F}}_n = \underline{\underline{A}}$, $n \geq 1$. This satisfies (1) but is not L^1-bounded !) That is why the condition (1) is of special interest for the present work.

The proof of this result is by contradiction, and is long and somewhat involved. The result for the martingale case has been proved by Chow [2]. Under the present hypothesis, his proof applies with simple modifications. So this will be omitted. Complete details and related results are given in ([7], Section IV.4). In the case $I = \mathbb{N}$, the natural numbers, a proof of the above result has been given by Chow himself ([3], Th. 3), and that will be sufficient for the work of the next section.

3. A DECOMPOSITION FOR NON L^1-BOUNDED SUBMARTINGALES

If a martingale is L^1-bounded, then Gundy [5] has obtained a very useful decomposition theorem for it. His result admits the following extension.

THEOREM 2. *Let* $\{f_n, \underset{=}{F}_n, n \geq 1\} \subset L^1(P)$ *be a (sub-) martingale and let* $\underset{\sim}{T}$ *be the set of all stopping times of* $\{\underset{=}{F}_n, n \geq 1\}$. *Suppose that*

$$\{\alpha_S : S \in \underset{\sim}{T}\} \subset \mathbb{R}^+ , \quad \alpha_S = \int_X f_S^+ \, dP . \tag{2}$$

Then for each $S \in \underset{\sim}{T}$, *and* $u > 0$, *there are a.e. convergent submartingale* $\{g_n^1, \underset{=}{F}_n, n \geq 1\}$ *and martingales* $\{g_n^j, \underset{=}{F}_n, n \geq 1\}$, $2 \leq j \leq 4$ *such that* $f_n = \sum_{i=1}^{4} g_n^i$, *with the following properties (here* g_n^1 *may be chosen independent of* u, *but not the others, and the decomposition is not unique):*

(i) $\{g_n^j, \underset{=}{F}_n, n \geq 1\}$, $j = 2, 3, 4$ *are* L^1*-bounded, but* $\{g_n^1, \underset{=}{F}_n, n \geq 1\}$ *is non* L^1*-bounded*;

(ii) *for each* n_1, *one has* :

$$uP[\sup_{1 \leq n \leq n_1} g_n^1 > u] \leq 2\alpha_S - \int_X f_1 \, dP + \int_X f_{n_1}^+ \, dP = \beta_S + \int_X f_{n_1}^+ \, dP \quad (\textit{say}) ;$$

(iii) $uP[\sup_n |g_n^2| > 0] \leq 4\beta_S$;

(iv) $\| \sum_{n=1}^{\infty} |g_n^3 - g_{n-1}^3| \|_1 \leq 4\beta_S$; $(g_0^3 = 0$ a.e.)

(v) $\|g_n^4\|_\infty \leq 4u$, $\|g_n^4\|_2^2 \leq 6u\beta_S$,

and

(vi) $\|g_n^j\|_1 \leq 2\beta_S$, $j = 2, 3, 4$.

Moreover, β_S is bounded by a constant iff the given (sub-) martingale is L^1-bounded.

Remark. The point of this decomposition is to split off a "large" non L^1-bounded (sub-) martingale from the given one so that the remaining part is L^1-bounded to which Gundy's result is applicable. Taking $f_n = g_n^1$ and $g_n^j = 0$, $2 \leq j \leq 4$, one gets a trivial, or a "non-efficient", decomposition. Thus, the decomposition is non-unique. In the non trivial case, the proof shows that all the component martingales are also non trivial. The martingale and submartingale cases are treated in that order for convenience. In the martingale case, g_n^1 is also a martingale and can be taken $= 0$ if $\{f_n , n \geq 1\}$ is L^1-bounded.

Proof. I. Suppose that the f_n-process is a martingale. Let $S \in \underset{\sim}{T}$ and $S_k = \min(S, k)$, $k \geq 1$. Then $\{S_k , k \geq 1\}$ in $\underset{\sim}{T}$ is a finite valued stopping time process. If $h_n = f_{S_n}$, then $\{h_n , \underline{\underline{F}}_n , n \geq 1\}$ is a martingale. Indeed, by definition, if $\bar{g}_n = f_n - f_{n-1}$ $(f_o = 0)$,

$$h_n = \sum_{k=1}^{n-1} f_i \chi_{[S=k]} + f_n \chi_{[S \geq n]} = \sum_{k=1}^{n-1} \bar{g}_k \cdot \chi_{[S \geq i]} \cdot \tag{3}$$

Since $E(\bar{g}_{k+1} | \underline{\underline{F}}_k) = 0$ by the martingale property of f_n's $([S > k] = [S \leq k]^c \in \underline{\underline{F}}_k)$, it follows that $E(h_{n+1} | \underline{\underline{F}}_n) = h_n$ a.e. from (3).

Also by the martingale property of h_n's , one has :

$$\int_X h_n \, dP = \sum_{k=1}^{n-1} \int_{[S=k]} f_k \, dP + \int_{[S \geq n]} f_n \, dP$$

$$(4) \qquad = \sum_{n=1}^{n-1} \int_{[S=k]} f_n \, dP + \int_{[S \geq n]} f_n \, dP = \int_X f_n \, dP \, .$$

Similarly since $\{|f_n|, \underline{\underline{F}}_n, n \geq 1\}$ is a submartingale, one gets

$$\int_X |h_n| \, dP \leq \int_\Omega |f_n| \, dP \, , \quad n \geq 1 \, .$$

Let $r_{k+1} = f^+_{k+1} - f^+_k$, a submartingale increment. Then

$$(5) \qquad f^+_S = \sum_{k=1}^{\infty} f^+_k \chi_{[S=k]} = \sum_{k=1}^{\infty} r_{k+1} \chi_{[S \geq k]} \, .$$

Here (2) is used to conclude that the above series is absolutely convergent for a.a. (x) , so that the rearrangement is legitimate.

To show that $\{h_n, \underline{\underline{F}}_n, n \geq 1\}$ is L^1-bounded, consider the submartingale $\{h^+_n, \underline{\underline{F}}_n, n \geq 1\}$. Thus

$$E(f^+_S | F_n) = h^+_n + \sum_{k \geq n+1} E(E(r_k \chi_{[S \geq k]} | \underline{\underline{F}}_{k-1}) | \underline{\underline{F}}_n)$$

$$= h^+_n + \sum_{k \geq n+1} E(\chi_{[S \geq k]} E(r_k | \underline{\underline{F}}_{k-1}) | \underline{\underline{F}}_n)$$

$$\geq h^+_n \, , \quad \text{a.e.,}$$

since $[S \geq k] \in \underline{\underline{F}}_{k-1}$, and $E(r_k | \underline{\underline{F}}_{k-1}) \geq 0$ a.e. by the submartingale property. Hence $\{h^+_n, \underline{\underline{F}}_n, n \geq 1\}$ is a submartingale which is closed on the right by the integrable random variable f^+_S . This implies

$$E(|h_n|) \leq 2E(h^+_n) - E(h_n) \leq 2E(f^+_S) - E(f_1) < \infty \, ,$$

by (2) and (4). Hence $\{h_n, \underline{\underline{F}}_n, n \geq 1\}$ is an L^1-bounded martingale.

II. Suppose now that $\{f_n, \underset{=}{F}_n, n \geq 1\}$ is a submartingale satisfying the given conditions. Let $S \in \underset{\sim}{T}$, $S_k = \min(S, k)$, $k \geq 1$ as before. Since only the discrete case is considered, one can apply the classical Doob decomposition to the f_n-process so that

(6) $$f_n = f_n^1 + a_n, \quad n \geq 1,$$

where $\{f_n^1, \underset{=}{F}_n, n \geq 1\}$ is a martingale and $a_n \geq 0$ is an increasing process such that a_n is $\underset{=}{F}_{n-1}$-adapted $(a_o = 0)$, and $\{a_n, \underset{=}{F}_n, n \geq 1\}$ is trivially a submartingale. Also $f_n \geq f_n^1$ for all $n \geq 1$. Hence $f_n^+ \geq (f_n^1)^+$ a.e. and by (2), $E(f_S^{1+}) \leq E(f_S^+) < \infty$, $S \in \underset{\sim}{T}$. Since $\lim_n E(a_n)$ is not necessarily finite, the martingale $\{f_n^1, \underset{=}{F}_n, n \geq 1\}$ is not necessarily L^1-bounded. However $E((f_S^1)^+) < \infty$, $S \in \underset{\sim}{T}$ so that by step I, there exists an L^1-bounded martingale $\{h_n^1, \underset{=}{F}_n, n \geq 1\}$ such that $h_n^1 = f_{S_n}^1$.

III. By theorem 1, $f_n \longrightarrow f_\infty$ a.e. in both cases. By the classical martingale convergence, the L^1-bounded martingale $h_n \longrightarrow h_\infty$ a.e., $(h_n^1 \longrightarrow h_\infty^1$ a.e.). If $g_n^1 = f_n - h_n$ in the martingale case, and $g_n^1 = f_n - h_n^1 = f_n^1 + a_n - h_n^1$ in the submartingale case, then $g_n^1 \longrightarrow g_\infty^1$ a.e., (but g_∞^1 may be infinite on a set of positive probability). $\{g_n^1, \underset{=}{F}_n, n \geq 1\}$ is a (sub-)martingale. Also $0 \leq a_n \uparrow a_\infty$ a.e. But the fact that $f_n^1 \longrightarrow f_\infty^1$ a.e. and $f_n \longrightarrow f_\infty$ a.e. implies $f_n - a_n \longrightarrow f_\infty^1$ a.e., so that the infinities should match. In all these cases therefore for the L^1-bounded process $\{h_n, \underset{=}{F}_n, n \geq 1\}$ (or $\{h_n^1, \underset{=}{F}_n, n \geq 1\}$), Gundy's decomposition is applicable and there exist martingales $\{g_n^j, \underset{=}{F}_n, n \geq 1\}$ $j = 2, 3, 4$ such that $h_n = g_n^2 + g_n^3 + g_n^4$ a.e. holds, $n \geq 1$. Thus putting all parts together, one has $f_n = \sum_{j=1}^{4} g_n^j$, and it is now easy to check, with the work of [5], that all the statements of the theorem obtain on using the submartingale maximal inequality, since the stated g_n^j are guarranteed by [5].

Remark. The use of this decomposition in harmonic analysis, particularly in extending the classical Littlewood-Paley inequalities is well-illustrated in [8].

It is also of interest in the study of limit theorems. Related discussion appears in [7].

4. SETS OF FINITENESS OF THE LIMIT AND APPROXIMATION

The pointwise a.e. convergence of the submartingale sequence given by Theorem 1, and used in the preceding section, is on X, with the limits having possibly infinite values on sets of positive probability. If the submartingale is L^1-bounded, then the classical theory implies the a.e. finiteness of the limit. In the non L^1-bounded case, it is therefore of interest to find sets on which the limit is finite. Let us introduce the necessary concepts now.

For each $0<\delta<1$ and an increasing sequence $\{\underline{\underline{F}}_n , n\geq 1\}$ of σ-subalgebras of $\underline{\underline{A}}$, let $S(B , \delta : n,n+1) = [P(B|\underline{\underline{F}}_n) \leq \delta]$, $B\in \underline{\underline{F}}_{n+1}$, where $P(.|\underline{\underline{F}}_n)$ is the conditional probability function relative to $\underline{\underline{F}}_n$. Then one can show the existence of a (maximal) set $B_o \in \underline{\underline{F}}_{n+1}$ such that $S(B , \delta : n , n+1) \subset S(B_o , \delta : n , n+1)$ a.e. for any $B\in \underline{\underline{F}}_{n+1}$. This latter set is a.e. uniquely defined, and is called the δ-splitting of $\underline{\underline{F}}_n$ relative to $\underline{\underline{F}}_{n+1}$ and essentially depends only on δ, $\underline{\underline{F}}_n$, $\underline{\underline{F}}_{n+1}$. So let $S(\delta : n , n+1) = S(B_o , \delta : n , n+1)$. If $\delta_k \searrow 0$ and $S = \bigcap_{k=1}^{\infty} \limsup_n S(\delta_k : n , n+1)$, then $X^{(r)} = X - S$ is called the <u>regular part</u> of X relative to $\{\underline{\underline{F}}_n , n\geq 1\}$ from $(X , \underline{\underline{A}} , P)$. It is, of course, possible that $X = S$ a.e., or $S = \emptyset$ a.e.

The following sufficient condition includes the known work obtained for a similar purpose.

THEOREM 3. <u>Let</u> $\{f_n , \underline{\underline{F}}_n , n\geq 1\}$ <u>be a submartingale on</u> $(X , \underline{\underline{A}} , P)$ <u>and</u> $X^{(r)}$ <u>be the regular part of</u> X <u>relative to</u> $\{\underline{\underline{F}}_n , n\geq 1\}$. <u>Then</u> $f_n(x) \longrightarrow f_\infty(x)$ <u>exists and</u> $|f_\infty(x)| < \infty$ <u>for a.a.</u> $x\in X_o$, <u>where</u>

$$X_o = X^{(r)} \cap ([\sup_n f_n < \infty] \cup [\inf_n f_n > -\infty]) . \tag{7}$$

[Of course, $X_o = \emptyset$ a.e. is possible, as the trivial example following Theorem 1 shows.]

The regular sets $X^{(r)}$ were introduced by Lamb in [6] for this purpose, and he proved the above result for martingales. The same argument works for submartingales, and so an outline will be included here for completeness, indicating the changes.

Thus for each $n \geq 1$, u real, define $T^u_{mn} = \min(T^u_m, n)$ where

$$T^u_n = \inf\{k \geq n : P([f_{k+1} > u] | \underline{\underline{F}}_k) > 0\} . \tag{8}$$

Then T^u_{mn} is a bounded stopping time of $\{\underline{\underline{F}}_n, n \geq 1\}$ and if $g_{mn} = f_{T^u_{mn}}$, then $\{g_{mn}, \underline{\underline{H}}_n, n \geq 1\}$ is a submartingale, closed on the right by $\max(f_m, u)$ by the classical optimal sampling theorem, so that $g_{mn} \longrightarrow h_m$ a.e. $(\leq \max(f_m, u))$ where $\underline{\underline{H}}_n = \underline{\underline{F}}_n$, or can also be $\underline{\underline{B}}_{T^u_{mn}}$ with $m \geq 1$ fixed. If $x_o \in X^r \cap [\sup_n f_n < \infty]$, then $(\sup_n f_n)(x_o) < \infty$ so that for some u_o $(= u_{x_o})$, $\sup_n f_n(x_o) \leq u_o$. Also $x_o \in X^{(r)}$ implies

$$x_o \in S^c = \bigcup_{k \geq 1} \bigcup_{j \geq 1} \bigcap_{n \geq j} S^c_n(\delta_k) ,$$

so there is a $\delta_o > 0$, $j_o \geq 1$ and $x_o \in S^c_n(\delta_o)$, $n \geq j_o$. By the definition of δ-splitting :

$$e_k(x_o) = P([f_{k+1} > u_o] | \underline{\underline{F}}_k)(x_o) > \delta \text{ or } = 0 , \quad k \geq j_o . \tag{9}$$

Let $C = [\sup_n f_n > u_o] \in \underline{\underline{F}}_\infty$. Then

$$0 \leq e_k(x_o) \leq P(C | \underline{\underline{F}}_k)(x_o) = E(\chi_C | F_k)(x_o) \longrightarrow \chi_C(x_o) .$$

by the martingale convergence, for a.a.(x_o). In particular if $x_o \notin C$, then $e_k(x_o) = 0$ for some $k \geq m \geq j_o$. So the set in $\{\ \}$ of (8) will be empty and hence $T^u_m(x_o) = \infty$. Similarly $T^n_m(x'_o) = \infty$ for $x'_o \in X^{(r)} \cap [\inf_n f_n > -\infty]$. Thus for a.a. $x \in X_o$, this holds. Since the given submartingale is bounded on this set, the existence of limit is obvious.

As noted above, the proof is simply that of Lamb's [6]. Finally, it is of interest to give a result on approximation of a given function by a martingale. The classical structure theorem says that every finite real measurable function is a pointwise limit of a sequence of measurable step (or simple) functions. On the other hand, if f is a function on $(X, \underline{\underline{A}}, P)$ such that $Q(A) = \int_A f\, dP$ defines a signed (or σ-finite) measure, then, for each sequence $\underline{\underline{F}}_n \subset \underline{\underline{F}}_{n+1} \subset \underline{\underline{A}}$ such that $\sigma(\bigcup_n \underline{\underline{F}}_n) = \underline{\underline{A}}$, the Andersen-Jessen theorem says that there is a martingale $\{f_n, \underline{\underline{F}}_n, n \geq 1\}$ such that $f_n \longrightarrow f$ a.e. In fact, $f_n = \frac{dQ_n}{dP_n}$ where $Q_n = Q|\underline{\underline{F}}_n$, $P_n = P|\underline{\underline{F}}_n$. [Cf. ([7], Sec. II.6) for a convenient reference for all these convergence results.] If the sequence $\{\underline{\underline{F}}_n, n \geq 1\}$ is restricted somewhat, then the integrability hypothesis of f can be dispensed with in the above. If moreover $\underline{\underline{A}}$ is countably generated, it is even possible to present a fixed "universal" martingale $\{f_n, \underline{\underline{F}}_n, n \geq 1\}$ such that every $\underline{\underline{A}}$-measurable real function is a pointwise limit of some subsequence of the above martingale. So the martingale itself cannot converge. These two results are due to Lamb [6], and because of their interest, they will be precisely stated here, refering the proofs to his paper [6].

Let $S(m, n) = S(\frac{1}{2}; m, n)$ be the $\frac{1}{2}$-splitting of $\underline{\underline{F}}_m$ relative to $\underline{\underline{F}}_n$, $m < n$. Then $\{\underline{\underline{F}}_n, n \geq 1\}$ is a (disintegrating or) d-<u>sequence</u> if for each $m \geq 1$, $\bigcup_{n=1}^{\infty} S(m, n) = \Omega$, a.e. Thus each set of $\underline{\underline{F}}_m$ is split by future σ-algebras of the sequence. Note that $S(m,n) \subseteq S(m,n+1)$ and if each $\underline{\underline{F}}_n$ is atomic, then for a d-sequence, no set of $\bigcup_{n \geq 1} \underline{\underline{F}}_n$ can be an atom of $\sigma(\bigcup_n \underline{\underline{F}}_n)$, so that the latter is "rich" enough.

The desired approximation results are given by :

THEOREM 4. (a) <u>Let</u> $\{\underline{\underline{F}}_n, n \geq 1\}$ <u>be a</u> d-<u>sequence of</u> σ-<u>subalgebras of</u> $(X, \underline{\underline{A}}, P)$

and let $\underline{\underline{A}} = \sigma(\bigcup_n \underline{\underline{F}}_n)$. Then given any $\underline{\underline{A}}$-measurable $f : X \longrightarrow \overline{\mathbb{R}}$, there is a martingale $\{f_n, \underline{\underline{F}}_n, n \geq 1\}$ such that $f_n \longrightarrow f$ a.e. and the limit is finite a.e. iff $|f(x)| < \infty$ for a.a. $x \in X^r$, the regular part of X .

(b) For the d-sequence above, suppose $\underline{\underline{A}}$ is countably generated. Then there is a fixed (universal) martingale $\{\tilde{f}_n, \underline{\underline{F}}_n, n \geq 1\}$ such that each $\underline{\underline{A}}$-measurable $f : X \longrightarrow \overline{\mathbb{R}}$ is a pointwise limit of some subsequence $\{\tilde{f}_{n_i}, \underline{\underline{F}}_{n_i}, i \geq 1\}$.

Remark. The peculiar behaviour of martingales reported in [1] and [4] are thus particular cases of the "universal martingale" above. The construction given in [6] of the "universal martingale" shows that one can get martingales which converge in distribution but not in probability also.

Finally, if $\{\underline{\underline{F}}_t, t \geq 0\}$ is a net of σ-algebras in $\underline{\underline{A}}$, call it a d-sequence if for some subsequence $0 \leq t_n \uparrow \infty$, $\{\underline{\underline{F}}_{t_n}, n \geq 1\}$ is a d-sequence, as defined above. (Thus the same holds for any other such t-sequence.) Then the above result extends immediately to the continuous parameter case. However, there are difficulties in extending these results for the direct indexed processes. One can present sufficient conditions with Vitali V_o hypothesis for the decomposition. But they seem complicated, and so the matters will have to rest at this point.

ACKNOWLEDGEMENT. This paper is prepared while the author is visiting the Département de Mathématique, Université de Strasbourg, with a UCR Sabbatical.

REFERENCES

[1] L. BÁEZ-DUARTE : "An a.e. divergent martingale that converges in probability", J. Math. Anal. Appl., 36 (1971), 149-150.

[2] Y.S. CHOW : "Martingales in a σ-finite measure space indexed by directed sets", Trans. Amer. Math. Soc., 91 (1960), 254-285.

[3] Y.S. CHOW : "Convergence theorems of martingales", Z. Wahrs., 1 (1963), 340-346.

[4] D. GRILAT : "Convergence in distribution, convergence in probability, and almost sure convergence of discrete martingales", Ann. Math. Statist., 43 (1972), 1374-1379.

[5] R.F. GUNDY : "A decomposition for L^1-bounded martingales", Ann. Math. Statist., 39 (1968), 134-138.

[6] C.W. LAMB : "Representation of functions as limits of martingales", Trans. Amer. Math. Soc., 188 (1974), 395-405.

[7] M.M. RAO : Stochastic Processes and Integration, Sijthoff & Noordhoff, (Alphen aan den Rijn) The Netherlands, 1978.

[8] E.M. STEIN : Topics in Harmonic Analysis, Princeton University Press, 1970.

Department of Mathematics
University of California
Riverside, Calif., 92521

ON THE DEFINITION AND DETECTION OF STRUCTURAL CHANGE

B. Rustem
Department of Economics
London School of Economics
Houghton St,. London WC2A 2AE, U.K.

K. Velupillai
Nationalekonomiska Institutionen
Lunds Universitet
220 05 Lund 5, Sweden

1. INTRODUCTION

To analyse the time-variation of the parameters of a linear econometric model, a Kalman filter may be used (see Athans [1], Rustem and Velupillai [19]) to obtain the recursive estimates of these parameters. The plots of these parameters over time sometimes exhibit suspiciously large jumps in their values. Such jumps may either be attributed to errors due to the mis-specification of the original model or to structural changes during the period of estimation in the actual system being modelled. In this paper, the detection of structural change is discussed with methods based on recursive parameter estimation. The original model is assumed to be correctly specified.

Thus, we intend to propose some general definitions in Sections 2 and 3. These definitions are relative to the more basic aim of analysing and detecting 'structural change'. In Section 4, analytical results are given on 'structural change' for the case of a continuous model. The Cameron-Martin-Girsanov (Girsanov [13]) transformation formula is used to prove the existence of a solution to a stochastic differential equation representing a continuous model of the parameter dynamics with discontinuous drift. It appears to be the case that this solution is the stochastic analogue of the problems discussed by Champsaur, Dreze, Henry [7] on the existence of solutions to deterministic differential equations with discontinuous right-hand sides. The Radon-Nikodym derivative implied in the Cameron-Martin-Girsanov transformation formula provides the link between the problem of detecting structural change and the estimation of structures. An observation arising from these considerations is that some popular definitions of structure in econometrics also include the definition of structural change in this paper. Sections 5 and 6 have been devoted to the discussion of recursive estimation and likelihood ratio tests of the detection of structural change.

2. GENERAL DEFINITIONS

In analysing economic problems and phenomena we are studying *one real entity* called *the system* or more precisely *the economic system*. This system is made up of various elemental units (households-firms, consumers-producers, etc.). These elemental units engage in various activities in their respective capacities - sometimes in groups (coalitions), at other times hierarchically, etc. It is in describing the relevant activities of the elemental units in their various capacities that we need to consider subsets of these units. The formation of subsets, in turn, depends on defining appropriate algebraic operations on the set of elemental units. But prior to this, it is necessary to define a *system*.

Definition 2.1

A *system* S will be defined as follows: (a 'double')

$$S \triangleq < A, \Omega_R > \tag{2.1}$$

where

A: a non-empty set A

Ω_R: a set of *relations* defined on A (or subsets of A).

Remark 2.1

As an example of an economic system (for a given country) the set A could be made up of consumers, producers, commodities, natural resources - i.e. a definition that will be exhaustive and exclusive. The definition must be such that any individual agent in any capacity or anything material (or not) that is relevant for the problem at hand is a member of the set A.

Remark 2.2

In the case of a *relation* some concept of order is involved - i.e. some sort of comparison between the elements of A ('greater than', 'equal to' etc.).

Definition 2.2

We define a *model* to be the triple:

$$M \triangleq < A, \Omega_0, \Omega_R > . \tag{2.2}$$

and the double

$$\mathcal{A} \triangleq < A, \Omega_0 > \tag{2.3}$$

an *algebra*, with

Ω_0 as a set of *operations* defined on A (and closure with respect to these operations is usually assumed), furthermore $\Omega_0 \cap \Omega_R = \phi$.

Remark 2.3

In the case of an *operation*, no concept of order is associated with it - i.e. no concept of *comparison* between any number of elements of a set; only a correspondence between a subset of elements of the set and another element of the same set. Familiar examples of operations are of course Unions, Intersections, Complements etc. (generating Boolean, σ - and other Algebras).

It can thus be seen that in the case of a *model* we may be able to discuss about the *relations* between only a subset of the elements of A (or between different subsets, i.e. relations between coalitions).

In the case of an Algebra, the operator and operation that defines it on any given set must be performable on *all* elements of the given set.

Thus Rational Structural Form, Polynomial Structural Form, Reduced Form, Final Form, etc., are all *models*, according to our definitions; 'Keynesian', 'Monetarist', 'Input-Output' are more familiar economic examples of *models*.

Finally, a *structure* is defined as:

Definition 2.3

$$S_t \triangleq < A, \Omega_o, \Omega_R, \Pi > \tag{2.4}$$

where,

Π: set of elements from a ring or a field.

The set of Operations and/or Relations on A are suitably augmented so as to preserve closure with respect to Π.

Remark 2.4

For example, given that our elemental units are endogenous, exogenous and other types of variables usually considered in econometrics, we have:

i) given an aggregation over these elemental units (i.e. given Ω_o);

ii) for any Ω_R we get a particular structure of a given model by estimating a subset of elements from Π, with respect to some criterion - i.e. the criterion determines a subset of Π for a given model;

iii) this estimated set of coefficients $\Pi^e \subset \Pi$ for the given model $< A, \Omega_o, \Omega_R >$ gives us a particular structure: $< A, \Omega_o, \Omega_R, \Pi^e >$.

In this paper we shall consider changes in structure due to changes in the set Π. This is rather an imprecise statement but it will be clarified in later sections. It is implicitly assumed that any $\Pi^e \subset \Pi$ associated with a given M is determined on the basis of optimization either at the individual element level or at some appropriate aggregated level. Thus observed variations in Π^e depend upon variations in M (i.e. in A, Ω_g or Ω_R or any combination of them). Our aim is to start with a postulated set of $\Pi^e \subset \Pi$ for a given M (determined, for example, by an initial econometric precedure) assuming constancy of A, Ω_o and Ω_R and check for the consistency of these assumptions by confronting them with the observed variations in Π^e. This implies that the members of the field Π^e determining a structure of a given M are themselves, at a 'second stage' reformulated in terms of the above (System → Model → Structure). In particular a linear stochastic dynamical model for the elements of Π^e will be developed.

The index set over which the elements of A (or those of Π^e) are allowed to vary determines whether the space over which the model and structure are defined is continuous or discrete. Typically, in economic problems, we have an interaction between a model (of a National Economy or sub-sectors of it) in continuous space and observations of the relevant elements of the model in discrete space. Discretization of the observation space is due not only to the problems underlying the meaning and nature of continuous observations, but more imperatively to the practical intractability of observing and processing continuously a large number of elements.

The theoretical basis of our detection and estimation problems must be therefore consistent in the following sense: it is only through observations, made at discrete points, that inference about the true model can be made. Any discontinuity in the observed phenomena must correspond to an analogous occurrence in the (continuous) model. Therefore, the model built for analysing observations must be based on an appropriate discrete approximation of the continuous model. The continuous model, by itself, must be flexible enough to incorporate the theoretical possibilities of the variations in, say Π^e, that we wish to consider. Since we would like to define *structural change* in forms of discontinuities in the model for Π^e, it must be theoretically possible to prove the existence (and uniqueness) of solutions to this model in the presence of the variations in Π. More about this will be presented in Section 4. In Diagram 1 an elementary schematic description of the nature of the problem is given. The increasing restrictions imposed on the successive representations when going from A to a structure entail the set inclusions.

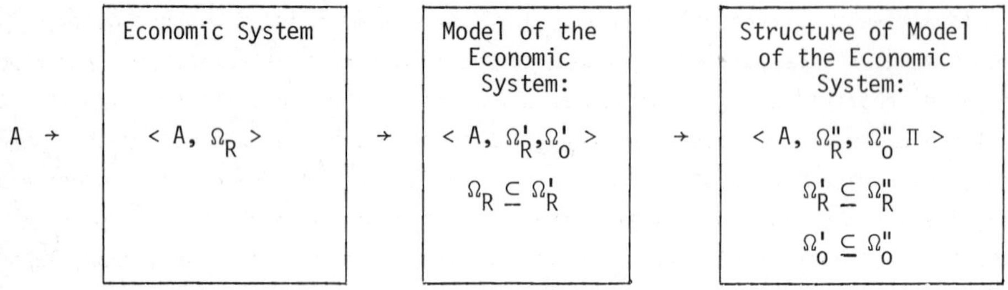

Diagram 1

3. CONTINUOUS AND DISCRETE REPRESENTATIONS

Economic activity of some sort is going on all the time. Production processes (steel plants, cement factories are typical examples but also service sectors - e.g. hospitals, telegraph services, etc. shipment, communications etc.) are basically continuous processes. Any discretization of this continuity can only take place due to accounting and/or other such practical - and obviously necessary - constraints.

Almost all decisions in the economic space or pertaining to elements of the set A of the economic system are subject to stochastic constraints. Traditionally economists have concentrated on distinguishing between 'static' and 'dynamic' in a deterministic space. However, in a deterministic space there is no qualitative distinction between *static* and *dynamic model* - especially within a non-conflicting framework, which is the type exploited by econometric modelling. The really important and qualitative distinction is between stochastic and deterministic models. Thus the economic system should ideally be defined over a continuous-stochastic space.

In subsequent sections a state-space model is used for the representation of the dynamics of structures (2.4). In this process all the elements of the state vector are taken to be continuous functions of time. The observations on the economic variables are given in discrete time. Analysis of the data when conducted in a discrete framework and subsequently employed for prediction and control purposes also implies an interaction between two discrete frameworks ("structures"). Thus, only the discussion in the next section will be conducted for a continuous state-space model. Due to computational limitations the remainder of this paper is devoted to the discussion of discrete state-space and discrete observations models.

4. DISCONTINUITIES IN STATE-SPACE STRUCTURES

Intuitively, structural change is implied by some form of discontinuity. Thus, given a model of the parameter system, if discontinuous time variations take place in the set Π^e characterizing a particular structure of the model, then we say that *the model has undergone structural changes*. A continuous variation in Π^e with respect to time (i.e. a dynamical system - cf. Hirsch, Smale [14] pp.159-160 for a precise definition) implies the existence of an appropriate mapping which can be incorporated into the model M by redefining Ω_R to include also this mapping. Analogous statements hold when the dynamical system is defined for random variables in Hilbert Spaces. Thus, the existence of solutions in models that are defined on stochastic spaces and also allow for some suitable discontinuity is the primary pre-requisite for our analysis of 'Structural Changes'.

A continuous state space model for the parameter system is taken in this section. We assume that the time variations in the parameters can be modelled by a set of stochastic (first-order) differential equations. Hence, given the set R of the parameters whose time variation is to be studied, $\Pi \supset R$, $\Pi^e \supset R$, R can be associated with a Δ'_o and a Δ'_R such that the model (2.2) of the parameters $m = < R, \Delta'_o, \Delta'_R >$ is defined by a set of stochastic (first-order) differential equations. Diagram 2 is a schematic representation of this 'secondary' modelling process. The analogy between this and Diagram 1 is apparent.

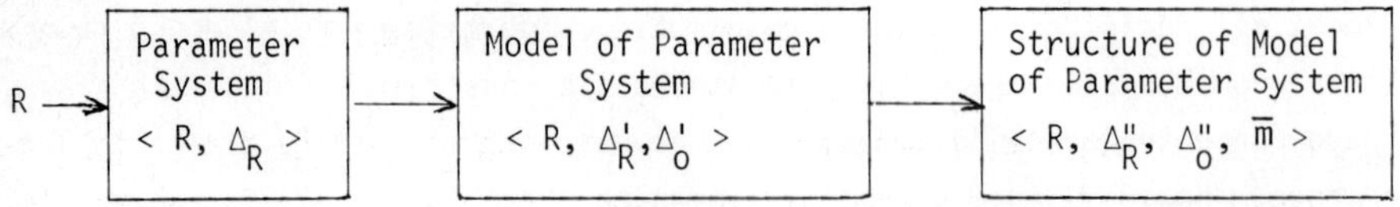

Diagram 2

We also use some results from Ito Stochastic Calculus in this section. All integrals in this section are Ito integrals. Within this framework, structural change defined by discontinuities in time variation of Π^e is to be confined to discontinuous changes in the local drift of the stochastic differential equations modelling the parameter system. It is then shown, using the Cameron-Martin-Girsanov transformation formula, that there exists a solution to the stochastic differential equation under these conditions - i.e. when the local drift is discontinuous. The economic meaning of the transformation formula and the solution is that the economic agents are now working with a new structure of expectations etc., i.e. in a new probability triple or a new stochastic space.

<u>Notations and formulation of the Model: $< R, \Delta'_R, \Delta'_o >$ for the Parameter System: $< R, \Delta_R >$</u>

Given, the triple $<\Omega, F, P>$ where, Ω : non-void set whose elements are the (basic) parameters, i.e. the 'non-aggregative' parameters, F : σ-algebra of subsets of Ω, i.e. parameters corresponding to aggregate 'economic' variables etc.,: e.g. Cobb-Douglas coefficients, 'marginal propensity to consume' (aggregature), 'capital-output' ratio etc., P : A probability measure defined on F.

Thus $$m \triangleq < R, \Delta'_o, \Delta'_R > \triangleq < \Omega, F, P > . \qquad (4.0)$$

<u>Definition 4.1</u>

A real-valued process in (s,T) is a one-dimensional Brownian motion if: (i) is a continuous process, (ii) $\beta(t) - \beta(s)$ has Gaussian distribution with zero mean and variance $q^2|t-s|$, (iii) β has independent increments, where q is a positive constant. When $q=1$, β is called a standard Brownian motion. A process $\underline{x}$ is said to have independent increments if $\forall\ t_o < t_1 < \ldots < t_n$ in [s,T] the random vectors $\underline{x}(t_o), \underline{x}(t_1) - \underline{x}(t_o), \ldots, \underline{x}(t_n) - \underline{x}(t_{n-1})$ are independent.

Definition 4.2

A process $\underline{\beta} = (\beta_1, \ldots, \beta_r)$ is an r-dimensional Brownian motion if the elements of $\underline{\beta}$ are independent 1-dimensional Brownian motions. Covariance of $\{\underline{\beta}(t) - \underline{\beta}(s)\}$ is diagonal with the ith element given by $q_i^2|t-s|$. (If $q_i = 1, \forall\, i$, then $\underline{\beta}$ is an r-dimensional Standard Brownian Motion.) Thus, as a model of the Parameter System, consider:

$$\frac{d\underline{x}}{dt} = \dot{\underline{x}} = \underline{f}(t, \underline{x}(t)) + G(t, \underline{x}(t))\underline{w}(t) \tag{4.1}$$

where, $\underline{x}$: an n-vector of parameters, $\underline{w} = \frac{d\underline{\beta}}{dt}$: and $\frac{d\beta}{dt}$ is the formal derivative of the Brownian motion (called "white noise"), $\underline{f}(t, \underline{x}(t))$: the 'local drift function'. Thus, rewriting (4.1) we get

$$d\underline{x} = \underline{f}(t, \underline{x}(t))dt + G(t, \underline{x}(t))\, d\underline{\beta} \tag{4.2}$$

where, now, $\underline{\beta}$ is a standard Brown motion vector of dimension r. A solution of (4.2) is to be interpreted as a solution of the (Ito) Stochastic Integral Equation:

$$\underline{x}(t) = \underline{x}(s) + \int_s^t \underline{f}(r,\underline{x}(r))dr + \int_s^t G(r,\underline{x}(r))d\underline{\beta}(r)$$
$$s \leq t \leq T \tag{4.3}$$

The existence and uniqueness conditions for equation (4.3) is a standard problem of the Ito calculus. What we are really interested in is the existence of a solution for (4.2) when the local drift is discontinuous.

Definition 4.3

$\underline{f}(t, \underline{x}(t))$ on $[s,T]$ is piecewise continuous if there exists a finite partition of (s,T) into intervals Z_i such that the restriction of $\underline{f}(t, \underline{x}(t))$ to Z_i is continuous for each i.

Definition 4.4

Any transformation $\eta : f_i \to f_j$ ($i \neq j$ and $j > i$, f_i denoting the restriction of $\underline{f}(t, \underline{x}(t))$ to Z_i) defines a structural change of the model given by (4.0) for the parameter system such that $f_i \neq f_j$. Economically, the above discontinuities of the local drift function $\underline{f}(t, \underline{x}(t))$ correspond to phenomena such as (i) sharp variations induced in savings coefficients with the introduction of pension funds (with appropriate lags); (ii) 'Oil price rises' etc.

As mentioned above, it can be shown, using a transformation formula of Cameron-Martin-Girsanov, that (4.2) has a solution even when the local drift function $\underline{f}(t, \underline{x}(t))$ is discontinuous - and above all, the transformation and the solution are exactly the ones we want, on the basis of the economics of the model of the parameter system.

We shall outline the nature of the solution and provide some interpretation, but for details reference should be made to Fleming, Rishel [11] or Gikhman, Skorokhod [12].

Consider, (i) Ω, F and an increasing family $\{F_t\}$ of σ-algebras for $t \in [s,T]$ (reflecting the fact that 'more information" or "new technology" etc. will be available as time progresses), (ii) the non-anticipative processes (cf. Flemming, Rishel [11], p. 108) $\underline{\tilde{f}}(r, \underline{\tilde{x}}(r))$ and $G(r, \underline{\tilde{x}}(r))$. For two processes $\underline{x}$ and $\underline{\tilde{x}}$ having the sample functions, let: $\underline{\tilde{x}}$ be a solution of:

$$d\underline{\tilde{x}} = \underline{\tilde{f}}(t, \underline{\tilde{x}}(t))dt + G(t, \underline{\tilde{x}}(t))d\underline{\tilde{\beta}} \tag{4.4}$$

where now: $\underline{\tilde{\beta}}$: a standard r-dimensional Brownian motion with respect to a probability measure $\tilde{P}$.

Find, then, the solution of:

$$d\underline{x} = \underline{f}(t, \underline{x}(t))dt + G(t, \underline{x}(t))d\underline{\beta} \tag{4.5}$$

where, due to structural change $\underline{\tilde{f}}$ is replaced by $\underline{f}$, but both $\underline{x}$ and $\underline{\tilde{x}}$ have the same sample functions, and $\underline{\tilde{\beta}}$ is replaced by a new Brownian motion (with respect to the probability measure P).

<u>Theorem 4.1</u>

Let $Q^o = (s,T) \times E^n$, where E^n is the n-dimensional Euclidean Space and let $\tilde{Q}^o$ be the closure of Q^o. Suppose now that

$$\underline{f}(t,\underline{x}) = \underline{\tilde{f}}(t,\underline{x}) + G(t,\underline{x})\ \underline{\alpha}\ (t,\underline{x})\ \forall\ (t,\underline{x}) \in \tilde{Q}^o \tag{4.6}$$

Assume now: (i) $\underline{\tilde{f}}(t,\underline{x})$, $G(t,\underline{x})$ satisfy the Ito conditions. (cf. Fleming and Rishel [11] p.118 or Gikhman and Skorokhod [12] ch.2.6) and that $G(t,\underline{x})$ is bounded, (ii) $\underline{\alpha}$ is bounded and Borel measurable, and, (iii) $E|\underline{x}(s)|^2 < \infty$. Let P be absolutely continuous with respect to $\tilde{P}$ with the Radon-Nikodym derivative:

$$\frac{dP}{d\tilde{P}} = \exp\left\{ \int_s^t \underline{\alpha}\ (r, \underline{\tilde{x}}(r))\ d\underline{\tilde{\beta}}(r) - \tfrac{1}{2}\int_s^t |\underline{\alpha}(r,\underline{\tilde{x}}(r))|^2 dr\right\}. \tag{4.7}$$

(Note, once again, that the above integrals are all Ito integrals.) Then, (a) $P(\Omega) = 1$, i.e. $\langle\Omega, F, P\rangle$ is a probability triple, (b) let $\underline{\beta}(t) = \underline{\tilde{\beta}}(t) - \int_s^t \underline{\alpha}(r,\underline{\tilde{x}}(r))dr$. Then $\underline{\beta}$ is a standard r-dimensional Brownian motion with respect to P. (c) Let $\underline{f} = \underline{\tilde{f}} + G\underline{x}$ as in (4.6). It follows then, that:

$$\underline{x}(t) - \underline{x}(s) = \int_s^t \underline{f}(r,\underline{x}(r)dr + \int_s^t G(r,\underline{\tilde{x}}(r))d\underline{\beta}(r) \tag{4.8}$$

is a solution for (4.5). [Proof can be found in Gikhman-Skorokhod, [12] p.90.] Girsanov's transformation is the basis for (b), (c) and that these follow from (a) is proved by Girsanov [13] pp.287-295. Economically, due to the discontinuities caused by, say oil price increases, innovations, pension funds etc. even though the same sample functions are realised, they now correspond to different probability spaces, $<\Omega, F, \tilde{P}>$ and $<\Omega, F, P>$ respectively, (or $< R, \Delta_0, \tilde{\Delta}'_R >$ and $< R, \Delta_0\ \Delta'_R >$ respectively). Now, when one recalls that the 'parameters' of an econometric model are usually behaviourally and technologically determined (aggregated from the basic individual space of agents and production processes) ; and that technological parameters, as a rule, are results of entrepreneurial choice of techniques of production - it becomes clear that the particular realization of the parameter set $\Pi^e \subset R$ is a result of expectations. In this sense, the absolutely continuous transformation of probability measures is related to an interesting and realistic economic interpretation. It corresponds to the fact that political and exogenous (technological, oil prices, discovery of off-shore oil etc.) actions (measures) have so 'shocked' the large mass of decision makers, that they have been forced to change the structure of their expectations; or, what comes to the same thing, they now operate in a different stochastic space. (We interpret probability from a subjective viewpoint - which seems to be the only possible interpretation here.) The solution is directly linked with estimation, in a discrete space, of the parameters of an econometric model (via an appropriate discretization of the Ito integrals of relevance), and with detecting, as quickly as possible, the discontinuities in the local drift function (i.e. structural changes) via the likelihood ratio interpretation of the Radon-Nikodym derivative given by equation (4.7). This implies that Ito integrals must be evaluated. It is also useful to remember the definition of conditional expectations in terms of Radon-Nikodym derivatives which also strengthens our above economic interpretation.

One of the popular definitions of structure in econometrics is that "... a structure is a set of autonomous relationships sufficient to determine uniquely the conditional probability distributions of the endogenous variables, given the values of the exogenous variables" (Christ [8] p.153) It can easily be seen from the definition of structural change (4.4) and the solution (4.8) of (4.5) that our definition of structural change also satisfies the above definition of structure. The existence of the solution (4.8) ensures the corresponding values for the endogenous variables once the exogenous values are given.

5. DISCRETE-TIME RECURSIVE ESTIMATORS

Accurate prediction and quick detection of changes are probably the most important elements of any system with random structure. Prediction and detection both imply models - in our case a so-called process model and an observation model of the parameter system. For computational purposes both have to be within a discrete framework. In addition, the stochastic differential equations of the previous section are restricted to linear stochastic difference equations in this section.

Consider the linear (state-space) model of the parameter system described by the (vector) difference equation:

$$\underline{x}_{k+1} = \phi_k \underline{x}_k + \Gamma_k \underline{\omega}_k \tag{5.1}$$

where, $\underline{x}_k$: n-vector of parameters at time k, $1 \leq k \leq N$, ϕ_k : n×n non-singular state transition matrix at k, Γ_k : n×r matrix, $\underline{\omega}_k$: r-vector of a white noise sequence ($\underline{\omega}_k \sim N(0,Q_k)$). Discrete linear observations of the model (5.1) of the parameter system are given by:

$$\underline{y}_k = H_k \underline{x}_k + \underline{v}_k \tag{5.2}$$

where, $\underline{y}_k$: m-vector of observations at time k, H_k : m×n matrix of 'observation' coefficients, $\underline{v}_k$: m-vector of a white noise sequence ($\underline{v}_k \sim N(0,R_k)$).

The series $\{\underline{v}_k\}$ and $\{\underline{\omega}_k\}$ are assumed to be independent. The 'outcomes' of (5.1) are observed through (5.2). The probability space of the random variables $\underline{x}_k$ is denoted by $<\Omega, X, P_x>$. However, since the outcomes of (5.1) are observed through (5.2), the probability space $<\Omega, Y, P_y>$ of the random variables $\underline{y}_k$ is the space through which the random variables $\underline{x}_k$ must be studied.

Definition (5.1):
The set of all square integrable random variables (i.e. with finite second moments) on $<\Omega, Y, P_y>$ is a Hilbert Space (with the usual definitions). The equivalence classes of random variables in this space is also a Hilbert space and is denoted by H. (cf. e.g., M.H.A. Davis [10], section 2.3.)

Furthermore: $H_K^y \triangleq$ subspace spanned by $\{\underline{y}_j | 1 \leq j \leq k\} \subset H$, $P_k \triangleq$ Projection onto H_k^y, then for $\delta > o$ and given $\{\underline{y}_j | 1 \leq j \leq k\}$, $\hat{\underline{x}}_{k+\delta} \triangleq P_k \underline{x}_{k+\delta}$ is the predicted estimate for $\delta > 0$, the filtered estimate for $\delta = 0$ and the smoothed estimate for $\delta < 0$.

As is clear from the above discussions in this section and in Section 4, only filtered estimates will be discussed in this paper and henceforth they will be simply referred to as estimates.

Definition 5.2:
Estimates are said to be recursive if $P_k \underline{x}_k$ is obtained by updating $P_{k-1} \underline{x}_{k-1}$ with $\underline{y}_k$; i.e. $\hat{\underline{x}}_k = P_k \underline{x}_k = f(\hat{\underline{x}}_{k-1}, \underline{y}_k)$. The projections are defined with respect to the

norm: $||\underline{x}|| = E^{\frac{1}{2}}\{\underline{x}^2\}$ and the inner product: $<\underline{x}, \underline{y}> = E\{\underline{xy}\}$. Using the orthogonal projection lemma (cf. e.g. Jazwinski [16] p.202 or Luenberger [18] p.51), the projection problem may be written as the minimum norm problem:

$$E\{(\underline{x}_k - \hat{\underline{x}}_k)^T (\underline{x}_k - \hat{\underline{x}}_k) = \min\{E\{(\underline{x}_k - \underline{x}_k')^T (\underline{x}_k - \underline{x}_k') | \underline{x}_k \in H_K^y\} \qquad (5.3)$$

The solution to this constrained optimization problem is the recursive minimum variance estimator which is also the Kalman-Bucy filter for the discrete estimation problem. The solution to (5.3) is the well known Kalman-Bucy Filter (see, Jazwinski [16], Kalman [17]).

6. DETECTION; TESTS FOR STRUCTURAL CHANGE; MARTINGALES AND JUMP PROCESS

In testing whether we are in regime $\underline{f}(,)$ or $\tilde{\underline{f}}(,)$ (Section 4) we may use the likelihood ratio interpretation of the Radon-Nikodym derivative (4.7). As mentioned in Section 5, the process (5.1) is observed through the observation model of the parameter system, (5.2); thus, whether these observations imply $\underline{f}$ or $\tilde{\underline{f}}$ may be checked by testing corresponding hypotheses on the matrix H.

Assume the following hypotheses: 0: $H_k = 0$ implied by (Ω, Y, P_{yo}); 1: $H_k = \bar{H}_k$ implied by (Ω, Y, P_{y1}); 2: $H_k = \bar{\bar{H}}$ implied by (Ω, Y, P_{y2}).

Hypothesis 0 along with $\phi_k = I$ in (5.1) implies the time invariant parameter case. This can be verified by setting $\phi_k = I$ and $H_k = 0$ in the Kalman-Bucy filter equations (see Jazwinski [16], Section 7.3).

The continuous version of the likelihood ratio test given by the Radon-Nikodym derivative would be expressed by:

$$\frac{dP_1}{dP_o} \begin{cases} > \rho, \text{ decide in favour of } P_{y1} \\ < \rho, \text{ decide in favour of } P_{yo} \end{cases}$$

for a given (subjectively determined) ρ. Similarly, for testing Hypotheses 1 versus 2 the following simple rule is adequate:

$$\frac{dP_1/dP_o}{dP_2/dP_o} = \frac{dP_1}{dP_2} \begin{cases} > \rho\text{: decide in favour of } P_{y1} \\ < \rho\text{: decide in favour of } P_{y2} \end{cases}$$

For the discrete case the likelihood ratio test is used as follows:

Let $p(\bar{H})$ denote the probability density over the samples

$$\{\underline{y}_k, k_\ell \leq k \leq k_u\} \text{ for } H_k = \bar{H} \text{ and } 1 \leq k_\ell < k_u \leq N.$$

Let $p(\bar{\bar{H}})$ be the probability density for $H_k = \bar{\bar{H}}$ and let $p(0)$ be the probability density for $H_k = 0$.

Then $\log \frac{p(\bar{H})}{p(0)} = -\frac{1}{2}\left(\sum_{k=k_\ell}^{k_u} \underline{z}_k^{o\,T} D_k^{-1} \underline{z}_k^o - \sum_{k=k_\ell}^{k_u} y_k^T R_k^{-1} y_k\right)$

$$- \tfrac{1}{2} \sum_{k=k_\ell}^{k_u} \log\,(\det D_k/\det R_k) \qquad (6.1)$$

where $D_k = E[\underline{z}_k^o\ \underline{z}_k^o],\ \underline{z}_{k+1}^o = \underline{y}_{k+1} - H_{k+1}\,\phi_k\,\hat{\underline{x}}_k$, (6.2)

and once again $\hat{\underline{x}}_k$ is an estimate of $\underline{x}_k$ at time k (see Balakrishnan [2], p.247).

Similarly for $H_k = \bar{\bar{H}}$ and $H_k = 0$, $\log \frac{P(\bar{\bar{H}})}{P(0)}$ may easily be computed.

Hence:

$$\log \frac{P(\bar{H})}{P(0)} / \log \frac{P(\bar{\bar{H}})}{P(0)} \begin{cases} > \rho: \text{ decide in favour of } \bar{H} \\ < \rho: \text{ decide in favour of } \bar{\bar{H}} \end{cases}$$

Now, as is clear from equation (6.2) an estimate for x_k is needed if meaningful decisions are to be made based on discrete observations. This is our most basic justification for treating not only the observation model but also the process model of the parameter system in discrete spaces. Brown, Durbin and Evans [6] have discussed some techniques for the purpose of detecting what we have called structural change. However, it should be noted that though the methodology of recursive least squares is common, the specific model for the parameter system that we have chosen in Section 5 differs from the models tested by Brown et.al [6].

We have mentioned at the beginning of Section 4 the possibility of augmenting the set of relations Ω_R on A if continuous variations are to be modelled. Some remarks about this is now in order: On the basis of (5.1) and (5.2) and thus the Kalman filter we would obtain a description of the time-variation of the model for the parameter system, i.e. the time-variation is plotted. If the plots show any clear pattern like an exponential decay for any one parameter, this can be taken account of in one or two ways:

Either, a) Operate directly on the raw data in such a way that distant past values are weighted to be appropriately negligible and recent values given extra weight. This compensates for "too good" estimates. Alternatively, using the theory of Limited Memory Filtering, old data can be discarded (see Jazwinski [16]; or

b) If the plot shows a graph with fluctuations and monotone tendencies in a continuous way, it is proposed to operate on the monotone part of the raw data as above, to reduce the raw data to a mean around the fluctuations. Once again the alternative is the Limited Memory Filter for the monotone part.

The Limited Memory Filter when incorporated to the K-B filter is equivalent to augmenting the set of relations Ω_R on A or Δ_R on R. If, on the other hand, discontinuous shifts in the parameters are shown on the graph then it would be necessary to return to the original model of the economic system to take account of such changes. Such discontinuities if detected or predicted would necessitate wholesale discarding of certain batches of samples (observations or realizations) and a re-specification and re-estimation of the original model of the economic system. Another idea accounting for discontinuous changes in the parameters involves postulating a non-identity structure for the coefficient matrix ϕ_k in (5.1).

The representation of the dynamics of a structure can be seen as a jump process. Structural change will usually be the result of a single jump. Jump processes have recently been studied in detail; their association with Martingales and the representation of such Martingales have been established (see Davis [9], Boel, Varia, Wong [5], Jacod [15]). In Section 4 the dynamics of a structure was represented by a change in probability measure (i.e. the Radon-Nikodym derivative and the likelihood ratio test) which itself is related to Martingales (see Jacod [15]. The control of models undergoing structural change may thus be formulated as the control of models whose structure is associated with appropriate jump processes. The use of Martingales for the control of jump processes has been explored by Benes [3], Boel and Varia [4]. The stochastic control problems for models undergoing structural change may hence be resolved by the adoption of a Martingale approach to stochastic optimal control. This seems to be an obvious field in which further research is required.

REFERENCES

[1] Athans, M. "The Importance of Kalman Filtering Methods for Economic Systems", A.E.S.M., Vol.3, 1, pp.49-64, (1974).

[2] Balakrishnan, A.V. Stochastic Differential Systems, Springer Verlag, Berlin, (1973).

[3] Benes, V. "Existence of Optimal Strategies Based on Specified Information, for a Class of Stochastic Decision Problems", SIAM J. Control, Vol.8, 3, pp. 179-188, (1970).

[4] Boel, R. and Varaiya, P. "Optimal Control of Jump Processes", SIAM J. Control and Optimization, Vol.15, 1, pp.92-119, (1977).

[5] Boel, R., Varaiya, P. and Wong, E. "Martingales on Jump Processes I: Representation Results", SIAM J. Control, Vol.13, 5, pp. 999-1021, (1975).

[6] Brown, R.L., Durbin, J. and Evans, J.M. "Techniques for Testing the Constancy of Regression Relationships over Time", JRSS, Ser. B, 2, pp.149-192, (1975).

[7] Champsaur, P., Dreze, J. and Henry, C. "Stability Theorems with Economic Applications", Econometrica, Vol.45, 2, pp.273-294, (1977).

[8] Christ, C.F. Econometric Models and Methods, John Wiley & Sons Inc., New York, (1966).

[9] Davis, M.H.A. "The Representation of Martingales of Jump Processes", SIAM J. Control and Optimization, Vol.14, 4, pp.623-638, (1975).

[10] Davis, M.H.A. Linear Estimation and Stochastic Control, Chapman and Hall, London,(1977).

[11] Fleming, W.H. and Rishel, R.W. Deterministic and Stochastic Optimal Control, Springer-Verlag, Heidelberg, (1975).

[12] Gikhman, I.I. and Skorohod, A.V. Stochastic Differential Equations, Springer-Verlag, Heidelberg, (1972).

[13] Girsanov, I.V. "On Transforming a Certain Class of Stochastic Processes by Absolutely Continuous Substitution of Measures", Theory of Probability and its Applications, Vol.5, pp.285-301, (1960).

[14] Hirsch, M.W. and Smale, S. Differential Equation, Dynamical Systems, and Linear Algebra, Academic Press, New York and London, (1974).

[15] Jacod, J. "Multivariate Point Processes: Predictable Projection, Radon-Mikodym Derivatives, Representation of Martingales", Z. Mahrscheinlichkeits theorie und Verw. Gebiete, Vol. 31, pp. 235-253, (1975).

[16] Jazwinski, A.H. Stochastic Processes and Filtering Theory, Academic Press, New York, (1970).

[17] Kalman, R.E. "A New Approach to Linear Filtering and Production Problems", Trans. ASME, Ser. D.J. Basic Eng. Vol.82, pp.394-400, (1960).

[18] Luenberger, D.G. Optimization by Vector Space Methods, John Wiley and Sons Inc., New York and London, (1969).

[19] Rustem, B. and Velupillai, K., "Recursive Parameter Estimation Using the Kalman Filter, (in preparation).

EXACT FILTERING IN EXPONENTIAL FAMILIES: DISCRETE TIME

Günther Sawitzki
Institut für Mathematik
Ruhr-Universität
D-4630 Bochum

Abstract: For partially observable processes (ξ_t, η_t) with conditional distributions within fixed (parametrized) exponential families for all times t, the parameters of the a-posteriori distributions $_{\xi_t}P(\,|\eta_1,\ldots,\eta_t)\,(\omega)$ can be calculated by a recursive algorithm. A method to find the algorithm in this situation is given.

1. Let X, Y be topological spaces, endowed with the σ-algebra of Borel sets, Ω a measurable space, Θ a parameter set. Let $(\xi_t, \eta_t)\colon \Omega \to X \times Y$ be a stochastic process with observable part (η_t), $t \in \mathbb{N}$. Let $\mathcal{P} = \{P(\ ;\theta)\colon \theta \in \Theta\}$, $\mathcal{P}' = \{P'(\ ;\theta)\colon \theta \in \Theta\}$ be parametrized families of probability distributions on Ω, X respectively, such that $_{\xi_t}P(\,|\eta_1,\ldots,\eta_t)\,(\omega) \in \mathcal{P}'$ for all $t \in \mathbb{N}$, $\omega \in \Omega$, and each $P \in \mathcal{P}$.

2. By an <u>exact filter</u> in this context we mean an algorithm $\varphi_t\colon \Theta \times Y \to \Theta$, $t \in \mathbb{N}$, such that for all $P \in \mathcal{P}$

i) $P = P(\ ;\theta) \Rightarrow {}_{\xi_1}P(\,|\eta_1) = P'(\ ;\varphi_1(\theta,\eta_1))$

ii) $_{\xi_t}P(\,|\eta_1,\ldots,\eta_t) = P'(\ ;\theta')$

$$\Rightarrow {}_{\xi_{t+1}}P(\,|\eta_1,\ldots,\eta_{t+1}) = P'(\ ;\varphi_{t+1}(\theta',\eta_{t+1}))$$

As usual in the theory of exponential families, we use the word exact in opposition to approximate and asymptotic.

For example, in (dynamic) linear models the Kalman filter algorithm is an exact filter in the case of (conditionally) gaussian noise, whereas it is not an exact filter in general for non-gaussian noise.

3. We assume that the parameter set Θ is endowed with a σ-field, that all parametrizations define transition probabilities, and φ_t is measurable. We do not mention sets of measure zero, so all statements about conditional distribution are to be understood for choice of appropriate versions.

4. Then for each $\theta \in \Theta$, an exact filter defines a transitive system of statistics with respect to (η_t) by $\theta_0 := \theta$, $\theta_t := \varphi_t(\theta_{t-1},\eta_t)$ such that for all t:

$$_{\xi_t}P(\,|\eta^t) = P'(\ ;\theta_t)$$

where $P := P(\ ;\theta) \in \mathcal{P}$; $\eta^t := (\eta_1,\ldots,\eta_t)$.

We are interested in determining exact filters in families of probability distributions admitting a (natural) finite dimensional parametrization. By a result of Koopman [Koopman, 1936] under regularity conditions the most general situation here is that of exponential families, that is families of distributions with densities of the form

$$C(\theta)\cdot h(.)\ \exp \langle T(.),\theta\rangle$$

with respect to any dominating probability measure. Here T is a (multi-dimensional) statistic, θ a (multi-dimensional) parameter, $\langle T,\theta\rangle := \Sigma T_i \cdot \theta_i$.

Note that most of the standard families (for example gaussian, poisson, standard beta,...) are exponential families. For a recent account of the theory of exponential families see [Barndorff-Nielsen, 1978].

5. <u>Distribution assumption</u>: We assume that $\mathcal{P}'$ is an exponential family, and that the distributions $_{\eta_t}P(\ |\xi_t = x)$ of the observations too belong to an exponential family $\mathcal{P}''$; possibly $\mathcal{P}' \neq \mathcal{P}''$.

6. Taking any $P'_o \in \mathcal{P}'$, $P''_o \in \mathcal{P}''$ resp. as dominating measure we can assume the weight function h to be constant = 1. To fix notation, let $\mathcal{P}' = \{P'(\ ;\theta) : \theta \in \Theta\}$ with densities

$$\frac{dP'(\ ;\theta)}{dP'_o}(x) = C'(\theta)\ \exp \langle T'(x),\theta\rangle$$

and let $\mathcal{P}'' = \{P''(\ ;\lambda) : \lambda \in \Lambda\}$ with densities

$$\frac{dP''(\ ;\lambda)}{dP''_o}(y) = C''(\lambda)\ \exp \langle T''(y),\lambda\rangle.$$

We have to describe the class of models in which we want to give the filtering algorithm. We prefer to give this description directly on the level of parametrized families.

7. Corresponding to the (predicted) development of our system we have a measurable transformation

$$\alpha_t : \Theta \to \Theta$$

and corresponding to the observation we have some measurable transformation

$$\lambda_t : X \to \Lambda.$$

The interpretation of α_t, λ_t is formalized with the help of the global family $\mathcal{P}$ as:

i) $P = P(\ ;\theta) \in \mathcal{P} \Rightarrow {}_{\xi_1}P = P'(\ ;\alpha_1(\theta))$

ii) for each $P \in \mathcal{P}$: ${}_{\xi_t}P(\ |\eta^t) = P'(\ ;\theta')$
$\Rightarrow {}_{\xi_{t+1}}P(\ |\eta^t) = P'(\ ;\alpha_{t+1}(\theta'))$.

iii) for each $P \in \mathcal{P}$: ${}_{\eta_t}P(\ |\xi_t = .) = P''(\ ;\lambda_t(.))$.

8. Independence assumption: We assume that the system process (ξ_t) is markov with respect to each $P \in \mathcal{P}$, and that the observation is interaction free, that is η_t is independent of $\eta_{t'}, \xi_{t'}$ for $t' \neq t$ with respect to each $P(\ |\eta_t = x)$, $P \in \mathcal{P}$, $x \in X$. For example, dynamic linear models with independent gaussian noise can be formulated within this framework.

From the independence assumption (8.) we get by theorem 3 of [Grigelionis, 1969]:
9. Lemma: Let $P = P(\ ;\theta) \in \mathcal{P}$ and (θ_t) as in (4.). (θ_t) is a transitive system of statistics with respect to (η_t) and has the markov property.

In the frame of our model, we can calculate the density of the a-posteriori distribution by Bayes' formula and get:

10. If $\xi_t P(\ |\eta^t = .) = P'(\ ;\theta_t)$ then $\xi_{t+1}P(\ |\eta^{t+1} = y^{t+1})$ is dominated by P' for any $y^{t+1} \in Y^{t+1}$ and has density

$$\frac{d\xi_{t+1}P(\ |\eta^{t+1})}{dP'_o}(x) = \frac{1}{N(\eta_{t+1},\overline{\theta}_{t+1})} C''(\lambda_{t+1}(x))\exp<\lambda_{t+1}(x) \oplus T'(x), T''(\eta_{t+1}) \oplus \overline{\theta}_{t+1}>$$

where $\overline{\theta}_{t+1} = \alpha_{t+1} \circ \theta_t$,

$$N(\eta_{t+1},\theta_{t+1}) = \int C''(\lambda_{t+1}(x))\exp<\lambda_{t+1}(x) \oplus T'(x), T''(\eta_{t+1}) \oplus \theta_{t+1}> P'(dx)$$

and $(a_1,\dots,a_n)^\tau \oplus (b_1,\dots,b_m)^\tau := (a_1,\dots,a_n,b_1,\dots,b_m)^\tau$; $<c,d> := \Sigma c_i d_i$.
With (10.) we can calculate stepwise the parameters of the a-posteriori distribution, which by assumption is a distribution belonging to $\mathcal{P}'$. But (10.) gives us the parameters with respect to the mixed statistics $(\lambda_{t+1} \oplus T')$, whereas what we want is the parameters with respect to the representation we have previously chosen for $\mathcal{P}'$ in (6.). So we still have to find an appropriate transformation of parameters connecting these representations. This is given by:

11. Lemma: Let $\tilde{\mathcal{P}}$ be an exponential family with two representations corresponding to some dominating measure P_o

$$\Theta \ni \theta \longmapsto P'(\ ;\theta) \in \tilde{\mathcal{P}}$$

such that

$$\frac{dP'(\ ;\theta)}{dP}(x) = C((\theta) \exp <T'(x),\theta>$$

and

$$\tilde{\Theta} \ni \tilde{\theta} \longmapsto \tilde{P}(\ ;\tilde{\theta}) \in \tilde{\mathcal{P}}$$

such that

$$\frac{d\tilde{P}(\ ;\tilde{\theta})}{dP}(x) = \tilde{C}(\tilde{\theta})\tilde{h}(x) \exp <\tilde{T}(x),\tilde{\alpha}(\theta)>$$

with continuous statistics $\tilde{T}, T'; \tilde{h} > 0$.

Let $\theta \to P'(\ ;\theta)$ be 1-1 onto, $T' : X \to \mathbb{R}^k$ with $1, T'_1, \ldots, T'_k$ linearly independent. Then there is a matrix A and a vector B such that

$$P'(\ ;\theta) = \tilde{P}(\ ;\tilde{\theta}) \Rightarrow 0 = A \cdot \tilde{\alpha}(\tilde{\theta}) + B.$$

Proof: By independence it is possible to chose points $x_o, \ldots, x_k$ in the common support of $\tilde{\mathcal{P}}$, such that the vectors $T'(x_1)-T'(x_o), \ldots, T'(x_k)-T'(x_o)$ are linearly independent. Hence the matrix $A_1 := (T'(x_1)-T'(x_o), \ldots, T'(x_k)-T'(x_o))$ is invertible. Let $A_2 := (\tilde{T}(x_1)-\tilde{T}(x_o), \ldots, \tilde{T}(x_k)-T(x_o))$ and set $A := (A_2 \cdot A_1^{-1})^T$.
Since $\theta \mapsto P'(\ ;\theta)$ is assumed to be 1-1 onto, the transformation looked for must exist. By comparison of the representations, there are vectors B_1, B_2 solving the linear equation

$$-\ln \tilde{h}(x_o) + \ln \tilde{h}(x) = \langle \tilde{T}(x) - \tilde{T}(x_o), B_1 \rangle + \langle T'(x) - T'(x_o), B_2 \rangle$$

for all $x \in X$. Set $B := A \cdot B_1 + B_2$; by direct comparison,

$$\frac{d\tilde{P}(\ ;\tilde{\theta})}{dP_o} = \frac{dP'(\ ;A \cdot \tilde{\alpha}(\tilde{\theta}) + B)}{dP_o}$$

for all θ, so the lemma holds. □

Now we can state the final result as:

12. Filtering in exponential families: Let $\mathcal{P}, \mathcal{P}', \mathcal{P}''$ as in the model described above. Let $\theta \mapsto P'(\ ;\theta)$ be a minimal parametrization with continuous statistics T'. Let the transformations λ_t be continuous. Then there is an exact filter φ_t of the form

$$\varphi_t(\theta, y) = A_t \cdot (T''_t(y) \oplus \alpha_t(\theta)) + B_t$$

where A_t, B_t can be determined by the equations given in the proof of (11.).

Proof: By (10.), for each $t \in \mathbb{N}$, the family $\mathcal{P}_t := \{\xi_t P(\ |\eta^t = y^t) : P \in \mathcal{P}, y^t \in Y^t\}$ is an exponential family; by assumption of the model $\mathcal{P}_t \subset \mathcal{P}'$. By minimality of the representation $\theta \mapsto P'(\ ;\theta)$, the restriction to $\Theta_t := \{\theta \in \Theta : P'(\ ;\theta) \in \mathcal{P}_t\}$ satisfies the conditions of lemma (11.). Take as representation to be compared that resulting of (1o.), that is

$$\tilde{\Theta}_t := \{T''_t(y) \oplus \alpha_t(\theta) : y \in Y, \theta \in \Theta_{t-1}\}$$

and representation

$$\frac{d\tilde{P}(\ ;\tilde{\theta})}{dP'_o}(x) = \frac{1}{N(\tilde{\theta})} \cdot \tilde{h}(x) \exp \langle \lambda_t(x) \oplus T'(x), \tilde{\theta} \rangle$$

where $\tilde{h}(x) := C''(\lambda_t(x))$ and $N(\tilde{\theta}) = N(y, \alpha_t(\theta))$ for $\tilde{\theta} = T''(y) \oplus \alpha_t(\theta))$.
Note that N is well defined. By induction (11.) gives the corresponding matrices A_t and vectors B_t for each $t \in \mathbb{N}$. □

REFERENCES

Barndorff-Nielsen, O.: Information and exponential families in statistical theory. Wiley, New York 1978

Grigelionis, B.: Sufficiency in the optimal stopping problems. Lietovskii Matehm. Sbornik 9(1969) 471 - 480

Koopman, B.O.: On distributions admitting a sufficient statistic. Trans AMS 39(1936) 399 - 409

LOWER ESTIMATION ERROR BOUNDS FOR GAUSS-POISSON PROCESSES

Adrian Segall
Department of Electrical Engineering
Technion - Israel Institute of Technology
Haifa, Israel

ABSTRACT

The paper considers the problem of estimation of a signal modulating the rate of an observed jump process. Representation formulas for the least squares estimate have been obtained in previous works, but the exact solution requires solving an infinite set of stochastic differential equations, so that one has to work with suboptimal estimates. In order to investigate their performance compared with the optimal estimate, bounds for the performance of the latter are useful. In this paper we apply a general method developed by Bobrovsky - Zakai to obtain lower bounds for the estimation error when the observed process is of the Gauss-Poisson type.

1. INTRODUCTION

The general mathematical model considered in this paper is motivated by the following communications problem. Messages arrive at nodes of a data - communication network and, after being processed, leave them either to adjacent nodes or to users of the network. We assume that the flows of messages consist of two types, one of relatively short messages and the other of longer ones. Dynamics of the network and fluctuations in the input rates will cause that the average flows in the nodes will change according to a dynamic stochastic equation. If we assume that the dynamics is linear and the disturbing fluctuations are white and Gaussian, we can model the vector of all flows of messages in the network as being drawn from a linear dynamic equation driven by white Gaussian noise,

$$dx(t) = A(t)\, x(t)dt + d\xi(t)$$
$$f^c(t) = C(t)\, x(t) \qquad\qquad f^d(t) = H(t)\, x(t)$$

where the various vectors and matrices are of appropriate dimensions, and f^c and f^d are the vectors of average flows of short and long messages respectively. For further details about the above medel see [1, Sec. IV].

The amounts $y^c(t)$ of bits for example, provided by short messages stored in the nodes at time t, is modelled to be a stochastic process around the mean $f^c(t)$ such that

$$dy^c(t) = f^c(t)dt + dw(t)$$

This work was supported by the Advanced Research Projects Agency of the U.S. Department of Defense, under Contract N00014-75-C-1183.

where $w(t)$ is a zero mean Wiener process independent of $\xi(t)$. The amounts $Y(t)$ of bits contributed by long messages in the nodes are modelled as Poisson-Gauss processes as defined in [2], namely the arrival-departure process is assumed to be Poisson, possibly nonhomogeneous, and the sizes of jumps, given by the size of the message arriving or departing, are taken to be Gaussian with mean $H(t)\,x(t)$. If we look at the total number $y(t)$ of bits stored in each of the nodes at time t, then we obtain the model treated in [2] and for which estimation and control algorithms have been obtained in [2] - [5]. It has been shown that the optimal estimators and optimal centralized and certain decentralized controllers are finite-dimensional, and explicit recursive algorithms for these problems have been obtained. On the other hand in order to evaluate the performance of the optimal estimators and controllers, it is necessary to solve an infinite-dimensional dynamic equation, so that the best one can hope for is bounds on their performance. Using certain matrix manipulations, Rhodes and Snyder obtain in [6] upper and lower bounds for the performance of these algorithms.

In the present paper, we address the same problem of obtaining bounds on the estimation performance for Gauss-Poisson processes using a different technique. The lower bounds are obtained using a generalized Cramer - Rao bound developed in [7] and applied there to diffusion processes. Although the two methods are quite different in nature, the lower bound obtained here is identical to the one in [6].

2. THE MODEL AND THE ESTIMATION PROBLEM

We consider here the signal and observation models introduced in [6], [2]:

$$dx(t) = A(t)\,x(t)dt + d\xi(t) \qquad x(o) = x_o \tag{1}$$

$$dy(t) = C(t)x(t)dt + d\theta(t) + dY(t) \tag{2}$$

where $x(t) \in R^n$, $y(t) \in R^m$, the vector x_o is Gaussian with zero mean and covariance matrix π_o and the processes $\xi(t)$, $\theta(t)$ are independent Wiener processes with zero-mean and nonsingular covariance matrices

$$E[d\xi(t)d\xi'(t)] = \Xi(t)dt, \qquad E[d\theta(t)d\theta'(t)] = \Theta(t)dt \quad . \tag{3}$$

Conditioned on $x(\cdot)$, the process $Y(t)$ is a Gauss-Poisson process as defined in [2]. Briefly, a Gauss-Poisson process conditioned on $x(\cdot)$ is a jump process whose jumps occur according to a Poisson process $N(t)$ independent of $x(\cdot)$ and with rate $\Lambda(t)$ and whose jump sizes are Gaussian, independent of each other and independent of $N(\cdot)$, with mean $H(t)\,x(t)$ and covariance $\Sigma(t)$. Here $H(\cdot)$ and $\Sigma(\cdot)$ are given matrices of dimensions $(m\times n)$ and $(m\times m)$ respectively, and it is assumed that $\Sigma(t)$ is nonsingular for all t. In other words, if we denote

$$\mathcal{B}_t = \sigma\{x(s),\, y(s),\quad s \leq t\}\ , \tag{4}$$

then

$$\text{Prob}\{Y(t)-Y(t-)\in[r,r+dr]\,\big|\,Y(t) \neq Y(t-),\ \ \mathcal{B}_{t-}\} = \frac{\lambda(t,r,x(t))}{\Lambda(t)}\,dr+o(dr) \tag{5}$$

where

$$\lambda(t,r,x) = \Lambda(t)(2\pi)^{-m/2}[\det\Sigma(t)]^{-1/2}\exp\{-\tfrac{1}{2}[r-H(t)x]^T\Sigma^{-1}(t)[r-H(t)x]\} \tag{6}$$

For future reference we shall also need the following notation : let Γ be a Borel set in R^m, then let $p(\Gamma,t)$ = number of jumps of $Y(\cdot)$ of size in Γ that occured up to and including time t; then we have

$$N(t) = \int_{R^m} p(dr,t) \tag{7}$$

$$Y(t) = \int_o^t \int_{R^m} r\, p(dr,d\tau) \tag{8}$$

and it follows from [11], [13, eq. (75)] that the processes

$$q(\Gamma,t) = p(\Gamma,t) - \int_o^t \int_\Gamma \lambda(\tau,r,x(\tau))drd\tau \tag{9}$$

$$\int_o^t \int_{R^m} q(dr,d\tau) = N(t) - \int_o^t \int_{R^m} \lambda(\tau,r,x(\tau)drd\tau = N(t) - \int_o^t \Lambda(\tau)d\tau \tag{10}$$

$$\int_o^t \int_{R^m} rq(dr,d\tau) = Y(t) - \int_o^t \int_{R^m} r\lambda(\tau,r,x(\tau))drd\tau = Y(t) - \int_o^t \Lambda(\tau)H(\tau)x(\tau)d\tau \tag{11}$$

are all martingales with respect to $\mathcal{B}(\cdot)$.

Consider now the problem of estimating $x(t)$ from

$$\mathcal{F}_t = \sigma\{y(s), \quad s \leq t\} . \tag{12}$$

Then it has been shown in [2], [6] that the filtered estimate and the conditional covariance of $x(t)$ given $\mathcal{F}_t$ satisfy finite-dimensional recursive stochastic equations. On the other hand, the unconditional covariance

$$P(t) = E[x(t) - \hat{x}(t)][x(t) - \hat{x}(t)]^T \tag{13}$$

cannot be calculated because it requires the solution of an infinite-dimensional equation. It is of interest therefore to obtain bounds on P_t and this is the main purpose of this paper.

3. THE INFORMATION MATRIX AND LOWER BOUND

Let μ be the measure induced by $\{x(t), y(t), o \leq t \leq T\}$ of (1), (2). Let $\{\phi_i(t), i = 1,2,\ldots\}$ be an orthonormal set of functions on $[o,T]$ taking values in R^n possessing continuous derivatives $\dot{\phi}_i(t)$. For a given $\varepsilon > o$ and a given i, let $\mu_{i,\varepsilon}$ be the measure induced by $\{x'(t), y'(t), o \leq t \leq T\}$, where

$$x'(t) = x(t) + \varepsilon\phi_i(t)$$

$$y'(t) = y(t) \; ; \; Y'(t) = Y(t) \tag{14}$$

It follows from [8], [9] that $\mu_{i,\varepsilon}$ and μ are mutually absolutely continuous and it has been shown in [7] that the information matrix $J = \{J_{ij}, i,j=1,2,\ldots\}$ defined by

$$J_{i,j} = \lim_{\varepsilon \to o} E\left\{\frac{1}{\varepsilon^2}\left[1 - \frac{d\mu_{i,\varepsilon}}{d\mu}\right]\left[1 - \frac{d\mu_{j,\varepsilon}}{d\mu}\right]\right\} \tag{15}$$

plays an important role in developing lower estimation bounds. The following theorem gives an explicit expression for J.

Theorem 1

$$\begin{aligned} J_{i,j} = {} & \phi_i^T(o)\, \pi_o^{-1} \phi_j(o) + \int_o^T [\dot{\phi}_i(t) - A(t)\phi(t)]^T \Xi^{-1}(t)[\dot{\phi}_i(t) - A(t)\phi(t)]dt + \\ & + \int_o^T \phi_i^T(t) C^T(t)\, \Theta^{-1}(t) C(t)\phi_j(t)dt + \\ & + \int_o^T \phi_i^T(t) H^T(t) \sum^{-1}(t) H(t)\phi_j(t)\Lambda(t)dt \; . \end{aligned} \tag{16}$$

Proof

First consider the case when $x_o = 0$ and $\phi_i(o) = 0$ for all i. From (9) and (1), (2) we have

$$dx'(t) = \varepsilon\cdot\dot{\phi}_i(t)dt + A(t)x'(t)dt - \varepsilon A(t)\phi_i(t)dt + d\xi(t)$$

$$dy'(t) = C(t)x'(t)dt - \varepsilon C(t)\phi_i(t)dt + dY'(t) \tag{17}$$

and if we define

$$\mathcal{B}_t' = \sigma\{x'(s), y'(s), s \leq t\} \; , \tag{18}$$

then

$$\begin{aligned} & \text{Prob}\{Y'(t) - Y'(t-) \; \varepsilon[r,r+dr] \,|\, Y'(t) \neq Y'(t-), \mathcal{B}_{t-}'\} = \\ & = \frac{\lambda(t,r,x'(t) - \varepsilon\phi_i(t))}{\Lambda(t)} dr + o(dr) \end{aligned} \tag{19}$$

Let

$$M(t) = \begin{bmatrix} \Xi(t) & 0 \\ 0 & \Theta(t) \end{bmatrix} \; ;$$

$$a_i(t) = M^{-1}(t)\cdot \begin{bmatrix} \dot{\phi}_i(t) - A(t)\; \phi_i(t) - \\ - C(t)\; \phi_i(t) \end{bmatrix} \; ; \qquad \eta(t) = \begin{bmatrix} \xi(t) \\ \theta(t) \end{bmatrix} , \tag{20}$$

and observe from (6) that

$$\int_o^T \int_{R^m} \lambda(t,r,x(t))drdt = \int_o^T \int_{R^m} \lambda(t,r,x(t) - \varepsilon\phi_i(t))drdt = \int_o^T \Lambda(t)dt . \tag{21}$$

The Radon-Nykodim derivative $d\mu_{i,\varepsilon}/d\mu$ is given then by [10]

$$\frac{d\mu_{i,\varepsilon}}{d\mu} = \exp \{\int_o^T a_i^T(t)d\eta(t) - \frac{1}{2}\varepsilon^2 \int_o^T a_i^T(t)\, a_i(t)dt \quad + $$

$$+ \int_o^T \int_{R^m} \log \frac{\lambda(t,r,x(t) - \varepsilon\phi_i(t))}{\lambda(t,r,x(t))} \; p(dr,dt) \} \tag{22}$$

and substituting from (6) and using (7), we have

$$\frac{d\mu_{i,\varepsilon}}{d\mu} = \exp\{\varepsilon[\int_o^T a_i^T(t)d\eta(t) + \int_o^T \int_{R^m} [r-H(t)x(t)]^T \Sigma^{-1}(t)H(t)\phi_i(t)p(dr,dt)]$$

$$- \frac{1}{2}\varepsilon^2[\int_o^T a_i^T(t)a_i(t)dt + \int_o^T \phi_i^T(t)H(t)\Sigma^{-1}(t)H(t)\phi_i(t)N(dt)] \} \tag{23}$$

Taking limits as $\varepsilon \to o$, we have

$$\lim_{\varepsilon \to o} \frac{1}{\varepsilon} \left(\frac{d\mu_{i,\varepsilon}}{d\mu} - 1 \right) = \int_o^T a_i^T(t)d\eta(t) + \int_o^T \int_{R^m} [r-H(t)x(t)]^T \Sigma^{-1}(t)H(t)\phi_i(t)p(dr,dt) \tag{24}$$

Moreover, since the function of ε

$$f(\varepsilon) = \frac{1}{\varepsilon} \{1 - \exp[\varepsilon m - \frac{1}{2}\varepsilon^2 n] \} \tag{25}$$

is monotone, it follows by the monotone convergence theorem [12] that

$$J_{i,j} = E\{[\int_o^T a_i^T(t)d\eta(t) + \int_o^T \int_{R^m} [r - H(t)x(t)]^T \Sigma^{-1}(t)H(t)\phi_i(t)p(dr,dt)]$$

$$. [\int_o^T a_j^T(t)d\eta(t) + \int_o^T \int_{R^m} [r - H(t)x(t)]^T \Sigma^{-1}(t)H(t)\phi_j(t)p(dr,dt)] \tag{26}$$

Using (3) and (A.3), expression (26) becomes

$$J_{i,j} = \int_o^T a_i^T(t)M(t)a_j(t)dt + \int_o^T \int_{R^m} \phi_i^T(t)H^T(t)\Sigma^{-1}(t)[r - H(t)x(t)][r - H(t)x(t)]^T \cdot$$

$$\cdot \Sigma^{-1}(t)H(t)\phi_j(t)\lambda(r,t,x(t))drdt$$

$$= \int_o^T a_i^T(t)M(t)a_j(t)dt + \int_o^T \phi_i^T(t)H^T(t)\Sigma^{-1}(t)H(t)\phi_j(t)\Lambda(t)dt \tag{27}$$

This completes the proof of (16) except for the initial conditions, that are incorporated in the same way as in [7, theorem 4].

The estimation lower bound is given in

Theorem 2

Consider the linear system

$$dx_1(t) = A(t)x_1(t)dt + d\xi_1(t) \qquad x_1(o) = x_{10}$$

$$dy_1(t) = \begin{bmatrix} C(t) \\ H(t) \end{bmatrix} x_1(t)dt + \begin{bmatrix} d\theta_1(t) \\ d\sigma(t) \end{bmatrix} \tag{28}$$

where $x_1(t) \in R^n$, $y_1(t) \in R^{2m}$, the Gaussian vector x_{10} has the same statistics as x_o, the processes $\xi_1(t)$, $\theta_1(t)$, $\sigma(t)$ are independent zero-mean Wiener processes with covariances $\Xi(t)$, $\Theta(t)$, $\Lambda^{-1}(t) \cdot \sum(t)$ respectively.

Let $P(t)$ denote the error covariance matrix for estimating $x(t)$ from $\{y(s), s \leq t\}$. Let $P_1(t)$ denote the error covariance matrix for estimating $x_1(t)$ from $y_1(t)$, namely $P_1(t)$ satisfies

$$\dot{P}_1(t) = A(t)P_1(t) + P_1(t)A'(t) + \Xi(t) -$$

$$- P_1(t)[B'(t)\ \Theta^{-1}(t)B(t)+\Lambda(t)H'(t)\textstyle\sum^{-1}(t)H(t)]P_1(t) \tag{29}$$

$$P_1(o) = \pi_o$$

Then

$$P(t) \geq P_1(t) \quad \text{for all } t. \tag{30}$$

Proof

Observing that (16) and [7, eq. 19] have the same form, the result follows from [7, theorem 6].

Note Observe that (29) is identical to the lower bound for the same problem obtained in [6] by different methods.

Appendix

If $p(\cdot,\cdot)$ and $q(\cdot,\cdot)$ are defined as in Section 2, then from [13, eq.(75)] follows that

$$v(t) = \int_o^t \int_{R^m} g(\tau,r,x(\tau))\ q(dr,d\tau) \tag{A.1}$$

is a martingale with respect to $\mathcal{B}(\cdot)$ as defined in (4) for any function g. If v_1 and v_2 are defined as in (A.1) with integrands g_1, g_2 respectively, then their quadratic covariation is from [13, eq. (77)]

$$\langle v_1,v_2\rangle_t = \int_o^t \int_{R^m} g_1(\tau,r,x(\tau))g_2(\tau,r,x(\tau))\lambda(\tau,r,x(\tau))drd\tau \tag{A.2}$$

and

$$E\ v_1(t)v_2(t) = E\langle v_1,v_2\rangle_t \tag{A.3}$$

Conclusion

A simple lower bound for estimation of Gaussian signals modulating the rate of a Gauss-Poisson process has been developed. The same method can be used for estimation of more general jump processes as shown in [14] - [15].

REFERENCES

1. A. Segall, The modelling of adaptive routing in data-communication networks, IEEE Trans. on Comm, Vol. COM-25, No.1, Jan. 1977.
2. A. Segall, Centralized and decentralized control schemes for Gauss-Poisson processes, IEEE Trans. on Autom. Control. Vol. AC-23, No.1, Feb. 1978.
3. D.L. Snyder & P.M. Fishman, How to track a swarm of fireflies by observing their flashes, IEEE Trans. on Infor. Theory, Vol. IT-21, Nov. 1975.
4. D.L. Snyder, I.B. Rhodes and E.V. Hovesten, A separation theorem for stochastic control problems with point process observations, Automatica, Vol. 13, Jan. 1977.
5. M. Vaca and D.L. Snyder, A measure transformation approach to estimation and decision for observations derived from martingales, Wash. Univ. School of Medicine, Mono. 271, May 1975.
6. I.B. Rhodes and D.L. Snyder, Estimation and control performance for space - time point process observations, IEEE Trans. Autom. Control. Vol. AC-22, No. 3, June 1977.
7. B.Z. Bobrovsky & M. Zakai, A lower bound on the estimation error for certain diffusion processes, IEEE Trans. Infor. Thry. Vol. IT-22, No. 1, Jan. 1976.
8. A.V. Skorokhod, Random processes with independent increments, DDC Report AD645769, Aug. 1966.
9. A.V. Skorokhod, On the differentiability of measures corresponding to random processes, II Markov processes, Theory Prob. Appl. (USSR), Vol. V, No.1, 1960(sec.4).
10. A. Segall & T. Kailath, Radon-Nikodym derivatives with respect to measures induced by discontinuous independent increment processes, Ann. of Prob., Vol. 3, No.3, June 1975.
11. A. Segall & T. Kailath, The modelling of randomly modulated jump processes, IEEE Trans. on Infor. Thry, Vol. IT-21, No.2, March 1975.
12. K.L. Chung, A course in probability theory, Harcourt, Brace & World, 1968.
13. A. Segall, Stochastic processes in estimation theory, IEEE Trans. Infor. Thry. Vol. IT-22, No. 3, May 1976.
14. A. Segall & T. Kailath, Martingales in nonlinear least-squares estimation theory, in E. Stear, Advances in Nonlinear Estimation, to appear.
15. A. Segall, On estimation error bounds for jump prcesses, in preparation.

SUR L'APPROXIMATION D'UN PROCESSUS DE TRANSPORT PAR UNE DIFFUSION

Rémis Sentis

Ceremade. Université Paris IX-Dauphine (75775 Paris Cédex 16)

et IRIA-Laboria

Abstract: We generalize the result of [2] on convergence of transport process to diffusion, to the case where the velocity is not bounded. And we give assumptions which imply that this diffusion is not degenerated.

1. INTRODUCTION

Nous étudions tout d'abord dans le §2, la solution u de l'équation de Poisson

$$Qu + f = 0$$

où Q est le générateur infinitésimal du processus Y_t qui sera la partie-vitesse du processus de transport, et f une fonction à croissance au plus linéaire (afin de l'appliquer au cas où f est linéaire). Considérons donc un processus stochastiquement continu Y_t sur un borelien S de $\mathbb{R}^N$ muni d'un mesure de probabilité r telle que:

$$(H_0) \qquad \int_S |y|^2 \; r(dy) < +\infty$$

En notant $\rho(t,y,A)[t \geq 0, y \in S, A \subset S]$ la fonction de transition de Y_t, faisons les hypothèses suivantes

$$(H_1) \qquad \begin{cases} \text{Il existe } \gamma > 0 \text{ et } \tau > 0 \text{ tels que:} \\ \rho(\tau,y,A) \geq \gamma r(A) \qquad \forall y \in S \quad \forall A \text{ borelien de } S. \end{cases}$$

$$(H_2) \qquad \int_S |z|^2 \rho(t,y,dz) = E_y |Y_t|^2 \leq D_0^2 + |y|^2 \qquad \forall t \quad (D_0 \text{ est une constante})$$

Nous donnons ci-dessous des exemples de processus vérifiant ces hypothèses. Notons T_t le semi-groupe d'opérateur (qui agit sur l'ensemble $\mathcal{B}$ où $\mathcal{B} = L^\infty(S,\mathbb{R})$) et Q le générateur infinitésimal de T_t (de domaine $\mathcal{D}$) associés à ce processus de Markov Y_t. Notons $\mathcal{B}_1$ l'ensemble des fonctions f de S dans $\mathbb{R}$ telles que:

$$\exists c \qquad f(y) \leq C + C|y| \qquad \forall y \in S \quad .$$

et $\mathcal{D}_1$ l'ensemble des fonctions f de $\mathcal{B}_1$ telles que:

$\lim\limits_{t\to 0} \frac{1}{t} [T_t f(y) - f(y)]$ existe et est une fonction de y qui est dans $\mathcal{B}_1$.

Si S est borné, (H_0) et (H_2) sont vérifiés et $\mathcal{B}_1 = \mathcal{B}$, $\mathcal{D}_1 = \mathcal{D}$.

Proposition 1 i) *Le processus* Y_t *admet une probabilité invariante* $\overline{P}$.

ii) *Si* $f \in \mathcal{B}_1$, *alors* $T_t f \in \mathcal{B}_1$ $\forall t$

iii) *Soit* $f \in \mathcal{B}_1$, *f continue, pour qu'il existe dans* $\mathcal{D}_1$, *une solution u de:*

$$\text{(1.1)} \qquad Qu + f = 0$$

il faut et il suffit que:

$$\text{(1.2)} \qquad \overline{P}(f) = 0$$

Et la solution u est donnée (à une constante additive près) par

$$\text{(1.3)} \qquad u(y) = \int_0^{+\infty} T_t f(y)\, dt$$

iv) *Il existe* λ *une constante strictement positive ne dépendant que de* γ *et* τ, *telle que pour tout f vérifiant (1.2) et u donné par (1.3), on a:*

(1.4) $$\int_S f(y)u(y)\overline{P}(dy) = \overline{P}(f\cdot\int_0^{+\infty} T_t f dt) \geq \lambda \operatorname{Min}\{\overline{P}(f^2), \frac{[\overline{P}(f^2)]^2}{\overline{P}(|Qf|^2)}\}$$

Nous considérons ensuite un processus de transport $(X_t^\varepsilon, Y_t^\varepsilon)$ sur $\mathbb{R}^N \times S$, qui dépend d'un paramêtre ε et qui est défini comme un processus de Markov de générateur infinitésimal:

(1.5) $$g = g(x,y) \mapsto \frac{1}{\varepsilon}\frac{\partial g}{\partial x} + \frac{1}{\varepsilon^2} Q_x g$$

où Q_x est, pour tout x fixé, le générateur infinitésimal d'un processus de Markov sur S, dont la fonction de transition $\rho_x(t,y,A)$ vérifie H_1 et H_2 (avec $\mathcal{D}$, τ, γ indépendant de x).

Notons $\overline{P}_x$ la probabilité invariante associée à ρ_x.

Supposons que les hypothèses suivantes soient vérifiées:

(H_3) $\forall f \in \mathcal{D}$; l'application de $\mathbb{R}^N$ dans $\mathcal{B}$: $x \mapsto Q_x f$ est très régulière.

(H_4) $\int_S y_i \overline{P}_x(dy) = 0 \qquad \forall i = 1,2,\dots,N \qquad \forall x \in \mathbb{R}^N$

Quand nous disons qu'une fonction est régulière cela signifie qu'elle est bornée et que toutes ses dérivées existent et sont bornées. Enonçons maintenant le résultat principal dont la démonstration est donnée au §3.

Théorème <u>i) Il existe une matrice $(a_{ij}(x))_{i,j=1,\dots N}$ définie non négative dépendant de x de façon régulière telle que, si g est une fonction régulière de $\mathbb{R}^N$ dans $\mathbb{R}$ et v^ε la solution de:</u>

(1.6) $$\begin{cases} \dfrac{dv^\varepsilon}{dt} = \dfrac{1}{\varepsilon}\, y \cdot \dfrac{\partial v^\varepsilon}{\partial x} + \dfrac{1}{\varepsilon^2} Q_x v^\varepsilon & (t,x,y) \in \mathbb{R}^+ \times \mathbb{R}^N \times S \\ v^\varepsilon(0,x,y) = g(x) \end{cases}$$

<u>Alors $v^{\varepsilon}(t,x,y) \to v(t,x)$ uniformement quand $\varepsilon \to 0$, où v est la solution de:</u>

$$(1.7)\quad \begin{cases} \dfrac{\partial v}{\partial t} = a_{ij} \dfrac{\partial^2 v}{\partial x_i \partial x_j} + b_i \dfrac{\partial v}{\partial x_i} & (t,x) \in R^+ \times R^N \\ v(0,x) \quad g(x) \end{cases}$$

ii) <u>De plus la matrice</u> $a_{ij}(x)$ <u>est uniformement strictement définie positive si on a:</u>

$$(H_5)\quad \begin{cases} \text{Il existe } \beta_0 \ (\beta_0 > 0) \text{ tel que} \\ \sum_{ij} [\int_S y_i y_j \overline{P}_x(dy)] \zeta_i \zeta_j \geq \beta_0 |\zeta|^2 \qquad \forall \zeta \in \mathbb{R}^N \end{cases}$$

Nous donnons le shéma de la démonstration dans le §3, celle-ci étant semblable à celle de [2].

<u>Corollaire</u> Le processus X_t^{ε} converge faiblement vers la diffusion X_t associée à (1.7).

La démonstration est semblable à celle donnée dans [2]. Voir [5] pour une application de ce résultat à un problème où se mêlent une approximation du type précédent et une homogénisation en x.

Donnons maintenant des exemples de processus vérifiant les hypothèses H_1 et H_2.

Notons $h(y) = |y|^2$.

<u>Exemple 1.</u> <u>Processus de saut pur.</u>

Soit S un fermé de $\mathbb{R}^N$ et r une mesure sur S tel que $\int_S |y|^2 r(dy < \infty)$. On considére le processus de saut Y_t défini par son intensité des temps de saut q et sa mesure de saut π vérifiant:

$$0 < q_0 \leq q(y) \leq q_1 \qquad \forall y$$

$$\pi(y,dz) = g(y,z) r(dz)$$

$$0 < g_0 \leq g(y,z) \leq g_1 \qquad \forall y \forall z$$

L'opérateur Q est alors:

$$Qf(y) = q(y)(\int f(z)\pi(y,dz) - f(y))$$

L'hypothèse H_1 est vérifiée car on a pour tout τ:

$$\rho(\tau,y,A) = e^{-q(y)\tau}\chi_A(y) + \int_0^s \int_S \pi(y,dz)P(\tau-\sigma,z,A)q(y)e^{-q(y)\sigma}d\sigma$$

$$\geq \int_0^s \int_S \pi(y,dz)e^{-q(z)(\sigma-\tau)}\chi_A(z)q(y)e^{-q(y)\sigma}d\sigma$$

$$\geq g_0 q_0 \tau e^{-q_1\tau} r(A)$$

Pour vérifier H_2, remarquons que le semi groupe T_t peut être défini de la façon suivante. Définissons les opérateurs:

$$T_t^{(0)} f(y) = e^{-q(y)t} f \qquad \forall f \in \mathcal{B}_1$$

$$T_t^{(n+1)} f(y) = \int_0^t \int_S q(y)e^{-q(y)(t-s)} T_s^{(n)} f(z)g(y,z)r(dz)ds(\forall f \in \ {}_1)$$

Alors: $T_t f = \sum_{n=0}^{\infty} T_t^{(n)} f$.

On vérifie successivement que (en posant $H = T_\sigma h$ où $0 < \sigma \leq s$):

$$|T_t^{(n)} f| \leq \frac{t^n}{n!} (q_1 g_1)^n e^{-q_0 t} r(|f|) + e^{-q_0 t}|f| \qquad \forall f \in \mathcal{B}_1$$

$$|T_t f| \leq e^{+(q_1 g_1 - q_0)t} r(|f|) + e^{-q_0 t}|f| \qquad \forall f \in \mathcal{B}_1$$

$$|T_{ns} H| \leq e^{(q_1 g_1 - q_0)s} \frac{1}{1-e^{-q_0 s}} r(h) + h \qquad \forall n \qquad \text{D'où } (H_2) .$$

Ici on a: $\mathcal{D}_1 = \mathcal{B}_1$.

Exemple 2 Diffusion sur le tore. Voir Bensoussan-Lions-Papanicolaou [1, Chap. III, §3.2].

§2 ETUDE DE L'ÉQUATION DE POISSON

Notations Soit $|\cdot|$ la norme de $\mathcal{B} = \mathcal{L}^\infty(S,\mathbb{R})$.

Soit (Z_n) une chaine de Markov sur S dont la fonction de transition est notée $p = p(y,A)$; $y \in S$, A borelien de S. Notons $p^{(k)}(y,A)$ la k-ième itérée de p. Notons également par p l'opérateur sur $\mathcal{B}$ défini par:

$$pf(y) = \int_S f(z)p(y,dz)$$

On a:

$$p^k f(y) = \int_S f(z)p^{(k)}(y,dz)$$

Rappelons la propriété de Doeblin (voir Doob [3, p. 197]):

Proposition 2 S'il existe un entier ℓ et une constante $\gamma (\gamma>0)$ tels que

(2.1) $$p^{(\ell)}(y,A) \geq \gamma r(A) \qquad \forall A \text{ borelien de } S$$

Alors la chaine de Markov Z_n admet une probabilité invariante $\overline{P}$ et on a:

(2.2) $$|p^{(k)}(y,A) - \overline{P}(A)| \leq (1-\gamma)^{(k/\ell)-1} \qquad \forall A \text{ borelien de } S$$

La proposition suivante en est une conséquence.

Proposition 3 Supposons que p vérifie (2.1).

i> Si $f \in \mathcal{B}$ on a:

(2.3) $$|p^k f - \overline{P}(f)|_0 \leq \frac{2}{1-\gamma}(1-\gamma)^{k/\ell}|f|_0$$

Si $f \in \mathcal{B}$ et $\overline{P}(f) = 0$ alors

(2.4) $$\sum_{k=0}^{\infty} p^i f \in \mathcal{B}$$

ii> Si $f \in \mathcal{B}$ et $\overline{P}(f) = 0$ alors

(2.5) $$\overline{P}(f \cdot \sum_{k=0}^{\infty} p^k f) \geq \frac{1}{2} \overline{P}(f^2)$$

Démonstration

i) Pour vérifier (2.3) il suffit de séparer les parties positives et négatives de la mesure $p^{(k)}(y,\cdot) - \overline{P}$.

ii) Comme $\overline{P}$ est probabilité invariante pour la chaine de Markov Z_n, on a

$$\overline{P}(p^i v \cdot p^{k+1} w) = \overline{P}(v \cdot p^k w) \qquad \forall v,w \in \mathcal{B} \quad .$$

Si $\overline{E}$ désigne l'espérance sachant que Z_0 est distribué selon $\overline{P}$, on vérifie que

$$\tfrac{1}{2}\overline{P}(f^2) + \sum_{k=1}^{\infty} \overline{P}(f \cdot p^k f) = \tfrac{1}{2} \lim_{n\to\infty} \overline{E}\{[\frac{1}{\sqrt{n}} \sum_{k=0}^{n-1} f(Z_k)]^2\} < +\infty$$

Comme le second membre est positif, le premier l'est aussi, d'où (2.5). C.Q.F.D.

Avant d'énoncer la proposition 4 qui sera l'analogue pour les chaines de Markov de la proposition 1, remarquons que si p vérifie (2.1) et:

(2.7) $$p^k h(y) \leq D_0^2 + |y|^2 \qquad \forall k \in \mathbb{N} \qquad \forall y \in S$$

où h est la fonction $h(y) = y^2$, alors on a:

(2.8) $$\overline{P}(h) \leq D_0^2$$

Et donc si f et g sont dans $\mathcal{B}_1$, $\overline{P}(f\cdot g)$ est borné.

Proposition 4 Supposons que p vérifie (2.1) et (2.7). Soit f appartenant à $\mathcal{B}_1$ et vérifiant $|f(y)| < C_1 + C|y|$. Alors on a :

i) $p^k f \in \mathcal{B}_1$ et $|p^k f(y)| \leq C_1 + CD_0 + C|y|$

ii) $|p^k f(y) - \overline{P}(f)| \leq \frac{2}{1-\gamma}(1-\gamma)^{k/2\ell}[C_1 + CD_0 + \overline{P}(f^2)^{\frac{1}{2}} + C|y|]$.

iii) Si de plus $\overline{P}(f) = 0$ on voit que $\sum_{k=0}^{\infty} p^k f \in \mathcal{B}_1$ et

$$\overline{P}(f \cdot \sum_{k=0}^{\infty} p^k f) \geq \tfrac{1}{2}\,\overline{P}(f^2)$$

Démonstration

Posons $f_n(y) = \mathrm{Inf}[n, \mathrm{Sup}(-n, f(y))]$.

i) Comme $|f_n|$ croit vers $|f|$, on peut vérifier que:

$$(2.12) \qquad p^k f^2 \leq \sup_n p^k f_n^2 \leq C_1^2 + 2CC_1(D_0 + h^{\frac{1}{2}}) + C^2 D_0^2 + C^2 h \leq (C_1 + CD_0 + Ch^{\frac{1}{2}})^2$$

Comme on a $|p^k f| \leq [p^k f^2]^{\frac{1}{2}}$, le résultat en découle.

ii) Pour k et y donné notons M_+ et M_- les supports des parties positives et négatives de la mesure $p_y^k - \overline{P}$ [on écrit p_y^k au lieu de $p^{(k)}(y,\cdot)$]. On a:

$$(2.13) \qquad |\int_{M_+} f(p_y^k - \overline{P})| \leq [(p_y^k - P)(M_+)]^{\frac{1}{2}} \cdot [\int_{M_+} f(p_y^k - P)]^{\frac{1}{2}} \leq \frac{(1-\gamma)^{k/2\ell}}{1-\gamma}[p^k f^2(y) + P(f^2)]^{\frac{1}{2}}$$

Donc en faisant de même pour M_- on obtient une majoration de $|p^k f - \overline{P}(f)|$ qui donne le résultat grâce à (2.12).

iii) Il suffit d'appliquer (2.5) aux fonctions f_n et de remarquer que $\overline{P}(f_n \sum_{k=0}^{\infty} p^k f_n^2)$ et $\overline{P}(f_n)$ sont majorés par des constantes indépendantes de n.

C.Q.F.D.

Démonstration de la proposition 1

Fixons un entier ℓ que l'on déterminera par la suite, et posons:

(2.14) $p(y,A) = \rho(\tau/\ell,y,A)$ $\forall y \in S$, $\forall A$ borelien de S

Alors p est la probabilité de transition d'une chaine de Markov Z_n qui vérifie (2.1)(où γ est le même que dans H_1) et (2.7). Et on a:

(2.15) $$p^k f = T_{\tau k/\ell} f \qquad \forall f \in \mathcal{B} .$$

i) Donc la chaine Z_n admet une probabilité invariante $\overline{P}$, et

(2.16) $$\overline{P}(T_{\tau k/\ell} f) = \overline{P}(f) \qquad \forall f \in \mathcal{B}, \quad \forall k \in \mathbb{N}$$

La chaine de Markov dont la fonction de transition est $\tilde{p}(y,A) = \rho(\frac{t}{m},y,A)$ vérifie (2.1) et admet une probabilité invariante $\overline{P}_m$. Donc on a:

$$\overline{P}_m(T_{\tau j/m} f) = \overline{P}_m(f) \qquad \forall f \in \mathcal{B} \quad \forall j \in \mathbb{N}$$

Donc on voit que $\overline{P}_m = \overline{P}$. D'où le résultat car on a:

(2.17) $$\overline{P}(T_t f) = \overline{P}(f) \qquad \forall f \in \mathcal{B}$$

pour t tel que t/τ est rationnel et donc, par continuité, pour tout t.

ii) D'après la prop. 4-i), si $f \in \mathcal{B}_1$ on sait $T_t f \in \mathcal{B}_1$ pour t tel que t/τ est rationnel, donc aussi pour tout t. Et d'après (2.17), on a:

$$\overline{P}(T_t f_n) = \overline{P}(f_n)$$

On vérifie que l'on peut passer à la limite en n et on obtient:

(2.18) $$\overline{P}(T_t f) = \overline{P}(f) \qquad \forall f \in \mathcal{B}_1 \qquad \forall t \in \mathbb{R}^+$$

iii) Supposons qu'il existe u solution de (1.1). On a alors

$$\lim_{t\to 0} \frac{1}{t}[T_t f(y) - f(y)] = -f(y)$$

Donc d'après (2.18) on a nécessairement $\overline{P}(f) = 0$.

Supposons maintenant que $P(f) = 0$ et que $f(y) \leq C_1 + C|y|$, alors d'après la prop. 4-ii), en posant $\eta = (1-\gamma)^{\frac{1}{2}}$ on a:

$$|T_t f(y)| \leq \frac{2}{1-\gamma} \eta^t [C_1 + CD_0 + \overline{P}(f^2)^{\frac{1}{2}} + C|y|]$$

pour t tel que $t/\tau \in Q$, donc aussi pour tout t. Et $u = \int_0^{+\infty} T_t f \, dt$ est une fonction de ${}_1$. Or on a:

$$\frac{1}{s}[T_s u(y) - u(y)] = \frac{1}{s} \int_s^{+\infty} T_t f(y)\, dt - \int_0^{\infty} T_t f(y)\, dt = -\frac{1}{s} \int_0^{s} T_t f(y)\, dt$$

Comme f est continue et que Y_t est stochastiquement continue on sait (DINKIN [4, p. 54]) que $T_t f(y) \to f(y)$ $\forall y$ quand $t \to 0$. Donc si on fait tendre s vers 0 on obtient:

$$Qu = -f$$

iv) Reprenons p défini par (2.14). Comme Y_t admet une probabilité invariante $\overline{P}$, on peut définir Y_t pour t négatif de telle sorte que le processus de Markov $(Y_t)_{t\in\mathbb{R}}$ sera stationnaire. Donc pour tout t réel on aura:

$$\text{(2.22)} \qquad P(f \cdot T_t g) = \overline{P}(T_{-t} f \quad g) \qquad \forall f,g \in \mathcal{B}$$

Notons $\overline{E}$ l'espérance sous la probabilité correspondant au processus Y_t avec Y_0 distribué selon $\overline{P}$. Posons:

$$\alpha = \overline{E}\int_0^{+\infty} f(Y_0)f(Y_t)\,dt = \overline{P}(f\cdot\int_0^{+\infty} T_t f\,dt) = \tfrac{1}{2}\overline{P}(f\cdot\int_{-\infty}^{+\infty} T_t f\,dt)$$

Posons: $s = \tau/\ell$ (ℓ étant défini en 2.14).

(2.23) $$\phi = \int_0^s T_{-t} f\,dt \qquad \phi_1 = \int_0^s T_t f\,dt$$

(2.24) $$\psi = \frac{1}{s^2}(\phi - sf) \qquad \psi_1 = \frac{1}{s^2}(\phi_1 - sf) \quad \Rightarrow \quad \phi = sf + s^2\psi$$

Comme $Qf \in \mathcal{B}_1$ on vérifie (grâce à (2.12)) qu'il existe une fonction G_f de $\mathcal{B}_1$ telle que: $T_t|Qf|^2 \leq (G_f)^2 \quad \forall t$

puis on vérifie que:

(2.25) $$|\psi(y)| \leq \frac{1}{s^2}\int_0^s\int_0^t T_\sigma |Qf|(y)\,d\sigma\,dt \leq \tfrac{1}{2}G_f(y)$$

En utilisant (2.22) et (2.23) puis (2.24) on obtient:

$$2\alpha = \overline{P}(\phi.\sum_{k=0}^{\infty} T_{ks} f) + \overline{P}(f.\sum_{k=0}^{\infty} T_{ks}\,\phi)$$

$$= s\,[\overline{P}(f\sum_{k=0}^{\infty} p^k f) + \overline{P}(\frac{\phi}{s}\sum_k p^k \frac{\phi}{s})] - s^3\,\overline{P}(\psi\sum_k p^k\psi) + s^2\,\overline{P}(f(\sum_{k=0}^{\infty} p^k\psi_1 - p^k\psi))$$

Or, d'après la proposition 4-iii), on a:

$$\overline{P}(f\cdot\sum_{k=0}^{\infty} p^k f) \geq \tfrac{1}{2}\overline{P}(f^2)$$

$$\overline{P}(\frac{\phi}{s}\cdot\sum_{k=0}^{\infty} p^k \frac{\phi}{s}) \geq \tfrac{1}{2}\overline{P}(\frac{\phi^2}{s^2}) \geq \tfrac{1}{2}\overline{P}(f^2) - s\overline{P}(|f|\cdot G_f)$$

Or d'après (2.18) on a $\overline{P}(\psi) = 0$, et en utilisant (2.13) puis (2.25) on a:

$$\overline{P}(\psi \cdot \sum_{k=0}^{\infty} p^k \psi) \leq \frac{2}{1-\gamma} \sum_{k=0}^{\infty} (1-\gamma)^{\frac{k}{2\ell}} \overline{P}(|\psi| \cdot [(p^k \psi^2)^{\frac{1}{2}} + (\overline{P}\psi^2)^{\frac{1}{2}}])$$

$$\leq \frac{1}{1-\gamma} \frac{4\ell}{\gamma} \quad \overline{P}(G_f^2) \qquad (\text{car } 1-e^{-\gamma/2\ell} \geq \frac{\gamma}{4\ell})$$

Comme $p^{k+1}\psi = p^k \psi$, on a : $\overline{P}(f \sum_k p^k \psi_1 - p^k \psi) = - \overline{P}(f\psi) \geq - \frac{1}{2} \overline{P}(|f| G_f)$

Et on obtient:

$$2\alpha \geq \frac{\tau}{\ell} \overline{P}(f^2) - \frac{1}{2}(\frac{\tau}{\ell})^2 [\overline{P}(f^2) + \lambda_0 \overline{P}(G_f^2)] \qquad \text{avec } \lambda_0 = 1 + \frac{8\tau}{\gamma(1-\gamma)}$$

$$\geq \frac{1}{2} \frac{\tau}{\ell} \overline{P}(f^2) \geq 4\lambda \frac{\overline{P}(f^2)^2}{\overline{P}(f^2) + \overline{P}(G_f^2)} \qquad \text{avec} \quad \lambda = \frac{\tau}{8(\lambda_0 + 1)}$$

sachant que l'on a choisit ℓ tel que:

$$\lambda_0 \quad [1 + \frac{\overline{P}(G_f^2)}{\overline{P}(f^2)}] \leq \frac{\ell}{\tau} \leq (\lambda_0 + \frac{1}{\tau})[1 + \frac{\overline{P}(G_f^2)}{\overline{P}(f^2)}]$$

D'où le résultat car d'après (2.18) on a: $\overline{P}(G_f^2) = \overline{P}(|Qf|^2)$.

C.Q.F.D.

§3 SCHÉMA DE LA DÉMONSTRATION DU THÉORÈME

Notons: H_i la fonction: $H_i(y) = y_i$

T_t^x le semi groupe associé au processus de générateur infinitésimal Q_x

On utilise la convention de sommation ($x_i y_i = \sum_i x_i y_i$).

i) Faisons le développement suivant de v^ε:

(3.1) $$v^\varepsilon = v + \varepsilon v_1 + \varepsilon^2 v_2 + u^\varepsilon$$

Si on reporte dans (1.6), il vient (avec $f_\varepsilon = \frac{\partial v_1}{\partial t} + \varepsilon \frac{\partial v_2}{\partial t} + y \frac{\partial v_2}{\partial x}$):

(3.2) $$\frac{du^\varepsilon}{dt} - \frac{y}{\varepsilon}\frac{\partial u^\varepsilon}{\partial x} - \frac{1}{\varepsilon^2} Q_x u^\varepsilon = -\frac{dv}{dt} + \frac{1}{\varepsilon} y \frac{\partial v}{\partial x} + \frac{1}{\varepsilon^2} Q_x v + y \frac{\partial v_1}{\partial x}$$

$$+ \frac{1}{\varepsilon} Q_x v_1 + Q_x v_2 + \varepsilon f_\varepsilon$$

Cherchons donc v indépendant de y (donc $Q_x v = 0$), v_1 et v_2 tels que

(3.3) $$Q_x v_1 + y_i \frac{\partial v}{\partial x_i} = 0$$

(3.4) $$\frac{dv}{dt} = y_i \frac{\partial v}{\partial x_i} + Q_x v_2$$

(3.5) $$v_1(0,x,y) = v_2(0,x,y) = 0$$

Comme $\bar{P}_x(y)\frac{\partial v}{\partial x} = 0$, d'après la proposition 1, l'équation (3.3) donne

$$v_1 = u_i \frac{\partial v}{\partial x_i} + \lambda(t) \qquad \text{où} \qquad u_i(x,y) = \int_0^{+\infty} T_\theta^x H_i(y)\,d\theta$$

λ indépendant de y.

Et pour qu'il existe v_2 solution de (3.4) il faut et il suffit que

(3.6) $$\frac{\partial v}{\partial t} = \bar{P}_x[H_i \frac{\partial}{\partial x_i}(u_j \frac{\partial v}{\partial x_j})] = a_{ij} \frac{\partial^2 v}{\partial x_i \partial x_j} + b_i \frac{\partial v}{\partial x_i}$$

(3.7) avec $$a_{ij} = \bar{P}_x(H_i . \int_0^{+\infty} T_s^x H_j ds) \qquad b_i = \bar{P}_x(H_j \frac{\partial}{\partial x_j}\int_0^{+\infty} T_s^x H_i ds)$$

On vérifie que les a_{ij} sont très réguliers et que la matrice a_{ij} est définie non négative, donc il existe une solution très régulière v de (3.6) avec la condition initiale $v(0,x) = g(x)$. Alors on peut trouver v_1 et v_2 très régulière et vérifiant (3.3),(3.4) et (3.5). Donc u^ε vérifie:

$$\frac{du^\varepsilon}{dt} = \frac{y}{\varepsilon}\frac{\partial u^\varepsilon}{\partial x} + \frac{1}{\varepsilon^2} Q_x u^\varepsilon + \varepsilon f_\varepsilon$$

$$u^\varepsilon(0,x,y) = 0$$

Donc on a: $u^{\varepsilon}(t,x,y) \to 0$ $\forall t,x,y$ quand $\varepsilon \to 0$.

ii) Pour tout ζ de $\mathbb{R}^N$, posons: $g_\zeta = \zeta_i H_i$. D'après (3.7), on a:

$$a_{ij}(x)\zeta_i\zeta_j = \overline{P}_x[g_\zeta \cdot \int_0^{+\infty} T_t^x g_\zeta dt]$$

Or d'après (H_5) on a: $\overline{P}(g_\zeta^2) \geq \beta_0 |\zeta|^2$.

Donc d'après la prop. 1-iv) on a:

$$a_{ij}(x)\zeta_i\zeta_j \geq |\zeta|^2 \lambda \operatorname{Min}[\beta_0, \frac{\beta_0^2}{\sum_i (Q_x H_i)^2}]$$

C.Q.F.D.

REFERENCES

[1] A. BENSOUSSAN-J.L. LIONS- G. PAPANICOLAOU. Asymptotic Analysis for Periodic Structures, Dunod, Paris, 1978.

[2] G. BLANKENSHIP-G. PAPANICOLAOU. Stability and control for stochastic systems with wide band noise disturbance, I. SIAM J. Appl. Math. 34 (1978), pp. 437-476.

[3] J.L. DOOB. Stochastic processes, J. Wiley, New York. 1953.

[4] E.B. DYNKIN. Markov processes, Springer, Berlin, 1965.

[5] R. SENTIS. Approximation and Homogenization of a Transport Process, to appear.

RESOLUTION OF MEASURABILITY PROBLEMS IN DISCRETE - TIME STOCHASTIC CONTROL

by

Steven E. Shreve
Department of Mathematical Sciences
University of Delaware
Newark, Delaware

December, 1978

ABSTRACT

The formulation of dynamic programming as given by Bellman did not address measurability difficulties. Blackwell later initiated a study of these problems in Polish spaces, and Blackwell, Freedman and Orkin subsequently showed that by relaxing Borel measurability requirements on policies, some known heuristic results could be rigorously obtained. This paper presents three types of measurability restrictions on policies which allow rigorous proofs of all the basic existence results and characterizations of optimal and nearly optimal policies. These types of measurability, all more general than that considered by Blackwell, Freedman and Orkin, correspond to three σ-algebras in Polish spaces. The σ-algebras are constructed by radically different methods and the relationships between them are still unclear.

I. MEASURABILITY CONSIDERATIONS IN DISCRETE-TIME STOCHASTIC OPTIMAL CONTROL

Let us consider a simple two-stage stochastic optimal control problem. An initial state $x_o \in R$ is given and a control $u_o \in R$ is to be chosen. A new state $x_1 \in R$ will be chosen according to the probability distribution $p(dx_1|x_o,u_o)$ on the Borel subsets of R. A control u_1 is to then be chosen, and a cost $g(x_1,u_1)$ is incurred. Let us assume that for each Borel set $B \subset R$, $p(B|x_o,u_o)$ is Borel measurable in (x_o,u_o), and let us also assume that g is bounded, real-valued, and Borel measurable. A solution to this problem is a specification of a pair of measurable functions $\pi = (\mu_o,\mu_1)$ such that

$$(1) \qquad J_\pi(x_o) = \int g(x_1,\mu_1(x_1))p(dx_1|x_o,\mu_o(x_o))$$

is minimized. We call J_π the <u>expected cost corresponding to π</u> and define the <u>optimal cost</u> by

$$(2) \qquad J^*(x_o) = \inf_\pi J_\pi(x_o),$$

where the infimum is over all appropriately measurable policies. A policy π is ε-optimal if $J_\pi(x_o) \le J^*(x_o) + \varepsilon \; \forall \, x_o \in R$, and π is <u>optimal</u> if it is ε-optimal with $\varepsilon = 0$.

The <u>principle of optimality</u> advanced by Bellman [1] says that an ε-optimal policy exists and can be obtained by choosing μ_1 to satisfy

$$(3) \qquad g(x_1,\mu_1(x_1)) \le J_1^*(x_1) + \varepsilon/2 \;\; \forall \; x_1 \in R,$$

where

$$(4) \qquad J_1^*(x_1) = \inf_{u_1 \in R} g(x_1,u_1),$$

and choosing μ_o to satisfy

$$(5) \qquad \int J_1^*(x_1)p(dx_1|x_o,\mu_o(x_o)) \le J_o^*(x_o) + \varepsilon/2 \;\; \forall \; x_o \in R,$$

where

$$(6) \qquad J_o^*(x_o) = \inf_{u_o \in R} \int J_1^*(x_1)p(dx_1|x_o,u_o).$$

Furthermore, $J^* = J_o^*$. If the infimum in (4) is attained for every $x_1 \in R$ and the infimum in (6) is attained for every $x_o \in R$, then an optimal policy exists and can be obtained by choosing $\pi = (\mu_o, \mu_1)$ to satisfy (3) and (5) with $\varepsilon = 0$. Although quite plausible, this principle requires verification in individual cases.

In the problem just outlined, the functions J_1^* and J_o^* can fail to be Borel measurable and there need not exist a Borel measurable policy $\pi = (\mu_o, \mu_1)$ satisfying (3) and (5). This leads to consideration of σ-algebras more general than the Borel σ-algebra. Let X be a topological space homeomorphic to a Borel subset of a complete separable metric space. We call such an X a Borel space and denote by $\mathcal{B}_X$ or simply $\mathcal{B}$ the Borel σ-algebra in X. Let P(X) be the space of probability measures on $(X, \mathcal{B})$. We will always take P(X) to be equipped with the weak topology, under which it is itself a Borel space [2,7]. For $p \in P(x)$, let $\mathcal{B}(p)$ denote the completion of $\mathcal{B}$ with respect to p and define the universal σ-algebra $\mathcal{U} = \bigcap_{p \in P(X)} \mathcal{B}(p)$. The universal σ-algebra has the property that if $E \in \mathcal{U}$ and $p \in P(X)$, then E is p-measurable, and $\mathcal{U}$ is the largest σ-algebra with this property. In our consideration of σ-algebras $\mathcal{F}$ more general than $\mathcal{B}$, we will want to consider only those for which

(U) $$\mathcal{F} \subset \mathcal{U}.$$

Given a system of sets $\{S(\sigma_1, \ldots, \sigma_n)\}$ indexed by finite sequences of positive integers, we define the result of operation (A) applied to the system as

$$\bigcup_{(\sigma_1, \sigma_2, \ldots)} \bigcap_{n=1}^{\infty} S(\sigma_1, \ldots, \sigma_n),$$

where the union is over all sequences of positive integers and is thus uncountable. If $\mathcal{F}$ is any collection of subsets of X, we denote by $\mathcal{S}(\mathcal{F})$ the collection of sets which can be obtained by applying operation (A) to systems taken from $\mathcal{F}$. By a theorem due to Lusin, if $\mathcal{F} \subset \mathcal{U}$, then $\mathcal{S}(\mathcal{F}) \subset \mathcal{U}$ [2,8]. The members of $\mathcal{S}(\mathcal{B})$ are called the analytic subsets of X. Given any collection of sets $\mathcal{F}$, we denote by $\sigma(\mathcal{F})$ the σ-algebra generated by $\mathcal{F}$. The σ-algebra of <u>analytically measurable</u> sets is $\sigma(\mathcal{S}(\mathcal{B}))$. If X and Y are Borel spaces and $\mathcal{F}$ is a σ-algebra on X, we say the function $f: X \to Y$ is $\mathcal{F}$-measurable if $f^{-1}(B) \in \mathcal{F}$ for every $B \in \mathcal{B}_Y$. If $f: X \to [-\infty, \infty]$ has the property that the set $\{x : f(x) \le \lambda\}$ is analytic for every real λ, we say f is <u>lower semianalytic</u>. It follows from the above discussion that every Borel measurable, extended real-valued function is lower semianalytic and every lower semianalytic function is analytically (and thus universally) measurable.

Returning to the control problem at the beginning of this section, it can be shown that whenever $f(x,y)$ is a lower semianalytic function on a product of Borel spaces $X \times Y$, then

$$f^*(x) = \inf_{y \in Y} f(x,y) \tag{7}$$

is also lower semianalytic [2,4]. (The functions f and f^* may assume the values $\pm \infty$.) As a direct consequence of this, J_1^* defined by (4) is lower semianalytic and the integrals in (5) and (6) are defined. Furthermore, whenever $f(x,y)$ is lower semianalytic and bounded and $t(dy|x)$ is in $P(Y)$ for fixed $x \in X$ and $t(B|x)$ is Borel measurable in x for fixed $B \in \mathcal{B}_Y$, then $g(x) = \int f(x,y)t(dy|x)$ is lower semianalytic. From this we see that J_o^* defined by (6) is lower semianalytic.

If $\mathcal{F}$ contains the analytic subsets of X, then the lower semianalytic functions on X are $\mathcal{F}$-measurable. In light of this observation and the lower semianalyticity of J_o^* and J_1^*, we will want to consider σ-algebras $\mathcal{F}$ on X for which:

(A) $\mathcal{F}$ contains the analytic subsets of X.

If $f(x,y)$ is a lower semianalytic function on the product of Borel spaces $X \times Y$, f^* is defined by (7), and $\varepsilon > 0$ is given, then there is an analytically measurable $\phi: X \to Y$ such that [2,4]

$$f(x,\phi(x)) \le \begin{cases} f^*(x) + \varepsilon & \text{if } f^*(x) > -\infty, \\ -1/\varepsilon & \text{if } f^*(x) = -\infty. \end{cases} \tag{8}$$

If $\mathcal{F}_X$ satisfies property (A), then ϕ is $\mathcal{F}_X$-measurable. In particular, if $\mathcal{F}_R$ satisfies property (A), then for each $\varepsilon > 0$, $\mathcal{F}_R$-measurable functions μ_o and μ_1 can be found which satisfy (3) and (5). If the infimum in (7) is attained for every $x \in X$, then there is a function $\phi: X \to Y$ which is the composition of two analytically measurable functions such that [2,5]

$$f(x,\phi(x)) = f^*(x) \qquad x \in X. \tag{9}$$

This leads us to consider σ-algebras $\mathcal{F}$ for which:

(C) Whenever X, Y and Z are Borel spaces and $\phi: X \to Y$ is $\mathcal{F}_X$-measurable and $\psi: Y \to Z$ is $\mathcal{F}_Y$-measurable, then $\psi \circ \phi: X \to Z$ is $\mathcal{F}_X$-measurable.

In stating property (C), we assume a definition of $\mathcal{F}_X$ for every Borel space X. For example, the "Borel σ-algebra" and the "analytic σ-algebra" have definitions in terms of the topology of Borel spaces and are consequently defined for every Borel space.

If $\mathcal{F}_X$ has both properties (A) and (C), then ϕ in (9) can be chosen to be $\mathcal{F}_X$-measurable. In particular, if $\mathcal{F}_R$ satisfies (A) and (C) and the infima in (4) and (6) are attained for each x_1 and x_o respectively, then $\mathcal{F}_R$-measurable functions μ_o and μ_1 can be found which satisfy (3) and (5) with $\varepsilon = 0$.

In light of the previous discussion, it is not difficult to verify that if $\mathcal{F}_R$ has properties (U), (A) and (C), and the infimum in (2) is over all $\mathcal{F}_R$-measurable policies (i.e., $\pi = (\mu_o,\mu_1)$, where μ_o and μ_1 are $\mathcal{F}_R$-measurable), then the principle of optimality as set forth above is correct. Furthermore, J^* is $\mathcal{F}_R$-measurable.

There is one additional property, related to Fubini's theorem, that is desirable in a σ-algebra $\mathcal{F}$:

(F) If f is a bounded, real-valued, $\mathcal{F}_{X\times Y}$-measurable function, $p(dy|x)$ is in $P(Y)$ for fixed x, and the function $x \to p(dy|x)$ is $\mathcal{F}_X$-measurable then

$$g(x) = \int f(x,y)p(dy|x)$$

is $\mathcal{F}_X$-measurable.

As in property (C), we assume in stating (F) that $\mathcal{F}$ is defined for every Borel space X. If $\mathcal{F}_R$ has properties (U), (A), (C), and (F), then not only is the principle of optimality valid, but for any $\mathcal{F}_R$-measurable policy π, J_π as defined by (1) is $\mathcal{F}_R$-measurable. In particular, the set $\{x_o : J_\pi(x_o) \leq J^*(x_o) + \varepsilon\}$ is $\mathcal{F}_R$-measurable. This observation is useful in more complicated problems when we wish to piece together policies which are ε-optimal on only part of the state space to obtain a policy which is ε-optimal on the whole space [2].

II. THREE USEFUL σ-ALGEBRAS

There are presently three σ-algebras known which have properties (U), (A), (C) and (F). The largest of these is the universal σ-algebra $\mathcal{U}$. The verification of these four properties for $\mathcal{U}$ is not difficult and can be found in [2]. The smallest σ-algebra with these four properties is the σ-algebra $\mathcal{C}$ of C-sets studied by Selivanovskij [9]. This σ-algebra can be defined as the intersection of all σ-algebras having properties (A) and (C), or, alternatively, can be constructed from the Borel σ-algebra by transfinite induction using operation (A). It is constructed and shown to have properties (U), (A), (C) and (F) in [2,10]. Finally, there is the Borel-approachable σ-algebra BA, which is the subject of the next section. Like $\mathcal{C}$, it is constructed by transfinite induction, but operation (A) is not used. It is known that

$$\mathcal{C} \subset BA \subset \mathcal{U},$$

and under the axiom of choice and the continuum hypothesis, $\mathcal{C} \neq \mathcal{U}$. Nothing more is known about the relations among these σ-algebras.

III. THE BOREL-APPROACHABLE SETS

Let X be a Borel space and denote by ω_1 the first uncountable ordinal [6]. A collection of functions $\{f_\alpha : \alpha < \omega_1\}$ mapping X into a bounded real interval is called an <u>approach</u> if

(10) $$\alpha \leq \beta \Rightarrow f_\alpha(x) \leq f_\beta(x) \quad \forall x \in X,$$

$$f_\alpha(x) = f_{\alpha+1}(x) \Rightarrow f_\alpha(x) = f_\beta(x) \quad \forall \beta \geq \alpha .$$

We define the limit of the approach to be

(12) $$f(x) = \sup_{\alpha < \omega_1} f_\alpha(x) \quad \forall x \in X.$$

If each f_α is Borel measurable, we say the approach is Borel and f is Borel approachable (BA for short). Every subset of X of the form $f^{-1}(B)$, where $B \in \mathcal{B}_R$ and f is BA is a BA set, and the collection of all BA sets forms the BA σ-algebra. It can be shown that a function mapping X into a bounded real interval is BA if and only if it is measurable with respect to the BA σ-algebra.

The BA sets and functions are discussed in [11], where a slightly different but equivalent definition is given. The BA sets contain the Borel-programmable sets of Blackwell [3], and these are known to satisfy properties (U), (A) and (C). It follows immediately that the BA sets have property (A). By arguments similar to those found in [3], the BA sets can be shown to have property (C), and we refer the reader to [11]. To give the reader the flavor of the arguments, we establish properties (U) and (F) for the BA sets here. The proof of (F) uses (C).

<u>Theorem 1</u>: The BA σ-algebra has property (U), i.e., $BA \subset \mathcal{U}$.

<u>Proof</u>: Let $\{f_\alpha : \alpha < \omega\}$ be a BA approach to f. Choose $p \in P(X)$ and define

(13) $$F_\alpha(p) = \int f_\alpha dp.$$

If $\alpha \le \beta$, $F_\alpha(p) \le F_\beta(p)$, and since the set $\{\alpha:\alpha < \omega_1\}$ is uncountable, there must exist some $\alpha < \omega_1$ for which $F_\alpha(p) = F_{\alpha+1}(p)$. This implies by (10) that $f_\alpha(x) = f_{\alpha+1}(x)$ for p-almost every x. From (11) we see that $f_\alpha(x) = f(x)$ for p-almost every x, and since f_α is Borel measurable, f is universally measurable. Q.E.D.

Theorem 2: The BA σ-algebra has property (F).

Proof: Let X and Y be Borel spaces and f a bounded, real-valued, BA function approached by $\{f_\alpha:\alpha < \omega_1\}$. For $p \in P(X \times Y)$, define

$$F_\alpha(p) = \int f_\alpha dp.$$

From the proof of Theorem 1 we see that $\{F_\alpha:\alpha < \omega_1\}$ is a Borel approach to

$$F(p) = \int f\, dp,$$

so F is BA. Now suppose $p(dy|x)$ is in $P(Y)$ for fixed x and the function $x \to p(dy|x)$ is BA-measurable. For $x \in X$, let p_x be the measure which assigns probability one to x. The mapping $\sigma:X \to P(X) \times P(Y)$ given by $\sigma(x) = (p_x, p(dy|x))$ is BA-measurable, and the mapping $\tau:P(X) \times P(Y) \to P(X \times Y)$ which maps a pair of measures into their product is continuous [2]. The function $g(x) = \int f(x,y)\, p(dy|x)$ is the composition $F \circ \tau \circ \sigma$, and this is BA by property (C). Q.E.D.

REFERENCES

[1] R. Bellman, Dynamic Programming, Princeton Univ. Press, Princeton, New Jersey, 1957.

[2] D. P. Bertsekas and S. Shreve, Stochastic Optimal Control: The Discrete Time Case, Academic Press, New York, 1978.

[3] D. Blackwell, "Borel-programmable functions," Ann. Prob. 6 (1978), 321-324.

[4] D. Blackwell, D. Freedman and M. Orkin, "The optimal reward operator in dynamic programming," Ann. Prob. 2 (1974), 926-941.

[5] L. D. Brown and R. Purves, "Measurable selections of extrema," Ann. Statist. 1 (1973), 902-912.

[6] F. Hausdorff, Set Theory, Chelsea, New York, 1957.

[7] K. Parthasarathy, Probability Measures on Metric Spaces, Academic Press, New York, 1967.

[8] S. Saks, Theory of the Integral, Stechert, New York, 1937.

[9] E. Selivanovskij, "Ob odnom klasse effektivnyh mnozestv (mnozestva C)", Mat. Sb. 35 (1928), 379-413.

[10] S. Shreve, "Probability measures and the C-sets of Selivanovskij", Pac. J. Math. (to appear).

[11] S. Shreve, "Borel-approachable functions," Working Paper, Dept. of Math. Sci., Univ. of Delaware, 1978.

OPTIMAL NON-EXPLOSIVE CONTROL OF A NON CONSTRAINED DIFFUSION AND BEHAVIOUR WHEN THE DISCOUNT VANISHES

R. Tarrès
Département de mathématiques
Faculté des Sciences et Techniques
29283 BREST CEDEX FRANCE
temporarily: Centre Universitaire TLEMCEN, ALGERIA

§0 INTRODUCTION, GENERAL ASSUMPTIONS AND NOTATIONS

0.1. Statement of the problem. Let us consider the stochastic differential equation of Ito type:

$$(1) \quad \xi(0)=x \ , \ d\xi(t)=p(\xi(t))dt+\rho dw(t)$$

where: w is a normalized brownian motion on the real line $\mathbb{R}$,

$\rho>0$ is a constant ($\rho=\sqrt{2}$ in order to simplify formulas),

$p\in\Lambda$: the control set Λ consists of all weakly growing functions $p:\mathbb{R}\mapsto\mathbb{R}$ (this means that there exist positive constants b_p and m_p such that for all $u\in\mathbb{R}$, $|p(u)|\leqslant b_p(1+|u|^{m_p})$) such that: 1) p is lipschitzian on every bounded interval

2) there exists a positive constant c_p such that $\frac{u}{|u|}p(u)\leqslant c_p(1+|u|)$ for each $u\in\mathbb{R}^*$.

We know that, for each initial state $x\in\mathbb{R}$ and for each control $p\in\Lambda$, this equation (1) has a solution $\xi_{x,p}$ defined on $[0,+\infty[$, unique in the sense of pathwise uniqueness on each interval $[0,T]$; $\xi_{x,p}$ is a non explosive diffusion process with diffusion coefficient $\rho^2=2$ and drift coefficient p (see [2],[5],[6],[12]).

For each constant s (s>0), $x\in\mathbb{R}$ and $p\in\Lambda$,the relation

$$(2) \quad J_s(x,p)=E\int_0^{+\infty} e^{-st}[g(\xi_{x,p}(t))+f(p(\xi_{x,p}(t)))]dt$$

defines the discounted cost of our problem; the functions $f\in C^2(\mathbb{R};\mathbb{R}_+)$ and $g\in C^1(\mathbb{R};\mathbb{R}_+)$ are given.

We are interested in the following two problems:

1) The problem $(P^{\Lambda'}_{x,s})$: to minimize $J_s(x,p)$, for $p\in\Lambda'$ $(\Lambda'\subset\Lambda)$

2) What is the behaviour of $(P^{\Lambda'}_{x,s})$ when the discount s vanishes ?

Remarks: 1) The controls are closed-loop deterministic ones.

2) $(P^{\Lambda'}_{x,s})$ is a stationary problem.

3) Constraints are imposed neither to the controls nor to the trajectories of the controlled diffusion: the controls are only non explosive ones, and the processes $\xi_{x,p}$ evolve on the non bounded set $\mathbb{R}$.

In 1975, J.M.Lasry (see [9],[10],[11]) studied the problems above in n-dimensional case, Λ' being the set of bounded controls; he supposed in addition that, either g was a periodic function, or the diffusion $\xi_{x,p}$ evolves on a bounded domain of $\mathbb{R}^n$, with reflection at the boundary; and he obtained the next interesting convergence results: in such cases, an optimal control p_s exists for $(P^{\Lambda'}_{x,s})$ (p_s is independant of the initial state x), for every $s>0$; and when s vanishes, p_s converges to a control p_0 which is optimal for the problem $(Q^{\Lambda'}_x)$ defined below; moreover, the optimal cost λ_0 of $(Q^{\Lambda'}_x)$ is independant of x and is the limit of $sy_s(x)$, where $y_s(x)$ is the optimal cost of $(P^{\Lambda'}_{x,s})$.

For each $x\in\mathbb{R}$ and $p\in\Lambda$,the relation

(3) $\mu(x,p)=\liminf_{\tau\to+\infty}\frac{1}{\tau}E\int_0^\tau [g(\xi_{x,p}(t))+f(p(\xi_{x,p}(t)))]dt$

defines the cost of the limiting stationary problem

$(Q^{\Lambda'}_x)$: to minimize $\mu(x,p)$, for $p\in\Lambda'$.

The present work originates from the following conjecture of J.M.Lasry: if we replace his additional hypotheses by sufficiently strong coercivity hypotheses on the functions g and f in the running cost, it should be possible to obtain similar convergence results. The idea of this conjecture is the next one: with such coercivity hypotheses, the optimal control is naturally rather centripetal, that is to say it tends to bring back the evolution of the process in the region where g takes small values; so that the situation is similar to the one corresponding to the case where the diffusion is reflecting at the boundary of a bounded domain, the centripetal aspect of the optimal control and of reasonable controls replacing the reflection phenomenon.

We shall give three solutions to the problems above stated: in theorems 1 and 2, we assume different coercivity hypotheses; theorem 3 is concerned with the bounded and periodical case. In these theorems, the problems are solved on certain subsets of Λ; more precisely, let us define Λ_i for i=1,2,3,4: Λ_i consists of all controls $p\in\Lambda$ which are centripetal in the sense of the next condition (C_i)

(C_1) for some constants $c_p\in\mathbb{R}_+$ and $\alpha_p\in[0,1[$, $\frac{u}{|u|}p(u)\leqslant c_p(1+|u|^{\alpha_p})$ in $\mathbb{R}^*$

(C_2) for some constant $c_p\in\mathbb{R}_+$, $\frac{u}{|u|}p(u)\leqslant c_p$ in $\mathbb{R}^*$

(C_3) for some constants $c_p\geqslant 0, d_p>0$ and $\alpha_p>0$, $\frac{u}{|u|}p(u)\leqslant c_p-d_p|u|^{\alpha_p}$ in $\mathbb{R}^*$

(C_4) for some constants $c_p\geqslant 0$ and $d_p>0$, $\frac{u}{|u|}p(u)\leqslant c_p-d_p|u|$ in $\mathbb{R}^*$

It is obvious that $\Lambda\supset\Lambda_1\supset\Lambda_2\supset\Lambda_3\supset\Lambda_4$.

0.2. Method of solution. We utilize the dynamic programming method (see [1],[3],[4],[7],[16]). The solving equation of problems $(P^{\Lambda'}_{x,s})$ is

(R_s) $-y''(u)+sy(u)+h(-y'(u))=g(u)$ for each $u\in\mathbb{R}$

where $h=f^*$ is the conjugate function of f (according to the convex analysis), defined by: $h(z)=\sup_{u\in\mathbb{R}}[zu-f(u)]$ for each $z\in\mathbb{R}$.

We assume that f satisfies the following coercivity hypothesis:

(H_1) for some constant $c_o>0$, $f''(u)\geq c_o$ for each $u\in\mathbb{R}$;

therefore, $h\in C^2(\mathbb{R};[-f(0),+\infty[)$ and $0<h''(u)\leq\frac{1}{c_o}$ for each $u\in\mathbb{R}$.

The solving equation of problems ($Q_x^{\Lambda'}$) is

(R_o) $-v''(u)+\lambda+h(-v'(u))=g(u)$ for each $u\in\mathbb{R}$

The unknown of (R_o) is the pair $(\lambda,v)\in\mathbb{R}\times C^2(\mathbb{R};\mathbb{R})$, for which we shall use the term of "relative uniqueness" in the next sense: if (λ_i,v_i), for i=1 and 2 are two solutions of (R_o), then $\lambda_1=\lambda_2$, v_1-v_2 is constant.

Remark: in the problems ($P_{x,s}^{\Lambda'}$) and ($Q_x^{\Lambda'}$) , with reflection on the boundary of a bounded domain (respectively in the periodical case), we have a limit condition of Neumann type on the boundary of this domain (respectively the periodical condition) to characterize the optimal cost among all the solutions of the solving equations; in our problems, we don't have such conditions, and this characterization is obtained by means of a "radiative condition" expressing the adequate centripetal aspect of the corresponding optimal control, in theorems 1 and 2 below.

§1. THE FIRST COERCIVE CASE. Theorem 1 below is generalized to n-dimentional case (to appear). The coercivity hypotheses concern g'.

1.1. Theorem 1: we make all the assumptions of §0 above.

a) If further g satisfies the growth and coercivity hypotheses

(H_2) g' is a weakly growing function

(H_3) for some positive constant A, $\frac{u}{|u|}g'(u)\geq -A$ for each $u\in\mathbb{R}^*$

then, for each fixed s>0, there exists one and only one solution $y\in C^2(\mathbb{R};\mathbb{R})$ of (R_s) satisfying the growth and radiative conditions:

1) y' is a weakly growing function

2) $h'(-y'(.))\in\Lambda_1$ ("weak radiative condition").

Let y_s denote this solution; and let $p_s=h'(-y_s'(.))$;

then, $p_s\in\Lambda_2$ and for each $p\in\Lambda_1$ and $x\in\mathbb{R}$, $y_s(x)=J_s(x,p_s)\leq J_s(x,p)$; in other words, for each $x\in\mathbb{R}$, $y_s(x)$ is the optimal cost for ($P_{x,s}^{\Lambda_1}$) and p_s is an optimal control (independant of x) for this problem.

b) If we replace (H_3) by the stronger hypothesis

$$(H_4)\begin{cases}\text{for some constants } \alpha_1\in]1,2] ,\ \theta\geq\frac{3-\alpha_1}{\alpha_1-1} ,\ A\geq0,\ B>0, K_1>0 \text{ and } \lambda_1>0,\\ \frac{u}{|u|}g'(u)\geq -A+B|u|^\theta \text{ for each } u\in\mathbb{R}^*\\ h''(u)\geq K_1|u|^{\alpha_1-2} \text{ for each } u\in\mathbb{R} \text{ satisfying } |u|\geq\lambda_1\end{cases}$$

then the equation (R_o) admits a relatively unique solution $(\lambda,v)\in\mathbb{R}\times C^2(\mathbb{R};\mathbb{R})$ satisfying the "strong radiative condition" $h'(-v'(.))\in\Lambda_4$.

Let (λ_o,v_o) be this solution of (R_o); and let $p_o=h'(-v_o'(.))$;

then, $p_o \in \Lambda_4$ and for each $p \in \Lambda_4$ and $x \in \mathbb{R}$, $\lambda_o = \mu(x,p_o) \leqslant \mu(x,p)$; in other words, for each $x \in \mathbb{R}$, λ_o is the optimal cost (independant of x) and p_o is an optimal control (independant of x) for $(Q_x^{\Lambda_4})$.

Let us consider y_s and p_s defined above; then, for each $s>0$, $p_s \in \Lambda_4$. Furthermore, when s vanishes, the problem $(P_{x,s}^{\Lambda_4})$ converges to the problem $(Q_x^{\Lambda_4})$ in the following sense: uniformly on each compact subset of $\mathbb{R}$, $\lim_{s\to 0} sy_s = \lambda_o$, $\lim_{s\to 0} y_s' = v_o'$, $\lim_{s\to 0} y_s'' = v_o''$ and $\lim_{s\to 0} p_s = p_o$.

1.2. Proof of theorem 1. (For details and other results, see [14])

a) Lemma 1: Let $y_s \in C^2(\mathbb{R};\mathbb{R})$ be a solution of (R_s); and suppose that y_s' is a weakly growing function; then, for each $p \in \Lambda$, $\tau \geqslant 0$ and $x \in \mathbb{R}$, $y_s(x) \leqslant E\int_0^\tau e^{-st}[g(\xi_{x,p}(t))+f(p(\xi_{x,p}(t)))]dt + e^{-s\tau}E(y_s(\xi_{x,p}(\tau)))$, and this relation becomes an equality if $p=p_s=h'(-y_s'(.)) \in \Lambda$.

Proof: this property is a consequense of the Ito formula applied to the process $\alpha_{s,x,p}$ defined by $\alpha_{s,x,p}(t)=e^{-st}y_s(\xi_{x,p}(t))$; then it is sufficient to write the mathematical expectations, using (R_s) and the definition of h.

Lemma 2: if $\varphi:\mathbb{R}\mapsto\mathbb{R}$ is a weakly growing and measurable function, and if $p \in \Lambda_1$, then $E(\varphi(\xi_{x,p}(.)))$ is a weakly growing function for all $x \in \mathbb{R}$

Proof: it is sufficient to verify the result when $\varphi(u)=u^{2n}, n \in \mathbb{N}^*$. Let Γ_p be the differential operator associated with equation (1): $\Gamma_p = \frac{d^2}{dx^2} + p\frac{d}{dx}$. Since $p \in \Lambda_1$, there exist $\nu \geqslant 0$, $\eta \geqslant 0$ and $\beta \in]0,1[$ such that, for each $x \in \mathbb{R}$, $\Gamma_p\varphi(x) \leqslant G(\varphi(x))$, where $G(u)=\nu u^\beta+\eta$ for all $u \in \mathbb{R}_+$.

It is well known that, if $m(t)=E(\varphi(\xi_{x,p}(t)))$, then m_d' exists on $\mathbb{R}_+$ and for each $t \in \mathbb{R}_+$, $m_d'(t)=E(\Gamma_p\varphi(\xi_{x,p}(t)))$ (see [6] and also [14] for details: our hypotheses are not exactly those of [6]).

Therefore $m_d'(t) \leqslant E[G(\varphi(\xi_{x,p}(t)))] \leqslant G(m(t))$ because of Jensen's inequality and concavity of the function G; consequently, $m(t) \leqslant r(t)$, where r is the maximal solution, defined on $\mathbb{R}_+$, of the differential equation $u'=G(u)$, with initial condition $u(0)=x^{2n}$ (for such results concerning differential inequalities, see [8]); the verification that r is a weakly growing function is easy and completes the proof.

Lemma 3: under the hypotheses of theorem 1,a, (R_s) has at least one solution $y_s \in C^2(\mathbb{R};\mathbb{R})$ such that y_s' is weakly growing and $h'(-y_s'(.)) \in \Lambda_2$

Proof: for each $s>0$ and $T>0$, let $y_{s,T} \in C^2([-T,T];\mathbb{R})$ be the solution of (R_s) on $[-T,T]$ such that $y_{s,T}'(\pm T)=0$ (we shall use sometimes the strong existence and uniqueness property concerning Neuman conditions for the equations (R_s) or (R_o); such a property can be proved, for instance, with the help of the fixed point theorem of Schaefer, starting from the same property for the linear equation $-y''(x)+sy(x)=F(x)$; see [13], [14]).

We have for $y_{s,T}$ and $y_{s,T}'$ the following estimates:

$(s_n)_{n\in\mathbb{N}}$ such that $\lim_{n\uparrow+\infty} s_n=0$, $\lim_{n\uparrow+\infty} y'_{s_n}=v'_o$ in $C^1([-U,U];\mathbb{R})$, and $\lim_{n\uparrow+\infty} s_n y_{s_n}=\lambda_o$ in $C^0([-U,U];\mathbb{R})$.

A solution (λ_o,v_o) of (R_o) in lemma 6 is such that v_o is weakly growing and $h'(-v'_o(.))\in\Lambda_4$; hence, because of lemma 5, if $p\in\Lambda_4$ (then if $p=p_o$), $\frac{1}{\tau}E(v_o(\xi_{x,p}(\tau)))\xrightarrow{\tau\uparrow+\infty}0$; the lemma 4 completes the proof of the results concerning $(Q_x^{\Lambda_4})$. The convergence properties follow from the construction of (λ_o,v_o) and the uniqueness property (easy to prove).

Remarks: 1) $\lambda_o=\mu(x,p_o)=\lim_{\tau\uparrow+\infty}\frac{1}{\tau}E\int_0^\tau[g(\xi_{x,p}(t))+f(p(\xi_{x,p}(t)))]dt$.

2) Let $(\lambda^{a,\varepsilon}_{o,T},v^{a,\varepsilon}_{o,T})\in\mathbb{R}\times C^2([-T,T];\mathbb{R})$ be the solution of (R_o) such that $v^{a,\varepsilon}_{o,T}{}'(T)=a\psi_\varepsilon(T)$ and $v^{a,\varepsilon}_{o,T}{}'(-T)=a\psi_\varepsilon(-T)$, defined for each $T>0$, $a\in\mathbb{R}$ and $\varepsilon\geqslant1$ (such a pair is unique, except for the addition of a constant for $v^{a,\varepsilon}_{o,T}$); if ε and a are the constants occuring in the proof of lemma 6 then we have the following convergence properties: for each $T>0$,

$\lim_{s\to0} s y^{a,\varepsilon}_{s,T}=\lambda^{a,\varepsilon}_{o,T}$, $\lim_{s\to0} y^{a,\varepsilon}_{s,T}{}'=v^{a,\varepsilon}_{o,T}{}'$, $\lim_{s\to0} y^{a,\varepsilon}_{s,T}{}''=v^{a,\varepsilon}_{o,T}{}''$, uniformly on $[-T,T]$; $\lim_{T\uparrow+\infty}\lambda^{a,\varepsilon}_{o,T}=\lambda_o$; and $\lim_{T\uparrow+\infty} v^{a,\varepsilon}_{o,T}{}'=v'_o$, $\lim_{T\uparrow+\infty} v^{a,\varepsilon}_{o,T}{}''=v''_o$ uniformly on each compact set.

3) In theorem 1,a, 2) implies 1) if $h''(u)\geqslant K_1|u|^{\alpha_1-2}$ $(\alpha_1\in]1,2])$.

§2. THE SECOND COERCIVE CASE. The coercivity hypotheses concern g .

2.1. Theorem 2: we make all the assumptions of §0 above.

a) If further g and h satisfy the coercivity hypothesis

$$(H_5)\begin{cases}\text{for some constants } \alpha_1\in]1,2],\ K_1>0,\ \lambda_1>0,\ \gamma>0,\ \beta>0,\ A_1\in\mathbb{R},\ A_2\in\mathbb{R},\\ B_1>0 \text{ and } B_2>0, \text{ with } \gamma\geqslant\beta\geqslant1+\frac{\gamma}{\alpha_1} \ (\text{then } 1+\frac{\gamma}{\alpha_1}\geqslant\frac{\alpha_1}{\alpha_1-1}\geqslant2),\\ h''(u)\geqslant K_1|u|^{\alpha_1-2} \text{ for each } u\in\mathbb{R} \text{ satisfying } |u|\geqslant\lambda_1\\ A_1+B_1|u|^\beta\leqslant g(u)\leqslant A_2+B_2|u|^\gamma \text{ for each } u\in\mathbb{R}\end{cases}$$

then, for all $s>0$ if $1+\frac{\gamma}{\alpha_1}<\beta$ (s $]0,s_o[$ for some $s_o>0$ if $1+\frac{\gamma}{\alpha_1}=\beta$) (R_s) admits one and only one solution $y\in C^2(\mathbb{R};\mathbb{R})$ such that $h'(-y'(.))\in\Lambda_1$.

Let y_s denote this solution; and let $p_s=h'(-y'_s(.))$; then $p_s\in\Lambda_3$ and for each $p\in\Lambda_1$ and $x\in\mathbb{R}$, $y_s(x)=J_s(x,p_s)\leqslant J_s(x,p)$ (p_s is optimal for $(P^{\Lambda_1}_{x,s})$).

b) If we replace (H_5) by the hypothesis

$$(H_6)\begin{cases}\text{consisting of } (H_5) \text{ with the additional existence of constants}\\ \alpha_2\in]1,2],\ K_2>0,\ \lambda_2>0, \text{ with } 1<\alpha_1\leqslant\alpha_2\leqslant2,\ \frac{\alpha_1}{\alpha_1-1}\leqslant1+\frac{\beta}{\alpha_2} \text{ and such that}\\ h''(u)\leqslant K_2|u|^{\alpha_2-2} \text{ for each } u\in\mathbb{R} \text{ satisfying } |u|\geqslant\lambda_2 .\end{cases}$$

then we conclude as in theorem 1,b (optimality for $(Q_x^{\Lambda_4})$, convergences).

2.2. Proof of theorem 2. This proof is similar to that of theorem 1; it is sufficient to replace lemmas 3 and 6 by

Lemma 7: under the hypotheses of theorem 2,a (respectively b) (R_s) (respectively (R_o)) has at least one solution $y_s\in C^2(\mathbb{R};\mathbb{R})$ (respectively $(\lambda_o,v_o)\in\mathbb{R}\times C^2(\mathbb{R};\mathbb{R})$) such that y'_s is weakly growing and $h'(-y'_s(.))\in\Lambda_3$

(respectively v_0' is weakly growing and $h'(-v_0'(.))\in\Lambda_4$).

Proof: Let us introduce a family $(\varphi_\delta)_{\delta>1}$ of functions $\varphi_\delta\in C^2(\mathbb{R};\mathbb{R})$ such that: if $u\to+\infty$, then $\varphi_\delta(u)\sim u^\delta$, $\varphi_\delta'(u)\sim\delta u^{\delta-1}$, $\varphi_\delta''(u)\sim\delta(\delta-1)u^{\delta-2}$

$$\varphi_\delta(u)=\varphi_\delta(-u)\geqslant 0,\ \varphi_\delta'(u)\geqslant 0 \text{ and } \varphi_\delta''(u)\geqslant 0 \text{ for each } u\in\mathbb{R}_+$$

(for example, $\varphi_\delta(u)=\int_0^u dv\int_0^v \eta_\delta(w)dw$, where η_δ is defined by: $\eta_\delta(u)=\delta(\delta-1)$ if $|u|\leqslant 1$, and $\eta_\delta(u)=\delta(\delta-1)|u|^{\delta-2}$ if $|u|\geqslant 1$).

For each $s>0$, $T>0$, $a\in\mathbb{R}$ and $\delta>1$, let $y_{s,T}^{a;\delta}\in C^2([-T,T];\mathbb{R})$ be the solution of (R_s) on $[-T,T]$, such that $y_{s,T}^{a;\delta\,\prime}(T)=a\varphi_\delta'(T)$ and $y_{s,T}^{a;\delta\,\prime}(-T)=a\varphi_\delta'(-T)$.

We have for $y_{s,T}^{a;\delta}$ and $y_{s,T}^{a;\delta\,\prime}$ the following estimates (under the hypotheses of theorem 2,b , without the condition $\frac{\alpha_1}{\alpha_1-1}\leqslant 1+\frac{\beta}{\alpha_2}$):

let $\delta\in[1+\frac{\gamma}{\alpha_1},\beta[$ if $1+\frac{\gamma}{\alpha_1}<\beta$ (respectively, let $\delta=\beta$) and let $\varepsilon\in]1,1+\frac{\beta}{\alpha_2}]$ (therefore $1<\varepsilon\leqslant 1+\frac{\beta}{\alpha_2}\leqslant 1+\frac{\gamma}{\alpha_1}\leqslant\delta\leqslant\beta$); then, for each $\bar{s}>0$ (respectively $\bar{s}\in]0,s_0[$ for some $s_0>0$), there exist $a>0, b>0, a'>0, b'\in\mathbb{R}, c>0$ and $T_0>0$ such that

(E_7) $\inf g-h(0)\leqslant s y_{s,T}^{a;\delta}(u)\leqslant a s\varphi_\delta(u)+c$ for each $s>0, T>0$ and $u\in[-T,T]$,

(E_8) $\frac{u}{|u|}(y_{s,T}^{a;\delta\,\prime}(u)-b\varphi_\varepsilon'(u))\geqslant 0$ and

(E_9) $\frac{u}{|u|}h'(-y_{s,T}^{a;\delta\,\prime}(u))\leqslant -a'|u|^{(\varepsilon-1)(\alpha_1-1)}+b'$

for each $s\in]0,\bar{s}]$, $T>T_0$ and $u\in[-T,-T_0]\cup[T_0,T]$.

(E_7) is more precise than (E_1) or (E_6) and is obtained in a similar way; as a matter of fact, this relation is useful for the proof of (E_8): for some constants $a>0$, $b\in]0,a[$ and $T_1>0$,

$$-y_{s,T}^{a;\delta\,\prime\prime}(u)+h(-y_{s,T}^{a;\delta\,\prime}(u))=g(u)-s y_{s,T}^{a;\delta}(u)\geqslant g(u)-\bar{s}a\varphi_\delta(u)-c\geqslant -v'(u)+h(-v(u))$$

for each $T>T_1$, $s\in]0,\bar{s}]$ and $u\in[-T,-T_1]\cup[T_1,T]$, where $v=b\varphi_\varepsilon'$, and $a|\varphi_\delta'(u)|\geqslant b|\varphi_\varepsilon'(u)|$ for each u satisfying $|u|\geqslant T_1$.

Let us now consider the differential equation $w'=h(-w)-V(u)$, where $V(u)=-b\varphi_\varepsilon''(u)+h(-b\varphi_\varepsilon'(u))$, for instance on $[-T,-T_1]$; the comparison of the solution v and the lower solution $y_{s,T}^{a;\delta\,\prime}$ on this interval ,taking the values of their initial conditions into account $(a\varphi_\delta'(-T)\leqslant b\varphi_\varepsilon'(-T))$, leads to $y_{s,T}^{a;\delta\,\prime}(u)\leqslant b\varphi_\varepsilon'(u)$ if $u\in[-T,-T_1]$.

(E_9) is a consequence of (E_8) and the above hypotheses concerning h. The hypotheses of theorem 2,a involve those of theorem 2,b without the condition $\frac{\alpha_1}{\alpha_1-1}\leqslant 1+\frac{\beta}{\alpha_2}$ (the above estimates were obtained by means of these last hypotheses) but with $\alpha_2=2$ because of (H_1); therefore, the application of (E_9) and the limit passage $T\uparrow+\infty$ leads to the existence of a solution y_s of (R_s) satisfying $h'(-y'(.))\in\Lambda_3$. Under the hypotheses of theorem 2,b , the application of (E_9) and the successive limit passages $T\uparrow+\infty$ and $s\to 0$, taking $\delta=\beta$ and $\varepsilon=\frac{\alpha_1}{\alpha_1-1}$ (then $(\varepsilon-1)(\alpha_1-1)=1$), leads to the existence of a solution (λ_0,v_0) of (R_0) satisfying $h'(-v_0'(.))\in\Lambda_4$.

As a matter of fact, the above estimates are not sufficient to apply the limit passages as in lemmas 3 and 6, because (E_8) and (E_9) do not cover the real line. The next estimate completes the proof of lemma 7 because it is a weakly growing and uniform (with respect to s and T) estimate of $y^{a;\delta}_{s,T}{}'$ on $\mathbb{R}$: under the hypotheses of theorem 2,a , for each $\delta>1$ and $a\geq 0$, there exist constants $d\geq 0$ and $q\in\mathbb{N}^*$ such that

(E_{10}) $|y^{a;\delta}_{s,T}{}'(u)|\leq u^{2q}+d$ for each $s>0$, $T>0$ and $u\in[-T,T]$.

Indeed, for sufficiently large constants d and q, and for all $\delta>1$ and $a>0$ $-y^{a;\delta}_{s,T}{}''(u)+h(-y^{a;\delta}_{s,T}{}'(u))=g(u)-sy^{a;\delta}_{s,T}(u)\leq g(u)+h(0)-\inf g\leq -v'(u)+h(-v(u))$ for each $T>0$, $s>0$ and $u\in[-T,T]$, where $v(u)=u^{2q}+b$, and $a\varphi_\delta'(T)\leq v(T)$ for each $T>0$.

Let us now consider the differential equation $w'=h(-w)-V(u)$, where $V(u)=-v'(u)+h(-v(u))$, on the interval $[-T,T]$; the comparison of the solution v and the upper solution $y^{a;\delta}_{s,T}{}'$ on this interval, taking account of $y^{a;\delta}_{s,T}{}'(T)=a\varphi_\delta'(T)\leq v(T)$ leads to $y^{a;\delta}_{s,T}{}'(u)\leq v(u)$ if $u\in[-T,T]$. The study of $-y^{a;\delta}_{s,T}{}'(u)\leq u^{2q}+d$ is similar and completes the proof of (E_{10}).

Remarks: 1) with some evident modifications, the remarks of §1.2.a and b are applicable to theorem 2.

2) It seems that the theorem 2 can not be generalized to the n dimensional case, except perhaps with important additional hypotheses, and evidently with another type of proof (the estimates (E_9), (E_{10}) being obtained by means of differential equations arguments).

§3. THE BOUNDED AND PERIODICAL CASE. ($(P^\wedge_{x,s})$ and $(Q^\wedge_x)$)

3.1. Theorem 3: we make all the assumptions of §0 above.

a) If further g is a bounded function, then (R_s) admits one and only one bounded solution $y\in C^2(\mathbb{R};\mathbb{R})$ such that y' is a weakly growing function and $h'(-y'(.))\in\Lambda$.

Let y_s denote this solution; and let $p_s=h'(-y_s'(.))$; then $p_s\in\Lambda$ and is bounded; and for each $p\in\Lambda$, $x\in\mathbb{R}$, $y_s(x)=J_s(x,p_s)\leq J_s(x,p)$.

b) If moreover g is a χ-periodic function, then

1) y_s is the unique χ-periodic solution $y\in C^2(\mathbb{R};\mathbb{R})$ of (R_s) .

2) (R_o) admits a relatively unique solution $(\lambda,v)\in\mathbb{R}\times C^2(\mathbb{R};\mathbb{R})$ such that v is a χ-periodic function.

Let (λ_o,v_o) be this solution of (R_o); and let $p_o=h'(-v_o'(.))$; then $p_o\in\Lambda$ and is χ-periodic; and for each $p\in\Lambda$, $x\in\mathbb{R}$, $\lambda_o=\mu(x,p_o)\leq\mu(x,p)$. The convergence properties are identical to those of theorem 1,b .

3.2. Proof of theorem 3:

a) The theorem 3,a is a consequence of lemma 1 and the existence of a solution $y_s\in C^2(\mathbb{R};\mathbb{R})$ of (R_s) such that y_s and y_s' are bounded; this existence property arises from the next estimates and the limit passage

$T\uparrow+\infty$ (as in lemma 3): under the hypotheses of theorem 3,a ,

(E_{11}) $\inf g-h(0)\leq sy_{s,T}(u)\leq \sup g-h(0)$ for each $s>0$, $T>0$ and $u\in[-T,T]$,

(E_{12}) for some constant $b\geq 0$, $|y'_{s,T}(u)|\leq b$ for all $s>0, T>0$ and $u\in[-T,T]$.

The proofs of (E_{11}) and (E_{12}) are respectively similar to those of (E_1) and (E_{10}).

Remark: The first remark of §1.2.a is applicable to theorem 3,a .

b) The existence of a χ-periodic solution $y_s\in C^2(\mathbb{R};\mathbb{R})$ of (R_s) can be proved with the help of the fixed point theorem of Schaefer (see [13],[14]). The existence property concerning (R_o) is obtained by means of the limit passage $s\to 0$, taking account of (E_{11}) and (E_{12}).

Remarks: 1) The first remark of §1.2.b is applicable to theorem 3,b.

2) Theorem 3 is generalized to n-dimentional case (3,a: to appear; 3,b: see[9],[10],[11]) with slightly stronger hypotheses. But it seems to be difficult to weaken the periodical hypothesis.

REFERENCES

1 . A.Bensoussan, E.Gerald Hurst, J.R. and B.Naslund: Management applications of modern control theory.North-Holland, 1974.

2 . A.Bensoussan, J.L.Lions: Equations différentielles stochastiques et équations aux dérivées partielles linéaires du 2e ordre. CMD 7701 (*)

3 . W.H.Fleming: Optimal continuous-parameter stochastic control. SIAM Review, vol. 11 n°4, oct 69, p 470-509.

4 . W.H.Fleming, R.W.Rishel: Deterministic and stochastic optimal control. Springer Verlag 1975.

5 . A.Friedman: Stochastic differential equations and applications. Vol. 1 and 2, Academic Press 1975.

6 . I.I.Gikhman,A.V.Skorohod: Stochastic differential equations. Springer Verlag, 1972.

7 . H.Kushner: Introduction to stochastic control. Holt, Rinehart and Winston, 1971.

8 . G.S.Ladde, V.Lakshmikantham, P.T.Liu: Differential inequalities and Ito type stochastic differential equations. Proc. "Equations différentielles et fonctionnelles non linéaires", ed by P.Janssens, J.Mawhin, N.Rouche; Hermann 1973.

9 . J.M.Lasry: Evolution of problems of stochastic control when the discount vanishes. CMD 7519 (*).

10. J.M.Lasry: Thesis. Univ. Paris Dauphine.

11. J.M.Lasry: Proc. "Congrès de contrôle optimal, I.R.I.A. 1974", Lecture notes in economics and mathematical systems n° 107, ed. by A.Bensoussan, J.L.Lions. Springer Verlag 1975 .

12. M.Métivier: Introduction au calcul différentiel stochastique, journées de théorie du contrôle, Gourette 1974. Univ. Bordeaux-Talence.

13. H.Schaefer: Über die methode der a priori Schranken. Math. ann. t 129, 1955, p 415-416.

14. R.Tarrès: Contrôle optimal d'une diffusion non contrainte et non explosive; comportement lorsque le taux d'actualisation du critère intégral s'annulle. Thèse de 3e cycle et CMD 7809 (*).

15. R.Tarrès:(to appear) Asymptotic evolution of a stochastic control problem when the discount vanishes. Journées sur l'analyse des systèmes, septembre 1978, Univ. Bordeaux 1. Astérisque.

16. M.Viot: Introduction aux problèmes de contrôle stochastique. Journées de théorie du contrôle, Seez 1975; Univ. 1 et 2 Grenoble.

(*) CMD: Cahiers de mathématiques de la décision, Univ. Paris Dauphine.

SEQUENTIAL ESTIMATION OF THE SOLUTION OF AN INTEGRAL EQUATION IN FILTERING THEORY

H. Walk

Universität Essen - Gesamthochschule
Fachbereich Mathematik
D 4300 Essen 1, Universitätsstraße 3
Bundesrepublik Deutschland

In the theory of optimal filters for linear systems in the one-dimensional case the integral equation

$$x(u,v)+\int_{[0,u]} x(u,w)q(w,v)a(w,v)dw-q(u,v)b(v) = 0, \quad (u,v)\in[0,1]^2,$$

appears, where $a\in C([0,1]^2)$, $b\in C[0,1]$ are known and $q\in C([0,1]^2)$ is given by $q(u,v):= E\tilde{Q}(u)\tilde{Q}(v)$ with a signal process $\tilde{Q}$ (see Bucy-Joseph [2], p. 53, and Arnold [1], p. 219). It is assumed that $\tilde{Q}$ is path-continuous with $E\sup_u|\tilde{Q}(u)|^2 < \infty$ and that an independent sequence of copies $\tilde{Q}_n(n\in\mathbb{N})$ of $\tilde{Q}$ is observable.

For sequential estimation of the root $\theta\in C([0,1]^2)$ of the equation, which uniquely exists under a certain spectral condition on the underlying kernel operator, a modified Robbins-Monro procedure will be defined which contains a kind of adaptation to the operator. For the sequence of $C([0,1]^2)$-valued random variables belonging to it an a.s. convergence result and an invariance principle are given (Theorem 1). The corresponding usual Robbins-Monro process a.s. converges under a sharpened assumption, and for $L^2([0,1]^2)$ as the state space a central limit theorem holds under weakened assumptions (Theorem 2). These results follow from a theorem on partial sums of independent random elements in $C([0,1]^2)$ (see [9]) and from results in the more general setting of a real separable Banach or Hilbert space (see [9] as to Theorem 1, and Theorem 3 as to Theorem 2). Supplementary to Theorems 2 and 3 a central limit theorem for the Banach space case is given (Theorem 4).

<u>Theorem 1.</u> Let $C([0,1]^2)$ be provided with the max-norm and $a,b,q,(\tilde{Q}_n)$ be given as above. Let the operators A, $H:C([0,1]^2)\to C([0,1]^2)$ and the operator $G:C([0,1]^2)\times C([0,1]^2)\to C([0,1]^2)$ be defined by

$A := A_q := I+G(\cdot,q)$ (I identity operator),

$$(G(x,y))(u,v) := \int_{[0,u]} x(u,w)y(w,v)a(w,v)\,dw,$$

$$(Hy)(u,v) := y(u,v)b(v).$$

There is assumed

$$c^* := \min\{\mathrm{Re}\lambda : \lambda \in \mathrm{spectrum}(A)\} > 0. \qquad (1)$$

Let the unique root of the equation $Ax-Hq = 0$ in $C([0,1]^2)$ be denoted by θ and the sequence of $C([0,1]^2)$-valued random variables X_n be defined by

$$X_{n+1} := X_n - \frac{c}{n}[X_n + G(X_n, \frac{1}{n}\sum_{j=1}^{n} Q_j) - HQ_n], \qquad n \in \mathbb{N},$$

with a constant $c > 0$, $Q_j(u,v) = \tilde{Q}_j(u)\tilde{Q}_j(v)$ and X_1 independent of $(\tilde{Q}_n)$.

a) There holds

$$X_n \to \theta \quad \text{a.s.} \qquad (2)$$

b) Let the assumptions be sharpened to

$$\tilde{Q}(0) \in L^4, \quad \underset{\bar{c}\in\mathbb{R}_+}{\exists} \quad \underset{u,u',u''}{\forall} \quad E(\tilde{Q}(u)-\tilde{Q}(u'))^2\tilde{Q}(u'')^2 \le \bar{c}|u-u'|, \qquad (3)$$

existence of a random variable $M \in L^4$ and of an $h: \mathbb{R}_+ \to \mathbb{R}_+$ such that

$$\underset{\alpha>0}{\exists} \qquad h(u) = O((\log\log \frac{1}{u})^{-1-\alpha}) \qquad (u \to +0), \qquad (4)$$

$$\underset{\delta>0}{\forall} \qquad w(\tilde{Q},\delta) := \sup_{|u-u'|\le\delta} |\tilde{Q}(u)-\tilde{Q}(u')| \le Mh(\delta), \qquad (5)$$

$$c^* > \frac{1}{2c}. \qquad (6)$$

Then the sequence of random elements Z_n in $C([0,1]^3)$ with max-norm, defined by

$$Z_n(t,u,v) := \frac{1}{\sqrt{n}} R_{[nt]}(u,v) + (nt-[nt])\frac{1}{\sqrt{n}}(R_{[nt]+1}(u,v) - R_{[nt]}(u,v))$$

with $R_n := n(X_{n+1}-\theta)$, converges in distribution to a Gaussian random element Z in $C([0,1]^3)$ with

$$Z(t,\cdot,\cdot) = cHW(t,\cdot,\cdot) + c\int_{(0,1]} e^{(\ln z)(cA-2I)}((I-cA)H - G(\theta,\cdot))W(tz,\cdot,\cdot)\,dz \qquad (7)$$

where the random element W in $C([0,1]^3)$ is a Gaussian process with

$$\underset{t,u,v}{\forall} \quad EW(t,u,v) = 0$$

$$\underset{t,u,v,t',u',v'}{\forall} \quad EW(t,u,v)W(t',u',v') = (E\tilde{Q}(u)\tilde{Q}(v)\tilde{Q}(u')\tilde{Q}(v') - q(u,v)q(u',v'))\min(t,t').$$

Remark 1. The spectral conditions (1), (6) concern the operator A continued to the corresponding complex Banach space in a natural way under preservation of norm; (1) in the case $a(u,v) \equiv 1$ is fulfilled for $\|q\| < 1$; (6) guarantees a.s. existence of the Bochner integral in (7). The random function $t \to W(t,\cdot,\cdot)$ in (7) is a Brownian motion in the Banach space $C([0,1]^2)$ (see e.g. Kuelbs [5]) where $W(1,\cdot,\cdot)$ is a Gaussian process with expectation zero and covariance function

$S:[0,1]^2 \times [0,1]^2 \to \mathbb{R}$ with

$$S(u,v,u',v') = E\tilde{Q}(u)\tilde{Q}(v)\tilde{Q}(u')\tilde{Q}(v') - q(u,v)q(u',v'). \tag{8}$$

Theorem 1, which immediately yields a functional central limit theorem for (X_n), is a consequence of two other theorems. The one theorem is an invariance principle for a sequence of partial sums of independent $C([0,1]^2)$-valued random variables - which can be generalized to the case of a martingale difference array of $C(K)$-valued random variables (K compact metric space) using the concept of metric entropy - , with a condition on variances and a continuity assumption as above which does not follow from the metric entropy conditions of Strassen-Dudley [7] and Giné M. [4] . The other theorem says that a functional central limit theorem for the sequence of partial sums of random elements in a real separable Banach space L together with a growth condition on their expected norms implies a corresponding result for the more general case of a class of Robbins-Monro processes in L with a spectral condition as before and also for a modified Robbins-Monro procedure which concerns a strongly consistent recursive estimation of the root of an equation in L of the above form. For further details see [9].

<u>Theorem 2.</u> Let the notations and general assumptions of Theorem 1 be used, but the sequence (X_n) be defined by

$$X_{n+1} := X_n - \frac{c}{n}[X_n + G(X_n, Q_n) - HQ_n], \quad n \in \mathbb{N} .$$

a) Under the assumptions of Theorem 1b, but with

$$c^* > (E\| G(\cdot, Q_1 - q)\|^2)^{1/2} \tag{9}$$

resp.

$$c^* > \frac{1}{2c} + (E\| G(\cdot, Q_1 - q)\|^2)^{1/2} \tag{10}$$

instead of (6), there holds

$$X_n \to \theta \text{ a.s. and in quadratic mean} \tag{11}$$

resp.

$$E\| X_n - \theta\|^2 = O(\tfrac{1}{n}) . \tag{12}$$

b) Let the X_n be considered as random elements in the Hilbert space $L^2([0,1]^2)$. Then (9) implies (11). If (6) and (9) hold, then (12) holds, and the sequence of random elements $\sqrt{n}(X_n-\theta)$ converges in distribution to a Gaussian process with expectation zero and with a square integrable covariance function

$K^*:[0,1]^2\times[0,1]^2 \to \mathbb{R}$ such that the function $F^*:[0,1]^2\times[0,1]^2 \to \mathbb{R}$ with

$$F^*(u,v,u',v') := ((cA - \frac{I}{2})K^*(\cdot,\cdot,u',v'))(u,v)$$

fulfils

$$F^*(u,v,u',v')+F^*(u',v',u,v) = S^*(u,v,u',v') \quad (u,v,u',v' \in [0,1]) ,$$

where S^* is the covariance function of $c(H-G(\theta,\cdot))(Q_1-q)$.

Theorem 2 is easily deduced from Theorem 3, where for the proof of Theorem 2a the relation

$$E\|\sum_{k=1}^{n} (Q_k-q)\|^2 = O(n)$$

(see [9]) is used.

Theorem 3. Let L be a real separable Banach space, N(L,L) the real separable Banach space of bounded linear transformations from L into L, $p \in L$, $A \in N(L,L)$, $((A_n,U_n))_{n\in\mathbb{N}}$ an independent sequence of identically distributed random elements in the product space $N(L,L)\times L$ and the random element X_1 in L be independent of this sequence. There is assumed

$$c^* := \min\{\mathrm{Re}\lambda : \lambda \in \text{spectrum } (A)\} > 0 \tag{1'}$$

and

$$E\|A_1\|^2 < \infty,\ EA_1=A,\ E\|U_1\|^2 < \infty,\ EU_1=0.$$

Let the unique root of the equation $Ax-p = 0$ in L be denoted by θ and the sequence of L-valued random variables X_n be defined by

$$X_{n+1} := X_n - \frac{c}{n}(A_nX_n - p - U_n), \quad n \in \mathbb{N} ,$$

with a constant $c > 0$.

a) Assume

$$E\|\sum_{k=1}^{n} (A_k-A)\|^2 = O(n) ,\quad E\|\sum_{k=1}^{n} U_k\|^2 = O(n) . \tag{13}$$

If

$$c^* > (E\|A_1-A\|^2)^{1/2} \tag{14}$$

resp.

$$c^* > \frac{1}{2c} + (E\|A_1-A\|^2)^{1/2}, \tag{15}$$

then

$$X_n \to \theta \text{ a.s. and in quadratic mean} \tag{11'}$$

resp.

$$E\| X_n - \theta \|^2 = O(\frac{1}{n}) . \tag{12'}$$

b) Let L especially be a Hilbert space. Then (14) implies (11').If

$$c^* > \frac{1}{2c} \tag{6'}$$

and (14) hold, then (12') holds, and the sequence of random elements $\sqrt{n}(X_n-\theta)$ converges in distribution to a Gaussian random element in L wi expectation zero and a covariance operator $\tilde{K}$ which is the unique solut of the equation $(cA-\frac{I}{2})\tilde{K}+\tilde{K}(cA'-\frac{I}{2}) = \tilde{S}$, where $\tilde{S}$ is the covariance operato of $c(U_1-(A_1-A)\theta)$.

Remark 2. It can be shown that in Theorem 3b relation (12') holds in the sharpened version $nE\|X_n-\theta\|^2 \to \text{trace}\,(\tilde{K})$.

Proof of Theorem 3. Without loss of generality we may assume c = 1.

a) We set

$$c^{**} := (E\|A_1-A\|^2)^{1/2}$$

and choose $\varepsilon^*>0$ such that $c":=c^*-c^{**}-2\varepsilon^* \in (0,\frac{1}{2})$ resp. $\in(\frac{1}{2},1)$ in the cas (14) resp. (15). Now we use the fact that for a bounded linear operator $B:L\to L$ with spectrum $(B)\subset\{\lambda\in\mathbb{C}:\mathrm{Re}\lambda>0\}$ there exists a second norm $\| \ \|^*$ on L defined by

$$\| x \|^* := (\int_{\mathbb{R}_+} \| e^{-sB}x\|^2 ds)^{1/2},\ x \in L$$

with corresponding operator norm such that $\| \ \|$ and $\| \ \|^*$ are equival and

$$\| I - \frac{1}{n}B\|^* \leq 1 - \frac{\tilde{c}}{n} + O(1/n^2) \tag{16}$$

for a suitable constant $\tilde{c} > 0$ (see [9]). This yields, according to the proof of Lemma 3 in [8],

$$\underset{c_1\in\mathbb{R}_+}{\exists}\ \underset{n\in\mathbb{N}}{\forall}\ \underset{k\in\{1,\dots,n-1\}}{\forall}\ \prod_{j=k+2}^{n} \|I - \frac{1}{j}A\| \leq c_1(\frac{k}{n})^{c^*-\varepsilon^*} . \tag{17}$$

Noticing

$$E\| I - \frac{1}{j}A_j \|^2 \leq (\| I - \frac{1}{j} A\| + \frac{1}{j} (E\| A_j - A\|^2)^{1/2})^2$$

$$\leq (1+ \frac{1}{j}(c^{**}+\varepsilon^*))^2 \| I - \frac{1}{j}A\|^2 \quad \text{for j sufficiently large,}$$

we now obtain

$$\underset{c_2\in\mathbb{R}_+}{\exists}\ \underset{n\in\mathbb{N}}{\forall}\ \underset{k\in\{1,\dots,n-1\}}{\forall}\ \prod_{j=k+2}^{n} E\| I - \frac{1}{j}A_j\|^2 \leq c_2(\frac{k}{n})^{2c"} . \tag{18}$$

Setting $X'_n := X_n-\theta$, $H_n := U_n - (A_n-A)\theta$ we have

$$X'_{n+1} = (I-\frac{1}{n}A_n)X'_n + \frac{1}{n} H_n \tag{19}$$

and (compare (12), (16), (40) in [8])

$$X'_{n+1} = \frac{1}{n}\sum_{k=1}^{n} H_k + \sum_{k=1}^{n-1} \frac{1}{k(k+1)}(I-\frac{1}{n}A_n)\cdots(I-\frac{1}{k+2}A_{k+2})(I-A_{k+1}) \sum_{j=1}^{k} H_j$$
$$+(I-\frac{1}{n}A_n)\cdots(I-A_1)X'_1 \qquad (n \in \mathbb{N}). \tag{20}$$

Setting

$$C_{nk} := \frac{1}{k} \prod_{j=k+2}^{n} \|I-\frac{1}{j}A_j\| \; \|I-A_{k+1}\| \quad (n \in \{2,3,\dots\}, k \in \{1,\dots,n-1\})$$

and regarding the independence assumptions, (17) and

$$E\|\sum_{k=1}^{n} H_k\|^2 = O(n),$$

which follows from (13), we obtain, with a suitable $c_3 \in \mathbb{R}_+$,

$$E\|X'_{n+1}\|^2$$
$$\le 3\, E\|\frac{1}{n} \sum_{k=1}^{n} H_k\|^2$$
$$+3E(\sum_{k=1}^{n-1} C_{nk}\|\frac{1}{k+1} \sum_{j=1}^{k} H_j\|)^2 + 3\, E\prod_{j=1}^{n} \|I-\frac{1}{j}A_j\|^2 E\|X'_1\|^2$$
$$\le c_3[n^{-1}+n^{-2c''}(\sum_{k=1}^{n} k^{c''-3/2})^2 + n^{-2c''}] \qquad (n \in \mathbb{N})$$
$$= O(n^{-2c''}) \text{ resp. } O(n^{-1}) \tag{21}$$

in the case (14) resp. (15), which yields the assertion on convergence, resp. rate of convergence, in quadratic mean.

We now show $X_n \to \theta$ a.s. Let the sequence (X''_n) of random elements in L be defined by

$$X''_1 := X'_1, \quad X''_{n+1} := (I-\frac{1}{n}A)X''_n + \frac{1}{n} H_n \qquad (n \in \mathbb{N}).$$

From

$$\frac{1}{n}\sum_{k=1}^{n} H_k \to 0 \text{ a.s.},$$

which follows from Mourier's strong law of large numbers (see Padgett-Taylor [6], pp. 41, 42), we obtain $X''_n \to 0$ a.s. This is obtained from a generalization of Lemma 2.1 of Fabian [3] to the case of a Banach space with an operator A satisfying (1'), where in the proof (16) with B=A or the analogue of (20) with A instead of the A_j is used. Now it remains to prove $X'_n - X''_n \to 0$ $(n \to \infty)$.

Because of the relation

$$X'_{n+1}-X''_{n+1} = (I-\frac{1}{n}A)(X'_n-X''_n)-\frac{1}{n}(A_n-A)X'_n \qquad (n \in \mathbb{N}) \tag{22}$$

and the argument just before it suffices to prove

$$\frac{1}{n}\sum_{j=1}^{n}(A_j-A)X'_j \to 0 \text{ a.s.}$$

But this follows, by the Kronecker lemma for the case of a Banach space, from the convergence of $\Sigma j^{-1}E\|A_j-A\|\,E\|X'_j\|$, which is established by (21).

b) We may restrict ourselves to the proof of the second part, because the first part follows from a) by noticing that for the Hilbert space L the general assumptions imply (13). Let X'_n, X''_n $(n \in \mathbb{N})$ be defined as in a). The assertion for $(\sqrt{n}X''_n)$ instead of $(\sqrt{n}X'_n)$ follows by taking the square in the definition of X''_n, noticing $E(X''_n,H_n)=0$ $(n \in \mathbb{N})$ and using (16) for $B=A-\frac{I}{2}$ and Chung's lemma (see Fabian [3] for references) resp. from [8] . Thus it suffices to prove

$$En\|X'_n-X''_n\|^2 \to 0 \quad (n \to \infty).$$

But this follows by taking the square in (22) and arguing as just before with

$$E((I-\frac{1}{n}A)(X'_n-X''_n),\ (A_n-A)X'_n) = 0 \qquad (n \in \mathbb{N})$$

and

$$E\|X'_n\|^2 \to 0 \qquad (n \to \infty).\rfloor$$

Theorem 4. Let L be a real separable Banach space resp. $C([0,1]^2)$; let the notations and assumptions of Theorem 3a with (14) and also

$$c^* > \frac{1}{2c} \tag{6"}$$

and

weak convergence of the distribution of $n^{-1/2}\sum_{k=1}^{n}(U_k-(A_k-A)\theta)$ to a mean-zero Gaussian measure μ on L, (23)

resp. of Theorem 2a with (9) and also (6) be used. Then the sequence of random elements $\sqrt{n}(X_n-\theta)$ in L converges in distribution to a Gaussian random element

$$c\bar{W}(1)+c(I-cA)\int_{(0,1]} e^{(\ln z)(cA-2I)}\bar{W}(z)\,dz = c\int_{(0,1]} e^{(\ln z)(cA-I)}d\bar{W}(z)$$

with Brownian motion $\bar{W}$ in L generated by μ, resp.to a path-continuous Gaussian process with expectation zero and covariance function as in Theorem 2b.

Proof. Because of a result in [9] it suffices to treat the general

Banach space case. We choose c=1 and use the notations of the proof of Theorem 3. The assertion for $(\sqrt{n}X_n'')$ instead of $(\sqrt{n}X_n')$ follows from Kuelbs [5], (6"), (16) and the argument in [8]. Thus it suffices to prove $E\sqrt{n}\| X_n'-X_n''\| \to 0$ $(n \to \infty)$. This relation follows from (22) together with analogues of (20), (16), (17) and from

$$C_n := E\| \frac{1}{n} \sum_{j=1}^{n} (A_j-A)\sqrt{j}X_j'\| \to 0 \quad (n \to \infty). \tag{24}$$

For proving (24) we set

$$D_n := E\| \frac{1}{n} \sum_{j=1}^{n} (A_{j+1}-A)j^{-1/2} \sum_{i=1}^{j} H_i\|$$

and first obtain $C_n=D_n + o(1)$ by partial summation, (19), once more partial summation, (13) and (11'). Then we show $D_n \to 0$ $(n \to \infty)$ by using the argument of Padgett-Taylor ([6], 5.1, 5.2) on partial sums of weakly uncorrelated random elements in a real separable Banach space which also works if, instead of identical distribution and integrability, it is only assumed that these random elements converge in distribution and have uniformly integrable norms, and if convergence in probability is replaced by convergence in first mean; for verifying these assumptions we notice general assumptions of Theorem 4 or Theorem 3 and (23) and (13).⌋

REFERENCES

[1] Arnold, L.: Stochastische Differentialgleichungen. München: Oldenbourg 1973.

[2] Bucy, R.S.; Joseph, P.D.: Filtering for Stochastic Processes with Applications to Guidance. New York: Interscience Publ. 1968.

[3] Fabian, V.: On asymptotic normality in stochastic approximation. Ann. Math. Statist. 39, 1327-1332 (1968).

[4] Giné M., E.: On the central limit theorem for sample continuous processes. Ann. Probability 2, 629-641 (1974).

[5] Kuelbs, J.: The invariance principle for Banach space valued random variables. J. Multivariate Analysis 3, 161-172 (1973).

[6] Padgett, W.J.; Taylor, R.L.: Laws of Large Numbers for Normed Linear Spaces and Certain Fréchet Spaces. Berlin: Springer 1973.

[7] Strassen, V.; Dudley, R.M. : The central limit theorem and ε-entropy. In: Probability and Information Theory (eds. M. Behara, K. Krickeberg, J. Wolfowitz), 224-231. Berlin: Springer 1969.

[8] Walk, H.: An invariance principle for the Robbins-Monro process in a Hilbert space. Z. Wahrscheinlichkeitstheorie verw. Gebiete 39, 135-150 (1977).

[9] Walk, H.: A functional central limit theorem for martingales in C(K) and its application to sequential estimates. To appear.

CAUSAL AND NON-ANTICIPATING SOLUTIONS OF STOCHASTIC EQUATIONS

M.P. Yershov

The aim of this paper is to give an example of concrete applications of general results obtained in [2] .

1. GENERAL AND STANDARD STOCHASTIC EQUATIONS. By stochastic equations (SE's), in the most general situation, we mean equations (algebraic, differential, integral, functional etc.) in which the data as well as the unknowns are random elements (with values in corresponding measurable spaces). Moreover, by random elements we will mean random elements in the wide sense, i.e. distributions.

Examples. 1) Equations with random parametres. Let f be a given function on $\mathbb{R}^3$, ξ and η be given random variables. Consider the equation (w.r. to $\xi(\cdot)$)

$$d\xi(t)/dt = f(t, \xi(t), \eta), \quad t \in T,$$

where T is the semi-axis $[0,\infty)$, say, with the initial condition

$$\xi(0) = \xi .$$

We can resolve it w.r. to ξ and η by rewriting it as the system of equations (w.r. to $(\xi(\cdot), \eta(\cdot))$):

$$\begin{aligned} \xi(t) - \int_0^t f(s, \xi(s), \eta(s))\,ds &= \xi \\ \eta(t) &= \eta \end{aligned}$$

or in the form:

$$F(\zeta(\cdot)) = \zeta$$

where

$$\zeta(t) = (\xi(t), \eta(t)), \quad \zeta = (\xi, \eta),$$

$$F((x(\cdot), y(\cdot)))|_t = (x(t) - \int_0^t f(s, x(s), y(s))\,ds, \, y(t)).$$

2) Stochastic differential equations (SDE's). Let f be a given function on $\mathbb{R}^2$, ξ be a random variable and $\eta(\cdot)$ be a Wiener process on $[0, \infty)$ independent of ξ . Consider the equation

$$d\xi(t) = f(t, \xi(t))\,dt + d\eta(t), \quad \xi(0) = \xi .$$

It is understood as an equivalent of the integral equation

$$\xi(t) = \xi + \int_0^t f(s, \xi(s))ds + \eta(t).$$

The latter, in turn, can be rewritten in the form

$$F(\xi(\cdot)) = \bar{\eta}(\cdot)$$

where $\bar{\eta}(\cdot)$ is a Wiener process "starting" from ξ ,

$$F(x(\cdot))\big|_t = x(t) - \int_0^t f(s, x(s))ds .$$

Thus, in both the cases, we dealt with stochastic equations of the form

$$F(\xi) = \eta$$

where η is a given and ξ is an unknown random element, F is a given mapping of a (function) space into another.

It is clear that it will be a more general problem if one replaces ξ and η by the corresponding distributions and F by the mapping of measures which is induced by F.

Here is a more precise explanation.

Let $(X, \mathscr{X})$ and $(Y, \mathscr{Y})$ be measurable spaces and F be a measurable mapping of $(X, \mathscr{X})$ into $(Y, \mathscr{Y})$. For any measure μ on $(X, \mathscr{X})$, denote the measure on $(Y, \mathscr{Y})$ defined by the formula

$$B \longmapsto \mu(F^{-1}(B)), \quad B \in \mathscr{Y},$$

by $F(\mu)$. Thus any measurable mapping $F: (X, \mathscr{X}) \to (Y, \mathscr{Y})$ defines (induces) a mapping which takes measures on $(X, \mathscr{X})$ to measures on $(Y, \mathscr{Y})$ (we denote the induced mapping also by F).

Return to equation

(1.1) $$F(\xi) = \eta .$$

Here η is a given random element with values in a measurable space $(Y, \mathscr{Y})$, ξ be an unknown random element with values in a measurable space $(X, \mathscr{X})$ and F be a measurable mapping of $(X, \mathscr{X})$ into $(Y, \mathscr{Y})$. Let ν be the distribution of η :

$$\nu(B) = \text{Prob.}\{\eta \in B\}, \quad B \in \mathscr{Y} .$$

Assume that we have found a solution ξ , and let μ be the distribution of ξ :

$$\mu(A) = \text{Prob.}\{\xi \in A\}, \quad A \in \mathscr{X}.$$

Then by definition

(1.2) $$F(\mu) = \nu.$$

Thus equation (1.2) (w.r. to μ) is a generalization of (1.1) in the sense that, if (1.1) has a solution, so does (1.2). However the converse is not alsways true. There is a class of solutions of (1.2) which enable constructing solutions of (1.1). This is the class of so-called strong solutions or - as is more preferable to call them - extreme solutions (see Remark below).

We shall call equations of the form (1.2) standard stochastic equations (SSE's). From the first glance it appears that the class of SSE's is rather narrow (they are always resolved w.r. to the given distribution). However one can show that practically any SE can be reduced to the form (1.2) by making spaces (X , $\mathcal{X}$) and (Y , $\mathcal{Y}$) more complicated. We have seen how it can be done in two simple examples. Other equations can be handled analogously although sometimes it requires ingenuity (e.g. for SDE's with non-trivial diffusion coefficients).

The following reasoning is an illustration.

The problem of solving practically any SE is described as follows: Given a measure (distribution) in one measurable space; construct a measure in another measurable space which is in a certain way connected with the first measure (this connection is expressed by the equation). Clearly, one can assume that the basic set in both measurable spaces is one and the same: otherwise one can take their Cartesian product with the cylindric "extensions" of the σ-algebras. Therefore our problem is imbedded into the following: Given a measure μ_0 on a σ-algebra $\mathcal{X}_0$ in X ; extend it to a wider σ-algebra so that extensions μ satisfy the constraints defined by the equation. The problem of extending μ_0 is equivalent to that of solving SSE (1.2) where $(Y, \mathcal{Y}, \nu) = (X, \mathcal{X}_0, \mu_0)$ and F is the identity mapping of X onto itself. The constraints for solutions of (1.2) can be of various kinds. For example, for SDE's it is the non-anticipation property (see below).

Remark. Note that whatever $F:(X, \mathcal{X}) \to (Y, \mathcal{Y})$ is, the induced mapping of measures is always linear! Moreover the set of solutions of (1.2) is convex and its extreme points μ are characterized by the relation

$$\mathcal{X} = F^{-1}(\mathcal{Y}) \quad (\mathrm{mod}\ \mu)$$

(cf. [1] , [4] , [3]). We shall call such solutions μ extreme.

2. CAUSALITY AND NON-ANTICIPATION. We formulate definitions and results of [2] in a slightly modified form.

Causality and non-anticipation are notions connected with SE's in which the random elements are stochastic processes; in other words, with SE's (1.2) in which X and Y are sets of functions on an interval of $\mathbb{R}^1$.

Definition. Let X be a set, T be a set linearly ordered by a relation $\leq$ and, for each $t \in T$, $\mathcal{X}_t$ be a σ-algebra in X. The family

$$\mathfrak{X} = \{\mathcal{X}_t\}_{t \in T}$$

is called a flow of σ-algebras in X (over T) if

$$s \in T,\ t \in T,\ s \leq t \Rightarrow \mathcal{X}_s \subset \mathcal{X}_t$$

(here $\subset$ is the non-strict inclusion).

A flow $\mathfrak{X}$ over T is said to be subordinate to a flow $\mathfrak{X}'$ over T:

$$\mathfrak{X} \prec \mathfrak{X}'$$

if

$$\forall t \in T \qquad \mathcal{X}_t \subset \mathcal{X}_t'.$$

Definition. Let X and Y be sets and $\mathfrak{X}$ and $\mathfrak{Y}$ be flows of σ-algebras in X and Y resp. over a T. A mapping $F: X \to Y$ is called causal (w.r. to $(\mathfrak{X}, \mathfrak{Y})$):

$$F: (X, \mathfrak{X}) \to (Y, \mathfrak{Y})$$

if

$$F^{-1}(\mathfrak{Y}) := \{F^{-1}(\mathcal{Y}_t)\}_{t \in T} \prec \mathfrak{X}.$$

Definition. Let $F: (X, \mathfrak{X}) \to (Y, \mathfrak{Y})$ be a causal mapping,

$$\mathcal{X} = \bigvee_{t \in T} \mathcal{X}_t, \quad \mathcal{Y} = \bigvee_{t \in T} \mathcal{Y}_t$$

and ν be a (probability) measure on $(Y, \mathcal{Y})$. Consider SE (1.2). Its solution μ_* will be called causal (w.r. to $(\mathfrak{X}, \mathfrak{Y})$) if

$$\mathcal{X}_t = F^{-1}(\mathcal{Y}_t) \pmod{\mu_*} \qquad \forall t \in T.$$

Remark. A causal solution is obviously extreme.

Proposition 1. Causality of μ_* is equivalent to the condition

$$\mu_*(A \mid \mathcal{X}_t) = \mu_*(A \mid F^{-1}(\mathcal{Y}_t)) \pmod{\mu_*} \qquad \forall A \in \mathcal{X} \quad \forall t \in T$$

where $\mu_*(\cdot \mid \cdot)$ is the conditional μ_*-probability.

Definition. A solution μ_* of (1.2) is non-anticipating (w.r. to $(\mathfrak{X}, \mathfrak{Y})$) if

$$\mu_*(F^{-1}(B)|\mathcal{X}_t) = \mu_*(F^{-1}(B)|F^{-1}(\mathcal{Y}_t)) \pmod{\mu_*} \quad \forall B \in \mathcal{Y} \quad \forall t \in T.$$

Remark. By Proposition 1, any causal solution is non-anticipating.

Proposition 2. Any extreme and non-anticipating solution is causal.

Remark. It follows from Proposition 2 that the two (completed w.r. to the basic probability) σ-algebras $\sigma(\xi_0^t)$ and $\sigma(W_0^t)$, in the Kailath innovation problem for SDE

$$d\xi_t = a(t, \xi_0^t)dt + dW_t ,$$

coincide for each t if so do the σ-algebras $\bigvee_t \sigma(\xi_0^t)$ and $\bigvee_t \sigma(W_0^t)$ only.

Corollary. The set of causal solutions is equal to the set of extreme and non-anticipating solutions.

Definition. Let $\mathfrak{F}$ be a set of measurable integrable real functions on $(Y, \mathcal{Y}, \nu)$. A solution μ_* of (1.2) is called $\mathfrak{F}$-non-anticipating (w.r. to $(\mathfrak{X}, \mathfrak{Y})$) if

$$E_{\mu_*}(f \circ F | \mathcal{X}_t) = E_{\mu_*}(f \circ F | F^{-1}(\mathcal{Y}_t)) \pmod{\mu_*} \quad \forall t \in T \quad \forall f \in \mathfrak{F}$$

where $E_{\mu_*}(\cdot|\cdot)$ is the conditional expectation w.r. to μ_* .

Examples. 1) If, e.g., $\mathfrak{F}$ contains the indicators of all sets from $\mathcal{Y}$, then $\mathfrak{F}$-non-anticipation is the same as non-anticipation.

2) Let $Y = C[0,\infty)$, $\mathcal{Y}_t$ be the σ-algebra in Y generated by cylindric sets over $[0,t]$ and ν be the Wiener measure (this is, e.g., the case of Example 1.2)). Let $\mathfrak{F}$ be the set of "coordinate" functions:

$$\mathfrak{F} = \{(f_t : Y \to \mathbb{R}^1) : f_t(y(\cdot)) = y(t) \ ; \ t \in [0,\infty)\}.$$

Then $\mathfrak{F}$-non-anticipation is the same as non-anticipation.

Problem. Let $F: X \to Y$ be a causal w.r. to $(\mathfrak{X}, \mathfrak{Y})$ mapping. Whether equation (1.2) (where $\mathcal{X}$ and $\mathcal{Y}$ are "maximal" σ-algebras of $\mathfrak{X}$ and $\mathfrak{Y}$ resp.) has a causal or a non-anticipating or, more generally, an $\mathfrak{F}$-non-anticipating solution for a set $\mathfrak{F}$ of integrable real functions on $(Y, \mathcal{Y}, \nu)$?

In [2] , a simple example is given in which (1.2) does have a solution but does not have any $\mathfrak{F}$-non-anticipating solution for all non-trivial $\mathfrak{F}$. The trouble is, as that example shows, that the F

has "too strong memory" in the sense that the past of the argument impose strong constraints on the future of its F-image. In this connection the notion of non-anticipating mappings was introduced in [2] and it was shown that this is in a certain sense a maximal class for which the above problem admits a positive solution.

Definition. A causal w.r. to ($\mathfrak{X}$, $\mathfrak{Y}$) mapping F is called ν-non-anticipating (w.r. to ($\mathfrak{X}$, $\mathfrak{Y}$)) if

$$\forall t \in T \quad \forall A \in \mathcal{X}_t \quad \forall B \in \mathcal{Y}: F(A) \subset B,$$
$$\exists B' \in \mathcal{Y}_t: F(A) \subset B' \ \& \ \nu(B' \setminus B) = 0.$$

Remark. The ν-non-anticipation property is obviously weaker than:

$$\forall t \in T \quad \forall A \in \mathcal{X}_t , \quad F(A) \in \mathcal{Y}_t(\nu)$$

but, in general, not weaker than:

$$\forall t \in T \quad \forall A \in \mathcal{X}_t , \quad F(A) \in \mathcal{Y}_t(\mathcal{Y};\nu)$$

(here $\mathcal{Y}_t(\nu)$ and $\mathcal{Y}_t(\mathcal{Y};\nu)$ are, resp., the Lebesgue completion of $\mathcal{Y}_t$ w.r. to ν and the completion of $\mathcal{Y}_t$ by ν-null sets from $\mathcal{Y}$).

3. THE EXISTENCE OF NON-ANTICIPATING SOLUTIONS. We formulate first basic assumptions under which an exestence theorem is proved in [2] (Theorem 4.3 and Corollary 4.6).

(i) X is an analytic metric space.

(ii) T is a set on the real line (with the usual order).

(iii) $\mathfrak{X} = \{\mathcal{X}_t\}_{t \in T}$ is a flow of σ-algebras in X , each $\mathcal{X}_t$ being generated by a family $\mathcal{G}_t$ of continuous functions $g: X \to \mathbb{R}^1$; $\mathcal{X} = \bigvee_t \mathcal{X}_t$ is the Borel σ-algebra in X .

(iv) Y is a metric space, $\mathfrak{Y} = \{\mathcal{Y}_t\}_{t \in T}$ is a flow of σ-subalgebras of the Borel σ-algebra in Y such that, for each $t \in T$, there exists a sequence $\{B_n\} \subset \mathcal{Y}_t$ with the property that the Lebesgue completion w.r. to ν of the σ-algebra generated by $\{B_n\}$ contains $\mathcal{Y}_t$; $\mathcal{Y} = \bigvee_t \mathcal{Y}_t$ is the Borel σ-algebra in Y .

(v) Denote by $\mathcal{F}_t$ $(t \in T)$ the set of all real ν-integrable continuous functions f on Y such that

$$E_\nu(f \mid \mathcal{Y}_t) = \Phi_{f,t} \pmod{\nu}$$

where $\Phi_{f,t}$ is a continuous function on Y .

Theorem. [2]. Let conditions (i) - (v) be satisfied. Let $F: X \to Y$ be a continuous mapping such that $\nu(F(X)) = 1$ *, F-pre-images of compacta are compact and F is ν-non-anticipating w.r. to ($\mathcal{X}$, $\mathcal{Y}$).

Then the stochastic equation

$$F(\mu) = \nu$$

has an $\mathcal{F}$-non-anticipating solution w.r. to ($\mathcal{X}$, $\mathcal{Y}$) where

$$\mathcal{F} = \bigcap_{t \in T} \mathcal{F}_t .$$

4. AN APPLICATION. Let $X = Y = C^m$ be the set of all continuous m-vector functions on $T = [0, \infty)$ "starting" at the origin: $x_i(0) = 0 \quad (i = 1, \ldots, m)$. Let, for each t, $\mathcal{X}_t = \mathcal{Y}_t = \mathcal{C}_t^m$ be the σ-algebra in C^m generated by cylindric sets over $[0,t]$:

$$\{ x(\cdot) \in C^m : x(s) \in B \}, \quad B \in \mathcal{B}(\mathbb{R}^m), \quad 0 \le s \le t,$$

where $\mathcal{B}(\mathbb{R}^m)$ is the Borel σ-algebra in $\mathbb{R}^m$.

The set C^m can be metrized as a complete separable space:

$$d(x(\cdot), x'(\cdot)) = \sum_n 2^{-n} \frac{\| x - x' \|_n}{1 + \| x - x' \|_n}$$

where

$$\| x \|_t = \sup \{ |x(s)| : 0 \le s \le t \} .$$

Hence, with this metric, X and Y are analytic, and it is easy to see that $\mathcal{C}^m = \bigvee_t \mathcal{C}_t^m$ is the Borel σ-algebra in C^m. It is also obvious that the σ-algebras $\mathcal{C}_t^m$ are generated by families of continuous functions into the Borel line and that they are of countable weight (countably generated).

Thus conditions (i) - (iv) of No.3 are satisfied.

Let ν be a measure on (Y, $\mathcal{Y}$) which is the distribution of a continuous m-dimensional martingale. Let $\mathcal{F}_t$, for each t, be one and the same set of all "coordinate" functions on Y:

---

x This condition, with the outer measure corresponding to ν instead of ν, is necessary for the existence of at least one solution of (1.2). In the case considered $F(X)$ is analytic and hence its outer measure coincides with ν (more precisely: with the Lebesgue completion of ν).

$$\mathcal{F}_t = \{ (f_s^i : Y \to R^1) : \; f_s^i(y(\cdot)) = y_i(s);\; i=1,\dots,m;\; 0 \le s < \infty \}.$$

By the martingale property,

$$E_\nu (f_s^i \mid \mathcal{Y}_t) = y_i (s \wedge t) \quad (\mathrm{mod}\ \nu)$$

so that $\mathcal{F} = \mathcal{F}_t \quad (0 \le t < \infty)$ satisfies condition (v) of No.3.

Let G be a continuous (in the metric introduced) mapping of X into Y such that

$$\forall t \qquad (x(s) = x'(s),\ 0 \le s \le t) \Rightarrow (G(x(\cdot))|_s = G(x'(\cdot))|_s,\ 0 \le s \le t)$$

and the set $G(X)$ is relatively compact in Y. Let I be the "identity" mapping of X onto Y: $I(x(\cdot))|_t = x(t)$, and define

$$F = I - G \qquad (F(x(\cdot)) = I(x(\cdot)) - G(x(\cdot))).$$

Consider the problem of finding an $\mathcal{F}$-non-anticipating w.r. to $(\mathcal{X}, \mathcal{Y})$ solution of the equation

$$F(\mu) = \nu.$$

Check the conditions of Theorem in No. 3.

We have seen that conditions (i) - (v) of No. 3 are fulfilled. It is clear that F is continuous and one can easily show that F is causal w.r. to $(\mathcal{X}, \mathcal{Y})$.

Let K be a compact in Y. Then

$$F^{-1}(K) = \{ x(\cdot) : I(x(\cdot)) - G(x(\cdot)) \in K \}$$
$$\subset \{ x(\cdot) : I(x(\cdot)) \in K + G(X) \}$$

(vector addition), so that $F^{-1}(K)$ is relatively compact and hence compact.

Let us check that F is $\mathcal{Y}$-non-anticipating and $\nu(F(X)) = 1$.

Assume that we had proved the following

<u>Lemma</u>. <u>For each</u> $t \ge 0$, <u>for each</u> $x(\cdot) \in X$ <u>and for each</u> $y(\cdot) \in Y$ <u>such that</u>

$$y(s) = F(x(\cdot))|_s, \quad 0 \le s \le t,$$

<u>there exists an</u> $x'(\cdot) \in X$ <u>such that</u>

$$x'(s) = x(s), \quad 0 \le s \le t,$$

<u>and</u>

$$F(x'(\cdot)) = y(\cdot).$$

Then $F(X)=Y$ (take $t=0$ in Lemma). For each $t\geq 0$ and $A\in\mathcal{X}_t$, any $B\in\mathcal{Y}$ such that $F(A)\subset B$ must contain, together with a function $y(\cdot)$, also any $y'(\cdot)$ coinciding with $y(\cdot)$ on $[0,t]$; so that $B\in\mathcal{Y}_t$, i.e. F is ν-non-anticipating.

It remains to prove the above Lemma.

We describe main points of the reasoning.

For each n, choose an increasing sequence $\{t_{nk}\}_{k=0,1,\dots}$ such that

$$t_{n0}=t,\quad t_{nk}\xrightarrow[k]{}\infty,\quad t_{n,k+1}-t_{nk}\leq\frac{1}{n}$$

and the oscillation of $G(x(\cdot))$ inside each interval $[t_{nk},t_{n,k+1}]$ does not exceed $1/n$ for each $x(\cdot)$. Define $x^n(\cdot)$ as follows:

$$x^n(s)=x(s)\qquad(0\leq s\leq t),$$

$$x^n(s)=x^n(t_{nk})+\frac{(s-t_{nk})}{(t_{n,k+1}-t_{nk})}\left(y(t_{n,k+1})-F(x^n(\cdot))\big|_{t_{nk}}\right)$$

$$(t_{nk}\leq s\leq t_{n,k+1}).$$

Causality of F implies that this definition is correct.

For each k,

$$F(x^n(\cdot))\big|_{t_{n,k+1}}=x^n(t_{n,k+1})-G(x^n(\cdot))\big|_{t_{n,k+1}}$$

$$=x^n(t_{nk})+\left(y(t_{n,k+1})-x^n(t_{nk})+G(x^n(\cdot))\big|_{t_{nk}}\right)$$

$$-G(x^n(\cdot))\big|_{t_{n,k+1}}=y(t_{n,k+1})+\left(G(x^n(\cdot))\big|_{t_{nk}}-G(x^n(\cdot))\big|_{t_{n,k+1}}\right)$$

so that

$$\left|F(x^n(\cdot))\big|_{t_{n,k+1}}-y(t_{n,k+1})\right|\leq\frac{1}{n}.$$

The supremum modulus and the modulus of continuity of $x^n(\cdot)$ on each segment $[0,u]$ are easily estimated from above uniformly in n by the corresponding characteristics of $y(\cdot)$ and all $y'(\cdot)\in G(X)$. So that this implies that the sequence $\{x^n(\cdot)\}$ has a limiting point $x'(\cdot)$. By the above proved and by continuity of F,

$$F(x'(\cdot))=y(\cdot);\quad x'(s)=x'(s)\quad(0\leq s\leq t).$$

<u>Example</u>. The SDE

$$d\xi(t)=g(t,\xi(\cdot))dt+dW(t),\quad \xi(0)=0,$$

where $g(t, x(\cdot))$ depends only on $x(s)$, $s \leq t$, has a "weak" solution (for any continuous martingale $W(\cdot)$) if, for some $\varepsilon > 0$,

$$\sup_{x(\cdot)} \int_0^t |g(s, x(\cdot))|^{1+\varepsilon} ds < \infty .$$

In fact, under this condition,

$$G : \qquad G(x(\cdot))|_t = \int_0^t g(s, x(\cdot)) ds$$

maps C^m onto a relatively compact set in C^m .

This case is not covered by the Girsanov theorem.

REFERENCES

1. Yershov M.P., The Choquet theorem and stochastic equations, Analysis Math. 1(1975), 259-271.

2. Yershov M.P., Non-anticipating solutions of stochastic equations, Proc. 3d Japan-USSR Sympos. Probab. Theory, Springer, Lecture Notes in Math. 550(1976), 655-691.

3. Yershov M.P., Second disintegration of measures, Univ. Linz, Institutsbericht 1978.

4. Yor M., Quelques resultats de representation integrale, Preprint 1978.